Complexity Science, Living Systems, and Reflexing Interfaces:

New Models and Perspectives

Franco Orsucci
University College London, UK & Institute for Complexity Studies, Italy

Nicoletta Sala
University of Lugano, Switzerland

Information Science
REFERENCE

Managing Director:	Lindsay Johnston
Book Production Manager:	Jennifer Romanchak
Publishing Systems Analyst:	Adrienne Freeland
Managing Editor:	Joel Gamon
Development Editor:	Myla Merkel
Assistant Acquisitions Editor:	Kayla Wolfe
Typesetter:	Lisandro Gonzalez
Cover Design:	Nick Newcomer

Published in the United States of America by
Information Science Reference (an imprint of IGI Global)
701 E. Chocolate Avenue
Hershey PA 17033
Tel: 717-533-8845
Fax: 717-533-8661
E-mail: cust@igi-global.com
Web site: http://www.igi-global.com

Library of Congress Cataloging-in-Publication Data

Complexity science, living systems, and reflexing interfaces : new models and perspectives / Franco Orsucci and Nicoletta Sala, editors.
    p. cm.
  Includes bibliographical references and index.
  ISBN 978-1-4666-2077-3 (hardcover) -- ISBN 978-1-4666-2078-0 (ebook) -- ISBN 978-1-4666-2079-7 (print & perpetual access) 1. Complexity (Philosophy) 2. Biocomplexity. I. Orsucci, Franco. II. Sala, Nicoletta.
  Q175.32.C65C654 2013
  577--dc23
                                    2012015948

British Cataloguing in Publication Data
A Cataloguing in Publication record for this book is available from the British Library.

All work contributed to this book is new, previously-unpublished material. The views expressed in this book are those of the authors, but not necessarily of the publisher.

List of Reviewers

Walter Ambrosetti, *CNR – Institute for Ecosystem Study, Italy*
Gabriele Cappellato, *Università della Svizzera Italiana, Switzerland*
Leonardo Castellano, *Matec Modelli Matematici, Italy*
Giovanni Degli Antoni, *Università degli Studi di Milano, Italy*
Alessandro Giuliani, *Istituto Superiore di Sanita, Italy*
Tullio Minelli, *University of Padova, Italy*
Rita Pizzi, *Università degli Studi di Milano, Italy*
Nicoletta Sala, *Università della Svizzera Italiana, Switzerland*

Table of Contents

Section 1
Living Systems and Information Technology

Section 2
Application Fields: From Networks to the Fractals

Detailed Table of Contents

Section 1
Living Systems and Information Technology

Chapter 1

> *Franco Orsucci, University College London, UK & Institute for Complexity Studies, Italy*

The author identifies the reflexing interfaces that can redefine different approaches in different disciplines in the new millennium. The chapter sets the scene for discussions presented by various subsequent authors.

Chapter 2

> *Terry Marks-Tarlow, Private Practice, USA*

The author describes fractal geometry as a bridge between the imaginary and the real, mind and matter, conscious and the unconscious. The chapter presents as fractals are multidimensional objects with self-similar detail across size and/or time scales.

Chapter 3

> *Franco Scalzone, Italian Psychoanalytical Society, Italy*
> *Gemma Zontini, Italian Psychoanalytical Society, Italy*

The authors present some interesting "similarities" between computer science and psychoanalysis. They formulate some hypotheses by "bringing closer" the statute of connectionism to the energetic model of the psychic apparatus as well as the OOP (Object Oriented Programming) to the object relations theory. They explore the "man/machine" theme, the way in which men relate to machines, especially "thinking machines," describing the fantasies they arouse.

Chapter 4

Liane Gabora, University of British Columbia, Canada
Maegan Merrifield, University of British Columbia, Canada

The authors describe new theoretical framework for the process by which human culture evolves inspired by the views of complexity theorists on the problem of how life began. The chapter also explores the implications of this new framework for culture on the transformative processes of individuals; addressing what this emerging perspective on cultural evolution implies for to go about attaining a sustainable worldview; that is, a web of habits, understandings, and ways of approaching situations that is conducive to the development of a sustainable world.

Chapter 5

R. Pizzi, Università degli Studi di Milano, Italy
S. Fiorentini, Università degli Studi di Milano, Italy
G. Strini, Università degli Studi di Milano, Italy
M. Pregnolato, Università degli Studi di Pavia, Italy

The authors present Microtubules (MTs) which are cylindrical polymers of the tubulin dimer, are constituents of all eukaryotic cells cytoskeleton and are involved in key cellular functions and are claimed to be involved as sub-cellular information or quantum information communication systems. They evaluated some biophysical properties of MTs by means of specific physical measures of resonance and birefringence in presence of electromagnetic field, on the assumption that when tubulin and MTs show different biophysical behaviours, this should be due to their special structural properties. Actually MTs are the closest biological equivalent to the well-known carbon nanotubes (CNTs), whose interesting biophysical and quantum properties are due to their peculiar microscopic structure.

Chapter 6

David Vernon, Canterbury Christ Church University, UK
Tammy Dempster, Canterbury Christ Church University, UK

The authors explore the use of neurofeedback training as a mechanism for altering human brain functioning and in turn influencing behaviour. The chapter highlights some of the findings from research, including clinical, peak performance, and functional validation studies. In addition, it delineates some important methodological issues that remain to be addressed. It is hoped that outlining these issues will serve a dual purpose. First, it will assist in the understanding of some of the theoretical and methodological limitations that may be holding the field back. Second, it is hoped that such information will stimulate researchers to work towards designing more efficient and effective research protocols and neurofeedback training paradigms.

Chapter 7

Hector Sabelli, Chicago Center for Creative Development, USA

Louis H. Kauffman, University of Illinois at Chicago, USA

The authors describe how the logic of physical and biological processes may be employed in the design and programming of computers. Quantum processes do not follow Boolean logic; the development of quantum computers requires the formulation of an appropriate logic. While in Boolean logic, entities are static, opposites exclude each other, and change is not creative, natural processes involve action, opposition, and creativity. Creativity is detected by changes in pattern, diversification, and novelty. Causally-generated creative patterns (Bios) are found in numerous processes at all levels of organization: recordings of presumed gravitational waves, the distribution of galaxies and quasars, population dynamics, cardiac rhythms, economic data, and music. Quantum processes show biotic patterns.

Section 2
Application Fields: From Networks to the Fractals

Chapter 8

Alessandro Giuliani, Istituto Superiore di Sanita, Italy

The author presents the notion of 'network' which is more and more widespread in all the fields of human investigation, from physics to sociology. He describes some applications of network based modelling will be presented so to both introduce the basic terminology of the emergent 'network paradigm' and to highlight strengths and limitations of the method.

Chapter 9

Francisco Torrens, Institut Universitari de Ciència Molecular, Universitat de València, Spain

Gloria Castellano, Universidad Católica de Valencia San Vicente Mártir, Spain

The authors present the definition of complexity related to Kolmogorov complexity and Shannon entropy measures. They describe a novel approach, presented by Lin, for assessing molecular diversity based on Shannon information theory. A set of compounds is viewed as a static collection of microstates that can register information about their environment. The method is characterized by a strong tendency to oversample remote areas of the feature space and produce unbalanced designs. The chapter demonstrates the limitation with some simple examples and provides a rationale for the failure to produce results that are consistent.

The authors propose a method for the estimation of the characteristic size and frequency of the typical structure in systems showing two dimensional spatial patterns. They use several indicators caught from the nonlinear framework for identifying the small and large scales of the systems. The indicators are applied to the images corresponding to the instantaneous realization of the system. The method assumes that it is possible to capture the main system's properties from the distribution of the recurring patterns in the image and does not require the knowledge of the dynamical system generating the patterns neither the application of any image segmentation method.

The authors describe a study designed to evaluate the spectrum of the residence time of the water at different depths of a deep lake, and to examine the mechanisms governing the seasonal cycle of thermal stratification and destratification, with the ultimate aim of assessing the actual exchange time of the lake water. The chapter describes the study which was performed on Lake Maggiore (depth 370m) using a multidimensional mathematical model and computer codes for the heat and mass transfer in very large natural water bodies. A 3D Eulerian time-dependent CFD (Computational Fluid Dynamics) code was applied under real conditions.

The author presents the notion of fractals and complex patterns in their use in computer-aided design and computer art. The chapter looks for answers to the following questions: How do we perceive fractals? Are fractals predominantly man-made or natural objects? How do fractals relate to the overall visual art experience of mankind? What are the main problems in using fractals in arts? What are the experiences from the visual art-history? Do Nature and artists use the same algorithm? What fractal experts can do to help artists?

The author describes a research project, developed by Map-Aria research team, that consists in applying automatic generative methods in design processes. The chapter presents a specific tool able to model the global structure of architectural objects through a morphological and semantic description of its finite elements. This discrete conceptual model was refined during the geometric modeling of the "Vieux Lyon" district, containing a high level of morpho-stylistic disparity.

The author presents the fractal geometry as a "tool" that can help to describe and to understand the natural shapes. The chapter describes important applications of fractals in computer science, for example to compress the images, to reproduce, in the virtual reality environments, the complex patterns and the irregular forms present in nature using simple iterative algorithms executed by computers. Recent studies apply this geometry for controlling the traffic in the computer networks (LANs, MANs, WANs, and the Internet) and in the realization of virtual worlds based on World Wide Web. The chapter presents the fractals, their properties (e.g., the self similarity) and their applications in computer science (starting from the computer graphics, to the virtual reality).

Foreword

Intelligent behavior is characterized by flexible and creative pursuit of endogenously defined goals. It has emerged in humans through the stages of evolution that are manifested in the brains and behaviors of other animals. Intentionality is a key concept by which to link brain dynamics to goal-directed behavior. The archetypal form of intentional behavior is an act of observation through time and space, by which information is sought for the guidance of future action. Sequences of such acts constitute the key desired property of free-roving, semi-autonomous devices capable of exploring remote environments that are inhospitable for humans. Intentionality consists of (a) the neurodynamics, by which images are created of future states as goals; (b) command sequences by which to act in pursuit of goals; (c) prediction of changes in sensory input resulting from intended actions (reafference); (d) evaluation of performance; and (e) modification of the device by itself in learning from the consequences of its intended actions. These principles are well known among psychologists, philosophers, and engineers (e.g., Merleau-Ponty, 1945; Ashby, 1952; Clark, 1996; Hendriks-Jansen, 1996).

What is new is the development of nonlinear mesoscopic brain dynamics (Freeman, 2000), by which to apply complexity theory in order to understand and emulate the construction of meaningful patterns of endogenous activity that implement the action-perception cycle (Merleau-Ponty, 1942) as exemplified by the perceptual process of observation.

The prototypic hardware realization of intelligent behavior is already apparent in certain classes of robots. The chaotic neurodynamics of sensory cortices in pattern recognition is ready for hardware embodiments, which are needed to provide the eyes, noses, and ears of devices for survival and intentional operation – as distinct from autonomous operation in connoting cooperation with the controller - in complex and/or unpredictable environments.

The three salient characteristics of intentionality as are (a) intent or directedness toward some future state or goal, (b) wholeness, and (c) unity. These three aspects correspond to current use of the term in psychology [with the meaning of purpose], in medicine [with the meaning of mode of healing and integration of the body], and in analytic philosophy [with the meaning of the way in which beliefs and thoughts are connected with ("about") objects and events in the world, also known as the symbol-grounding problem].

Intent comprises the endogenous initiation, construction, and direction of behavior into the world. It emerges from brains. Humans, animals, and autonomous robots select their own goals, plan their own tactics, and choose when to begin, modify, and stop sequences of action. Humans at least are subjectively aware of themselves acting, but consciousness is not a necessary property of intention. Unity appears in the combining of input from all sensory modalities into Gestalts, in the coordination of all parts of the body, both musculoskeletal and autonomic, into adaptive, flexible, yet focused movements. Subjectively, unity appears in the awareness of self and emotion, but again this is not intrinsic to or requisite for intention. Wholeness is revealed by the orderly changes in the self and its behavior that constitute the development, maturation, and adaptation of the self, within the constraints of its genes or design principles, and its material, social, and industrial environments. Subjectively, wholeness is revealed in the remembrance of self through a lifetime of change, although the influences of accumulated and integrated experience on current behavior are not dependent on recollection and recognition. In brief, simulation of intentionality should be directed toward replicating the mechanisms by which goal states are constructed, approached, and evaluated, and not toward emulating processes of consciousness, awareness, emotion, et cetera, in machines.

Chaotic dynamics has proved to be extremely difficult to harness in the service of intelligent machines. Most studies that purport to control chaos either find ways to suppress it and replace it with periodic or quasiperiodic fluctuations, or to lock two or more oscillators into synchrony sharing a common aperiodic wave form, often as an optimal means for encryption and secure transmission. The aim in this book is to employ chaotic dynamics as the means for creating novel and endogenous space-time patterns, which must be the means to achieve any significant degree of autonomy in devices that must operate far from human guidance, where in order to function they must make up their courses of action as they go along. We know of no other way to approach a solution to the problem of how to introduce creative processes into machines, other than to simulate the dynamics we have found in animal brains. To be sure, there are major unsolved problems in this approach, chief among them that we know too little about the dynamics of the limbic system. Hence we find it necessary to restrict the development of hardware models to the stage of brain-world interaction that we know best, which is the field of perception. In brief, what are the problems in giving eyes, ears, and a nose to a robot, so that it might learn about its environment in something like the way that even the simpler animals do - by creating hypotheses and testing them through their own actions?

Formation of a world-view by which the device can guide its explorations for the means to reach its goals depends on the integration of the outputs of the several sensory systems, in order to form a multisensory percept known as a gestalt.

The sequential frames deriving from sampling the environment must then be integrated over time and oriented in space.

It is also clear that such devices were first built by the pioneer of intentional robotics, W Grey Walter (1953), and are now in advanced development to meet the challenges of extraterrestrial exploration with intentional robots (Huntsberger, 2001; Huntsberger et al., 2006; Kozma, 2007). The proper path of future management will not be by techniques of passive memory installation or of training and aversive conditioning, but by education, with inculcation of desired values determined by the manufacturers that will govern the choices that must by definition be made by the newly intentional and quasi-autonomous mechanical devices.

This book is a logical continuation and the widening of *Reflexing Interfaces: The Complex Coevolution of Information Technology Ecosystems* (2008). It is providing both a toolbox and mapping for the exploration of new landscapes of the human techno-cultural environment.

Walter J. Freeman
University of California Berkeley, USA
July 2011

xiv

Walter J. Freeman *studied Physics and Mathematics at M.I.T., Electronics in the Navy in World War II, Philosophy at the University of Chicago, Medicine at Yale University, Internal Medicine at Johns Hopkins, and Neuropsychiatry at UCLA. He has taught Brain Science in the University of California at Berkeley since 1959, where he is Professor of the Graduate School. Dr. Freeman received his M.D. cum laude in 1954, and he has more than 20 awards, among which are the Bennett Award from the Society of Biological Psychiatry in 1964, a Guggenheim in 1965, the MERIT Award from NIMH in 1990, and the Pioneer Award from the Neural Networks Council of the IEEE in 1992. He was President of the International Neural Network Society in 1994, is Life Fellow of the IEEE, and Chair, IEEE Oakland-East Bay Section, EMBS, 2006. He has authored over 450 articles and 4 books: "Mass Action in the Nervous System" 1975, "Societies of Brains" 1995, "Neurodynamics" 2000, and "How Brains Make up Their Minds" 2001.*

REFERENCES

Ashby, W. R. (1952). *Design for a brain*. London, UK: Chapman and Hall.

Clark, A. (1996). *Being there: Putting brain, body, and world together again*. Cambridge, MA: MIT Press.

Freeman, W. J. (2000). *Neurodynamics. An exploration of mesoscopic brain dynamics*. London, UK: Sprinter.

Hendriks-Jansen, H. (1996). *Catching ourselves in the act: Situated activity, interactive emergence, evolution, and human thought*. Cambridge, MA: MIT Press.

Huntsberger, T. (2001). Biologically inspired autonomous rover control. *Autonomous Robots, 11*, 341–346.

Huntsberger, T., Tunstel, E., & Kozma, R. (2006). Onboard learning strategies for planetary surface rovers. In Howard, A., & Tunstel, E. (Eds.), *Intelligence for space robotics* (pp. 403–422). San Antonio, TX: TCI Press.

Kozma, R. (2007). Neurodynamics of intentional behavior generation. In Perlovsky, L., & Kozma, R. (Eds.), *Neurodynamics of cognition and consciousness*. Heidelberg, Germany: Springer Series on Understanding Complex Systems.

Merleau-Ponty, M. (1942/1963). *The structure of behavior* (Fischer, A. L., Trans.). Boston, MA: Beacon Press.

Merleau-Ponty, M. (1945/1962). *Phenomenology of perception* (Smith, C., Trans.). New York, NY: Humanities Press.

Walter, W. G. (1953). *The living brain*. New York, NY: W. W. Norton.

Preface

...it's a Looking-glass book, of course! -Lewis Carroll

This book is a logical continuation and the widening of the editors' *Reflexing Interfaces: The Complex Coevolution of Information Technology Ecosystems* (2008).

Since the first production of tools at the beginning of human presence on earth, human evolution is linked to the invention of new tools, usually combined with new environmental adaptations.

The symbiosis of man with tools and environments represents one of the main factors in human evolutionary processes. It is evident how this coupling is based on the *biophysics* of our bodies and the development of the social memory system called *culture*.

In recent times, computing devices, molecular biology, and new media (all members in different ways of the Information Communication Technology set) are redesigning the human embodiment and its ecological niche.

The studies on interfaces, forming a common boundary between adjacent regions, bodies, substances, or phases, seem located at the core of these new developments (Jonassen & Land, 2000). It is there, at the junction, sometimes originating a projection, or an incorporation, that human new embodied identity evolves. New interfaces are actively reflexive and extend in more and more subtle ways the reflexivity naturally embedded in our bodies.

The cognitive neuroscience of the *reflexive function* can be one of the main keys to understand how the emergence of new interfaces yields new ways of extending and change the human presence and consciousness in the world.

The embodied mind emerges and grows (bottom-up) on the basic reflexive function as an order parameter in biological processes. Some authors use these terms synonymously but, the editors prefer to use the different terminology to stress the conceptual and factual difference. Reflexivity will be direct and non-conceptual: it implies an immediate capacity of awareness without effort, or intellectualization. Reflectivity is a meta-cognitive process of higher order, implying secondary self-observation, denotation and conceptualisation (Gladwell, 2005; Siegel, 2007).

In reflexivity the interface is "under your skin," as we might remind that the embryological origin of skin, brain, and mind is the same. The *ectoderm*, our primary interface, is the outermost of the three primary germ layers of an embryo and the source of the epidermis, the nervous system, the eyes and ears: i.e. interfaces. Reflexions happen at a very pre-cognitive stage, before any higher order metacognition might be established. Primary reflexivity is based on massive nonlinear dynamics and it is probably the basic property of living matter, whose ultimate extension is consciousness. Modern advancements in complexity theory from Henry Poincare to Walter J. Freeman and Stuart Kauffman point in this direction and beyond. Fractal mathematics has extended the *isomorphism* capabilities in space and time for our techno-cultural niche (Thelen & Smith, 1994; Orsucci, 1998, 2006; Orsucci & Sala, 2005, Sala, 2006).

The current debate on cyborg identity is, by this perspective, relocated to a more familiar (though maybe not less disconcerting) perspective (Marcuse, 1962; Hayles, 1999; Gray, 2001). Our thesis is that man is a cyborg by default as human intelligence and embodied technology are just as in a Möbius strip: you can change perspective, they might look different, but the surface is the same. Ancient Greek and Hindi tales describing strange half-flesh/half-metal creatures, golems, talking heads, homunculi, and modern cyborgs are just expressions of the same effort, for our intellectual Egos, to understand and adapt to this natural evolutionary line.

ORGANIZATION OF THE BOOK

The book is divided in two sections. The first section, organized in seven chapters, explores theoretical perspectives. The second section, including the last seven chapters, presents a series of examples of applications in different fields.

Chapter 1 is titled "Reflexing Interfaces." Franco Orsucci identifies the reflexing interfaces that can redefine different approaches in different disciplines in the new millennium. The chapter sets the scene for discussions presented by various subsequent authors. In particular, it identifies how the cognitive neuroscience of the reflexive function can be a key to understand how the emergence of new interfaces links new ways of projecting human presence and consciousness in the world. In substance, Information Science and Technology are accumulating ground for new possible evolutionary jumps. Computing devices, molecular biology, and new media are redesigning the human embodiment and its environment. An integrated approach, which should include the latest advancements in neuroscience, can draw the map of new possible human evolutions.

Chapter 2 is "Fractal Geometry as a Bridge Between Realms." Terry Marks-Tarlows describes fractal geometry as a bridge between the imaginary and the real, mind and matter, conscious and the unconscious. Fractals are multidimensional objects with self-similar detail across size and/or time scales. Jung conceived of number as the most primitive archetype of order, serving to link observers with the observed. Whereas Jung focused upon natural numbers as the foundation for order that is already conscious in the observer, the author offers up the fractal geometry as the underpinnings for a dynamic unconscious destined never to become fully conscious. Throughout nature, fractals model the complex, recursively branching structures of self-organizing systems. When they serve at the edges of open systems, fractal boundaries articulate a paradoxical zone that simultaneously separates as it connects. When modeled by Spencer-Brown's mathematical notation, full interpenetration between inside and outside edges translates to a distinction that leads to no distinction. By occupying the infinitely deep "space between" dimensions and levels of existence, fractal boundaries contribute to the notion of intersubjectivity, where self and other become most entwined. They also exemplify reentry dynamics of Varela's autonomous systems, plus Hofstadter's ever-elusive "tangled hierarchy" between brain and mind.

Chapter 3 is titled "Thinking Animals and Thinking Machines in Psychoanalysis and Beyond." Francesco Scalzone and Gemma Zontini examine some interesting "similarities" between computer science and psychoanalysis formulating some hypotheses by bringing closer the statute of connectionism to the energetic model of the psychic apparatus as well as the OOP (object-oriented programming) to the object relations theory. They also describe the relation existing between the functioning of mnemic systems and human temporalities as dynamic structures/processes which might be represented as complementary images of each other. The authors make some remarks on the machine and people theme, the way in which men relate to machines, especially "thinking machines," describing the fantasies they arouse. In order to do this the authors use Tausk's classic (1919/1933) "On the Origin of the 'Influencing Machine' in Schizophrenia," as well as some of Freud's writings.

Chapter 4 is "Dynamical Disequilibrium, Transformation, and the Evolution and Development of Integrated Worldviews." Liane Gabora and Maegan Merrifield begin by outlining a promising, new theoretical framework for the process by which human culture evolves inspired by the views of complexity theorists on the problem of how life began. Elements of culture, like species, evolve over time; that is, they exhibit cumulative change that is adaptive in nature. By studying how biological evolution got started, it is possible to gain insight into not just the specifics of biological evolution, but also general insights into the initiation of any evolutionary process that may be applicable to culture. The authors then explore the implications of this new framework for culture on the transformative processes of individuals. Specifically, they address what this emerging perspective on cultural evolution implies for to go about attaining a *sustainable worldview*; that is, a web of habits, understandings, and ways of approaching situations that is conducive to the development of a sustainable world.

Chapter 5 is "Exploring Structural And Dynamical Properties Microtubules By Means Of Artificial Neural Networks." Rita Pizzi, Silvia Fiorentini, Giuliano Strini, and Massimo Pregnolato describe Microtubules (MTs), cylindrical polymers of the tubulin dimer, which are constituents of all eukaryotic cells cytoskeleton and are involved in key cellular functions and are claimed to be involved as sub-cellular information or quantum information communication systems. The authors evaluate some biophysical properties of MTs by means of specific physical measures of resonance and birefringence in presence of electromagnetic field, on the assumption that when tubulin and MTs show different biophysical behaviours, this should be due to their special structural properties. Actually MTs are the closest biological equivalent to the well-known carbon nanotubes (CNTs), whose interesting biophysical and quantum properties are due to their peculiar microscopic structure. The experimental results show a physical behaviour of MTs in comparison with tubulin. The dynamic simulation of MT and tubulin subjected to electromagnetic field was performed via MD tools. Their level of self-organization was evaluated using artificial neural networks, which resulted to be an effective method to gather the dynamical behaviour of cellular and non-cellular structures and to compare their physical properties.

Chapter 6 is titled "Neurofeedback: Refining the Methodology of Brain-Computer Interface Training." David Vernon and Tammy Dempster explore the use of neurofeedback training as a mechanism for altering human brain functioning and in turn influencing behaviour. The chapter outlines the notion that such training provides a plausible mechanism by which an individual may be able to learn to alter and control specific aspects of his electro-cortical activity. The chapter highlights some of the findings from research, including clinical, peak performance and functional validation studies. In addition, it delineates some important methodological issues that remain to be addressed. It is hoped that outlining these issues will serve a dual purpose. First, it will assist in the understanding of some of the theoretical and methodological limitations that may be holding the field back. Second, it is hoped that such information will stimulate researchers to work towards designing more efficient and effective research protocols and neurofeedback training paradigms.

Chapter 7 is "The Biotic Logic of Quantum Processes and Quantum Computation." Hector Sabelli and Louis H. Kauffman explore how the logic of physical and biological processes may be employed in the design and programming of computers. Quantum processes do not follow Boolean logic; the development of quantum computers requires the formulation of an appropriate logic. While in Boolean logic entities are static, opposites exclude each other, and change is not creative, natural processes involve action, opposition, and creativity. Creativity is detected by changes in pattern, diversification, and novelty. Causally-generated creative patterns (Bios) are found in numerous processes at all levels of organization: recordings of presumed gravitational waves, the distribution of galaxies and quasars, population dynamics, cardiac rhythms, economic data, and music. Quantum processes show biotic patterns. Bios is generated by mathematical equations that involve action, bipolar opposition, and continuous transformation. These features are present in physical and human processes. They are abstracted by lattice, algebras, and topology, the three mother structures of mathematics, which may then be considered as dynamic logic. Quantum processes as described by the Schrödinger's equation involve action, coexisting and interacting opposites, and the causal creation of novelty, diversity, complexity, and low entropy. In addition to 'economic' (not entropy producing) reversible gates (the current goal in the design of quantum gates), irreversible, entropy generating, gates may contribute to quantum computation because quantum measurements as well as creation and decay, are irreversible processes. quantum gates and circuits may provide an opportunity to incorporate the pattern of quantum processes into the logical structure of the computer, and thereby employ rules for reasoning that take into account the pattern of quantum processes as well as that of many other natural processes.

The second section is organized in seven chapters.

Chapter 8 is titled "Networks: A Sketchy Portrait of an Emergent Paradigm." Alessandro Giuliani presents the notion of 'network,' which is more and more widespread in all the fields of human investigation, from physics to sociology. Network based approaches gave very brilliant results in fields like biochemistry where the consideration of the whole set of metabolic reactions of an organism allowed us to understand some very important properties of the organisms that cannot be appreciated by the simple enumeration of the single biochemical reactions. Nevertheless, appreciation networks are modelling tools and not real entities, which could be detrimental to the exploitation of the full potential of this paradigm. Some applications of network based modelling are presented so to introduce the basic terminology of the emergent 'network paradigm,' to highlight strengths and limitations of the method, and to put sketch the strong relation linking network based approach to other modelling tools.

Chapter 9 is "Complexity, Emergence, and Molecular Diversity via Information Theory." Francisco Torrens and Gloria Castellano present the *complexity* and its definition. The definition here is related to *Kolmogorov complexity* and *Shannon entropy* measures. However, the price is to introduce context dependence into the definition of complexity. Such context dependence is an inherent property of complexity. Scientists are uncomfortable with such context dependence that smacks of subjectivity, which is the reason why little agreement is found on the meaning of the terms. In an article published in *Molecules*, Lin presented a novel approach for assessing molecular diversity based on Shannon information theory. A set of compounds is viewed as a static collection of microstates that can register information about their environment. The method is characterized by a strong tendency to oversample remote areas of the feature space and produce unbalanced designs. This report demonstrates the limitation with some simple examples and provides a rationale for the failure to produce results that are consistent.

Chapter 10 is titled "Recurrence Indicators for the Estimation of Characteristic Size and Frequency of Spatial Patterns." Chiara Mocenni and Angelo Facchini propose a method for the estimation of the characteristic size and frequency of the typical structure in systems showing two dimensional spatial patterns. In particular, the authors use several indicators caught from the nonlinear framework for identifying the small and large scales of the systems. The indicators are applied to the images corresponding to the instantaneous realization of the system. The method assumes that it is possible to capture the main system's properties from the distribution of the recurring patterns in the image and does not require the knowledge of the dynamical system generating the patterns neither the application of any image segmentation method

Chapter 11 is: "The Residence Time of the Water in Lake MAGGIORE: Through an Eulerian-Lagrangian Approach." Leonardo Castellano, Nicoletta Sala, Angelo Rolla, and Walter Ambrosetti describe a study designed to evaluate the spectrum of the residence time of the water at different depths of a deep lake, examining the mechanisms governing the seasonal cycle of thermal stratification and destratification, with the ultimate aim of assessing the actual exchange time of the lake water. The study was performed on Lake Maggiore (depth 370m) using a multidimensional mathematical model and computer codes for the heat and mass transfer in very large natural water bodies. A 3D Eulerian time-dependent CFD (Computational Fluid Dynamics) code was applied under real conditions, taking into account the effects of the monthly mean values of the mass flow rates and temperatures of all the tributaries, mass flow rate of the Ticino effluent, and meteorological, hydrological, and limnological parameters available from the rich data-base of the CNR-ISE (Verbania Pallanza, Italy).

Chapter 12 is titled "Possibility of Fractal Aesthetics." Ljubiša M. Kocić considers the fast development of computer networking contributes to the global spreading and popularizing of the notion of fractals and complex patterns in their use in computer-aided design and computer art. He looks for answers to the following questions: "How do we perceive fractals?" "Are fractals predominantly man-made or natural objects?" "How do fractals relate to the overall visual art experience of mankind?" "What are the main problems in using fractals in arts?" "What are the experiences from the visual art-history?" "Do Nature and artists use the same algorithm?" "What fractal experts can do to help artists?"

Chapter 13 is "Parametric Generator for Architectural and Urban 3D Objects." Renato Saleri Lunazzi presents a research project, developed by Map-Aria research team, which consists in applying automatic generative methods in design processes. The Map-Aria research team of the School of Architecture of Lyon develops modeling assistants within the process of architectural conception. They run specific heuristics dramatically reducing time-consuming tasks of wide scale architectural and urban modeling by the implementation of bio-mimetic and/or parametric generative processes. Prior experiments implemented rule-based generative grammars with interesting results. The author describes a specific tool able to model the global structure of architectural objects through a morphological and semantic description of its finite elements. This discrete conceptual model - still in study - was refined during the geometric modeling of the "Vieux Lyon" district, containing a high level of morpho-stylistic disparity. Future developments should allow for increasing the genericity of its descriptive efficiency, permitting even more sparse morphological and\or stylistic varieties. Its general purpose doesn't consist in creating a "universal modeler," but to offer a simple tool able to quickly describe a majority of standard architectural objects compliant with some standard parametric definition rules.

Chapter 14 is "Fractals, Computer Science, and Beyond." Nicoletta Sala describes the fractal geometry as a recent "tool," which can help us to understand the Nature and its shapes (e.g., clouds, trees, shells, river basins, mountains), exceeding the limits imposed by Euclidean geometry. The author presents some applications of fractals and their properties in computer science, e.g. for image compression, in landscape modelling, in computer networks and in the creation of virtual worlds based on the Web technologies.

The chapter highlights that the self-similarity property that characterizes some fractal objects is a unifying concept. In fact, it is an attribute of many laws of nature and it is present in different fields of computer science, for example in Fractional Brownian motion, which has been observed for controlling traffic in computer networks (LANs, MANs, WANs, and the Internet), and in the creation of virtual worlds using procedures based iterative fractal algorithms.

CONCLUSION

In the Kubrick's movie *2001: A Space Odyssey* (1968), a savannah-dwelling ape has a eureka-like flash of inspiration in realizing the awesome power of the bone tool in his hands. He tosses it skyward, where it morphs into a space station at the dawn of this millennium (Ambrose, 2001).

This book, logical continuation and the widening of *Reflexing Interfaces: The Complex Coevolution of Information Technology Ecosystems* (2008), is a multifaceted mirror on how human evolution has had a constant psychobiological link with the development of new tools and environmental changes. Discoveries and technological innovations in Information & Communication Science and Technology (ICST) are paving the ground for new evolutionary steps. Computer devices could play a central role in this evolution, as Giovanni Degli Antoni (1988) affirms: "Computers become mirrors in which the real lives his new reality beyond space and the time."

In the book: *Through the Looking-Glass* (1872), sequel of *Alice's Adventures in Wonderland* (1871), Lewis Carroll described many mirror experiences lived by Alice. Alice's adventures beyond the mirror could be considered a metaphor for ICST realities. If Alice was a modern child, certainly her mirror could be a computer screen. She would be used to experience how actions in a real world are transformed in other actions in the virtual world, and vice versa. These transformations follow interesting mathematical and physical processes which Lewis Carroll would certainly be interested into: Degli Antoni named these new processes as *bi-causality* (Pizzi, 1989).

The isomorphism between bio-cognitive structures and the ICST niche we inhabit is progressively blurring boundaries between *res cogitans* and *res extensa*. Our new insights in neuro-cognition and the multiple reflexions implied in our sensory-perceptive processes are leading to new interfaces and new media. Reflexing interfaces are extensions of human embodiment just as the bone tool tossed skyward by a savannah-dwelling ape. Time flows, always different yet similar.

As Francisco Varela distilled aphoristically: "Readiness-for-action is a micro-identity and its corresponding level a micro-world: we embody streams of recurrent micro-world transitions" (1991).

We are flowing in and we are the flow of micro and macro worlds, nested and intermingled. The stream of time flows here and there, generating multiple cascades, reflexing in billions of infinitesimal mirrors, radiating in what we use to call consciousness.

REFERENCES

Ambrose, S. H. (2001). Paleolithic technology and human evolution . *Science, 291,* 1748–1753.

Degli Antoni, G. (1988). Il computer, il reale, l'artificiale. *Note di Software, 41.*

Gladwell, M. (2005). *Blink: The power of thinking without thinking.* Little, Brown.

Gray, C. H. (2002). *Cyborg citizen: Politics in the posthuman age*. London, UK: Routledge.

Hayles, N. K. (1999). *How we became posthuman: Virtual bodies in cybernetics, literature, and informatics*. Chicago, IL: University of Chicago Press.

Jonassen, D. H., & Land, S. M. (2000). *Theoretical foundations of learning environments*. Mahwah, NJ: Lawrence Erlbaum Associates Inc.

Kubrick, S. (1968). *2001: A space odyssey*. Hollywood, CA: Warner Brothers.

Marcuse, H. (1962). *Eros and civilization: A philosophical inquiry into Freud*. New York, NY: Vintage Books.

Orsucci, F. (Ed.). (1998). *The complex matters of the mind*. Singapore: World Scientific.

Orsucci, F., & Sala, N. (2005). Virtual reality, telemedicine and beyond . In Carbonara, D. (Ed.), *Technology literacy applications in learning environments* (pp. 349–357). Hershey, PA: Idea Group.

Orsucci, F. (2006). The paradigm of complexity in clinical neuro-cognitive science. *The Neuroscientist, 12*(4), 1–10.

Pizzi, R. (1989). Through the looking glass: Una metafora della realtà artificiale. *Verso la comunicazione elettronica* (pp. 7-16), Milano, Italy: Sole 24 HTE (High Tech and Education).

Sala, N. (2006). Complexity, fractals, nature and industrial design: Some connections . In Novak, M. M. (Ed.), *Complexus Mundi: Emergent pattern in nature* (pp. 171–180). Singapore: World Scientific.

Siegel, D. J. (2007). *The mindful brain: Reflection and attunement in the cultivation of well-being*. New York, NY: Norton.

Tausk, V. (1919). Uber die Entstehung des Beeinflussungsapparates. *Inter.Zeitsch.Psychoan, 5*.

Thelen, E., & Smith, L. B. (1994). *A dynamic systems approach to the development of cognition and action*. Cambridge, MA: MIT Press.

Varela, F. J., Thompson, E., & Rosch, E. (1991). *The embodied mind: Cognitive science and human experience*. Cambridge, MA: MIT Press.

Acknowledgment

The editors would like to acknowledge the contributions of all people involved in the project, collation, and review process, without whose support the book could not have been satisfactorily completed.

Our gratitude goes to all the authors, whose creativity added multiple reflexing perspectives to this looking-glass book. We wish to thank all of the authors for their insights and excellent contributions to this book. We also want to thank all of the people who assisted us in the reviewing process, and for their suggestions for improving our book quality: Mauro Annunziato (Enea - Ente Nazionale Energia Elettrica, Rome, Italy), Gabriele Cappellato (Università della Svizzera Italiana, USI, Mendrisio, Switzerland), Giovanni Degli Antoni (Università degli Studi di Milano, Milan, Italy), Walter J. Freeman (University of California at Berkeley, Berkeley, USA), Mario Fulcheri (Università degli Studi di Chieti, Chieti, Italy), Mario Reda (Università degli Studi di Siena, Siena, Italy), Marco Tomassini (University of Lausanne, Lausanne, Switzerland),

Special thanks also go to all the staff at IGI Global, whose contributions throughout the whole process from inception of the initial idea to final publication have been invaluable.

Finally, we want to thank our families for their love and support throughout this project.

Franco Orsucci
University College London, UK & Institute for Complexity Studies, Italy

Nicoletta Sala
University of Lugano, Switzerland

Section 1
Living Systems and Information Technology

Chapter 1
Reflexing Interfaces

Franco Orsucci
University College London, UK & Institute for Complexity Studies, Italy

ABSTRACT

Since the first production of tools at the beginning of human presence on earth, evolutionary jumps mark human development. Sometimes, these punctuations were triggered by inventions of new tools, combined with new environmental adaptations. Affordances, as specialized forms of symbiotic embodiment with tools and environments, represent one of the main factors for human evolutionary processes. The cognitive neuroscience of the reflexive function can be one of the main keys to understand how the emergence of new interfaces yields new ways of projecting the human presence and consciousness in the world.

1. PRELUDE

In the movie 2001: A Space Odyssey (Ambrose 2001), a savannah-dwelling ape has a eureka-like flash of inspiration in realizing the awesome power of the bone tool in his hands. He tosses it skyward, where it morphs into a space station at the dawn of this millennium.

Since the first production of tools at the beginning of human presence on earth, evolutionary jumps mark human development. Sometimes these punctuations were triggered by inventions of new tools, combined with new environmental adaptations.

Affordances, as specialized forms of symbiotic embodiment with tools and environments, represent one of the main factors for human evolutionary processes.

The cognitive neuroscience of the reflexive function can be one of the main keys to understand how the emergence of new interfaces yields new ways of projecting the human presence and consciousness in the world.

In recent times, Information Science and Technology are accumulating ground for new possible evolutionary jumps. Computing devices, molecular biology, and new media (all members in different ways of the ICT set) are redesigning the human embodiment and its environment. An integrated approach of ICT and neuroscience can design a map for new possible human evolutions.

DOI: 10.4018/978-1-4666-2077-3.ch001

2. SETTING

Stone tool technology, robust australopithecines, and the genus Homo appeared almost simultaneously 2.5 Ma. Once this adaptive threshold was crossed, technological evolution continued to be associated with increased brain size, population size, and geographical range. Traits of behaviour, economy, mental capacities, neurological functions, the origin of grammatical language, and socio-symbolic systems have been inferred from the archaeological record of Palaeolithic technology (Ambrose 2001).

Homo Habilis is, obviously, considered the first toolmaker. The contiguity in the brain of Broca's area, involved in oro-facial fine motor control and language, to the area for precise hand motor control might be more than casual. The hand of *Homo Habilis* resembles that of modern humans. Its brain was significantly larger (600 to 800 cm3) than that of earlier and contemporary australopithecines and extant African apes (450 to 500 cm3), and its teeth were relatively small for its body size, suggesting a relation between tool use, quality of diet, and intelligence.

The production of tools and artefacts is linked to the development of language, culture and cognitive functions. This happened as tools and artefacts were, just as other socio-linguistic processes, *mediating and reflexing interfaces* in environmental and social interactions.

We need to know more about the ways in which speaking, tool-using, and sociality are interwoven into the texture of everyday life in contemporary human groups.

The birth of *technique* was incubated in the complex system of material resources, tools, operational sequences and skills, verbal and nonverbal knowledge, and specific modes of work coordination that come into play in the fabrication of material artefacts. It is a process, a complex *interplay* of *reflexivity* between sensory-motor skills, symbolic cognition, tools, artefacts and environment.

James J. Gibson (1979), in this context, originally proposed the concept of *affordance* to refer to "all action possibilities" latent in a specific environment, objectively measurable, and independent of the individual's ability to recognize those possibilities. Further, those action possibilities are dependent on the physical capabilities of the agent. For instance, a set of steps with risers four feet high does not afford the act of climbing, if the actor is a crawling infant. Therefore, we should measure affordances along with the relevant actors.

Donald Norman (1988) introduced the term affordance in Human Machine Interaction, which made it a very popular term in the Interaction Design field. Later (Norman 1999) he clarified he was actually referring to a perceived affordance, as opposed to an objective affordance. This new definition clarified that affordances are determined not only by the physical capabilities of the agent, but also by the individual and social knowledge embedded in objects and interactions of everyday life.

For example, if an agent steps into a room with a chair and a book, Gibson's definition of affordance allows a possibility that the agent may look at the chair and sit on the book, as this is objectively possible. Norman's definition of perceived affordance captures the likelihood that the actor will sit on the chair and look at the book, because of the embodiment and social knowledge embedded as affordance in these objects.

As the figure above clearly presents, affordances are rooted in motor schemes and neuro-cognitive dynamics.

3. FOCUS

The significance of evolutionary theory to the human sciences cannot be fully appreciated without a better understanding of how phenotypes in general, and human beings in particular, modify significant sources of selection in their environments, thereby

Figure 1. Neuro-cognitive dynamics in affordance, for example grasping a mug (Arbib 2002)

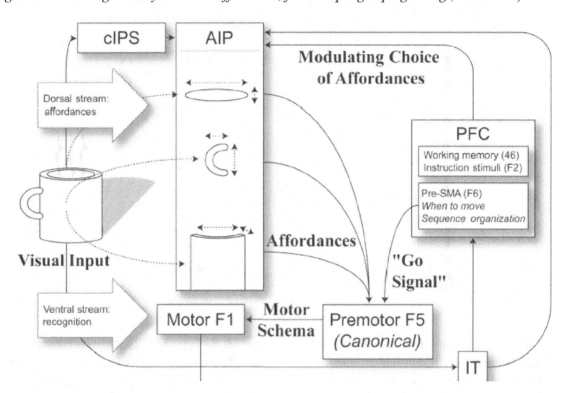

co-directing subsequent biological evolution. Empirical data and theoretical arguments suggest that human techno-cultural activities have influenced human genetic evolution by modifying sources of natural selection and altering genotype frequencies in some human populations (Bodmer & Cavalli-Sforza 1976). Techno-cultural traits, such as the use of tools, weapons, fire, cooking, symbols, language, and trade, may have also played important roles in driving hominid evolution in general and the evolution of the human brain in particular (Aiello & Wheeler 1995). It is more than likely that some cultural and scientific practices in contemporary human societies are still affecting human genetic evolution.

Modern molecular biologists do interfere with genes directly on the basis of their acquired scientific experiences, though this practice might be too recent to have already had an enduring impact on human genetic evolution. In any case, it already brings a new reflexive loop in our development.

Other evolutionary biologists maintain that culture frequently does affect the evolutionary

process, and some have begun to develop mathematical and conceptual models of gene-culture coevolution that involve descriptions not only of how human genetic evolution influences culture but also of how human culture can drive, or co-direct, some genetic changes in human populations (Feldman & Laland 1996). These models include culturally biased non-random mating systems, the treatment of human sociocultural or linguistic environments as sources of natural selection (Aoki & Feldman 1987), and the impact of different cultural activities on the transmission of certain diseases (Durham 1991). The common element among these cases is that *cultural processes change the human selective environment and thereby affect which genotypes survive and reproduce.*

Culture works on the basis of various kinds of transmission systems (Boyd & Richerson 1985), which collectively provide humans with a second, non-genetic "knowledge-carrying" inheritance system.

Niche construction from all ontogenetic processes modifies human selective environments,

Figure 2. Evolutionary dynamics involving genes and techno-culture (Laland et al. 2000)

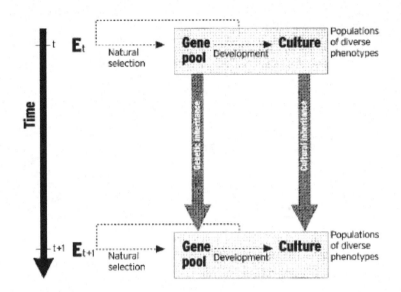

generating a legacy of modified natural selection pressures that are bequeathed by human ancestors to their descendants. This figure best captures the causal logic underlying the relationship between biological evolution and cultural change. (Laland et al. 2000).

If the techno-cultural inheritance of an environment-modifying human activity persists for enough generations to produce a stable selective pressure, it will be able to co-direct human genetic evolution.

For example, the culturally inherited traditions of pastoralism provide a case in point. Apparently, the persistent domestication of cattle, sheep etc., and the associated dairying activities, did alter the selective environments of some human populations for sufficient generations to select for genes that today confer greater adult lactose tolerance (Durham 1991).

Although other species of animals have their "proto-cultures" (Galef 1988), it has generally been assumed that Homo sapiens is the only extant species with a techno-cultural transmission stable enough to co-direct genetic evolution

(Boyd & Richerson 1985). We may conclude that our techno-culture is part of our *ecological niche*.

Building on ideas initially developed by Lewontin (1983), Laland has previously proposed that biological evolution depends not only on natural selection and genetic inheritance but also on *niche construction* (Laland et al. 1996a). Niche construction refers to the activities, choices, and metabolic processes of organisms, through which they define, choose, modify, and partly create their own niches. It consists of the same processes that Jones et al. (1997) call "*ecosystem engineering.*"

For example, to varying degrees, organisms choose their own habitats, mates, and resources and construct important components of their local environments such as nests, holes, burrows, paths, webs, dams, and chemical environments. Many organisms also partly destroy their habitats, through stripping them of valuable resources or building up detritus, processes we refer to as negative niche construction.

Organisms may niche construct in ways that counteract natural selection, for example, by digging a burrow or migrating to avoid the cold, or they may niche construct in ways that

Table 1. Techno-cultural niche construction (Laland et al. 2000)

Table 1. Niche construction resulting from population genetic processes, information-acquiring ontogenetic processes, and cultural processes, can influence both biological evolution and cultural change (the point is illustrated by a single example in each cell)

Source of niche construction	Feedback to biological evolution	Feedback to cultural change
Population genetic processes	Web spiders marking web or building dummy spiders (Edmunds 1974)	Sex differences in human mating behaviour (Barkow et al. 1992; Daly & Wilson 1983)
Information acquiring ontogenetic processes	Woodpecker finch, by learning to grub with a tool, alleviates selection for a woodpecker's bill (Alcock 1972; Grant 1986)	Learning and experience influence the adoption of cultural traits (Durham 1991)
Cultural processes	Dairy farming selects for lactose tolerance (Feldman & Cavalli-Sforza 1989)	Invention of writing leads to other innovations such as printing, libraries, e-mail

introduce novel selection pressures, for example, by exploiting a new food resource, which might subsequently select for a new digestive enzyme. In every case, however, niche construction modifies one or more sources of natural selection in a population's environment.

One theoretical construct that captures some, but not all, of the consequences of niche construction is Dawkins's (1982) *extended phenotype*. Dawkins argues that genes can express themselves outside the bodies of the organisms that carry them. For example, the beaver's dam is an extended phenotypic effect of beaver genes. Like any other aspect of the phenotype, extended phenotypes play an evolutionary role by influencing the chances that the genes responsible for the extended phenotypic trait will be passed on to the next generation. Dawkins emphasises this single aspect of the evolutionary feedback from niche construction.

However, the beaver's dam sets up a host of selection pressures, which feed back to act not only on the genes responsible for the extended phenotype, but also on other genes that may influence the expression of other traits in beavers, such as the teeth, tail, feeding behaviour, susceptibility to predation or disease, social system, and many other aspects of their phenotypes. It may also affect many future generations of beavers that may "inherit" the dam, its lodge, and the altered river or stream, as well as many other species of organisms that now have to live in a world with a lake in it.

An example of contemporary environmental niches in IT can be obviously found in the computer mouse and its related iconic desktop interface. An evolution of the creation of virtual spaces which can change the way we perceive and interact with other dimensions of our realities is presented in new commercial and experimental interfaces. It is clear that every human interface tends to use biomechanical and physiological properties of the human body in order to reach a possible "perfect symbiosis" between man and machine. Wearable computing is one of the most meaningful buzzwords in this direction.

The result is the possibility of a real time interaction with a real or a conceptual object within a learning environment based on augmented reality adding new dimensions to our usual everyday reality and, at the same time, giving a new reality to scientific "mind objects".

Similar, and already commercial, pointing devices are the Wii Remotes for videogames, controllers as inviting as sophisticated, fusing the familiarity of a remote control with motion or neurophysiologic sensing technology.

Other experimental devices or prototypes might be interesting examples: eye movements, and brain waves and other bio-signals are captured

Figure 3. Interacting with a physico-mathematical structure in augmented reality, the Roessler attractor (courtesy of Studierstübe)

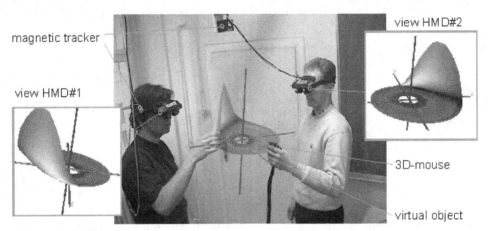

and amplified to translate bio-signals into useful logic commands and neural-signal interpretation (such as emotions).

4. MIRRORS

In "Language within our grasp", Rizzolatti and Arbib (1998) showed that the mirror system in monkey is the homologue of Broca's area, a crucial speech area in humans, and argued that this observation provides a neurobiological "missing link" for the long-argued hypothesis that primitive forms of communication based on manual gesture preceded speech in the evolution of language. "Language readiness evolved as a multimodal manual/facial/vocal system with proto-sign (manual-based protolanguage) providing the scaffolding for proto-speech (vocal-based protolanguage). There was the "neural critical mass" to trigger the emergence of language (Arbib 2002 and 2005) via the mirroring between neurons at the dendrite and axon level. The neurodynamic result of this critical mass was the possibility to reach the threshold, in terms of dynamical systems number of degrees of freedom necessary for effective psychodynamics (Freeman 1975; Orsucci 1998).

The "*Mirror System Hypothesis*" states that the matching of neural code for execution and observation of hand movements in the monkey is present in the common ancestor of monkey and human. It is the precursor of the crucial language property of parity, namely that an utterance usually carries similar meaning for speaker and hearer. *Imitation* plays a crucial role in human language acquisition and performance: brain mechanisms supporting imitation were crucial to the emergence of *Homo Sapiens*.

Rizzolatti & Arbib (1998) hypothesize several stages of this evolution:

a.   Grasping
b.   A mirror system for grasping (i.e., a system that matches observation and execution),
c.   A simple imitation system for grasping,
d.   A complex imitation system for grasping,
e.   A manual-based communication system,
f.   Speech, characterized as being the open-ended production and perception of sequences of vocal gestures, without implying that these sequences constitute a language
g.   Verbal language.

A mirror system for grasping in the monkey has been found in area F5 of premotor cortex,

Figure 4. Neurodynamics of mirror systems during an observed action (Rizzolatti & Arbib 1998)

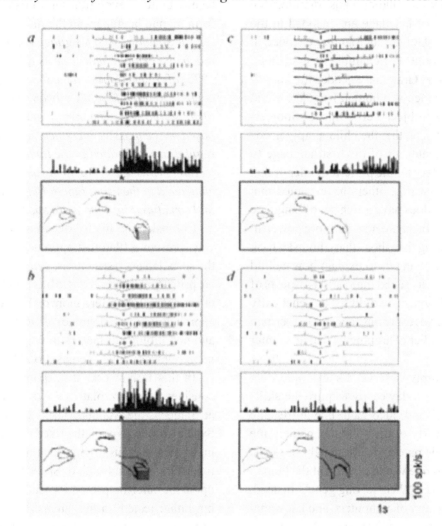

while data have been found consistent with the notion of a mirror system for grasping in humans in Broca's area, which is homologous to monkey F5 but in humans is most often thought of as a speech area. Following their findings and hypothesis, *language evolved from a basic mechanism not originally related to communication: the mirror system with its capacity to generate and recognize a set of actions.*

Anyway, there are some difficult questions posed by the interaction between new media and the mirror system. The different kinds of reality experience produced by new media might activate,

via direct perception, presentations or action-like brain effects, enduring plasticity effects. We are not referring just to the banal imitation induction we might experience after an immersive movie, but also to the longer lasting moulding of the brain by the mirroring induced by all the most various contents provided by new media. It is a problem older generations never encountered, and the spreading of diagnoses such as Attention Deficit Hyperactivity Disorder can be related to this (as we will se later on).

The linguist Noam Chomsky (e.g., 1975) has argued that since children acquire language rapidly despite the "poverty of the stimulus" therefore the basic structures of language are encoded in the brain, forming a Universal Grammar encoded in the human genome. For example, it is claimed that the Universal Grammar encodes the knowledge that a sentence in a human language could be ordered as Subject-Verb-Object, Subject-Object-Verb, etc., so that the child simply needs to hear a few sentences of his first language to "set the parameter" for the preferred order of that language. Against this, others have argued that in fact the child does have a rich set of language stimuli, and that there are now far more powerful models of learning than those that Chomsky took into account, allowing us to explain how a child might learn from its social interactions aspects of syntax which Chomsky would see as genetically pre-specified. The reader may consult Lieberman (1991) for a number of arguments which counter Chomsky's view.

Here we simply observe, for example, that many youngsters today easily acquire the skills of "Web surfing" and video-game playing despite a complete poverty of the stimulus, namely the inability of their parents to master these skills. We trust that no one would claim that the human genome contains a "Web-surfing gene"! Instead, we know the history of computers, and know that technology has advanced over the last 55 years to take us from an interface based on binary coding to a mouse-and-graphics interface so well adapted to human sensorimotor capabilities that a child can master it.

We reject Chomsky's view that many of the basic alternatives of grammatical structure of the world's current languages are already encoded in the human genome, so that the child's experience merely "sets parameters" to choose among pre-packaged alternative grammatical structures. The experimental evidence of this hypothesis, years after it was proposed, it is still weak. The different view, which I support, holds that the brain of the first Homo sapiens was "language-ready" but that it required many millennia of invention and

techno-cultural evolution for human societies to form human languages in the modern sense.

The structure of a language-ready brain had reached a critical neural mass action (Freeman 1975) *of connections and feedback redundancies capable to provide reflexivity and the emergence of consciousness. The mirror neurons finding is based on the massive increment of feedbacks and regulations embedded in the human brain architecture. In this sense, mirroring and reflexivity are embedded in the usual functioning of all neurons and structured in some more specialised ones.*

Chomsky and his followers instead, in some way, present a Platonist approach claiming that the so called deep structures, symbols and genes, are primary and antecedent to bio-psycho-physical experiences. We prefer a more realistic complexity approach which recognizes different biological and non biological factors in language development (Orsucci 2002; Tomasello 2003).

In this framework, it is quite interesting to consider how Rizzolatti & Arbib propose that at Stage 5, the Manual-Based Communication System, broke through the fixed repertoire of primate vocalizations to yield a combinatorial open repertoire, so that Stage 6, Speech, did not build upon the ancient primate vocalization system, but rather rested on the "invasion" of the vocal apparatus by collaterals from the communication system based on F5/Broca's area. In discussing the transition to Homo sapiens, they stress that our predecessors must have had a relatively flexible, open repertoire of vocalizations but this does not mean that they, or the first humans, had language.

They hold that human language (as well as some dyadic forms of primate communication) evolved from a basic mechanism that was not originally related to communication: the capacity to recognize actions.

Psychoanalytical studies highlight the important perspective of mirroring in emotional development. The reflexive function is central also in the definition of identity and relations. Freud (1920) had focused on a children play, after becoming famous as the *fort-da*, in which a mirror can be used by the child to represent the disappearance of the caregiver. Lacan (1937) proposed a specific stage in child development, called *le stade du miroir*, in which the child reaches recognition of her image in a mirror. This stage, linked to a crucial step in the integration of the Central Nervous System, is evident also in some primates and was considered crucial in the establishment of a self conscious identity. Gaddini (1969) explored imitation as a primary form of identification. Winnicott (1987) extended this notion to reflexive responsiveness a child can receive from the caregiver, the family and the extended social environment. Fonagy & Target (1997) state that reflective function is the developmental acquisition that permits the child to respond not only to other people's behavior, but to his conception of their beliefs, feelings, hopes, pretense, plans, and so on. "Reflective function or mentalization enables children to "read" people's minds". Paulina Kernberg (2006) recalls how the mirror function of the mother is expanded to the idea of attunement between mother and child (Stern 1983), resonating affectively, visually, vocally and by movement and touch.

5. EVOLUTION

Judging from the anatomical and cultural remains left by hominids and early humans, the most important evolutionary steps were concentrated into a few transition periods when the process of change was greatly accelerated, and these major transitions introduced fundamentally new capacities.

Merlin Donald (1997), within the same research line, proposes some evolutionary punctuation in the development of the human embodied mind.

The first transition is mimetic skill and auto cueing. The rationale for the first transition is based on several premises: (a) the first truly human cognitive breakthrough was a revolution in motor skill - mimetic skill - which enabled hominids to use the whole body as a representational device; (b)

this mimetic adaptation had two critical features: it was a multimodal modelling system, and it had a self-triggered rehearsal loop (that is, it could voluntarily access and retrieve its own outputs); (c) the sociocultural implications of mimetic skill are considerable, and could explain the documented achievements of Homo erectus; (d) in modern humans, mimetic skill in its broadest definition is dissociable from language-based skills, and retains its own realm of cultural usefulness; and (e) the mimetic motor adaptation set the stage for the later evolution of language.

Mimesis can be just an emergent property of the mass action in the nervous system as the mirror function is a specialization of the arousal and feedback neural processes. The embodiment of mind processes becomes, in this way, a neurobiological necessity.

As the whole body becomes a potential tool for expression, a variety of new possibilities enter the social arena: complex games, extended competition, pedagogy through directed imitation (with a concomitant differentiation of social roles), a subtler and more complex array of facial and vocal expressions, and public action-metaphor, such as intentional group displays of aggression, solidarity, joy, fear, and sorrow. *The emergence of religious practice could be also considered, in its animistic beginnings, as an inclusive extension of mimetic functions to the living and non-living environment.*

The second transition is the lexical invention. The rationale for the second transition is briefly as follows: (a) since no linguistic environment yet existed, a move towards language would have depended primarily on developing a capacity for lexical invention; (b) phonological evolution was accelerated by the emergence of this general capacity for lexical invention, and included a whole complex of special neuronal and anatomical modifications for speech; (c) the language system evolved as an extension of lexical skill, and gradually extended to the labelling of relationships between words, and also to the imposition of more and more complex meta-linguistic skills that govern the uses of words; and (d) the natural collective product of language was narrative thought, (essentially, storytelling) which evolved for specific social purposes, and serves essentially similar purposes in modern society; (e) further advanced product are technical jargons and mathematical notations. These new representational acts, speech and mimesis, both are performed covertly as well as overtly.

Covert speech has been called inner speech or inner dialogue to stress how it is equivalent to the activation of the central aspects of articulation, without actual motor execution. The mental operation we call "imagination" can similarly be seen as mimesis without motor execution of imagined acts and situations. The control of mimetic imagination (probably even of visual generative imagery, which is facilitated by imagined self-movement) presumably lies in a special form of kinematical imagery. Auto-retrievability is just as crucial for covert imaginative or linguistic thought as it is for the overt or acted-out equivalent. Thus, given a lexicon, the human mind became able to self-trigger recall from memory in two ways: by means of mimetic imagination, and by the use of word-symbols, either of which could be overt or covert.

Third transition is grammar and other meta-linguistic skills. According to the "competition" model proposed by Bates & MacWhinney (1987), the whole perisylvian region of the left hemisphere is diffusely dedicated to language, function words and grammatical rules being stored in the same tissue as other kinds and aspects of lexical entries. However, we readily admit that this issue, like many others in this field, is still not conclusively resolved; there is electrophysiological evidence that function words—those most relevant to grammar—might have a different cerebral representation from open-class words (Neville, 1992).

6. SYNCHRONIZATIONS

In the classical sense, the word *synchronization* (literally, from ancient Greek, "sharing time") means: "adjustment or entrainment of frequencies of periodic oscillators due to a weak interaction". Synchronization is a basic nonlinear phenomenon in physics, discovered in interactions between pendulums at the beginning of the modern age of science. More recently Maturana & Varela (1980), had suggested that sync is a form of structural coupling, a process which occurs when two structurally plastic systems repeatedly perturb one another's structure in a non-destructive way over a period of time. This leads to the development of structural 'fit' between systems. There is an intimate relationship between this process and the emergence of 'appropriate' behaviour from the interplay between interacting systems, because the structure of a system determines its responses to perturbing environmental events. Maturana (2002) stressed this dynamical approach in semiotic terms within a co-evolutionary perspective: "Language is a manner of living together in a flow of coordination of coordinations of consensual behaviours or doings that arises in a history of living in the collaboration of doing things together".

This dynamical systems' approach leads to control and synchronization in chaotic or complex systems. Pecora & Carroll (1990) and Ott, Grebogi & Yorke (1990) opened a new and reliable way to contemporary research on control and synchronization of complex systems.

We have been investigating sync during natural conversations, finding that it is a quite complex phenomenon happening at the same time at the nonverbal, phonetic, syntactic and semantic levels (Orsucci 1999; 2004; 2006). The statistical tool we consider most suitable for this kind of study is Recurrence Quntification Analysis (Eckman et al. 1987; Webber & Zbilut 1994; Marwan 2003) Co-ordination between conversation partners occurs at multiple levels, including choice of syntactic structure (Branigan et al. 2000). A number of outstanding questions concerning the origin of this coordination require novel analytic techniques.

Our research can be considered complimentary with a study by Shockley et al (2003), in which interpersonal coordination during conversation was based on recurrence strategies, to evaluate the shared activity between two postural time series in a reconstructed phase space.

In a study on speech and rhythmic behaviour Port et al. (1999) found that animals and humans exhibit many kinds of behaviour where frequencies of gestures are related by small integer ratios (like 1:1, 2:1 or 3:1). Many properties like these are found in speech, as an embodied activity considered as an oscillator prone to possible synchronizations.

Our findings in the synchronization of conversation dynamics can be relevant for the general issue of structural coupling of psychobiological organizations. Implications are related with psycho-chrono-biology research and the clinical field. Data on synchronization suggest that this dynamic behaviour can be evident also in semiotic and cognitive dynamics, besides the well established research on biological oscillators. For example, Dale & Spivey (2006) used this method to explore lexical and syntactic coordination between children and caregivers in conversation.

Results indicate that children and caregivers coordinate sequences of syntactic classes, and that this coordination diminishes over development. Similar studies highlight synchronization of eye movements in conversations (Richardson & Dale 2005).

Synchronization is a crucial area of studies in order to bridge biophysics, neuroscience and information technologies. Sharing time, in different timeframes, is critical for neurodynamics, consciousness and cooperation with humans and non-humans (machines included).

We might cite, for example, applications from several research groups some key areas of the current research in information science and technology in which synchronization is so important, though it might be not fully recognised:

a.   **Robotic Life:** How to build cooperative machines that work and learn in partnership with people

b.   **Object-Based Media:** How to create communication systems gaining an understanding of the content they carry and use it to make richer connections among users.

c.   **Sociable Media:** How to create better online environments and interfaces for human communication.

Figure 5. Synchronization during a natural conversation (Orsucci et al 2004)

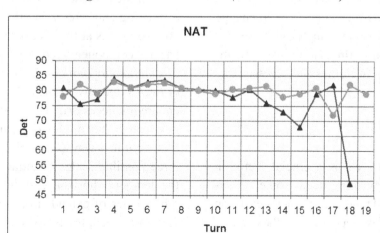

d.   **Biomechatronics:** How technology can be used to enhance human physical capability.
e.   **Tangible Media:** How to design seamless interfaces among humans, digital information, and the physical environment.
f.   **Software Agents:** How software can act as an assistant to the user rather than a tool, by learning from interaction and by proactively anticipating the user's needs.
g.   **Ambient Intelligence:** How ubiquitous, personalized interfaces can be responsive to our interests and expand our minds.
h.   **Society of Mind:** How various phenomena of mind emerge from the interactions among many kinds of highly evolved brain mechanisms.
i.   **Smart Cities:** How buildings and cities can become more intelligently responsive to the needs and desires of their inhabitants.
j.   **Future of Learning:** How to redefine and expand the conceptual framework and language of learning by creating new technologies and spheres of practice.
k.   **Responsive Environments:** How sensor networks augment and mediate human experience, interaction and perception.
l.   **Mobile Dynamics:** How to make mobile devices socially aware.
m.   **Affective Computing:** How computational systems can sense, recognize, and understand human emotions and respond.
n.   **Learning Environments:** How to engage people in creative learning experiences.
o.   **Wearable Computing:** How to embed computing devices in clothes and accessories.

7. REFLEXIONS

Time, as we have seen, is a crucial factor in synchronization. Mirroring needs some coincidences, in space and time, though their definition can be quite complex: depending on the context, the framing of sync can change. Subjective, and neuro-cognitive, time in experience is quite different from time as measured by a clock. Time in experience presents itself not only as linear but also as having a *complex texture* (evidence that we are not dealing with a "knife-edge" present) a texture that dominates our existence to an important degree (Varela in Petitot, 1999).

This overall approach to cognition is based on *situated embodied agents*. Varela (Varela, 1991; Thompson, 2001) has proposed the adjective *enactive* to designate this approach more precisely. It comprises two complementary aspects:

1.   Ongoing coupling of the cognitive agent, a permanent coping that is fundamentally mediated by sensory-motor activities;
2.   Autonomous activities of the agent whose identity is based on emerging, endogenous configurations (or self-organizing patterns) of neuronal activity.

Enaction implies that sensory-motor coupling modulates, but does not determine, an ongoing endogenous activity that it configures into meaningful world items in an unceasing flow.

From an enactive viewpoint, any mental act is characterized by the concurrent participation of several functionally distinct and topographically distributed regions of the brain and their sensory-motor embodiment. From the point of view of the neuroscientist, it is the complex task of relating and integrating these different components that is at the root of temporality. These various components require *a frame or window of simultaneity that corresponds to the duration of lived subjective present*. These kinds of present are not necessarily conscious, often they are not, though they might not be unconscious in the folk Freudian way (Orsucci 2006b). There are three possible scales of duration to understand the temporal horizon just introduced (though other scales of extended present, considered in chrono-biology, might considered):

- Basic or elementary events (the "1/10" scale);
- Relaxation time for large-scale integration (the "1" scale);
- Descriptive-narrative assessments (the "10" scale).

The first level is already evident in the so-called *fusion interval* of various sensory systems: the minimum distance needed for two stimuli to be perceived as non-simultaneous, a threshold that varies with each sensory modality. These thresholds can be grounded in the intrinsic cellular rhythms of neuronal discharges, and in the temporal summation capacities of synaptic integration. These events fall within a range of 10 ms (e.g., the rhythms of bursting inter-neurons) to 100 ms (e.g., the duration of an EPSP/IPSP sequence in a cortical pyramidal neuron). These values are the basis for the 1/10 scale.

Behaviourally, these elementary events give rise to *micro-cognitive phenomena* variously studied as perceptual moments, central oscillations, iconic memory, excitability cycles, and subjective time quanta. For instance, under minimum stationary conditions, reaction time or oculo-motor behaviour displays a multimodal distribution with a 30-40 ms distance between peaks; in average daylight, apparent motion (or "psi-phenomenon") requires 100 ms.

This leads naturally to the second scale, that of long-range integration. Component processes already have a short duration, about 30-100 ms; how can we understand such experimental psychological and neurobiological results, at the level of a fully constituted, normal cognitive operation? A long-standing tradition in neuroscience looks at the neuronal bases of cognitive acts (perception-action, memory, motivation, and the like) in terms of cell assemblies or, synonymously, neuronal ensembles. A cell assembly (CA) is a distributed subset of neurons with strong reciprocal connections.

The diagram depicts the three main time frames considered here. A cognitive activity (such as head turning) takes place within a relatively incompressible duration, a *cognitive present*. The basis for this emergent behaviour is the recruitment of widely distributed neuronal ensembles through increased frequently, coherence in the gamma (30-80 Hz) band. Thus, we might depict the corresponding neural correlates of a cognitive act as a synchronous neural hypergraph of brain regions undergoing bifurcations of phase transitions from a cognitive present content to another.

Recently this view has been supported by widespread findings of oscillations and synchronies in the gamma range (30-80 Hz) in neuronal groups during perceptual tasks. Thus, we have neuronal-level constitutive events that have a duration on the 1/10 scale, forming aggregates that manifest as incompressible but complete cognitive acts on the 1 scale.

This completion time is dynamically dependent on a number of dispersed assemblies and not on a fixed integration period; in other words, it is the basis of the origin of duration without an external or internally ticking clock.

Nowness, in this perspective, is therefore presemantic in that it does not require a remembering in order to emerge. The evidence for this important conclusion comes, again, from many sources. For instance, subjects can estimate durations of up to 2-3 seconds quite precisely, but their performance decreases considerably for longer times; spontaneous speech in many languages is organized such that utterances last 2-3 seconds; short, intentional movements (such as self-initiated arm motions) are embedded within windows of this same duration.

This brings to the fore the third duration, the 10 scale, proper to descriptive-narrative assessments. In fact, it is quite evident that these endogenous, dynamic horizons can be, in turn, linked together to form a broader temporal horizon. This temporal scale is inseparable from our descriptive-narrative assessments and linked to our linguistic capacities. It constitutes the "narrative centre of gravity" in

Figure 6. Windows of time (Varela et al. 1991)

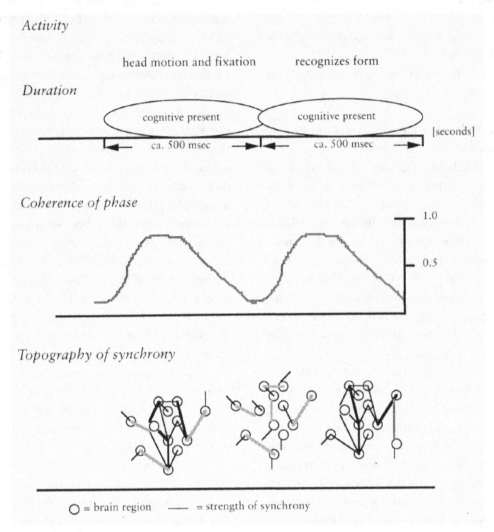

Dennett's metaphor (Dennett, 1991), the flow of time related to personal identity.

It is the continuity of the self that breaks down under intoxication or in pathologies such as schizophrenia or Korsakoff's syndrome. As Husserl (1980) points out, commenting on similar reasoning in Brentano: "We could not speak of a temporal succession of tones if … what is earlier would have vanished without a trace and only what is momentarily sensed would be given to our apprehension" To the appearance of the just-now one correlates two modes of understanding and examination (in other words, valid forms of donation in the phenomenological sense):

1. Remembrance or evocative memory
2. Mental imagery and fantasy.

The Ur-impression is the proper mode of nowness, or in other words, it is where the new appears; impression intends the new. Briefly: impression is always presentational, while memory or evocation is re-presentational.

These neurophysiologic events are correlated to micro-cognitive phenomena and behavioral elements variously studied as perceptual moments, central oscillations, iconic memory, excitability cycles, and subjective time quanta: the elementary particles of reflexions we can share with humans and media. Coupling and sharing between humans and machines are happening at this level, when meta-cognitive and mental skills are certainly unusual. It is the *a-conscious* level and modality, preliminary to any unconscious or preconscious modes. The kind of reflexivity implied in these processes concerns the embodied mind. It is a kind of cognitive capacity fully incorporated in bodily actions and re-actions. These kinds of processes involve a presentational intentionality, not a representational intellect. It is a form of direct cognition, not a self conscious meta-cognition.

The embodied mind emerges and grows (bottom-up) on the basic *reflexive function* as a direct parameter in biological processes. *Reflection* is a meta-cognitive function (top-down): "the overall reflective process can embed more conceptual and

linguistic functions in the brain than the reflexive component alone" (Siegel 2007). Some authors use the terms synonymously but, we prefer to use a different terminology to stress a conceptual and factual difference. Reflexivity will be direct and non-conceptual: it implies an immediate capacity of awareness without effort, or intellectualization. In reflexivity the interface is just under your own skin, and it is useful to remind that the embryological origin of skin, brain and mind is the same. The *ectoderm*, our primary interface, is the outermost of the three primary germ layers of an embryo and the source of the epidermis, the nervous system, the eyes and ears: i.e. interfaces.

Reflexions happen at a very pre-cognitive stage, before any higher order metacognition might be established. We have been exploring some important implications of mirror neuron research. New findings by Benjamin Libet (1993; 1999) on the so-called readiness potential extend our perspectives on this matter.

Figure 7. Libet (1999)

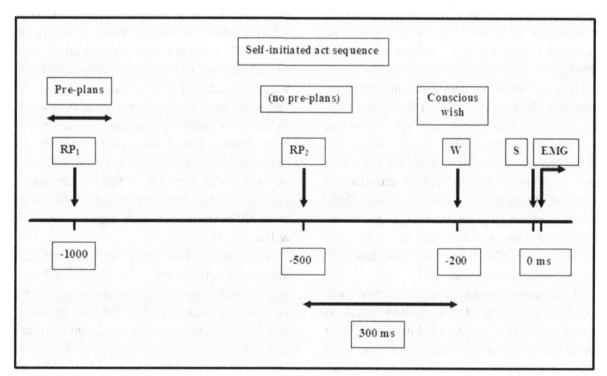

Kornhuber e Deecke (1965) had found that all actions are preceded by a slow potential easily detected in an EEG. They gave this potential a German name, *Bereitschaft-potential* but nowadays it is more frequently called in English: *Readiness Potential or RP*. A question was quite immediate: as the RP was happening at about 550 milliseconds before action, in which timing (and maybe causal) sequence was it placed with representations and decisions concerning that same action? It was found that every conscious representation and decision of acting (or not) were placed at just 200 msec. before action, so they were following the RP at about 300 msec. Benjamin Libet, an American neuro-physiologist has been expanding research in this area both in the sensory and the motor fields, including some possible psychological and philosophical implications (Libet, 1993; 1999). His vantage point might be summarized in this way: we don't have free-will but we do have free-denial. We have the possibility to facilitate or stop an action after it has been started, in an *aconscious* way. Recent advancements in the complex neurodynamics of time could provide seminal contributions in advancing our understanding of ethical issues on personal responsibility of actions (Gazzaniga 2005).

It is not surprising then that some recent research is showing evidence on how new media have a direct neurocognitive impact, including probable long term evolutionary results (Chan & Rabinowitz 2006). New media are exploiting our physiological capacity of direct sensation and reaction, through aconscious interactions. New media constitute a techno-cultural niche, an enriched or enhanced environment, based on forms of direct knowledge. A knowledge not mediated by intellectual representations.

Every generation has raised concerns regarding the negative impact of media on social skills and personal relationships. The Internet and other new media types are reported to have important social and mental health effects on everyone, especially on adolescents probably because they are heavy users and their brains and psychology are still very mouldable.

Video-game playing, for example, enhances the capacity of visual attention and its spatial distribution. Video-game training enhances task-switching abilities as well as decreasing the attention blink. Thus, both the visual and a-modal bottlenecks identified during temporal processing of visual information are reduced in video game players. Clearly, these individuals have an increased ability to process information over time; however, whether this is due to faster target processing, such as faster selection and stabilization of information in memory, or to an increased ability to maintain several attention windows in parallel, cannot be determined from our current data.

By forcing players to simultaneously juggle a number of varied tasks (detect new enemies, track existing enemies and avoid getting hurt, among others), action-video-game playing pushes the limits of three rather different aspects of visual attention. It leads to detectable effects on new tasks and at untrained locations after only 10 days of training. Therefore, although video-game playing may seem to be rather mindless, it is capable of radically altering visual attention processing. There are several ways by which video-game training could lead to such enhancements. Changes in known attention bottlenecks is certainly a possibility; however, speeded perceptual processes and/or better management of several tasks at the central executive level are also likely to contribute. It will be for future studies of the effect of video-game practice to determine the relative contribution of these different factors to skill learning Green CS & Bavelier D (2003)

For example, has been reported a statistical association between television viewing and obesity, attention disorders, school performance, and violence (Mathiak & Weber 2006). A significant relationship between Internet use and attention deficit hyperactivity disorder (ADHD) has also been shown in elementary school children (Yoo et al. 2004). The relationship between video games and Attention Deficit Hyperactivity Disorder is unknown. The incidence of ADHD continues to rise and it is a significant challenge on medical, financial, and educational resources. ADHD is a complex disorder that often requires input from the affected child or adolescent, teachers, parents, and physicians in order to be diagnosed correctly and treated successfully. Adolescents who play more than one hour of console or Internet video games a day may have more or more intense symptoms of ADHD or inattention than those who do not (Straker 2006).

New media, new reflexions, are already part of the techno-cultural niche of our age: this is part of a new evolutionary step we can better understand considering studies on learning and enriched environments. At Harvard, David Hubel and Torsten Wiesel studied cats raised blind in one eye, and by 1962 they had demonstrated that such deprivation caused profound structural changes in the cats' visual cortex. Hubel and Wiesel's work made it clear that severe deprivation during critical developmental periods could have catastrophic effects on a growing brain, but the question of whether the opposite was true remained suspended for a while. By 1964, the Berkeley team led by Mark Rosenzweig completed a series of experiments that began to answer those questions. They found that rats raised in an "enriched" environment, with toys and nice social activities, were not only smarter than rats raised in impoverished environments, but that the improvement in performance correlated with an increase in the weight of the rats' cerebral cortex. The idea that the brain, like a muscle, might respond to "cerebral exercise" with physical growth was surprising to many, and gave strength to an increasingly powerful theory suggesting that all aspects of the mind - from memory, to dreams, to emotions - have physical correlates. The classical statement by William James (now in 1967) has found an experimental validation: "Experience is remoulding us at every moment: Whilst we think, our brain changes".

Studies on enriched environments are still growing, but they have already established evidence that the brain modifies its structure (not necessarily its size) depending from the kind of niche that Rosenzweig called Environmental Complexity and Training. These studies are now extended to human learning environments (Carbonara 2005; Orsucci & Sala 2005).

8. FINALE

From the neurodynamic point of view adopted in our explorations on human interfaces, human subjects are fully embodied in brain-body dynamics, in a comprehensive *biophysical identity*. This approach is an evolution of the metaphoric conceptions of *embodiment* (Varela, Thompson, & Rosch, 1991), *proto-self* (Damasio, 1999), *synaptic self* (LeDoux, 2002).

We proposed a Mind Force theory aimed at providing a comprehensive biophysical framework for embodiment (Orsucci, 2009).

Mind Force (MF) is the expression of scaling dynamical networks of oscillators organized by waves of synchronization. As it is based on oscillator dynamics, and oscillators are present at different scales, MF spans through molecular, neural, cognitive and socio-cultural domains. We might consider MF "vertical" waves ranging across different scales/domains, and "horizontal" waves within a single domain.

The usage of this integrated biophysical approach represents a benefit for human interface studies and their applications.

A definition of Mind Force would be as *the dynamical resultant formed by networks of synchronized oscillators coupled in waves spanning trough heterogeneous domains* (Orsucci, 2009).

Within the myriad of bio-psychosocial oscillators some act as master hubs, others as slave or free (Kauffman, 1993; 1995; 2000; Kelso, 1995) nodes within the MF hyperstructure dynamics. Waves of massive and heterogeneous transient

Figure 8. Rossi (1996)

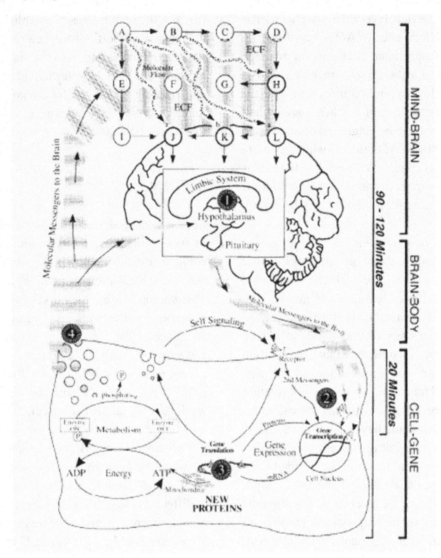

entrainment self-organize in attractors, waves and fields. These waves of massive synchronizations can propagate through different media, domains and scales. MF transient or steady fields interfere and interact, producing MF resultants and forming MF dynamical landscapes.

In conclusion, to use an expression coined by Douglas Hofstadter (2007: 39) Mind Force is the result of "the causal potency of collective phenomena" and pattern

The basic modeling for Mind Force is grounded in dynamics within networks of oscillators. To start, a pair of oscillators interacting through phase differences satisfies equations of the form

$$\theta_1^l = \omega_1 + H_1(\theta_2 - \theta_1),$$
$$\theta_2^l = \omega_2 + H_2(\theta_1 - \theta_2).$$

Here θ_i are the phases of the oscillators, ω_i are the frequencies of the uncoupled oscillators, and H_i are smooth 2π-periodic functions of the phase differences.

Figure 9. Somers & Kopell (1995)

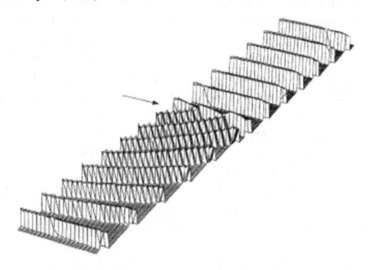

From a more abstract viewpoint, synchronization has been identified as a generic form of collective behavior in ensembles of dynamical systems with long range coupling. Several models that capture the essence of synchronization phenomena have been thoroughly studied over the last few decades. An ensemble of N coupled phase oscillators can be governed by the equations

$$\phi_i(t) = \Omega_i + \frac{\varepsilon}{N} \sum_{j=1}^{N} \sin(\phi_j - \phi_i),$$

i = 1,...,N, where $\varepsilon > 0$ is the strength of coupling. In the absence of coupling, $\varepsilon = 0$, each oscillator *i* performs a uniform angular motion with its natural frequency Ω_i. For $\varepsilon \neq 0$, the oscillators are globally coupled in the sense that the strength of the pair interaction does not depend on their relative position, but only on their relative state. In other words, each oscillator interacts with the rest of the system through global averages only.

Within the limit $N \to \infty$, exists a critical value ε_c of the coupling intensity such that, for $\varepsilon > \varepsilon_c$, a sub-ensemble of oscillators becomes entrained in periodic orbits with the same frequency, whereas other oscillators remain unsynchronized.

A great deal of attention has been paid to the synchronization of ensembles formed by identical elements, especially in the case where the individual dynamics is chaotic. Both continuous and discrete-time dynamics have been considered. Kaneko (1994) has introduced globally coupled chaotic maps as a mean-field model of lattice maps, which are extensively used to model complex extended systems (Kaneko, 1993).

For an ensemble of *N* maps whose individual dynamics is governed by the equation w (t + 1) = f [w(t)], global coupling is introduced as

$$w_i(t+1) = (1-\varepsilon)f[w_i(t)] + \frac{\varepsilon}{N} \sum_{j=1}^{N} f[w_j(t)]$$
$$= (1-\varepsilon)f[w_i(t)] + \varepsilon\overline{f(w)},$$

i = 1,...,N, with ε Î [0, 1]. While for $\varepsilon = 0$ the elements evolve independently, for $\varepsilon = 1$ they become fully synchronized after the first time step.

Full synchronization is understood here as a situation where the individual states of all the elements in the ensemble coincide, i.e. where the trajectory of the system in phase space is restricted to the subspace $w_1 = w_2 = ... = w_N$. In this situation, the evolution of all the elements coincides with that of an independent element. The state of full synchronization can be asymptotically approached as the system evolves even for $\varepsilon < 1$. It has been shown that, if the individual dynamics is chaotic, full synchronization is linearly stable for $\varepsilon > \varepsilon_c$, where the critical value ε_c is related to the maximal Lyapunov exponent λ_M of the individual dynamics, as $\varepsilon_c = 1 - \exp(-\lambda_M)$. For nonchaotic individual dynamics where $\lambda_M < 0$, full synchronization is a stable state for any $\varepsilon > 0$. The connection between ε_c and λ_M makes it clear that the transition to full synchronization in chaotic systems, which has the character of a critical phenomenon, results from the competition between the stabilizing effect of global coupling and the inherent instability of chaotic orbits. Note carefully that the critical value ε_c does not depend on N, so that the synchronization threshold is the same for any size of the coupled ensemble.

For coupling strengths just below ε_c the system evolves asymptotically to a state of partial synchronization in the form of *clustering*, where the elements become divided into groups. Within each cluster the elements are fully synchronized but different clusters have different trajectories.

For large systems, the dynamics in the clustering regime is highly multi-stable and exhibits glassy-like features. In contrast with the critical value ε_c, the stability properties of the clustering regime are strongly dependent on the system size (Abramson, 2000).

Cross-Coupled Extended Systems provide a versatile collection of models for a wide class of complex natural phenomena, ranging from pattern formation in physicochemical reactions, to biological morphogenesis, to evolutionary processes.

It is therefore interesting to consider how these systems behave under the effect of mutual interactions and, in particular, study the synchronization properties of their co-evolution when they are mutually coupled by algorithms similar to the scheme of coupling already presented (Zanette & Morelli, 2003).

P.M. Gleiser and D.H. Zanette (2006) analyzed the interplay of synchronization and structure evolution in an evolving network of phase oscillators. An initially random network is adaptively rewired according to the dynamical coherence of the oscillators, in order to enhance their mutual synchronization. They showed that the evolving network reaches a small-world structure. Its clustering coefficient attains a maximum for an intermediate intensity of the coupling between oscillators, where a rich diversity of synchronized oscillator groups is observed. In the stationary state, these synchronized groups are directly associated with network clusters.

Their model consists of an ensemble of N coupled phase oscillators, whose individual evolution is given by

$$\phi_i = \omega_i + \frac{r}{M_i} \sum_{j=1}^{N} W_{ij} \sin(\phi_j - \phi_i),$$

$i = 1,...,N,$ where ω_i is the natural frequency of oscillator I and r is the coupling strength. The weights W_{ij} define the adjacency matrix of the interaction network: $W_{ij} = 1$ if oscillator i interacts with oscillator j, and 0 otherwise. The number of neighbors of oscillator i is $M_{ij} = S_j W_{ij}$. The adjacent matrix is symmetric, $W_{ij} = W_{ji}$, so that the network is a non directed graph.

A definition of Mind Force would be as the dynamical hyperstructure formed by networks of synchronized oscillators coupled in waves of synchronization, spanning trough heterogeneous domains. Mind Force theory is based on the integration of 4 main pillar-theories: Complexity theory; Synchronization theory; Network theory; Field theory. Mind Force is the result of the causal power of collective phenomena and patterns. The new theory of Mind Force represents an integration of different biophysical and cognitive domains considered as components of a dynamical hyper-network.

It can produce breakthrough advancements in consciousness studies, psychosocial and clinical applications. It might lead to new pathways in science and epistemology.

This book is a multifaceted mirror on how human evolution has had a constant psychobiological link with the development of new tools and environmental changes. Discoveries and technological innovations in Information & Communication Science and Technology are paving the ground for new evolutionary steps.

Our new insights in neuro-cognition and the multiple reflexions implied in our sensory-perceptive processes are leading to new interfaces and new media. The isomorphism between bio-cognitive structures and the ICST niche we inhabit is progressively blurring boundaries between *res cogitans* and *res extensa*. Reflexing interfaces are extensions of human embodiment just as the bone tool tossed skyward by a savannah-dwelling ape.

Time flows, always different yet similar. We are flowing in, and we are the flow of, micro and macro worlds, nested and intermingled. The stream of time runs here and there, generating multiple cascades, reflexing in billions of infinitesimal mirrors.

REFERENCES

Abramson, G. (2000). Long transients and cluster size in globally coupled maps. *Europhysics Letters, 52*(6), 615–619.

Aiello, L. C., & Wheeler, P. (1995). The expensive-tissue hypothesis. *Current Anthropology, 36,* 199–221.

Ambrose, S. H. (2001). Paleolithic technology and human evolution. *Science, 291,* 1748.

Aoki, K., & Feldman, M. V. (1987). Toward a theory for the evolution of cultural. *Proceedings of the National Academy of Sciences of the United States of America, 84,* 7164–7168.

Arbib, M. A. (2002). The mirror system, imitation, and the evolution of language. In Nehaniv, C., & Dautenhahn, K. (Eds.), *Imitation in animals and artifacts.* The MIT Press.

Arbib, M. A. (2005). From monkey-like action recognition to human language: An evolutionary framework for neurolinguistics. *The Behavioral and Brain Sciences, 28,* 105–167.

Bates, E., & MacWhinney, B. (1987). Competition, variation and language learning. In MacWhinney, B. (Ed.), *Mechanisms of language acquisition.* Erlbaum.

Bodmer, W. F., & Cavalli-Sforza, L. L. (1976). *Genetics, evolution and man.* Freeman.

Boyd, R., & Richerson, P. J. (1985). *Culture and the evolutionary process.* University of Chicago Press.

Branigan, H. P., Pickering, M. J., & Cleland, A. A. (2000). Syntactic co-ordination in dialogue. *Cognition, 75,* B13–B25.

Carbonara, D. (Ed.). (2005). *Technology literacy applications in learning environments.* Hershey, PA: Idea Group.

Chan, P. A., & Rabinowitz, T. (2006). A cross-sectional analysis of video games and attention deficit hyperactivity disorder symptoms in adolescents. *Annals of General Psychiatry, 5,* 16.

Chomsky, N. (1975). *Reflections on language.* New York, NY: Pantheon.

Dale, R., & Spivey, M. J. (2006). Unravelling the dyad: Using recurrence analysis to explore patterns of syntactic coordination between children and caregivers in conversation. *Language Learning, 56,* 391–430.

Damasio, A. R. (1999). How the brain creates the mind. *Scientific American, 281,* 112–117.

Dawkins, R. (1982). *The extended phenotype.* Freeman.

Dennett, D. C. (1991). *Consciousness explained.* Boston, MA: Little, Brown and Co.

Donald, M. (1997). Origins of the modern mind: Three stages in the evolution of culture and cognition. *The Behavioral and Brain Sciences, 16*(4), 737–791.

Eckmann, J.-P., Kamphorst, S. O., & Ruelle, D. (1987). Recurrence plots of dynamical systems. *Europhysics Letters, 5,* 973–977.

Feldman, M. W., & Laland, K. N. (1996). Gene-culture coevolutionary theory. *Trends in Ecology & Evolution, 11,* 453–457.

Fonagy, P., & Target, M. (1997). Attachment and reflective function: Their role in self-organization. *Development and Psychopathology, 9,* 679–700.

Freeman, W. J. (1975). *Mass action in the nervous system.* New York, NY: Academic Press.

Freud, S. (1920). *Beyond the pleasure principle. Standard Edition, 18,* 1-64. London, UK: Hogarth Press.

Gaddini, E. (1969). On imitation. *The International Journal of Psycho-Analysis, 50,* 475–484.

Gazzaniga, M. S. (2005). *The ethical brain.* USA: The Dana Press.

Gibson, J. J. (1979). *The ecological approach to visual perception.* New Jersey, USA: Lawrence Erlbaum Associates.

Gleiser, P. M., & Zanette, D. H. (2006). Synchronization and structure in an adaptive oscillator network. *Europhysics Journal B, 53,* 233–238.

Green, C. S., & Bavelier, D. (2003). Action video game modifies visual selective attention. *Nature, 423.*

Griffiths, M. (2000). Does internet and computer "addiction" exist? Some case study evidence. *Cyberpsychology & Behavior, 3*(2), 211–218.

Hofstadter, D. (2007). *I am a strange loop.* New York, NY: Basic Books.

Husserl, E. (1980). *Collected works.* Boston, MA: The Hague

James, W. (1967). *The writings of William James* (McDermott, J. J., Ed.). New York, NY: Random House.

Kaneko, K. (1993). *Theory and applications of coupled map lattices.* Chichester, UK: Wiley.

Kaneko, K. (1994). Relevance of clustering to biological networks. *Physica D. Nonlinear Phenomena, 75*(1-3), 55–73.

Kauffman, S. A. (1993). *The origins of order, self organization and selection in evolution.* New York, NY: Oxford University Press.

Kauffman, S. A. (1995). *At home in the universe. The search for laws of self-organization and complexity.* New York, NY: Oxford University Press.

Kauffman, S. A. (2000). *Investigations.* Oxford, UK: Oxford University Press.

Kelso, J. A. S. (1995). *Dynamic patterns: The self-organization of brain and behavior.* Cambridge, MA: MIT Press.

Kernberg, P. F. (2007). *Beyond the reflection: The role of the mirror paradigm in clinical practice.* New York, NY: Other Press.

Kornhuber, H. H., & Deecke, L. (1965). Hirnpotentialänderungen bei Willkürbewegungen und passiven Bewegungen des Menschen: Bereitschaftspotential und reafferente Potentiale. *Pflügers Arch. ges. Physiol, 284,* 1–17.

Lacan, J. (1937). The mirror stage. In *Ecrits.* W. W. Norton, new edition (2005)

Laland, K. N., Odling-Smee, J., & Feldman, M. W. (2000). Niche construction, biological evolution, and cultural change. *The Behavioral and Brain Sciences, 23,* 131–175.

LeDoux, J. E. (2002). *Synaptic self: How our brains become who we are.* New York, NY: Viking.

Lewontin, R. C. (1983). Gene, organism, and environment. In Bendall, D. S. (Ed.), *Evolution from molecules to men.* Cambridge University Press.

Libet, B. (1993). *Neurophysiology of consciousness: Selected papers and new essays.* Boston, MA: Birkhauser.

Libet, B., Freeman, A., & Sutherland, K. (1999). *The volitional brain: Towards a neuroscience of free will.* Thorverton, UK: Imprint Academic.

Lieberman, P. (1991). *Uniquely human: The evolution of speech, thought, and selfless behavior.* Cambridge, MA: Harvard University Press.

Marwan, N. (2003). *Encounters with neighbours.* Doctoral dissertation, University of Potsdam.

Mathiak, K., & Weber, R. (2006). Toward brain correlates of natural behavior: fMRI during violent video games. *Human Brain Mapping, 27*(12), 948–956.

Maturana, H. (2002). *Autopoiesis, structural coupling and cognition: A history of these and other notions in the biology of cognition.* Instituto Matriztico, Internet publication.

Maturana, H. R., & Varela, F. J. (1980). *Autopoiesis and cognition, the realization of the living.* Dordrecht, Holland: D. Reidel Pub. Co.

Norman, D. A. (1988). *The design of everyday things.* New York, NY: Doubleday.

Norman, D. A. (1999). Affordances, conventions, and design. *Interaction, 6*(3), 38–41.

Orsucci, F. (Ed.). (1998). *The complex matters of the mind.* Singapore: World Scientific.

Orsucci, F. (2006b). The paradigm of complexity in clinical neuro-cognitive science. *The Neuroscientist – SAGE, 12*(4), 1-10.

Orsucci, F. (2009). *Mind force: On human attractions.* River Edge, NJ: World Scientific Publishing.

Orsucci, F., Giuliani, A., Webber, C., Zbilut, J., Fonagy, P., & Mazza, M. (2006). Combinatorics & synchronization in natural semiotics. *Physica A: Statistical Mechanics and its Applications, 361,* 665–676.

Orsucci, F., Giuliani, A., & Zbilut, J. (2004). Structure & coupling of semiotic sets. *Experimental Chaos, American Institute of Physics. AIP Proceedings, 742,* 83–93.

Orsucci, F., & Sala, N. (2005). Virtual reality, telemedicine and beyond. In Carbonara, D. (Ed.), *Technology literacy applications in learning environments* (pp. 755–757). Hershey, PA: Idea Group.

Orsucci, F., Walters, K., Giuliani, A., Webber, C. Jr, & Zbilut, J. (1999). Orthographic structuring of human speech and texts. *International Journal of Chaos Theory and Applications, 4*(2), 80–88.

Ott, E., Grebogi, C., & Yorke, J. A. (1990). Controlling chaos. *Physical Review Letters, 64*(11), 1196.

Pecora, L. M., & Carroll, T. L. (1990). Synchronization control of chaos. *Physical Review Letters, 64,* 821.

Petitot, J. (1999). *Naturalizing phenomenology, issues in contemporary phenomenology and cognitive science.* Stanford, CA: Stanford University Press.

Port, R., Tajima, K., & Cummins, F. (1999). *Nonlinear analysis of developmental processes* (van der Maas, L. J., & van Geert, P., Eds.). Amsterdam, The Netherlands: Elsevier.

Richardson, D. C., & Dale, R. (2005). Looking to understand: The coupling between speakers' and listeners' eye movements and its relationship to discourse comprehension. *Cognitive Science, 29,* 39–54.

Rizzolatti, G., & Arbib, M. A. (1998). Language within our grasp. *Trends in Neurosciences, 21,* 188–194.

Rossi, E. L. (1996). The psychobiology of mind-body communication: The complex, self-organizing field of information transduction. *Bio Systems, 38,* 199–206.

Shockley, K., Santana, M.-V., & Fowler, C. A. (2003). Mutual interpersonal postural constraints are involved in cooperative conversation. *Journal of Experimental Psychology. Human Perception and Performance, 29,* 326–332.

Siegel, D. J. (2007). *The mindful brain.* New York, NY: Norton.

Somers, D., & Kopell, N. (1995). Waves and synchrony in networks of oscillators of relaxation and non-relaxation type. *Physica D. Nonlinear Phenomena, 89,* 169–183.

Stern, D. (1985). *The interpersonal world of the infant.* New York, NY: Basic Books.

Straker, L. M., Pollock, C. M., Zubrick, S. R., & Kurinczuk, J. J. (2006). The association between information and communication technology exposure and physical activity, musculoskeletal and visual symptoms and socio-economic status in 5-year-olds. *Child: Care, Health and Development, 32*(3), 343–351.

Thompson, W. I. (1996). *Coming into being: Artefacts and texts in the evolution of consciousness.* New York, NY: St. Martin's Press.

Tomasello, M. (2003). *A usage-based theory of language.* Cambridge, MA: Harvard University Press.

Varela, F. J., Thompson, E., & Rosch, E. (1991). *The embodied mind, cognitive science and human experience.* Cambridge, MA: MIT Press.

Webber, C. L. Jr, & Zbilut, J. P. (1994). Dynamical assessment of physiological systems and states using recurrence plot strategies. *Journal of Applied Physiology, 76,* 965–973.

Winnicott, D. W. (1987). *The child, the family, and the outside world.* Reading, MA: Addison-Wesley Pub. Co.

Yoo, H. J. (2004). Attention deficit hyperactivity symptoms and internet addiction. *Psychiatry and Clinical Neurosciences, 58*(5), 487–494.

Zanette, D. H., & Morelli, L. G. (2003). Synchronization of coupled extended dynamical systems. *International Journal of Bifurcation and Chaos in Applied Sciences and Engineering, 13*(4).

Chapter 2
Fractal Geometry as a Bridge between Realms

Terry Marks-Tarlow
Private Practice, USA

ABSTRACT

This chapter describes fractal geometry as a bridge between the imaginary and the real, mind and matter, conscious and the unconscious. Fractals are multidimensional objects with self-similar detail across size and/or time scales. Jung conceived of number as the most primitive archetype of order, serving to link observers with the observed. Whereas Jung focused upon natural numbers as the foundation for order that is already conscious in the observer, I offer up the fractal geometry as the underpinnings for a dynamic unconscious destined never to become fully conscious. Throughout nature, fractals model the complex, recursively branching structures of self-organizing systems. When they serve at the edges of open systems, fractal boundaries articulate a paradoxical zone that simultaneously separates as it connects. When modeled by Spencer-Brown's mathematical notation, full interpenetration between inside and outside edges translates to a distinction that leads to no distinction. By occupying the infinitely deep "space between" dimensions and levels of existence, fractal boundaries contribute to the notion of intersubjectivity, where self and other become most entwined. They also exemplify reentry dynamics of Varela's autonomous systems, plus Hofstadter's ever-elusive "tangled hierarchy" between brain and mind.

INTRODUCTION

Any distinction is wholly eyemaginary, an act of creation, an act of the imagination. Each proof that convinces is a proof that uses imaginary values to reason to a true answer... Mathematics is about the consequence of making a distinction,

DOI: 10.4018/978-1-4666-2077-3.ch002

as if there were such a thing as a distinction. It is all imaginary and only the imaginary is real!
— *Louis Kauffman*

The capacity to make distinctions between *this* and *that* lies at the base of human consciousness. Throughout the lifespan a key distinction involves discerning inner from outer processes. That is, we must distinguish products of imagination, memory and dreams from outside objects, people and events in the environment. British psychoanalyst Donald Winnicott (1974) introduces the significance of childhood play for creating/discovering inner versus outer realms of experience, by speculating that symbol, self and culture all emerge in the "transitional space" between mother and child. Likewise Australian psychiatrist Russell Meares (2006) details developmental processes by which young children shuttle back and forth between incorporating outside objects into imaginary play, and breaking away from play to attend to goings on in the immediate environment. Through this

shuttling of attention an ever moving boundary is established between the interior dialogue of a personal self and the exterior dialogue of a social self. Figure 1 illustrates the play of imagination as it exists between inner and outer realms.

Whereas children's inner focus dictates the perspective of the observer, their outer focus illuminates objects and territory under observation. We might assume clear distinctions exist between observers and observed, but this is not necessarily the case. When a schizophrenic can't tell the difference between an object hallucinated and one that exists in reality, fuzzy boundaries between

Figure 1. The play of imagination as it exists between inner and outer realms (Courtesy of the author)

inner and outer realms become the stuff of psychosis. Yet similar fuzzy boundaries also characterize the mindsets of visionaries able to make their dreams come true. Clean boundaries between inner and outer realms, imply a Cartesian split as represented by the true/false, either/or distinctions of classic Aristotelian logic. According to this view, something *either* exists inside the observer *or* outside, but not in both places at once. By contrast, fuzzy boundaries offer more choices, with fuzzy logic permitting an infinite number of distinctions between true and false. This is illustrated by the fuzzy logic cube in Figure 2. If 1 and 0 represent true and false respectively, then the cube's corners are anchored by binary sets that characterize traditional logic. Inside the cube, a variety of fuzzy sets express degrees of truth, with the center point occupying the completely ambiguous, if not paradoxical, position of being just as true as it is false.

Writing about that magical, ambiguous zone between observer and observed, Lou Kauffman examines various systems of logic and mathematics. As the epigraph above indicates, Kauffman highlights paradox as he underscores the hidden action of the imaginary in bringing forth the "real" world of everyday distinctions. This chapter fol-lows in the paradoxical spirit of Winnicott and Kauffman by investigating the play between imaginary/real, observer/observed as detectable within fractal geometry. I argue for the importance of fractal dynamics to model entangled relations between observer and observed, where each fully interpenetrates the other. By understanding the broad foundation of fractal geometry as it involves infinite recursion on the imaginary plane, we can enhance our understanding of reality as finitely perceived in nature. Conversely, by comprehending how fractals manifest ubiquitously at the joints in nature, we can expand our understanding of the infinitely extending, self-referential nature of mind. Of special interest here is the "deep relativity" that exists between observer and observed at all scales of observation, such that the closer we look, the more we can see. I introduce self-similarity as a newly discovered symmetry in nature that represents the sign of identity. Explored semiotically, self-similarity can be seen as a distinction that leads to no distinction. I relate this paradoxical equivalence of change and no-change to the operation of cancellation within Spencer-Brown's arithmetic of first distinctions, as well as to Varela's reentry dynamics characteristic of autonomous systems. My main thesis is that fractal boundaries—whether between inside/outside, self/other, subjective/objective levels or conscious/unconscious underpinnings of experience—represent an imaginary/real foundation for the entangled co-creation of world and psyche.

Number as the Archetype for Conscious Order

If ... a group of objects is deprived of every single one of its properties or characteristics, there still remains, at the end, its number, which seems to indicate that number is something irreducible ... [something which] helps more than anything else to bring order into the chaos of appearances. — Carl Jung

Figure 2. Fuzzy logic cube (Courtesy of the author, from Marks-Tarlow, 2008)

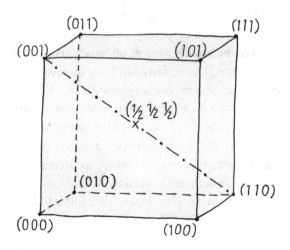

Swiss psychiatrist Carl Jung came to view number as the most primitive quality of existence. By crafting an archetypal theory, his theory of number doubled over as a theory of mind. Jung attributed to number the power to bring order into the chaos of *appearances,* referring to material existence *not as objectively conceived,* but rather *as subjectively perceived by an observer.* Here number links observers and observed, inner and outer worlds in a way parallel to second-order cybernetics. In the footsteps of Margaret Mead and Heinz von Foerster, this viewpoint is carried forth eloquently by the "Musings" of Ranulph Glanville, e.g., "the whole point of Second Order Cybernetics is that it asserts there is no observation without an observer. There is nothing spoken without a speaker, there is no action without an actor" (Glanville, 1998, p. 85).

Jung viewed number as the realm where mind and matter meet, sometimes referred to as the *psychoid level* of existence and at other times the *Unus Mundus.* Jung intuited that the realm of mathematical abstraction is discovered, in so far as it uncovers quantitative "facts" about the workings of the external world. At the same time, it is invented as an abstraction in the mind, indicating something qualitative about the subjective realm of meaning. For Jung, number serves as the most fundamental structure of perceived reality, the place where observers and observed merge at the level of synchronicity, symbol and meaning. In building a bridge between mind and matter, Jung and his dedicated follower, Marie-Louise von Franz, were interested primarily in the counting numbers as symbols and founts of inexhaustible metaphor during the production of conscious experience. Whether in dream, mythology or art, the number *one* tends to symbolize undifferentiated unity; *two* signifies the first distinction or duality; *three* indicates dynamic change and movement away from the static opposition, and *four* suggests stable manifestation.

In this chapter I depart from the natural numbers that interested Jung to number as manifested *naturally* in what Benoit Mandelbrot (1977) calls the *fractal geometry of nature.* I argue for a link between imaginary numbers as iterated recursively on the complex plane and self-reflexive underpinnings of the dynamic unconscious. A precedent for my approach exists in the work of Jungian psychologist and mathematician Robin Robertson (1989). Robertson advances Jung's search for the archetype of order by tracing a history of the qualitative development of human consciousness based on the evolution of quantitative, mathematical discovery. Robertson identifies four stages of evolution, which I describe next, before placing fractal geometry into the context of the fourth.

The first stage involves knowledge of the counting numbers, as relates to primitive consciousness characteristic of many traditional tribes and young children. Here, the inner contents of the unconscious are unwittingly projected into outer, conscious experience. In cybernetic terms, observer and observed are unconsciously merged during the act of making/discovering distinctions in ongoing experience. Translated into the language of contemporary neuroscience, this stage depends upon procedural and implicit memory whose capacity is hard-wired into the primitive brain. This type of memory is *unconscious,* in the more contemporary meaning of the word, embraced by neuroscientists like Jaak Panksapp, Allan Schore, and Daniel Siegel. Whereas Freud's unconscious consists of repressed knowledge *dynamically* pushed beneath the surface of conscious awareness, contemporary neuroscientists view much of the brain's work as unconscious in a different sense. The self-organization of autonomic and limbic systems occurs subcortically, beneath the threshold of consciousness, operating on time scales too rapid *ever* to reach conscious awareness. This distinction between material pushed out of awareness and that which awareness can never reach becomes critical to my later assertion of fractal geometry as the abstract formalization for the ever-receding threshold between conscious and unconscious processes.

During stage two of collective human consciousness, zero emerges as a symbol around the dawn of the Christian era. Within Peircean semiotics, zero represents an important *portmanteau*, a sign that carries double meaning, in this case, by embodying paradox. Zero is a symbol form of *no-thing* that also means *some-thing*. In modern number notation zero serves as a placeholder that enables us endlessly to recycle the same ten digits. By eliminating the need for a different symbol to represent each new number, zero provides an invisible, underground unity to the number system. Here we see early glimmerings of Kauffman's virtual logic—the play of imagination that sharpens focus on "real" distinctions. Recycled digits brought the first formal sign of fractal dynamics within mathematics, albeit in inchoate form, because full arithmetic expression involves self-similar, nested structure on ever-grander scales of magnitude across the 10's, 100's, 1000's number columns. Whereas modern number notation represents a somewhat trivial example of self-similarity, in that it lacks the fractional dimensionality of true fractal form, SUNY philosophers Patrick Grim, Gary Mar, and Paul St. Denis (1998) assert significantly that all of mathematics and logic can be modelled on the computer as an infinitely expanding fractal system. Figure 3 illustrates one aspect of their system: how paradoxes of self-reference can be iterated on the computer.

The classic liar states, "This sentence is false." In the interpersonal version Socrates asserts, "Plato speaks falsely," while Plato counters, "Socrates speaks truly." Fuzzy logic allows infinite-valued variations, starting with the following two assertions:

Figure 3. Self-reference can be iterated on the computer (Courtesy of Patrick Grim, Group for Logic & Formal Semantics, Department of Philosophy, SUNY at Stony Brook)

x: x is as true as y,

y: y is as true as x is false

The assertions are translated mathematically as follows:

$$x_{n+1} = 1 - \text{Abs}(y_n - x_n)$$

$$y_{n+1} = 1 - \text{Abs}((1 - x_n) - y_n)$$

As these equations then are iterated on the computer, fractal images appear when escape time diagrams are colored according to how long it takes various pairs of points to cross certain thresholds.

Robertson's third stage in the evolution of modern consciousness emerged during the Renaissance with the formal introduction of infinity. Using zero as an anchor, humans flew to previously unseen heights of abstraction. The discovery/invention of calculus independently by Newton and Leibniz captured both symbols of zero and infinity concretely within the single concept of a *limit*. Calculus permits the human mind to delve ever more flexibly under the surface of moving and irregular processes into the chaos of imaginary waters, in order to resurface with a new perception of order. The simultaneous invention of perspective in art, plus René Descartes' method of analytic geometry, gave humankind an even sharper, downright 3-dimensional view of distinctions in the natural world.

During this third stage, human beings stopped projecting the contents of inner processes into the outer world. Or at least, this is what they believed they were doing. Beginning with the Renaissance, all attention became fixated on how to categorize perceptible objects. The world of appearances became privileged over that of the imagination, and tools of science and math aided in this mission of *objectifying* perception. With everyone acting as if observers could be separated from processes of their observation, this period of collective consciousness accompanied the development of classical science, while anticipating the emergence of first-order cybernetics.

The fourth and current stage of self-reflexive consciousness arose during the nineteenth century, when previous seeds of recursion became concretely embedded into mathematical technique. Georg Cantor's introduction of the "pigeon-hole technique," by which numbers are paired one-to-one with subsets of themselves, brought recognition of multiple sizes of infinity. Eventually, the number of infinities proliferated until an infinite variety was unveiled.

At the same time that conscious understanding of recursion became ever-more deeply embedded in abstract systems of symbolization, human consciousness was beginning to circle back around to conceptualize imaginative bases for its own unconscious processing. This is evident in the work of South American psychologist, Ignacio Matte Blanco, who uses the seeming *illogic* of infinite sets to characterize the nature of unconscious thinking (e.g., Matte Blanco & Raynor, 1998). The hallmark of infinite sets—that their subsets equate to the whole—is apparent psychologically whenever we generalize a single encounter to every case. This occurs, for example, in the immature psyche of young children fond of calling all women "mommy." It also occurs in the immature psyche of adults guilty of stereotyping, racial bias or misogyny. By contrast, Matte Blanco claims that consciousness of everyday distinctions rests on the mathematics of finite sets. Here, thinking is tethered to deductive methods of concrete discovery. Objects either exist or do not, as deduced by minute-to-minute experience, and guided by Boolean and Aristotelian logic devoid of wild inductive leaps.

Matte Blanco's brand of virtual logic, inspired by properties of infinite sets, anticipates this author's intrapsychic interpretation of fractal dynamics (Marks-Tarlow, 1995; 1999; 2002; 2008). As mathematically defined, fractals are partially infinite and partially finite. While their Euclidean dimension anchors and bounds them in the real world, they also partake of the infinite, which is necessary to calculate fractional dimensionality. As elaborated upon shortly, fractals occupy a

Figure 4. a)Escher's drawing, The Art Gallery, and b) a portrays self-reference as a canvas within a canvas (Courtesy of the author, from Marks-Tarlow (2008))

a)

b)

twilight existence *between* "real" and idealized dimensions. Here the symmetry of identity—self-similarity —paradoxically exhibits parts as complex and infinitely detailed as their whole.

Observers Observing Themselves: Imaginary Numbers and Hidden Dimensions

The shortest path between two truths in the real domain passes through the complex domain. — Jacques Hadamard

By self-reflexively using numbers to code and reflect upon other numbers, Austrian mathematician Gödel brought this fourth stage of human self-reflexive consciousness to full fruition in the mid-twentieth century. Enter second-order cybernetics plus symbol makers using symbols to symbolize the symbolizing process itself plus inherent limitations therein. Like an eyeball attempting to twist around to view its own mechanism, Gödel's mathematics plus the cybernetics of cybernetics make obvious that no observer can

ever hope to observe the observation process fully, without either receiving an incomplete view or becoming mired in paradox.

Figure 4 illustrates how paradoxes of self-reference appear in the work of two different artists. The left frame portrays the author's rendition of Maurice Escher's famous drawing, *The Art Gallery.* An observer looks at a picture of a gallery that includes the observer himself. The perspective is continuous, as it wraps from outside towards inside the observer. Yet a point of discontinuity remains in the form of a blank spot in the center. The blank spot indicates a singularity forming where all order breaks down and the image dissolves recursively into internal contradiction. The right-hand frame, inspired by a David Hockney drawing, portrays self-reference as a canvas within a canvas, implying a discontinuous relationship between external observation and the embedded nature of the self as observer. Just as a different "picture" on the lens can emerge with the next blink of an eye, this form of discrete representation displays crisp edges between embedded levels.

31

While I won't claim that fractals represent a symbol at the same level that zero and infinity do, I will assert that the system of notation ushered in by fractal geometry represents a portmanteau embodying infinite/finite, continuous/discontinuous methods of symbolization. Here, recursive iteration on the imaginary plane reveals yet another level of complexity both in nature and collective consciousness. Here, observers are even more complexly, self-reflexively and consciously entangled in the observed. This fleshes out further Jung's intuition that number brings "order into the chaos of appearances." Within fractals, not only does what you see depend upon the scale of observation, but also the closer you look, the more there is to see.

As a prelude to fractals, let's consider imaginary numbers, which appear as a vital link between complicated order manifest in nature and in the human mind. Discovered in the seventeenth century by Italian mathematician Jerome Cardano, imaginary numbers involve two independent, or orthogonal, axes, one real and one imaginary, and the seemingly impossible square root of -1. As their name suggests, these numbers originally were considered entirely fanciful, even though they kept cropping up in equations of the form, $X^2 = -1$. As often occurs with even the most far-out seeming mathematical abstractions, unexpected practical uses are eventually found, sometimes in the strangest, most apparently magical places. For example, although non-Euclidean geometry was originally thought impractical and contradictory to everyday perception, its rather strange geometry perfectly models Einstein's four-dimensional curvature of spacetime. Generally within mathematical equations, the square root of -1 represents invisible, extra, or hidden dimensionality. In electrical engineering it models reversed polarities of alternating currents. In Einstein's famous equation, $E = mc^2$, the square root of -1 represents the fourth dimension of time, added to the three customary dimensions of space: length, width, and depth. As modeled geometrically by Kauffman (2001), imaginary numbers also crop up in quantum mechanics, another field spawned by Einstein's discoveries, where they capture (or fail to capture) immeasurable, non-local aspects of electron behavior known as *wave functions*.

Jung and his followers play with the idea that imaginary numbers serve to unify inner and outer worlds. As Robertson (2000) notes, Jung mistakenly calls them "transcendent numbers," and names a corresponding psychological function – the *transcendent function* – after them. Jung interprets real and imaginary aspects of the complex plane in terms of the union of conscious and unconscious contents of the psyche. This union for Jung constitutes the essence of individuation, the process by which we come most fully into ourselves. During individuation, the "little self" of the conscious ego aligns and balances with the "big Self" of the unconscious whole: The part of the known coincides with the whole of the unknown.

Physicist and psychologist Arnold Mindell (2000) believes that all mathematics is a code for linking observers with the observed. Mindell upholds imaginary numbers to represent qualitative, subjective aspects of experience, or what he calls "nonconsensual reality," his thinking influenced by Wolfgang Pauli, a physicist whose psychoanalysis also inspired Jung. Pauli's most famous dream involved an inner music teacher who conceptualized imaginary numbers as the key to unifying physics and psychology (see Wolf, 1994). Geometrically, by signifying a phase shift of 90 degrees in the complex plane to represent orthogonal dimensions, Kauffman (2001) characterizes *i* as the most primal distinction in the observer. Generally, it appears that those artificially constructed *fictions* called complex numbers, which possess both a real and an imaginary component, tend to emerge in the very same, self-reflexive places where the observer is increasingly detectable within the observed.

Figure 5. A Mandelbrot set and its zoom levels (Courtesy of Nicolas Desprez, from Marks-Tarlow, 2008)

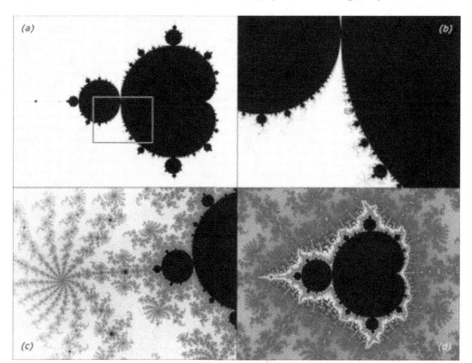

Fractal Geometry

If you like fractals, it is because you are made of them. If you can't stand fractals, it's because you can't stand yourself. It happens. — Homer Smith, Computer Engineer, Art Matrix

Fractal geometry represents the full mathematical fruition of the fourth stage of self-reflexive consciousness, where imaginary numbers are concretized in nature simultaneously to co-create world and self. Computer-generated fractals provide one of the most successful tools ever discovered/invented for simulating highly complex forms in nature. With fractals comes the cyber-semiotic recognition of how the infinite becomes finitely embodied in nature. When the computer is used as a microscope on the complex plane to zoom in on ever-smaller scales of the nonlinear Mandelbrot set ($z \rightarrow x^2 + c$), iteration exhibits unceasing complexity, shifting dynamically with the perspective of the observer. This is illustrated

in the Mandelbrot zoom within Figure 5, where each box represents a magnification of a small area within the previous box.

The benchmark of fractals is self-similarity, a newly discovered, self-reflexive symmetry in which parts of a fractal object resemble the whole. Sometimes this resemblance is approximate and statistical, as is the case with the nonlinear Mandelbrot set. Other times self-similarity is exact, such as with linear fractals. Figure 6 illustrates a linear fractal called the Koch snowflake. In this figure, we easily see how each iteration brings greater complexity. While the area within the snowflake remains finitely bounded, the edges of the Koch curve grow infinitely complex. Whether we consider the linear or nonlinear variety of fractal, not only is the whole greater than the sum of its parts—the hallmark of organic as compared to purely mechanistic systems—but the whole is also paradoxically embodied within the very parts themselves.

Figure 6. Koch's snowflake (Courtesy of Nicolas Desprez, from Marks-Tarlow, 2008)

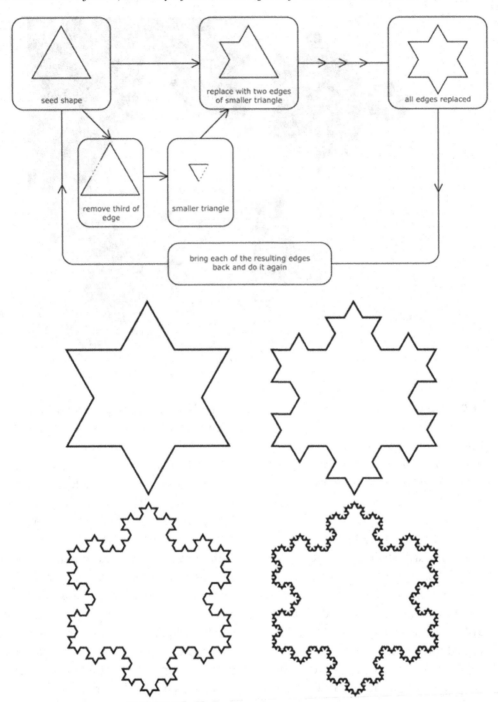

Everywhere they arise, fractals occupy the *boundary zone between dynamic, open processes in nature*. This quality of *betweenness* is illuminated by a technical understanding of fractal dimensionality. Since imaginary numbers model hidden dimensionality, in the case of fractals, this consists of infinite expanses, or imaginary frontiers that lurk *in the spaces between* ordinary, Euclidean dimensions.

Clouds can be conceived as 0-dimensional points that occupy 3-dimensional space. Coastlines are 1-dimensional lines that occupy 2-dimensional planes. Mountains are 2-dimensional surfaces draping a 3-dimensional world. Quaternions are products of the hypercomplex plane consisting of one real and three imaginary axes, as is illustrated in Figure 7. If imaginary numbers do relate to abstract processes in consciousness, and more specifically to the fuzzy zone between mind and body, inner and outer processes, then because they are 3-dimensional shadows of 4-dimensional space, quaternions may provide some clues as to the internal landscape of higher dimensional thought. To understand this, imagine a pink elephant dancing, and you will be manipulating a 3-dimensional image through the 4th dimension of time.

To calculate fractal or Hausdorf dimension (one of a number of ways to measure fractal dimensionality) a log/log relationship estimates the rate at which more information becomes available as we shrink the size of our measuring device. Here a kind of magic becomes evident in the unexpected relationship that emerges between the observer and observed, that is, between measuring stick and that which is measured. Unlike finite objects, where resolution of measurement is possible, because fractal objects partake of the infinite, they exhibit a paradoxical quality: the smaller the measuring stick, the larger the measurement, as illustrated in Figure 8. Because the quantity of measure continually alters relative to the size of the yardstick, fractal dimension is *not only a measurement of quantity* as we usually conceive it. Instead, fractal dimension represents a portmanteau that also indicates the *quality of relations between observer and observed.* Since fractal dimensionality signals what remains constant as we change scales, another paradox soon becomes evident. Fractal pattern simultaneously appears on *all* scales, at the same time that it demonstrates no characteristic scale – a quality called *scale invariance* (Figure 9).

Paradoxical Boundaries

The imaginary numbers are a wonderful flight of God's spirit; they are almost an amphibian between being and not being. —Gottfried Wilhelm Leibniz

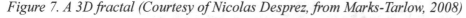

Figure 7. A 3D fractal (Courtesy of Nicolas Desprez, from Marks-Tarlow, 2008)

Figure 8. Compass rule to determine the fractal dimension of a Koch's curve (Adapted from Eglash, 1999, from Marks-Tarlow, 2008)

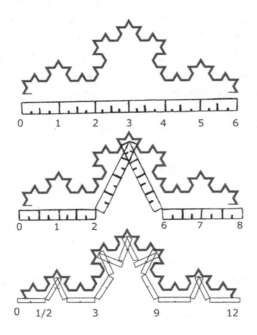

Figure 9. A fractal set (Adapted from Gleick, 1987, from Marks-Tarlow, 2008)

Although mountains and rivers appear to be stable *things* to our Western minds, they are actually continually moving processes that evolve dynamically on various time scales. The fiction of stability and *thingness* is reified by the English language with its predominance of nouns acting on and acted upon by verbs. The dynamism of fractals as processes-in-nature seems much more consistent with American Indian languages, where features such as lightning and coastlines are described using verbs.

As embodied in nature, fractals occupy the complex interface between chaotic forces, such as wind, water and heat comprising the weather. They represent the place where time gets etched into structure through process (see Kauffman, 1980). Fractal dynamics pervade our bodies (e.g., Iannaccone & Khokha, 1996), occupying zones of openness, communication and transportation between various subsystems of the body, as well as between the body and the outside world (Marks-Tarlow, 2002). Blood circulates throughout the body in the fractal branching of arteries and veins. The lungs cycle oxygen in and carbon dioxide out through fractal bronchioles. Even the ion channels in our cells and the neural pathways in the brain, our main organ for perception and communication, are fractal. Self-similar dynamics also pervade psychophysics, in that physical stimuli outside our bodies often follow power laws, which transmute into "just noticeable differences" in sensation and perception.

In human physiology generally, as in nature broadly, fractals function in open systems as boundary keepers, both by separating and connecting various subsystems and levels of being. Skin pores, wrinkles and other markings on the *sacks* in which humans and other animals are enclosed are usually fractally distributed. Facial wrinkles are a good example of how time can get etched into space through fractal form at the outer edge of our bodies. Whereas babies all have smooth faces, older people get uniquely lined. Brows furrowed with worry and mouths framed by laugh lines allow

us to "read" the social history of a person. In this way, self-similar wrinkles engrave characteristic muscle patterns related to emotional response and expression throughout life.

Wrinkles reveal fractals at the interface between mind and body, psychological and physical levels. Likewise, fractals in the brain's neuronal branches and recursively embedded circuits mediate similar *space between* subjective and objective processes. Mathematician Manford Schroeder (1991) opened a door for analyzing fractals symbolically, through which cyberneticist Ron Eglash, among others, now walks. Eglash describes self-similar patterns in Dogon culture, based upon the human form as the unit of meaning (1989), as well as illustrates fractals in African settlement patterns (1999). Physicist-cyberneticist Nicoletta Sala demonstrates that fractal geometry, in particular the self-similarity, is present as an aesthetic property in all cultures, for example in African, Mesoamerican, Western, Japanese, Chinese, Hindu and Islamic cultures (Sala, 2004). She also analyzed the fractal components in different architectural styles as unconscious or conscious acts of design (Sala, 2002). This kind of geometry finds application for generating virtual worlds (Sala, 2010).

Elsewhere (Marks-Tarlow, 1999, 2002) I have detailed the existence of fractals at a more abstract, symbolic level within the human psyche. In the paradoxical, intersubjective space between self and other, fractal dynamics become evident in human behavior, as personality traits manifest in self-similar patterns at multiple scales of social observation. An aggressive person may push others aside verbally with overtalk, push ahead of others physically in bank and other lines, while pushing self-oriented needs ahead of others' in significant relationships. In the clinical sphere, fractals are evident in the frequent mirroring of content in process, as well as within common therapist lore that the entirety of a patient session or even psychoanalysis can be gleaned from a first utterance or dream (e.g., Levenson, 1983;

Marks-Tarlow, 2008). The fractal self is multiply embedded within different scales of social observation (Marks-Tarlow, 1999). Each of us has a proto-self that is biologically driven and precedes consciousness. We have an intrapsychic self, revealed by dreams and unique patterns within our intrapsychic landscape. We possess an interpersonal self, brought into social existence through interaction with others. We have a cultural identity that enables us to share the language and customs of like others. And we possess a national identity that contrasts with people from other countries. Possibly, we possess a global identity opened up by high-tech communication that allows instant access the world over.

Generally speaking, self-similar dynamics appear in the joints, in the space between levels. Not only does identity in nature appear fundamentally fractal, where self-similarity captures scale-invariant patterns as well as scale-variant irregularities and discontinuities, but also, fractals are prevalent in the psyche, where identity is constituted intersubjectively by endless feedback loops in the space between self and other, inside and outside. Within the psyche, scale invariance allows us to operate psychologically on all size and time scales, while self-similarity carries our characteristic stamp of uniqueness and wholeness to each facet of symbolic and social operations.

Seeking Semiotic Seams

It appears as if different, successively larger levels are connected and intercross at the point where the constituents of the new lower level refer to themselves, where antinomic [contradictory] forms appear, and time sets in. We recognize this fact in ordinary speech. When trying to convey a description of a new domain we often construct an apparent antinomy to induce the listener's cognition in a way such as to compel his imagination towards the construction of a larger domain where the apparent opposites can exist in unity. (A moral example: once you lose everything, you

have everything; a philosophical one: a being is when it ceases to be). — Francisco Varela

I have argued that self-similarity spans the full range of existence, from the most concrete, material levels to the most highly abstract and psychological ones. Viewed semiotically, I believe this newly discovered symmetry represents the sign for identity in nature, *the pattern of patterning,* by which essences actually precede evolution and biological reproduction. Due to self-similarity, wholes in nature can dynamically inform the shaping of self-similar parts.

Consider symmetry semiotically as a distinction that leads to no distinction. Within the search for universal scientific laws, this makes sense, because symmetry functions as a formal transformation that results in invariant operations. The idea of a distinction leading to no distinction also links back to the operation of *cancellation* within Spencer-Brown's primitive arithmetic (1969, 1979). Here, at the level of first distinctions, before space and time become established as clear dimensions, symmetry can be viewed as a double-crossing that annihilates the original distinction. An everyday example would be to rotate an object through a mirror axis of symmetry and then back, without any detectable difference.

At the level of first distinctions, where the act of marking is inseparable from the mark itself, a paradox appears: We can't tell the difference between a second crossing that, at less primitive levels, brings us deeper into marked space, over into unmarked territory, or right back to where we started. Formally, all three possibilities are equivalent (as shown in Figure 10).

This is easily visualized with the help of nested versus adjacent circles. Begin with the first distinction indicated by a circle that brackets off insides as *marked* from outsides as *unmarked* (a.). Now consider three recursively-nested circles, each inside the next (b.). Here, to cross twice represents penetration into a deeper level of marked space. In the case of two adjacent circles

Figure 10. Courtesy of the author, from Marks-Tarlow, 2005

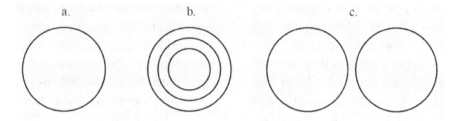

(c.), to cross twice represents entry into an entirely different marked space. Finally in the case of only a single circle (again, a.), to cross twice is to leave and reenter the original marked area. The single circle (a.) represents the basic inner/outer distinction of the self; the three nested circles (b.) represent degrees of interiority of the self; while two adjacent circles (c.) represent the two subjectivities of self and other. The impossibility of formally distinguishing between these three conditions establishes their imaginal, paradoxical foundations at the level of first distinctions. This inability definitively to distinguish between realms of self, world and other carries far-reaching implications.

In the *Laws of Form*, logician Spencer-Brown moved from the duality implied by first distinctions, to paradox that sometimes stems from the self-referential capacity of a system to reenter itself. Varela (1975) notes the brilliance of Spencer-Brown's interpretation of the paradox of reentry as an oscillation, or "an *imaginary* state in the form seen in *time* as an alteration of the two states of the form" (p. 20, emphasis in original). Spencer-Brown's "discovery" of time implicitly links paradoxical form to imaginary numbers on the complex number plane. By asserting reentry as a third value in its own right, Varela agrees with Spencer-Brown that self-referential dynamics establish the presence of time. With Kauffman, Varela went further to assert that paradox becomes embodied at the most basic level, *in the very process dynamics of form itself* (Kauffman & Varela, 1980).

Perhaps the primal confusion surrounding first distinctions, where a double-crossing sometimes leads back to the original marked area and at other times does not, helps explain why Varela's reentry dynamics sometimes lead to paradox and at other times do not. This primal confusion between inside/outside, self/other, organism/world becomes even clearer where second-order cybernetics dovetails with clinical psychology. In this territory, we find a persistent, fundamental inability to distinguish between the deepest recesses of our own subjectivity, versus the intersubjectivity of others, versus the "objectivity" of a world that exists outside of the organism. The notion of primal confusion helps explain the *felt-reality* of dreams and psychoses, and legitimates the controversy surrounding psychoanalytic concepts, such as introjection (the subjective reality of an idealized other as "swallowed whole"), or projective identification (an aspect of the therapist's experience considered as a *disowned* piece of the patient's psyche). Finally, it lends a kind of *imaginative reality* to the apparent *out-there-ness* of everyday experience as well as to the "objective stance" of classical science.

In a previous article for *Cybernetics & Human Knowing* (Marks-Tarlow, Robertson & Combs, 2002), I, with colleagues, speculate on the psychological significance of Varela's recursive dynamics, by examining the individuation process as lifelong, self-reflexive cycles of reentry. Psychological birth is preceded by the paradoxical union of opposites within the unconscious, as we begin our mental life with good/bad, you/me, inside/outside melded together. In order to make first distinctions, nascent consciousness must separate each pole from its opposite. Yet, complete psychological evolution requires that we bring together, blend and balance all opposites. Inner development requires that we leave ourselves in order to get deeper inside. In fact, spiritual advancement can be characterized as the use of self-reflection to achieve increasing objectivity. Yet most spiritual paths aimed towards objectivity move in the opposite direction, e.g., using methods of meditation, to delve yet further *inside* one's inner life. To reframe this primal confusion in terms of fractal boundaries between mind and body, conscious and unconscious elements of experience, provides a new reading of Douglas Hofstadter's (1979) seminal book, *Gödel, Bach and Escher*. Within his proposed *tangled hierarchy*, the "software tangle" of symbols as supported by the brain's "hardware tangle" is easily re-conceptualized in terms of fractal boundaries. Such thinking receives empirical support from the research of Carl Anderson (e.g., Anderson et al., 1998) on the role of rapid eye movement (REM) sleep in fetal and neonatal brain development. Periods of *nuchal atonia* (loss of neck muscle tone) during REM sleep appear organized into self-similar patterns of phasic EMG bursts. From this and related studies, Anderson theorizes that the foundations of consciousness are based on the vertical convergence of $1/f$ power law dynamics, from ion channels to behavioral states (Anderson & Mandell, 1996).

More broadly, I propose that fractals comprise reentry dynamics within Varela's (1979) realm of *autonomous functioning*, typified by borders that are functionally closed yet structurally open. Whether in organic or inorganic forms, autonomous systems appear supported by inherently contradictory underpinnings, which allow recursive cycles of reentry to etch temporal dynamics into spatial form. In the epigraph at the beginning of this section, Francisco Varela (1975) offers self-reference as "the hinge upon which levels of serial inclusiveness intercross" (p. 12). It is easy to view

the universe in terms of successively larger levels of serial inclusiveness. As a crude example, from a semiotic perspective, we might say that physics is embedded within chemistry, which is embedded within biology, which is embedded within psychology. Fractal boundaries help us to conceptualize how Varela's levels of serial inclusiveness connect and intercross. The primal confusion that arises when discontinuous, finite distinctions are made in systems that are embedded in infinite, continuous dynamics suggests why paradox so often arises at the seams in nature.

Whether existing in symbolic or physical form or comprising ordered attractors beneath chaotic forces in nature, fractals negotiate the boundary zone, a place where levels contain the antinomy of opposites both unified and separated. Because fractals span all scales of observation, both to divide and connect them at boundary points, these dynamics might help to bridge traditional levels of analysis, from the purely physical level of Prigogine's far-from-equilibrium thermodynamics, through biological levels of reentry in Maturana and Varela's autopoietic systems, to higher order social and cultural levels implied by Peirce's concept of historical drift and praxis.

CONCLUSION: A FINAL WORD ABOUT CYBERSEMIOTICS

This chapter suggests fractal geometry as an important archetype of order, the pattern of nature's patterning, as a bridge between finite and infinite dimensions, real and imaginary processes, as well as material and psychological levels of existence. One irony is this: While we use *unnatural* or mechanical means, such as computers, to discover and illuminate the workings of fractals, what we illuminate extends beyond and beneath the postmodern mirrors that reflect infinite regression in forms of human production and reproduction. Ranulph Glanville rails against the cybernetic nightmare of machines controlling human beings, presenting instead the second-order cybernetic alternative of the controller controlled by the controllee. Fractal geometry helps us move away from the paradigm of control entirely. By illuminating fractals, we self-reflexively illuminate wholes in nature where the observer appears in the observed during the co-creation of both.

That we need the computer to help us visualize fractals suggests the importance of cybersemiotics to psychological development. While it takes a community to raise a child, by providing multiple subjectivities necessary for full cultural and social awareness, ironically it takes the mechanism of a computer to develop the potential for greater self-awareness and connectivity back to nature. Because the mathematics of fractals depends upon infinite, recursive iteration, humankind had but a glimpse of this geometry during the nineteenth century, in the form of *monster curves* and Julia sets. The ability to represent the granddaddy of all Julia sets – the full Mandelbrot set – plus higher dimensional offshoots – like quaternions – required the speed and tremendous parallel processing capabilities of the computer, which was not possible until the end of the twentieth century.

Whereas first-order cybernetics purports to represent reality as it exists outside of observers, second-order cybernetics twists around recursively to represent the observers themselves, using the computer as metaphor and mind modeled as mechanism. With fractal geometry, the metaphor comes full circle back to its organic bases. A unity between mind, machine, and nature becomes apparent when self-similarity is regarded as nature's sign of identity. This insight dovetails with the frequent spiritual vision of all of creation as a self-reflexive expression of self into form in order to know, share and lovingly reunite with Self. Indeed fractals are evident in religious images and architecture throughout the world (see Jackson, 2004). The notion of fractals unifying mind, machine and nature also dovetails with the position of neurological positivism espoused by philosopher and psychologist Larry Vandervert (1990).

Vandervert claims that evolution itself proceeds self-reflexively, culminating in the most complex object in the known universe, the human brain. As we use our brains self-reflexively to examine ourselves, our models grow more sophisticated and ever closer to the fractal stuff of which our minds, brains and nature at large is composed.

Semiotically, the ubiquitous presence of fractals and self-similar dynamics in mind, body, and nature as revealed by modern computing, offer exciting possibilities for new metaphors of unity between mind, machine and nature. By allowing us to see deeper into the unconscious bases of our own experience, fractals point the way to the invisible, interconnected ground of all being, giving rise to observer and observed, mind and body, inside and outside, subjective and objective experience alike. Here we glimpse the fabric of the infinite whole as it is sewn into each finite part.

In sum, whereas Jung speculated about the archetypal significance of the *natural* numbers, in this essay I explore number as manifested *naturally* in the fractal geometry of nature. Whereas Jung speaks of number as an archetype of order *which has become conscious*, I present fractal geometry as deep order under chaos, *which is yet to become conscious and impossible ever fully to do so*. With fractals as a new metaphor of mind, we no longer need to deify or defile mechanism as metaphor.

Instead we can use mechanism as a tool. As we continue to use the recursive formulas of chaos, complexity, fractal geometry and cellular automata to simulate the natural world, we see across multiple, nested levels of serial inclusiveness, how self-similar fractal dynamics recur as a meta-pattern.

Cycles of reentry continually oscillate between creating and erasing the seam where observer and observed, perceiver and perceived, inner and outer, self and other, intersect and self-cross paradoxically. At these semiotic seams, self and world appear mutually co-determining. Meanwhile, fractals represent another level of abstraction in human consciousness, suggestive of the dynamic underpinnings of the unconscious. In this elusive seam where the unconscious and conscious minds touch, we forever seek the means by which brains cobble minds that study brains. Here, the physiological act of making a distinction creates the world as we perceive it, while the world brings distinction to the consciousness of the perceiver.

REFERENCES

Anderson, C., & Mandell, A. (1996). Fractal time and the foundations of consciousness: Vertical convergence of 1/f phenomena from ion channels to behavioral states. In Mac Cormac, E., & Stamenov, M. (Eds.), *Fractals of brain, fractals of mind* (pp. 75–126). Amsterdam, The Netherlands: John Benjamin.

Anderson, C., Mandell, A., Selz, K., Terry, L., Robinson, S., & Wong, C. (1998). The development of nuchal atonia associated with active (REM) sleep in fetal sheep: Presence of recurrent fractal organization. *Brain Research, 787*(2), 351–357.

Eglash, R. (1999). *African fractals: Modern computing and indigenous design*. New Brunswick, NJ: Rutgers University Press.

Eglash, R., & Broadwell, P. (1989). Fractal geometry in traditional African architecture. *Dynamics Newsletter*, June.

Glanville, R. (1998). A (Cybernetic) musing: The gestation of second order cybernetics, 1968-1975 – A personal account. *Cybernetics & Human Knowing, 5*(2), 85–95.

Grim, P., Mar, G., & St. Denis, P. (1998). *The philosophical computer: Exploratory essays in philosophical computer modeling*. Cambridge, MA: The MIT Press.

Hofstadter, D. (1979). *Gödel, Escher, Bach: An eternal golden braid*. New York, NY: Vintage.

Iannaccone, P., & Khokha, M. (Eds.). (1996). *Fractal geometry in biological systems*. New York, NY: CRC Press.

Jackson, W. (2004). *Heaven's fractal net: Retrieving lost visions in the humanities*. Bloomington, IN: Indiana University Press.

Kauffman, L. (2001). Virtual logic – Reasoning and playing with imaginary Boolean values. *Cybernetics & Human Knowing, 8*(3), 77–85.

Kauffman, L., & Varela, F. (1980). Form dynamics. *Journal of Social and Biological Structures, 3*, 171–206.

Levenson, E. (1983). *The ambiguity of change*. New York, NY: Basic Books.

Mandelbrot, B. (1977). *The fractal geometry of nature*. New York, NY: W. H. Freeman.

Marks-Tarlow, T. (1995). The fractal geometry of human nature. In R. Robertson & A. Combs (Eds.), *Proceedings from the First Conference of the Society for Chaos Theory in Psychology and the Life Sciences*. Mahweh: NJ: Erlbaum.

Marks-Tarlow, T. (1999). The self as a dynamical system. *Nonlinear Dynamics Psychology and Life Sciences, 3*(4), 311–345.

Marks-Tarlow, T. (2002). Fractal dynamics of the psyche. In B. Goertzel & A. Combs (Eds.), *Dynamical psychology: An international, interdisciplinary e-journal of complex mental affairs*. Retrieved from http://www.goertzel.org/dynapsyc/2002/FractalPsyche.htm

Marks-Tarlow, T. (2005). Semiotic seams: Fractal dynamics of reentry. *Cybernetics & Human Knowing, 11*(1), 49–62.

Marks-Tarlow, T. (2008). *Psyche's veil: Psychotherapy, fractals and complexity*. New York, NY: Routledge.

Marks-Tarlow, T., Robertson, R., & Combs, A. (2002). Varela and the Uroboros: The psychological significance of reentry. *Cybernetics & Human Knowing, 9*(2), 31–47.

Matte Blanco, I., & Raynor, E. (1998). *The unconscious as infinite sets.* London, UK: Karnac Books.

Meares, R. (2006). *The metaphor of play.* New York, NY: Routledge.

Mindell, A. (2000). *Quantum mind: The edge between physics and psychology.* Portland, OR: Lao Tse Press.

Robertson, R. (1989). The evolution of number: Self-reflection and the archetype of order. *Psychological Perspectives, 20*(1), 128–141.

Robertson, R. (2000). The evolution of Jung's archetypal reality. *Psychological Perspectives, 41,* 66–80.

Sala, N. (2002). The presence of the self-similarity in architecture: Some examples. In Novak, M. M. (Ed.), *Emergent nature* (pp. 273–283). Singapore: World Scientific.

Sala, N. (2004). Fractal geometry in the arts: An overview across the different cultures. In Novak, M. M. (Ed.), *Thinking in patterns: Fractals and related phenomena in nature* (pp. 177–188). Singapore: World Scientific.

Sala, N. (2010). Fractals in architecture, hyper-architecture …and beyond. *Chaos and Complexity Letters. International Journal on Dynamical System Research, 4*(3), 147–180.

Schroeder, M. (1991). *Fractals, chaos, power laws.* New York, NY: Freeman.

Spencer-Brown, G. (1969). *Laws of form.* London, UK: Allen and Unwin.

Spencer-Brown, G. (1979). *Laws of form* (rev. ed.). New York, NY: E. P. Dutton.

Vandervert, L. (1990). Systems thinking and neurological positivism: Further elucidations and implications. *Systems Research, 7*(1), 1–17.

Varela, F. (1975). A calculus for self-reference. *International Journal of General Systems, 2,* 5–24.

Varela, F. (1979). *Principles of biological autonomy.* New York, NY: North Holland.

Winnicott, D. (1974). *Playing and reality.* Harmondsworth, UK: Penguin.

Wolf, F. (1994). *The dreaming universe: A mind expanding journey into the realm where psyche and physics meet.* New York, NY: Simon and Schuster.

Chapter 3
Thinking Animals and Thinking Machines in Psychoanalysis and Beyond

Franco Scalzone
Italian Psychoanalytical Society, Italy

Gemma Zontini
Italian Psychoanalytical Society, Italy

ABSTRACT

In this chapter, the authors examine some similarities between computer science and psychoanalysis, and formulate some hypotheses by bringing closer the statute of connectionism to the energetic model of the psychic apparatus as well as the OOP (object-oriented programming) to the object relations theory. The chapter also describes the relation existing between the functioning of mnemic systems and human temporalities as dynamic structures/processes which might be represented as complementary images of each other. The authors make some remarks on the machine and people theme, the way in which men relate to machines, especially "thinking machines," describing the fantasies they arouse. In order to do this, the chapter uses Tausk's classic (1919/1933) "On the Origin of the 'Influencing Machine' in Schizophrenia"[1], as well as some of Freud's writings.

PSYCHOANALYSIS AND ARTIFICIAL INTELLIGENCE: A NEW ALLIANCE?

In this chapter we describe, with a panoramic view, some similarities between computer science and psychoanalysis and we will formulate some hypotheses by bringing closer the statute of connectionism to the energetic model of the psychic apparatus as well as the OOP (Object Oriented Programming) to the object relations theory. Finally we will make some remarks on the machine and people theme, the way in which men relate to machines, especially "thinking machines," describing the fantasies they arouse and we will then propose a psychoanalytical interpretation. In order to do this we will use Tausk's classic (1919/1933) "On the Origin of the 'Influencing Machine' in Schizophrenia," as well as some of Freud's writings.

DOI: 10.4018/978-1-4666-2077-3.ch003

CONNECTIONISM

Computers are not appropriate models of brain, but they are the most powerful heuristic tool we have with which to try to understand the matter of the mind. (Edelman, 1992, p. 194)

As Turkle(1988) points out, what we may call classic artificial intelligence (AI) is too often viewed only as computation or as procedures for information processing; it is therefore mainly connected to cognitivism. Such conceptual collocation has driven away from AI the interests of many psychoanalysts, notwithstanding many attempts, such as Erdelyi's (1985), Bucci's (1997) and others', to build a bridge between psychoanalysis and cognitive psychology.

AI studies intelligence in an indirect way, trying to build machines capable of intelligent behaviour but without paying too much attention to the peculiar features of human intelligence. Its method is the programming of calculators so that they may show some intelligent capabilities. We may say that there are essentially two ways to try and simulate intelligent human processes through computer modelling: either we start from the symbolic functions of a higher level then trying to break them down into lower level subfunctions (top-down method) or we start from the attempt to reproduce low level functions, or even the hardware, to then make our way up to high level symbolic functions.

Edelman (1992), with his neural Darwinism theory, shows us just how our brain is able, through neural group segregation (TNGS), to operate in a bottom-up mode, that is to say able to self-learn and self–organise when faced with an unlabelled world. We can say that the first method to simulate cognitive processes is the one carried out by classic AI, which some would like to merely call cognitive simulation, and the second one is the one by emergent AI.

If we consider the reductionistic position which homologises mind and calculator, we see that, for the time being, the only mental activities which can be simulated on a calculator are the perceptive cognitive and logical ones. As it is known, the latter are the simplest ones to simulate through ad hoc algorithms, while much harder, for instance, is the simulation of perceptive processes.

We witness the apparent paradox of how the ones which appear as mental activities difficult for men to carry out, such as complex mathematical calculations, are rapidly performed by computers. On the contrary, psychological functions, which we deem as simple, (common sense*)*, which we are all capable of performing without even realising it but which pertain subjectivity and can't be so easily expressed in as formalised a way through an algorithm, entail extreme processing complexity and a difficult theoretical explanation as well as the impossibility, at least for now, of being simulated on a computer.

AI has found remarkable difficulties every time it has been faced with the solution of aleatory problems, as in the simulation of vision in order to recognise forms with irregular contours, or in analogical reasoning etc. Also emotions are indirect and secondary products of the functioning of the structure and of the way in which it is organised and they cannot be reproduced through an effective procedure, through a programme. What a machine would be lacking is the qualitative character of the conscious experience (qualia*)*. They, the emotions, can be found in no place and in no particular level, they too are distributed functions and emerge from the complexity of the structural organisation.

Another difficulty is the fact that human mathematical skills also possess the non-algorithmic capacity to recognise mathematical truths, which would spring from some sort of intuition which would not use physical symbols manipulated by following algorithmical procedures.

Nowadays calculators are able to simulate mainly logical thinking–the type of system which, according to Basch-Kahre (1985), is innate to the brain; in fact she assumes that a primitive form of logic has existed since the gestation period of the foetus. We are saying this to underline how the forms of thinking which at times seem to be the most fully developed, that is logical thinking, can probably be also very ancient and perhaps they seem to be more connected to the physical structure of the brain (hardwired) than other types of mental functioning. A Boolean network for instance, that is, nonintentional system, is already able to solve self-learning problems by using logical functions. But one must also say that our brain, when performing logical thinking and using logical language, neither reveals nor operates on the low level of the neural network but on the high levels of a sophisticated symbolic functioning and with a symbolic language.

Already von Neumann (1958) wrote that the external forms of our mathematical language are absolutely irrelevant in the evaluation of the logical or mathematical language actually used in the central nervous system. Furthermore, the brain, unlike calculators and boolean networks, is a system capable of intentional self-organisation.

Taking into account what we have said and pushing inferences a little forward, we can say that the computational aspects of the mind (considering their higher accessibility to being simulated on a calculator, though considered as superior functions) show a higher feasibility both by using for instance a machine with a von Neumann-like architecture, Turing machine[2], and by using a neural network architecture working with parallel processing. The functioning of the second type is certainly more similar to the functioning of the brain-machine, especially as regards the part which we would call the unconscious.

The term simulation is employed in computer science with many different shades of meaning ranging from the possibility to build perfect sequences of symbolic thinking, like the one about the logic processes of thought, until the possibility to deceit, through which the naive spectator is fooled when showed that the machine has intelligence and a relational skill similar to the human

being's but which, at least for the time being, it does not possess. By simulation here we do not mean simulation of the mind expressed through computer programmes, for example the one shown by programmes such as PARRY by Colby or ELIZA[3] by Weizebaum which look more like artefacts to us, if not funny and sophisticated bluffs. Programmes like ELIZA, which in its section called DOCTOR simulates a rogersian psychotherapist, only simulate the initial and final parts of human behaviour and therefore, like the Turing test deal with mind just as if it were a black box. By studying merely the initial conditions, the inputs, and the final ones, the outputs, they reduce the whole test to the utilisation of verbal behaviour. Such method is unacceptable because one cannot reduce intelligence and emotionality to being expressed only verbally. In fact, Weizenbaum underlined, when rightly criticising his disciple Colby's programme PARRY which simulates a paranoid mind, that when the programme was having some trouble, it would shut down thus refusing to answer and confirming to the interlocutor a kind of behaviour which showed anxiety of the persecutory type. Therefore, a programme which were completely passive and in which the interlocutor found himself facing a dumb screen, would have perfectly represented the simulation of an autistic patient.

Simulations are not simply and only supposed to reproduce phenomena, but they must try to reproduce the mechanisms and processes which lie behind phenomena; they are another way of expressing theories without turning to symbols. Furthermore they are useful also to formulate some empirical previsions and then verify them: they realize an experimental laboratory in which virtual phenomena occur within an artificial reality. The simulations which we are referring to are made possible by the presence of the computer. The advantages in using simulations are manifold: for instance, they allow to study phenomena which, due to physical and temporal reasons, cannot be studied any other way or phenomena impossible to reproduce for ethical reasons, and so forth.

Moreover, they are extremely useful in order to study complex systems which present strong unpredictability and irrepeatability otherwise difficult to face and whose theories are as complex.

By simulation we here mean, according to the connectivism paradigm, simulating the functioning of the brain and therefore of the mind, including its internal structural organisation, just the way they operate perhaps in real people. It is true that there is the risk of excessive reductionism but which is highly sophisticated and therefore very different from the reductionism of classic AI. But simulation techniques are only in their early stages and we shall have to wait for future development to fully appreciate their real possibilities.

For a long time now, an interest in a different field of AI has been resurfacing: connectionism. It employs the calculator not by using programmes which work in a sequential way according to instructions and rules provided by the programme to manipulate data, but by using software which simulates the neural network, that is, neural networks, which perform parallel processing; that, in a way, is much more similar to the operational mode of the brain. A neural network is a set of neurons linked by connections which carries out feedback when the cells are stimulated. When Hebb in 1949 put forward such model, scientists had little knowledge of the real connections present in the brain. One may also utilise proper parallel-architecture machines in which there is a high number of *processors* operating in parallel: such architecture speeds up processing in a remarkable way. Within connectionism information processing is carried out by the interaction of a great number of simple units appropriately connected. The architecture of most digital calculators, instead, is the classic one by von Neumann (1958) in which the memory and the central processing unit (CPU) are separated. In order to perform a programme, data are called back by memory, processed within the central unit and then reallocated into the memory: this is a sequential architecture because operations are carried out one at a time and the process then can

hardly be speeded up over certain limits because of the existence of bottlenecks which slow down the performing of programmes.

We must particularly underline one characteristic which differentiates traditional programming from neural network-programming. In classic AI the machine must be explicitly programmed by man who provides the instructions for the performing of a certain procedure; this is obtained through one or more algorithms which will be written in a chosen programming language and which will form the programme. Instead, in connectionism man provides, randomly, a series of weights entered into the input units of the network, and then the network is able to modify itself by performing self-learning based on experience. All of this will determine the behaviour of the network; in other words, the network is able to find by itself those weights on the connections which will allow it to realise the performance required, and therefore it is able to self-organize.

It is interesting to report here a passage by Freud (Breuer & Freud, 1892-1895, p. 291) that exemplifies the functioning of conscience:

For there is some justification for speaking of the "defile" of consciousness. The term gains meaning and liveliness for a physician who carries out an analysis like this. Only a single memory at a time can enter ego-consciousness. A patient who is occupied in working through such a memory sees nothing of what is pushing after it and forgets what has already pushed its way through. If there are difficulties in the way of mastering this single pathogenic memory–as, for instance, if the patient does not relax his resistance against it, if he tries to repress or mutilate it–then the defile is, so to speak, blocked. The work is at a standstill, nothing more can appear, and the single memory which is in process of breaking through remains in front of the patient until he has taken it up into the breadth of his ego. The whole spatially-extended mass of psychogenic material is in this way drawn through a narrow cleft and thus arrives in consciousness cut up, as it were, into pieces or strips. It is the psychotherapist's business to put these together once more into the organization which he presumes to have existed. Anyone who has a craving for further similes may think at this point of a Chinese puzzle.

Conscious processes then, also according to Freud, are processed in a sequential way and therefore conscience would work along the lines of an architecture similar to von Neumann's. Unconscious, instead, would work in parallel, a mode which is much more similar to the neural network processing one. Here, the parallelism is meant as the spatial development of a complex performing algorithm and not as several independent processes in a simultaneous performance. Therefore parallel time has a limit because it is bound to sequential space and thus the series of intermediate data, which must be periodically memorised, represents the space needed to solve the problem.

In the final part of the above-mentioned quotation by Freud, we can see how the mass of psychic materials, in order to be used by conscience, must first be translated into words and then processed and conveyed, as it occurs, for instance, in the conscious work of an analysis, and must then be "drawn through a narrow cleft and thus arrives in consciousness cut up, as it were, into pieces or strips." It is evident here the evocation of the paper tape of the sequential functioning in a Turing Machine. Freud had attributed the difference between *Ucs* and *Prec* to the fact that preconscious representation is linked to language, that is, to word representation. He therefore believed that for unconscious contents (thing representations) to become conscious it needed linking to word representation, and therefore such linkage to language, as a matter of fact, made consciousness a typically sequential process (AI).

Returning to our subject, other machines, instead, have a parallel architecture; that is, they are made up of many microprocessors, functioning

simultaneously, which are each provided with their own memory. The processing is thus remarkably speeded up compared to von Neumann-designed machines.

Nowadays, neural networks can be realised on a calculator, networks of simple elements which simulate a network of neurons and which can be implemented both on parallel processing machines and on normal personal computers: they simulate the nervous system of an organism or artificial life which uses genetic algorithms. The networks are made up of three components: input units connected to internal units and these ones to output units. These simulations or these parallel machines, when they simulate a mind, have a functioning which is more similar to the functioning of the Ucs system in which several processes operate in parallel simultaneously. In the case of artificial life we also have the simulation of the environment in which the organism lives. A neural network is a simulated system which transforms patterns of activation of neurons into other patterns of activation of neurons; therefore, there are no symbols.

We have here spoken about feed-forward neural networks whose characteristics are limited, because for example there is no representation of time. In order to realise this we need recurrent networks, that is networks in which there are paths of ascending and descending or recurring information, as in the brain, thanks to which they are able to have some sort of short-term memory. A network of this type can generate complex successions of activation vectors even without any input. But the true innovation is when not only the software, but also the hardware is structured through platforms specialised for the processing of particular algorithms (neuronal chip). This allows not to limit oneself to using simple simulations programmed on a serial machine, which is however slow, but real hardware networks able to carry out the parallel distributed calculation at high speed.

For the paradigm of strong AI, then, the properly programmed calculator is a mind because it possesses cognitive states. Conversely, weak AI considers the calculator only as a powerful work-tool to study the mind.

Classic AI studied mental functioning trying to reproduce procedures which might provide the same results of mental operations, neglecting the architecture of the physical device: functionalism. The important element is the software, the set of algorithmic procedures implemented in the biological hardware, without any interest either in the machine or in the processes occurring inside of it, therefore not even inside of the person.

Emergent AI, on the contrary, strives to reproduce also the neural organisation in which the brain is structured and therefore it can investigate the birth of the microstructure of the cognitive processes of the system to then get to the macrostructure as the set of emerging properties. Cognitivism tried to reproduce only the external results of mental workings; connectivism, instead, tries to reproduce the mechanisms and the internal functioning mode. That is, it tries to reproduce not only the functioning of the mental machine but also its physical correlate and its organisational architecture. Finally, classic AI operates by simulating a type of top-down knowledge, which means starting from highly symbolic levels, while neural networks proceed in the opposite way, bottom-up, starting, that is, from the level of sub or presymbolic configuration; Freud would say, in the "Project for a scientific psychology" (1895/n.d.-b), starting from quantity to get to quality, that is, to the conscious being.

The connectionistic idea that the quantity of the weight can be viewed as a measure of the conductivity of the relative connection makes us think of the Freudian idea, once again expressed in the "Project" and regarding the description of the functioning of the neuronic apparatus, about the facilitations that the nervous impulse may encounter in the passing through the contact-barriers of the neurons of ψ system, which is connected to memory. As we know, when the passing of excitation from one neuron to the other through the contact barriers causes a permanent diminishing of resistances, there will be a facilitation so that excitation will in the future choose the path which has been facilitated. We would like to remind our readers that for Freud, the mnestic trace is nothing but a particular configuration of facilitations. Both processes, the connectionistic one and the psychoanalytical one, are then referred to the construction of a memory by means of the organisation of neuronic configurations in which certain circuits and certain neuronal groups, more stable because facilitated, are favoured compared to others when meeting, in the future, signals of a similar type. Long-term changes of the forces of synapses then supply the basis to learning and memory.

Freud, also in the case of memory, does not always present to us the same ideas; sometimes he seems to be talking of a localised, static, addressed memory, based on set memory traces which once activated produce memories, and at other times he presents to us a much more developed picture of a dynamic memory, arranged in a distributed structure and capable of constant recategorizations, which he described in a letter to Fliess (Masson, 1985) as a "rearrangement" in accordance with fresh circumstances–to a retranscription. The categorisation indicates the possibility to generalise, to enter perceived objects into preconstituted empty forms. Recategorization means that the recalling of a particular categorical response does not occur in the form in which it occurred the first time (even though such possibility cannot be excluded). The response, that is, memory, in general is modified and enriched by the ongoing changes. This type of memory is both associative and inaccurate, unlike the replicative memory of computers, but it is dynamic and capable of generalisations, because founded upon probabilistic perceptive categorisations based upon values, and continuous recategorizations.

We are here going to sum up some of the fundamental characteristics of the functioning of networks. Firstly, we would like to highlight the subformal, subsymbolic approach of the system which brings it closer to the functioning of the unconscious: it is capable of producing an internal representation of the quantitative-type concept. The organisation of knowledge (perception, memory) is distributed and not localistic, this means that it is represented by a set of network units, while with classic AI knowledge is conceived in terms of symbolic representation and information processing in accordance with sequential programmes founded upon rules which manipulate data, just like in cognitivism, which utilises a computational model of the mind. Memory is neither localized nor simply addressed, but it is a procedural and distributed memory thus being able to be continually recategorized; it is a property of the system. It is then a nonreplicative memory which depends for its form on the dynamics of degenerative and associative networks. Such a characteristic about distributed functions allows the system to react to lesions without replying with a breakdown of the system itself but only with a slow decaying of the net due to its tolerance to defaults, as it occurs with the brain. Finally, we would like to underline the capacity to learn through experience, not by resorting to the transmission either of data in the form of information, or of programmes which reveal how to process them, but by using procedures which assess any aleatory perturbation from the outside and then process them according to its own purposes.

Learning can be carried out, for instance, according to the backpropagation[4] learning method or by means of simulated annealing[5]. The system has therefore the possibility to self-organise and evolve in an adaptive way.

Connectionism does not limit itself to studying the mind with models inspired to the brain, but it studies both the mind and the brain, as particular cases of a larger class of systems characterised by a large number of simple elements which are in intersection among themselves according to nonlinear and complex dimensions. This means that the dualism between mind and brain is overcome not by simply reducing the former to the latter but by including the study of both into the more general study on a particular class of phenomena of nature, or if you wish, of reality.

This initial approach to AI, the one of the connectionistic type, can be compared to the energetic drive model of psychoanalysis, because we can compare, for instance, the quantitative concept of weight or value to the one of charge. During the training of neural networks, as we said, patterns of activation are assigned to the input units and then the correctness of the output patterns will be verified.

ROAMING THROUGH MEMORY IN PSYCHOANALYSIS: MNESTIC SYSTEMS DYNAMICS

In this paragraph we try to give an example concerning the two different models of the psychic functioning in psychoanalysis, the localized one and the distributed one. For this purpose, we will try to highlight Freud's two different conceptions of memory. The first one is based upon a localistic model and serial processing: memories are stored in a fixed and static way and therefore, they can be retrieved one at a time and cannot be changed or rearranged in a different way. The second model, on the contrary, was based on a connectionistic conception and parallel processing: memory is a distributed function and can be continuously reorganized and recategorized, because of the registration of new external or internal inputs. In fact, Freud sometimes appears to be talking about memory as static, localized, based on fixed memory traces which, when activated, produce memories; at other times he presents the picture of a dynamic memory, arranged in a distributed way and capable of constant recategorizations. Actually, in our brain there are no specific memories; there are only tools for reorganizing past impressions. As we have already said, a memory of such a type is both associative and inaccurate–that is, reminiscences–unlike the replicative memory of computers.

The underlying fil rouge of the paragraph is represented by the relation existing between the functioning of mnemic systems and human temporalities as dynamic structures/processes which might be represented as complementary images of each other. We may also say that primary fantasies (innate elements), individual memory (acquired elements) and temporality function as a self-referential three-fold structures able to generate a world and provide it with a meaning. The Nachträglichkeit (deferred action) is its main dynamic mechanism which, with its continual functioning–just like the flying shuttle of a loom–constantly corrects the warp through a temporal-spatial to-and-from movement of the desire thread.

There might therefore arise the need to individuate in the same subject different chronotypes, not only on a diachronic level but also on a synchronic one. It is possible, by grasping the mismatch between noncongruent historical times which exist in the same chronological present, to get to envision a temporal multiversum, a time with many dimensions, all present, an intertwining of different time planes, a counterpoint of temporal unbalances in the same individual who still lives in a single and shared chronological time.

Man is a caducous system which, through primary fantasies and his tending towards the object, encompasses, concealed in himself, a sort of unlimited time, whether projected towards the past or towards the future.

We can find useful descriptions of the organization and functioning of memory in *Studies on hysteria*, where Freud (Breuer & Freud, 1893-1895) describes the complexity of the arrangement of mnemic traces which unfold through mnemic chains. We have so far been talking about memory in order to clarify, obviously, how closely connected it is to the organization and temporal processing of psychism.

Let's quote Freud, (1896/ n.d.-c):

From a single scene two or more memories are reached at the same time, and from these again side-chains proceed whose individual links may once more be associatively connected with links belonging to the main chain. Indeed, a comparison with the genealogical tree of a family whose members have also, intermarried, is not at all a bad one. (p. 198)

Later on, in the last part of "The psychotherapy of hysteria" (Breuer & Freud, 1893-1895), Freud will extensively deal with the description of the arrangement of psychic material in a severe neuroses: a structure in several dimensions which organizes itself in three different ways. By following the description of such a complex pathological organization of part of the mental apparatus, and precisely the repressed material, we may see, as if through a torn curtain, the structuring of part of the unconscious systems (repressed unconscious). We will use this description to show the organization of mnemic systems in a spatial-temporal sense: see Figure 1[6].

To sum up, we will say that there exists a nucleus consisting in memories of events or trains of thought in which the traumatic factor has culminated or the pathogenic idea has found its purest manifestation. All around such a core there is an 'atmosphere' of mnemic material arranged in a threefold order.

1.   If we call theme the grouping of homogeneous memories into a linearly stratified plurality, the first arrangement will present itself according to a linear chronological order, like in a dossier; the first memory is what Freud called the outer cover of the dossier.

2.   The second type of morphological arrangement of the themes will be the concentric mode which develops around the central pathogenic nucleus in strata of equal degree of resistance, though gradually increasing when approaching the centre. This type

Figure 1. Organization of the pathogenic material of a severe hysteric neurosis

ORGANIZATION OF THE PATHOGENIC MATERIAL OF A SEVERE HYSTERIC NEUROSES

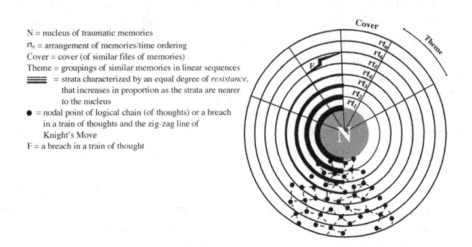

N = nucleus of traumatic memories
rt_0 = arrangement of memories/time ordering
Cover = cover (of similar files of memories)
Theme = groupings of similar memories in linear sequences
▬▬▬ = strata characterized by an equal degree of *resistance*,
     that increases in proportion as the strata are nearer
     to the nucleus
● = nodal point of logical chain (of thoughts) or a breach
     in a train of thoughts and the zig-zag line of
     Knight's Move
F = a breach in a train of thought

Picture of the Pathogenic Psychical Group

of arrangement is simultaneously morphological and chronological, because the most superficial themes are the most recent ones as well as the ones presenting less resistance. Moreover, it is an arrangement of the energetic type because resistances are provided with a countercharge regulated by its distance from the repressed: a defensive countercatexis.

3.   And finally, an arrangement according to thought-content, the linkage made by a logical thread which reaches as far as the nucleus and tends to take an irregular and twisting path, different in every case: a dynamic arrangement. (Breuer & Freud, 1893-1895, pp. 288-290).

This logical connection might be graphically represented with a network of lines, that is mnemic chains, which meet in/branch out of nodal points, thus intersecting, uniting or diverging in all directions, as if to form a web. The first type of arrangement seems to hint at an almost localistic description of fixed mnemic traces. The type of arrangement which appears to be the most inter-esting is the dynamic one, arranged according to logical threads. This arrangement is structured like a network, made up of *connection tracts* and *exchange nodes*, tri-dimensionally expanding around the *pathogenic nucleus* according to a spatial representation which we imagine as being spherical.

Taking into account Freud's quotation (Freud, 1918/n.d.-f) when he says: "I have therefore been obliged to put it together from even smaller fragments than are usually at one's disposal for purposes of synthesis. This task, which is not difficult in other respects, finds a natural limit when it is a question of forcing a structure which is itself in many dimensions on to the two-dimensional descriptive plane." (p. 72) and of the limits he denounces, we may imagine the graph not as a bidimensional structure, but as a pluridimensional structure.

Connections are established, for instance within therapy, by free associations. In this case, for the exploration of the network of the mnemic traces, at times this is resolutive "the zig-zag line in the solution of a Knight's Move" with which it is possible to enter ever-new paths transversal and transradial, leading to key-memory, always of a sexual nature.

We may therefore access memories both through temporal sequences (sequential access) and at random (random access) as Freud (1923) said relating how one should proceed in the dream interpretation technique. The organisation of the associative paths of the memory, as well as language and dream together with condensation and shifting, indicate all the mechanisms of thought movements according to the rules of its functioning.

We may then assume that memory thus organized is not allocated, within exact locations, but rather lies in a state which we might define as being distributed. This type of allocation, or better still, of organization, is completely different from the initial two which Freud himself called morphological. Memory is dynamically distributed throughout the system and therefore enjoys some peculiarities. The dynamic allocation of memories, or of the material able to organize and re-organize memories–or better still recategorize within time, both spontaneously and by evocation–does not belong to an only block or neuronal map. The possibility for a memory to be evoked, therefore, also depends on the mnemonic complex of which it is part and therefore it can, for instance, be available within a certain mnemic context, within a given circuit, and conversely inaccessible within others because it can be repressed, uncathected and therefore un-facilitated. In therapy, this will be fundamental for the retrieval of repressed memories and for the overcoming of resistances. The subject experiences itself in multiple temporal dimensions, of which only one at a time may appear within consciousness and occupy it, thus giving the impression of being the only one, and excluding the others: that particular one will be the conscious dimension of the present at that given moment.

Finally, the psyche must retain a recording of its own functioning and of its unfolding in time at the very moment they occur. Memory turns the past into a sort of endlessly explorable virtual world, and such explorations become themselves elements of memory: a second grade memory, that is. memory of memories, a sort of metaverse.

Man is a complex system for adaptive reasons, that is to adapt himself to the complexity of the external world, of which, somehow, his own memory is part; such complexity he himself constantly tends to increase.

The graph in Figure 1 visually and structurally recalls the representations of the Greek and Christian Universe, but also the ones of the Keshvar of the Mazdea imaginary geography (see Corbin 1979) and cosmos of Dante Alighieri, as he presented it in the Divine Comedy (see Patapievici 2004), or even the mnemonic wheels by Giordano Bruno (see Mino 2001), true thinking machines (logic machine): that is alphabet-wheeled mnemonic machines.

The significance that mnestic systems and the mnestic function have in the functioning of self-organising systems is evident, so much so that some believe that the mind functions as a simple mapping machine and that also a high level function such as intelligence may be nothing but a good management of row memory.

To conclude these reflections upon memory we will use the following quotation still to show other aspects of the Freudian representation of memory in relation to time. In "Civilization and its Discontents" Freud (1930/n.d.-i, p. 71) uses three metaphors to illustrate some characteristics of the psychic organism and stresses similarities to and differences from other systems: 1) The metaphor of the evolution of animal species, 2) The one regarding the evolution of the Eternal City and 3) that one of the development of the body of an animal or a human being. All three recall the idea of an evolution, though they are lacking, as he himself tells us "[...] that only in the mind is such a preservation of all the earlier stages alongside of the final form possible, and that we are not in a position to represent this phenomenon in pictorial terms."

For reasons of space we need to limit ourselves and only consider the Eternal City evolution metaphor.

Let us listen to Freud (1930/ n.d.-i, pp. 68-71)

But have we a right to assume the survival of something that was originally there, alongside of what was later derived from it? Undoubtedly. There is nothing strange in such a phenomenon, whether in the mental field or elsewhere. [...]

This brings us to the more general problem of preservation in the sphere of the mind. The subject has hardly been studied as yet;1 but it is so attractive and important that we may be allowed to turn our attention to it for a little, even though our excuse is insufficient. Since we overcame the error of supposing that the forgetting we are familiar with signified a destruction of the memory-trace—that is, its annihilation—we have been inclined to take the opposite view, that in mental life nothing which has once been formed can perish—that everything is somehow preserved and that in suitable circumstances (when, for instance, regression goes back far enough) it can once more be brought to light. Let us try to grasp what this assumption involves by taking an analogy from another field. We will choose as an example the history of the Eternal City. [...]

Now let us, by a flight of imagination, suppose that Rome is not a human habitation but a psychical entity with a similarly long and copious past—an entity, that is to say, in which nothing that has once come into existence will have passed away and all the earlier phases of development continue to exist alongside the latest one. This would mean that in Rome the palaces of the Caesars and the Septizonium of Septimius Severus would still be rising to their old height on the Palatine and that the castle of S. Angelo would still be carrying on its battlements the beautiful statues which graced it until the siege by the Goths, and so on. But more than this. In the place occupied by the Palazzo

Caffarelli would once more stand—without the Palazzo having to be removed—the Temple of Jupiter Gapitolinus; and this not only in its latest shape, as the Romans of the Empire saw it, but also in its earliest one, when it still showed Etruscan forms and was ornamented with terracotta ante-fixes. Where the Coliseum now stands we could at the same time admire Nero's vanished Golden House. On the Piazza of the Pantheon we should find not only the Pantheon of to-day, as it was bequeathed to us by Hadrian, but, on the same site, the original edifice erected by Agrippa; indeed, the same piece of ground would be supporting the church of Santa Maria sopra Minerva and the ancient temple over which it was built. And the observer would perhaps only have to change the direction of his glance or his position in order to call up the one view or the other.

There is clearly no point in spinning our phantasy any further, for it leads to things that are unimaginable and even absurd. If we want to represent historical sequence in spatial terms we can only do it by juxtaposition in space: the same space cannot have two different contents. Our attempt seems to be an idle game. It has only one justification. It shows us how far we are from mastering the characteristics of mental life by representing them in pictorial terms. [...]

The fact remains that only in the mind is such a preservation of all the earlier stages alongside of the final form possible, and that we are not in a position to represent this phenomenon in pictorial terms.

We wish to underline the difficulty Freud finds here, which is being able to represent in spatial terms, and therefore visual, the simultaneous presence of mnemic traces belonging to different historical times: different chronotypes (see Fachinelli, 1979). Such a situation may be better illustrated today by using a spatial representation based upon the concept of memory maps or transitory activation patterns or circuits. Retrieving a memory entails the activation of some portions of global maps. In the same neuronal map there are various possibilities of carving out different neuronal groups, which once activated, give rise to different memories. The same ψ neuron present in a map–neuron here is meant as a virtual structure and not an anatomical one–can join different activation patterns, and therefore different memories, according to the pattern which has been activated there and then. This is why if we imagine ancient Rome as a unique map, though provided with numerous and different activation patterns, we may spatially picture what was already stated by the Freudian model itself. As a matter of fact, within the same map there coexist many transitory patterns, all on stand by, ready to be activated and capable of giving rise to a memory, without the single memory itself being stored as an engram or fixed image somewhere into the cerebral tissue. Thus indeed (Freud, 1901/ n.d.-d): [...] the observer would perhaps only have to change the direction of his glance or his position in order to call up the one view or the other." (see above) and, by changing the activated pattern, the outcome would be that within psyche, the same space might have two different contents. There can be endless states of memory, overlapping and coexisting, without there being any overprinting, and therefore numberless configurations. The brain truly appears to be a "magic loom."

We must now add to this description of the mnestic systems organisation and of memories, already in themselves complex, a further element of complexity represented by the existence of a particular kind of memories: screen memories which somehow falsify our memory. They can be of three types of "chronological relation between the screen memory and the content which is screened off by it." (ibidem, p. 44).

There are different types of *screen memories*: *retroactive* or *retrogressive, pushed ahead* or *displaced forward* and *contemporary* or *contiguous.*

However, the memory map can be modified in certain points due to resistances, therefore (1899/ n.d.-c, p. 307) "[...] instead of the mnemic image which would have been justified by the original event, another is produced which has been to some degree associatively displaced from the former one." The shifting is of a spatial-temporal nature. As Freud stresses, the process, which occurs in the psychic life both of psycho-neurotic subjects, because of a conflict, and in normal subjects is:

conflict → repression → substitution involving a compromise

In such cases the modification of the spatial-temporal representation of memory is due to the fact that, in such occurrences, repressed fantasies tends to pass into a mnestic trace of childhood scene which has some points of contact with the former, which leads to a falsification of memory. One last but very important thing is that (Freud, 1899, p. 319): "[...] what provides the intermediate step between a screen memory and what it conceals is likely to be a verbal expression."

But in these cases too the falsified memory is the first that we become aware of: the raw material of memory-traces out of which it was forged remains unknown to us in its original form. (Freud, ibidem, p. 322).

Freud (1891/n.d.-a, p. 56) wonders:

What then is the physiological correlate of the simple idea emerge and re-emerging? Obviously nothing static, but something in the nature of a process. This process is not incompatible with localization. It stats at a specific point in the cortex and from there spreads over the whole cortex and along certain pathways. When this event has taken place it leaves behind a modification, with the possibility of a memory, in the part of cortex affected. [...] Yet whenever the same cortical state is elicited again, the previous psychic event re-emerges as a memory. We have, of course, not the slightest idea how animal tissue can possibly undergo, and differentiate, so many various modifications.

If we now piece together both quotations, the one relating nucleuses of pathogenic matter and the one concerning the analogy with the Eternal City, we see that Freud shows us a very complex organization of memory in which, to the three spatial dimensions, the dimension of time is added. For this reason it will be impossible for him "to represent historical sequence in spatial terms" but it will not be unimaginable. It is true that it is not possible to portray it, as "the same space cannot have two different contents," but only if we use a static representation. If, instead, we use a dynamic representation through moving images, then we can see all the various eras flowing on a screen without the images of the past being erased by images of the present: we only need to underline and fix the images which at a certain time constitute the present. We can control anything but the past and the one of all those who are in our "cone of past."

Just a few remarks about phylogenetic memory. The idea is as early as "Studies on Hysteria." In "Totem and Taboo" (1913/ n.d.-e, p. 157), Freud hypothesized "the existence of a collective mind, in which mental processes occur just as they do in the mind of an individual." Probably he made such an hypothesis in the attempt to search for an hidden variable which might function also as an unknown determinant of the consequences of fantasized traumatic events, that is, primary phantasies.

After the formulation of the second topic, the phylogenetic memory found its well-defined collocation within the psychic apparatus and it acquired a fundamental function in the development of an individual. The id became the depositary of the archaic heritage (inheritance) of individuals.

We would like to conclude these observations on the psychoanalytic model of memory by noticing that in our view, the interminability of analysis results from the fact that investigation of the unconscious in general, and therefore also of dreams, generates its object at the same time as it explores it: we, then, find ourselves in the presence of a transfinite. This process activates a multiplier of meanings, so that the reservoir of meanings does not shrink with the progress of interpretative activity. Instead, the boundary between the analyzed and the analyzable 'shifts constantly forward', resulting in a Zuider Zee that can never be completely drained. Moreover, every interpretation throws light on a new part of the dream to be interpreted but, to make the work of interpretation inexhaustible, it is not necessary for this part of the dream to be uninterpretable, but only for it to be interpreted in such a way as to generate new parts to be interpreted in turn, and so on in an interminable process (see Scalzone & Zontini, 2001), which is not human life, that is submitted to the laws of open, dissipative systems; therefore it has a natural ending.

Also here we may notice the presence of an interminable inscribed into a finite because we must observe, as Ilya Prigogine said (1988), that to the illusion-time of Einstein's irreversibility and to the degradation time of enthropy we must add the creative time: the constructive time of complex systems.

OBJECTS

Another point of convergence between AI and psychoanalysis, another analogy, is found by Turkle (1988), on the one hand, in OOP and on the other in the object relations theory.

Both postulate particular entities or agents inside the system: objects, though obviously not superimposable, can be viewed as analogous and can be, besides plain omophony, a different and common way to approach the organisation and the functioning of inner reality. We will briefly try and touch upon the aspects the two concepts may share.

We know that in psychoanalysis the objects theory is becoming increasingly articulated and that there are by now several theories of objects, because scholars at times put forward very different concepts of what is meant by an object. Here we will accept the extensive definition given by Greenberg and Mitchell (1983) who talk about the object relations theory as theories concerning the study of relations between external real people and internal images and residues of relations with them, and the significance these residues have for psychic functioning. As for object relations instead, they speak of interactions of individuals with other internal and external people (real and imaginary) and of the relation between their inner and outer object worlds.

The object is a module with an interface. Object-based programming is then a modular programming of the bottom-up type with predisposed basic modules operating on the data. Modules (objects) are built from the bottom towards the top and thus the stage regarding the choosing of low-level modules is very important. The object is an abstract type of datum. Modules are predisposed through a clearly defined interface in which, though, the data structure is concealed within the module which appears as a black box and therefore the user (or the subject, the person) knows the interface but not the data structure. Similarly, the internal objects of psychoanalytical theory and their dynamics inform us of their state, their interactions with the individual's internal world, that is, the other objects, and with the external one represented by inter-personal relationships. Psychoanalytical objects can also be nested inside each other, as we can see in some versions of the Kleinian theory (see Wisdom 1961).

In OOP, as a programming technique, it is important to take some concepts into consideration: the *class* to which objects belong, the hereditariness of the characteristics (data and functions), polymorphism, modularisation and information hiding. These classes of objects can, for instance, define the state in which objects are at a particular moment. Due to their modularity, objects cannot be manipulated directly but only through the functions which constitute the interfacing with the rest of the system and with the external environment.

Already many attempts have been made in psychoanalysis to theorise mixed models of the mind to try to harmonise the drive model and the object model but, for the time being, no satisfactory results have been achieved.

In psychoanalysis, however, object theory still risks being a theory which slides into a homunculus conception of psyche and therefore it may lead to an endless regression because the subject constantly escapes individuation and thus only the relations with other objects are left to investigate: on the whole, it will be about a inter-personal relations theory both in its external and in its interiorised dimension.

Also the self can be seen as an object among many and therefore either the subject is defined as an emergence from the complex organisation of the interaction between objects, a mere representation, or is defined as a deus ex machina coming down from above when we find ourselves faced with theoretical difficulties. Are internal objects in psychoanalysis homunculi with their own personality, their own memory, their own feelings and thoughts? Or are they assimilable with simplified models of a part of the total individual and of some functions of the internalised exterior ones and therefore they are necessitated not only to interact with the other objects of the internal world but also, for instance, to draw upon central memory and upon a single thinking apparatus? Conversely, can they think or even think themselves: that is, can they be a thought of thought? Is the self a simple internal representation or is it an autonomous agent? The questions which need answering could multiply immeasurably.

The object theory in psychoanalysis, however, while placing the drive theory in the back seat though without necessarily refusing it, lends itself to a dialogue with emergent AI and perhaps to a simulation on the calculator.

Finally, also internal objects are assimilable to modules which cannot be attacked in a direct way but, as for the whole mental set, allow only for an indirect access through particular routes and functions. Therefore we may consider objects as modules, and the mind as a modular mind (see Fodor, 1983; Minsky, 1985).

For example, we may consider internal objects as incapsulated modular agents forming a matrix in which the Self is immersed; agents, that is, able to operate a pre-processing of emotions before being totally recognised as an integral part of the self.

They too, the objects, like units of sense, would in their turn be incapsulated modules, probably made up of smaller modules more or less integrated among themselves: partial objects.

Such an organisation would be used to avoid that the true and proper self, as a narcissistically organised central system, may excessively affect the inner world with its emotional setup, which already existed when the internal objects appeared. If we then consider internal objects as a sort of doubles of the external ones, we may assume that there existed a preobject state of psychism and that, following the maturation process, a sort of internal virtual reality was organised in which objects are utilised to relate oneself to the external world and to experience, through an informational redundance, new configurations and emotional (ideative) responses, without altering by a short circuit the individual's emotional setup. It is as if the individual could mentally experiment with more solutions before taking on the responsibility of the definitive decision about situations he is faced with in his relational life, and not as if he had to function just to react to stimuli. Yet, we must always take into account the reference to the existence of the real machine, which is placed under the virtual machine and which allows the latter to exist; obviously in our case it is constituted by the neuronal network of the brain. We may then either side with those who consider virtual reality as reality tout court, therefore able to provide real sensations, or with

those who see the real machine (hardware) as the only reality (reductionism) and virtual reality as a plain phenomenal reality or simulation: therefore it is always a question of levels of reality. But in both cases the effects of virtual reality will be real effects when considering both the "magical" link between psyche and external world and the one between psyche and soma.

Freud in his "Project for a Scientific Psychology" (1895/n.d.-b) tried to actually start from the neuronal level characterised by movements of quantity (energy) to then reach the conscience capable of recognising the quality of the mental set, but he himself was not as presumptious as to think he had solved the problem and claimed:

No attempt, of course, can be made to explain how it is that excitatory processes in the ω neurones bring consciousness along with them. It is only a question of establishing a coincidence between the characteristics of consciousness that are known to us and processes in the ω neurones which vary in parallel with them. And this is quite possible in some detail. (p. 311)

But we would like to point out that, especially at the beginning of his studies, Freud prevented the hardware—the brain—from becoming absorbed, therefore invisible in respect of the software, psyche. Only later on, as it is well known, did he opt for psychological enquiry, but he never wanted to unhook psychoanalysis from the somatic bedrock for fear of wandering too far away from other sciences.

We must finally underline, so that there may not be any misunderstanding, that obviously the modular model of the mind and the distributed one are almost irreconcilable, as are the drive model and the object one in psychoanalysis. Yet we have dealt with it here in order to show the availability of more than one model of mental functioning which might be used, for instance, for different cerebral hemisphere (right or left), different functional areas or for different periods of mental maturation. We must also say that the modular organisation of objects in AI could be arranged in its internal part as a neural network and the objects could be connected among themselves with a network-like distributed organisation. Then, the distributed model could be likened to a type of primary functioning of the mind preceding the operational closure of the modules when there is still a strong transmodularity, while the object-oriented modular model could be likened to the more mature functioning of the individual when both sensory modules and the object ones are closed to the conditioning of central systems–to the self. Also in the mature individual, objects could live in a drive atmosphere and seek pleasure through object relations; but maybe this chapter is still to be written. However, we know that the two functioning modes may still keep on coexisting all through one's life without maturation suppressing any of the two, even though the former mode gets probably concealed by the latter.

REGARDING "BEEINFLUSSUNGAPPARATES" (INFLUENCING MACHINE) AND THINKING MACHINES: AN EXAMPLE DRAWN FROM PSYCHOANALYTICAL LITERATURE

Over the last few years the issue concerning the relation between man and machine has been present more than ever. We will now make some remarks on how men view machines, we will describe the fantasies they arouse and we will then put forward an interpretation. In order to achieve such purpose we will use the classic work by Tausk (1919/1933) "On the Origin of the Influencing Machine in Schizophrenia," as well as some of Freud's works.

Tausk (1919/1933) talks of delusions of influence which sometimes present themselves in psychoses, and in particular, in schizophrenia and which are enacted through an influencing machine which would have characteristics drawn from the technical and scientific knowledge of the time; it would be structured in an articulate and complex way and it would influence individuals through levers, beams and various devices. It would also be responsible for visions, stimulations and various bodily sensations.

Tausk claims that the influencing machine represents the projection of the genital organs of the human body. The stimuli coming from such organs are perceived as something threatening and unfamiliar–erection, for instance–which are out of ego's control. The excitement deriving from them is felt as being outlandish and therefore menacing and is then projected into the machine which thus takes on a threatening and alien aspect. But the influencing machine can also represent a projection of the whole body, meant as a pregenital body or even as a nongenital body. The entire body, and the sensations deriving from it, are perceived as something which the ego cannot control and are therefore projected outside the individual and attributed to the machine.

From an evolutive moment onwards a swift technological development will start which, through exteriorisation processes of a series of functions and operational programmes, will lead to the ever–increasing liberation of time which will then become spare time. The possibility to exteriorise the motor brain into tools will pave the way to a lengthy process towards the realisation of machines and, later on, to the exteriorisation of memory and of logic-mathematical thought (symbolic thought). However, while tools are the material prolongation of an organ, the effectiveness of which is thus increased, the machine is a more or less a complex system built by man in order to carry out various operations through the use of some form of energy. Scientific discoveries themselves always need an instrument to be realised and made applicable. Later on we will dwell particularly on the computer which allows men extraordinary calculation skills. Also these machines belong to those phenomena of externalisation of human mental faculties which developed through a long and complex evolutive process which began with the invention of the abacus as an externalisation of calculation faculties and which constitutes the base for the realisation of new writing techniques, of immense electronic memories, of audio-visual systems, of communicational cyberspaces[7] and so forth. Every time men provide themselves with new artificial organs, whether they act as sensory detectors or as performing machines, they integrate into their system another part of the world and they must deal, also emotionally, with the consequent change. Regarding this topic, we would like to underline that the more powerful the machine is, the more outlandish and alien it appears, and all the more so it lends itself to being the target of projections: the more powerful it is, the more frightening.

From such evolutive process feelings seem to be left out, if we did not consider that they too are exteriorised all the same through the mechanism of the projection onto people and objects.

We will now examine how such projections manifest themselves, for instance, not only in our patients, but also in the life of clinically sane individuals in their fantastic relation with machines.

FINAL REMARKS ON MACHINE AND PEOPLE: FANTASIES OF OMNIPOTENCE, *COMPUTERPHILIA*, AND *COMPUTERPHOBIA*

The calculator-machine, as we know, is almost always seen as a mechanism capable of logical operations but, in any case, uncannily devoid of emotions and restraint. This particular characteristic easily turns it into a persecutory or protective object, as the expression of the other face of the same fantasy, therefore highly threatening because it arouses the fear it might escape rational control over drive: as if having feelings were in itself a warranty for goodness. In order to refute this assumption we must draw the reader's attention to three robotics rules invented by Asimov (1950), in his sci-fi novel *I, Robot*, which strictly forbid

automata to commit acts which might be harmful to men: robots are therefore subjected to a sort of cybernetics taboo. Probably their features make the machine, on the one hand alien but, on the other, disquietingly similar to us–a replica. In fact, both the idea that suddenly the robot could come alive like a *golem*[8] and the fear that man might lose his feelings and be regulated by a plain mechanism that is, turn out to be a cold machine, an automaton, is uncanny.

In our view, however, it is not just the lack of emotions to represents the difference between calculator-machine (artificial machine) and man (natural machine), but also the radically different way of treating symbols, and therefore having or not having a symbolic thought. Furthermore, machines have no or very little tolerance for contradictions, for uncertainties, or ambiguity; they have neither initiative, common sense nor opinions. Finally they do not have any intentionality nor any self-organisational skills. Our brain, unlike other machines, uses processes which modify the brain itself: the mind is a complex system.

Machines, as we said, are unable to understand the meaning of the symbols they manipulate while men, conversely, by understanding their meaning, can operate with the instrument of thought; they possess, therefore, a "sixth sense-organ": conscience. Conscience is a nonspecialised sense; a sort of universal processing and perceptive faculty. Moreover, men are able to free themselves of the testimony of senses through developing representations and logical thinking and can operate some sort of mental experiments (*Gedankenexperimente*) as a test for the subsequent getting into action. Riedl (1988) rightly notices that the advantage consists of the fact that instead of jeopardising one's life, man can put at risk only a mental experiment; the assumption may die, instead of he who formulated it.

But now let us get back to the texts. In the article by Freud "The Uncanny" (1919/n.d.-g) we come across Olimpia Spallanzani's daughter; "a mysteriously laconic and still doll," unmistakably a sign of a narcissistic vocation; she is nothing but an automaton. The fact that Nathaniel, the main character in Hoffman's short story, falls for her shows us the charm which a machine may exercise, all the more so when it has feminine features.

It is our opinion that one of the attractions some programmes simulating human beings have, at least at the start and for little experienced people, is the one about being able to pretend to posses the capacity to manipulate verbal symbols, to have some sort of linguistic behaviour from which the presence of a mental activity may be inferred, though only testified by the capacity to communicate by writing on a screen. Actually thought is a peculiar capacity of the human being which, as a matter of fact, the machine does not yet possess; it does not possess an apparatus to think thoughts because it is unable to understand the meaning of words it uses, though it is able to manipulate them in a syntactically correct way. (see Searle, 1981). And already Turing in 1948 wrote that possessing a human (so to say) cortex would be virtually useless if no attempt were made to organise it.

Simulation in machines even of the plain human exterior aspect increases the interlocutor's disorientation. That's the reason why, a human being's exact copy, though artificial, capable of imitating all types of behaviour and not just the linguistic ones, would seriously embarrass us in case we had to decide, for instance, whether or not to assign it the capacity to think and to suffer or experience any other kind of feeling, that is, to be a person. The fact is that we must consider ourselves content with indirect signs, the same ones we use when dealing with other people as we do not yet have at our disposal any direct and error-proof heuristic which might reveal to us the existence or the non-existence of consciousness, or rather intentionality, as one would say nowadays, provided we were able to define it in an exact way.

At this point we are faced with the troubling issue of thinking machines; upon it we would like to dwell, though very briefly. We are about to approach the subject in a rather vague fashion in order to talk of the problems facing analysts when the possibility arises of comparing, if not even defining, man or his mind as a machine—a mechanism—though of a very particular kind.

However, saying that the brain is a calculator is not like saying that man can be likened to a machine because it all depends on what we mean by machine. We would like to remind how Varela speaks of man as of an ontologic machine, Dawkins as (genetic) "machines of survival," Maturana and Varela talk of living beings, and therefore also man, as being self-poietic machines and so forth. Thus, they are convinced that such definition does not belittle human's dignity but, on the contrary, it opens up new studying opportunities and, watch out!, not only regarding the body as an ontologic machine, but also the mind-brain: the body-mind unity

We must not then prejudicially be scared off by such an eventuality, if first we do not provide a definition of the word *machine* which can be acceptable also to psychoanalysts.

Even Freud in a letter to Fliess in 1895 wrote (Masson, 1985)

Now listen to this. During an industrious night last week, when I was suffering from that degree of pain which brings about the optimal condition for my mental activities, the barriers suddenly lifted, the veils dropped, and everything became transparent—from the details of the neuroses to the determinants of consciousness. Everything seemed fall into place, the cogs meshed, I had the impression that the thing now really was a machine that shortly would function on its own. (p. 146)

Here, by "machine" Freud meant a system made up of well-identifiable parts and with a precise and predictable functioning, still within the limits of what is possible, which could be studied through concepts drawn from natural sciences.

Surely we can date back to Descartes the idea of describing the body as a machine (*res extensa*), at least in its more modern conceptualisation. Later on, early AI scholars wondered about the possibility of finding intelligent behaviour, or even a mind, in machines or calculators. Today we may explore the idea that mind is a machine, though of a very particular type. Although we do not believe that the brain is a calculator, we may not only utilise the calculator to simulate parts of the brain, but we may even assume, at least in principle, the possibility of building an artefact even endowed with conscience, as Edelman claims. Then, whether or not we are able to carry out such project with the technologies currently available is quite another matter.

Machines make us think of predictable and precise systems provided with mechanisms and operating processes which are easily individuated and, moreover, studied through natural laws, especially physics. Now, human beings are not mechanical, because they are not simple systems, but complex ones which present unpredictable behaviours, are capable of learning and of adapting and so forth.

A remarkable significance along this scientific route has been taken on by the Turing test which, invented by an outstanding English mathematician, is a procedure to test any given machine capable of manipulating fully-developed symbols in order to decide whether or not it has an intelligent kind of behaviour, if not even a mind. In brief, The inventor would set into communication a man and a calculator, ruling out any possibility of using eyesight, through a keyboard and a printing machine with which questions could be sent and answers received. One has to be able to find out whether the interlocutor is a man or a machine. An endless number of articles have been written both in favour and against this original way of testing machines, which its inventor oddly called The Imitation Game; and we would like to add in a Gaddini sort of way; imitation *in order to be*.

We would like to specify, here, that the test would need a significantly long time of execution because it is easy to deceit the interlocutor on a short amount of time and yet so far no simulation programme on computers has ever overcome the Turing test.

At this point, we have to say something regarding the issue of consciousness and the possibility of its implementation onto the machine, referring our readers to other texts for an in-depth study on the subject.

For instance, if we take into account what Edelman (1992) claims, we see that he distinguishes between two types of conscience: primary consciousness and higher-order consciousness, that is, the consciousness of being conscious. It is important to remember that also Edelman claims that conscience is a function emerging from the bottom-up self-organisation of the neural network. He likens primary conscience to a sort of remembered present resulting from processes of self-categorisation of the brain obtained by matching past perceptive categorisations which originate in the thalamus-cortical system with systems of value coming from the brainstem and limbic system connected by means of re-entrant rings. Instead, the higher-order consciousness is possible thanks to a symbolic memory and is closely connected to language in its phonological, semantical and syntactical aspects. We would like to remind the reader that also Freud, who defines consciousness as an "organ of sense for the perception of psychic qualities," closely connected the becoming conscious of mental contents to the possibility of being verbally expressed, that is, to language. Therefore conscious representation consists, according to Freud, of the representation of (unconscious) thing plus word representation.

If we now move on to the possibility of implementing conscience into machines, as part of the system's awareness, we may use, for instance, Trautteur's (1987) proposal, which, also by drawing upon Jaynes's (1976, 1995) ideas, hypothesizes an algorithm which might realize, at least theoretically, a functional, but not analogical, simulation of the nervous system.

First of all, Trautteur views algorithms as physical systems, as effective procedures, located where their symbols are and therefore to be deemed as material processes, as well as mental processes whenever they are performing; they, as widespread and active entities, belong then both to *res cogitans* and to *res extensa* (Trautteur, 1997). He takes into consideration the realisation of a system which includes three identical systems, yet distinguishable according to their differentiated activities. There would then be a speaker, a listener and a third element, a witness, injected at a later moment into the speaker, able to witness and record what is happening and to recursively and dynamically recall itself. In this sense there would be a bystander, internalised by now, whose behaviour would be the same, or better isomorphic, to the description from the outside. Thus there would take place some sort of doubling of identity which reiterates itself in the following calls of the system which will later be recorded in some stack[9]. The first call would have the character of an analyser and the second would constitute the internal bystander: interiority. The realisation of this "one and trine" algorithm would be able to carry out in the machine something very similar to awareness because it is able, for example, to answer questions of a personal type.

However, there would still be left to specify whether the machine is able to understand the meanings of the symbols it manipulates, as Searle (1981) and others highlight raising this fundamental issue, or it is limited to the display of linguistic behaviour which is only externally meaningful. Searle's criticism, expressed in the experiment of the Chinese chamber[10], consists of underlining that the kind of syntax calculator programmes have is not sufficient to determine semantics, which is what characterises human minds. The human mind is not a plain computational mind, as cognitivism would state, which manipulates symbols only in an algorithmic fashion, but it does it also in a semantic way. In any case, also this kind of

criticism is, in its turn, criticised because of the doubt about the existence of an intrinsic meaning.

A completely different possibility would be to train a neural network by means of self-learning and at a certain point be able to verify, once reached the critical mass in the complex system, the possibility that this machine is able to talk to us about itself and therefore testify the emerging of intentionality. Regarding this alternative hypotheses might be helpful, and perhaps even more interesting for analysts, as the ones by Edelman (1976) who, starting from TNGS indicates to us how it is possible from neurons, ascending then through the production of re-entrant maps and categorisations and recategorizations and so forth, to get to the birth of a primary conscience and then, through semantic self-elevation with the advent of language, to the appearance of a higher-order consciousness. These models, at least in principle, can be implemented on an evolved parallelism computer: then a simulation can be realised. However there still remains the fact that neural network learning always needs a human operator who establishes at least the initial instructions in order to carry out the learning rules; that is, it is not based, as in brain development, on selection; on an autonomous neural Darwinism.

For the time being, we may say that a thinking machine does not yet exist and perhaps it never will, if by mental activity and its product, thought, we mean what a man's mind is able to elaborate. The fact is, however, that there can be a series of activities which can be processed by a machine or attributed to it by our activity, for instance by our fantasy. The human mind is able to avail itself of the calculator and of machines in general, as a prolongation, prothesis or simple tool for an *exteriorised* function of itself. Such possibility may allow to build worlds which mirror the mind's fantasies to then make them independent realities to be shared with others, as before was done only with films and books. However, while cinema is only passively enjoyed, virtual reality and cyberspace are modifiable by the operator, can be shared with others, and are navigable. Furthermore one experiences, through virtual realities, real sensations, though, here, there is the risk that sensory experiences of assimilation and extension of the self may turn into sensual experiences mediated by an erotisation of the process. Part of the human mental activity can be implemented onto the machine and one can make it run: that means that one can follow its functioning and modify it. One of the dangers might be to utilise all this in a magically and omnipotently defensive way in order to reduce the surrounding environment, that is, external reality, to being a plain *extension* of the Self at the magical service of the self with the intention of avoiding persecutory anxieties which would entail recognising the other from the self.

However, for analysts, maybe, it is not so interesting to establish whether machines have a mind as to establish whether the mind is a machine. The problem, then, is not just the technical realisation of building a conscious and intelligent machine, but succeeding in defining, in a way that can be shared, what intelligence is and what consciousness is and, we would add, the strategies to diagnose the entities which possess them through definite heuristics; it is essentially this that keeps us away from building an intelligent artificial system: the lack of an explicative theory about intelligent entities, and not the irrealisability of an artificial intentionality, or the limits of silicon compared to carbon. After having done this, one should similarly move on to the definition of emotions and to the possibility of diagnosing them and simulate them on models of mental machines. The main problem is exactly having a good theory of consciousness, or at least an acceptable one.

Through consciousness we become aware of the phenomenal present. We can state, as we have already said, that mental processes take place in parallel, or rather we can say that conscious processes are serial and the unconscious ones, instead, are parallel. Concerning this aspect, Johnson-Laird (1988) lists three types of machines: Cartesian machines which are incapable of using symbols and of being self-aware; Craikian automaton

which are capable of building symbolic models of the world and of basic awareness; and finally machines which possess the recursive capacity of including models within models, of having a model of their own operating system and which are able to apply the one to the other: these systems would also be self-reflective and intentional. But all this would still be not sufficient to make sure that such a machine is provided with consciousness, like the human one. For the time being, a machine supplied with conscience does not exist, but this does not mean that it will be possible when our technology will be more refined.

The decisive fact which still blocks us is that we do not possess a sure heuristics which can help us claim whether or not a system has any consciousness, and therefore even if there were a machine with consciousness we would not be able to easily demonstrate it. For this reason perhaps we may say, parodying Dennett (1978), that in the meantime it is better to avoid kicking calculators... they might kick us back.

Therefore, the thinking machine, that is, the calculator, can be experienced also in a persecutory way, like a Tauskian influencing machine which can take our powers away from us and take them on itself, thus making us totally helpless and subjected to it. We then move from a tolerant disparagement of the calculator to a really delusional "computerphobia," whereas "computerphilia" is the other side of the coin. We cannot forget that also in this case we must consider the role played by sexuality and sexual organs in order to retrace an interpretative route. Tausk (1919/1933) also writes that: "*Indeed, the machines produced by man's ingenuity and created in the image of man are unconscious projections of man's bodily structure. Man's ingenuity seems to be unable to free itself from its relation to the unconscious.*" (p. 555).

Furthermore:

The evolution by distortion of the human apparatus into a machine is a projection that corresponds to the development of the pathological process which converts the ego into a diffuse sexual be-ing, or–expressed in the language of the genital period–into a genital, a machine independent of the aims of the ego and subordinated to a foreign will. It is no longer subordinated to the will of the ego, but dominates it. Here, too, we are reminded of the astonishment of boys when they become aware for the first time of erection. And the fact that the erection is shortly conceived as an exceptional and mysterious feat, supports the assumption that erection is felt to be a thing independent of the ego, a part of the outer world not completely mastered. (p. 556).

Thus, as erection can be perceived by the child as an autonomous and uncontrollable process, but powerful and magic, also the machine, onto which the genital projection has been made, may escape, as mind itself, the control of the mind: the endogenous excitation is then perceived as being aroused from the outside; some sort of real seductive suggestion which, being no longer controllable, becomes persecutory.

After all, Freud reminds us how the gods inherited just from the genitalia their divine functions of omnipotence and omniscience.

We may here try to hypothesise the following process: initially man, through technology, externalises cortical functions by building different kinds of tools, among which the calculator. This technical process is accompanied by a fantastical psychical activity through which he projects, onto the structure of the machine, his genitals and the relative functions which still enjoy divine worship as the legacy of animism and of the fantasy of realising the omnipotence of thought, which is conveyed to all the new activities learned by the same men, including the capacity of processing by means of calculators. It seems to us that thinking machines exercise great seductive power and that one of the reason for this fascination consists of an idealisation of their capacity of processing which gives the illusion, by manipulating and controlling them, of being able to magically realise,

even though only through their help, the ancient dream of omniscience, through the omnicomprehensiveness of information archives, of mastering multiplicity and of the computational and logic omnipotence of thought. We have to highlight, here, the distinction which must be taken into account between the magical use of magic thought and the magical use of logic thought: they are very similar but still there is a difference. The latter is more treacherous, and therefore more dangerous, because it can more easily be mistaken for real scientific thinking while, instead, it does nothing but convey a very primitive animistic thought with defensive purposes.

With the passing of time, when the idealisation of machines began to fade away because men realised it cannot keep the promise about an impossible omnipotence, man repossesses the divine part which is now summed up by pure mental activity and the rest, that is, the technical instrument calculator as genital organ, falls prey to contempt, thus paving the way to persecutory delusions. Only a few madmen remain slave of the machine which, as the Tauskian one, is the menacing heir of the power of genitalia by now perceived as being prey only to the instinctual component no longer restrained by reason. This means that problems arise when there is a splitting of the rational parts from the instinctual ones and a drive defusion with the consequent freeing of a destructive element which rebels against the individual along the lines of a dynamics of the persecutory type. It is such despised rest, split and projected, that unleashes persecutory anxieties, only at times denied and concealed with a rationalised and reassuring depreciation of the machine-persecutor. The fact is that the invention and the use of the machine gives the illusion of a greater control over one's emotional life: that is, avoiding the recognition of the other and the encounter with separation anxieties, by actively generating confusion between the inside and outside and between subject and object through the narcissistic relation with a mechanised object.

Delusion, as well as the extreme technological competence, obey the same need about controlling the huge, and therefore feared, power of the primary object. This is the reason why the delusion of the paranoid person represents the extreme defensive attempt from the intrusion of the object into one's mind. Moreover, we have to notice that the calculator can become, in somebody's fantasy, either a fetish, a symbolic substitute for the maternal penis which might help to deny castration anxieties or, worse, an autistic object which helps protect against unthinkable anxieties of fragmentation and separation and their tragic consequences. In actual fact, even the calculator is not a real thinking machine, but at most is a machine devoid of any initiative and creativity and which can only be programmed by man, as already Lady Lovelace in the 19th century had understood. Therefore, though presently things are already changing and some neural networks are able to show some sort of unpredictable behaviour (very limited, actually), the calculator is able to process or think only the thought the programmer projects into it, just the way it happens with delusion of influence. The fact that many fear the calculator makes people demential (as well as an excessive masturbation) because it carries out operations which should be accomplished by man who in his turn is impoverished every time he uses such proxy, is an idea which finds its reasons only within persecutory fantasies about psycho-physical harm. In actual fact, the calculator takes on the task of performing mainly those long, repetitive and monotonous calculations which would waste our time and, by freeing ourselves of this burden, it allows us to deal with more creative things: obviously only as long and as far as we are capable of it.

Threats coming from machines (computers) therefore do not derive from their inhumanity; on the contrary, they are the product of the far too human tendency, which we have inserted into machines, mostly in those built by fantasy, and which these machines, when they are capable of it, provide on their part to develop and potentiate.

The fact is that the clash is not between man and machine, but between man and man or between man and their inner world.

REFERENCES

Asimov, I. (1950). *I, robot*. Boston, MA: Gnome Press.

Basch-Kahre, E. (1985). Patterns of thinking. *The International Journal of Psycho-Analysis, 66*(4), 455–470.

Breuer, J., & Freud, S. (1976). Studies on hysteria. In J. Strachey (Ed. & Trans.), *The standard edition of the complete psychological works of Sigmund Freud* (Vol. 2). London: Hogarth Press. (Original work published 1893-1895).

Bucci, W. (1997). *Psychoanalysis and cognitive science*. New York, NY: Guilford Press.

Corbin, H. (1979). *Spiritual body and celestial earth: From Mazdean Iran to Shi'ite Iran*. Princeton, NJ: Princeton University Press.

Dennett, D. C. (1978). *Brainstorms*. Cambridge, MA: MIT Press/Bradford Books.

Edelman, G. M. (1992). *Bright air, brilliant fire. On the matter of the mind*. London, UK: Penguin Group.

Erdelyi, M. H. (1985). *Psychoanalysis: Freud's cognitive psychology*. New York, NY: W. H. Freeman & Company.

Fodor, J. A. (1983). *The modularity of mind*. Cambridge, MA: MIT Press.

Freud, S. (1891). *(n.d.-a). On aphasia: A critical study*. New York, NY: International University Press.

Freud, S. (n.d.-b). Project for a scientific psychology. In Strachey, J. (Trans. Ed.) *The standard edition of the complete psychological works of Sigmund Freud* (*Vol. 1*, pp. 295–391). London, UK: Hogarth Press. (Original work published 1895)

Freud, S. (n.d.-c). The aetiology of hysteria. In Strachey, J. (Trans. Ed.) *The standard edition of the complete psychological works of Sigmund Freud* (*Vol. 3*, pp. 187–221). London, UK: Hogarth Press. (Original work published 1896)

Freud, S. (n.d.-c). Screen memories. In Strachey, J. (Trans. Ed.) *The standard edition of the complete psychological works of Sigmund Freud* (*Vol. 3*, pp. 301–322). London, UK: Hogarth Press. (Original work published 1899)

Freud, S. (n.d.-d). Psychopathology of everyday life. In Strachey, J. (Trans. Ed.) *The standard edition of the complete psychological works of Sigmund Freud* (*Vol. 6*). London, UK: Hogarth Press. (Original work published 1901)

Freud, S. (n.d.-e). Totem and taboo. In Strachey, J. (Trans. Ed.) *The standard edition of the complete psychological works of Sigmund Freud* (*Vol. 3*, pp. 187–221). London, UK: Hogarth Press. (Original work published 1913)

Freud, S. (n.d.-f). From the history of an infantile neurosis. In Strachey, J. (Trans. Ed.) *The standard edition of the complete psychological works of Sigmund Freud* (*Vol. 17*, pp. 1–124). London, UK: Hogarth Press. (Original work published 1918)

Freud, S. (n.d.-g). The 'uncanny. In Strachey, J. (Trans. Ed.) *The standard edition of the complete psychological works of Sigmund Freud* (*Vol. 17*, pp. 217–256). London, UK: Hogarth Press. (Original work published 1910)

Freud, S. (n.d.-h). Remarks on the theory and practice of dream-interpretation. In Strachey, J. (Trans. Ed.) *The standard edition of the complete psychological works of Sigmund Freud* (*Vol. 19*, pp. 107–122). London, UK: Hogarth Press. (Original work published 1923)

Freud, S. (n.d.-i). Civilization and its discontents. In Strachey, J. (Trans. Ed.) *The standard edition of the complete psychological works of Sigmund Freud* (*Vol. 21*, pp. 57–146). London, UK: Hogarth Press. (Original work published 1930)

Gaddini, E. (1989). Fenomeni PSI e processo creativo. In *Scritti*. Milan, Italy: Cortina. (Original work published 1969)

Gaddini, E. (1992). On imitation. In Limentani (Ed.), *A psychoanalytic theory of infantile experience*. London, UK: Routledge. (Original work published 1969)

Galatzer-Levy, R. (1988). On working through: a model from artificial intelligence. *Journal of the American Psychoanalytic Association, 38*(1), 125–151.

Greenberg, J. R., & Mitchell, S. A. (1983). *Object relations in psychoanalytic theory*. Cambridge, MA: Harvard University Press.

Jaynes, J. (1976). *The origin of consciousness in the breackdown of bicameral mind*. New York, NY: Houghton Mifflin.

Jaynes, J. (1995). The diacronicity of consciousness. In G. Trautteur (Ed.), *Consciousness: Distinction and reflection*. Napoli, Italia: Bibliopolis, 1995.

Masson, J. M. (Ed.). (1985). *The complete letters of Sigmund Freud to Wilhelm Fliess 1887-1904*. Cambridge, MA: Belknap.

Mino, G. (Ed.). (2001). *Bruno G. Corpus iconographicum*. Milan, Italy: Adelphi.

Minsky, M. (1985). *The society of mind*. New York, NY: Simon & Schuster.

Patapievici, H.-R. (2004). *Ochii Beatriceii. Cum arata cu adevarat lumea lui Dante?* Bucuresti, Romania: Humanitas.

Scalzone, F., & Zontini, G. (2001). The dream's navel between chaos and thought. *The International Journal of Psycho-Analysis, 82*(2), 263–282.

Searle, J. R. (1980). Minds, brains, and programs. *The Behavioral and Brain Sciences, 3*, 417–424.

Tausk, V. (1933). On the origin of the "influencing machine" in schizophrenia. *Psychoanalytic Quarterly, 2*, 519-556. (Original work published 1919)

Trautteur, G. (1987, February). *Intelligenza umana e intelligenza artificiale.* Paper presented at Centro Culturale San Carlo of Milano, Milan.

Trautteur, G. (1997-1998). Distinzione e riflessione. *ATQUE, 16*, 127–141.

Turing, A. M. (1964). *Minds and machines.* Englewood Cliffs, NJ: Prentice Hall. (Original work published 1950)

Turkle, S. (1988). Artificial intelligence and psychoanalysis: A new alliance. *Daedalus, 117*(1), 241–268.

von Neumann, J. (1958). *The computer and the brain.* London, UK: Yale University Press.

Wisdom, J. O. (1961). A methodological approach to the problem of hysteria. *The International Journal of Psycho-Analysis, 42*, 224–237.

ENDNOTES

1. Tausk's paper was published, oddly enough, in the same year, 1919, in which Freud published "The Uncanny."
2. By the name of Turing machine is usually meant the conception of a machine which is abstract but which can actually be realized.
3. Programmes like Weizenbaum's ELIZA, which in its DOCTOR section simulates a rogersian psychotherapist, simulate only the initial and final parts of human behaviour and therefore, on a par with the Turing test, treat the mind as if it were a black box.
4. Backpropagation is a technique of learning by or training of neural networks obtained through correcting weights on the connections along an antidromic route.
5. Simulated annealing is a technique for the training of neural networks consisting of simulating the process through which, in metallurgy, metals are tempered, by means of heating and cooling, or rather "freezing," in order to free them of any impurities.
6. The graphic in figure 1 has been processed by Franco Scalzone and carried out by Mrs. Claudia Vignale.
7. Cyberspace is a word coined by the sci-fi author William Gibson. It indicates a new parallel universe created by global networks of communication via computer.
8. The Golem is a legendary figure created by Rabbi Löw from Prague.
9. The stack is a type of data structure ordered according to L.I.F.O. (last in first out) arrangement (set of rules), that is, the last element enters the structure and the first one exits it.
10. The Chinese chamber experiment allows us to swiftly manipulate formal symbols, the Chinese characters, and to answer incoming questions in Chinese, by using only the instructions and rules written in our language, but without us ever understanding the meaning neither of what we are being asked nor of what we are answering, still in Chinese, though the entire operation is carried out correctly from a grammatical and syntactical point of view.

Chapter 4
Dynamical Disequilibrium, Transformation, and the Evolution and Development of Sustainable Worldviews

Liane Gabora
University of British Columbia, Canada

Maegan Merrifield
University of British Columbia, Canada

ABSTRACT

This chapter begins by outlining a promising, new theoretical framework for the process by which human culture evolves inspired by the views of complexity theorists on the problem of how life began. Elements of culture, like species, evolve over time; that is, they exhibit cumulative change that is adaptive in nature. By studying how biological evolution got started, it is possible to gain insight into not just the specifics of biological evolution, but also general insights into the initiation of any evolutionary process that may be applicable to culture. The authors, thus, explore the implications of this new framework for culture on the transformative processes of individuals. Specifically, they address what this emerging perspective on cultural evolution implies for to go about attaining a sustainable worldview; that is, a web of habits, understandings, and ways of approaching situations that is conducive to the development of a sustainable world.

HOW DOES AN EVOLUTIONARY PROCESS GET STARTED?

In attempting to gain insight into the origins of transformative processes in individuals, it is instructive to look at the transformative processes by which the earliest forms of life evolved. Research into how life began is stymied by the improbability of a spontaneously generated structure that replicates itself using a self-assembly code such as the genetic code. Something so complex as this is unlikely to emerge out of the blue! Hoyle (1981) infamously compared it to the probability that a tornado blowing through a junkyard would assemble a Boeing 747.

DOI: 10.4018/978-1-4666-2077-3.ch004

This has led to widespread support for different versions of the proposal that the earliest self-replicating structures were autocatalytic sets of molecules (Bollobas, 2001; Bollobas & Rasmussen, 1989; Dyson, 1982, 1985; Gabora, 2006; Kauffman, 1986, 1993; Morowitz, 1992; Segré, Ben-Eli, & Lancet, 2000; Segré, et al, 2001a, b; Wäechtershäeuser, 1992; Weber, 1998, 2000; Williams & Frausto da Silva, 1999, 2002; Vetsigian *et al.*, 2006). A set of molecules is *autocatalytic* if every molecule in the set can be regenerated through chemical reactions occurring amongst *other* molecules in the set. (The term 'autocatalytic' comes from the fact that the molecules speed up or *catalyze* the reactions by which other molecules are formed.) Reactions between molecules generate new, different molecules. As the number of different molecules increases, the number of reactions by which they can interconvert increases even faster (Cohen, 1988; Erdös & Rényi, 1960). Thus some subset of them reaches a critical threshold where there is a reaction pathway to the formation of every molecule in the set.

At this point, the parts can reconstitute the whole in a piecemeal manner, through bottom-up interactions rather than top-down interpreting of a genetic code (Kauffman, 1993; for summary see Gabora, 2008). The hydrophilic (water-loving) molecules orient toward the periphery, forming a spherical vesicle that encloses the more hydrophobic (water-avoiding) molecules. This kind of spherical vesicle made up of collectively self-replicating parts is sometimes referred to as a *protocell*. It is prone to fission or budding, wherein part of it pinches off, and it divides in two. So long as there is at least one copy of each polymer in each of the two resulting vesicles, they can self-replicate, and continue to do so indefinitely, or until their structure changes drastically enough that self-replication capacity breaks down, and by that point there will exist other self-replicating sister-lineages. The process is sloppier and more haphazard than the self-replication that occurs in modern day organisms. Some raise the concern that, at least with respect to some versions of this theory, replication occurs with such low fidelity that evolvability breaks down (Vasas, Szathmary, & Santos, 2009). Nevertheless, there is broad consensus that such a structure remains sufficiently intact over generations for stable evolution (Schuster, 2010). A key thing to note here is that with this kind of self-replication there is nothing to prohibit the inheritance of acquired characteristics. A change to any one part of the structure persists after fission occurs, and this may cause other changes that have a significant effect further downstream.

Evolution of these early life forms occurs through horizontal exchange (i.e. not restricted to vertical transmission from parent to offspring) of "innovation-sharing protocols" (Vetsigian *et al.*, 2006). It was not until the genetic code came into existence—and the process in which self-assembly instructions are copied (meiosis) became distinct from developmental processes—that acquired characteristics could no longer be passed on to the next generation (Gabora, 2006). The work of Woese and his colleagues indicates that early life underwent a transition from this fundamentally cooperative process horizontal evolution through communal exchange, to a fundamentally competitive process of vertical evolution by way of the genetic code. This transition is referred to as the *Darwinian threshold* (Woese, 2002) or *Darwinian transition* (Vetsigian et al., 2006) because it marks the onset of what we think of as conventional Darwinian evolution through natural selection. Kalin Vetsigian (pers. comm.) estimates that the period between when life first arose and the time of the Darwinian threshold spanned several hundred million years.

Thus we have two kinds of self-replication (Gabora, 2004). *Coded self-replication,* such as is seen in present-day organisms, uses self-assembly instructions as proposed by von Neumann. This ensures they replicate with high fidelity, and acquired characteristics are not inherited. *Uncoded self-replication,* such as is seen in protocells, involves autocatalysis. This is a low fidelity means of replication, and there is nothing to prohibit inheritance of acquired characteristics. Note that it is sometimes said that because acquired traits are inherited in culture, culture cannot be described in evolutionary terms. It is ironic that scientists working on the problem of how life began have shown that this is also the case with respect to the earliest stage of biological life itself. These origin of life scientists have however resolved the problem of how culture could evolve despite inheritance of acquired characteristics by showing that it is possible for an evolutionary process to get underway and for adaptive, cumulative change to take place *without* natural selection.

In sum, there is increasing evidence that the very earliest life forms were self-organized metabolisms that self-replicated rather haphazardly through duplication of their catalytic components. They evolved through a non-Darwinian (Lamarckian) process involving piecemeal transformation and communal exchange, as opposed to the competitive exclusion or 'survival of the fittest' that characterizes natural selection.

HOW DOES HUMAN CULTURE EVOLVE?

Over time our widgets have become more complex and our art has become more varied, leading many to suggest that human culture evolves. However it has not been definitively established in what sense culture constitutes an evolutionary process. To do so is the overarching goal of the various strands of my research. I aim to bring forward a theoretical framework for cultural evolution that is as sound as our theoretical framework for biological evolution, and apply it to the tasks of reconstructing our past, exploring possible futures, and furthering human wellbeing.

It is sometimes assumed that the self-replicating units of cultural evolution are artifacts (tools, fashions, etc.) or the ideas or 'memes' that give rise to them, and that they evolve, like modern-day organisms do, through natural selection. But

as pointed out earlier, von Neumann showed that the key feature of self-replication in biology is not mere self-copying, but self-copying using a code (such as the genetic code) that functions both as a self-description (passively transmitted to offspring during the process of reproduction) and as self-assembly instructions (actively interpreted to build the organism during the process of development). It is because of this division of labour that in biological evolution, acquired traits are not inherited (e.g., you do not inherit your mother's tattoo). However, there is nothing in cultural evolution that functions both as self-description and self-assembly instructions. That is why acquired characteristics are transmitted. For example, if you are told a joke and you think of a funnier version of the joke it is probably your version that you tell to someone else; the new trait acquired by the joke is transmitted. This is one reason why natural selection does not provide an adequate explanatory model of cultural evolution.

An alternative to the notion that culture is Darwinian is the proposal that the transformative, evolutionary, adaptive processes of culture are structurally similar to those of the earliest life forms (Gabora, 2000, 2004, 2008, in press; Gabora & Aerts, 2009). It is proposed that in human culture what evolves is not discrete ideas or artifacts but minds, or more specifically, peoples' internal models of the world, including knowledge and how it has been made sense of, as well as ideas, hopes, attitudes, beliefs, values, predispositions, and habitual patterns of thought and behavior. This internal model of the world is referred to as a *worldview*. Worldviews evolve in the same haphazard sense as these earliest life forms, not through competition for survival of the *fittest* as modern-day life, but through transformation of *all*. In other words, the assemblage of human worldviews changes over time not because some replicate at the expense of others, as in natural selection, but because of ongoing mutual interaction and modification.

A human worldview has the following properties. It is self-organizing in the sense that one constantly uses newly acquired information to update one's general understanding of people and things and how they are related. It is self-mending in the sense that just as a body spontaneously heals itself when wounded, if something unexpected happens one can't help but try to figure out why, i.e. to revise one's worldview to accommodate this unexpected event. A worldview is also autopoietic, i.e. the whole emerges through interactions amongst the parts. As a young child thinks through how the different bits of information it learns are related to one another it comes to have an integrated understanding of the world it lives in and his or her relationship to that world.

We saw that an important component of an evolutionary process is self-replication—basically, making a copy of oneself. An adult shares ideas, stories, and attitudes with children (and other adults), influencing little by little the formation of other worldviews. Of necessity, a worldview acquires and expresses cultural information in the form of discrete units (e.g. gestures or artifacts), but the processing of it (i.e., the process by which it acquires characteristics) reflects its own multifaceted web of knowledge, experience, needs, and perspectives. Different situations expose different facets of a worldview (much like cutting a fruit at different angles exposes different parts of its interior). Elements of culture (such as rituals, customs, beliefs, and artifacts) reflect the current evolutionary states of the worldviews that generate them. People influence the contexts by which the potential of their worldviews is realized, either externally, by influencing their environments, or internally, by generating their own contexts (e.g. fantasy, rumination, counterfactual thinking).

Implications of the Theory for Personal Transformation

This theory of cultural evolution has significant implications for the individual's process of therapeutic self-transformation, which it is argued is a creative process that arises due to the *self-organizing, self-mending* nature of a worldview. In other words, the ruminative, associative thought processes that one engages in when in a state of emotional upheaval or internal dynamical disequilibrium reflects the natural tendency of a worldview to seek integration or consistency amongst both its pre-existing and newly-added components, including ideas, attitudes, or bits of knowledge (Gabora, under revision). Each idea or interpretation of a situation that the individual comes up with is a different expression of the same underlying core network of understandings, beliefs, and attitudes. A worldview has a characteristic structure, and the individual's behavior reflects the (to some extent) unique architecture of this web of understandings.

The individual's behavior and other outputs are like footprints in the snow, suggesting the 'shape' and dynamics of the underlying worldview that gave rise to them but which we never see directly. The individual's behavioral outputs are thus integrally related to one another and potentially pave the way for one another (Gabora, 2010; Gabora, O'Connor, and Ranjan, in press). They also pave the way for the transformative processes of others who interact with that individual and/or his or her creative outputs, and thereby the transformative process of each individual contributes to the global process of the human cultural evolution.

It is proposed that what drives this is a sense of fragmentation or dynamical disequilibrium. This may be externally generated, i.e. it may arise due to life problems, knowledge or ideas that do not cohere, unexpected situations, injustices, and so forth. Alternatively, the dynamical disequilibrium may be internally generated, *i.e.*, it may arise through intrinsically motivated play or exploration, perhaps driven by curiosity or restlessness. Because a human worldview is self-organizing, people influence the contexts by which the potential of their worldviews is realized, and thereby respond to and 'mend' the state of disequilibrium. Though imagination, fantasy, rumination, and 'what if' type thinking, further play and exploration, or trying things out, a worldview is exposed to contexts that may transform to a more integrated state. The individual thereby regains dynamical equilibrium (absence of major life problems, knowledge and ideas more or less cohere, unexpected situations explained, injustices put right, and so forth).

Thus, the therapeutic self-transformation arises as a result of the propensity of an internal model of the world to respond to dynamical disequilibrium with ruminative, associative processes aimed at self-reorganization. The transformative processes may take place in an informal setting, through reflection, perhaps aided by discussion, or an experience of nature. It may also occur in a formal setting such as through art therapy. The American Art Therapy Association (2008) defines art therapy as a clinical practice "being dedicated to the belief that making art is healing and life enhancing." It is based on the idea that there is an inherent healing power in the creative process and that art making provides access to things that are difficult or impossible to verbalize. Art therapists believe that there are two processes going on during the act of creating: 1) the work produced through art making within the clinical sessions, and 2) its accompanying emotional catharsis or connection. The creative work can provide a springboard for discussion between the client and therapist, and it can also be analyzed for symbolic meaning and used in assessment (Malchiodi, 2007).

Art therapy is comprehensive in its objectives. Some goals of art therapists are to help people find healthier ways of dealing with their personal internal processes, other people, their community, and their environment (Dunn-Snow & Smellie, 2011). Therapy can help build on skills activated in the past (Riley, 1999). Clinical experience indicates that creating art is a way to manage intense feelings as a result of emotional work (Moon, 1999). Experimental studies of emotion and creativity indicate that higher levels of creativity are correlated with positive affect (Hennessey & Amabile, 2010). Clinical practitioners of art therapy note that imagery and creative engagement can deepen communication between the client and therapist (Moon, 2009). A primary goal of therapy is to equip clients with skills that transfer to other settings, including communication skills. It can also offer a way for the clients to achieve insights into situations and behaviors that could not be obtained by thinking and speaking in a logical manner (Moon, 2009). Art can thereby open doors to healing and create a free and safe space to express emotional experience.

The honing theory of creativity can also be applied to art therapy. Honing theory places equal emphasis on the externally visible creative outcome and the internal cognitive restructuring brought about by the creative process. Art therapy has the potential to address this self-mending process. Honing involves drawing associations, reorganizing understandings, and working through emotions. The more experiences one has or tensions one has to face, the more ingredients one has to draw upon in this process. Artistic expression can be seen as the manifestation of deeper hidden structures, and as a means of accessing personal history that would not be available through verbalization (Karkou & Sanderson, 2006). The process of creating can result in new associations and understandings that pave the way toward more constructive attitudes, and thus enhanced mental health. This can lead to better coping. Through the use of art in a therapeutic context, the individual can restructure negative thoughts and experiences into positive ones. Art therapy (as well as related therapies such as music therapy and dance therapy) can thus provide a structured way for people to respond to and challenge beliefs and attitudes, and develop an integrated worldview.

EDUCATION AND THE COMPARTMENTALIZATION OF KNOWLEDGE

What are the implications of this new view of personal transformation founded on a scientific perspective on the manner in which culture evolves? One such implication has to do with how we teach children about the world they live in. The view of reality that is presented to children both aids and constrains how that child's worldview develops. We present the world to children in a compartmentalized fashion. Spontaneous deviations from the daily school routine are not tolerated because curricula would not be covered, and scores on standardized tests would fall. Even the weekends offer little possibility for spontaneously playing with, exploring, and discovering for oneself an understanding of the world that strays from the compartmentalized version of reality we are handed down. Moreover, if children do discover something new for themselves, they are often discouraged from exploring it further. As a child, one of the authors of this chapter (for simplicity, hereafter referred to as "I") developed a "framework for all things". It included: things that repeatedly go back and forth unchanged (such as a pendulum or metronome), things that repeatedly go back and forth but change (such as night and day, or a spiral), things that just go up and down (such as a ball thrown into the air), things that go up and down but with a change (such as the feelings you have about a story during and after reading it). I was made to feel like what I had arrived at was not the correct way of classifying elements of life. I had gotten it all wrong. The "correct" way was in terms of the subjects you learn at school, and the jobs adults have: math, art, biology, social studies, and so forth.

It wasn't until much later that I started to question to what extent these conventional categories objectively capture something *real* about the world (and to wonder why no one else seemed to find this important.) Most of my friends at the time were computer scientists working in the entertainment industry developing equations and algorithms to render animated creatures in life-like, artistically appealing, socially acceptable ways. So much for the view that math, art, biology, and social studies are distinct and separate domains! Life doesn't *come* compartmentalized; *any* way one goes about carving up reality involves a degree of arbitrariness.

A Sustainable Worldview is an Integrated Worldview

It is useful, sometimes essential, to categorize and compartmentalize in order to accomplish particular tasks. But if we take any sort of compartmentalization seriously, that is, if we assume it to be a faithful representation of what really exists, it distorts how we see the world, which in turn distorts how we act in it. Behind a sustainable world lies a sustainable worldview. By *sustainable worldview*, we mean a way of seeing the world and being in the world that incorporates how different systems are interconnected and mutually affect one another, an internal model of the world that is *ecological* in character. Sustainability requires not just understanding and solutions; it requires the laying down of new habitual patterns of thinking and acting that foster sustainable outcomes, and that over time become second nature (Clayton & Brook, 2005; Gifford, 2006; Koger & Winter, 2010; Kurz, 2002 Nickerson, 2003; Vlek & Steg, 2007; Winter & Koger, 2004). The compartmentalization of knowledge may lead to an artificially compartmentalized view of the world, which may in turn interfere with our capacity to think about the multifaceted downstream consequences of our actions.

If knowledge is *presented* in compartmentalized chunks, then our youth may end up with a compartmentalized understanding of the world. If knowledge were presented more holistically, a more integrated kind of understanding may be possible. Exposure to a wide range of creative opportunities such as dance, painting, pottery, or creative writing allows for divergent thinking and novel connections to be made, thus encouraging integration of many experiences into a cohesive view. It may be that our potential for a deeply ecological worldview in a modern context is just beginning to be exploited, through ventures such as the Learning through the Arts program, in which students, for example, learn mathematics through dance, or learn about food chains through the creation of visual art. This program originated in Canada but is now being adopted abroad. Such activities can contribute to the therapeutic self-transformation of the individual by providing new narrative structures forging a more reliable, resilient, and empathic connection between the various parts of oneself, and the world in which one lives.

REFERENCES

American Art Therapy Association. (2008). *About us*. Retrieved from http://www.americanartthera-pyassociation.org/aata-aboutus.html

Bollobas, B. (2001). *Random graphs*. Cambridge, UK: Cambridge University Press.

Bollobas, B., & Rasmussen, S. (1989). First cycles in random directed graph processes. *Discrete Mathematics*, *75*(1-3), 55–68.

Clayton, S., & Brook, A. (2005). Can psychology help save the world? A model for conservation psychology. *Analyses of Social Issues and Public Policy (ASAP)*, *5*, 1–15.

Dunn-Snow, P., & Joy-Smelie, S. (2011). Teaching art therapy techniques: Mask-making, a case in point. *Art Therapy*, *17*(2), 125–131. doi:doi:10.1080/07421656.2000.10129512

Dyson, F. (1982). A model for the origin of life. *Journal of Molecular Evolution*, *18*, 344–350.

Dyson, F. (1985/1999). *Origins of life*. Cambridge, UK: Cambridge University Press.

Gabora, L. (2000). Conceptual closure: Weaving memories into an interconnected worldview. In G. Van de Vijver & J. Chandler (Eds.), *Closure: Emergent organizations and their dynamics: Annals of the New York Academy of Sciences*, *901*, 42-53.

Gabora, L. (2006). Self-other organization: Why early life did not evolve through natural selection. *Journal of Theoretical Biology*, *241*(3), 443–450.

Gabora, L. (2008). The cultural evolution of socially situated cognition. *Cognitive Systems Research*, *9*(1-2), 104–113.

Gabora, L. (2010a). Revenge of the 'neurds': Characterizing creative thought in terms of the structure and dynamics of human memory. *Creativity Research Journal*, *22*(1), 1–13.

Gabora, L. (2010b). Recognizability of creative style within and across domains: Preliminary studies. *Proceedings of the Annual Meeting of the Cognitive Science Society* (pp. 2350-2355). August 11-14, 2010, Portland, Oregon.

Gabora, L. (2011). Five clarifications about cultural evolution. *Journal of Cognition and Culture*, *11*, 61–83.

Gabora, L. (under revision). *The honing theory of creativity*, in press.

Gabora, L., & Aerts, D. (2009). A model of the emergence and evolution of integrated world-views. *Journal of Mathematical Psychology*, *53*, 434–451.

Gabora, L., O'Connor, B., & Ranjan, A. (in press). *The recognizability of individuals styles within and across domains*. Submitted.

Gifford, R. (2006). *Environmental psychology: Principles and practice*. Optimal Books.

Gifford, R. (in press). *The dragons of inaction: Psychological barriers that limit climate change mitigation and adaptation.*

Hennessey, B. A., & Amabile, T. (2010). Creativity. *Annual Review of Psychology, 61,* 569–598. doi:doi:10.1146/annurev.psych.093008.100416

Hoyle, F. (1981). Hoyle on evolution. *Nature, 294,* 105.

Karkou, V., & Sanderson, P. (2006). *Arts therapies: A research based map of the field.* London, UK: Elsevier Churchill Livingstone.

Kauffman, S. (1986). Autocatalytic sets of proteins. *Journal of Theoretical Biology, 119,* 1–24.

Kauffman, S. (1993). *Origins of order.* New York, NY: Oxford University Press.

Koger, S., & Winter, D. D. (2010). *The psychology of environmental problems: Psychology for sustainability* (3rd ed.). New York, NY: Taylor & Francis.

Kurz, M. (2002). The psychology of environmentally sustainable behavior: Fitting together pieces of the puzzle. *Analyses of Social Issues and Public Policy (ASAP), 2*(1), 257–278.

Malchiodi, C. (2007). *The art therapy sourcebook.* New York, NY: McGraw-Hill.

Moon, B. (1999). The tears make me paint: The role of responsive artmaking in adolescent art therapy. *Art Therapy: Journal of the American Art Therapy Association, 16*(2), 78–82. doi:doi:10.1080/07421656.1999.10129671

Moon, B. (2009). *Existential art therapy: The canvas mirror.* Springfield, IL: Charles C. Thomas Publisher, Ltd.

Morowitz, H. J. (2002). *The emergence of everything: How the world became complex.* New York, NY: Oxford University Press.

Nickerson, R. S. (2003). *Psychology and environmental change.* Mahwah, NJ: Lawrence Erlbaum Associates.

Riley, S. (1999). Brief therapy: An adolescent intervention. *Art Therapy: Journal of the American Art Therapy Association, 16*(2), 83–86. doi:doi:10.1080/07421656.1999.10129669

Schuster, P. (2010). Origins of life: Concepts, data, and debates. *Complexity, 15*(3), 7–10.

Segré, D., Ben-Eli, D., Deamer, D. W., & Lancet, D. (2001). The lipid world. *Origins of Life and Evolution of the Biosphere, 31,* 119–145.

Segré, D., Ben-Eli, D., & Lancet, D. (2000). Compositional genomes: Prebiotic information transfer in mutually catalytic noncovalent assemblies. *Proceedings of the New York Academy of Science USA, 97,* 4112–4117.

Segré, D., Shenhav, B., Kafri, R., & Lancet, D. (2001). The molecular roots of compositional inheritance. *Journal of Theoretical Biology, 213,* 481–491.

Vasas, V., Szathmáry, E., & Santos, M. (2009). Lack of evolvability in self-sustaining autocatalytic networks: A constraint on metabolism-first path to the origin of life. *Proceedings of the National Academy of Sciences of the United States of America, 107*(4), 1470–1475.

Vetsigian, K., Woese, C., & Goldenfeld, N. (2006). Collective evolution and the genetic code. *Proceedings of the New York Academy of Science USA, 103,* 10696–10701.

Vlek, C., & Steg, L. (Eds.). (2007). Human behavior and environmental sustainability. *The Journal of Social Issues, 63*(1), 1–231.

Wächtershäuser, G. (1992). Groundwork for an evolutionary biochemistry: The iron-sulfur world. *Progress in Biophysics and Molecular Biology, 58,* 85–201.

Weber, B. H. (1998). Emergence of life and biological selection from the perspective of complex systems dynamics. In van de Vijver, G., Salthe, S. N., & Delpos, M. (Eds.), *Evolutionary systems: Biological and epistemological perspectives on selection and self-organization.* Dordrecht, The Netherlands: Kluwer.

Weber, B. H. (2000). Closure in the emergence and evolution of life: Multiple discourses or one? In J. L. R. Chandler & G. Van de Vijver (Eds.), *Closure: Emergent organizations and their dynamics, Annals of the New York Academy of Sciences, 901,* 132-138.

Weber, B. H., & Depew, J. D. (1996). Natural selection and self-organization. *Biology and Philosophy, 11*(1), 33–65.

Williams, R. J. P., & Frausto da Silva, J. J. R. (1999). *Bringing chemistry to life: From matter to man.* Oxford, UK: Oxford University Press.

Williams, R. J. P., & Frausto da Silva, J. J. R. (2002). The systems approach to evolution. *Biochemical and Biophysical Research Communications, 297,* 689–699.

Williams, R. J. P., & Frausto da Silva, J. J. R. (2003). Evolution was chemically constrained. *Journal of Theoretical Biology, 220,* 323–343.

Winter, D. D., & Koger, S. M. (2004). *The psychology of environmental problems* (2nd ed.). Mahwah, NJ: Lawrence Erlbaum Associates.

Woese, C. R. (2002). On the evolution of cells. *Proceedings of the National Academy of Sciences of the United States of America, 99*(13), 8742–8747.

Woese, C. R. (2004). A new biology for a new century. *Microbiology and Molecular Biology Reviews, 68*(2), 173–186.

Chapter 5
Exploring Structural and Dynamical Properties Microtubules by Means of Artificial Neural Networks

R. Pizzi
Università degli Studi di Milano, Italy

S. Fiorentini
Università degli Studi di Milano, Italy

G. Strini
Università degli Studi di Milano, Italy

M. Pregnolato
Università degli Studi di Pavia, Italy

ABSTRACT

Microtubules (MTs) are cylindrical polymers of the tubulin dimer, are constituents of all eukaryotic cells cytoskeleton and are involved in key cellular functions and are claimed to be involved as sub-cellular information or quantum information communication systems. The authors evaluated some biophysical properties of MTs by means of specific physical measures of resonance and birefringence in presence of electromagnetic field, on the assumption that when tubulin and MTs show different biophysical behaviours, this should be due to their special structural properties. Actually, MTs are the closest biological equivalent to the well-known carbon nanotubes (CNTs), whose interesting biophysical and quantum properties are due to their peculiar microscopic structure. The experimental results highlighted a physical behaviour of MTs in comparison with tubulin. The dynamic simulation of MT and tubulin subjected to electromagnetic field was performed via MD tools. Their level of self-organization was evaluated using artificial neural networks, which resulted to be an effective method to gather the dynamical behaviour of cellular and non-cellular structures and to compare their physical properties.

DOI: 10.4018/978-1-4666-2077-3.ch005

INTRODUCTION

Background

Microtubules

Microtubules (MTs) are key constituents of all eukaryotic cells cytoskeleton. They are involved in the regulation of essential cellular functions such as the transport of materials within the cell, the movement of cytoplasmic organelles or vesicles and the cell division (Hyams & Lloyd, 1994).

MTs are stiff cytoskeletal filaments characterized by a tubelike structure. The building block of a MT is a 110-kDa heterodimeric protein said tubulin, that is the association product of two different subunits, designated α and β tubulin (Postingl, Krauhs, Little, & Kempf 1981, Krauhs, Little, Kempf, Hofer-Warbinek, Ade, & Postingl 1981) and encoded by separate genes. The word tubulin always refers to the αβ heterodimer, that is usually considered as one unit, although the association is only due to non-covalent interactions. Each monomer of α and β tubulin is a compact ellipsoid of approximate dimensions 46 x 40 x 65 A° (width, height, and depth, respectively); while dimensions of α β-heterodimer are 46 x 80 x 65 A°. Both α- and β- tubulin is composed of approximately 450 amino acids.

Recently important information about tubulin conformational changes during the MTs polymerization have been obtained through X-ray crystallography (Ravelli, Gigant, Curmi, Jourdain, Lachkar, Sobel, & Knossow 2004).

The general structure of MTs has been established experimentally (Amos & Amos 1991, Chrétien & Wade 1991). MTs have been considered as helical polymers and they are built by the self-association of the αβ-heterodimer through a process of polymerization and depolymerization.

This dynamic nature makes MTs sensitive to several pharmacological agents, i.e. some classes of anticancer agents that are able to destroy or stabilize their structure.

The polymerization occurs in a two-dimensional process that involves two types of contacts between tubulin subunits. The first process involve head-to-tail binding of heterodimers and it results in polar protofilaments that run along the length of the MT. The second process involve lateral interactions between parallel protofilaments and it completes the MT wall to form a hollow tube (Nogales, Whittaker, Milligan & Downing 1999). The longitudinal contacts along protofilaments appear to be much stronger than those between adjacent protofilaments (Mandelkow, Mandelkow, & Milligan 1991).

All protofilaments in a MT have the same orientation.

Assembly mechanism of α- and β- tubulin gives rise *in vitro* to a variety of cylindrical structures that differ by their protofilament and monomer helix-start numbers (Binder & Rosenbaum, 1978, Burton & Himes 1978, Chrétien, Metoz, Verde, Karsenti & Wade 1992, Linck & Langevin 1981, Pierson, Burton & Himes 1978, Chrétien 2000). In contrast, most MTs assembled *in vivo* seem to be composed of 13 protofilaments, although many exceptions have been noted in different species and cell types.

The lengths of MTs vary but commonly reach 5-10 μm dimensions; and their diameter depends on the protofilament number. For example in the case of 13 protofilaments the tube has an outer diameter of 23 nm and an inner diameter of roughly 15 nm.

Microtubules Quantum Theories

In the last decade many theories and papers have been published concerning the biophysical properties of MTs including the hypothesis of MTs implication in coherent quantum states in the brain evolving in some form of energy and information transfer.

The most discussed theory on quantum effects involving MTs has been proposed by Hameroff and Penrose that published the OrchOR Model in 1996 (Hameroff & Penrose, 1996,Hameroff & Penrose, 1996).

They supposed that quantum-superposed states develop in tubulins, remain coherent and recruit more superposed tubulins until a mass-time-energy threshold, related to quantum gravity, is reached (up to 500 msec). This model has been discussed and refined for more than 10 years, mainly focusing attention to the decoherence criterion after the Tegmark critical paper of 2000 (Tegmark, 2000a, Tegmark, 2000b) and proposing several methods of shielding MTs against the environment of the brain (Woolf & Hameroff, 2001, Hagan, Hameroff & Tuszynski, 2002, Hameroff, 2007a). In the Hameroff model MTs perform a kind of quantum computation through the tubulins working like cellular automata. The MTs interior works as an electromagnetic wave guide, filled with water in an organized collective states, transmitting information through the brain (Hameroff, 2007b).

In the same years Nanopoulos et al adopted the string theory to develop a so called QED-Cavity model predicting dissipationless energy transfer along MTs as well as quantum teleportation of states at near room temperature (Nanopoulos & Mavromatos, 1996).

Mavromatos 2000, Mavromatos, Mershin & Nanopoulos, 2002). The Tuszynski approach is based on the biophysical aspects of MTs. Tubulins have electric dipole momeCNTs due to asymmetric charges distribution and MTs can be modeled as a lattice of orientated dipoles that can be in random phase, ferroelectric (parallel-aligned) and an intermediate weakly ferroelectric phase like a spin-glass phase (Tuszynski, Hameroff, Satarić, Trpišová & Nip, 1995, Trpišová, Sept & Satarić,1997, Tuszynski, Brown & Hawrylak, 1998). The model has been sustained by Faber, Portugal & Rosa (2006), who considered a MT as a classical subneuronal information processor.

In 1994 Jibu Hagan, Hameroff, Pribram and Yasue (1994) suggested that the Fröhlich dynamics of ordered water molecules and the quantized electromagnetic field confined inside the hollow MTs core can give rise to the collective quantum optical modes responsible for the phenomenon of superradiance by which any incoherent molecular electromagnetic energy can be transformed in a coherent photon inside the MTs. These photons propagate along the internal hollow core as if the optical medium were transparent and this quantum theoretical phenomenon is called "self-induced transparency".

A decade before, applying quantum field theory (QFT), Del Giudice, Doglia, Milani, Vitiello (1982, 1983) reported that electromagnetic energy penetrating into cytoplasm would self-focus inside filaments whose diameter depend on symmetry breaking (Bose condensation) of ordered water dipoles. The diameter calculated was exactly the inner diameter of MTs (15 nm).

In any case, all phenomena occurring within the brain, both at macroscopic or microscopic level, can be related to some form of phase transition and a number of authors (Pessa, 2007, Alfinito, Viglione, & Vitiello, 2001) pointed out the inconsistence of a quantum mechanical framework based only on traditional computational schemata. It is to be recalled, in this regard, that these schemata have been introduced to deal with particles, atoms, or molecules, and are unsuitable when applied to biological phenomena. In particular Pessa suggested that adopting a wider framework of QFT and, in particular, the dissipative version of it, relying on the doubling mechanism, we could achieve a generalization of QFT able to account for change phenomena in the biological world (Vitiello, 1995, Pessa & Vitiello, 2004, Freeman & Vitiello, 2006).

Carbon Nanotubes and Microtubules

The electronics industry is going to evolve from the technology based on silicon towards innovative materials with new physical properties. These new materials include the carbon nanotubes which currently represent one of the most promising alternatives to overcome the current limits of silicon.

Currently, with a large commitment of academic and industrial scientists, the research is developing nanoscale materials with extremely advanced and useful properties, as they can act both as semiconductors and as superconductors. Thanks to the structure of these materials, their properties are not restricted to classical physics, but presents a wide range of quantum mechanical effects. These may lead to an even more efficient tool for information transfer.

In particular, carbon nanotubes (CNTs) display a wide range of physical effects among them electronic properties are particularly attractive Quantum transport properties of CNTs has been reviewed by Roche, Akkermans, Chauvet, Hekking, Issi, Martel, Montambaux, & Poncharal (2006) both from a theoretical and experimental view. Recently has been described the low-temperature spin relaxation time measurement in a fully tunable CNT double quantum dots. This is an interesting study for new microwave-based quantum information processing experiments with CNTs (Sapmaz, Meyer, Beliczynski, Jarillo-Herrero & Knowenhoven, 2006).

According to Pampaloni & Florin (2008) CNTs are the closest equivalent to MTs among the known nanomaterials. Although their elastic moduli are different, MTs and CNTs have similar mechanical behaviours. They are both exceptionally resilient and form large boundless with improved stiffness.

Nanobiotechnology can move towards a next generation of materials with a wide range of functional properties. As suggest by Michette, Mavromatos, Powell, Holwill, and Pfauntsch (2004), MTs associated with carbon chemistry will allow to build complex macromolecular assemblies for sharing the exciting electronic properties of semi- and super-conductors

Purpose of this Work

Taking into account the connection between structural and physical properties in CNTs and their structural similarity to MTs, our basic assumption in this research was that when tubulin and MTs show different biophysical behaviours, this should be due to the special structural properties of MTs.

In the study of the physical properties of MTs compared with those of CNTs, it is desired to search and analyze a possible reaction to microwaves, observing any ability of MTs to absorb or emit like antennas. The MTs, as well as CNTs, may behave as oscillators, this could make them superreactive receivers able to amplify the signals.

In order to validate this hypothesis we carried out a set of *in vitro* experiments on MTs and tubulin, then we explored the possible meaning of the obtained findings by simulating and comparing the dynamic evolution of MTs, tubulin and CNTs. To this purpose two different procedures based on Artificial Neural Networks models were developed and applied. This paper describes and discussed both procedures and the achieved results.

METHODS

Resonance and Birefringence Experiments

Antennas are devices capable to transform an electromagnetic field into an electrical signal, or to radiate, in the form of electromagnetic field, the electrical signal they are fed by. When powered by an electrical signal to their ends, antennas absorb energy and return it in the surrounding space as electromagnetic waves (transmitting antenna), or absorb energy from an electromagnetic wave and generate a voltage to their ends (receiving antenna). On theoretical bases any conductive object acts as an antenna, regardless of the electromagnetic wave frequency they are hit or the signal that is fed by. In particular, any tubular conductor cable, resonating mechanically, acts as a cavity antenna.

The magnitude of the effect becomes significant when the frequency corresponds to the resonance frequency and in this case the output voltage can be used for receiving and transmitting radio waves.

Resonance is a physical condition that occurs when a damped oscillating system is subjected to a periodic solicitation with a frequency equal to the system oscillation. A resonance phenomenon causes a significant increase in the extent of the oscillations that corresponds to a remarkable accumulation of energy within the oscillator.

The other physical property taken into account in this research is *birefringence*. Birefringence is an optical property of materials that arises from the interaction of light with oriented molecular andstructural components (Huang & Knighton, 2005). Birefringence is the decomposition of a beam of light into two rays that occurs when the light crosses specific anisotropic media depending on the polarization of the light. The interaction between light and magnetic field in a medium results in the rotation of the plane of polarization proportional to the intensity of the magnetic field component in the direction of the beam of light (Faraday effect).

Recent observations and experiments on CNTs have led to the development of an array of CNTs able to act as antennas (Wang, Kempa, Kimball, Carlson, Benham, Li, Kempa, Rybczynski, Herczynski & Ren, 2004). These, instead to transmit and receive radio waves (measured in meters), due to their scale capture wavelengths at the nanoscale (measured in nanometers).

Our group carried out an experiment (Pizzi, Strini, Fiorentini, Pappalardo & Pregnolato, submitted) intended to verify the existence of mechanical resonance in MTs, in analogy with the CNTs, at the frequency that amplifies the wave.

During the experiment we identified a difference in the peak amplitude of the solution with MTs at a frequency of 1.510 MHz, whereas the solution with tubulin and the control solution did not show any reaction. The lack of response in tubulin and control can be considered a hint that the peculiar structure of microtubules could be the cause of the observed signal.

Considering the nanoscopic size of MTs, the resonance analysis would be more effective if carried out on much higher frequencies (up to 100 GHz), with suitable instrumentation. But the presence of a small but sharp resonance effect at a low frequency could be the hint of a much evident effect at higher frequencies.

To assess the physical behaviour of MTs under the effect of electric and magnetic fields we performed *in vitro* birefringence experiments (Pizzi, Strini, Fiorentini, Pappalardo & Pregnolato, submitted) on different samples of MTs and tubulin.

By means of a polarized light and a suitable detection apparatus, it is possible to observe the associated birefringence and, therefore, the index of orientation of MTs subjected either to transverse electric fields and to transverse and longitudinal magnetic fields (Oldenbourg, Salmon & Tran, 1998).

MTs and tubulin were put in stabilizing buffer solution, and we measured the polarization under controlled conditions in order to determine different effects in the interaction of almost static electromagnetic fields. For our comparative experiments the variation of the refraction index is important because it is a function of the wavelength of the electromagnetic radiation and the nature of the crossed material.

Behavioural differences observed between samples of tubulin and MTs, would lead us to understand weather the cavity structure in the MT reacts in a peculiar way in response to specific stimuli or not.

Actually, the analysis of the results of birefringence experiment highlights that the MTs react to electromagnetic fields in a different way than tubulin. In particular, electric field and longitudinal magnetic field show opposite effects in the two types of proteins. Anyway in spite of the effect under electric field is the same as with no field, an unexpected and interesting effect is shown in the case of longitudinal magnetic field.

The achieved results, supported by statistical significance, suggest that the tubular structure of MTs might be responsible for the different behaviour in respect to free tubulins.

Dynamical Simulation

In order to constitute a significant progress in the comprehension of the hypothesized peculiar properties of MTs, the experimental findings must match the estimations of a consistent model.

To this purpose, we performed a dynamic simulation of the molecular structures of tubulin and MTs subjected to different levels of electromagnetic field and in the absence of field, compared with the similar behavior in terms of carbon nanotubes (CNTs) and buckyballs (BBs), globular nanostructured elements (Kroto, Heath, O'Brien, Curl & Smalley, 1985). whose relationship with CNTs can be compared to the relationship between tubulin and MTs.

We adopted the simulation environment Ascalaph (Ascalaph, website): due to the possibility to perform simulations for wide molecular structures with a large number of parameterizations. The simulations were carried out as follows:

- 1st simulation: zero electric field, A = 0
- 2nd simulation: A = 2 V/cm, F = 90 Hz
- 3rd simulation: A = 90 V/cm, F = 90 Hz

The structures were immersed in water at 298.15 °K. The simulation duration was 7000 ps. We adopted the AMBER (Assisted Model Building and Energie Refinement) default force field.

The tertiary structure of tubulin was obtained from Protein Data Bank (Protein Data Bank, website), MTs from the website of the

NANO-D) research group at INRIA Grenoble-Rhone-Alpes (NANO-D, website), BBs and CNTs were directly obtained from Ascalaph.

After the end of simulation and a suitable dynamical optimization, the graphical visualization of the structures appears as in Figure 1.

Artificial Neural Network Processing

In order to evaluate the results of the dynamical simulations, we conceived a novel methods based on Artificial Neural Networks (ANNs). ANNs are intrinsically non-linear models able to classify complex patterns. In particular, the self-organizing networks as the Kohonen's Self Organizing Map (SOM) is well-known as a natural non-linear classifiers (Kohonen, 1990, Ritter, & Schulten 1988).

We submitted the structural data obtained by the MD evolution to two different SOM-based models, then compared their results.

The first adopted model was SONNIA. SONNIA is a powerful Artificial Neural Networks environment, very useful in the field of drug discovery and protein prediction (SONNIA, website). It allows to classify a series of data sets, providing both supervised and unsupervised learning.

The output maps are represented by a set of colored boxes, one for each output neuron. The boxes configuration highlightes two interesting parameters:

1. Occupancy, i.e. the number of patterns that have been mapped onto the same neuron, indicating similarities in the input domain.
2. Conflicts or conflict neurons, i.e. neurons that refer to inputs belonging to different classes.
3. In general, there are always at least a few conflicts such as with any other modeling technique there are false positives or false negatives.

Figure 1. 3D visualization of the structures after dynamical simulation under A= 90 V/cm electric field: a) tubulin, b) MT, c) BB, d) NT

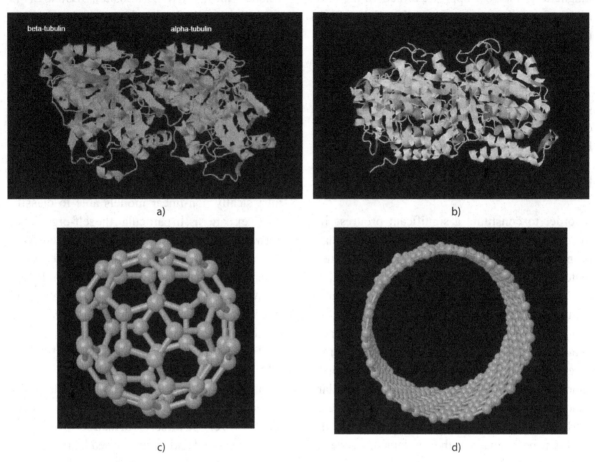

a)

b)

c)

d)

For our case study we chose a Kohonen rectangular network structure with 9x6 neurons and a random initialization.

Besides, we used another self-organizing artificial network developed by our group, the ITSOM (Inductive Tracing Self-Organizing Map), to discriminate the dynamical behaviour of the structures under investigation, on the basis of the chaotic attractors determined by the sequences of its winning neurons (Pizzi, Inama, Durin & Pedrinazzi, 2007).

In fact an analysis on the SOM has shown that such a sequence, provided to keep the learning rates steady (instead of gradually decreasing them), constitutes chaotic attractors that repeat "nearly" exactly in time with the epochs succeeding, and that, once codified by the network, univocally characterize the input element that has determined them.

An attractor can be defined as a generalization of the steady state point, and represents the trajectory in a portion of state space where a dynamical system is attracted to (Ruelle,1981).

We tried to highlight the presence of dynamical attractors in the described structures using MATLAB and its SIMULINK module for the dynamical systems simulation.

In the following (Figure2, Figure 3) we show a comparison of the two different visualizations (SONNIA and ITSOM).

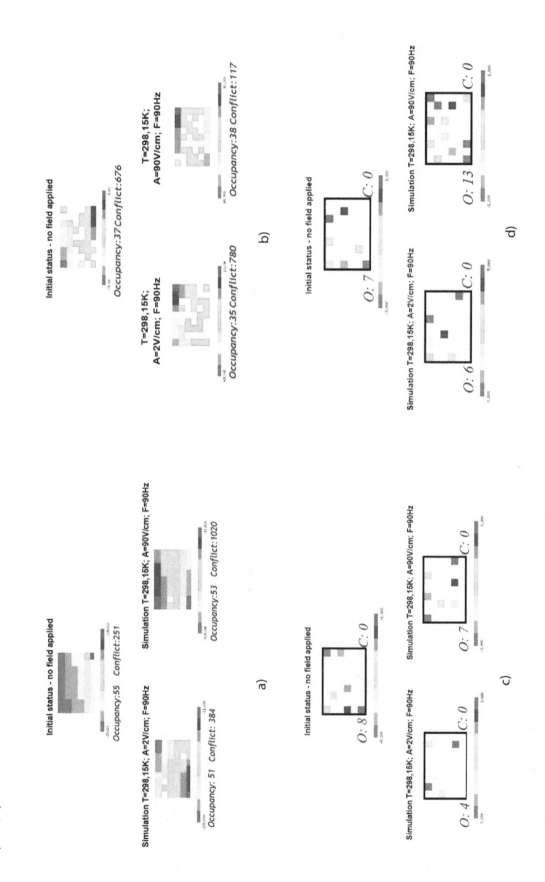

Figure 2. SONNIA visualization. Dynamical evolution without electric field (A=0), with A=2V/s, with A=90V/cm. a) tubulin, b) MT, c) BB, d) NT.

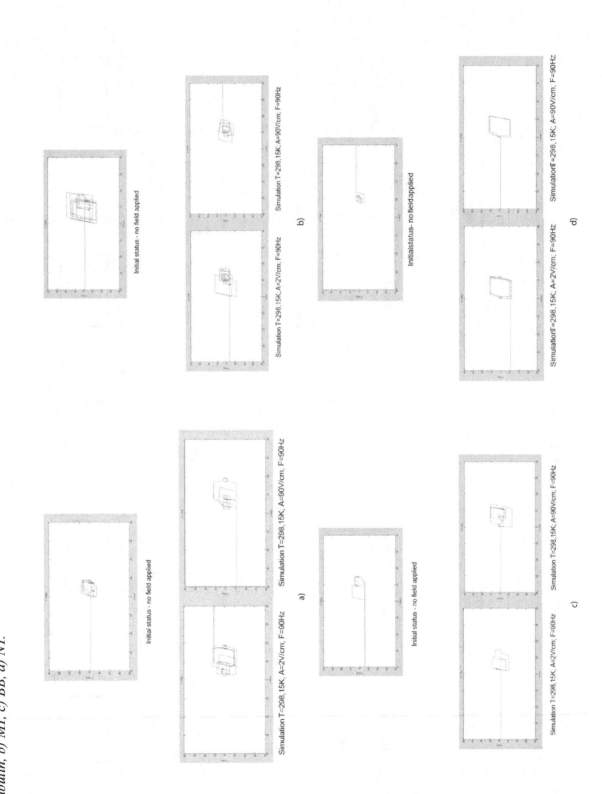

Figure 3. ITSOM visualization with MATLAB – Simulink. Dynamical evolution without electric field (A=0), with A =2V/s, with A=90V/cm. a) tubulin, b) MT, c) BB, d) NT.

RESULTS

In the conditions of zero field the tubulin shows a high occupancy value, and a rather consistent number of conflicts.

The stabilization of the neural network is achieved with the greatest difficulty with respect to all other examined structures, to highlight a lack of native dynamic organization in relationship to the other structures.

By applying a weak electric field the tubulin tends to restrict its configuration space, while maintaining similar rates of occupancy and conflict with respect to the absence of field.

With a 90 V/cm field the configuration space and the occupancy don't change, but the number of conflicts is increased.

In absence of field the MT shows a much more restricted occupancy than tubulin, especially considering that its dimensions are much greater. The configuration space is well confined. With weak electric field the situation does not change, the MT appears spatially and structurally stable.

With a stronger electric field the occupancy does not change, while decreasing the number of conflicts.

The low occupancy values and the absence of conflicts in all configurations of BB and NT is due to the low number of their components if compared to the size of the network and to their extremely regular structure.

By applying a weak electric field to the BB, occupancy tends to decline, the BB tends to stabilize in a range of values. The spatial configuration tends to shrink. But as the electric field grows, the occupancy tends to return to the same levels as in the absence of field.

Although the NT structure is bigger than that of a BB, the occupancy is low and similar to the BB one, symbolizing the strong stability of the structure.

With weak electric field the situation does not change, even though there is a spatial displacement of the structure.

With higher field the structure tends to go back to the positions obtained without field, although in a more distributed way, as occupancy tends to be more distributed.

CONCLUSION AND FUTURE TRENDS

This research presents a novel use of Artificial Neural Networks in the evaluation of the dynamical organization of MTs versus tubulin and CNTs. After performing a MD simulation, we compared it with the evolution of two different models of self-organized neural networks.

The results obtained by SONNIA reflect the same behaviour observed during the Ascalaph dynamical simulation. In fact during the dynamical simulations we observed that both BBs and CNTs move with a dynamic axial motion, which becomes a real pulse in the presence of electric field.

The NT, which in the dynamic evolution at zero field tends to move off its initial position, with the influence of the electric field tends to return to the starting position and to stabilize.

The behavior of the neural network reflects this trend, which shows the extreme regularity of these nanostructures and an interesting already known behavior of NT in the presence of electric field.

The tubulin, despite its symmetric structure, seems to have different internal forces that tend to resist a dynamic stabilization. However, in the presence of electric field, although it tends to squash, it does not show any particular reaction.

The dynamic simulation confirms the lack of specific characterization. The neural simulation shows final graphs that clearly indicate a MTs dynamic organization much stronger than the tubulin one, that is not altered by the presence of electric field even in its spatial configuration.

However, the significant reduction of conflicts indicates a dramatic increase in the spatial organization. On the other hand, the graphs obtained by the ITSOM network confirm the SONNIA neural network analysis and the dynamic simulations. The attractors generated by BB both in the absence of field and with low electric field are extremely cyclical and regular, even though with higher field it tends to present a regular compactness, and to broaden its values, as described by the SONNIA output.

The attractor regularity is clearly present even in the CNTs, and the electric field tends to increase both spatial range and regularity. The tubulin, which is initially well-structured (although with a much more complex pattern of NT and BB), maintains a structured shape even in presence of electric field, although with an increase of disorder. The MTs, however, despite their structural complexity, show a strong dynamic stability, which the electric field, after an initial transient, improves significantly. The field increase further stabilizes the structural dynamics and the spatial configuration of MTs.

It is worth noting that all three methods converge in emphasizing the dynamic stability of these four structures, but show that only CNTs and MTs exhibit a significant behavior in presence of electric field, in the direction of a stronger structural and spatial organization.

These results confirm those already obtained in the cited previous experiments on real samples of tubulin and MTs in conditions of resonance and birefringence.

For this reason, the research on these interesting structures will continue with further studies.

However, the use of simulation methods can help to motivate at a microscopic level the experimental evidences and justify the agreement with theoretical assumptions.

These positive results encourage us to continue also our experimental research. In particular we will carry out in the future a replication of the already performed tests on MTs and tubulins interacting with different ligands.

The experimental results will be coupled with the MD simulation of the protein folding binding different ligands, to study the emerging conformational differences. These studies would support hypotheses on the origin of the different biophysical behaviour in relationship with conformational changes.

ACKNOWLEDGMENT

PRIN 2009 project on tubulins is acknowledged. We thank D. Rossetti, M. Eng., and Dr. S. Manziana, Università degli Studi di Milano, for their valuable work.

REFERENCES

Alfinito, E., Viglione, R., & Vitiello, G. (2001). *The decoherence criterion*. Retrieved from http://arxiv.org/PS_cache/quant-ph/pdf/0007/0007020v2.pdf

Amos, L. A., & Amos, W. B. (1991). *Molecules of the cytoskeleton*. London, UK: MacMillan Press.

Amos, L. A., & Schlieper, D. (2005). Microtubules and MAPs. *Advances in Chemistry, 71*, 257.

Ascalaph. (n.d.). Retrieved from http://www.agilemolecule.com/Products.html

Binder, L. I., & Rosenbaum, J. L. (1978). The in vitro assembly of flagellar outer doublet tubulin. *The Journal of Cell Biology, 79*, 500–515.

Burton, P. R., & Himes, R. H. (1978). Electron microscope studies of pH effects on assembly of tubulin free of associated proteins. *The Journal of Cell Biology, 77*(1), 120–133.

Chrétien, D. (2000). Microtubules switch occasionally into unfavorable configuration during elongation. *Journal of Molecular Biology, 298*, 663–676.

Chrétien, D., Metoz, F., Verde, F., Karsenti, E., & Wade, R. H. (1992). Lattice defects in microtubules: Protofilament numbers vary within individual microtubules. *The Journal of Cell Biology, 117*(5), 1031–1040.

Chrétien, D., & Wade, R. H. (1991). New data on the microtubule surface lattice. *Biology of the Cell, 71*(1-2), 161–174.

Del Giudice, E., Doglia, M., & Milani, M. (1982). Self-focusing of Fröhlich waves and cytoskeleton dynamics. *Physical Review Letters, 90A*, 104–106.

Del Giudice, E., Doglia, S., Milani, M., & Vitiello, G. (1983). Spontaneous symmetry breakdown and boson condensation in biology. *Physical Review Letters, 95A*, 508–510.

Faber, J., Portugal, R., & Rosa, L. P. (2006). Information processing in brain microtubules. *Bio Systems, 83*(1), 1–9.

Freeman, W. J., & Vitiello, G. (2006). Nonlinear brain dynamics as macroscopic manifestation of underlying many-body field dynamics. *Physics of Life Reviews, 3*(2), 93–118.

Fukushige, T., Siddiqui, Z. K., Chou, M., Culotti, J. G., Gogonea, C. B., Siddiqui, S. S., & Hamelin, M. (1999). MEC-12, an α-tubulin required for touch sensitivity in C. elegans. *Journal of Cell Science, 112*, 395–403.

Hagan, S., Hameroff, S. R., & Tuszynski, J. A. (2002). Quantum computation in brain microtubules: Decoherence and biological feasibility. *Physical Review E: Statistical, Nonlinear, and Soft Matter Physics, 65*, 061901–061911.

Hameroff, S. R. (2007a). The brain is both neurocomputer and quantum computer. *Cognitive Science, 31*, 1035–1045.

Hameroff, S. R. (2007b). Orchestrated reduction of quantum coherence in brain microtubules. *NeuroQuantology, 5*(1), 1–8.

Hameroff, S. R., & Penrose, R. (1996a). Orchestrated reduction of quantum coherence in brain microtubules: A model for consciousness. *Mathematics and Computers in Simulation, 40*, 453–480.

Hameroff, S. R., & Penrose, R. (1996b). Conscious events as orchestrated space-time selection. *Journal of Consciousness Studies, 3*, 36–53.

Huang, X.-R., & Knighton, R. W. (2005). Microtubules contribute to the birefringence of the retinal nerve fiber layer. *Investigative Ophthalmology & Visual Science, 46*(12), 4588–4593.

Hyams, J. S., & Lloyd, C. W. (Eds.). (1994). *Microtubules*. New York, NY: Wiley-Liss.

Jibu, M., Hagan, S., Hameroff, S. R., Pribram, K. H., & Yasue, K. (1994). Quantum optical coherence in cytoskeletal microtubules: Implications for brain function. *Bio Systems, 32*, 195–209.

Kohonen, T. (1990). The self-organizing map. *Proceedings of the IEEE, 78*, 1464–1480.

Krauhs, E., Little, M., Kempf, T., Hofer-Warbinek, R., Ade, W., & Postingl, H. (1981). Complete amino acid sequence of β-tubulin from porcine brain. *Proceedings of the National Academy of Sciences of the United States of America, 78*, 4156–4160.

Kroto, H. W., Heath, J. R., O'Brien, S. C., Curl, R. F., & Smalley, R. E. (1985). C_{60}: Buckminsterfullerene. *Nature, 318*, 162–163.

Linck, R. W., & Langevin, G. L. (1981). Reassembly of flagellar B (αβ) tubulin into singlet microtubules: Consequences for cytoplasmic microtubule structure and assembly. *The Journal of Cell Biology, 89*, 323–337.

Lowe, J., & Amos, L. A. (1998). Crystal structure of the bacterial cell-division protein FtsZ. *Nature, 391*, 203–206.

Lowe, J., Li, H., Downing, K. H., & Nogales, E. (1998). Refined structure of αβ-Tubulin at 3.5 A° resolution. *Journal of Molecular Biology, 313,* 1045–1057.

Mandelkow, E. M., Mandelkow, E., & Milligan, R. A. (1991). Microtubules dynamics and microtubules caps: A time-resolved cryoelectron microscopy study. *The Journal of Cell Biology, 114,* 977–991.

Mavromatos, N. (2000). *Cell microtubules as cavities: Quantum coherence and energy transfer?* Retrieved from http://arxiv.org/pdf/quant-ph/0009089

Mavromatos, N., Mershin, A., & Nanopoulos, D. V. (2002). *QED-cavity model of microtubules implies dissipationless energy transfer and biological quantum teleportation.* Retrieved from http://arxiv.org/pdf/quant-ph/0204021

Michette, A. G., Mavromatos, N., Powell, K., Holwill, M., & Pfauntsch, S. J. (2004). Nanotubes and microtubules as quantum information carriers. *Proceedings of the Society for Photo-Instrumentation Engineers, 522,* 5581.

NANO-D. (n.d.). Retrieved from http://nano-d. inrialpes.fr/

Nanopoulos, D. V. (1995).Theory of brain function, quantum mechanics and superstrings. Retrieved from http://arxiv.org/abs/hep-ph/9505374

Nanopoulos, D. V., & Mavromatos, N. (1996). *A non-critical string (Liouville) approach to brain microtubules: State vector reduction, memory coding and capacity.* Retrieved from http://arxiv. org/abs/quant-ph/9512021

Nogales, E. (1998). Structure of the αβ-tubulin dimer by electron crystallography. *Letters to Nature, 391,* 192–203.

Nogales, E., Whittaker, M., Milligan, R. A., & Downing, K. H. (1999). High-resolution model of the microtubule. *Cell, 96,* 79–88.

Oldenbourg, R., Salmon, E. D., & Tran, P. T. (1998). Birefringence of single and bundled microtubules. *Biophysical Journal, 74,* 645–654.

Pampaloni, F., & Florin, E. L. (2008). Microtubule architecture: inspiration for novel carbon nanotube-based biomimetic materials. *Trends in Biotechnology, 26*(6), 302–310.

Pessa, E. (2007). Phase transition in biological matter. In Licata, I., & Sakaji, A. (Eds.), *Physics of emergence and organization* (pp. 165–228). Singapore: World Scientific.

Pessa, E., & Vitiello, G. (2004). Quantum noise induced entanglement and chaos in the dissipative quantum model of brain. *International Journal of Modern Physics B, 18*(6), 841–858.

Pierson, G. B., Burton, P. R., & Himes, R. H. (1978).Alterations in number of protofilameCNTs in microtubules assembled in vitro. *The Journal of Cell Biology, 76,* 223–228.

Pizzi, R., Inama, G., Durin, O., & Pedrinazzi, C. (2007). Non.invasive assessment of risk for severe tachyarrhythmias by means of non-linear analysis techniques. *Chaos and Complexity Letters, 3*(3).

Pizzi, R., Strini, G., Fiorentini, S., Pappalardo, V., & Pregnolato, M. (in press). Evidences of new biophysical properties of microtubules. [in press]. *NanoBiotechnology.*

Postingl, H., Krauhs, E., Little, M., & Kempf, T. (1981). Complete amino acid sequence of α-tubulin from porcine brain. *Proceedings of the National Academy of Sciences of the United States of America, 78,* 2757–2761.

Protein Data Bank. (n.d.). Retrieved from http:// www.rcsb.org/pdb/home/home.do

Ravelli, R., Gigant, B., Curmi, P. A., Jourdain, I., Lachkar, S., Sobel, A., & Knossow, M. (2004). Insight into tubulin regulation from a complex with colchicine and a stathmin-like domain. *Letters to Nature, 428,* 198–202.

Ritter, H., & Schulten, H. (1988). Convergence properties of Kohonen's topology conserving maps: Fluctuations, stability, and dimension selection. *Biological Cybernetics, 60,* 59–71.

Roche, S., Akkermans, E., Chauvet, O., Hekking, F., Issi, J.-P., & Martel, R. ... Poncharal, P. (2006). *Transport properties. understanding carbon nanotubes.* In A. Loiseau, P. Launois, P. Petit, S. Roche, & J.-P. Salvetat (Eds.), *Lecture Notes in Computer Science, 677,* 335–437.

Ruelle, D. (1981). Small random perturbations of dynamical systems and the definition of attractors. *Communications in Mathematical Physics, 82,* 137–151.

Sapmaz, S., Meyer, C., Beliczynski, P., Jarillo-Herrero, P., & Knowenhoven, L. P. (2006). Excited state spectroscopy in carbon nanotube double quantum dots. *Nano Letters, 6*(7), 1350–1355.

Savage, C., Hamelin, M., Culotti, J. G., Coulson, A., Albertson, D. G., & Chalfie, M. (1989). MEC-7 is a β-tubulin gene required for the production of 15-protofilament microtubules in Caenorhabditis elegans. *Genes & Development, 3,* 870–881.

SONNIA. (n.d.). Retrieved from http://www.molecular-networks.com/

Tegmark, M. (2000a). The importance of quantum decoherence in brain processes. *Physical Review E: Statistical Physics, Plasmas, Fluids, and Related Interdisciplinary Topics, 61*(4), 4194–4206.

Tegmark, M. (2000b). Why the brain is probably not a quantum computer. *Information Science, 128*(3-4), 155–179.

Tuszynski, J., Hameroff, S. R., Satarić, M. V., Trpišová, B., & Nip, M. L. A. (1995). Ferroelectric behavior in microtubule dipole lattices: Implications for information processing, signaling and assembly/disassembly. *Journal of Theoretical Biology, 174,* 371–380.

Tuszynski, J. A., Brown, J. A., Crawford, E., & Carpenter, E. J. (2005). Molecular dynamics simulations of tubulin structure and calculations of electrostatic properties of microtubules. *Mathematical and Computer Modelling, 41,* 1055–1070.

Tuszynski, J. A., Brown, J. A., & Hawrylak, P. (1998). Dielectric polarization, electrical conduction, information processing and quantum computation in microtubules: Are they plausible? *Philosophical Transactions of the The Royal Society of London A, 356*(1743), 1897–926.

Tuszynski, J. A., Trpišová, B., Sept, D., & Satarić, M. V. (1997). The enigma of microtubules and their self-organization behavior in the cytoskeleton. *Bio Systems, 42,* 153–175.

Vitiello, G. (1995). Dissipation and memory capacity in the quantum brain model. *International Journal of Modern Physics B, 9*(8), 973–989.

Wang, Y., Kempa, K., Kimball, B., Carlson, J. B., Benham, G., & Li, W. Z. (2004). Receiving and transmitting light-like radio waves: Antenna effect in arrays of aligned carbon nanotubes. *Applied Physics Letters, 85*(13), 2607–2609.

Woolf, N. J., & Hameroff, S. R. (2001). A quantum approach to visual consciousness. *Trends in Cognitive Sciences, 5*(11), 472–478.

Chapter 6
Neurofeedback:
Refining the Methodology of Brain–Computer Interface Training

David Vernon
Canterbury Christ Church University, UK

Tammy Dempster
Canterbury Christ Church University, UK

ABSTRACT

This chapter explores the use of neurofeedback training as a mechanism for altering human brain functioning and in turn influencing behaviour. It outlines the notion that such training provides a plausible mechanism by which an individual may be able to learn to alter and control specific aspects of his electro-cortical activity. The chapter highlights some of the findings from research, including clinical, peak performance, and functional validation studies. In addition, it delineates some important methodological issues that remain to be addressed. It is hoped that outlining these issues will serve a dual purpose. First, it will assist in the understanding of some of the theoretical and methodological limitations that may be holding the field back. Second, it is hoped that such information will stimulate researchers to work towards designing more efficient and effective research protocols and neurofeedback training paradigms.

INTRODUCTION

This chapter provides an outline of some of the applications for neurofeedback training (NFT) and in doing so highlights some key unresolved methodological issues. The first section describes how your brain produces a constant stream of electrocortical activity which can be recorded and then separated into a range of pre-set frequency components. This is followed by a brief overview of NFT which is based on a standard operant conditioning paradigm and can enable you to learn how to use computer based technology to alter specific aspects of your brain wave activity. The chapter then provides a brief outline of the main rationales that have been put forward for conducting such training. This is followed by a section which focuses on some of the outstanding

DOI: 10.4018/978-1-4666-2077-3.ch006

methodological issues that pertain to NFT. These are: the range of spectral components that may be altered using NFT, how to identify whether someone has learnt to alter their EEG via NFT, what measures should be used when exploring possible changes in the EEG as a result of NFT, how the reward threshold level should be set, whether there is a particularly efficient strategy that has been identified, and what effect the participant's motivation level may have on the outcome of such training. By highlighting these issues, which relate to the methodology of NFT, we hope to stimulate future researchers to address them empirically and in doing so improve the efficiency and effectiveness of the NFT protocol. The final section of the chapter outlines the possible future trend of using full scalp recording along with simultaneous feedback of multiple frequency components across multiple sites to provide a more comprehensive training approach.

THE ELECTROENCEPHALOGRAM

It was Richard Caton who, in the late 19th century, first discovered that it was possible to record the weak electrical signals emanating from the brains of living animals. This work was later extended and developed by Hans Berger to encapsulate the recording of such signals from human participants. Since then the electroencephalogram (EEG) has become an integral part of the modern clinician's battery and provided research scientists with a plethora of intriguing links between your behaviour and the activity of your brain.

The EEG is a non-invasive technique and is invariably recorded by placing sensors across the scalp using an agreed placement system. This is commonly referred to as the montage and follows a preset pattern on the scalp according to an international EEG nomenclature called the 10-20 system and is based on the relationship between the location of an electrode and the underlying area of cerebral cortex (Jasper, 1958). It is called

the 10-20 system because the sensors are placed at distances of either 10% or 20% apart from each other or set points across the scalp. In addition to this each site is identified by a letter, which corresponds to the underlying cortical region, and another letter or number to denote the location. For example, the letters F, T, C, P, and O refer to the Frontal, Temporal, Central, Parietal and Occipital regions. In addition to this any accompanying even numbers (2,4,6,8) refer to the right hemisphere and odd numbers (1,3,5,7) refer to the left hemisphere, with the letter z denoting a sensor placed on the midline. Thus, the position Cz refers to the central region of the scalp along the midline whereas C3 refers to the central position of the scalp on the left. See Figure 1 below for an illustration of some the commonly used scalp locations.

Though the EEG may be recorded by a single sensor it is important to realise that such a measure necessarily represents the gross brain activity and function from millions of cells beneath that sensor (see e.g., Davidson, 1988). According to Barlow (1993) the EEG represents the summation of excitatory and inhibitory postsynaptic potentials in the pyramidal cells of the cerebral cortex. As such, the EEG recorded from your scalp represents the current flow associated with summed post-synaptic potentials in synchronously activated, vertically oriented, pyramidal cells. In addition to this, the rapid changes which can be seen in the rhythm of the EEG, from slower to faster and vice versa, are believed to reflect the unique properties of thalamocortical circuits (see Sterman, 1996).

The raw EEG trace recorded from each active sensor can be separated into a range of pre-defined frequency components. Much in the same way as white light can be 'split' by a prism into its spectral components of red, orange, yellow etc, your raw EEG trace can be divided into a range of frequency components using a Fast Fourier Transform (FFT), see Figure 2.

Figure 1. Showing EEG sensor placement according to the 10-20 system

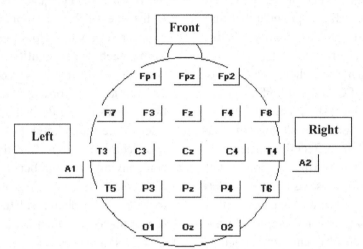

Traditionally the raw EEG trace has been divided into five main frequency bands. These are delta (1-4Hz), theta (4-7Hz), alpha (8-12Hz), beta (13-30Hz) and gamma (35+Hz) (see e.g., Andreassi, 2000). Though some have suggested that these bandwidths themselves can be further subdivided and can also be defined based upon the dominant frequency of each individual's brain activity rather than a standard pre-set frequency range (see e.g., Klimesch, Schimke, Ladurner, & Pfurtscheller, 1990; Klimesch, Schimke & Pfurtscheller, 1993). Nevertheless, once isolated each spectral component of your EEG can be examined in terms of its frequency, amplitude and/or coherence. Where frequency refers to the number of oscillations of EEG activity occurring each second, whilst amplitude is measured as half

the distance between the high and low points of an oscillation and coherence refers to how much the EEG recorded from two separate active sites on your scalp are synchronised, such that the crests and troughs of the waves occur simultaneously, see Figure 3.

NEUROFEEDBACK

Neurofeedback represents a sophisticated form of EEG-biofeedback based on specific aspects of your brain activity. The aim of neurofeedback is to encourage you to learn how to modify some aspect of your brain activity, which may include learning to change the amplitude, frequency and/or coherence of distinct spectral components. The

Figure 2. Showing the conversion of the raw EEG trace into four of the classic frequencies (i.e., delta, theta, alpha and beta)

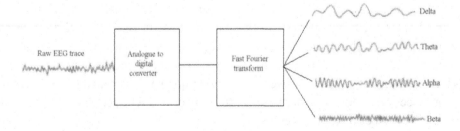

Figure 3. Showing amplitude, frequency and coherence of the EEG

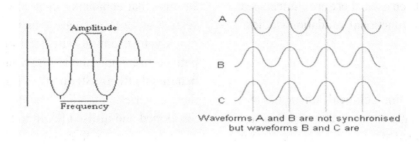

goal of neurofeedback training is to teach you what specific states of cortical arousal feel like and how to re-activate such states voluntarily. During such training your EEG is recorded and the relevant target components are extracted and fed back to you using an online feedback loop in the form of audio, visual or combined audio-visual information. For instance, it may be that your aim is to enhance the amplitude of your alpha EEG frequency and simultaneously inhibit the surrounding theta and beta frequencies. As such, each of these frequency components may be represented on a computer screen as coloured bars, with the amplitude of the relevant frequency component represented by the size of the bar, such that the higher the bar the greater the amplitude. Given this, your task would then be to increase the size of the training-frequency bar (alpha) and simultaneously decrease the size of the bars representing the inhibitory-frequencies (theta and beta). You attempt to do this by trying to remember and re-create the thoughts and feelings you had when the bar was high. Such training can provide you with the opportunity to learn to alter a range of brain wave activity.

Neurofeedback as a technique to enable humans to control their brain activity was developed back in the 1960's when Joe Kamiya examined how different states of consciousness were associated with distinct patterns of electrical activity in the brain. In particular he was interested in the activity of the alpha frequency, as this was associated with a calm resting state. He conducted a two part study examining whether an individual could influence their brain activity when such information was fed back to them (Kamiya, 1968). In the first part of his study participants were seated with eyes closed and when a tone sounded were asked to say whether they thought they were producing alpha waves or not. He found that some individuals could learn to identify when their brain was producing alpha waves and as a consequence were able to increase their production. In the second part of the study, subjects were asked to go into alpha when a bell rang once and not go into the state when the bell rang twice. Once again some of the participants' were able to enter the state on command. Others, however, could not control it at all. Nevertheless, the results were significant and very attractive, showing for the first time that it was possible for someone to voluntarily control the production of a particular aspect of cortical activity.

RATIONALE FOR NEUROFEEDBACK TRAINING

Ever since Kamiya (1968) first suggested that it was possible for individuals to learn to obtain a degree of conscious control over the production of their own brainwave activity there has been interest in how such training could influence behaviour. To date there are three main areas for which NFT has been used, these are clinical, peak performance and functional validation studies.

Clinical

The use of NFT within a clinical domain has been based predominantly on observations of abnormal pathology exhibited by a particular clinical group. Two good examples of this are those suffering from epilepsy and those diagnosed with attention deficit hyperactivity disorder (ADHD).

Individuals diagnosed with epilepsy often suffer recurrent fits and seizures which are caused by abnormal electrical discharges in the grey matter of the brain and can be characterised by partial or generalised seizures. A partial seizure is restricted to one region of the brain whereas a generalised seizure may spread to other areas. For example, an individual suffering a *grand mal* generalised seizure may experience a fit that results in him falling to the ground unconscious with muscles contracting whilst arms and legs remain rigid. Other generalised seizures include the *petit mal* where the individual may experience a blank period, remaining completely unaware of what is happening and what is going on around them. There are many causes of epilepsy, including viruses, neurotoxins, tumors and head injury (see e.g., Berkovic, Mulley, Scheffer & Petrou, 2006). However, these epileptic seizures are often associated with bursts of high amplitude EEG spikes, which are apparent in the EEG during an attack (Cohen, Navarro, Clemenceau, Baulac & Miles, 2002). For many these seizures remain intractable to current medical and/or surgical therapies and as such NFT offers a potentially useful alternative for reducing the impact of these seizures based on self-modulation of the EEG. The idea for utilising NFT as a treatment for patients with epilepsy is based on the early work of Barry Sterman who found that cats trained to enhance the sensorimotor rhythm (SMR) of their EEG exhibited a considerably later seizure onset when exposed to rocket

fuel. It was this early work which led Sterman to surmise that enhancing their SMR had reduced seizure onset for the cats, which in turn spurned a study to examine whether training epileptic patients to enhance their SMR would have similar beneficial effects (Sterman & Friar, 1972). Since then a variety of NFT techniques have been developed and utilised to aid in the treatment of patients suffering from epilepsy, including the entrainment of slow cortical potentials (SCPs) and in particular the higher-frequency sensorimotor rhythm (see Monderer, Harrison & Haut, 2002 for a review). Many of these studies have since shown that the motor seizure incidence of epileptic patients may be lowered significantly by training them to enhance their SMR using NFT (Sterman, 1973, 2000; Sterman & Macdonald, 1978; Sterman, Macdonald, & Stone, 1974). Indeed, a meta-analysis examining the effects of NFT as a treatment for epilepsy recently concluded that NFT produced a significant reduction on seizure frequency (Tan, Thornby, Hammond, Strehl, Canady, Arnemann & Kaiser, 2009).

In contrast, ADHD can be seen as an enduring disorder characterised by persistent symptoms of inattention alone or in combination with hyperactivity and impulsivity (American Psychiatric Association, 1994). These symptoms have been shown to significantly impair an individual's ability to function effectively at home, school and in the workplace (Friel, 2007). It was the early findings of Sterman and colleagues that led Joel Lubar to wonder whether NFT to enhance the SMR, which required the individual to remain mentally alert but motorically quiet, would aid in the reduction of some of the hyperactive/impulsive behaviours exhibited by children with ADHD (Lubar & Shouse, 1976). Early research produced some positive findings showing improvements in both the behaviour and academic performance of those diagnosed with ADHD (Linden, Habib, & Radojevic, 1996; Lubar, Swartwood, Swartwood, & O'Donnell, 1995; for a review see Vernon, Frick, & Gruzelier, 2004). Additional support for the use of NFT to treat those diagnosed with ADHD comes from the quantitative electroencephalographic (QEEG) analyses of such patients showing clear abnormalities in the EEG of a large proportion of those diagnosed with ADHD (Chabot, di Michele, Prichep, & John, 2001) which have been suggested to be directly implicated in its cause (see e.g., Sterman, 1996). For instance, when compared to non-clinical controls children with ADHD exhibit an excess of slow theta activity, predominantly in the frontal regions, and lower levels of the faster beta activity (Clarke, Barry, McCarthy, & Selikowitz, 1998; Clarke, Barry, McCarthy, Selikowitz, & Brown, 2002; Mann, Lubar, Zimmerman, Miller, & Muenchen, 1992). These findings have led to a new range of neurofeedback training protocols aimed at training children with ADHD to inhibit the excessive slow wave theta activity and simultaneously attempt to enhance the faster beta activity (Monastra, Monastra, & George, 2002; Thompson & Thompson, 1998). Reviews of this treatment intervention have produced results ranging from 'probably efficacious' (Monastra et al., 2005, p.6) to 'comparable to that of stimulant medication' (Friel, 2007, p.146). With a recent meta-analysis concluding that NFT as an intervention for ADHD can be 'considered efficacious and specific with a large effect size for inattention and impulsivity and a medium effect size for hyperactivity' (Arns, de Ridder, Strehl, Breteler & Coenen, 2009, p.180).

Thus, it is clear that NFT can be regarded as a clinically useful intervention for; *inter alia*, those suffering from epilepsy or ADHD.

Peak Performance

Outside of the clinical arena NFT has also been utilised as a performance enhancement technique (see e.g., Vernon, 2005; 2008; 2009; Vernon & Gruzelier, 2008; Vernon et al., 2009). In general, the rationale for using such a technique to enhance performance has been based on the associations reported between specific frequency components of the EEG and particular physical and/or cognitive behaviours. For instance, Vernon et al (2009) recently made a case for the use of alpha NFT as a plausible mechanism to potentially inhibit non-essential processing which in turn would lead to facilitated cognitive performance on tasks utilising such activity. To date NFT has been utilised as a possible mechanism for enhancing sporting performance, a range of cognitive abilities and artistic performance (see Vernon, 2005; 2009).

For instance, one group of researchers examined whether neurofeedback training to enhance low frequency activity prior to the execution of a physical skill would benefit performance (Landers et al., 1991). Landers et al (1991) examined the performance of two groups of pre-elite archers receiving neurofeedback training. The NFT required one of the groups to increase the low frequency activity in their left temporal region. This was based on the assumption that an increase in low frequency activity represented a reduced level of cognitive activation which would result in a reduced level of covert verbalisations of the left-brain, allowing the visual-spatial processing of the right-hemisphere to become more dominant. The second neurofeedback group was included to control for motivational or expectancy effects associated with the use of the neurofeedback equipment and as such received the same type of training over their right temporal region. Both groups completed 27 shots at a target positioned 45m distant, with the level of performance measured as the distance between the arrow and the centre of the target. This was followed by a number of neurofeedback training sessions, which continued until each participant reached a pre-set criterion with regard to changes in the amplitude of their EEG. Then both groups completed a further 27 target shots. They found that those trained to enhance low frequency activity in their left-temporal region showed a significant improvement in their performance. In contrast, those trained to enhance low frequency activity in their right-temporal region performed significantly worse following the neurofeedback training. These findings led Landers et al (1991) to conclude that neurofeedback training may be used as a method of enhancing the performance of pre-elite archers.

Research has also examined whether neurofeedback training to alter the faster beta frequencies can influence the cognitive abilities of healthy participants (Egner & Gruzelier, 2001; Rasey, Lubar, McIntyre, Zoffuto, & Abbott, 1996; Vernon et al., 2003). For instance, Egner and Gruzelier (2001) trained a group of 22 participants to enhance their low beta activity in the 12-15Hz over the right central region of the brain and 15-18Hz range over the left central region, whilst simultaneously inhibiting the surrounding lower theta (4-7Hz) and higher beta (22-30Hz) frequencies. The participants completed a total of ten NFT sessions whilst pre and post measures of cognition were examined using a computerised continuous performance task (CPT) (Greenberg, 1987) and an event related potential (ERP) measure of attention. The continuous performance task involved presenting a range of stimuli on screen, some of which were 'targets' which required the participant to respond to as quickly and as accurately as possible, and some of which were 'lures' or non-targets. In this instance the participant was required to refrain from responding. The ERP task involved presenting a range of tones to the participant which changed in pitch and the participant was required to actively monitor and detect such changes whilst his EEG was recorded. They found that, following the NFT, participants showed a significant improvement on the CPT task and an increase in the amplitude of a generalised P3b ERP component that is thought to represent an updating of information in working memory (Donchin & Coles, 1988). They also found some correlations between changes in participants EEG as a function of NFT and improvements in cognitive processing. This led them to conclude that the results represented a 'successful enhancement of attentional performance in healthy volunteers through EEG operant conditioning techniques' (p.9).

More recently Vernon et al. (2003) found that NFT to enhance the low beta (12-15Hz) frequency can influence semantic working memory performance. They trained two groups to enhance a range of different EEG frequencies and then examined the effect of such training on a range of cognitive tasks. The first group trained to enhance slow theta (4-8Hz) activity whilst simultaneously inhibiting the surrounding delta (1-4Hz) and alpha (8-12Hz) frequencies. The second group underwent NFT to enhance the amplitude of their low beta (12-15Hz) whilst simultaneously inhibiting theta (4-8Hz) and high beta (18-22Hz). All participants completed a range of cognitive tasks designed to measure attention and semantic working memory, followed by eight sessions of NFT, with the sensor placed on the central position of the scalp, and then repeated the measures of cognitive performance. Contrary to expectations it was found that those training to enhance their theta activity actually showed a marginal reduction of theta and exhibited no change in their cognitive performance. In contrast, those training to enhance their low-beta showed significant changes in their EEG in line with the NFT protocol. In addition to this the low-beta training group also showed a significant improvement in semantic working memory. An attempt was made to account for this by suggesting that enhancing 12-15Hz aids the maintenance of the working memory representation utilised in semantic working memory.

With regard to artistic performance research has reported on two successive experiments aimed at utilising neurofeedback to enhance music performance (Egner & Gruzelier, 2003). In the first experiment Egner and Gruzelier report on a group of music students who underwent NFT to enhance a combination of frequency ranges, including low beta (12-15Hz and 15-18Hz) and theta (5-8Hz) at different scalp locations. Pre and post NFT all participants were required to play a piece of music for 15 minutes, which was recorded. Their performance was assessed internally by a panel of judges from the Royal College of Music and externally by a set of experts examining the video recordings of each performance. They found that the NFT resulted in marginal improvements in musical performance. These findings led them to conduct a second experiment which utilised a similar design but had a separate group of participants undergo NFT to enhance the level of their theta activity over that of their alpha activity (commonly referred to as alpha-theta training). Here they found that when participants post-training musical performance were examined they showed significant improvements in overall quality, musical understanding, stylistic accuracy and interpretative imagination. This led Egner and Gruzelier (2003) to conclude that NFT can benefit the musical performance of healthy individuals.

Functional Validation

A third and potentially useful, yet little explored, avenue for NFT is the idea that it may be used as a mechanism to validate the functional role of the various EEG components. For example, there is a great deal of research outlining the various associations between specific spectral components of the EEG and particular aspects of cognition (see Klimesch, 1999 for a review). However, much, if not all of this research is based on correlating changes in behaviour with changes in electro-cortical activity, which it has been suggested makes it difficult to rule out the notion that other cognitive processes may be influencing the EEG and thereby acting as a possible confound (Keizer, Veerschoor, Verment & Hommel, 2010). Thus, the idea here is that NFT may be used as a mechanism to investigate the functional relevance of a particular component of the EEG by having participants learn to directly synchronise or desynchronise activity within a specific frequency range and monitor how this influences cognitive behaviour. For example, perception of a visual scene has been shown to rely upon distributed neural networks encoding and representing the various properties of the scene. Given this, Treis-

man (1996) has pointed out that some mechanism is needed to bring together the disparate aspects of such a scene and bind the information relating to each object whilst simultaneously distinguishing it from others. One plausible candidate mechanism that has been proposed to coordinate this binding is the temporal synchronous firing of the various neural networks within the gamma frequency band of the EEG (see Engel & Singer, 2001). Keizer et al (2010) tested this idea by using NFT to alter the power of the gamma band EEG to investigate what changes this would have on an individual's ability to bind disparate features within a visual scene. They found that eight 30-minute sessions of NFT aimed at enhancing power within the gamma (36-44Hz) frequency range at position Oz were sufficient to elicit increases in gamma power and that these increases were directly related to a reduction in the amount of time taken to bind visual feature conjunctions. A similar pattern was reported by Keizer, Verment and Hommel (2010) who found that an increase in synchronous gamma (36-44Hz) band activity via NFT elicited greater episodic binding of shape and location information. Such findings have led to the conclusion that NFT provides 'a powerful method for studying the functional relevance of frequency specific bands in the EEG' (Keizer et al., 2010, p.7).

Given the findings outlined above from the clinical, peak performance and functional validation literature it would seem that NFT represents a useful mechanism for providing you with the ability to alter your brain activity and in doing so change your behaviour. However, whilst this evidence is encouraging there are a number of issues, in particular relating to the methodology of NFT, which limit our understanding of its use and its acceptance in the wider field. These include the scope of EEG frequencies that may be altered using NFT and whether changes in such frequency components are purely a localised phenomenon. Furthermore, it is unclear at present what the criteria should be for deciding whether an individual has learnt to alter their EEG or not and what dependent measures may be best used to provide an index of learning. In addition, there are questions concerning the reward threshold that is set during NFT and how this may influence the outcome of the training. There are also issues of strategy and motivation, where it is not clear whether a specific strategy can be identified as useful during NFT and also whether it is only those who are 'highly motivated' that will be able to learn to alter their EEG using NFT and as a consequence only highly motivated people should take part. Each of these issues is explored in more detail below.

ISSUES

Scope and Effect

As outlined above the principle aim of NFT is to enable you to learn to alter specific aspects of your own electro-cortical activity and in doing so influence your behaviour. However, one question that has been raised is whether it is possible to alter all aspects of your EEG. That is, is it possible for you to learn to alter only some or all of the components of your EEG and are these effects specifically localised to the region of training?

An examination of previous research suggests that the range of NFT effects is widespread and may include all aspects of the EEG. For example, as outlined above the raw EEG signal can be separated into five main frequency bands: delta (1-4Hz), theta (4-7Hz), alpha (8-12Hz), beta (13-30Hz) and gamma (35+Hz) (Andreassi, 2000). Research utilising NFT has shown that it is possible for people to learn to alter the amplitude and/or level of activity of most of these frequencies. This includes theta (3-7Hz) (Beatty, Greenberg, Diebler & O'Hanlon, 1974), alpha (8-13Hz) (Angelakis et al., 2007; Dempster & Vernon, 2009; Fell et al., 2002), which also includes sub-components of the alpha frequency range (see e.g., Bazanova & Lubomir, 2006; Hanslmayr, Sauseng, Doppelmayr,

Schabus & Klimesch, 2005), and individually based alpha rhythms determined by identifying the difference in peak alpha amplitude between eyes closed and eyes open using a broader range of 6-14Hz (Bazanova, Verevkin & Shtark, 2007). In addition, changes have also been reported in the sensorimotor rhythm (SMR) (12-15Hz) (Vernon et al., 2003), combined SMR and low-beta (12-18Hz) (Fuchs et al., 2003), beta (16-20Hz) and gamma (36-44Hz) (Keizer, Verschoor et al., 2010). Alongside the changes in single frequency ranges researchers have also been able to show that NFT is capable of helping you modify one frequency in relation to another: with alpha-theta NFT (Egner, Strawson & Gruzelier, 2002). Alpha-theta NFT represents an attempt to increase the level of your theta activity over that of your alpha in an attempt to induce a hypnogogic state which has traditionally been associated with creativity (see Gruzelier, 2009). Furthermore, NFT has also been shown to elicit changes in slow cortical potentials (Kotchoubey, Schleichert, Lutzenberger & Birbaumer, 1997; Landers et al., 1991). Slow cortical potentials (SCPs) represent changes in the polarisation of the EEG occurring within the frequency range below 1-2 Hz and can persist over several seconds to produce either a negative or positive shift. Negative shifts have been associated with cortical excitation whilst positive shifts reflect inhibition (see, Birbaumer, 1999). Such research would seem to provide a strong indication that NFT is capable of eliciting changes in many, if not most, aspects of cortical activity. Nevertheless, such training may elicit changes outside the boundaries of the frequencies trained and beyond the location where the training occurred. For instance, Egner, Zech and Gruzelier (2004) found that NFT aimed at enhancing low beta (12-15Hz) in the right central area (C4) led to decreased low-beta activity in the pre-frontal region (which included FP1; FP2; F7 and F8). In addition, NFT aimed at enhancing theta to alpha ratios at the central posterior region (Pz) was associated with reduced frontal beta activity (region

F3; Fz and F4). More recently Keizer, Verment and Hommel (2010) found that NFT aimed at enhancing beta (12-20Hz) resulted in an increase in coherence between frontal (Fz) and occipital (Oz) regions in the gamma (36-44Hz) frequency range. Such results challenge the assumption that NFT of a specific frequency component will result in changes *only* in that component and *only* at the location where the training is conducted. As such, it is clear that NFT is capable of eliciting changes in many aspects of the EEG however, what remains unclear at present is the precise nature and location of such changes.

Learners vs. Non-Learners

As can be seen above it would seem that it is possible for you to elicit changes in most if not all aspects of your electro-cortical activity via NFT. However, what is not clear is whether everyone can do this or not. That is, is it possible for everyone to learn to alter their EEG using NFT or will only some be able to do this and if so what are the criteria that can be used to identify such 'learners'? Unfortunately this is an area that is particularly under researched with many simply identifying learners as those who exhibit the desired changes in their EEG following NFT. Whilst such changes in the EEG are essential it would be more helpful to have a clearly defined criterion or set of criteria that provide a standard way of assessing whether you have learnt to alter your EEG via NFT or not.

This is clearly an issue that has been around for some time as Kamiya (1968) stated early on that it may be that only certain types of people are able to learn to control their EEG with NFT. Indeed, when examining changes in EEG to classify people as learners or non-learners some have reported that only about 50% of the sample receiving the NFT showed evidence of learning (see e.g., Hanslmayr et al., 2005). Hence, not everyone may be able to learn to use this technique and by grouping together potential learners and non-learners any possible effects elicited by the training could be reduced and may even be washed out, leading to the possible erroneous conclusion that NFT has no effect.

Given that the aim of NFT is to elicit changes in the EEG it would seem an obvious and essential point that those who subsequently exhibit changes in their EEG be identified as learners (see, Vernon, 2005). However, it needs to be made much clearer where such changes need to occur, which also raises the issue of distinguishing between a *responder* and a *learner*. For example, Hanslmayr et al., (2005) identified those who exhibited a change in their EEG *during* the NFT in line with the goal of the training as *responders*. More recently Weber, Koberl, Frank and Doppelmayr (in press) go some way to extend and clarify this by suggesting that a *responder* is someone who exhibits an increase in target frequency amplitude of 8% from the beginning to the end of the training and shows consistent changes in amplitude in the desired direction across 'all' training sessions. Something we consider to represent a good first step in addressing this issue. However, we would go one step further and propose that the person undergoing the NFT also needs to exhibit the ability to alter his EEG in the desired direction without the need for any feedback, and by doing this he would truly be classified as a *learner*. Hence, changes within and across the training session would lead to the person being classified as a *responder* whereas these changes along with changes that occur outside of the training session and without the need for feedback would lead to the more stringent classification of *learner*. We recognise that this represents a more conservative criterion for identifying potential learners, as well as helping to make the fine discrimination between responders and learners but as suggested elsewhere (Vernon et al., 2009) it would provide a clear indication of the level of control achieved by the individual undergoing the NFT.

Index of Learning

How learning is measured is also a crucial point to decide on. If researchers all measure changes in participants' performance in different ways it makes it difficult to compare studies. For instance, if one study assesses learning by examining participants' changes in amplitude from one session to another and another categorises learning as time spent above the reward threshold during the NFT then it may be difficult to know whether any differences found in outcome (i.e., changes in behaviour) are a result of differences in the training procedure itself, or whether they are related to changes in a particular measure. In other words, if studies all use different methods for measuring performance and assessing learning it makes it difficult to spot possible trends and correlations which could help identify the specific elements of the NFT that affect the outcome. For instance, if changes in cognition can be produced using NFT it needs to be made clear whether such changes are the result of alterations in amplitude or the amount of time spent over a particular threshold level, or both. In addition, it also needs to be made clear whether such changes need to occur concurrently from one session to the next, or just within the training session itself. In sum, what are the indices of learning which should be used to measure performance during NFT to help identify learners? Clearly this question has two elements: how are changes in the desired frequency components measured and how is learning defined? Three of the more common ways of measuring changes in the desired frequency component are amplitude (e.g. Vernon et al., 2003), percent time (e.g. Angelakis et al., 2007) or a combination of the two. With regards to how successful learning is defined there are two main methods: across session changes (e.g. Egner & Gruzelier, 2003), i.e. changes from one NFT session to another, and within session changes (e.g. Egner, Strawson & Gruzelier, 2002), i.e. changes which occur during the NFT session itself. Both of which can be ana-

lysed in relation to a resting baseline or not, with baseline referring to the relevant measure of the desired frequency component when participants are not trying to influence it. For example, the amplitude of their SMR (13-15Hz) before they start that day's training.

Until some standardization is seen in the measures used it is unclear whether it is changes in amplitude, percent time, or a combination of the two which is the crucial element of learning. It is also unclear whether these changes need to be seen within sessions, across sessions, or both. It has been suggested that it depends on the measure used as to how successful NFT is found to be (Ancoli & Kamiya, 1978). It would therefore seem crucial to establish an index or indices of learning in order to be able to compare studies and spot trends and thus identify the crucial aspects of NFT which elicit the desired outcomes (e.g. changes in cognition). In order to help establish some standardisation within the field we have recommended the use of a within sessions compared to baseline analysis incorporating both amplitude and percent time as two distinct measures rather than an integrated measure which combines them both (see Dempster & Vernon, 2009).

Reward Threshold

Given that feedback is invariably given during NFT *only* when a participant's target EEG component exceeds a pre-set threshold, it would seem obvious to point out that when attempting to increase the amplitude of an EEG component the higher the threshold the more difficult would be the task. Furthermore, reward thresholds can remain fixed or change along with the training. Unfortunately, it is not always made clear why a particular reward threshold has been chosen and in some cases such information is not reported (e.g., Angelakis et al., 2007; Beatty, 1971; Hardt & Gale, 1993; Johnson & Meyer, 1974; Konareva, 2006; Wacker, 1996). Nevertheless, when such information is reported there is little consistency in its use. For instance, the most common measures reported are amplitude, as measured in microvolts, and measures based on a ratio of the amount of EEG activity seen when at rest. However, reward thresholds based on amplitude range from $10\mu V$ up to $40\mu V$ (e.g., Ancoli & Green, 1977; Hardt & Kamiya, 1976; Holmes, Burish & Frost, 1980; Kuhlman & Klieger, 1975; Nowlis & Kamiya, 1970; Valle & DeGood, 1977) with some setting additional upper limits of $75\mu V$ and $100\mu V$ (Marshall & Bentler, 1976; Tyson, 1982). There is a similar level of variety when using thresholds based on a proportion of resting EEG activity, with thresholds set at between 50% and 85% of the amount of alpha seen when at rest (e.g., Cram, Kohlenberg & Singer, 1977; Cho et al., 2008; Norris et al., 2001; Prewett & Adams, 1976; Travis, Kondo & Knott, 1974; 1975).

Clearly, identifying an optimal reward threshold would seem an essential aspect of NFT because it needs to be set at a level that ensures an adequate amount of feedback information is provided allowing you to identify states, feelings and cognitions which elicit the required activity. If the threshold is set too low, making the task very easy, there may be little motivation and/or need for you to do anything in order to elicit positive feedback. In contrast, if it is set too high insufficient feedback information will be provided and you are likely to become frustrated. Both scenarios could potentially inhibit your ability to learn to alter your EEG via NFT. Unfortunately there is very little guidance identifying optimal reward thresholds. For instance, Knox (1980) suggested that for a threshold to be relevant participants need to exhibit between 25-75% above threshold activity during an eyes closed resting baseline period. If they exhibit less than 25% above threshold activity it is likely that too little information would be provided for the feedback loop to operate effectively. However, this leaves a broad range open for possible use and it is likely that a threshold based on resting activity which

is only exceeded by 25% would be substantially more difficult, and may involve distinct processes, than one that is exceeded by 75%.

Furthermore, it is likely that thresholds based on a ratio of resting EEG activity are more meaningful and possibly more effective than those based on an arbitrary level of amplitude. This is because each threshold would then relate directly to your natural resting level of EEG activity. For example, Knox (1980) measured the amount of alpha exhibited by participants that exceeded an arbitrary fixed threshold of $15\mu V$ when resting with their eyes closed. She found that the majority of participants (68%) exhibited less than 25% of alpha when using this cut-off point and argued against the use of such arbitrary fixed thresholds based simply on level of amplitude. Thus, setting a reward threshold that fails to relate to your resting EEG activity may make the task of NFT more difficult and in doing so reduce its effectiveness. As such, additional research is needed to identify an optimal level, or range, of reward thresholds, ideally comparing fixed versus variable thresholds as well as directly comparing the effectiveness of the different measures used, to establish an optimum threshold level.

Motivation

The large variability in training ability seen in NFT has led to suggestions that it is not just the methodology used which influences training success but also individual variables relating to the participants themselves (e.g. Konareva, 2006). In particular, participants' levels of motivation has been cited by those such as Ancoli and Kamiya (1978) as being particularly important with regard to how successful the participants are in learning to train the desired frequency component via NFT. If this is true it would be expected that the more motivated the participant the more successful they would be likely to be at such training. The question then becomes, how can motivation be assessed/predicted and is there any way it can be increased in order to try and maximise participants' learning success?

Money is a common method of recruiting participants (e.g. Weber et al., in press) and has been suggested to increase participants' motivation and therefore performance (e.g. Brolund & Schallow, 1976). However, when Regestein, Pegram, Cook and Bradley (1973) compared the difference between giving a monetary reward of $2.50 for each hour of criterion alpha (8-13Hz) produced to giving no reward at all they found no difference in participants' performance. Although no specific measure of motivation was taken this would suggest that payment made no difference to participants' performance. However, work by Kondo, Travis and Knott (1975) suggests that the possible reason for this lack of effect is likely due to the payment being too small to be motivating. In their research, Kondo et al. (1975) paid 40 students $2 an hour to enhance their alpha (8-13Hz) at Oz. In addition, 10 of those participants were offered a $10 bonus if the alpha in each of their last 5 trials reached 120% of that of their alpha in their 1st trial, 10 participants were offered $5 for the same, 10 were offered $2.50, and 10 were not offered any bonus at all. Whilst the $5 and $10 bonus participants enhanced their alpha to the required levels the $2.50 and no bonus groups did not. This led the authors to suggest that whilst offering money may be a motivating force which can influence participants' neurofeedback performance it has to be of a sufficient amount to be motivational and to therefore make a difference to training.

Even if motivation does influence training success, simply assuming that money alone is enough in itself to motivate participants may be a mistake. For instance, Weber et al. (in press) paid each of their participants 250 Euros for taking part but still categorised approximately 50% of their participants as non-learners, suggesting that money in itself may not be enough of a motivational force to produce a learner. Arguably, monetary rewards may well encourage participants

to turn up and complete the required training but it does not necessarily mean that they will try any harder than those who have not been paid. In actual fact, Ancoli and Green (1977) suggested that unpaid volunteers would perform better than paid volunteers because they were more likely to be internally rather than externally motivated and therefore more likely to want to do well. Of course, there are methods other than money which have been used to try and increase participants' motivation. For instance, Cho et al. (2008) told their participants that the NFT could reduce anxiety levels and improve their ability to learn. However, they reported only limited success with regards to changes in the EEG as a result of using such a strategy.

Whilst it makes intuitive sense that the more motivated participants may make more of an effort and as a consequence may be more likely to exhibit changes in their EEG, researchers to date have tended to employ fairly generic methods to increase participants' motivation but have not actually devised a way of measuring it. If motivation is indeed an influencing factor in participants' ability to learn it would seem useful to come up with a clear and accurate way of measuring it. Moreover, researchers could then use such a measure to ensure that only highly motivated participants are selected.

Strategies

Whilst the measures used to examine participants' performance and their levels of motivation may be important, the difference between learners and non-learners may also reflect the strategies that are used to train the required element of a particular frequency component(s). For instance, whilst the goal of neurofeedback is the same for each participant, to learn to exert a conscious control over some aspect of their cortical activity, there are two ways they could achieve this. The first is to wait for the desired feedback to occur and then try and learn what it is they are thinking/feeling/

doing when this happens. The second is to try out various strategies and see which appears to elicit a greater level of feedback. Either way it is usually left to the participant to work out what works for him/her and it is unusual for studies to report precisely what strategies their participants used, or look for differences between those who were deemed successful and those who were not as a function of the various strategies employed.

Of those who have tried to explore the effects of different strategies no definitive approach emerges as the most ideal. For instance, Peper and Mullholland (1970) asked their participants what they were doing to turn the feedback tone 'on' and 'off' during the training. They found that it depended on whether participants had particularly high or low resting baseline levels of alpha before they started the training. High alpha participants found relaxation helped them increase their alpha and tension helped them to suppress it, but low alpha participants reported the opposite pattern, which could indicate that individual differences could impact the effectiveness of a particular strategy. The authors did suggest that losing awareness of their surroundings appeared to be related to enhancing alpha which is intriguing because this is something which has also been suggested by others (see e.g., Lynch & Paskewitz, 1971; Nowlis & Kamiya, 1970). Interestingly, Nowlis and Kamiya (1970) also found that success during NFT depended on whether participants' eyes remained open or closed during the training and this interacted with the strategies reported as being particularly successful, which suggests that a particular strategy may be influenced by the specific training methodology (e.g. eyes open vs. eyes closed NFT). On a related point, just because a strategy is found to be successful for training one particular frequency (e.g. alpha) does not necessarily mean that it would be successful for training other frequency components of the EEG. Likewise, it is also unknown whether the area of the brain that is the focus of the NFT, the specific montage used (i.e. monopolar vs. bipolar) or the measure used to underlie the training require

different strategies. Ultimately, there is no clear agreement yet as to whether an optimum strategy exists for NFT. Indeed, Plotkin (1976) has suggested that what participants are not doing may be just as important as what they are.

If it is the case that there are specific strategies which are more effective for training particular frequency components, as opposed to distinct strategies working for different people as a result of individual differences, then this would be useful not just for optimising participants' ability to learn during NFT but also for helping them to exert the desired effect over a particular target frequency during their daily lives as opposed to restricting it to the training period only. In order for this to be established, however, more research clearly needs to be conducted.

FUTURE TRENDS

Although NFT has been around for some time now its popularity in recent years has grown, not only in clinical practice and peak performance training but also as a mechanism to validate the functional role of the EEG. Nevertheless, most if not all NFT neurofeedback training is still conducted using single or dual sensors placed using either a referential or sequential montage. Such an approach whilst useful has its limitations in terms of what can be trained and where. As our understanding of the nature and complexity of the brain improves and our ability to build computers that are capable of processing more information at faster speeds evolves the NFT of the future may be very different from the type of training undertaken today. Instead of attempting to enhance a set frequency range recorded from a single sensor placed at a fixed location we may be able to train a whole range of distinct frequency components, recorded from across the whole scalp. Full cap NFT with multiple frequencies being fed back to the participant in real time may open up a whole new range of possibilities concerning what can be trained and what effect this may have on behaviour.

CONCLUSION

Neurofeedback training represents an interesting example of human–computer interaction that has evolved over time to be used in a range of different settings. The use of a computer to provide you with specific information regarding particular aspects of the electrical activity of your brain, of which you were previously unaware, provides a mechanism which enables you to obtain some degree of conscious control over the activation of the various EEG frequencies and by doing so alter specific aspects of your behaviour. It remains the domain of future researchers to provide a detailed and comprehensive understanding of the possible effects such training may have.

REFERENCES

American Psychiatric Association – APA. (1994). *Diagnostic and statistical manual of mental disorders*. Washington, DC: Author.

Ancoli, S., & Green, K. F. (1977). Authoritarianism, introspection, and alpha wave biofeedback training. *Psychophysiology, 14*(1), 40–44.

Ancoli, S., & Kamiya, J. (1978). Methodological issues in alpha biofeedback training. *Biofeedback and Self-Regulation, 3*(2), 159–183.

Andreassi, J. L. (2000). *Psychophysiology: Human behaviour and physiological response* (4thed.). Mahweh, NJ: LEA.

Angelakis, E., Stathopoulou, S., Frymiare, J. L., Green, D. L., Lubar, J. F., & Kounios, J. (2007). EEG neurofeedback: A brief overview and an example of peak alpha frequency training for cognitive enhancement in the elderly. *The Clinical Neuropsychologist, 21*(1), 110–129.

Arns, M., de Ridder, S., Strehl, U., Breteler, M., & Coenen, A. (2009). Efficacy of neurofeedback treatment in ADHD: The effects on inattention, impulsivity and hyperactivity: A meta-analysis. *Clinical EEG and Neuroscience, 40*(3), 180–189.

Barlow, J. S. (1993). *The electroencephalogram: Its patterns and origins*. Cambridge, MA: MIT Press.

Bazanova, O. M., & Lubomir, A. (2006). Learnability and individual frequency characteristics of EEG alpha activity. *Vestnik Rossiiskoi Akademii Meditsinskikh Nauk, 5*(6), 30–33.

Bazanova, O. M., Verevkin, E. G., & Shtark, M. B. (2007). Biofeedback in optimising psychomotor reactivity: II. The dynamics of segmental alpha-activity characteristics. *Human Physiology, 33*(6), 695–700.

Beatty, J. (1971). Effects of initial alpha wave abundance and operant training procedures on occipital alpha and beta wave activity. *Psychosomatic Science, 23*(3), 197–199.

Beatty, J., Greenberg, A., Diebler, W. P., & O'Hanlon, J. F. (1974). Operant control of occipital theta rhythm affects performance in a radar monitoring task. *Science, 183*(4127), 871–873.

Berkovic, S. F., Mulley, J. C., Scheffer, I. E., & Petrou, S. (2006). Human epilepsies: Interaction of genetic and acquired factors. *Trends in Neurosciences, 29*, 391–397.

Birbaumer, N. (1999). Slow cortical potentials: Plasticity, operant control, and behavioural effects. *The Neuroscientist, 5*(2), 74–78.

Brolund, J. W., & Schallow, J. R. (1976). The effects of reward on occipital alpha facilitation by biofeedback. *Psychophysiology, 13*(3), 236–241.

Chabot, R. J., di Michele, F., Prichep, L., & John, E. R. (2001). The clinical role of computerized EEG in the evaluation and treatment of learning and attention disorders in children and adolescents. *The Journal of Neuropsychiatry and Clinical Neurosciences, 13*(2), 171–186.

Cho, M. K., Jang, H. S., Jeong, S., Jang, I., Choi, B., & Lee, M. T. (2008). Alpha neurofeedback improves the maintaining ability of alpha activity. *Neuroreport, 19*(3), 315–317.

Clarke, A. R., Barry, R. J., McCarthy, R., & Selikowitz, M. (1998). EEG analysis in attention-deficit/hyperactivity disorder: A comparative study of two subtypes. *Psychiatry Research, 81*(1), 19–29.

Clarke, A. R., Barry, R. J., McCarthy, R., Selikowitz, M., & Brown, C. R. (2002). EEG evidence for a new conceptualisation of attention deficit hyperactivity disorder. *Clinical Neurophysiology, 113*(7), 1036–1044.

Cohen, I., Navarro, V., Clemenceau, S., Baulac, M., & Miles, R. (2002). On the origin of interictal activity in human temporal lobe epilepsy *in vitro*. *Science, 298*, 1418–1421.

Cram, J. R., Kohlenberg, R. J., & Singer, M. (1977). Operant control of alpha EEG and the effects of illumination and eye closure. *Psychosomatic Medicine, 39*(1), 11–18.

Davidson, R. J. (1988). EEG measures of cerebral asymmetry: Conceptual and methodological issues. *The International Journal of Neuroscience, 39*(3), 71–89.

Dempster, T., & Vernon, D. (2009). Identifying indices of learning for alpha neurofeedback training. *Applied Psychophysiology and Biofeedback, 34*, 309–318.

Donchin, E., & Coles, M. G. H. (1988). Is the P300 component a manifestation of context updating. *The Behavioral and Brain Sciences, 11*, 406–425.

Egner, T., & Gruzelier, J. (2003). Ecological validity of neurofeedback: Modulation of slow wave EEG enhances musical performance. *Neuroreport, 14*(9), 1221–1224.

Egner, T., & Gruzelier, J. H. (2001). Learned self-regulation of EEG frequency components affects attention and event-related brain potentials in humans. *Neuroreport, 12*(18), 4155–4159.

Egner, T., Strawson, E., & Gruzelier, J. H. (2002). EEG signature and phenomenology of alpha/theta neurofeedback training versus mock feedback. *Applied Psychophysiology and Biofeedback, 27*(4), 261–270.

Egner, T., Zech, T. F., & Gruzelier, J. (2004). The effects of neurofeedback training on the spectral topography of the healthy electroencephalogram. *Clinical Neurophysiology, 115*, 2452–2460.

Engel, A. K., & Singer, W. (2001). Temporal binding and the neural correlates of sensory awareness. *Trends in Cognitive Sciences, 5*(1), 16–25.

Fell, J., Elfadil, H., Klaver, P., Roschke, J., Elger, C. E., & Fernandez, G. (2002). Covariation of spectral and nonlinear EEG measures with alpha biofeedback. *The International Journal of Neuroscience, 112*, 1047–1057.

Friel, P. N. (2007). EEG biofeedback in the treatment of attention deficit/hyperactivity disorder. *Alternative Medicine Review, 12*(2), 146–151.

Fuchs, T., Birbaumer, N., Lutzenberger, W., Gruzelier, J. H., & Kaiser, J. (2003). Neurofeedback treatment for attention-deficit/hyperactivity disorder in children: A comparison with methylphenidate. *Applied Psychophysiology and Biofeedback, 28*(1), 1–12.

Greenberg, L. (1987). An objective measure of methylphenidate response: Clinical use of the MCA. *Psychopharmacology Bulletin, 23*(2), 279–282.

Gruzelier, J. (2009). A theory of alpha/theta neurofeedback, creative performance enhancement, long distance functional connectivity and psychological integration. *Cognitive Processing, 10*(1), 101–109.

Hanslmayr, S., Sauseng, P., Doppelmayr, M., Schabus, M., & Klimesch, W. (2005). Increasing individual upper alpha power by neurofeedback improves cognitive performance in human subjects. *Applied Psychophysiology and Biofeedback, 30*(1), 1–10.

Hardt, J. V., & Gale, R. (1993). Creativity increases in scientists through alpha EEG feedback training. *Proceedings of the Association for Applied Psychophysiology and Biofeedback*, 24th Annual Meeting, Los Angeles, CA, March 25-30.

Hardt, J. V., & Kamiya, J. (1976). Conflicting results in EEG alpha feedback studies: Why amplitude integration should replace percent time. *Biofeedback and Self-Regulation, 1*, 63–75.

Holmes, D. S., Burish, T. G., & Frost, R. O. (1980). Effects of instructions and biofeedback on EEG-alpha production and the effect of EEG-alpha biofeedback training for controlling arousal in a subsequent stressful situation. *Journal of Research in Personality, 14*, 212–223.

Jasper, H. H. (1958). Report of the committee on methods of clinical examination in electroencephalography. *Electroencephalography and Clinical Neurophysiology, 10*, 370–375.

Johnson, R., & Meyer, R. (1974). The locus of control construct in EEG alpha rhythm feedback. *Journal of Consulting and Clinical Psychology, 42*(6), 913.

Kamiya, J. (1968). Conscious control of brain waves. *Psychology Today, 1*, 57–60.

Keizer, A. W., Verment, R. S., & Hommel, B. (2010). Enhancing cognitive control through neurofeedback: A role of gamma-band activity in managing episodic retreival. *NeuroImage, 49*(4), 3404–3413.

Keizer, A. W., Vershoor, M., Verment, R. S., & Hommel, B. (2010). The effect of gamma enhancing neurofeedback on the control of feature bindings and intelligence measures. *International Journal of Psychophysiology, 75*(1), 25–32.

Klimesch, W. (1999). EEG alpha and theta oscillations reflect cognitive and memory performance: A review and analysis. *Brain Research. Brain Research Reviews, 29*(2-3), 169–195.

Klimesch, W., Schimke, H., Ladurner, G., & Pfurtscheller, G. (1990). Alpha frequency and memory performance. *Psychophysiology, 4*, 381–390.

Klimesch, W., Schimke, H., & Pfurtscheller, G. (1993). Alpha frequency, cognitive load and memory performance. *Brain Topography, 5*(3), 241–251.

Knox, S. S. (1980). Distribution of 'criterion' alpha in the resting EEG: Further argument against the use of an amplitude threshold in alpha biofeedback training. *Biological Psychology, 11*, 1–6.

Konareva, I. N. (2006). Correlations between the psychological peculiarities of an individual and the efficacy of a single neurofeedback session. *Neurophysiology, 38*(3), 201–208.

Kondo, C. Y., Travis, T. A., & Knott, J. R. (1975). The effect of changes in motivation on alpha enhancement. *Psychophysiology, 12*(4), 388–389.

Kotchoubey, B., Schleichert, H., Lutzenberger, W., & Birbaumer, N. (1997). A new method for self-regulation of slow cortical potentials in a timed paradigm. *Applied Psychophysiology and Biofeedback, 22*, 77–93.

Kuhlman, W. N., & Klieger, D. M. (1975). Alpha enhancement: effectiveness of two feedback contingencies relative to a resting baseline. *Psychophysiology, 12*(4), 456–460.

Landers, D. M., Petruzzello, S. J., Salazar, W., Crews, D. J., Kubitz, K. A., & Gannon, T. L. (1991). The influence of electrocortical biofeedback on performance in pre-elite archers. *Medicine and Science in Sports and Exercise, 23*(1), 123–129.

Linden, M., Habib, T., & Radojevic, V. (1996). A controlled study of the effects of EEG biofeedback on cognition and behaviour of children with ADD and LD. *Biofeedback and Self-Regulation, 21*(1), 35–49.

Lubar, J. F., & Shouse, M. N. (1976). EEG and behavioral changes in a hyperkinetic child concurrent with training of the sensorimotor rhythm (SMR): A preliminary report. *Biofeedback and Self-Regulation, 1*(3), 293–306.

Lubar, J. F., Swartwood, M. O., Swartwood, J. N., & O'Donnell, P. H. (1995). Evaluation of the effectiveness of EEG neurofeedback training for ADHD in a clinical setting as measured by changes in T.O.V.A. scores, behavioural ratings, and WISC-R performance. *Biofeedback and Self-Regulation, 20*(1), 83–99.

Lynch, J. J., & Paskewitz, D. A. (1971). On the mechanisms of the feedback control of human brain wave activity. *The Journal of Nervous and Mental Disease, 153*(3), 205–217.

Mann, C. A., Lubar, J. F., Zimmerman, A. W., Miller, C. A., & Muenchen, R. A. (1992). Quantitative analysis of EEG in boys with attention-deficit-hyperactivity disorder: Controlled study with clinical implications. *Pediatric Neurology, 8*(1), 30–36.

Marshall, M. S., & Bentler, P. M. (1976). The effects of deep physical relaxation and low-frequency-alpha brainwaves on alpha subjective reports. *Psychophysiology, 13*(6), 505–516.

Monastra, V. J., Lynn, S., Linden, M., Lubar, J. F., Gruzelier, J., & La Vaque, T. J. (2005). Electro-encephalographic biofeedback in the treatment of attention deficit/hyperactivity disorder. *Journal of Neurotherapy, 9*(4), 5–34.

Monastra, V. J., Monastra, D. M., & George, S. (2002). The effects of stimulant therapy, EEG biofeedback and parenting style on the primary symptoms of attention deficit/hyperactivity disorder. *Applied Psychophysiology and Biofeedback, 27*(4), 231–249.

Monderer, R. S., Harrison, D. M., & Haut, S. R. (2002). Neurofeedback and epilepsy. *Epilepsy & Behavior, 3*, 214–218.

Norris, S. L., Lee, C., Burshteyn, D., & Cea-Aravena, J. (2001). The effects of performance enhancement training on hypertension, human attention, stress, and brain wave patterns: A case study. *Journal of Neurotherapy, 4*(3), 29–44.

Nowlis, D. P., & Kamiya, J. (1970). The control of electroencephalographic alpha rhythms through auditory feedback and the associated mental activity. *Psychophysiology, 6*(4), 476–484.

Peper, E., & Mullholland, T. (1970). Methodological and theoretical problems in the voluntary control of electroencephalographic occipital alpha by the subject. *Kybernetik, 7*(1), 10–13.

Plotkin, W. B. (1976). On the self-regulation of the occipital alpha rhythm: Control strategies, states of consciousness, and the role of physiological feedback. *Journal of Experimental Psychology. General, 105*(1), 66–99.

Prewett, M. J., & Adams, H. E. (1976). Alpha activity suppression and enhancement as a function of feedback and instructions. *Psychophysiology, 13*(4), 307–310.

Rasey, H. W., Lubar, J. F., McIntyre, A., Zoffuto, A. C., & Abbott, P. L. (1996). EEG biofeedback for the enhancement of attentional processing in normal college students. *Journal of Neurotherapy, 1*(3), 15–21.

Regestein, Q. R., Pegram, G. V., Cook, B., & Bradley, D. (1973). Alpha rhythm percentage maintained during 4- and 12- hour feedback periods. *Psychosomatic Medicine, 35*(3), 215–222.

Sterman, M. B. (1973). Neurophysiologic and clinical studies of sensorimotor EEG biofeedback training: some effects on epilepsy. *Seminars in Psychiatry, 5*(4), 507–525.

Sterman, M. B. (1996). Physiological origins and functional correlates of EEG rhythmic activities: Implications for self-regulation. *Biofeedback and Self-Regulation, 21*(1), 3–33.

Sterman, M. B. (2000). Basic concepts and clinical findings in the treatment of seizure disorders with EEG operant conditioning. *Clinical EEG (Electroencephalography), 31*(1), 45–55.

Sterman, M. B., & Friar, L. (1972). Suppression of seizures in an epileptic following sensorimotor EEG feedback training. *Electroencephalography and Clinical Neurophysiology, 33*(1), 89–95.

Sterman, M. B., & Macdonald, L. R. (1978). Effects of central cortical EEG feedback training on incidence of poorly controlled seizures. *Epilepsia, 19*(3), 207–222.

Sterman, M. B., Macdonald, L. R., & Stone, R. K. (1974). Biofeedback training of the sensorimotor electroencephalogram rhythm in man: Effects on epilepsy. *Epilepsia, 15*(3), 395–416.

Tan, G., Thornby, J., Hammond, D. C., Strehl, U., Canady, B., Arnemann, K., & Kaiser, D. A. (2009). Meta-analysis of EEG biofeedback in treating epilepsy. *Journal of Clinical EEG & Neuroscience, 40*(3), 173–179.

Thompson, L., & Thompson, M. (1998). Neurofeedback combined with training in metacognitive strategies: Effectiveness in students with ADD. *Applied Psychophysiology and Biofeedback, 23*(4), 243–263.

Travis, T. A., Kondo, C. Y., & Knott, J. R. (1974). Parameters of eyes-closed alpha enhancement. *Psychophysiology, 11*(6), 674–681.

Travis, T. A., Kondo, C. Y., & Knott, J. R. (1975). Alpha enhancement research: A review. *Biological Psychiatry, 10*(1), 69–89.

Treisman, A. (1996). The binding problem. *Current Opinion in Neurobiology, 6*(2), 171–178.

Tyson, P. D. (1982). The choice of feedback stimulus can determine the success of alpha feedback training. *Psychophysiology, 19*(2), 218–230.

Valle, R. S., & DeGood, D. E. (1977). Effects of state-trait anxiety on the ability to enhance and suppress EEG alpha. *Psychophysiology, 14*(1), 1–7.

Vernon, D. (2005). Can neurofeedback training enhance performance? An evaluation of the evidence with implications for future research. *Applied Psychophysiology and Biofeedback, 30*(4), 347–364.

Vernon, D. (2008). Neurofeedback: using computer technology to alter brain functioning. In Orsucci, F., & Sala, N. (Eds.), *Reflexing interfaces: The complex coevolution of information technology systems* (pp. 94–108). New York, NY: Information Science Reference.

Vernon, D. (2009). *Human potential: Exploring techniques used to enhance human performance.* London, UK: Routledge.

Vernon, D., Dempster, T., Bazanova, O., Rutterford, N., Pasqualini, M., & Andersen, S. (2009). Alpha neurofeedback training for performance enhancement: Reviewing the methodology. *Journal of Neurotherapy, 13*(4), 214–227.

Vernon, D., Egner, T., Cooper, N., Compton, T., Neilands, C., Sheri, A., & Gruzelier, J. (2003). The effect of training distinct neurofeedback protocols on aspects of cognitive performance. *International Journal of Psychophysiology, 47*(1), 75–85.

Vernon, D., Frick, A., & Gruzelier, J. (2004). Neurofeedback as a treatment for ADHD: A methodological review with implications for future research. *Journal of Neurotherapy, 8*(2), 53–82.

Vernon, D., & Gruzelier, J. (2008). Electroencephalographic biofeedback as a mechanism to alter mood, creativity and artistic performance. In DeLuca, B. N. (Ed.), *Mind-body and relaxation research focus* (pp. 149–164). Nova Science.

Wacker, M. S. (1996). Alpha brainwave training and perception of time passing: Preliminary findings. *Biofeedback and Self-Regulation, 21*(4), 303–309.

Weber, E., Koberl, A., Frank, S., & Doppelmayr, M. (in press). Predicting successful learning of SMR neurofeedback in healthy participants: methodological considerations. *Applied Psychophysiology and Biofeedback.*

Chapter 7
The Biotic Logic of Quantum Processes and Quantum Computation[1]

Hector Sabelli
Chicago Center for Creative Development, USA

Louis H. Kauffman
University of Illinois at Chicago, USA

ABSTRACT

This chapter explores how the logic of physical and biological processes may be employed in the design and programing of computers. Quantum processes do not follow Boolean logic; the development of quantum computers requires the formulation of an appropriate logic. While in Boolean logic, entities are static, opposites exclude each other, and change is not creative, natural processes involve action, opposition, and creativity. Creativity is detected by changes in pattern, diversification, and novelty. Causally-generated creative patterns (Bios) are found in numerous processes at all levels of organization: recordings of presumed gravitational waves, the distribution of galaxies and quasars, population dynamics, cardiac rhythms, economic data, and music. Quantum processes show biotic patterns. Bios is generated by mathematical equations that involve action, bipolar opposition, and continuous transformation. These features are present in physical and human processes. They are abstracted by lattice, algebras, and topology, the three mother structures of mathematics, which may then be considered as dynamic logic. Quantum processes as described by the Schrödinger's equation involve action, coexisting and interacting opposites, and the causal creation of novelty, diversity, complexity and low entropy. In addition to 'economic' (not entropy producing) reversible gates (the current goal in the design of quantum gates), irreversible, entropy generating, gates may contribute to quantum computation, because quantum measurements, as well as creation and decay, are irreversible processes.

DOI: 10.4018/978-1-4666-2077-3.ch007

INTRODUCTION

Quantum gates and circuits may provide an opportunity to incorporate the pattern of quantum processes into the logical structure of the computer, and thereby employ rules for reasoning that take into account the pattern of quantum processes as well as that of many other natural processes.

This article explores the possibility for a logical design of computers that matches the logic inherent in natural processes. There are natural creative processes that are evident in biological organisms and also found in physical processes, including quantum ones. These biotic processes could become the basis for the working of a machine. We speculate on the possibility of harnessing these biotic processes for computation. Such logic would be natural and empirically based. In most mathematical systems, the axioms that we take are carefully abstracted from a certain aspect of experience. Quantum processes do not follow Boolean logic (Birkhoff and von Neumann, 1936), and therefore the development of quantum computation involves the development of quantum logic.

Adapting our humanly-conceived computer hardware and software to the actual logic of nature, one would hope to model mathematical, natural, and mental processes more directly and accurately. Of course we do not know what the "actual logic of nature" is, but we have a proposal based on physical and biological considerations. The founders of science and philosophy regarded biological processes as useful models for the cosmos; Aristotle noted that *"the heavens are high and far off and of celestial things the knowledge that our senses give is scanty and dim"* while *"living creatures are at our door and we may gain ample and certain knowledge of each and all"* (quoted by Prigogine, 1980). Cybernetics, Chaos and Complexity were largely inspired by biology, and Bios was found in human physiology before it was demonstrated in physics. The objective of this chapter is to sketch the general principles of a system of logic that incorporates the biotic complexity of quantum processes, hoping that it will be useful in quantum computation.

We focus on quantum processes because they are particularly relevant to the development of quantum computers. This will allow the full use of quantum processes for computation. Employing quantum processes directly could be extremely helpful to understanding them. Processing, transmitting and storing information encoded in systems with quantum properties will provide practical advantages as illustrated by the factoring of large numbers (Shor, 1997).2 A number of physical systems for quantum computation hardware (Ladd et al, 2010), and software (Nielsen & Chuang, 2000) are being developed.

Here we address a complementary task, to formulate the logic of quantum processes. A key new element that we bring into physics, logic and computation is the existence of causal creativity at all levels of organization including fundamental physical and biological processes (Sabelli, 2005). As a result, quantum processes as well as cosmological ones display life-like (biotic) patterns (Sabelli and Kovacevic, 2003, 2006; Thomas et al. 2006; Sabelli et al, forthcoming) as illustrated in Figure 1 for the wave function of an electron confined to a well. The same pattern is observed for purported gravitational waves presumably originating in the Big bang, and at processes at multiple levels of organization (see later). The Schrödinger equation originally was intended to portray the movement of electrons; it was later on interpreted by Born as the probability of finding the electron in a given place, but such 'probability' changes in time, hence the Schrödinger equation portrays a process, the temporal change of the distribution of the electron.3

We speculate on the possibility of harnessing biotic processes at the quantum level in quantum computers. This speculation is worth exploring because there are creative recursive processes that are not hard to specify. Causal creative processes can be generated by simple mathematical recur-

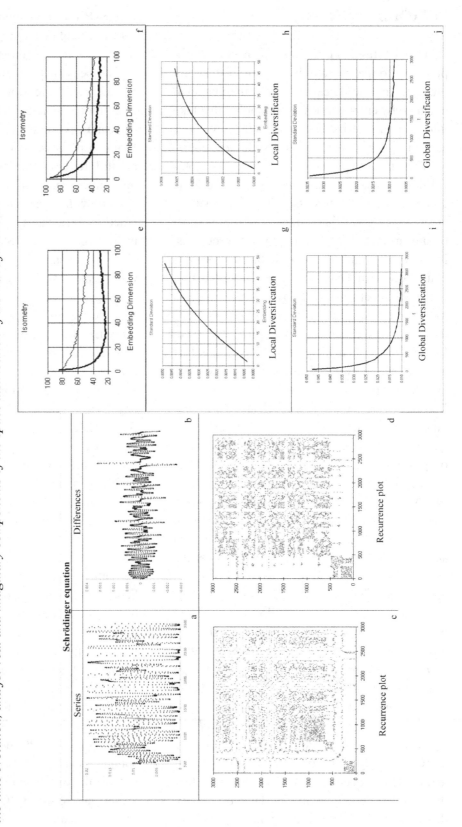

Figure 1. Biotic pattern in the Schrödinger equation: time evolution of the real and imaginary components of the wave function for an electron to a box. Black lines: data. Blue lines: shuffled data. . Left column: the analysis of the time series detects creative features: changes in pattern, with grouping of recurrences in "complexes" separated by recurrence-free intervals, lower rate of recurrence isometry than in randomized copies (novelty), asymmetric distribution lowering entropy, and increase variance at higher embedding (local diversification). Global diversification (increase variance with time) is not found. These results are obtained with biotic series and with random walks but not with random or chaotic series. Right column: finding pattern in the series of differences between consecutive terms demonstrates causal, non-random generation; this differentiates Bios from random walks. The results are qualitatively the same for the imaginary component of the time evolution, and for real and imaginary components of the space distribution of the wave function.

sions (Kaufmann & Sabelli, 1998; Sabelli & Kaufmann, 1999) and may in principle be used to construct logical circuits. At this time we have shown that the wave function for certain quantum processes is biotic, but we do not yet see how this bios could be detected by a physical measurement. If we knew how to physically measure quantum bios, then it would be directly possible to harness Bios in quantum computing. Thus we are not finished with this project!

To employ biotic processes as a basis for the working of a computer is a speculation, since we have not proven that a biotic approach to logic has advantages over a purely Boolean approach, but studies of physical, biological and psychological processes reviewed later point in this direction.

FOUNDATIONS

Action, information and matter appear to be the fundamental components of reality at all levels of organization (Figure 2). The scheme of physical entities as composed of core particles surrounded by energetic and informational fields, inspired in Whitehead's model of the solar system, offers a realistic interpretation of the particle-wave duality central to quantum physics.

Figure 2. Three components of natural processes. Systems have a material core, a larger energetic field and a larger and expanding informational field (top left) as illustrated by Whitehead portrait of the solar system (top right). These three aspects of natural processes repeat at all levels of organization including mathematical structures (bottom left) and quantum processes (bottom right).

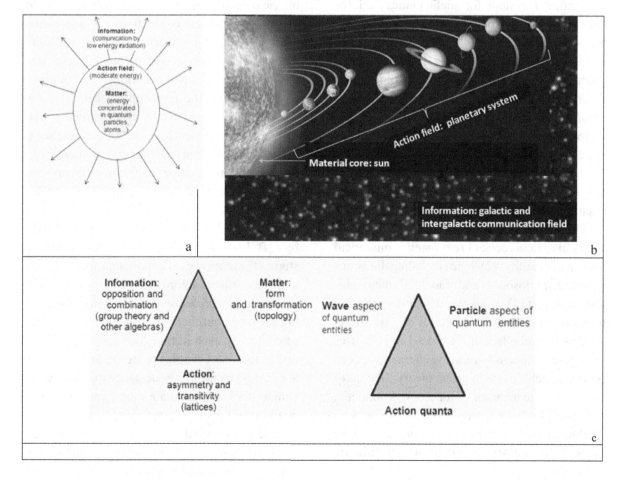

Mathematical structures capture essential aspects of these three components of reality. In this article we consider first mathematical structures as the foundation of mathematical logic and computation, physical processes as the material substrate of all reality, and biological processes because the brain is the material substrate of reasoning. Hence neurobiology may contribute to guide the development of logic (Sabelli, 1989; Kauffman, 2004).

Logic and Mathematics

To develop logic, it is rational to start with mathematics because physical and mental processes embody mathematical structures as advanced by Pythagoras and Galileo. Further, mathematics is the ideal example of reasoning.

Set theory is the most commonly accepted foundational system for mathematics and for logic. Expanding from set theory, the Bourbaki School4 identified three "mother structures" of mathematics: *lattice* theory that studies sequential order and asymmetry, *algebra*, including *group* theory that studies opposition and symmetry, and *topology* that studies transformations such as biological development and the evolution of material systems. The Bourbaki School did not apply this concept to logic, but Piaget (1950) found that these structures are equivalent to the basic patterns of cognition developing in childhood.

The actual "mother structures" of mathematics are its historical roots: (1) *arithmetic* –numerical order and quantity; (2) *logic* (including dialectics in Greek philosophy and Tao in Chinese philosophy); and (3) *geometry*, which is applicable to many processes and structures beyond space. Arithmetic embodies lattice order. Logic focuses on negation, opposition and the interaction of opposites which links it to group theory. Geometry is the concrete ancestor of topology. Arithmetic, logic and geometry are thus further abstracted by the three "mother structures" of mathematics. This higher level of abstraction may allow us to apply these concepts to logic.

Lattices, groups and topologies are three self-determining, autonomous mathematical structures that were developed independently. Lattice theory (Birkhoff, 1967) studies ordered elements, including sets, ordinal numbers and temporally-ordered processes of change. The defining features of order are asymmetry and transitivity. This relation defines partially ordered sets (posets) and allows one to construct unions ($A < A \cap B > B$) and intersections ($A > A \cap B > B$). Lattices are posets where any two elements have a lowest and a highest element. Since actions are asymmetric (time unidirectionality) and transitive (causation of effects), lattice theory naturally relates to basic physics.

Algebras such as group theory abstract interactions. Group theory, formulated by Galois in the 1830s, is described as the study of symmetry, but interactions involve opposites that may be symmetric or asymmetric. Every element of a group has an inverse, an opposition that represents a fundamental symmetry, as its most essential feature. Opposition is fundamental in logic– true and false, assertion and negation— and in physics, where group theory occupies a central place. The algebraic character of group structure can be extended to systems where, for each element, there two others that together complement it; an example of this is color, a structure that appears from quantum mechanics to vision and to color symbolism.

The term "Topology" was introduced in 1847 by J. B. Listing. Expanding geometry Topology studies the properties of a space that are preserved under continuous deformations. Transformations of structures preserve some connections and break others, but there are fundamental features of continuity even in transformations that break up connections. Complex processes and structures are formed by the same substance that makes the simple ones that generate them, and thus must contain their essential characteristics.

These mathematical disciplines were regarded as "structures." The term structure refers to stable patterns and relationships between entities. In earlier thought, "form" often plays a role comparable to that of structure in contemporary language. Mathematicians (and mathematical philosophers such as Plato) naturally regard ideas ("idea" meaning form in Greek) as primary and timeless forms that shape the physical world. Things are as they are, and cannot be changed. As mathematics was for a long time the only scientific basis for knowledge, this way of thinking has guided science for centuries. But modern science emerged with calculus, the study of change, developed by Newton and Leibnitz. Notwithstanding, up to the 19th century, our ideas were dominated by a focus on the stable, nay, the eternal– not only in religion but also in physics, biology, social organization, and human nature. Even world-wide travel and the discovery of entire continents in the modern era did not shake these beliefs.

A focus on stable ideas and operations dominated logic since its origination by Aristotle to Boole's mathematical formulation. Shannon (1938) discovered the possibility of mapping Boolean logical functions onto simple electronic gates. Boolean logical functions thus allowed the mathematization and thereby the mechanization of logic, i.e. computation. Logic has gone beyond a descriptive and normative science of thinking to become an engineering tool for computing, calculating, communicating, ordering, and organizing. The computers that organize our work, communication, travel, commerce, finances, medical care, scientific research, even our wars, are ruled by the logic of stable structures at odds with the scientific and personal evidence of ever-present change.

To move beyond static logic based on set theory, Sabelli (1989) proposed that the fundamental mathematical structures described by Bourbaki may be regarded as patterns of processes (Figure 2) rather than fixed structures. As mathematical structures, natural processes also involve asymmetric action (time is unidirectional as lattice order is asymmetric), bipolar interactions (electromagnetic force, sexuality and many other natural processes are bipolar as group inverses are

symmetric) and transformations with continuity (development of spatial forms and systems as in topology. Since the same fundamental structures described by Bourbaki in mathematics and by Piaget (1950) in cognition are also found in physical, biological and neurological structures constructed by evolution, they should be regarded as abstractions of fundamental natural processes rather than purely mathematical postulates.

We regard action, information, and form and transformation as the three physical embodiments of lattices, groups and topology (see later). Energy, matter, and information are often regarded as the three essential components of reality. Matter exists as discrete entities in the continuum of the "vacuum" of space which is apparently formless but filled with energy. Energy is inseparable from change and hence time, so action provides a more accurate description of physical reality. Information is contained in difference, distinction, and internal and external opposition. Thus lattice, group, and topological structures may be the starting point and the motor of physical and biological evolution (Sabelli, 2003) and of process logic.

A starting point is such if it is followed by further development. Arithmetic offers to logic more than lattices. Trigonometric analysis reveals much about opposition beyond group theory. The mathematical analysis of patterns in empirical time series (non-linear dynamics) enriches topology. Logic requires greater complexity than set theory. While Russell envisioned logic as the foundation of mathematics, we regard mathematics as fundamental and mathematical logic as a chapter in mathematics. But logic is not a purely mathematical discipline. Logic was conceived by Aristotle as a descriptive and normative study of reason. So it was seen again by Boole, who called his book *The Laws of Thought*. In our times, the term "logic" has four distinct uses: the logic of nature (Heraclitus), the science of reasoning (Aristotle), mathematical logic (Boole), and computer logic (Shannon) in decreasing order of extension.

Logic and Natural Science

The term logic derives from "logos," the term used by Heraclitus to indicate that the organization of nature corresponds to that of human reason. Nature is rational, not random or chaotic. In the context of modern science, one would express this idea by stating that nature has a mathematical structure (Galileo). Rationality consists in thinking according to the mathematical structure of nature. It is thus desirable, even necessary to consider physics and biology as foundations for mental and computational logic.

What are the scientific principles that should guide logic?

The universe is creative and life-like (biotic), proposed the Greek founders of science. Change and opposition are universal (Heraclitus); evolution is fueled and organized by the interaction of opposites (Empedocles). The coexistence of opposites in nature demands a method of reasoning in which opposition plays a central role, as in Socrates' Dialectics, which is the foundation and context of Aristotle's Logic. Three essential tenets of Aristotelian Logic have been consistently ignored by his medieval followers and by later thinkers: first the existence of a third open value (neither true nor false) for what has not yet come to pass, thus allowing for creativity; second, the superiority of states of coexisting opposites (the "Golden Middle"); and third, the *local* character of the principle of no contradiction: opposites do not coexist at the same time, at the same place and in the same context, but opposites can otherwise coexist. Thus true Aristotelian logic is compatible with process concepts; in fact, Aristotle pioneered the notion of development based on his studies of biological development. In contrast, standard contemporary logic has adopted the static perspective of medieval logic, excluding third values, and rendering non-contradiction an absolute, universal principle.

Modern science was initiated and developed in the context of a process philosophy. Galileo inaugurated modern science by establishing that inertia– the conservation of movement— not rest, was natural. Newton developed calculus as the foundation of physics. Leibniz independently developed calculus as a foundation for logic, and envisioned the embodiment of reasoning in mechanical devices; mechanism flourished in England and France. The origin of feelings and thoughts on material processes, recognized in antiquity (Hippocrates, Democritus) was reborn in modern times with the French philosophers (Gassendi, Descartes,5 La Mettrie, d'Holbach, Diderot) and physicians (Leroy, Cabanis and Lamettrie).

The notions of change and progress emerged with the development of industry and science, and became dominant with the French revolution.6 Change and progress became the new philosophy of an enlightened generation that incorporated industrialization, the idea of a republic, and freedom from church, king, and tradition. The concept of evolution became a practical subject of study. The notion of change through the interaction of opposites was reformulated by the German philosopher G.W. F Hegel. Biology gave rise to evolutionary theory –Linnaeus (sexuality as major factor in biological transformation), Erasmus and Darwin (biological evolution), Lamarck (continuity of biological and physical processes, active role of organisms), Bernard (constancy of the internal milieu), Pasteur (cosmic asymmetry), Darwin and Wallace (competition and selection as motors of change), Kropotkin (synergy as important as conflict in evolution), Mendel (conserved structures that allow the conservation of evolutionary change) and, on the twentieth century, Oparin and Haldane hypotheses and the Miller and Urey experiments on the origin of life. The notion of development was transferred from biology into sociology, economics, and psychology. Change and progress became the core of several contradictory social philosophies (e.g. racism, imperialism, democracy, and communism) and psychological theories (e.g., Freud's psychoanalysis and Moreno's psychodrama). Twentieth century physics supported the notion of creative evolution, starting with Einstein's discovery of the transformation of energy and matter, the expansion (Friedman, Lemaitre, Hubble) and evolution of the universe, the evolution of atoms from hydrogen (Payne), and Prigogine's thermodynamics of processes far from equilibrium.

Even in our modern era beliefs about stability have not been shaken; a majority of economists and a substantial number of psychologists still believe that there are unchangeable laws of human behavior (e.g. that seeking profit and the Oedipus conflict are common to all humans in all societies). Until the beginning of the twentieth century, physicists believed that their "laws" were eternal. For example, Einstein did not want to believe in the expansion of the universe. But the expansion of the universe revealed physical and cosmic evolution just as biology had convincingly demonstrated the evolution of living things.

This evolutionary perspective does not deny the mathematical structure of reality. Number abstracts quantity, quality, and complexity. Forms shape actions: processes are shaped and channeled by mathematical forms (temporal unidirectionality, the rotation of opposites, the tridimensional geometry of material structures, fractality, chaos, bios, and many more). Thus, following Boole Pierce, Russell, and Shannon initiated the development of mathematical logic which led to computation. Nonlinear dynamics now provides tools to expand Boolean logic.

As the science of reason, logic necessarily goes beyond particular attempts to formalize it and cannot be based on one branch of mathematics. The notion that one can formulate logical norms without attending to the physics of nature and the psychobiology of thinking seems at best overconfident. In any case, Boolean-Russell logic fails to describe reality— an example is its inability to describe quantum phenomena as well as natural reasoning— and to provide the sufficient bases for arithmetic (Gödel's theorem).

Static two-value logic based on set theory fails as a science of reason by:

1. Advancing a static concept of identity A=A that does not describe either physical actions or personal identity, both of which continually change and evolve. Change is modeled in mathematics (calculus, recursions) but not modeled in Boolean logic; recursions have not been directly used in logic per se.

2. Postulating the separation and mutual exclusion of opposites. Certainly in mathematics and other fields of science this concept may apply, but either-or reasoning in general is a distortion of reality that is not only false but also fosters depression, conflict, aggressive behavior, and even torture, from the burning alive of Bruno and Servetus to modern times.

3. Portraying entities and properties as spatial and separate atomic-like entities rather than as actions and interactions in the context of larger systems. Gödel's incompleteness theorem proving the existence of formally undecided statements within any consistent theory indicates that the essence of a theory must lie outside of its bounds. This shows that mathematical theories themselves cannot be taken in isolation. Each theory or formal structure is only meaningful through its interactions with all the rest of the science. This is the essence of this criticism of static logic. There are many uses for static logic (elementary syllogisms, circuit design) but such a logic taken in isolation is a false picture of the world in all its shadings, complexity and temporal evolution. It is thus necessary to examine the context and consequences of logical postulates.

In contrast to standard logic, physical processes *involve* three fundamental patterns: (1) *Asymmetric action*, such as inertial action that accounts for gravitational attraction. (2) *Bipolar interactions*, such as electromagnetic communication across galaxies and between nerve and muscle cells. (3) *Material form and transformations, including creative processes*. These principles suggest how we should develop logic.

Action

Action is a fundamental concept in physics, biology, economics and psychology. All that exists is action; significantly "actual" and "action" share the same root. The concept of action implies change: For all **At** there is a **At + n** such that **At + n** is not equal to **At**. It also captures the concept of becoming associated with process philosophy. Nothing is static; to be is to become. Prigogine (1980) pointedly called his book "From Being to Becoming". Time appears in physics as "a mere geometrical parameter" (d'Alembert, Lagrange, Minkowski); physical equations are invariant to time inversion. But irreversible processes are real and play a constructive role (Prigogine, 1980) as evident in biological, social and psychological evolution.

Action is the one and sole constituent of the universe proposed Sabelli (2005). Just as inertia, not rest, is intrinsic to mechanical movement, action (not energy, matter, or ideas) is the simplest component of reality. The universe is a uni-verse, a flow in one direction. *Asymmetry* is fundamental: energy, time, mass and information vary in quantity but there is no negative energy, time, mass or information.

Action requires time: there are no instantaneous interactions at a distance. Energy continually transforms itself, but its quantity is conserved. Conservation and change are inseparable aspects of action. Order and creativity are deeply associated (Bohm and Peat, 1987).

In physics, action A is the change of energy E in time t: $A = E * t$. Time is unidirectional, asymmetric, unipolar, and irreversible.[7] Ordered in time, actions form lattices.[8] Energy is conserved; it is neither created nor destroyed (first law of thermodynamics[9]). Energy is transformed and transmitted, so actions cause change. Conversely, since energy is not created, there cannot be events without cause ("chance").[10] *All processes are causal*; random events are impossible.

Both energy E and frequency 1/t are always present. Regardless of their diversity, the various definitions of action show time and energy as inseparable; they do not change independently of each other. We can extend this definition of action to all levels of organization. For instance, cardiac action involves force and time (timing, duration, and frequency) of contraction. In psychological processes, mania is characterized by high energy fast processing while depression is characterized by low energy and motor retardation (Sabelli, 2005).

In the context of mechanics, the function (called the Lagrangian) that summarizes the dynamics of the system is the kinetic energy of a mechanical system minus its potential energy. Action is the integral of differences. This is a noteworthy union of opposites.[11]

Universal Opposition: Coexistence, Circulation, and Interaction of Opposites

The term "opposite" means both "partner" and "antagonist." This ambiguity of meaning reflects the inseparability of these two opposites. The opposition of right and left extremities is essential for waking, swimming, or flying. The opposition of the thumb shows that opposition is essential for human dexterity. Procreation reminds us that opposition is fundamentally creative.[12]

All fundamental processes contain pairs of matching and contrasting complementary opposites according to Heraclitus and Lao-tzu. The universality of opposition is corroborated by modern science in quantum phenomena. The proton and the electron, and more generally positive and negative charge, exemplify physical opposites. Opposition is also represented in physics (Newton's action-reaction law where the mutual forces of action and reaction between two bodies are equal, oppositional, and collinear; bipolarity and bidimensionality in electromagnetic force; color and anti-color in nuclear forces) and in quantum physics (quantum conjugates such as energy and time, the wave–particle duality of energy and matter). Opposition is also central in biology (sexual reproduction, synergism, and competition in evolution), economics (supply and demand), sociology (cooperation and class struggle as per Thierry, Guizot, and Marx) and psychology (Freud's conflict, Jung's animus and anima and other paired archetypes). Obviously these are very diverse forms of opposition.

Metabolism exemplifies the inseparability of opposites. It involves the continual synthesis of more complex, larger molecules (anabolism) and their split into simpler components (catabolism). The two processes are linked and interdependent. This dual movement from simple to complex and from complex to simple is the engine of life. Similar "biotic engines" function in the planet– e.g. the water and the calcium cycles— drive the evolution of the planet rather than maintaining it in a constant state. Thus, opposition between the simple and the complex involves cycles that function as biotic engines. These biotic engines drive the overall ascending and decaying phases of the life hemicycle of an individual, and also propel the overall process of evolution that includes episodes of involution but also overall progress.

There is opposition in energetic, informational, and material processes at all levels of organization. The bipolarity of electrical charge is a coexistence of opposites that generates electromagnetic radiation. Electromagnetic waves carry information among distant galaxies and electromagnetic currents carry information in brain and computers. Information, so fundamental in genetics and computer science does not need to appear as a separate dimension in physics: *electrical charge is information*. As charge, information is bipolar (1 and −1). The sine wave form of electromagnetic waves provides a practical way to represent the coexistence and separation of opposites in computation.

Opposition produces change creating pattern. The process and diversifying recursions (Figures 3 and 4) illustrate how oppositions generate bifurcations rather than neutralizing each other in equilibrium or dialectic synthesis; two poles are necessary to generate bios, even if both are of the same sign. In turn bifurcations generate opposites in 2N periodicities, chaos, bios and beyond, atoms, and organisms. Bifurcations generate periodic and chaotic patterns, not the "splitting" of one trajectory into two.

Opposition also arrests change and creates structure. Electrical charge carries information but also generates complex patterns and constructs structures from atoms to organisms. Matter, often described as neutral, is actually bipolar. Atoms are made of positive nuclei and negative electrons; their mutual attraction and separation form structure. Atomic nuclei may also be formed by polar interactions, but in this case the quarks that combine to form protons and neutrons have three colors each paired with an anti-color.

Creativity

Continuous transformations create structures beginning with the minimum of tridimensional matter, such as the formation of units by nucleation of multiple copies of simpler ones (e.g. protons and neutrons by the nucleation of quarks, atomic nuclei by the nucleation of protons and neutrons). The creativity of natural processes is central to physical, biological and human evolution. Physical processes include nucleation (e.g. synthesis of atoms and formation of galaxies) and expansion (e.g. expansion of intergalactic space and thereby of the universe), the formation of systems (molecules, cells, multicellular organisms), folding (of proteins, membranes and neurological structures), and many others. Cosmic processes create macroscopic forms such as galaxies and novel structures such as atoms that make only the core of stars.

The notion of creative processes is fairly recent and it is not widely accepted. The currently dominant scientific views are determinism in

Figure 3. Process equation. Top row: Sequence of patterns generated by the process equation as the parameter g increases: steady state, bifurcation, period 2, bifurcation tree, chaos, bios. At g = 2n * π, there are leaps to new values followed by a new bifurcation cascade into bios. Second row: changes in the % of isometric recurrences and of consecutive isometric recurrences show the drastic difference between Chaos and Bios. Third row: power spectrum analysis demonstrates that Chaos is similar to random series (slope near 0) while Bios is similar to random walks (slope near 2 as in Brownian noise).

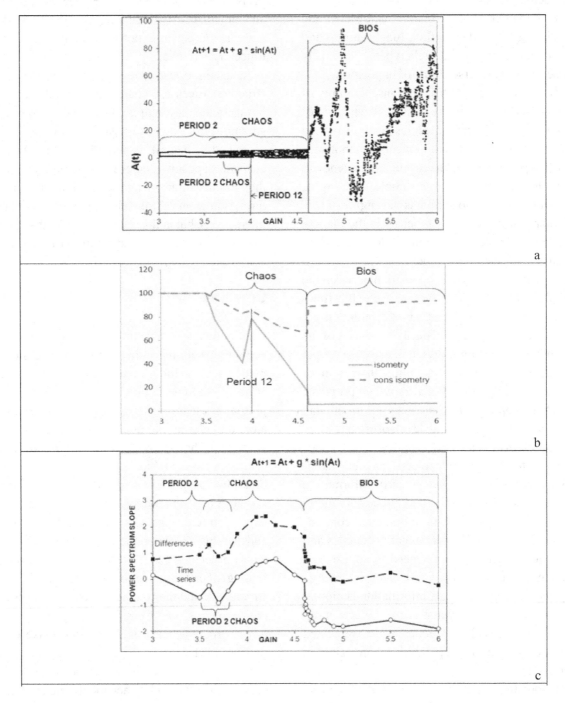

Figure 4. Trigonometric equations with variable parameters increasing as a function of time: gt = k * t and jt = k * t. Top row: process equation: parameter g represents gain (energy). Second row: diversifying equation: parameter j accelerates frequency. Third row: A recursion combining g and j.

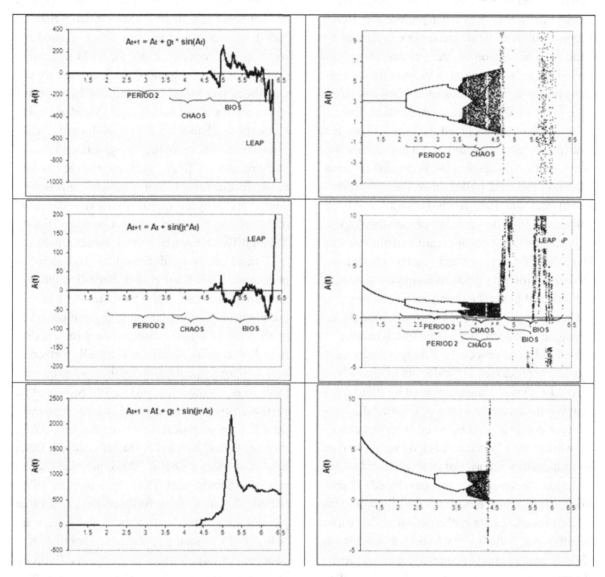

mechanics, sociology (biological and economic), and psychology (psychoanalysis, behaviorism), random change (from quantum physics to genetics and economics), and unavoidable decay towards entropy and disorder (thermodynamics). Creativity gained attention relatively recently. In the Middle Ages, creation was regarded as divine *creatio ex nihilo* ("creation out of nothing"). Only in the Renaissance, artistic creativity began to be recognized. New ideas of economic and social progress born in the 18th century led to Hegelian dialectics and to theories of biological and social evolution.

The notion of creativity was inherent in the work of Hegel, Lamarck, Darwin, and Marx, but these thinkers did not spell out the idea. Thus Darwinists came to regard chance as the source of novelty and Marxists stressed economic determinism.

At the turn of the 20th century, creativity in science began to be discussed by Łukasiewicz, Poincaré, Helmholtz, Wallas, and Wertheimer. Shortly afterwards, the French philosopher Henri Bergson initiated the discussion on creativity in nature, but his notion of creative evolution was limited because he separated biology from physics by repeating the old idea of a hypothetical life force (élan vital) separate from physical forces. Although Bergson received the Nobel Prize, his concept of creative evolution did not capture the attention of most scientists, but inspired the French paleontologist and philosopher Pierre Teilhard (1955) and the British mathematician Alfred Whitehead (1947) to formulate process theologies.

A scientific notion of creative evolution was developed first by psychiatrist and psychodramatist Jacob Moreno (1953) to formulate practical methods and general a theory of psychotherapy, and later on by the chemist and chaos theorist Ilya Prigogine (1984) to propose thermodynamics of non-equilibrium processes. Prigogine's concept of creative processes as "order out of chaos" (in Nietzsche's vivid expression used by Prigogine) captured the attention of many scientists13; creativity was said to arise between order and chaos.

Inspired by Moreno and Prigogine, as well as by 19th century theories of biological and social evolution, our research group developed (1) analytic methods that demonstrate causal creativity in natural processes, (2) a mathematical model (Bios) (Kauffman & Sabelli 1998; Sabelli & Kauffman, 1999) for causal creation, and (3) a general theory of processes (Sabelli, 1989, 2001, 2003, 2005) here applied to quantum physics and logic.

BIOS THEORY

Evidence for Bios in Empirical Data

Creativity is operationally defined by time series analyses (Sabelli, 2000, 2001; Sabelli & Abouzeid, 2003; Sabelli & Kauffman, 2004; Sabelli et al, 2004 (a); Sabelli et al 2004 (b); Sabelli et al 2004 (c); Sabelli et al, 2005) that demonstrate non-stationarity, temporal transformations of pattern or "temporal complexity" (Sugerman & Sabelli, 2003), a lower rate of repetition than its randomized copy, i.e. "novelty" (Sabelli, 2001), increasing diversity or "diversification", i.e. increase variance with time (Sabelli and Abouzeid, 2003), f-n power spectrum (Patel and Sabelli, 2003), and relatively low entropy (Sabelli, 1994; Sabelli et al, 2004). These methods, computer programs and exemplary results are freely available online (Sabelli et al, forthcoming). Non-random causation is demonstrated by an organized pattern in the series of differences between consecutive terms (Figure 5) that differentiates Bios from random walks.

Causal creativity defines Bios (Carlson-Sabelli et al, 1994; Kauffman & Sabelli, 1998; Sabelli and Kauffman, 1999; Sabelli, 2005). Bios is a non-periodic, non-stationary pattern observed at all levels of organization: prime numbers (Sabelli, forthcoming; Kauffman & Sabelli, forthcoming), temporal distribution of galaxies and quasars (Sabelli & Kovacevic, 2003, 2006; Sabelli et al, forthcoming), gravitational waves (Sabelli, 2008)14, geographical structures (Sabelli, 2005), meteorological processes (Sabelli, 2005), DNA base sequences (Sabelli, 2005), heartbeat series (Carlson-Sabelli et al, 1994; Sabelli et al, 1995; Sabelli & Lawandow, forthcoming) and other physiological processes (Sabelli & Carlson-Sabelli, 2005), animal populations (Sabelli & Kovacevic, 2008), human populations (Sabelli, 2005), economic processes (Patel & Sabelli, 2003; Sugerman & Sabelli, 2003; Levy-Carciente et al, 2004; Sabelli & Carlson-Sabelli, 2005; Sabelli & Kovacevic, forthcoming), and musical compositions (Levy et al, 2006; Sabelli et al, forthcoming). Creativity is also evident in human processes, from anatomy to language: faces, life stories, and dialogs are always unique. These observations indicate that biotic processes repeat at all levels of organization, in a fractal fashion.

Figure 5. Novelty and other evidence of pattern in the series of differences reveal non-random causation in Bios, as contrasted to random walks. Black lines: data. Blue lines: shuffled data

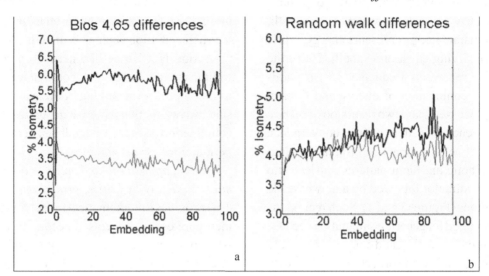

Evidence for Bios Theory

Bios theory is based on mathematical analysis of empirical data and on cybernetic mathematical models (Kauffman and Sabelli, 1998), and formulated in the light of process philosophy (Sabelli and Kauffman, 1999). Without the use of methods that detect novelty and causality, biotic patterns are described as random walks or as chaos, and creativity is described as variability and non-stationarity. The demonstration of Bios in empirical data and in mathematical series (such as the prime numbers, Sabelli, accepted for publication) results from the introduction of new analytic methods which are illustrated in Figure 1 and referenced in this chapter:

1. Measures of action: Wavelets. Recurrence plots. Changes in recurrence measures (temporal complexity) in Bios (Figure 5). Measures of non-stationarity (diversification) and of asymmetry (e.g. mean−median). Evidence for causation: non-random series of differences between consecutive terms (Figure 1, right column and Figure 6) and

long lasting changes by changes in initial value (Figure 6).

2. Measures of opposition: Diamond of opposites. Helicoid analysis of material networks and processes. Trigonometry portrays of the relation between linear order and (quasi) circular order (rotation). Complement plots, trigonometric walks, 3 D trigonometric walk (to be included in cretivebios.net)

3. Measures of creativity and complexity: embedding plots (plots of recurrences measures at low and high embedding to depict simple and complex patterns). Entropy. Novelty (1/recurrence). Arrangement.

With these methods it was possible to demonstrate Bios in many processes at all levels of organization.

Mathematical Generators of Bios

The other foundation of Bios theory is mathematical. Bios is generated by mathematical recursions that involve action (recursion), bipolar opposition (e.g. trigonometric functions), and change with conservation (Figures 3 and 4). These recursions model bipolar feedback, which is a cybernetic realization of the concept of co-creating opposites. In the process equation (Kauffman & Sabelli, 1998), the parameter **g** represents energy, while in the diversifying equation (Sabelli, 2005) the parameter **j** represents frequency 1/t. In parallel with the conjugation of energy and time in quantum processes, these two recursions generate similar sequences of pattern in time: convergence to a point attractor, cascade of bifurcations into periodic, chaotic, and biotic patterns, and leap into a new point attractor followed by a new cascade of bifurcations (Figures 3 and 4). Such recursions provide a method for generic computation because creative processes, action, and opposition actually exist in natural and human processes at every level of organization.

Bios is not reversible (Figure 7).

The process equation and the diversifying equation are cybernetic models for harmonic and creative dialectics (see later). Several other equations generate Bios including the Schrödinger equation.

Bios is also generated by the addition of sine waves. This probably accounts for the widespread occurrence of Bios because the universe is richly inhabited by sine waves.

Bios Theory of Processes

Bios theory (Sabelli & Kauffman, 2004; Sabelli, 2005; Sabelli et al, 2005) advances the hypotheses (1) *action, opposition and creation are universal*; and (2) *action and opposition create novelty and complexity*. Therefore causal creativity accounts for physical (Sabelli, 2008; Sabelli et al., forthcoming), biological (Sabelli, 2008; Sabelli & Kovacevic, 2006; 2008) and social (Sabelli, forthcoming) evolution. Paradigmatic of action is gravitation, the result of the distortion of space-time by mass, which is unipolar (attractive). Paradigmatic of opposition is the electromagnetic force that is attractive and repulsive, and bidimensional (electrical and magnetic). Creation spans from the nucleation of quarks to make protons and neutrons to artistic creation such as Botticelli's Venus.

Action is a lattice-like network, matter is a tridimensional form, and communication is a trigonometric form ranging from electromagnetic sine waves to the patterns generated by their combination as sum or feedback (equilibrium, periodicities, chaos and bios).

Action, opposition, and creation are modeled mathematically by lattice, groups and topology. This provides a mathematical model for logic that incorporates the concepts of becoming and coexisting opposites of dialectics and adds the notion of causal creation. But how shall we understand the term "structure" in this context? The term "structure" implies permanence and mathematical structures are static, but physical reality and rational thinking are in continual flow. We must then interpret lattice, groups, and topology as patterns of change. Some standard expressions appear to contradict this view: to state that action is stationary, the conflict inherent in the coexistence of opposites, and the continuity of topological transformations. To state that action is stationary (always minimal or maximal) is true, but stationarity does not capture the essence of action, which is change. The interaction of opposites includes conflict but also synergy and its essence is the co-creation of novelty and complexity. Topology involves continuity but continuity does not capture the essence of topology, which is change of form and discontinuities such as bifurcations.

Creativity generates new levels of complexity, in which simpler processes have priority and complex processes acquire supremacy. Biotic logic is being developed (Kauffmann, 2004; Sabelli, 1984; 1995; 2005) around four principles: action, universal opposition, co-creation, and priority/supremacy.

BIOTIC LOGIC

Action as Dynamic Identity

Logic must incorporate the universality of change, and its coexistence with partial conservation. Physical action may serve as a principle of dynamic identity, i.e. becoming which is required to understand the continuity of identity through time (e.g. the evolution of a tree from acorn to oak) and the multiple expressions of identity in different contexts (e.g. the behavior of a person at work and at home). Action is self-referential: action produces interactions, and change. Static identity A=A is valid only for abstract entities and for short periods of time for macroscopic entities. Reflexivity A=A implies idempotence; self-interaction does not produce change: A and A = A, and A or A = A. In the case of dynamic identity, reflexivity means self-transformation, so A(t) implies A(t+1). Dynamic identity implies transformation (not equality) and temporal asymmetry (not symmetry). "To be" is "to become." Beyond the copula "to be" and "if-then" implication, we may also include in logic other actions, e.g. active verbs such as "to do."

The various properties of action have significant implications regarding computation. To introduce action and change in logic, it is useful to employ recursions. Interactions are processes of mutual feedback. Feedback is an important component of creative biotic processes. Information is contained in the message, the sequence of terms, the sentence, not the letters. Lattice Theory describes important aspects of logic processes. Implication displays the properties of the partial order relation <. Any lattice has a dual, as A < B implies B > A.

Logical Opposition

Natural and human processes involve a large number and a wide range of oppositions—waves, superposition, duality, co-creation—but seldom if ever the mutual exclusion of opposites as in Aristotelian and Boolean logic. Logic must then incorporate the universality of bipolarity within an opposition between each entity, process, and system. Sine waves provide a model for incorporating the unity and duality of opposites. Their unity and duality is abstracted in mathematics by lattice asymmetry and group symmetry, corresponding to asymmetric time and physical oppositions. But at an intuitive level, classic logic focuses on *either/or* thinking, which in real life leads to conflict, in contrast to the dialectic *both\and* that in real life leads to harmony and creativity but also to ambiguity, and is compatible with quantum concepts such as the particle/wave duality of light (Einstein) and of matter (as proposed by Prince Louis de Broglie).

Opposition is a fundamental form of symmetry, but equally fundamental are asymmetric opposites, such as the mass differences between protons and electrons and the differences between sexes. Likewise in logic, assertion and negation are asymmetric. Differences are directional, not commutative; going from A to B is the opposite—not the same as—of going from B to A, and A − B is not equal to B − A. Even straightforward implication is not always symmetric.15

Opposition, negation, refutation are central to logic because opposition is universal in natural processes (*law of universal opposition*). Just as opposition is universal in energetic and material processes, opposition is also central to informational processes. Opposition embodies information: two values are necessary and sufficient to encode information. Complexity is the increase in the quantity and density of information generated by successive bifurcations of processes or their union. From the perspective of logic, distinctions embody information. Difference or change carries information according to Bateson (1979) but only in a static system; in changing processes, it is repetition that conveys pattern (Sabelli, 2005). Distinction involves either change or repetition. Both repetition and difference carry information.

For instance, messengers such as light are characterized by periodic repetition at a given frequency. Distinction requires asymmetry (Sabelli, 2005); partition alone is not sufficient. In fact distinction does not require a partition into separate classes, as in Aristotelian and Boolean logic, set theory, or the theory of form (Spencer-Brown, 1979).

Groups offer a fruitful model for negation: rotation separates and connects opposites. While Logic and Dialectics focus on 2, it seems necessary to develop a 2N valued logic, starting with the quaternity: the cross or square of opposites that emerges from the repetition of bifurcation.

Physicists have considered the coexistence of opposites from the perspective of oriental philosophy. The Taoist dialectics of the complementarity of opposites was seen by Bohr as being central to quantum physics (Capra, 1975) and explored as a logic of systems (Xu & Li, 1989; Sabelli, 1989; 1998) but computation has not made use of this concept thus far.

The set theory notion of complement formalizes the traditional notion of mutually exclusive opposites and thereby misrepresents reality. The opposite of *man* is not the set of all things that are not man– hippopotamus, triangles, quarks, and an infinity of other things- but very specifically *woman*. The dialectical notion of contradiction and the notion of distinction in the theory of form focus on abstract concepts developed by human minds and abstracted from nature, which are secondary to the more basic oppositions such as positive and negative electrical charge and biological sexes. These opposites coexist without contradiction. A logical contradiction between abstract objects of mathematics indicates a failure of reasoning.

Mathematization needs not imply the reductionist assumption that all science could be reduced to physics, all physics explained by mathematics, and the entire edifice of mathematics be founded upon simple and universal laws of logic. Such mathematization increases rigor by sacrificing meaning. For instance, negation is reduced to its simplest form, the complement, in set theory.

Complementation generates meaningless aggregates unless the complement is defined within a narrow universe of discourse (e.g. "non-red" includes hippopotamus, hippocampus, triangles, and blue objects). A negation must always be a concrete negation (Hegel) that includes the other (e.g. the negation of "man" is "woman"; the negation of "going to the movies" implies a possibility of going).

In Boolean logic, the simple definition of negation leads to paradoxes of self-reference such as "I am lying" (or its equivalent, Russell's paradox) which is nothing more than period 2, an alternation of opposites.

Actually mathematics provides models for more complex forms of negation, such as positive vs. negative, real vs. imaginary numbers in arithmetic, the inverse in group theory, and oppositely directed vectors in algebra. Each of these models captures some facets of the hierarchy of simple and complex forms of negation that obtain in human discourse. It is important not only to find the simplest form of negation, but also its various fundamental forms.

Dialectics: Chinese, German, Medical, and Mathematical Dialectics

The concepts of becoming and complementarity of opposites was pioneered in the East by Lao-tzu and in the West by Heraclitus. Following the rediscovery of Heraclitus's texts, the notions of fundamental opposition was adopted by Hegel through the idea of the *dialectic*. Hegelian dialectics is based on natural processes (e.g. the law of quantity and quality based on changes in the state of matter with temperature), and yet it is often interpreted as "idealistic." More materialist versions were formulated by Dietzgen (2010), Marx and Engels (Tucker, 1978) and Politzer (1928, 1948). Lefebvre (1969) highlighted the value of dialectics and its differences with formal logic.

In Hegelian-Marxist dialectics the coexistence of opposites is transient, and their interaction conflictual leading to their synthesis or to their mutual annihilation; synthesis which ends and completes an opposition and generates a new one.

From the perspective of medicine, Antonio Sabelli (1952) developed a different notion toward the coexistence and interaction of opposites. In Sabellian *"medical dialectics"*16, opposites are fundamentally *similar*, i.e. proton and electron are both charged particles; woman and man are human beings. At the same time, opposites are also fundamentally *different*. Opposites are synergic as they help form each other in a process of continuous, mutual, and bipolar (positive and negative) feedback. Opposites imply each other, and convert into each other. Through this *mutual implication* and *mutual conversion* of opposites, their coexistence and their interaction is permanent. For instance, love and self-love are continually interacting feelings, not stages as described by Freud. Further, the interaction of opposites creates new entities (co-creation, see later), as exemplified by sexual reproduction. Hence there are multiple possible paths for development, not one determined course of action as in Marxian, Freudian and biological theories.

These concepts resonate with cybernetics. The interaction of complementary opposites such as positive and negative particles, male and female, supply and demand, abuse and abuser, are significant cases of *mutual and bipolar feedback*. Bipolar feedback generates Bios (Sabelli, 2005). Mutuality generates processes of circular causality that highlight the role of feedback in complex systems and even in simple ones, departing from the mechanistic view of unidirectional causation that still dominates much scientific reasoning. "Circular causality" is essential in cybernetics (von Foerster, 1953); the significance of circular causality had been recognized before by a number of thinkers in different disciplines (not always under that name).

As a physician, Antonio Sabelli adhered to a biological, i.e. material approach to dialectics. Nevertheless he attended to the dialectic of love and self-love, art and reality, and other fundamental psychological issues. From the perspective of psychology, Riegel (1979), and others have developed dialectics as a research and clinical tool.

Dialectics and formal logic are sometimes posed as two oppositional forms of reasoning. Dialectical logic has been proposed as an alternative to standard logic (Lefebvre, 1969; Planty-Bonjour, 1965; Joja, 1969). Philosophical dialectics provide a threat of Ariadne that guides us beyond static views but its verbal formulation allows for abuses in reasoning (as illustrated by the rejection of quantum mechanics by Soviet Marxists). For the same reason, dialectical logic has not been used in computation.

Others regard dialectics and Logic as complementary forms of reasoning. Formal logic is appropriate for reasoning about static properties of separate non-interacting objects while dialectics deals with change and interaction. But formal logic has been extended in the course of history; for instance Lawvere's work in category theory and topos theory (Lawvere and Schanuel, 1982, 1996) and temporal logic (Rescher, 1996) deal with processes.

Likewise some aspects of dialectics have been mathematized. In contrast to Hegel's negative attitude regarding mathematics, Marx explored calculus (Gerdes, 1983). Some attempts have been made to develop a *mathematical dialectics* (Gauthier, 1984; Kosok, 1984) including various attempts to develop a scientific notion of the dialectical interaction of opposites (Sabelli, 1971; 1989; 1984; 1995).

Biotic logic mathematizes the concepts of process and interacting opposites of dialectics (Sabelli, 2005), but adds the concept of causal creative processes and its generation by the interaction of opposites (co-creation). It also reformulates opposition in terms of the sinusoidal pattern of electromagnetic and other waves, pairs of elementary particles, and information. Electromagnetic attraction forms atoms and many molecules, and electromagnetic energy is the carrier of information across galaxies (light) and across cells (action currents). The sinusoidal form of electromagnetic waves thus constitutes the ultimate case of opposition, far more general and fundamental than dialectic contradiction and Darwinian conflict. Formulating opposition in terms of sinusoidal waves implies a *harmonic dialectics*, Table 1 sketches some similarities and differences between Biotic, Boolean and Dialectic logic.

Catastrophes

Thom's *catastrophes* provide an important model for opposition. According to Thom (1980), the universe can be understood in terms of structures that are momentarily stable, and which are not of an infinite variety but are drastically constrained by factors of space and time. According to Thom's theorem, we need to consider only a few control forms17. The limited number of archetypal morphologies that Thom identified is assumed to be universal. Catastrophe forms appear in many natural and human processes (Thom, 1983, 1994; Carlson-Sabelli et al, 1992b; Guastello & Bond, 2007; Smerz and Guastello, 2008). Certainly forms are created and constrained by physical factors that also extend across the chemical, biological, social, and psychological domains. But processes that generate catastrophes do so only within limits beyond which they generate more complex patterns (Sabelli, 2005).

Catastrophes are mathematical structures that are the simplest of the complex structures generated by interacting opposites. Given simultaneous attraction and repulsion, their difference is information that determines the choice (selection or rejection), and the sum of the attraction and repulsion gives the energy of the choice. For simple fold catastrophes, the energy (the sum of opposites) is the bifurcating factor while the information (provided by the difference of opposites) is the asymmetric factor. This relation between energy, information and opposites may

also apply to more complex situations, such as the formation of structures in nature.

Some forms of opposition, including negation, may be modeled by catastrophes. Thom gives a constructive and a destructive interpretation to each catastrophe. For instance, the fold represents to begin and to end; the cusp represents to engender or unite and to capture and to break; the butterfly represents to give and to receive, as well as to exfoliate. Thom (1983) and others have explored how catastrophes can be used to model active verbs representing actions, as contrasted to Boolean logic that only models the non-active copula "to be." To be is to become; there is existence without change. To be is, as equality, reflexive, symmetric and transitive. To become is transitive, not reflexive, and may be symmetric in time (At goes to At+n and At+n goes to At+n+o) or asymmetric.

Thom's catastrophes provide a good starting point to go beyond the standard 'and' and "or" gates. A fold catastrophe abstracts or-exclusive (A or B but not both) while A and no-A may be modeled by bifurcation. Butterfly catastrophes generate three possible outcomes and may thus relate to creative processes. Catastrophes may serve to implement some forms of dialectic reasoning: given A, find no-A by increasing or decreasing a catastrophe parameter. This is accomplished by considering a phase space of opposites.

Phase Plane of Opposites

As opposites are primarily forces rather than different classes in physical processes, opposition and negation should be so regarded in logic. The phase plane provides a useful portrait of the interaction of opposites (Figure 8).

Any process involves the interaction of forces that can be represented by vectors, and that are in part synergistic and in part antagonistic. These forces share dimensions of energy and time, and often many other properties, since they participate in the same process. They are additive in some

Table 1. Biotic, Boolean, and dialectic logic

	Logic		
	Biotic	**Boolean**	**Dialectic**
Formulation	Physical and mathematical (lattice, group and topology)	Mathematical: set theory	Verbal
Identity	Physical action, the integral of temporal change in energy	Static A = A valid for mathematical entities	Dynamic, as evident in sociology and psychology
Substance	Substance monism, starting from, and always based on, action (energy, time and matter).	Compatible with materialism or idealism or dualism	Monism: idealist (Hegel) or matter (Marx)
Negation	Multiple forms: Lattice dual, Group inverse, Topological bifurcations	Set theory complementation.	Sublation: to end and simultaneously conserve.
Opposites	Similar, synergic and / or antagonistic. Sine waves. 22 bifurcations. Sexes.	Twoness. Differences stressed. Black or white thinking.	Twoness. Similarities or differences stressed in different contexts.
Implication and exclusion of opposites	Mutual implication of opposites. Exclusion of identical fermions (Pauli)	Mutual implication of complementary sets. Mutual exclusion of opposites in Logic.	Contradiction (Hegel) and conflict (Marx) are universal.
Contradiction	Aristotle's local principle of no contradiction (exclusion for same place, time and context)	Absolute principle of no contradiction	Contradiction as conflict resolved by either synthesis or destruction of one
Verbs modeled	Catastrophes, chaos, bios and leaps as models for active verbs	To be, to imply	No formal models
Logical values	Opposite signs and varying quantities: N and − N for bifurcations	0 and 1	Not formalized but implicit opposites of varying quantities.
Third value	Triads. Quantum chromodynamics. Categories. Aristotelian third value (open to future). Sarkovskii's theorem.	Exclusion.	Polarization excludes intermediate classes.
Information	Information = opposition as in repetition or difference	Probabilistic information theory uses logical values 0 and 1	No specific formulation
Graphic re-presentation	Phase space of opposites	Venn diagram	None
Negation of the negation	At < At+2, A < no-no-A Ubiquitous period 2 in time, space, context. Helicoid model.	Identical: A = no-no-A.	Third term (synthesis) similar but superior to thesis. Ubiquitous period 2 in time, space, context.
Logical operations	Iterated negation, catastrophes	And, Or, Negation	Dialectic synthesis, no formal model
Quality	Dimensions	Classes	Classes (e.g. socioeconomic)
Quantity and Quality	Quantitative parameters of catastrophes, chaos, bios and leaps.	Regarded as separate categories.	Necessary and non-linear relation between them. Dialectic leaps.
Simplicity and complexity	Priority of the simple and supremacy of the complex	Focus on simplicity; complex analyzed into simple components	Focus on single composition, material (Marx) or ideal (Hegel)
Logical properties included	Asymmetry and symmetry, non-commutativity, direct and indirect transitivity	Reflexive identity, asymmetric negation, directly transitive implication	Not formalized but implicit asymmetry and direct and indirect transitivity
Exclusions	Extreme, absolute values excluding their opposite	Third values, middle value	
Heuristic	Homology across levels. Refutation of refutation as confirmation.	Proof by refutation of the opposite. Confirmation by induction.	Dialectic of proof and refutation (Lakatos)
Computation	Developing biotic logic for digital and quantum computers	Developing computers with Boolean logic and quantum computers with Boolean logic and quantum physics.	No specific computer application
Innovation processes	Causal and creative development by synergy and conflict (bipolar and asymmetric feedback	Mechanical determinism. Innovation only by chance.	Innovation by synthesis. Frequent use of deterministic models.
Human processes	Sociatry (collective psychotherapy). Bio-socio-psychological medicine.	Unchanging human nature. Competition leading to conflict (Malthus, standard economics, Social Darwinism, racism).	Conflictual models (Darwinian evolution, Marxian class war, Freudian Oedipal conflict).

Table 2. Logical categories, traditional logic, and biotic logic

Logical Categories	Traditional logic	Biotic logic
Identity	$A \equiv A$	$A(t) \rightarrow A(t+1)$
Opposition	A if and only if (iff) No (No-A)	A iff No-A
Exclusion	Middle, and other third values	Poles (pure A or pure No-A)
Implication	$A \subseteq B$	$B(t+1) \subseteq A(t+1)$

dimensions and subtractive in others. We thus represent the process in term of opposite forces. Opposites are similar; what distinguishes them is sign (information). Electron and positron annihilate each other but their mass is converted to energy. Each of the two opposite vectors should then be decomposed into two orthogonal components, one corresponding to the properties they share and the other portraying their differences and antagonism. To represent opposition requires at least two orthogonal dimensions. This is the phase plane of opposites (Figure 9), a method that was devised to collect and analyze empirical data (Carlson-Sabelli and Sabelli, 1992 a, b; Sabelli, 1995).

Opposites such as supply and demand, cooperation and competition, attraction and repulsion, are plotted using orthogonal axes, thus creating a phase plane where we can plot trajectories in time. The plane allows representation of linear as well as nonlinear, complementary and partial opposites, and shows similarities and differences between them. The concept also provides an interpretation for phase portraits and return-maps both in terms of opposition and of energy and information. For instance these two-dimensional plots reveal and measure how opposite motivations and interpersonal feelings co-exist and may be positively correlated or uncorrelated, not inversely proportional or mutually exclusive as implicit in the linear scales standard in psychology and sociology. The diamond of opposites allows quantity, change, and the coexistence of opposites to be considered in all classes.

Plotting a concept or an entity Q in a phase plane of opposites A by no-A means that B is neither pure A nor pure no-A. The phase plane of opposites excludes these extremes (i.e. the exclusion of opposites) in sharp contrast to standard logic that excludes the coexistence of opposites (Table 2).

A preliminary understanding of the diamond of opposites is to regard its four quadrants as a 2 by 2 table (iterated negation). But a 2 by 2 table classifies entities into 4 mutually exclusive classes, while the diamond offers a two-dimensional field within which processes flow gradually from one point to another. Moreover, the opposites coexist in all cases, including those in the two quadrants in which one opposite predominates and the neutral cases in which neither appears to dominate over the other. The phase plane allows one to examine how the interaction of opposites produces different outcomes or choices (Carlson-Sabelli et al, 1992). The phase plane of opposites allows one to examine many practical issues, and it is used clinically in psychology particularly by psychodramatists. Issues and relations in the contradictory corner are particularly meaningful and most likely to lead to creative outcomes, while those on the extreme left or right are likely to be distorted and harmful perceptions that phase plane plots help to correct. In addition to portraying interactions between persons (e.g. in marital therapy) that are distorted by either-or logic, it also reveals patterns of thinking (Figure 7) such as linear and bifurcating personalities. Given simultaneous attraction and repulsion, their difference is information that determines the choice (selection or rejection), and the sum of the attraction and repulsion gives the energy of the choice (see later Catastrophes); plotting catastrophes in a phase plane of opposites often reveals fundamental dynamics (Figure 10).

The unipolar vertical axis of the phase plane represents the energy of the couple of opposites, and the bipolar horizontal axis portrays their information. Maximal energy and the maximal and most symmetric coexistence of opposites occur at the vertex. This is observed in the logic of language: terms such as "sanction", that are highly emotionally charged, also have opposite meanings (to sanction as approval or to sanction as punishment).

Twoness, Threeness, Quaternity

Twoness is a simple and familiar form of opposition, and it is widely used to encode information. Twoness is the numerical form that captures the most essential property of opposition. Logic and Dialectics focus on twoness. There is twoness in every process, but there are no mutually exclusive opposites like true and false of standard logic in either natural or human processes. A bifurcation that splits a process into two lines generates 2^2, 2^3, ...2^N lines of development.

Iterated negation (Sabelli, 1979; 1984; 1989) expands the use of Boolean logic. We start by constructing a 2 by 2 table in which one side of the table is one action (present or absent) and the other is its opposite (present or absent). In other words, we generate a four-valued logic by iterating the standard two-valued negation. Iterated negation thus generates four values: A, its opposite A-1, both, and neither. While in two valued logic A = 1 implies no-A = 0 and conversely A = 0 implies no-A = 1, we admit the relative independence of opposites so in a given situation both may exist A = 1 and no-A =1 (contradiction, ambivalence or complexity) or neither may be present (neither A nor no-A). Iterated negation represents the second step in a cascade of bifurcations.

Quaternity – the cross or square of opposites that emerges from the repetition of bifurcation-- plays a role at many levels of organization from quantum physics (e.g. the two pairs of conjugated opposites, the fundamental structure of the qubit, the group SU(2) which is central to the quantum mechanics of spin, see later) up to psychology.[18] Spacetime is four dimensional. At least four factors are necessary for the generation of biotic expansion, novelty, diversification, and complexity (Sabelli and Carlson-Sabelli, 2005). The four values generated by the bifurcation of a bifurcation allows for iterated negation and the incorporation of dialectic contradiction in Boolean logic (see later).

There can be 2N even 3, 5 ... opposites. In fact opposites can even be contained in an asymmetry within a unity, such as the direction of an action, the polarity of a magnet, or the spin of a quantum. Asymmetry is an internal union of opposites.

Actually, every process gives and receives energy and information from many others. Also any communication between 2, 3 and more entities occurs in the context of larger systems.

"Dialogs" between two entities are common and fundamental, but so are triads. Physics includes fundamental triadicity in the 3 dimensions of space, the CGS system of dimensions, and the color of quarks in quantum physics. A chromatic organization also exists at higher levels of complexity, including visual colors, and their emotional and symbolic associations. Cognitive processes such as the three basic cognitive structures described by Piaget, and emotional processes such as conflict behavior and the corresponding emotions (anger, fear and submission) involve triads (Sabelli, 1989; Sabelli & Carlson-Sabelli, 1991).[19] While dialectic thinking focuses on the interaction of opposites in creativity, the interaction of three or more agents is crucial to creativity, as illustrated by the ability of three kinds of quarks to create matter, three primary colors to generate all colors, and period three to imply all others (Sarkovskii's theorem).

Thus logic needs to incorporate *threeness*. How does one generate a third in logic? Quantitative logics (including fuzzy logic) postulate a third between opposites. Traditional dialectics regard the third as the synthesis of opposites. There is of course a third in the undifferentiated state that precedes a distinction. But Aristotle suggested a more interesting third, the open value for the future.

A third alternative complements and opposes both opposites. This differs radically from a "center" such as the "golden middle". One may create such third alternative by considering what is common to both opposites and negating it (just as one primary color is the opposite of the secondary color generated by the combination of the other two primaries). This is the neither/nor case (Shaffer's stroke), a logical function that can by itself generate the entire Boolean logic. For instance, a theory of creative processes negates both determinism and indeterminism, both of which imply that nothing new and more complex is generated and that humans have no control: change and conservation are both needed for innovation. A *third value as the negation of both opposites* is a practical notion when confronted with an undesirable alternative, as it is often the case in politics. While in the oppositional scheme of dialectics, the third alternative is a synthesis of the two opposites, a third primary color is the negation of both opposites, which makes it altogether new and different.

Tripolarity is not a three valued logic, and the third value is not the synthesis or a transition between the other two. To portrait triadic interactions we can use a phase space of opposites, which has been used to study the changes in the three emotional behaviors associated with conflict (Sabelli at al. 1995; Sabelli, 2005, page 169) and visualize it in a *cube of colors* (Figure 10). The chromatic representation is meaningful because quarks are organized in achromatic fashion.

Negation: Bifurcation, Polarity, and Boundaries

Oppositions are actions. Bifurcations from a common origin generate opposites that alternate with each other (periodically or aperiodically); bifurcations do not create dichotomies that separate opposites; they create cycles that contain and connect opposites. These cycles may be periodic, chaotic, or biotic. Groups thus offer a fruitful model for negation: rotation separates and connects opposites.

Opposites also interact, influencing each other and co-creating new entities. Bifurcation involves an increase in diversity from periodic to chaotic to biotic patterns.20 Thus bifurcation creates multiple qualities and structures.

Oppositions often determine boundaries in social processes, and negation is commonly represented by boundaries in logic. Opposites are defined by their differentiation, with or without separation into two entities. The Möbius ribbon, the Klein bottle and fractals further illustrate that opposites are not determined by boundaries. In Boolean logic, classes are separated by boundaries, but in reality boundaries may be fuzzy and interpenetrating (dialectics); in modern dynamics, boundaries may be fractal.

The extensional character of set theory logic is represented by Venn diagrams21 that draw sharp boundaries between opposites to define classes. Some mathematicians, aware of the complexities involved, may interpret that such boundaries join the domains they separate, and that Venn diagrams include the notion of domain and complementary domain, as well as an order derived from all domains being part of a universal domain. But many others interpret Venn diagrams as dividing classes, excluding the coexistence of opposites, and limiting hierarchical order to purely extensional cases.

In the Spencer-Brown notation, one has the mark <> that makes an ordered (inside to outside) distinction in a line space or a plane space. One could see Spencer-Brown's partition as separating not connecting opposites, and describing unipolarity (0 and 1) rather than bipolarity (1 and -1). On the other hand, Kauffman regards the mark as both joining and separating the two sides that it delineates; then order, polarity and connection are conjoined in the one distinction. This Laws of Form approach to logic/mathematics encounters infinity or infinitely many values in two ways: One way -- consider most elementary recursion X ---> <X> and write enfolded form J = <J> (as in a computer instruction to replace J by <J>). Taking the equality sign directly one has J = <J> = <<J>> = <<<J>>> = ... and so we "could" write "J = <<<<<...>>>>>" and certainly this is a true equation about the infinitely descending nest of marks. Entities such as @ = <<<<<...>>>>> are one way to go to values beyond true and false, by entering into a process. Another way is to deny the equation ◇◇=◇. Then one has numbers ◇,◇◇,◇◇◇,◇◇◇◇,... and a system of arithmetic if one wants to elaborate it. In this way one sees that numbers arise from NOT taking the redundancy of repeated naming. Yet another way is to deny the equation <◇> = . Then we have "SETS" ◇ empty set <◇> set whose member is the empty set <◇<◇>> set whose members are ◇ and <◇> etc. Here <<A><B><C>> has members <A>, <B> and <C>.

The patterns of classical logic all come out or along with this in a natural way by interpreting the mark of distinction as an operator (active versus passive) that connotes the change from the value indicated on its inside to the value indicated on its outside. Thus one can read ◇ as meaning "cross from the unmarked state" (hence becoming marked) and <◇> can be read as "cross from the marked state" (hence becoming unmarked). Hence <◇> = (unmarked). Similarly ◇◇ can be read as redundant, with the second mark naming again the value of the outside of the first mark. Hence ◇◇ = ◇. The equational patterns that come from these two equations generate a precursor to

Boolean algebra and one can match with standard logic by interpreting <a>b as "a implies b" with ◇ as true, <◇> as false, ab as " a or b", <a> as "not a" and (De Morgan's Law) <<a><b>> as "a and b". But this means that Spencer-Brown Laws of Form approach is a precursor to Boolean algebra, not to a logic of process, opposition, and creation.

Polarity is the quantitative aspect of opposition. Boolean logic and information theory describe opposition as unipolar. This denies the qualitative differences between opposites. Bipolarity is often portrayed as the coexistence of opposite poles in a linear relation, but true oppositions (such as synergy and conflict) involve two different, orthogonal dimensions. Opposites are *orthogonal*, similar and/or synergic in some dimensions and different and/or antagonistic in others. This is portrayed in the phase plane and the phase space of opposites.

Refutation, Negation of the Negation, Helices, and Helicoids

An important case of opposition in logic is refutation, which Popper made central in 20th century logic of science. Popper (1992; 2003) proposed that a theory should be considered scientific if and only if it is falsifiable. This led him to dismiss Darwinism ("Darwinism is not a testable scientific theory, but a metaphysical research program"), psychoanalysis, and Marxism as scientific, both also relativity and quantum mechanics were in contradiction with important facts at the start. Kuhn (1962) argued that falsification methodologies would make science impossible; some criterion of 'improbability' or of 'degree of falsification' is required. Also, Popper's stress on falsifiability did not prevent him from advancing notoriously controversial biological and political ideas. Biologists and particularly psychiatrists take issue with his theory of mind as a separate physical substance, while social scientists have deplored his radical denial of historical causation, his distrust of programs of social reform, and his espousal of the economic views of Friedrich Hayek, Milton Friedman, Ludwig von Mises.

In his modern classic, "Proofs and Refutations," Popper's former student Lakatos (1976) offers a heuristic in which a counterexample is used to improve the original conjecture, thus unifying proofs and refutations in a single dialectic process of creation. The refutation (falsification) of the refutation of a hypothesis serves as its confirmation as an alternative to the inductive definition of confirmation that leads to Hempel's paradox22 (Sabelli, 1989). Lakatos' view is grounded on the helical view of processes.

In nature many changes are cyclical-- --as in day/night, breathing in/breathing out, first one side dominates, then the other–but these cycles do not come back exactly to where they started; they don't make a perfect circle. Instead, change occurs in spiral fashion (Figure 12). The fundamental place of helices in natural processes is evident (e.g. proteins, DNA). The most immediate portrait of such processes are helical processes and helical structures such as the simple helices of proteins, the circulation of blood (Harvey), Descartes vortex, Fourier's analysis, spin (Pais, 1989), the helical shape of proteins (Pauling) the double helix (Watson & Crick, 1953, based on Rosalind Franklin's work), and the multiple irregular, creative, biotic patterns of biological processes. In a similar fashion, the law is embodied in the sequence from egg to bird to egg, and so on, and in historical processes. Evolution occurs through a chain of qualitative changes from one stage to another which is in some way the opposite (antithesis) of the preceding one (thesis), and then to another stage which is in some way the opposite of the second, and hence a partial return to the first one. In a conversation, first one person talks, then the other, then again the first person who has now listened to the second person ideas so he incorporates them in his new speech. This pattern also occurs with successive negations in logic. Period 2 captures this important aspect of negation. Static logic captures this periodicity by making - (-1) equal 1.

The dialectic law of the *negation of the negation* states that the negation of the negation is only similar to the original assertion, only a partial return, thus connecting with the spiral pattern widely observed in nature. Dialectics highlights the hierarchical character of the apparent period 2, so negation is more powerful than assertion. Dialectics also postulates that the negation of the negation is the synthesis of the preceding opposites (thesis and antithesis) so negation has a constructive role. This is a seminal but vague concept. To be more precise, the law of the negation of the negation should be formulated as a law of the sublation of the sublation. For Hegel, negation means more than 'No'; when one statement which is "negated" by another, the first is not simply "eliminated" but continues as a subordinate part of the new, "higher" truth; it is terminated and simultaneously preserved (Aufhebung, literally "out/up" or "lifting", meaning to conserve, negate and supersede, which is translated into English as "overcoming" or "sublation").

A hypothesis is sublated by a refutation (such as a counterexample) because it not only contradicts the thesis but also because empirical evidence is stronger than a hypothesis. This notion is modeled by *helicoids* (Figure 13), lattice-like sets with two colors that alternate (Sabelli, 1972). Opposites may also alternate in non-periodic fashion, such as chaotic and biotic patterns, and helicoids of three or more colors may be considered. By alternating in space and/or time, opposites coexist globally while remaining separated locally.

Helicoids are sets ordered by a relation sublation $\downarrow$. A two-colored helicoid is a relational structure $\langle H, \downarrow \rangle$ where H is a non-empty set and $\downarrow \subseteq H \times H$ is a non-empty binary relation called *sublation* satisfying the following axioms:

$(\forall a,b \in H)$, if $\langle a,b \rangle \in \downarrow$, then $\langle b,a \rangle \notin \downarrow$ (asymmetry)

$(\forall a,b, c, d \in H)$ if $<a,b>$, $<b,c>$ and $<c,d> \in \downarrow$,

then $<a,c> \notin \downarrow$ and $<a,d> \in \downarrow$ (indirect transitivity).

From these postulates we can infer

For no a, $a \downarrow a$ (non-reflexivity).

If $<a \downarrow b>$ and $<b \downarrow c>$, then $a \leq c$.

Thus c is similar (in color) and stronger than a. The elements of H are divided into 2 "colors" (Figure 11).

Sublation is also exemplified by physiological and pharmacological antagonisms (Sabelli, 1972). Regarding neuronal states, rest $\downarrow$ excitation $\downarrow$ inhibition. Rest and inhibition have the same output, but excitation can overcome rest but not inhibition. If neuron A inhibits neuron B and neuron B inhibits neuron C, then A is synergic to C and its activation represents a return to C.

Similarly, we can identify different types of drugs that act on different types of synapse. For a particular type of synapse, where the pre-synaptic neuron mediates its effect by the release of one specific neurotransmitter (e.g. acetylcholine), the following hierarchy applies: release of endogenous neurotransmitter < depleter < mimetic of endogenous neurotransmitter < blocker of the postsynaptic receptor. Combining such drug hierarchy with the ordered sequence of neurons in brain structures (as represented by McCulloch and Pitts' neuronal networks),23 one can make inferences regarding the anatomical relation between two or more types of neurons (e.g. those that use acetylcholine versus those that use norepinephrine as a neurotransmitter) (Sabelli, 1964; 1970); e.g., if atropine (an acetylcholine blocker) prevents the effect of epinephrine (a norepinephrine mimetic) on a given function, then the norepinephrine neurons come before acetylcholine neurons in the corresponding pathway). This empirical method illustrates a practical use of the concept of helicoids.

Helicoids clarify the meaning of the law of the negation of the negation. Neither Engels nor the few later Marxist philosophers I read, describe this law other than by example. Engels considered Hegel's notion of the negation of the negation so important that he made it into a fundamental law of dialectics; likewise Stalin judged it so fundamental that he erased from the article on dialectic materialism in the Encyclopedia of Philosophy published in the Soviet Union, because it implied the return from socialism to a capitalist-like state, as it indeed happened.

Co-Creation

The interaction of processes creates new forms, patterns and structures. Form and transformation are abstracted by topology, and its ancestor, geometry. Geometry highlights the metric and tridimensionality of actual physical space, i.e. of matter and void. Topology focuses on continuous transformations of form. This is illustrated by the sequence of patterns up to (Figures 3 and 4), and within Bios (Figure 6). As energy and matter are the minimum of existing, complexity transformation implies creativity. In this light, we must also consider the negative implication of not recognizing creativity: to channel action into the repetition of development in a linear fashion.

Creativity is often regarded something that is entirely a matter of judgment, not subjected to measurement, and limited to human activity. "Apparent" creativity in natural processes is attributed to random accidents or to increases in variance without net increase in complexity. We take changes in pattern (temporal complexity), novelty, diversification, and reduction of entropy as an operational definition of creativity that allows one to recognize and study creative natural processes. In this manner one can identify processes in which creativity is causally generated.

Figure 6. Bios and Chaos. Top: Changes in pattern with time in a biotic series and uniformity of pattern in chaos. Second row: The chaotic trajectory remains inside one cycle of the sine wave generator (0 to π) while trajectory spans beyond it. Third row: Chaos displays local sensitivity to initial conditions. Fourth row: Bios shows global sensitivity to initial conditions.

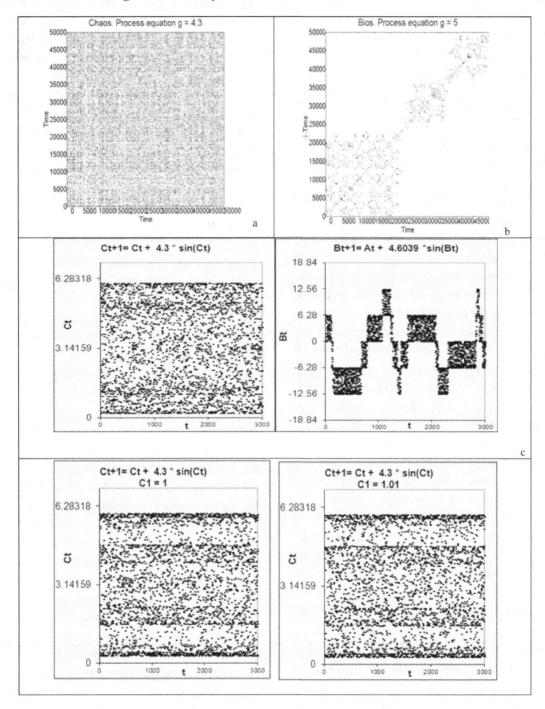

Figure 7. Biotic processes are not mathematically reversible (Sabelli, 2005)

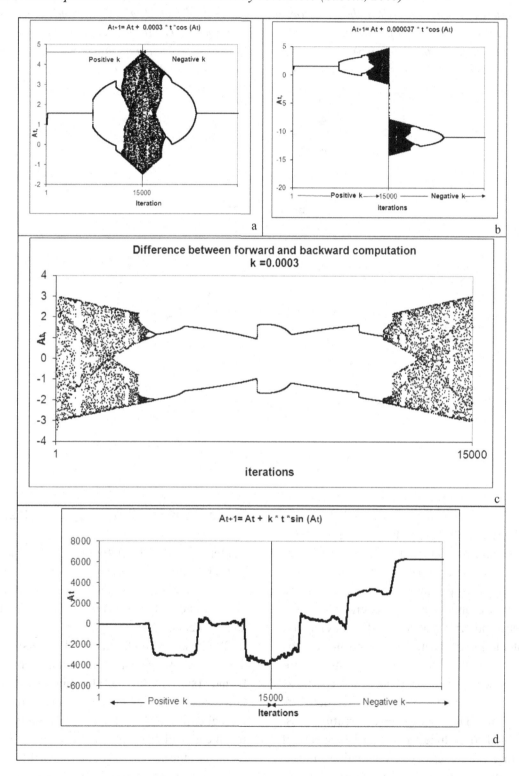

Figure 8. Two models of opposition. Phase Plane of Opposites is a bidimensional representation of opposites that allows one to represent the trajectory of processes as observed empirically and to relate these observations to underlying opposite forces and to physical theory. The difference between opposites P and N provides the information $\mathbf{I(S) = g [P - N]}$, *and the energy of both contributes to the total energy E of the system S, which for symmetric opposites is simply* $\mathbf{E(S) = \sqrt{(P2 + N2)}}$.

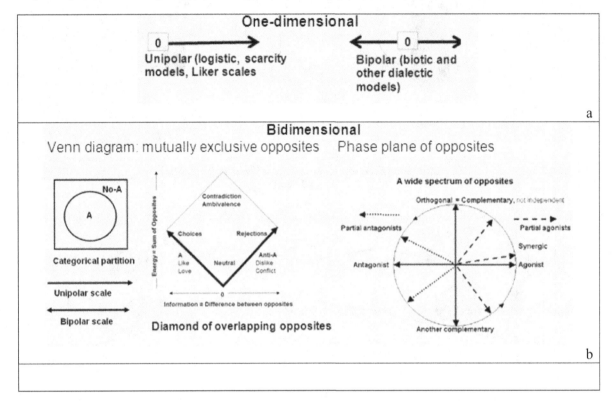

The *co-creation hypothesis* (Sabelli et al, 1997; Sabelli, 2001) states that processes create opposites (e.g. bifurcation cascades) and opposites co-create each other and co-create processes and structures. The opposites must be asymmetric as symmetric opposites such as group inverses annul each other: A and A-1 = Identity element. The interaction of asymmetric opposites can be creative while the interaction of symmetric opposites is destructive, i.e. reduces the complexity to the common denominator of all members of the group. The concept of co-creation must be enlarged to include triads and larger sets of interacting processes, even interacting entities that are otherwise unconnected. Also, the DNA double helix exemplifies co-creation from one strand to its opposite.

Matter: Space, Structure, and Classes

Matter consists of relatively stable structures. But structures are not static. They are engines, creative engines, such as enzymes that synthetize proteins and accelerators that create new particles and elements.

Processes create structures. Material structures are formed by nucleation around centers, not as bounded systems; this fact alone indicates the limitation of sets, classes and systems as fundamental logical entities. The fundamental centers are the tridimensional baryons (protons and neutrons) formed by the nucleation of quarks of three colors (quantum chromodynamics) and the nucleation of baryons as atomic nuclei.

Figure 9. Diamond of opposites, a clinical application of the phase plane of opposites. Top row: The diamond of opposites plots positive and negative motivations and feelings in orthogonal axes. Right: The relation between opposition, energy and information in the diamond of opposites. Rows 2 and 3 present the results obtained in two patients for their relation with a parent and with their closer friends and co-workers. This way of plotting the data allows one to differentiate two modes of thinking, linear and bifurcating.

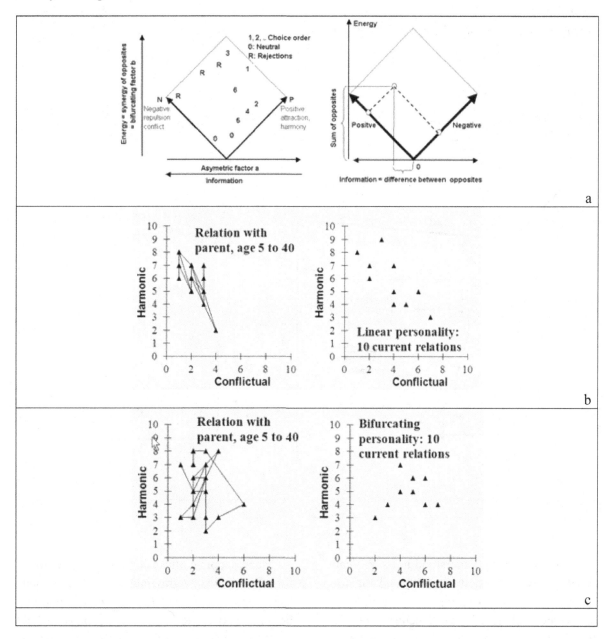

Figure 10. The phase plane of opposites may be interpreted as a catastrophe. Top row: Simple catastrophe (left) and the plotting of opposites (right). Lower row: Left: A simple catastrophe generated by the competition of two attractors (P and N). The outcome (choice, plotted in the third dimension) is determined by the relative power of the opposite attractors. The bifurcating parameter of the catastrophe is the energy resulting from the sum of the opposites, and the asymmetric parameter is the difference between the two opposites. Right: The catastrophe may be interpreted as the simplest case if co-creation of complexity. When the trajectory reaches one pole or another, the state of the system is simple. Greater complexity occurs at the fold, when there is "ambivalence" between the two poles.

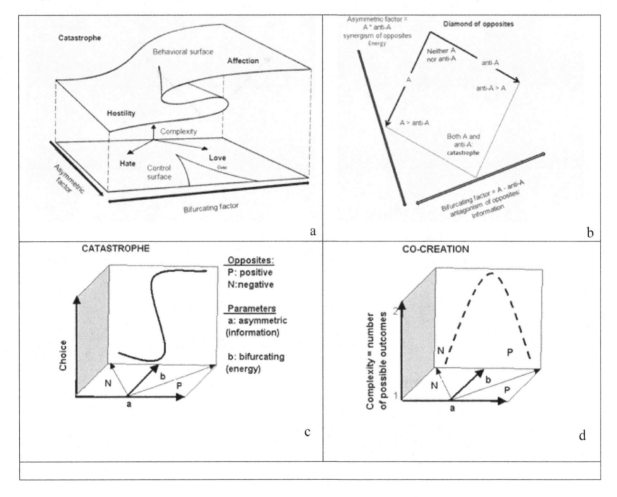

There is a poorly understood but significant relation between triadicity, stability and transformation. Protons are extremely stable –their decay has not been observed-, while neutrons outside the nucleus are extremely unstable, and it is the conversion between protons and neutrons via the weak force that creates higher forms of matter.

Macroscopic matter is organized in complex forms generated by gravitation in 4-dimensional space time. At this level, organization involves both nucleation and its opposite, expansion.

Both actions and structures carry information. They manifest as properties (qualities) from the viewpoint of isolated entities and as relations

Figure 11. Triadic opposition: Color

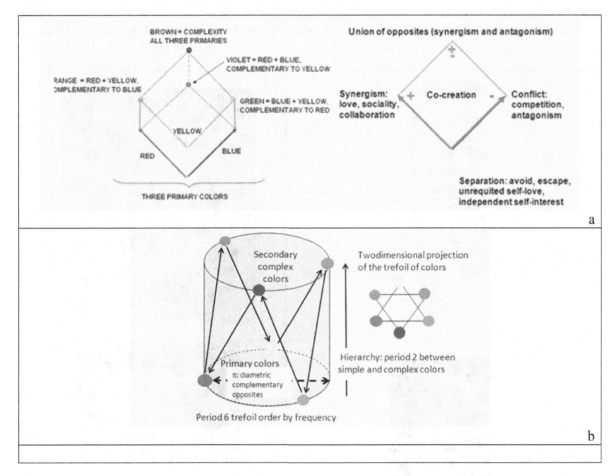

when regarded in context. Although properties and classes of processes and of material structures are correlated, there is no exact overlap between them. There are women and men, and there is masculinity and femininity, but both sexes partake, in different proportions of both sets of qualities. Properties such as being red cannot be defined by the set of red things. Classes cannot be defined qualities. Opposite properties are statistically but not absolutely divided in separate classes.

The logic of classes is itself a complex matter. Kauffman (2002; 2004) is developing a "Bio-logic" where he explores the boundary between biology and the study of formal systems (logic).

He arrives at a summary formalism, a chapter in "boundary mathematics" where there are not only containers <> but also extainers ><, entities open to interaction and distinguishing the space that they are not.

The boundary algebra of containers and extainers is to bio-logic what Boolean algebra is to classical logic. He shows how this formalism encompasses significant parts of the logic of DNA replication, the Dirac formalism for quantum mechanics, formalisms for protein folding and the basic structure of the Temperley Lieb algebra at the foundations of topological invariants of knots and links.

Figure 12. Schematic representation of the sequential repetition of action, interaction and creation pattern at multiple levels of organization (top left). Double helix nebulae (top right), right handed alpha helix of proteins (bottom upper left), DNA double helix (bottom middle), Helix pomatia (bottom upper right) and Inner ear helix (bottom lower right).

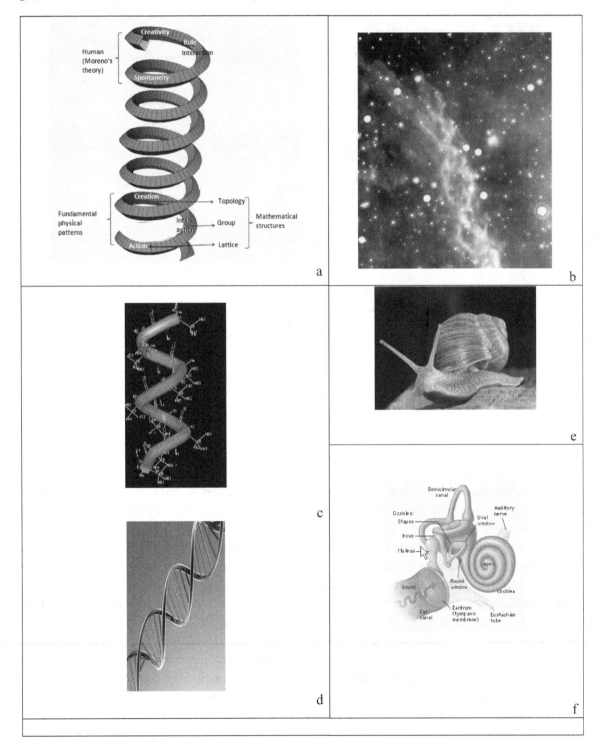

Figure 13. Helicoids

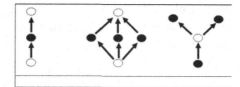

Causal Creation and Thermodynamic Decay

Progress and creation also include decay and destruction; in fact, decay and destruction are inseparable from creation. But the concept of progressive and causal creation refutes the thermodynamic notion of universal tendency to decay postulated by standard interpretation of the second law of Thermodynamics.

The Clausius-Boltzmann interpretation of entropy as disorder has become an issue in computer science. Claude Shannon adopted the de Moivre equation employed by Boltzmann to measure the probability of the occurrence of a signal as a definition and measure of information (Shannon, 1940). For equal probabilities $pi = p$, the information entropy H is

$$H = K \ln(1/p)$$

where K is a constant which determines the units of entropy; if the units are bits, then $K=1/\ln(2)$. Shannon omitted the Boltzmann constant that has the physical dimensions of heat and temperature that make the measurement of entropy relevant to physical processes. Nevertheless, John von Neumann advised Shannon to call his measure of information entropy because "nobody knows what entropy is," thereby inaugurating fifty years of confusion. It was subsequently assumed that the second law of thermodynamics applies to informational entropy. Yet one cannot simply assume that a law of physics applies to processes that are not physical; one would have to demonstrate such conjecture.

Clausius defined entropy as the energy that is not available to perform work and Boltzmann interpreted entropy as a measurement of the disorder in a system. The identification of entropy with disorder is meaningless without a definition of order such the mathematical model offered by Lattice Theory. Note also that there can be hidden order, such as the apparently random sequence of π digits. What is call disorder in thermodynamics may many times be hidden order. Randomization often increases entropy but this does not imply that entropy measures disorder. Entropy increases in many processes.

Clausius and Boltzmann portrayed the maximization of entropy as spontaneous, natural, and unavoidable decay towards maximal disorder; this concept still permeates physics and information science. Elementary texts appeal to purportedly intuitive examples –e.g. glasses break but they never spontaneously form. This neglects the fact that glasses must have been formed before they can be broken. The notion of monotonic decay implies that the universe started in a state of maximal organization, which is unlikely and certainly unproven.

Entropy is a measurement defined mathematically; the concept of entropy as disorder and decay is a philosophical overlay that does not derive from its mathematical definition, and that is unsupported by empirical observations. Alternative interpretations include chance, uncertainty, complexity, and diversity. Born and Gell-Mann (1994) attribute thermodynamic irreversibility to "ignorance." Entropy has become a popular word implying any type of disorder, disorganization, waste, or uncertainty. Outside the context of thermodynamics, entropy is largely a metaphor that has been stretched far beyond its breaking point (Cohen & Steward, 1994). The concept of entropy is applied to computation but in often contradictory ways; for instance, in Shannon's view, entropy is the opposite of information, but topological entropy (Adler et al, 1965) is information and measures the complexity of the system.

One way to resolve this morass of interpretations is to look directly at the mathematical equation that defines entropy, and at the results of empirical measurements. Measurements quantify what they actually measure, not what they are expected to measure. Defining entropy as a measure of disorder, decay, uncertainty, or complexity, does not make it so. This use of the term "entropy" is determined by history, custom, and authority, but in science, the only valid definitions are those that emerge from what is actually measured. When we measure entropy as a function of the number of bins employed in its calculation, entropy is shown to measure symmetry and diversity, not uncertainly or disorder. This is demonstrated by measuring the entropy of time series with increasing number of bins, 2, 3, …, 128, and plotting the value of entropy as a function of the logarithm of the number of bins (Figure 14).

A monotonic decay would prevent evolution; hence this interpretation has been questioned since the nineteenth century up to our times (Gal-Or, 1972; Georgescu-Roegen 1971). Physicists, biologists and economists have objected to the interpretation of a regularity about heat exchange should be regarded as a universal law about simple and complex processes. Schrödinger asked himself, how does biological evolution consistently overcome the dire prediction of entropic decay? He proposed that importing high-quality energy (low entropy) materials from outside their bodies may account for the evolution of life. Organisms feed on "negative entropy".

Prigogine came to a complementary solution of Schrödinger's paradox: the excretion of high entropy materials as waste. For instance, organisms excrete entropy through the skin (heat), respiration (CO_2), urination (metabolites), and defecation (gastrointestinal secretions and unabsorbed food). Both Schrödinger's intake of low entropy food and Prigogine's excretion of high entropy waste decrease the internal entropy of organisms by increasing the entropy of their environment. The entropy still increases overall.

The emergence of Bios illustrates another process that may account for the reduction of entropy in creative processes. The lower entropy of many empirical series that demonstrate creative features, and of bios and random walks among mathematical models, suggests that there is a third mechanism for the lowering of entropy in living organisms: creative processes such as the synthesis of low entropy biomolecules and biotic processes (Figure 14).

More important, entropy increases in constructive processes, not only with decay and disorder. Entropy and complexity increase together with evolution from equilibrium to periodicity, chaos and bios (Figure 14), but there is a greater increase in complexity and a proportionally lesser increase in entropy as the series evolves from chaos to bios.

Dimensions

We conceptualize qualities, i.e. information, as dimensions (Sabelli, 1989) rather than as classes. The traditional focus on classes has been extremely useful regarding the classification of elementary particles, chemical elements and biological species. Classes are used by philosophers to encode qualities by the extension of the entities that manifest a given property at least since Aristotle, but dimensions can also provide quantitative information (e.g. not only that X is red but also how red it is) and also encode the coexistence of qualities (e.g. X is so much red and so much green). Using dimensions also solves some simple conundrums, such as "does the American flag belong to the class of red objects or to the class of non-red objects?"

Figure 14. The increase in entropy in patterned processes and the relative reduction in biological organism and other creative processes. Left: Top row: measuring Shannon's entropy with multiple 2, 3, ...bins shows that entropy measures symmetry and diversity. Second row: entropy is higher in random and chaotic series than in mathematical Bios or in the time series generated by the Schrödinger's equation. Right: Entropy of the time series generated by the process equation. Entropy is maximal during the chaotic phase and in leaps, and there is a lesser decrease in entropy in the biotic phase. Bottom: Complex processes such as biological organisms bypass the second law of thermodynamics by ingesting low entropy materials (Schrödinger), by and excreting high entropy waste (Prigogine), and by creative processes such as Bios and the synthesis of biomolecules.

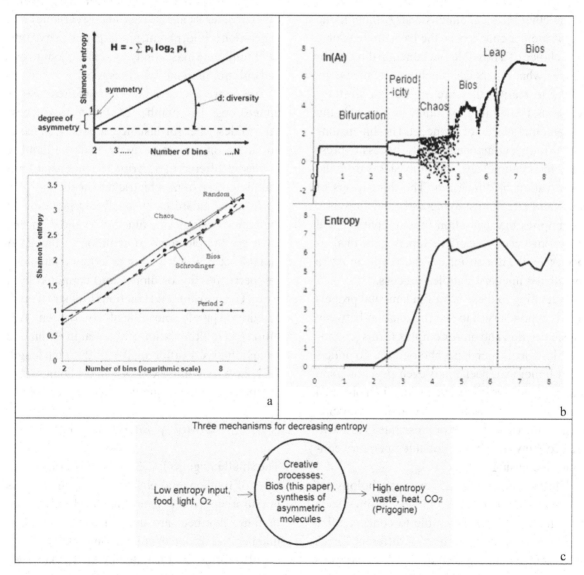

Dimensions encode qualities. In physics, which for good reasons is the model reference science, properties are represented as dimensions.24 The concept of dimension involves quantity and quality, and thus formalizes their essential unity (Galileo, Hegel, Engels), which is the foundation of modern science insofar as it hinges on measurement. Current stress on qualitative science and scale-free phenomena, while valuable in themselves, should not obscure the dialectic unity of quantity and quality. Additionally, involving quantity (measurement) and quality (properties and relations), dimensional analysis in physics involves a theoretical system. All fundamental physical processes can be expressed in terms of combinations of three basic dimensions, mass (M), length (L), and time (T), which allows us to define other physical dimensions (Although one may use other concepts as the basic dimensions, each choice of a possible fundamental dimension implies what others can be chosen. Dimensions belong to reality; they are not human arbitrary decisions.) Attending to dimensions reveals the fundamental aspects of a concept. The dimensions of the simpler components are by necessity present in their composites. Causality stems from the conservation of dimension. The dimensions of cause and effect must by necessity be the same: this implies that causation must be natural and deterministic; never can it be supernatural or aleatory. Also, the dimensions of the simple must be considered in every complex process.

Attending to these most fundamental properties of action serves to see the relation between physical action and more complex forms (chemical, biological, social, psychological). To understand biological, social and even psychological processes it is necessary to consider their physical dimensions–how would we practice medicine without measuring fever or pulse rate? How will the economy fare if the global temperature continues increasing?

Biology, sociology,25 and psychology of course also involve more complex qualities, such as form,26 which is desirable to conceptualize as dimensions –new forms, not different forces or substance than physical ones. We do not possess as yet a system of dimensions to organize and measure these complex processes, but this does not mean that biological and psychological dimensions do not exist.27

Dimensional analysis is the conceptual tool we apply to understand physical situations involving a mix of different kinds of physical quantities. We may generalize its use to all sciences to replace extensional logic based on set theory. To define a system of fundamental dimensions for human processes, as it has been done in physics, it is cogent to start with social dimensions as these are fewer and older than psychological ones. We thus first consider as age (a continuous variable) and generation (child, parent, grand-parent), sexuality (femininity and masculinity,), socioeconomic role, and cultural/national/religious roots.

There are no barriers to the practical use of dimensions. The number of dimensions necessary to describe, for instance, a person's race is no larger, only more accurate, than the number of classes offered to describe it. Dimensions are routinely used in psychiatric diagnosis.

In the standard extensional interpretation of mathematical logic, the function 'A and B' means what are the elements in common to the set A and the set B. But we often refer to the intension (property, quality or dimension) connoted by a word. Using arithmetic functions to abstract 'and' captures in part the meaning of 'co-creation'. Addition and multiplication are similar in arithmetic but qualitatively different: $2 + 2 = 2 \times 2$ but length $2x + 2x = 4x$ while $2x \times 2x = 4 x2$. Dimensions and polarity encode quality and complexity.

Number: Quantity, Order, and Form

The small integers (1, 2, 3, 4) portray crucial features of fundamental physical processes. This is not surprising as actions are quantized and ordered in time; numbers are unit quantities (cardinal numbers) and ordered (ordinal numbers). Numbers are also forms, as illustrated by the Pythagorean arrangements of dots and by the complement plots of integers.

The small numbers and π are numerical archetypes (Jung, 1971; Robertson, 1995), meaning they are generic forms present at multiple levels

The Biotic Logic of Quantum Processes and Quantum Computation

Table 3. Fundamental numerical archetypes

Form	Integer archetypes	Mathematical archetypes	Physical archetypes	Dimensions of physical archetypes
Action: oneness, units, asymmetry	1	φ self-similar asymmetry	Planck constant h	Frequency 1/t
Rotation of opposites: twoness, symmetry	2	$\sqrt{2}$, π circular symmetry, $e i\pi + 1 = 0$	Speed of light c	Velocity space/time
Tridimensional space: matter	3	$\sqrt{3}$, $i2 = j2 = k2 = ijk = -1$	Newton's universal gravitational constant G	r3 * m-1 * t-2 length cubed, divided by mass and by time squared

of organization (Pythagoras; Galileo; Pierce). At all levels there are units, pairs and triads. At all levels there is unidirectionality, symmetry, and spatial organization. At all levels there is a linear flow in time, two-way transformations, and hierarchical feedbacks. At all levels there is oneness of substance, partitions into opposite classes, and hierarchy of three levels. Triadicity is a fundamental form that repeats in many processes at multiple levels of organization, as illustrated by macroscopic physical space, π atomic orbitals, DNA codons, family triads, conceptual triads, and symbolic triads including Trinitarian concepts of God. Triads are fundamental also because Sarkovskii's theorem (Peitgen et al, 1992) that shows in a mapping with a point of period 3, this point is at the end of an ordered series of periodicities, including flights to infinity. This theorem is central to modern nonlinear dynamics. The infinity of periodicities implied by period 3 have been interpreted as chaos, and in fact gave the name to this field. While logic and dialectics focus on twoness, and others propose instead a three valued logic, we consider it necessary to include both twoness and triadicity. Indeed hexadic forms are found at multiple levels of organization (quarks, benzene rings, primary and secondary visual colors). Lattices model asymmetric unidirectional order (such as action, that is universal), hence oneness. Groups model opposition and symmetry, hence twoness. Topology models space-like form, hence includes

threeness. We propose to seek these numerical forms at each level and in each process (Sabelli & Carlson-Sabelli, 1996). They may reveal laws of formation beyond standard topologies. A starting point is Kauffman and Varela concept of "re-entry."

Prominent among numerical archetypes are the irrational and imaginary numbers that describe fundamental mathematical and physical processes (Table 3).

Number: Quantity, Quality, and Complexity

Numbers do not only measure quantity but also model quality. In fact, quantity and quality are inseparable (Aristotle). Changes in quantity generate changes in quality (Hegel), classically illustrated by the changes in state between ice, water and vapor, and the changes in processes between towns and cities. This is not the product of chance but the result of the fact that numbers have form. During much of the twentieth century, many scientists dismissed qualitative changes as reducible to quantitative ones; the importance of qualitative measurements is now widely recognized by leading scientists. Quantitative models that neglect qualitative change appear scientific but they are not.

The law of quantity and quality is expanded to include the three aspects of entities (Figure 15), and the hierarchy of complexity (Figure 16).

Figure 15. The law of quantity and quality applies to the changes from material core to energetic filed to informational range

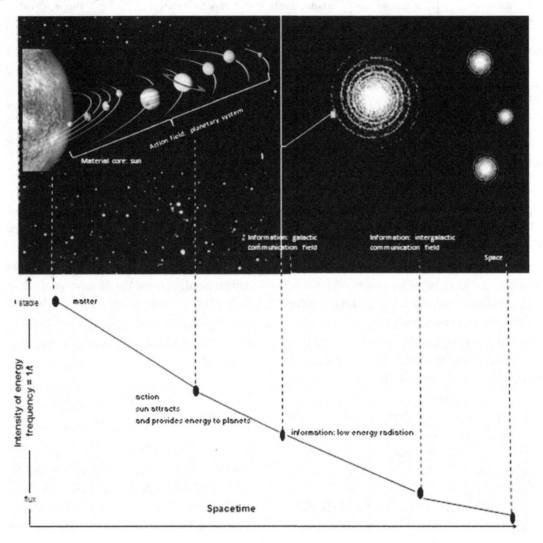

Hegel had proposed that changes in quantity generate qualitative changes. Expanding this concept, *changes in sequential order or in quantity* can *generate changes in quality and increases in complexity* (Sabelli, 2005). Change in order or quantity generate quality, diversity, and novelty. Gradual quantitative changes generate qualitative changes by leaps because numbers encode form. The sequence of patterns in time generated by recursions such as the process and the diversifying equations (convergence, steady state, bifurcations, chaos, bios, leaps) illustrate the relation between changes in quantity, quality and complexity.

Complexity is maximal at moderate size and temperature: living organism are neither sub-atomic nor cosmic, and exist only at moderate temperatures. The greatest known complexity, the human brain, is of moderate size (some animals have larger brains) and functions at 370.

Figure 16. Priority and supremacy: numbers also encode complexity

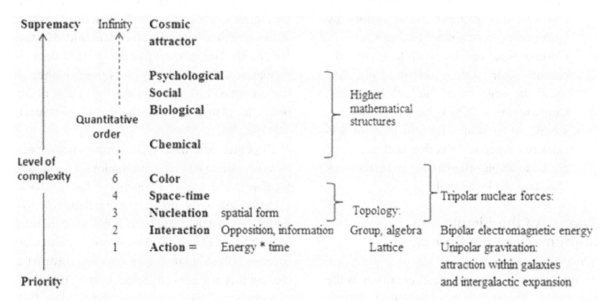

Creativity in Logic

The concept of co-creation has practical applications. In psychotherapy the therapist and the patient co-create; therapy in fact in fact hinges on the ability of the therapist to elicit creative behavior in the patient. More evident, marital and family therapy hinge on the ability of the therapist to elicit co-creative behavior in the couple or the family. Co-creation is likewise essential to peace. We survived the Cold War because the leading protagonists co-created it to maintain peace. Illustrating the educational application of the concept of co-creation, an online program for clinical training and supervision for psychiatric nurses has been developed at a major American medical center allowing students to collaborate and teach each other. The aim is competency, not competition. An additional objective is congruence. The student needs to learn to see her or himself as others see them to learn how to take care of a patient, as well as of working with others. Empathy teaches us who we are. This is Socratic imperative: Know Thyself. It also incorporates Heraclitus's justice of opposites. The matching of opposites – self and other – is not an equilibrium point, but promotes empathic, ethical, and effective behavior. One of the features of the program has been to create a virtual community that encompasses teachers and students from many universities.

The co-creation concept came to light in 2000 for business when the Internet altered the relationship between individuals and institutions. In the early 2000s, consultants and companies deployed co-creation as a tool for engaging customers in product design. Value will be increasingly co-created by the firm and the customer, they argued, rather than being created entirely inside the firm (Prahalad & Ramaswamy, 2000).

The notion of co-creation supports a number of logical strategies:

- **Dialectic Paradigm:** Given A, find no-A. Find how A and no-A coexist (and/or approach) rather than exclude each other (either/or approach).
- **Combination:** Unite opposites such as envisioned by dialectic synthesis.
- **Co-creation Paradigm:** find how A and no-A determine each other through pro-

cesses of mutual feedback, and how they co-create new patterns and/or entities by such processes of mutual feedback.

- **Co-negation:** negating both terms of a dichotomy can create a new third possibility as the negation of the both opposites. Constructing a third option is highly desirable when both sides had positive and negative aspects. Rejecting both terms of an undesirable alternative is better than choosing the lesser evil

Priority of the Simple and Supremacy of the Complex

An unavoidable consequence of creativity is the generation of complex processes from simple ones. Simple processes are widespread. They precede, create, make up, enclose, and outlast the complex patterns they generate. Simpler levels predominate globally because they have temporal priority, and more energy, more extension, more duration, and greater mass (*priority of the simple*). Complex processes are short-lived and local; they predominate locally over the simple processes that generate and constitute them via their greater informational content, greater energy flow density, and greater creativity (*supremacy of the complex*).

Exemplary of this process, in the central nervous system, newer and more complex structures (e.g. cerebral cortex) develop from, and integrate, inhibit and control the activity of older and simpler structures (e.g. spinal cord), which, in turn, serve as the input and output for the higher ones. There is hierarchy of levels (spinal < rhomboencephalic < mesencephalic < diencephalic < cortical) that interact with each other in continual processes of mutual and hierarchical feedback. Each neurological level represents a phase in biological evolution. Likewise, levels of organization in nature represent phases in the evolution of the universe (Figure 16).

As in the central nervous system, also in nature the higher levels control the bottom levels, while at the same time are themselves determined by the lower ones. Notably, the free energy flow density increases with complexity: it is much higher in human brain (150,000 ergs sec-1 g-1) than in the body, the planet, or even the sun (2 ergs sec-1 g-1) (Chaisson, 2001).

Together, bottom-to-top and top-to-bottom actions constitute a cycle, a continuously operating feedback. The two components of the feedback cycle, priority and supremacy are qualitatively different. For instance, the heart is not a specialized organ that enables us to carries out a particular function. If the heart stops functioning properly, the result is not a less efficient human, deprived of some specialized functions; the result is that the organism dies.

Processes at each level of organization are in part endogenous and in part co-determined by processes at simpler or more complex levels. For instance, the physical and biological environment has priority in economic processes, while the social, economic and legal systems have supremacy in determining the environment. Economic motivations largely predetermine our ideas and moral values; knowledge and moral values determine what we consider economically or legally sound.

Complex processes emerge later and also last for a short period of time. Simple processes not only emerge early but also persist; in fact complex processes depend on the simultaneous existence of simpler ones. Thus simple processes have priority in time and at each time. As a result, an increase in complexity represents an increase in variance, the simple still existing, and the complex being added; there always is a large majority of small and simple organisms. Notably, some interpret the observed increase in variance (Carroll, 2001) to dismiss progress in evolution although there is been an increase in the maximum level of complexity over the history of life.

The concept of the priority of the simple is a non-reductive form of materialism, as it includes the supremacy of the ideal, the perceived and the spiritual.

The Priority of Physics

Physics is regarded as the model for all sciences. Biological processes are to be explained by chemical laws, which in turn are explained by physics, and in turn physics is a realization of mathematical relations. The extraordinarily successful reductionist approach of present day physics exemplifies materialist philosophy. Lamarck regarded evolution (including mind) as arising from physical processes. In last instance, all processes are generated by quantum processes, at each time and at the start of time in Lemaitre's primordial atom (often referred to as the "Big bang"). In time, the expansion of the universe separates its various regions. There is priority of quantum priority and supremacy of cosmic processes.

Physicist George Ellis (2005) highlights that the reductionism of current physics is based on the concept of an isolated system, yet no real physical is isolated and in particular biological systems are open systems (Campbell, 1974; 1991) so context matters as much as laws. The physics approach tends to ignore three crucial features that enable the emergence of biological complexity out of the underlying physical substratum (Ellis 2004; 2005), namely top-down action in the hierarchy of complexity that affects both the operational context and nature of constituent parts, the causal efficacy of stored information ('memory effects'), and the origin of biological information through evolutionary adaptation. These features enable the causal efficacy of emergent biological order, described by phenomenological laws of behavior at each level of the hierarchy. Thus what occurs is *contextual emergence* of complexity (Ellis, 2005). According to Ellis, "the higher levels in the hierarchy of complexity have real autonomous causal powers, functionally independent of lower-level processes. The underlying physics both enables and constrains what is possible at the higher levels, creating the possibility space of outcomes, but does not enable us to actually predict events in the everyday world around us."

These concepts are explicit in the notion of priority of the simple (physical, material, energetic) and supremacy of the complex (informational) which also adds the notion of bipolar and hierarchical feedback as a process for the creation of complexity from simpler origin. In contrast, the concept of *emergence,* widely applied in discussions of *complexity* and embraced by Ellis, does not provide a mechanism for creation. Of course "emergence" refers to the possibility of complex structures arising from simpler known structures, and it does not exclude causation. The most extreme version of emergence includes a violation of laws that regulate the lower-level (Meehl & Sellars 1956; Campbell, 1974).

In the feedback relation between theory and experiment, physical reality has priority and theory supremacy. Theories have no effect on physical reality, but they have a strong effect on our relationship with physical reality. Our knowledge of quantum physics affects our ability to channel the energy of physical reality. The observer does not determine physical reality, but, by setting up a particular way to make an experiment, the observer determines "what" can be measured and the observations. The observer sets a physical context. The observer does not determine how physical reality will fill in that context. The feedback loop relating the observer and the physical reality gives freedom for the observer to choose ways of observation and the physical reality responds to this by giving the observer corresponding results. These results then feedback and affect the structure of the theory. The theory has any influence on the structure of the physical reality itself. It only affects our interaction with that reality. This means that in order to know physical reality, we must engage in the bipolar feedback of theory and experiment.

Figure 17. Priority and supremacy as complementary opposite components of biotic feedback

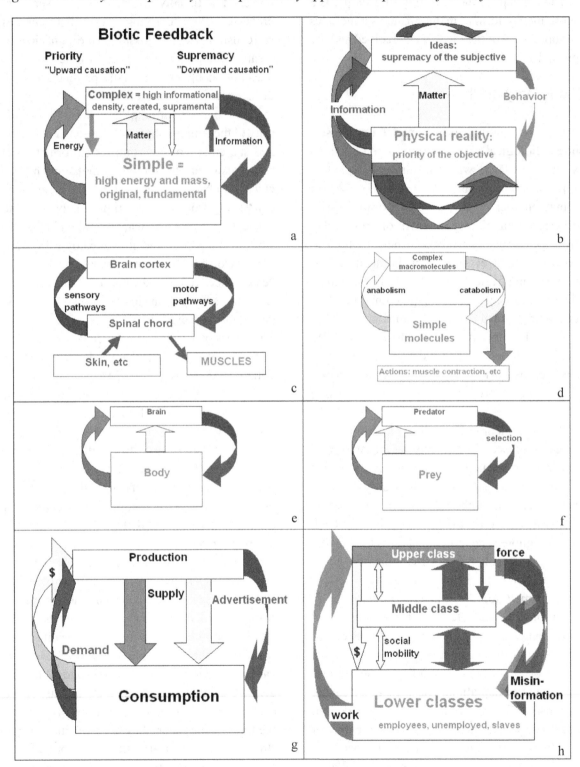

Otherwise, we shall not come to understand that which is independent of our particular theorizing. In this way our understanding of the nature of physical reality is in a constant state of evolution.

Priority of the Global and Supremacy of the Local

Simple physical processes are global, develop earlier, and generate biological processes which in turn generated social and psychological processes. The operation and even the existence of complex processes depend on lower level processes. Complex processes, i.e. processes rich in information, have less energy, duration and mass, while simple processes are larger, rich on energy and matter, and last longer, preceding and outlasting the complex processes that depend on them.

Complexity does depend on both number and differentiation of components. Process complexity depends on individuality: complexity is embodied in the number and differentiation of individual terms. There are hence two complementary forms of complexity. Systems complexity depends on the size of the system: in general, the larger the system, the greater the complexity. Molecules are more complex than the atoms that form them. However, often the smaller the component, the greater the complexity: a sand pile is simpler than the atom; the enormous distant universe is simpler than the smaller nearer universe. This is because the larger universe is dominated by global, relatively simpler, physical processes, where locally life and mind have developed. In this local system, the complex processes have supremacy, while global processes dominate everywhere for reasons of priority, extension and duration.

This concept of global priority and local supremacy has implications for human processes, such as medical care and institutional governance. Global physical processes overcome local social processes, witness the power with which global warming is destroying our ecological and eco-nomic system. But global warming is the product of human actions –supremacy of the complex.

Priority and Supremacy in Logic

The great intellectual revolution that created science in ancient Greece was the search for natural causes i.e. the upward causation from the simple to the complex. Rationalism is intimately associated with materialism. Analysis (chemical, social, psychological), i.e. the reduction of complex processes to its component parts, is the leading scientific method, and has met with extraordinary success in studies ranging from elementary particles to DNA. Cybernetics was born as an effort to account for complex behaviors through the action of simpler mechanical devices. Later on, cyberneticians established the existence of downward actions as real and causally efficient. The notion of hierarchical feedback allows one to assert the priority of natural cause without denying the local supremacy of downward causation. Priority and supremacy are co-creators, two sides of the feedback loop, so upward and downward causation alternate; at times complex processes have priority. Thus upward and downward causation can be reversed just as the sides of a Möbius strip. But different processes are involved in upward causation (temporal priority, energetic and material processes) and in downward causation (informational complexity, later action, supremacy).

The concept of priority of the simple and supremacy of the complex indicates that logic as a science of reason cannot be purely mathematical but must incorporate empirical knowledge and psychological insight. The reductionist program regarded all science as reducible to physics, physics reducible to mathematics, and, in Russell's magnificent encore, mathematics reducible to logic. Gödel showed that nothing simpler than arithmetic would be sufficient to account for it. Gödel's results show that formal systems that are rich enough to be consistent and handle basic arithmetic are incomplete. That is, there are theorems expressible in such a formal system that are not provable within the systems, but are provable in reasoning about the system (outside it) under the assumption that the formal system is consistent. The reasoning performed outside the system is not inherently different from any other mathematical reasoning, but exceed set theory. Thus mathematical logic cannot be reduced to set theory. The priority supremacy duality indicates that mathematical logic must encompass all of mathematics. There is a big difference between mathematics actively practiced, and the notion of a formalized set theory or a formalized number theory. In practice, mathematics is not contained in a specific formal system where all the reasoning must be part of that system. It is these constraints that lead to the incompleteness results. Finally, it is clear that formalized logics are part of formalized mathematics and not the other way around. Advances in mathematics are advances in (the use of) reason.

Logic and reason cannot be reduced to set theory or to any formalized logic. There is a big difference between mathematics actively practiced, and the notion of a formalized set theory or a formalized number theory. In practice, mathematics is not contained in a specific formal system where all the reasoning must be part of that system. It is these constraints that lead to the incompleteness results. Finally, it is clear that formalized logics are part of formalized mathematics and not the other way around. Advances in mathematics are advances in (the use of) reason. Regarding the relationship between classical logic and mathematics, classical logic had no notion of using infinity (mathematical induction) as a mode of reasoning. Basic mathematics uses the principle of mathematical induction and other properties of simple countable infinity to get its results. These are matters of reasoning that go beyond classical logic. Each new mathematical advance is an advance in logic. It is interesting to see how woven with normal practice is the use of infinity. For example

$$S = 1 + a + a2 + a3 + ...,$$

then $S = 1 + a(1 + a + a2 + a3 + ...)$

$$S = 1 + aS$$

$$S(1-a) = 1$$

$$S = 1/(1-a).$$

This is reasoning using the reentering property of an infinite row. It gives the correct answer in general for "formal power series" and needs the convergence condition $|a|<1$ for numerical series. It is fun to see what "crazy" identities one can derive outside the domains of convergence. For example, let $A = 2$. Then we get $-1 = 1/(1-2) = 1 + 2 + 22 + 23 + 24 + 25 + ...:-)$. Of course this does have a meaning since $-1 = 1 + 2 + 22 + 23 + ... + 2n + [-2(n+1)]$ and we have "pushed" the $22(n+1)$ off to infinity even though it is not going to zero.

Reduction of complex problems and processes to their simple components is a fundamental strategy in science. But Pasteur's cosmic asymmetry illustrates *complexity inference* (Sabelli, 1989), the development of a hypothesis about simple processes based on consideration of complex processes related to the simple process. In the studies reported here, methods to analyze complex non-stationary processes were developed in the context of medicine, causal creativity was first demonstrated in biological time series (hence the term "Bios") and subsequently Bios was found in physical processes.

THE BIOTIC LOGIC OF QUANTUM PROCESSES

- What are the principles of quantum physics that should guide logic and computation?

• What are the principles of quantum physics that should guide logic and computation?

First, quantum entities are processes. The Schrödinger function ψ is a function of t. It can collapse with measurement, but it disperses again. The *quantum of action* is the most fundamental concept in quantum physics. Incorporating the quantum of action, into logic would transform process philosophy into physics-based science. Beyond, the quantum concept of action also incorporates the fundamental role of number in nature and implies a discrete physics (Kauffman, 2004).

The Planck constant was first described as the proportionality constant between the energy of a photon and the frequency of its associated electromagnetic wave. Planck conjectured correctly that energy must be some multiple of a very small quantity ("quantum"). Einstein explained the photoelectric effect by assuming that light quanta were actual particles, which he called photons. Quanta are the units of action in nature. For all A, A is equally or larger than the Plank constant h, the quantum of action

$$(\forall A)\, A > h,$$

an equation proposed by Planck for the special case of the energy of the atoms in a cavity when they interact with light; considered as a *"purely formal assumption"*. Einstein made this concept concrete by postulating that radiation consists of quanta (photons), and that A > h apply to individual photons, a very different law indeed (Farmelo, 2002).28

Just as quantum physics establishes proportionality between the energy and frequency. Correspondingly, both changes energy (process equation) and in time (diversifying equation) produce similar sequences in pattern (Figures 3 and 4). In quantum physics, action actually involves two orthogonal pairs of conjugated opposites: energy and time, position and momentum. Position and time are locations in 4-dimensional spacetime, while energy and momentum represent self-causing, self-changing action.

The Principle of Least Action describes action as an integral quantity used to determine the evolution of a physical system between two defined states, i.e. a change of energy in time; imbued of the economic spirit, the principle requires the action to be least.29 Students, who conserve their critical faculties, question how natural processes "know" how to evolve in such economic fashion. In Feynman's quantum model, an entity does not follow a single path, but its behavior depends on all imaginable paths and the value of the actions of each path (Feynman, 1974).30

Quantum implies *discreteness*, e.g. quantum leaps of electrons between orbitals. The wavefunction ψ is continuous and permits the calculation of a most probable (expectation) value of a given variable. For a free particle, ψ is a sine wave implying a precisely determined momentum and a totally undetermined position.

The fact that measurements of energy and time, or of position and momentum, are related has been interpreted as uncertainty, because the more precisely one property is measured, the less precisely the other can be measured. According to Heisenberg, it is impossible to determine simultaneously both the position and velocity of an electron or any other particle with any great degree of accuracy or certainty, not as result of our limitations to measure particular quantities of a system, but as a consequence of the nature of quantum processes. However, we can know exactly the position of a macroscopic moving object but we cannot simultaneously know its velocity to arbitrary precision. The more precisely we know the position of macroscopic moving object or of a quantum particle, the less we can know about its velocity, and the more we know about the velocity, the less we can know about its instantaneous position. The reason for these macroscopic restrictions is that measurements are fundamentally discrete. In order to measure velocity, we cannot simply fid the instantaneous velocity. That is a fiction. We must, instead, give the system an increment of time, allow it to move and find the difference in start and end positions. But then there is an uncertainty in the position. We can only claim an exact velocity as an idealization for infinitely short distances and infinitely short times. Nobody would claim that a macroscopic object does not have an exact velocity and position, and neither should we claim it for quantum particles. What we measure or cannot measure does not change reality. It only changes what we know or do not know.

The fact is that instantaneous energy and time are not measurable: only changes in energy and time can be measured. Likewise position and momentum are not measurable in moving entities; only their change is. We can measure the integral of changes in time, energy, position and momentum in quantum mechanics. "Uncertainty" arises from the attempt to measure instantaneous values for changing variables, such as in a non-relativistic view of simultaneity. In the context of relativity, whether two events occur at the same time—is not absolute, but depends on the observer's reference frame.

The uncertainty principle is often interpreted to mean that we cannot know reality because we alter it by observation: the measurement of position necessarily disturbs a particle's momentum, and vice versa. Heisenberg and Bohr interpreted uncertainty as an observer effect because they adhered to logical positivism. The observer is part of the observed system; he is no longer external and neutral, but through the act of measurement he becomes himself a part of observed reality. In a similar manner, Einstein's relativity principle has been interpreted as philosophical and moral relativism. Such philosophical speculations are detrimental to understanding of the human implications of attending to reality. If we regard reality as that which can be observed, reality is created by the observer; literally, a patient has no cancer until diagnosed.

The Copenhagen interpretation has been interpreted to mean that a quantum entity has not a determined position until observed; when observed, the wavefunction collapses and thereby the observation determines the outcome of the measurement. But is the observation or the physical act (e.g. the impact of the photon on the electron) that determines the outcome of the measurement? Is there really a time in which a quantum particle does not interact? Certainly not, but interaction and measurement are different processes in quantum mechanics. A measurement is an interaction that results in a permanent macroscopic record such as a position of a needle in a meter, or a click on a Geiger counter, and for this it is necessary for it to be an irreversible interaction. In contrast there are other interactions that may be reversible and these are modeled by the solutions in time of the Schrodinger or Dirac equations. We essentially never have complete knowledge about a measurement, only knowing the way it is set up and the resulting information that it provides. Thus the physics is divided into quantum processes that can be construed as reversible interactions that do not leave records, and measurement interactions that do leave records.

Also in macroscopic processes the result of an observation is determined by both the external reality and the process of observation; e.g. the color of an object depends also on the eye that sees it, and different species have different retinal pigments. The Bohr-Heisenberg interpretation challenges the objective reality of quantum processes. This issue has enormous implications, particularly as quantum formalism applies to the whole of physics; thus, if there is no quantum reality, there is no reality at all (Penrose, 2005). Adhering to a realistic interpretation, the irreversibility of the measuring process, not the observation, determines the collapses of the wavefunction.

In the usual terminology that physicists use, reversible interactions are called "quantum processes", but this is just terminology. Prigogine (1980) highlighted that irreversible processes are as real as reversible ones, and that they play a constructive role, or a destructive one. Both creative and destructive processes are irreversible.

Periodic, chaotic, and biotic processes increase entropy. Entropy does not increase only with decay, as sometimes stated; in fact the greatest increase in entropy occurs with linear increases (or decreases) in quantity, such as leaps in biotic equations and in nature. Indeed all processes involve irreversible components in the sense that the second law of thermodynamics describes the unidirectional and hence irreversible increase in entropy. Computations are processes, and therefore they increase entropy. In the quantum realm, wave-function collapsing measurements are irreversible interactions.

The Copenhagen interpretation implies a quantum superposition, the combination of all the possible states of a system that undergoes collapse into a definite state only at the exact moment of measurement. Schrödinger refuted the uncertainty principle with a simple thought experiment (Schrödinger's cat) in which an indeterminacy originally restricted to the atomic domain becomes transformed into macroscopic indeterminacy, which can then be resolved by direct observation. Notably, many still take the idea of dead-and-alive cat seriously. On the contrary, Schrödinger intended the paradox as a reductio ad absurdum.31

The quantum concept of action relates energy and frequency as its inseparable components; in turn both of these two complementary opposites involve bipolarity –energy as polarity and as attraction and separation, and time as oscillation and cyclicity.

Second, quantum physics highlights the *complementarity of opposites* including the wave-particle duality, the superposition of opposites, and Schrödinger's interpretation of quantum physics as wave mechanics --waves involve an oscillation between opposites.

All the information about a particle is encoded in its wave function, which evolves according to the Schrödinger equation. But particle-like behavior is evident in quantum mechanical mea-surements. Upon measuring the location of the particle, the wave-function will "collapse" to a sharply peaked function at some location, and the measurement will return a well-defined position, a property traditionally associated with particles.

Wave–particle duality is the concept that all matter exhibits both wave and particle properties.32 This phenomenon has been verified for elementary particles, atoms and even molecules. Realistic interpretations of quantum mechanics explain wave-particle duality as a fundamental property of the Universe.33 As illustrated in Figure 2, there are realistic interpretations of the wave-particle duality.

Quantum electrodynamics provides a physical embodiment of information for computation. As charge, information is bipolar (1 and −1). At the quantum level, there are many properties that can also encode information, such as spin, nuclear spin, and color, all of which can in principle be measured simultaneously.

Spin was postulated by Goudsmit and Uhlenbeck to account for the magnetic properties of electrons by the fact that electrons are charged and rotating electrical charges generate magnetic fields (Pais, 1989). Spin state represent a direction in one dimension in physical space. The top and bottom perspective of the spin is equivalent to rotation in opposite directions.

The spin has only two values, ½ and −½, for electrons. Pauli's exclusion principle states that two identical fermions (electrons, protons, neutrons, quarks) cannot simultaneously occupy the same quantum state. If two fermions 1 and 2 are in states a and b respectively, the corresponding wavefunction ψ is

$$\psi = \psi 1 \, (a) \, \psi 2 \, (b) - \psi 1 \, (b) \, \psi 2 \, (a)$$

This anti-symmetric wave function requires two such entities located in the same place (e.g. two electrons in the same orbital) to have opposite spin. In a way Pauli's principle updates Aristotle's

Figure 18. Quaternity, the two fundamental pairs of conjugate variables in quantum mechanics

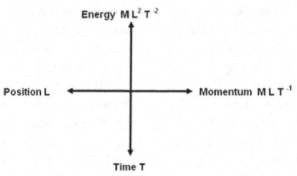

principle of local no contradiction, and thereby introduces dialectics.

The spin is continually and rapidly changing in the three dimensions of space. Thus, even when the initial state (such as up) is specified, it will change over time. When we measure the spin of an electron in one dimension, we necessarily affect its spin every other dimension of space. A property such as spin must be expressed by two complex Schrodinger-Dirac equations, thus four real numbers at every point in space. A measurement process for spin in one dimension (e.g. Stern and Gerlach experiment34) filters the system into two distinguishable states, up (+½ spin) and down (−½ spin) in physical space. Although the terms up and down mean linear opposition, in quantum mechanics they are used to refer to orthogonal states that we can combine in various proportions. The quantum state

$$|\psi> = \alpha |0> + \beta |1>$$

is usually described as a superposition of opposite orthogonal basis states.35 Actually there is no difference between basis and intermediate states other than what we choose as a basis in which to measure. "Superposition" means nothing other than taking the linear combination of orthogonal states. Although a given measurement selects a basis and we can determine only the fraction in each basis state |0> or |1>, the intermediate

states have real, verifiable consequences, which are significant for computation. We learn partial information about the complex numbers α and β. The qubit is thus described by four real numbers constrained by the absolute square of the wave function being constant. The qubit thus resides on the surface of a 3-sphere and is locally described by a three dimensional subspace, involving three orthogonal diameters, three pairs of opposites. Spin continually changes direction.

Hamilton's Quaternions serve as the group SU(2) to understand the quantum mechanics of spin. Hamilton's Quaternions are an algebraic structure on four dimensional space that turns out to have far reaching consequences for the structure of rotations in three-space and for many applications in physics including quantum mechanics (see later).

Quantum physics demonstrates that twoness is both fundamental and incomplete. Moreover, at the quantum level two particles that have interacted continue determining each other even after they are separated (entanglement), no matter how distant they are from each other (quantum non-locality).

Entanglement appears to play a key role in the design of protocols for transmitting quantum information in quantum cryptography and in quantum computing. In these cases one wants to design processes that will transmit quantum states without changing them. The transmission is accomplished by the use of entangled states in a "teleportation" procedure that involves a combination of measurements and correcting quantum processes. See (Nielsen & Chuang, 2000 for more details about teleportation). Entanglement may play a key role in quantum communication between different qubits and different computers.36

Spin state can be thought as representing a direction in one dimension in physical space. The spin is continually and rapidly changing in the three dimensions of space. Thus, even when the initial state is specified (such as up), over time it will change. When we measure the spin of an electron in one dimension, we necessarily affect its spin every other dimension of space. A property such as spin must be expressed by two complex Schrodinger-Dirac equations, thus four real numbers at every point in space. A measurement process for spin in one dimension filters the system into two distinguishable states, up ($+\frac{1}{2}$ spin) and down ($-\frac{1}{2}$ spin) in physical space. Although the terms up and down mean linear opposition, in quantum mechanics they are used to refer to orthogonal states that we can combine in various proportions. The quantum state

$$|\psi> = \alpha\,|0> + \beta\,|1>$$

is usually described as a superposition of opposite orthogonal basis states. Actually there is no difference between basis and intermediate states other than what is what we choose as a basis in which to measure. "Superposition" means taking the linear combination of orthogonal states. Although a given measurement selects a basis and we can determine only the fraction in each basis state $|0>$ or $|1>$, the intermediate states have real, verifiable consequences, which are significant for computation. We learn partial information about the complex numbers α and β.

The discovery of spin solved the contradiction between Pauli's exclusion principle (only one electron can occupy a given state) and the coexistence of two electrons in one atomic orbital ("duplexity"). Two electrons with opposite spins coexist in one orbital.

Such coexistence has implications regarding "uncertainty." Is there really a time in which a two electrons sharing one orbital quantum particle do not interact? Or do they separate from each other into different sides of an orbital as in the "split-p-orbital" model (Dewar & Sabelli, 1962).

If electrons restricted to an orbital (or an atom, a black body cavity, or a cable in an electrical circuit) interact with multiple entities such that it receives multiple inputs from many directions (spherical or "random" distribution), then its movement may be determined and possible chaotic or biotic, as these are the patterns generated by bipolar feedback. The demonstration of "erratic", locally diversifying, novelty generating, "biotic" pattern in the wave function of an electron restricted to a limited space (e.g. to a particular orbital of an atom) could be accounted for these interactions, particularly by interactions with paired electrons, similar in all respects but of opposite spin. We hypothesize that the spinning of quantum particles such as electrons may account for biotic patterns. Also, because each electron is negatively charged, it is in interaction with a positive "hole" in the vacuum (the positron).

Third, *quantum processes create structures* such as nucleons. Further, at least some quantum processes display biotic patterns (Sabelli & Kovacevic, 2003; 2006; Thomas et al, 2006; Sabelli & Thomas, 2008; Sabelli et al, forthcoming). The wave function of an electron in a box as described by Schrödinger's equation shows non-stationarity, temporal complexity, novelty, diversification, f-n power spectrum and relatively low entropy (Figure 1). Note, however, that we have not as yet observed biotic patterns in empirical data. Indirect evidence for creative features in quantum processes are the gravitational waves reaching us from all directions of space, which must therefore originate in LeMaitre's primordial "atom", before the formation of atoms as we know them.

Bios theory generalizes quantum processes as generic dynamics present at all levels of organization (Sabelli, 2005). Generalizing the notion of action quanta, we propose unipolar discrete action at all levels of organization (e.g. action potentials, cardiac contractions, individual persons). Generalizing quantum electrodynamics, we derive the notion that information is bipolar and that fundamental opposites exist at each level of organization, as illustrated by sex; cooperation and conflict; abundance and scarcity; true and false. Generalizing from the weak nuclear force and the strong nuclear force (quantum chromodynamics), we seek and find connectedness and tridimensionality at all levels of organization. At all levels there will be the three dimension of physical space, because all is material, as well as specific differences between these dimensions such as the tripolarity of quarks and of visual colors.

In summary, we speculate that quantum mechanics involves three fundamental regularities: (1) the collective of action quanta (where 'collective' means a set of energetic-material entities); (2) the collective of interacting opposites (charge, spin); and (3) novelty generating diversifying, complexity generating biotic patterns, the collective result of multiple bipolar interactions.

5. QUANTUM PHYSICS AND QUANTUM LOGIC

Many presentations of quantum physics imply that nature is "illogical", entities are in no specific state unless observed, the coexistence of contradictory properties must be accepted without question, and changes occur without cause. Einstein, Schrödinger and Bell, among others, found this formulation objectionable. Interpretations do not emerge from nature alone; they are processed by humans immersed in a given culture. Thus the task of developing quantum logic also involves the formulation of a realistic and rational interpretation of quantum phenomena.

Quantum processes have features sharply different from those of standard Boolean logic, so the possibility of developing quantum logic has been explored, starting with the 1936 paper by Birkhoff and von Neumann who addressed the inconsistency of commutativity in Boolean logic with the non-commutativity of complementary variables in quantum mechanics. Energy and time, and position and momentum do not commute. Heisenberg interpreted non-commutativity as uncertainty. However, in Bohr's view, non-commutativity implies a complementarity of opposites, which we have already encountered in macroscopic physics.

The distributive law of p and (q or *not q*) = (p and q) or (p and *not q*) applies in propositional logic, where p *and* q are propositional variables, but it can fail in quantum processes, where the symbols p and q refer to particles. For instance, if p = "the particle is moving to the right" and q = "the particle is in the interval [-1,1]" then the proposition "q or *not q*" is true, and so is p and (q or *not q*) = p. But the propositions "p and q" and "p and *not q*" may both be false, since they assert tighter restrictions on simultaneous values of position and momentum than is allowed by the uncertainty principle. So, "(p and q) or (p and *not q*)" is false.

Several definitions and models for "quantum logic" have been advanced including a Hilbert lattice (the set of closed subspaces of an infinite dimensional complex Hilbert space).[37] The basic idea of quantum logic is that propositions are replaced by subspaces of a Hilbert space. These subspaces correspond to subspaces of state vectors that correspond to certain physical conditions and to the possibility of observing those conditions corresponding to projection to that subspace. The background to this replacement is the basic structure of quantum theory where a state of a physical system corresponds to a vector in the

Hilbert space, and a physical process corresponds to a unitary (angle preserving) transformation of the Hilbert space.

The Hilbert space is endowed with a notion or perpendicularity (orthogonality) and negation is replaced by orthogonal complement. Thus we could write

~A = Perp(A) where Perp(A) is the set of vectors perpendicular to A. Then we have

~ ~ A = A just as in ordinary logic of negation.

The logical function 'and' $\cap$ and the logical function 'or' are defined as follows:

A $\cap$ B = the intersection of the subspaces A and B. This is again a subspace.

A $\cap$ B = the span of the subspaces A and B. This means all linear combinations of vectors from A and B. Again A or B is a subspace. The formal of logic of this way of defining words "not", "or" and 'and' is quite different from Boolean logic. For example, it is no longer the case that 'and' distributes over "or". This lack of distributivity is directly related to complementarity, but we will not go into that relationship here. The point about standard quantum logic is that it attempts to replace the use of the words 'not', 'or' and 'and' by new uses that correspond to how these words mean in describing the quantum world.

A qubit is a unit of quantum information with additional dimensions associated to the properties of quantum processes. The qubit is described by a state vector in a two-level quantum-mechanical system, which is formally equivalent to a two-dimensional vector space over the complex numbers. The qubit is described by four real numbers constrained by the absolute square of the wave function being constant. The qubit thus resides on the surface of a 3-sphere and is locally described by a three dimensional subspace, involving three orthogonal diameters, three pairs of opposites. The physical construction of a quantum computer is itself an arrangement of entangled atoms, and the qubit represents] both the state memory and the state of entanglement in a system. A quantum computation is performed by initializing a system

of qubits (a physical process that puts the system into an entangled state.)

The various properties of quantum action have significant implications regarding computation. First, macroscopic energy flow produces heat, and interactions produce decoherence of quantum superposition. Second, inter-actions are not instantaneous; they are communications via messengers and therefore they involve time.

At the quantum level, there are many oppositions that encode information, such as charge, spin, nuclear spin, color, etc., all of which can in principle be measured simultaneously. ,

Multiple dimensions enter in mathematics without any difficulty, and quantum processes are described in Hilbert space (a Euclidean-like space of infinite dimensions). The multidimensional space of quantum physics offers a natural realization for a multidimensional logic.

Obviously there are many dimensions that we have not defined, but the existence of which is made evident by time series analyses (e.g. correlation dimension, embedding dimension, etc.); instead of considering them as convenient mathematical conventions, we regard them as abstract representations of real dimensions, and. more specifically, as dimensions of form. Taking dimensionality as complexity, we interpret creativity as dimensiogenesis (Sabelli, 2005).

From a logical perspective, we note (1) the number of dimensions; (2) the nature of these dimensions; and (3) the polarity of each dimension (apolar, unipolar, bipolar).

To construct a general logic of quality, we propose as a general principle that for each level of organization there must be dimensions homologous38 to unidirectional action, bidimensional and bipolar information, a tridimensional space with different quality in each direction (like color), and the more complex forms generated by them. Starting with the concept of action, entities are represented in phase space, and the portrait of opposites requires a plane rather than a one-dimensional scale.

The basic idea of quantum logic is that propositions are replaced by subspaces of a Hilbert space. These subspaces correspond to subspaces of state vectors that correspond to certain physical conditions and to the possibility of observing those conditions corresponding to projection to that subspace. The background to this replacement is the basic structure of quantum theory where a state of a physical system corresponds to a vector in the Hilbert space, and a physical process corresponds to a unitary (angle preserving) transformation of the Hilbert space.

The Hilbert space is endowed with a notion of perpendicularity (orthogonality); negation is replaced by orthogonal complement. Thus we could write

$\sim V = Perp(V)$ where $Perp(V)$ is the set of vectors perpendicular to V. Then we have

$\sim\sim V = V$ just as in ordinary logic of negation. We also need and $\wedge$ and or V. These are defined as follows:

$V \wedge W$ = the intersection of the subspaces V and W. This is again a subspace.

$V \vee W$ = the span of the subspaces V and W. This means all linear combinations of vectors from V and W. Again V v W is a subspace. The formal of logic of this sort of negation, or and and is quite different from Boolean logic. For example, it is no longer the case that and distributes over or. This lack of distributivity is directly related to complementarity, but we will not go into that relationship here. The point about standard quantum logic is that it attempts to replace the use of the words 'not', 'or' and 'and' by new uses that correspond to how these words mean in describing the quantum world. We define the addition of vectors:

$v = (a_1, a_2, ..., a_n)$

$w = (b_1, b_2, ..., b_n)$

$v + w = (a_1, a_2, ..., a_n) + (b_1, b_2, ..., b_n) = (a_1 + b_1, a_2 + b_2, ..., a_n + b_n)$

and the scalar multiplication of vectors:

$v = (a_1, a_2, ..., a_n)$

$kv = (ka_1, ka_2, ..., ka_n)$

Given standard basis vectors:

$e_1 = (1, 0, 0, 0, ..., 0, 0)$

$e_2 = (0, 1, 0, 0, ..., 0, 0)$

$e_3 = (0, 0, 1, 0, ..., 0, 0)$

...

$e_n = (0, 0, 0, 0, ..., 0, 1),$

every vector is a unique superposition of standard basis vectors:

$(a_1, a_2, ..., a_n) = a_1 e_1 + a_2 e_2 + ... + a_n e_n$. A subspace W of R^n is a set of vectors that is closed under addition and scalar multiplication. Note that since k=0 is a scalar, O is always in any subspace. The intersection $W \wedge Z$ of any two subspaces is a subspace.

The span $W + Z = \{w + z \mid w$ is in W and z is in Z\} is a subspace if W and Z are subspaces.

Dot Product:

$v = (a_1, a_2, ..., a_n)$

$w = (b_1, b_2, ..., b_n)$

$<v|w> = a_1 b_1 + a_2 b_2 + ... + a_n b_n.$

(This is sometimes denoted $<v|w> = v.w.$)

Two vectors v and w are said to *perpendicular* if $<v|w> = 0$.

Given a subspace W, let

$\sim W = \{v \mid v$ is perpendicular to all vectors in W\}.

Proposition. If W is a subspace of R^n, then $\sim\sim W = W$. (proof omitted).

Let R, S and T be subspaces. Then

$$(R + S) + T = R + (S + T),$$

and $(R^\wedge S)^\wedge T = R^\wedge(S^\wedge T)$.

$$R + R = R.$$

$$R^\wedge R = R.$$

$$O^\wedge R = O.$$

$$O + R = R.$$

Let I denote the whole space R^n. Then

$$I^\wedge R = R$$

$$I + R = I.$$

And of course

$$I^\wedge O = O = O^\wedge I.$$

$$I^\wedge I = I$$

$$O^\wedge O = O$$

$$I + I = I$$

$$O + O = O$$

$$\sim O = I$$

$$\sim I = O.$$

As we see, O and I form a Boolean algebra, but the full algebra of subspaces is NOT Boolean. In particular, the distributive law does not hold. Let $S[v_1,...,v_r] = \{a_1 v_1 + ... + a_r v_r\}$

denote the subspace generated by the set of vectors $\{v_1,...,v_r\}$. Consider

$R = S[e_1]$, $S = S[e_2]$, and $V = S[e_1 + e_2]$. Then

$$V^\wedge R = O$$

$$V^\wedge S = O$$

But $V^\wedge(R + S) = V$. Thus $V^\wedge(R + S)$ is not equal to $V^\wedge R + V^\wedge S$.

To illustrate this non-distributivity, let e_1 and e_2 be the perpendicular basis vectors for R^2. Then we have, as above with $R + S = 1$ so that $V^\wedge(R+S) = V^\wedge 1 = V$, but $V^\wedge R = V^\wedge S = 0$.

Abstracting from quantum logic, Kauffman (2001) presented a logic that is naturally associated to linear spaces (vector spaces) as presented in Figure 15. A typical example of a linear space is the n-dimensional Euclidean space R^n whose elements are the vectors $\mathbf{v} = (a_1, a_2,...,a_n)$ where the a_i are real numbers. We will detail these notions in the sections to follow. Given a linear space V, it has not just vectors, but subspaces W. For example, if $V = R^3$, then V is a subspace of itself and there are the two-dimensional subspaces that are planes through the origin (The origin is the vector $O = (0,0,...,0)$.), the one dimensional sub-

Figure 19. R2 depiction

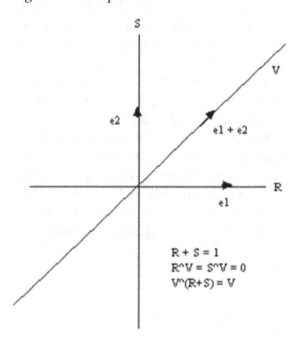

spaces consisting in lines through the origin, and the zero dimensional subspace consisting in the origin itself. We have also the notion of the collection of vectors that are perpendicular to a given vector or to all the vectors in a given subspace. We write ~W to denote the set of vectors perpendicular to the subspace W. If W and Z are two subspaces, then we let W^Z denote the intersection of W and Z, the set of all vectors that are common to both W and Z. If W and Z are two subspaces, we let W + Z denote the span of W and Z, the set of all sums of vectors from W and Z. The logic we are concerned with is the logic whose operations are:

1.   ~W (a form of negation)
2.   W^Z (a form of and)
3.   W + Z (a form of or).

Thinking of and (^) or (+) and not (~) in this way, leads to a geometrical logic that has different properties from standard Boolean logic. Because of its history we shall call the logic so produced quantum logic. In quantum logic any two possibilities (vectors) produce (by the process of addition or superposition) an infinite number of "intermediate" possibilities. Thus given vectors **v** and **w**, we can make all the superpositions $av + bw$ where a and b are real numbers. Quantum logic is a logic of possibilities with a distinctly geometric flavor. It differs from Boolean logic and it is related to human situations as well as quantum mechanical situations.

In quantum physics, vectors correspond to states of a quantum system. Perpendicular vectors correspond to complementary aspects (such as position and momentum). However, this kind of geometric logic may be applicable to domains that are not necessarily quantum mechanical.

Priority Supremacy Relations

Measurement in quantum physics, and hence in quantum computation, involves the priority of the quantum phenomena and the supremacy of the macroscopic measuring instrument. More generally, there is a priority of the quantum phenomena and the supremacy of the context.

In interpreting measurements, we must attend to the priority of reality and supremacy of interpretation. According to the Copenhagen interpretation of quantum mechanics, observations and observers determine physical reality. An observer in no way determines physical reality, but what does the observer determines? By setting up a particular way to make an experiment (e.g. phosphor screen for observing local interactions) the observer determines the form of the observations. The observer determines "what" can be measured. The observer sets a physical context. The observer does not determine how physical reality will fill in that context. The feedback loop relating the observer and the physical reality gives freedom for the observer to choose ways of observation and the physical reality responds to this by giving the observer corresponding results. These results then feedback and affect the structure of the theory. In physics there is no evidence whatsoever that the theory has any influence on the structure of the physical reality itself. The theory only affects our interaction with that reality. It is a confusion to think that the physical reality changes when the theory changes. In fact, in a certain sense, we can define physical reality to be that aspect of our experience that is independent of our theorizing. Note that our theories do change, and our ways of holding contexts and our languages do change. These are all aspects of our reality that change in relation to our theorizing and so these aspects are not in and of themselves part of the physical reality. This means that in order to know physical reality, we must engage in the bipolar feedback of theory and experiment. Otherwise, we shall not come to understand that which is independent of our particular theorizing. In this way our understanding of the nature of physical reality is in a constant state of evolution.

Cybernetic Logic and Quantum Gates

Computers are cybernetic machines. Cybernetics as well as logic study information at a higher level of complexity than Shannon's formulation of information in terms of entropy. Originally Cybernetics was regarded as the study of regulatory systems that serve to control. But, as the term *kybernētēs* (steersman, governor, pilot, helm, or rudder) indicates, steering includes decision, even creation, not simply control. While originally control, negative feedback, and homeostasis were the focus in Cybernetics, creation is brought to the fore by the generation of Bios (Sabelli, 2005) and Homeobios (Sabelli et al, in press) by bipolar (positive and negative) feedback.

The "general purpose" digital computer is constructed from electrical circuits connecting logical gates that represent Boolean logic functions (Figure 20, left). Boolean logic functions correspond to a mechanical, static, non-evolutionary worldview in which opposites exclude each other (principle of no contradiction). As a result, complex problems such as economic plans and predictions fail to be solved, and random changes are advanced as bet-

ter models than causal models. We envision the development of computers (Figure 20, right) that incorporate a world view focused on processes, evolution, and the creation of complexity via the interaction of opposites (such as quantum states). This involves three different problems: a logic, a cybernetic realization of such logic (as Shannon found for Boolean logic in electrical circuits), and the actual construction of such circuitry. The development of a logic that fits natural processes, including quantum phenomena, is the only issue addressed here, but the cybernetic realization of such logic seems feasible.

Quantum gates may use the superposition of quantum opposites to generate complex logical functions beyond those of Boolean logic. A quantum logical gate operates on a small number of qubits (one or two qubits, just like the common classical logic gates operate on one or two bits). Quantum logic gates can be described by 2×2 or 4×4 unitary matrices.

Quantum gates (Nielsen & Chuang, 2000) offer rich models for oppositions. While in standard logic opposition leads to one operation, negation, mechanized by the NOT gate in standard computers, quantum computation already involves several types of one-qubit gates that can model the implication of opposites.

To approach the complexity of nature, computers may need to use multiple types of gates, including complex gates. There may be Boolean

Figure 20. Digital and quantum computers

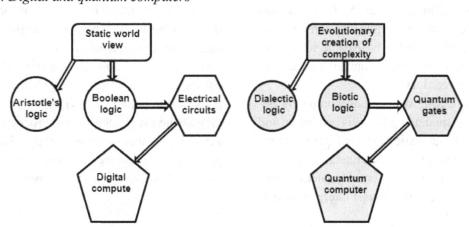

like gates channeling action, as they form lattices ordered in spacetime; also, by necessity, every quantum computer must include macroscopic connections.

The observation of biotic patterns in the wave function of an electron in a box as described by Schrödinger's equation may provide a starting point for biotic gates in quantum computation. Biotic processes can be useful as a model for logic because biotic patterns exist at all levels of organization. As quantum processes generate biotic patterns, we propose to develop quantum devices as logical gates. Biotic gates may be based on catastrophes, biotic equations, the generation of chaos in Newtonian equations (Poincaré), expansion in relativity equations (Friedmann, Lemaitre), and Schrödinger's and Dirac's equations.

The actual construction of quantum computers is an altogether different matter. Only quantum states of a few qubits have been prepared; sufficiently accurate quantum gates have not as yet been demonstrated. At this time, quantum computing still is a subject of academic rather than practical interest. Qubit manipulation increases the size of the computer and is costly so at this time there is no general speed advantage for quantum computers (Knill, 2010). Quantum computation faces enormous technical difficulties, starting with working at single-atom and single-photon scales, and then putting quantum gates together into circuits and preventing decoherence. All over the world many scientists are developing many different physical implementations for quantum computers, including photons (Zeilinger et al 2005). Quantum dots allow to one to employ single electrons. Recent experiments show that it is feasible to operate single-electron spins in quantum dots as quantum bits (Koppens et al, 2006).

The engineering of quantum computers depends on how quantum physics is conceived and developed. Probabilistic models of quantum processes are taught as fact, but the fundamental equations of quantum physics are entirely deterministic; this is compatible with a causal interpretation of physics à la Einstein and Schrödinger rather than with stochasticity. An important implication is that quantum processes always are in specific states. Being actions, quantum entities are in continual, spontaneous change, until an interaction (such as a measurement) determines, i.e. fixes one parameter. Many physicists question whether or not a quantum entity is in a particular state if nobody observes it (Wheeler, 1957). A qubit is said by some to exist in more than one state, until measuring causes that superposition to "collapse" into one state or the other. Also Schrödinger's cat is said to exist in more than one state until we open the cage. With apologies to many authors who misquote Schrödinger, we must let the cat out of the bag: he intended, and in our opinion succeeded, to refute the notion that the state of a physical system is "undefined" until observed by the fact that the cat is alive or dead regardless of our knowing it. Claiming that quantum particles are in no particular state unless observed pushes us into metaphysical idealism akin to that of Bishop Berkeley, who doubted whether or not a falling tree makes a sound when nobody hears it. In the case of the quantum system the state is defined exactly by the Schrodinger or Dirac equations. Measurement of the state elicits an aspect of the actuality.

Another practically important issue is energetic. Quantum processes do not generate heat and entropy; electrons moving in atomic orbitals do not heat up and radiate. Could then reversible gates work like Maxwell's demons, generating information without increasing entropy? Even if this could be possible, computation involves macroscopic processes such as measurement. Although information can be expressed in different ways (e.g. as voice, written words, or action potentials in brain neurons) without changing it, they all involve macroscopic processes in irreversible time that increase entropy. Macroscopic physical processes are not reversible. Computers cannot work like Maxwell's demons.

In physical processes, there is immense information involved in quantum superposition which is not communicated; communication reduces it to two complementary opposites. This is relevant to quantum computation: we can process much at the quantum level without producing heat (entropy) until we measure it. At the psychobiological level, there is an immense amount of information at the biological level that remains largely unconscious, and only the small tip of the iceberg becomes conscious. The existence of two levels of information in both natural and mental processes indicates an interesting parallel between them. The existence of two levels of information seems a very general phenomenon. For instance the chemical properties of an atom are given by the valence electrons, not by the core electrons and the nucleus.

One needs to perform computations using quantum processes and reduce as much as possible the number of macroscopic interactions such as measurement and communication with the human operator. A current focus in quantum computing is the design of logically reversible gates which could minimize energy cost (Landauer's principle, 1961) and prevent loss of information. Note, however, that irreversibility emerges also from creation not only from destruction. A dynamic logic by necessity must include logically irreversible gates. Irreversibility is a sine qua non of creativity. It also appears in simpler processes. Although equilibrium is often highlighted as emblematic of reversibility, equilibration is an irreversible process: once trajectories reach the attractor, we cannot know their point of origin. The Schrödinger equation generates bios, and biotic processes are not mathematically reversible (Sabelli, 2005).

The current focus on reversible quantum gates is driven by the need to protect information and the difficulty in attaining reversibility. But, based on the irreversibility of quantum measurements as well as of creative and destructive processes, we conclude that irreversible, entropy generating, gates may contribute to quantum computation in addition to 'economical' (not entropy producing) reversible gates, the current goal in the design of quantum gates. In fact, quantum computational processes are currently divided into reversible unitary gates and irreversible acts of measurement. These acts of measurement are irreversible processes and can be regarded as irreversible gates. In a fully quantum mechanical view of the world, the acts of measurement are also described by irreversible quantum processes, and the irreversibility of these measurements is a matter of ignorance on the part of the observer. This is the texture of an external view of the quantum world. If, on the other hand, we think about actual quantum processes such as the adiabatic transition from high energies and a soup of quarks and gluons to a world of protons and atoms, then it is natural to describe such a transition as irreversible. Taking such a view, one can ask to find irreversible quantum processes more structured than abstract measurements of states that will yield quantum information and effect the development of quantum computers. Such processes are used – for example the averaging measurements in NMR quantum computing. We speculate that the discovery of such irreversible quantum gates can lead to significant new developments in quantum computing, and perhaps such gates will open the door to the use of biotic patterns in quantum computing.

The real power of quantum computation has been the development of new algorithms that allow exploitation of quantum superposition. As a result we can now solve problems such as factorization, and come up with new methods to deal with encryption. We propose here to make further use of quantum superposition to develop a logic that is dynamic rather than static, dialectic rather than oppositional, and creative rather than classificatory.

A qubit has two distinguishable configurations, just as 0 and 1 in Boolean logic, but the qubit's states can be in any combination or superposition of these configurations (Knill, 2010).

Quantum processes provide in principle a way to move from to a dynamic biotic logic that incorporates mathematical structures, physical principles and psychological insights far beyond philosophy.

Biotic Logic, Quantum Logic, and Quantum Computation

The empirical success of quantum mechanics calls for a transformation of logic itself, and is connected with a realistic interpretation of quantum mechanics. We propose a creative logic grounded on quantum physics for classic and quantum computation which involves the following concepts: (1) action as dynamic identity; (2) opposition as a fundamental twoness which is self-referential (opposites overlap and separate, cooperate and conflict, persist and bifurcate); (3) tridimensional conceptual space; (4) generation of higher levels of complexity (information) that are homologous (new forms of action, opposition, space and generation); (5) mutual feedback between simpler actions that have priority and complex levels that have the supremacy of higher density of information. In summary, quantum logic is thus dialectic, chromatic, and biotic.

The implementation of a complex logic is not a matter of choice. Lattices, Groups, Topology and even more complex mathematical structures are needed to portray nature.

As discussed earlier, maximal energy and the maximal and most symmetric coexistence of opposites occur at the vertex of the diamond of opposites. One may thus initialize a high energy, high bipolarity gate.

Quantum computation may not only increase speed. We propose a different use for quantum computation: to provide a mechanism to generate new hypotheses. A question may be the starting point of scientific research, but to advance one needs testable hypotheses. Hence the generation of a set of hypotheses that can be tested and compared is a fundamental step in scientific research and in social planning.

Here we outline a new approach that adapts the logic of the computer to the logic of nature as embodied by both quantum computing devices and by natural and human processes. Regarding quantum physics as the fundamental logic of nature demands to consider its theory as logical principles. To find a logical interpretation to quantum principles should not be regarded as a proposal or a matter of choice, but as a task to be accomplished. While we are far from attaining it, such goal can be reached. The continuity of evolution requires that the same fundamental forms must be expressed at all levels of organization, so the principles of quantum physics and the principles of rational thinking must be homologous.

Logic (mathematical, computational, and philosophical) develops in a tension between the logic of nature–quantum and classic physics, and the logic of human behaviour– socioeconomics and psychology. Both the physical and the human logic each involves at least two levels. Even from the perspective of physics, computation involves quantum processes that have priority and macroscopic interactions that have supremacy. Material realities –physical and economic—have priority, while ideological and psychological interpretations have supremacy. Thus electrons are in particular states, albeit continuously changing, regardless of whether we observe them or not, and quantum computers are designed according to ideological presuppositions, not simply as determined by quantum physics. Strict adherence to the different meaning of terms in common language and in the various disciplines is required for interdisciplinary communication and for clear thinking.

Attending to both physical and human processes, both of which are at least biotic, and often much more complex, we propose a biotic logic that may be implemented by quantum computers. But even before the enormous engineering problems involved in this enterprise are solved, biotic logic can guide current computers. Conversely, models for biotic logic may help one to develop quantum computation. They may also help us to integrate multiple levels of organization in our conception of nature and of society. The concept of co-creation supports a healthier, more tolerant and more creative approach to personal and social behavior.

ACKNOWLEDGMENT

We are thankful to the Society for the Advancement for Clinical Philosophy (SACP) for its support, and to Mrs. Maria McCormick for her gifts to SACP. We are thankful to Lazar Kovacevic for his work in the early part of this research, to Gerald H. Thomas for further research and co-authoring the first version of his chapter, to Valerie Bush-Zurlent, Jerry Konecki and Linnea Carlson-Sabelli for fruitful discussion of this article, and to Atoor Lawandow for technical support.

REFERENCES

Adler, R. L., Konheim, A. G., & McAndrew, M. H. (1965). Topological entropy. *Transactions of the American Mathematical Society, 114*, 309–319.

Bateson, G. (1979). *Mind and nature: A necessary unity.* Toronto, Canada: Bantam.

Birkhoff, G. (1967). *Lattice theory.* Providence, RI: American Mathematical Society.

Bohm, D., & Peat, F. D. (1987). *Science, order, and creativity.* New York, NY: Bantam.

Bourbaki, N. (1952). *Éléments de mathématique.* Paris, France: Actualités Scientifiques et Industrielles.

Campbell, P. J. (1974). Biological reference materials in microampoules. *Journal of Biological Standardization, 2*, 269–270.

Capra, F. (1975). *The Tao of physics.* Boulder, CO: Shambhala.

Carlson-Sabelli, L. (2005). Co-creation practice: Education, nursing and psychodrama. In H. Sabelli (Ed.), *Bios: A study of creation* (609-618). Singapore: World Scientific.

Carlson-Sabelli, L., & Sabelli, H. (1992 a). Phase plane of opposites: A method to study change in complex processes, and its application to sociodynamics and psychotherapy. *The Social Dynamicist, 3*, 1–6.

Carlson-Sabelli, L., Sabelli, H., Patel, M., & Holm, K. (1992 b). The union of opposites in sociometry: An empirical application of process theory. *The Journal of Group Psychotherapy, Psychodrama and Sociometry, 44*, 147–171.

Carlson-Sabelli, L., Sabelli, H., Zbilut, J., Patel, M., Messer, J., & Walthall, K. … Zdanovics, O. (1994). How the heart informs about the brain. A process analysis of the electrocardiogram. In R. Trappl, (Ed.), *Cybernetics and Systems `94.* Singapore: World Scientific.

Carroll, S. B. (2001). Chance and necessity: the evolution of morphological complexity and diversity. *Nature, 409*, 1102–1109.

Chaisson, E. J. (2001). *Cosmic evolution.* Cambridge, MA: Harvard University Press.

Cohen, J., & Stewart, I. (1995). *The collapse of chaos.* New York, NY: Penguin.

Dewar, M. J. S., & Sabelli, N. L. (1962). The split p-orbital (SPO) method. *Physical Chemistry, 66*, 2300–2316.

Dietzgen, J. (1906). *The positive outcome of philosophy* (Unterman, E., Trans.). Chicago, IL: Charles H. Kerr & Company.

Dietzgen, J. (2010). *The nature of human brain work: An introduction to dialectics.* Oakland, CA: PM Press.

Ellis, G. F. R. (2004). *Science in faith and hope: An interaction.* Philadelphia, PA: Quaker Books.

Ellis, G. F. R. (2005). Physics, complexity and causality. *Nature, 435,* 743.

Farmelo, G. (Ed.). (2003). *It must be beautiful.* London, UK: Granta Books.

Feynman, R. P. (1996). *Feynman lectures on computation* (Hey, A. J. G., & Allen, R. W., Eds.). Reading, MA: Addison-Wesley.

Feynman, R. P. (1998). *Statistical mechanics: A set of lectures.* Boulder, CO: Westview Press.

Foerster von, H. (1953). Cybernetics: Circular causal and feedback mechanisms in biological and social systems. *Southern Medical Journal, 46,* 726–737.

Gal-Or, B. (1972). The crisis about the origin irreversibility and time anisotro. *Science, 176,* 11–17.

Gauthier, Y. (1984). Hegel's logic from a logical point of view . In Cohen, R. S., & Wartofsky, M. W. (Eds.), *Hegel and the sciences* (pp. 303–310). New York, NY: D. Reidel Publishing.

Gell-Mann, M. (1994). *The quark and the jaguar.* Amherst, MA: Owl Books.

Georgescu-Roegen, N. (1971). *Entropy: A new worldview.* New York, NY: Bantam Books.

Gerdes, P., & Arrancar, O. (1983). *Karl Marx: Arrancar o véu misterioso à matemática.* Maputo, Mozambique: Universidade Eduardo Mondlane.

Guastello, S., & Bond, R. W. (2007). A swallowtail catastrophe model for the emergence of leadership in coordination-intensive groups. *Nonlinear Dynamics Psychology and Life Sciences, 11,* 235–251.

Hempel, C. G. (1945). Studies in the logic of confirmation I. *Mind, 54,* 1–26.

Hempel, C. G. (1945). Studies in the logic of confirmation II. *Mind, 54,* 97–121.

Joja, A. (1969). *La lógica dialéctica y las ciencias* (Pérez, M. S., Trans.). Buenos Aires, Argentina: Juárez.

Jung, C. G. (1971). *Four archetypes* (Hull, R. F. C., Trans.). Princeton, NJ: Princeton University Press.

Kauffman, L. (2001). *Knots and physics.* Singapore: World Scientific.

Kauffman, L. (2004). Non-commutative worlds. *New Journal of Physics, 6,* 173–210.

Kauffman, L., & Sabelli, H. (1998). The process equation. *Cybernetics and Systems, 29,* 345–362.

Kauffman, L., & Sabelli, H. (2003). Mathematical bios. *Kybernetes, 31,* 1418–1428.

Kauffman, L., & Sabelli, H. (forthcoming). Riemann's zeta function displays a biotic pattern of diversification, novelty, and complexity. *Cybernetics and Systemics Journal.*

Kauffman, L. H. (2004). Bio-logic. *AMS Contemporary Mathematics Series, 304,* 313–340.

Knill, E. (2010). Quantum computing. *Nature, 463,* 441–443.

Koppens, F. H. L., Buizert, C., Tielrooij, K. J., Vink, L. T., Nowack, K. C., & Meunier, T. (2006). Driven coherent oscillations of a single electron spin in a quantum dot. *Nature, 442,* 766–771.

Kosok, M. (1984). The dynamics of Hegelian dialectics, and nonlinearity in the sciences. In R. S. Cohen & M. W. Wartofsky (Eds.), *Hegel and the sciences* (311-348). New York, NY: D. Reidel Publishing.

Kuhn, T. S. (1962). *The structure of scientific revolutions.* Chicago, IL: University of Chicago Press.

Ladd, T. D., Jelezko, F., Laflamme, R., Nakamura, Y., Monroe, C., & O'Brian, J. L. (2010). Quantum computers. *Nature, 464,* 45–53.

Lakatos, I. (1976). *Proofs and refutations*. New York, NY: Cambridge University Press.

Landauer, R. (1961). Irreversibility and heat generation in the computing process. *IBM Journal of Research and Development, 3*, 183–191.

Lang, K. R., & Gingerich, O. (1979). *A source book in astronomy and astrophysics, 1900-1975*. Cambridge, MA: Harvard University Press.

Lanyon, B. P., Weinhold, T. J., Langford, N. K., Barbieri, M., James, D. F. V., Gilchrist, A., & White, A. G. (2007). Experimental demonstration of a compiled version of Shor's algorithm with quantum entanglement. *Physical Review Letters, 99*, 250505–3.

Lawvere, F. W. (1996). Unity and identity of opposites in calculus and physics. *Applied Categorical Structures, 4*, 167–174.

Lawvere, F. W., & Schanuel, S. H. (1982). *Categories in continuum physics: Lectures given at a workshop held at SUNY, Buffalo 1982*. New York, NY: Springer.

Lawvere, F. W., & Schanuel, S. H. (1997). *Conceptual mathematics: A first introduction to categories*. New York, NY: Cambridge University Press.

Lefebvre, H. (1969). *Logique formelle, logique dialectique*. Paris, France: Editions Anthropos.

Levy, A., Alden, D., & Levy, C. (2006). Biotic patterns in music presented at the society for chaos theory in psychology & life sciences. 16th Annual International Conference 4-6 August 2006 Baltimore MD, USA.

Levy-Carciente, S., Sabelli, H., & Jaffe, K. (2004). Complex patterns in the oil market. *Intersciencia, 29*, 320–323.

Lu, C. Y., Browne, D. E., Yang, T., & Pan, J. W. (2007). Demonstration of a compiled version of Shor's quantum factoring algorithm using photonic qubits. *Physical Review Letters, 99*, 250504–250508.

Marx, K., & Engels, F. (1978). *The Marx and Engels reader* (Tucker, R. C., Ed.). New York, NY: Norton and Company.

McCulloch, W. S., & Pitts, W. (1943). A logical calculus of the ideas immanent in nervous activity. *The Bulletin of Mathematical Biophysics, 5*, 115–133.

Nielsen, M. A., & Chuang, I. L. (2000). *Quantum computation and quantum information*. New York, NY: Cambridge University Press.

Pais, A. (1989). George Uhlenbeck and the discovery of electron spin. *Physics Today, 42*, 30–40.

Papa, M. A. (2008). Progress towards gravitational wave astronomy. *Classical and Quantum Gravity, 25*, 114009–11401.

Patel, M., & Sabelli, H. (2003). Autocorrelation and frequency analysis differentiate cardiac and economic bios from 1/F noise. *Kybernetes, 32*, 692–702.

Peitgen, H. O., Jurgens, H., & Saupe, D. (1992). *Chaos and fractals*. New York, NY: Springer.

Penrose, R. (2005). *The road to reality*. New York, NY: Knopf.

Piaget, J. (1950). *Introduction à l'épistémologie génétique*. Paris, France: Presses Universitaires de France.

Planty-Bonjour, G. (1965). *Le categories du materialisme dialectique*. Paris, France: Presses Universitaires de France.

Politzer, G. (1928). *Critique des fondements de la psychologie*. Paris, France: Le Editions Rieder.

Politzer, G. (1948). *Principes élementaires de philosophie*. Paris, France: Messidor Scandéditions.

Popper, K. R. (1992). *The logic of scientific discovery*. New York, NY: Routledge.

Popper, K. R. (2003). *Conjectures and refutations: The growth of scientific knowledge*. New York, NY: Routledge.

Prahalad, C. K., & Ramaswamy, V. (2000, January 1). Co-opting customer competence. *Harvard Business Review, 78*(1), 79–87.

Prigogine, I. (1980). *From being to becoming*. San Francisco, CA: Freeman.

Prigogine, I. (1984). *Order out of chaos*. Boston, MA: Shambhala Publications.

Rescher, N. (1996). *Process metaphysics*. Albany, NY: State University of New York.

Riegel, K. (1979). *Foundations of dialectical psychology*. London, UK: Academic Press.

Robertson, R. (1995). *Jungian archetypes*. York Beach, ME: Nicholas-Hay.

Sabelli, A. (1952). *Escritos*. Private edition, Buenos Aires.

Sabelli, H. (1964). A pharmacological strategy for the study of central modulator linkages. In Wortis, J. (Ed.), *Recent advances in biological psychiatry* (pp. 145–182). New York, NY: Plenum Press.

Sabelli, H. (1971). An attempt to formalize some aspects of dialectic logic, Beyer. In R. Wilhelm (Ed.). *Hegel-Jahrbuch* (211-213). Meisenheim am Glan, Germany: Verlag Anton Hain.

Sabelli, H. (1972). A pharmacological approach for modeling neuronal nets. In Drischeland, H., & Dattmar, P. (Eds.), *Biocybernetics* (pp. 1–9). Jena, Germany: Veb Gustav Fischer Verlag.

Sabelli, H. (1984). Mathematical dialectics, scientific logic and the psychoanalysis of thinking. In Cohen, R. S., & Wartofsky, M. W. (Eds.), *Hegel and the sciences* (pp. 349–359). New York, NY: D. Reidel Publishing.

Sabelli, H. (1989). *Union of opposites: A comprehensive theory of natural and human processes*. Lawrenceville, NJ: Brunswick.

Sabelli, H. (1994). Entropy as symmetry: Theory and empirical support. In B. Brady & L. Peeno (Eds.), *Proceedings International Systems Society 38th Annual Meeting* (pp. 1483-1496).

Sabelli, H. (1995). Non-linear dynamics as a dialectic logic. *Proceedings of International Systems Society* (pp. 101-112).

Sabelli, H. (1998). The union of opposites: From Taoism to process theory. *Systems Research, 15*, 429–441.

Sabelli, H. (2000). Complement plots: analyzing opposites reveals Mandala-like patterns in human heartbeats. *International Journal of General Systems, 29*, 799–830.

Sabelli, H. (2001). Novelty, a measure of creative organization in natural and mathematical time series. *Nonlinear Dynamics Psychology and Life Sciences, 5*, 89–113.

Sabelli, H. (2001). The co-creation hypothesis. In Ragsdell, G., & Wilby, J. (Eds.), *Understanding complexity*. London, UK: Kluwer Academics Publishers.

Sabelli, H. (2003). Mathematical development: A theory of natural creation. *Kybernetes, 32*, 752–766.

Sabelli, H. (2005). *Bios. A study of creation*. Singapore: World Scientific.

Sabelli, H. (2008). Bios theory of innovation. *The Innovation Journal: The Public Sector Innovation Journal, 13*. Retrieved September 1, 2010, from http://www.innovation.cc/scholarly_style-articles.htm

Sabelli, H. (2008). How medicine informs informatics: Information is asymmetry, not entropy. *The Open Cybernetics and Systemics Journal, 2*, 93-108. Retrieved from http://www.bentham.org/open/tocsj/openaccess2.htm

Sabelli, H. (forthcoming). The biotic pattern of prime numbers. *Cybernetics and Systemics Journal*.

Sabelli, H. (forthcoming). Biothermodynamics. *Open Cybernetics and Systemics Journal*.

Sabelli, H., & Abouzeid, A. (2003). Definition and empirical characterization of creative processes. *Nonlinear Dynamics Psychology and Life Sciences, 7*, 35–47.

Sabelli, H., & Carlson-Sabelli, L. (1991). Process theory as a framework for comprehensive psychodynamic formulations. *Genetic, Social, and General Psychology Monographs, 1*, 5–27.

Sabelli, H., & Carlson-Sabelli, L. (1996). *As simple as one, two, three. Arithmetic: A simple, powerful, natural and dynamic logic* (pp. 543–554). Louisville, Kentucky: Proceedings International Systems Society.

Sabelli, H., & Carlson-Sabelli, L. (2005). Bios, a process approach to living system theory. *Systems Research and Behavioral Science, 23*, 323–336.

Sabelli, H., Carlson-Sabelli, L., Patel, M., Zbilut, J., Messer, J., & Walthall, K. (1995). Psycho-cardiological portraits: A clinical application of process theory . In Abraham, F. D., & Gilgen, A. R. (Eds.), *Chaos theory in psychology* (pp. 107–125). Westport, CT: Greenwood.

Sabelli, H., & Kauffman, L. (1999). The process equation: Formulating and testing the process theory of systems. *Cybernetics and Systems, 30*, 261–294.

Sabelli, H., & Kauffman, L. (2004). Bios and bipolar feedback: Mathematical models of creative processes. *Journal of Applied System Studies, 5*, 21–34.

Sabelli, H., Kauffman, L., Patel, M., Sugerman, A., Carlson-Sabelli, L., Afton, D., & Konecki, J. (1997). How is the universe, that it creates a human heart? Part II. Co-creation, evolution and entropy. In Y. P. Rhee & K. D. Bailey (Eds.), *Systems thinking, globalization of knowledge, and communitarian ethics: Proceedings of the International Systems Society* (pp. 924-935). Seoul, South Korea.

Sabelli, H., & Kovacevic, L. (2003). *Biotic expansion of the universe*. International Conference on Advances in Internet, Processing, Systems, and Interdisciplinary Research. Electronic Publication IPSI-2003.

Sabelli, H., & Kovacevic, L. (2006). Quantum bios and biotic complexity in the distribution of galaxies. *Complexity, 11*, 14–25.

Sabelli, H., & Kovacevic, L. (2008). Biotic complexity of population dynamics. *Complexity, 13*, 47–55.

Sabelli, H., & Kovacevic, L. (forthcoming). Economic bios. *Kybernetes*.

Sabelli, H., & Lawandow, A. (forthcoming). Homeobios: The pattern of heartbeats in newborns, adults, and elderly persons. *Nonlinear Dynamics Psychology and Life Sciences*.

Sabelli, H., Lawandow, A., & Kopra, A. R. (2010). Asymmetry, symmetry and beauty. *Symmetry, 2*, 1591–1624.

Sabelli, H., Patel, M., & Sugerman, A. (2004 b). Flux and action: Process statistics. *Journal of Applied System Studies*, *5*, 54–66.

Sabelli, H., Patel, M., Sugerman, A., Kovacevic, L., & Kauffman, L. (2004). Process entropy, a multidimensional measure of diversity and symmetry. *Journal of Applied System Studies*, *5*, 129–143.

Sabelli, H., Patel, M., & Venkatachalapathy, V. K. (2004 c). Action and information: Repetition, rise and fall. *Journal of Applied System Studies*, *5*, 67–77.

Sabelli, H., Sugerman, A., Kovacevic, L., Kauffman, L., Carlson-Sabelli, L., Patel, M., & Konecki, J. (2005). Bios data analyzer. *Nonlinear Dynamics Psychology and Life Sciences*, *9*, 505–538.

Sabelli, H., & Thomas, G. (2008). The future quantum computer: Biotic complexity. In Orsucci, F., & Sala, N. (Eds.), *Reflecting interfaces: The complex coevolution of information technology ecosystems*. Hershey, PA: IGI Global.

Sabelli, H., Thomas, J., Kovacevic, L., Lawandow, A., & Horan, D. (2010). Biotic dynamics of galactic distribution, gravitational waves, and quantum processes. A causal theory of cosmological evolution. In A. D. Wachter & R. J. Propst (Eds.), *Black holes and galaxy formation*. New York, NY: Nova Science Publishers. Retrieved from https://www.novapublishers.com/catalog/product_info.php?products_id=19328

Sabelli, H., Zarankin, S., & Carlson-Sabelli, L. (2004 a). Opposition: The phase space of opposites in psychology, sociology and economics. *Journal of Applied System Studies*, *5*, 78–93.

Saunders, P. T. (1980). *An introduction to catastrophe theory*. New York, NY: Cambridge University Press.

Shannon, C. E. (1940). *A symbolic analysis of relay and switching circuits*. Massachusetts Institute of Technology, Department of Electrical Engineering.

Shor, P. W. (1997). Polynomial-time algorithms for prime factorization and discrete logarithms on a quantum computer. *SIAM Journal on Scientific Computing*, *26*, 1484–1509.

Smerz, K. E., & Guastello, S. (2008). Cusp catastrophe model for binge drinking in a college population. *Nonlinear Dynamics Psychology and Life Sciences*, *12*, 205–224.

Spencer-Brown, G. (1979). *Laws of form*. New York, NY: E. P. Dutton.

Sugerman, A., & Sabelli, H. (2003). Novelty, diversification and nonrandom complexity define creative processes. *Kybernetes*, *32*, 829–836.

Thom, R. (1983). *Mathematical models of morphogenesis*. Chichester, UK: Ellis Horwood.

Thom, R. (1994). *Structural stability and morphogenesis*. Boulder, CO: Westview Press.

Thomas, G. H. (2006). *Geometry, language and strategy*. Singapore: World Scientific.

Thomas, G. H., Sabelli, H., Kovacevic, L., & Kauffman, L. (2006). *Biotic patterns in Schrödinger's equation and the evolution of the universe*. Retrieved April 26, 2011, from http://www.necsi.edu/events/iccs6/papers/b7794439db-c6b0515c7659d6088d.pdf

Vandersypen, L. M. K., Matthias, S., Gregory, B., Yannoni, C. S., Sherwood, M. H., & Chuang, I. L. (2001). Experimental realization of Shor's quantum factoring algorithm using nuclear magnetic resonance. *Nature*, *414*, 883–887.

Watson, J. D., & Crick, F. H. C. (1953). A structure for deoxyribose nucleic acid. *Nature*, *171*, 737–738.

Wheeler, J. A. (1957). Assessment of Everett's "relative state" formulation of quantum theory. *Reviews of Modern Physics, 29*, 463–465.

Xu, L. D., & Li, L. X. (1989). Complementary opposition as a systems concept. *Systems Research, 6*, 91–101.

Zeilinger, A., Weihs, G., Jennewein, T., & Aspelmeyer, M. (2005). Happy centenary, photon. *Nature, 433*, 230–238.

ENDNOTES

1.   This chapter extends "The Future Quantum Computer: Biotic Complexity" co-authored by Sabelli and Thomas, published in the first edition of this book.

2.   The algorithm first finds the period of a function, and then finds the period using the quantum Fourier transform. Shor's algorithm is important because it can be used to break a widely used public-key cryptography scheme.

3.   ψ does not describe a probability because it involves negative and complex numbers and it generates cancellations (destructive interference) while probabilities are neither negative nor complex, and they cannot generate cancellation (Penrose 2004).

4.   Nicolas Bourbaki was the pseudonym adopted during the 1930s by a group of young French mathematicians who undertook the collective writing of an up-to-date treatise of mathematical analysis. Bourbaki's books became classic in many areas of mathematics and in which their concepts and nomenclature were adopted as standard. Bourbaki's influence was strong in topology and algebra but not in logic.

5.   In his physics, separating it completely from his metaphysics, Descartes invested matter with self-creative power viewed matter and as the only basis of being and perceiving. Descartes was still living when Leroy transferred to the human soul the Cartesian construction of animals, and explained the soul as a mode of the body and ideas as mechanical movements. Leroy even believed that Descartes had dissembled his real opinion. Descartes protested, but he had good reasons to hide his beliefs from the church.

6.   Prigogine, in *Order out of Chaos* (p. 116), describes: "It is generally accepted that the problem of time took on a new importance during the nineteenth century. Indeed, the essential role of time began to be noticed in all fields – in geology, in biology, in language, as well as in the study of human social evolution and ethics. But it is interesting that the specific form in which time was introduced in physics, as a tendency toward homogeneity and death [i.e., entropy], reminds us more of ancient mythological and religious archetypes than of the progressive complexification and diversification described by biology and the social sciences. The return of these ancient themes can be seen as a cultural repercussion of the social and economic upheavals of the time. The rapid transformation of the technological mode of interaction with nature, the constantly accelerating pace of change experienced by the nineteenth century, produced a deep anxiety. This anxiety is still with us and takes various forms, from the repeated proposals for a 'zero growth' society or for a moratorium on scientific research to the announcement of 'scientific truths' concerning our disintegrating universe."

7.   Time is irreversible not only from the perspective of biology but also in physics. Charge, parity and time together are conserved (CPT invariance), but the observed violation of CP invariance implies that time is not reversible, although time reversibility is claimed as "fact" in many descriptions of

8.   classic, relativistic and quantum mechanics, and in theoretical discussions of quantum computation (see later).

8.   The partial, rather than total, order of lattices corresponds to the limitations in the definition of simultaneity implicit in Relativity Theory.

9.   Energy is conserved in all physical processes, and this fact is more basic than thermodynamic decay.

10. We thus challenge the usual statistical interpretation of quantum mechanics that takes quantum probability theory as a genuine doctrine of chances.

11. Newton's use of the term action, currently dismissed as "obsolete", calls attention to the inseparability of action and counter-action at the simplest level.

12. 'Creation" comes from the Latin 'creare' meaning "to give birth'.

13. Erich Jantsch (1975) developed the concept of self-organization, Stuart Kauffman (1993) studied non-random processes of evolution, Ben Goertzel (1997) applied the concepts of complexity science to explain human creativity, and psychiatrist Charles Johnston (1986) spoke of a 'creative imperative' as a 'paradigm shift' (in Popper's sense of the term). Indeed, recognizing the causal creation appears to be a major shift from both classic determinism and current stochastic models.

14. Are LIGO recordings really gravitational waves? Many scientists think so. Others regard the results as "null". Scientists and engineers from LIGO and other research institutes around the world have done a fantastic job of eliminating artifacts such human "noise". Caution is advisable in this important matter, and the LIGO scientists have been very prudent regarding how certain they are about the actual detection of gravitational waves. But from the perspective of learning about the prevailing patterns in nature, it is equally important to analyze what comes to our planet from all directions of space, whether it is predominantly gravitational waves from the Big bang or from other sources of spacetime variation, or variations of matter in spacetime.

15. Blunden (1984) states: Marx pays great attention to this differing of the roles of the left and right sides of equations. Equations are used by mathematicians as instruments for cognition, and their meaning resides in their use in true social practice, not in their abstract definition. "If we translate '=' as 'is', we would correctly conclude that 'x = 7' does not imply '7 = x', although within a strictly -defined context such implication would have formal truth. The falsity lies in misrepresenting the movement, from x to 7. Formal interpretation of this law, of course, denies the movement of cognition, since to formalism all the propositions of a theory are contained within its premises."

16. The term was coined by Günther to refer to this work.

17. "(T)*he number of qualitatively different configurations of discontinuities that can occur depends not on the number of state variables, which is generally very large, but on the control variables, which is generally very small. In particular, if the number of control variables is not greater than four, then there are only seven types of catastrophes, and in none of these more than two state variables are involved*" (Saunders, 1980.)

18. Psychologically, quaternity corresponds to concepts of justice according to Jung (see Robertson, 1995).

19. Classic theories portray conflict behaviors as choices between opposite alternatives. According to Freud, anger can be turned outward, as aggression, or inward, as depression; the union of opposites suggests that inwardly directed and outwardly directed anger coexist and reinforce each other. For

Cannon, conflict leads to fight or flight, a dichotomy modeled as a catastrophe (Zeeman, 1977): when a subject experiences both anger and fear simultaneously, these opposites do not cancel each other (as in quantitative theories of opposition), but rather one motion predominates. The subject either fights or flees. Actually, mammals confronted with conflict may also display submission, which normally terminates the aggressive behavior of the other, avoiding intra-species killing, and generating social hierarchies. Conflict thus poses a trifurcation: fight, flight or surrender. These behaviors may be mutually exclusive, but alternate, intertwine, and replace each other, according to circumstances. Their subjective components—anger, fear, and sorrow—coexist, consciously or unconsciously, because conflict is their common trigger. The conflict theory of affect (Sabelli, 1989; Sabelli and Carlson-Sabelli, 1991) postulates that rage, anxiety, and depression are pathological manifestations of these three innate responses to conflict, brought about by external conflicts, and/or triggered by dysfunctions in the metabolism of the neurhormones that mediate these emotional behaviors—in this case, the manifested hostile and depressive behaviors can create interpersonal conflict.

20. Bifurcation cascades generate increasingly diverse periodic series, then chaos and bios. Chaotic series show local sensitivity to initial conditions (change in trajectory) and diversification (increase in variance with embedding) only at low embedding dimensions. Biotic series show global sensitivity to initial conditions (change in the range of trajectories) and diversification (increase in variance with embedding) at low and high embedding dimensions.

21. The name given to the diagrams introduced by Euler in 1768.

22. Defining confirmation as the empirical demonstration of a case, the hypothesis "All ravens are black" is supported by finding a red shoe, as 'All A are B" is equivalent, in standard logic, to "No non-B is an A."

23. Neuroscientist McCulloch and logician Walter Pitts (1943) tried to understand how the brain could produce highly complex patterns by using many basic cells ("neurons") that are connected together.

24. A dimension (Latin, "measured out") is a parameter required to describe the relevant characteristics of an object or process as its position within a physical or conceptual *space* —where the *dimensions* of a space are the total number of different parameters used for all possible entities objects that must be considered. A Cartesian coordinate system is used to uniquely determine each point in the plane through two numbers, in space using three coordinates, and in higher dimensions with as many parameters as necessary. In this manner we can plot changes in quantity and quality. A Euclidean space (also called *Cartesian space*) is a generalization that applies Euclid's concept of distance, and the related concepts of length and angle, to a coordinate system in any number of dimensions. A Hilbert space is a generalization of Euclidean space that is not restricted to finite dimensions. Hilbert spaces are of crucial importance in the mathematical formulation of quantum mechanics. Differential geometry provides a different type of generalization to spaces that are locally Euclidean, but whose large scale properties are not flat. A sphere is a good example of this since at very small distances it appears flat, but at large scale the curvature is evident. Differential geometry allows coordinates that are not Cartesian. A general coordinate system specifies the distance ds between neighboring points xa and xa_{+dxa} in terms of a metric gaqb, which

is a matrix of numbers, and a prescription for calculating such small distances in terms of the product of the coordinate distances and the matrix:

$ds = \sqrt{\sum_{a,b} g_{ab} dx^a dx^b}$. The prescription is to

multiply the product of the shown distances by the indicated metric element and sum over all the possible directions of the space. The resultant distance is the square root of this quadratic form. By considering new coordinates that are linear combinations of the original, a new quadratic form can be formed; it is always possible to make a choice so that the resultant form is either Euclidean, or more generally a diagonal form in which some squares are added and some subtracted. Spaces that are not Euclidean are called Minkowski spaces. Newtonian physics is formulated for a Euclidean space whereas Einstein's physics is formulated for Minkowski space with time being treated differently from the space dimensions.

25. Regarding qualities as dimensions instead of as classes has evident implications for sociology where age, sex, socioeconomic and national classes play an important role. Dividing people as belonging to one race increases discrimination and conflict, and is false. (Most "Blacks" are largely "White"; "Hispanics" are of any color; Italian or Jewish brothers can become one "Hispanic" and the other "White" if born in different places.) The reality is that a person is female to some degree and male to some other, shares several races and cultures, continuously changes age, and relates in three ways regarding socioeconomic class: over some, under others, and at the same level as many others.

26. Physics focuses on generic processes rather than on the specific form of physical mountains or galaxies.

27. The fact that we still have not agreed upon units to measure biological or psychological dimensions is an incentive to define them clearly, not an objection against conceptualizing them as dimensions. Dimensions are not the same as units. Dimensionless quantities may have units, for example, angles. Dimensions are objective facts of nature.

28. Regarding the difference between Planck and Einstein's formulation of the quantum law ($\forall$A) A $\geq$ h, consider standard logic, where a property P is universal because for all x, P(x), so locality and globality are intimately related while in Biotic logic, locality and globality are related but not identical properties. Global and local diversification are related but local diversification does not always imply global diversification (Figure 1).

29. Actually action must be at a minimum, a maximum, or a saddle point for small perturbations about the true evolution. The derivative of the function equals zero; this is described as "extremal" or "stationary" meaning that the mean, variance and autocorrelation do not change over time.

30. Hamilton's view of action provides a connection to the view that classical physics provides a geometric optics approximation to the real world of quantum phenomena, identifies the variables that are conjugate, and demonstrates that they fundamentally do not commute. In general, the kinetic energy is a quadratic function of the velocities: $T = \sum m_{jk}\left(q_j\right)\dot{q}_j\dot{q}_k$. The system will be composed of many components, each with its own position in space, so the totality of unconstrained coordinates will be large. The coefficients may depend on these coordinates. The generalized space determined by the unconstrained coordinates can be given a metric suggested by this form of the kinetic energy: $ds = \sum m_{jk}\left(q_j\right)dq_j dq_k$.

Hamilton studied the behavior of physical systems by studying their motion in this space, and wrote his principle of least action using this measure for distance: $\Delta \int \sqrt{T} ds = 0$. The principle of least action is homologous to the principle applied to light traveling through a material with an index of refraction $\sqrt{T}$. Though light is a wave, when the wave length of light is sufficiently small compared to the size of the optical medium in which it travels, light take the path of least time subject to the proviso that its speed in a medium is determined by the index of refraction. Feynman formulates the behavior of light is in terms of the Lagrangian (as opposed to the Hamiltonian). It incorporates the view that light consists of quanta, and that the behavior of physical processes is described by the integration of the complex number $e^{iS/\hbar}$ over all possible paths, where the rate of change of the phase S with time is the Lagrangian function, $dS/dt = L$. The phase is Lagrange's action. In this view, the principle of least action arises when the actions are sufficiently larger than the unit of action, Planck's constant $\hbar$. This is the limit of geometrical optics, which we now apply to all phenomena, not just light.

31. *"One can even set up quite ridiculous cases. A cat is penned up in a steel chamber, along with the following device (which must be secured against direct interference by the cat): in a Geiger counter, there is a tiny bit of radioactive substance, so small that perhaps in the course of the hour, one of the atoms decays, but also, with equal probability, perhaps none; if it happens, the counter tube discharges, and through a relay releases a hammer that shatters a small flask of hydrocyanic acid. If one has left this entire system to itself for an hour, one would say that the cat still lives if meanwhile no atom has decayed. The psi-function of the entire system would express this by having in it the living and dead cat (pardon the expression) mixed or smeared out in equal parts."* Notably, many took the idea of dead-and-alive cats seriously. On the contrary, Schrödinger intended the paradox as a reductio ad absurdum.

32. A debate over the nature of light and matter dates back to antiquity. Aristotle proposed that light was a wave-like disturbance in the air while Democritus argued that all things in the universe, including light, were composed of indivisible atoms. In the 1600s, Descartes and Huygens offered a wave description of light, while Newton championed a corpuscular hypothesis. The wave theory prevailed when Maxwell discovered that visible light, ultraviolet light, and infrared light were all electromagnetic waves of differing frequency. But the corpuscular hypothesis was buttressed by the rise of atomic theory with Lavoisier who deduced the conservation of mass and categorized many new chemical elements and compounds, Proust who showed that elements combined in definite proportions, Dalton's resurrection of Democritus' atom, and the subsequent work of Avogadro and Mendeleev. The work of Planck, Albert Einstein, de Broglie, Compton, Bohr, and many others, inaugurated the current scientific theory according to which that all particles also have a wave nature, and vice versa.

33. The complementarity of opposites, such as wave-particle duality was interpreted by Bohr (who adhered to positivism) in an idealistic fashion. Einstein regarded the wave-particle duality as an ingenious and amazingly successful interpretation that appeared to him as only a temporary way out.

34. In the Stern-Gerlach experiment a beam of particles is sent through an inhomoge-

neous magnetic field and their deflection is observed. The results show that particles possess an intrinsic angular momentum that is analogous to the angular momentum of a classically spinning object, but that takes only certain quantized values. The experiment demonstrates that electrons and atoms have intrinsically quantum properties, and how measurement affects the system being measured.

35. The notation |X> is due to the Dirac equations and refers to a vector in the appropriate quantum space (Hilbert Space) with the label X. Thus if we study an electron with SPIN +½ and -1/2, then we can consider the states |+1/2> AND |-1/2> for this electron. A superposition of these states is in the form A|+1/2> + B|-1/2> and the formalism using |0> AND |1> is just a neutral formalism for an entity that has states labeled 0 and 1.

36. When Shor's algorithm was implemented by a group at IBM, who factored 15 into 3 × 5, using a quantum computer with 7 qubits (Vandersypen et al., 2001), no entanglement was observed, but entanglement was observed when Shor's algorithm using photonic qubits (Lu et al., 2007; Lanyon et al., 2007).

37. In *Mathematical Foundations of Quantum Mechanics*, von Neumann noted that projections on a Hilbert space can be viewed as propositions about physical observables. The set of principles for manipulating these quantum propositions was called *quantum logic* by von Neumann and Birkhoff.

38. In biology, homology indicates that two anatomical structures, physiological processes or or behavioral traits in different organisms originated from a structures, processes or traits of a common ancestral organism, although they may not necessarily perform the same function in each organism, and may even have become unused and therefore vestigial.

Section 2
Application Fields:
From Networks to the Fractals

Chapter 8
Networks:
A Sketchy Portrait of an Emergent Paradigm

Alessandro Giuliani
Istituto Superiore di Sanita, Italy

ABSTRACT

The term 'network' is more and more widespread in all the fields of human investigation from physics to sociology. It evokes a systemic approach to problems able to overcome the limitations reductionist approaches evidenced since some decades. Network based approaches gave brilliant results in fields like biochemistry where the consideration of the whole set of metabolic reactions of an organism allowed us to understand some very important properties of the organisms that cannot be appreciated by the simple enumeration of the single biochemical reactions. Nevertheless, the lack of appreciation networks are modelling tools and not real entities could be detrimental to the exploitation of the full potential of this paradigm. On a separate but related note, not discovering the model-like nature of networks severely limits the recognition of the substantial identity between networks and other mathematical models so hampering the power of network-like thought.

Some applications of network based modelling are presented so to introduce the basic terminology of the emergent network paradigm to highlight strengths and limitations of the method and to sketch the strong relation linking network based approach to other modelling tools.

INTRODUCTION

The network paradigm is the prevailing metaphor in nowadays natural sciences. We can read about gene networks (De Jong 2002, Gardner & Faith 2005), protein networks (Bork et al. (2004)),

metabolic networks (Nielsen 1998, Palumbo et al. 2005), ecological networks (Lassig et al. 2001) and so forth. This metaphor went well outside the realm of natural science so to invade most 'humanistic' and less formalized fields like sociology or psychology (McMahon et al. 2001).

The network paradigm is an horizontal construct (Palumbo et al. 2006), basically different

DOI: 10.4018/978-1-4666-2077-3.ch008

Figure 1. Waddington's epigenetic landscape, genome-wide regulatory network, and cell fate switching in an attractor landscape

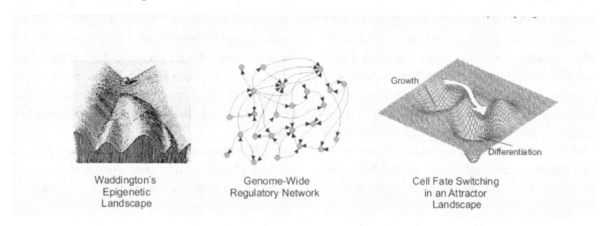

Waddington's
Epigenetic
Landscape

Genome-Wide
Regulatory Network

Cell Fate Switching
in an Attractor
Landscape

from the classical top-down paradigms of modern science, dominating the theoretical scene until not so many years ago (and still more or less unconsciously shaping the way of thinking of the large majority of scientists), in which there was a privileged flux of information (and a consequent hierarchy of explanation power) from more basic atomisms (fundamental forces in physics, DNA in biology) down to the less fundamental phenomenology (condensed matter organization, physiology).

The general concept of network as a collection of elements (nodes) and the relationships among those (arcs), cannot be separated by the definition of a "system" in dynamical systems theory, where the basic elements (nodes) are time varying functions and relationships are differential or difference equations. In this respect, the two definitions are very similar, while the emphasis of the term 'network' is on topology (i.e. the static wiring diagram of the modelled reality), the term 'dynamical system' refers to the dynamics emerging from the interaction of components, i.e. to the actual behaviour of the network when observed in time. This analogy is at the root of the recently renewed interest for systems biology (Klipp et al. 2005). The following sketch (Figure 1) comes (with permission) from a recent paper by Donald Ingber (Ingber D.E. (2006)).

On the left of Figure 1 the Conrad Waddington's cartoon of epigenetic landscape is depicted: it is a very famous and effective model of embryological development in which the differentiation trajectories of cell populations are depicted as a marble rolling across a rugged landscape of peaks and valleys following a 'least-action' trajectory driving the cell from an unstable undifferentiated stem state (top of the landscape, first embryonic development phases) to the definitive cell fates (bottom of the landscape, correspondent to mature, definitive tissues) following the 'valleys' generated by the regulation of genes expression (epigenetic control) (Waddington CH (1956)). In the fifties the Waddington's model was nothing more than a genial metaphor, in the XXI century this metaphor was filled by 'reality' by the discovery the epigenetic landscape was nothing more nothing less than the image of the stable states of a very connected network of interacting genes giving rise to an energy field in which the different cell kinds correspond to the potential minima. Even if we are still very far to understand the 'nature' of this differentiation 'energy, nevertheless we are able to sketch the phenomenological features of such landscapes (Felli et al 2010). It is worth considering how the network model was in this case a sort of 'transit paradigm' from a metaphorical to a fully dynamical and measurable way to model complex systems.

On another side psychology, as well as other soft sciences, are not new to 'systems' approach, the names of Von Bertalanffy, Wiener and so forth are not new to sociology and psychology students. The 'cultural' scene from 40's to 70's was dominated by metaphors borrowed from systems science like 'feedback' or 'stability' and 'trajectory'. This systemic approach came to an eclipse when apparently more fascinating metaphors came from hard sciences or, better, from what appeared to be the most innovative technology around. When the charisma of 'most powerful technology' shifted from servomechanisms to digital computers, anything stopped to be a 'dynamical system' and became a 'sequential machine' whose operational behaviour was embodied into a suitable memory and a processor able to read along the correct steps. Nowadays the 'fascination' comes from the world wide web that is unanimously considered the most powerful and innovative object around, thus it is not strange anything must be equated to a network and thus provoking a reprise of the dynamical metaphors of the fifties.

In the subsequent part of this work we will try and go beyond this idolatric way of thinking and to understand how and when the network based metaphors and modelling can be useful in day-by-day research work.

DISCUSSION

What a Network is

As we said before, a network is simply a set of nodes connected by arcs as in Figure 2 that depicts a portion of the metabolic network of a cell.

The nodes in the case of a biochemical pathway as the one depicted in the figure are metabolites but they can be airports in the case of airway transport systems, people in the case of a social network or any element sharing a meaningful relation with some other entities of the same kind. Consequently the arcs represent a meaningful

relation between the nodes, in the case of biochemical pathways an arc between node i and node j simply means that metabolite i can be transformed into metabolite j, in the case of airway transportation the arc points to the fact there is a direct flight between airport i and airport j, while in the case of the social network the arc implies a friendship relation between the two connected nodes.

The important thing for a network model to be useful (instead of a pure rhetorical exercise) is that we can derive some relevant information on the general behaviour of the modelled system by the sole knowledge of network wiring diagram (who is connected with whom).

It is important to stop and think about the previous statement: in the case of dynamical system theory we do not only need information about the topology of the system but, more important, we need information about the nature and strength of the arcs (the relations between the elements of the system). In other words, in order to build a differential equation based model, it is not sufficient to say molecule i is transformed into molecule j, or airport i is connected to airport j by a direct flight: we need to know in advance the rate of formation of j starting from i (and *viceversa*) and the time needed to fly from i to j. This requirement is at the basis of the substantial failure of dynamical system analysis of complex systems: simply we cannot give all the needed information because or they are outside the reach of empirical investigation or because they cannot assumed to be invariant during the system actual functioning. The shift from dynamical system approach to networks is then an admission of our limits of going in deep into complex system fine structure. The only way to recover a dynamical 'flavour' from the network approach is, like in the model depicted in figure 1, to forget about the single microscopic relations at the basis of the energetic landscape and concentrate on a mesoscopic approach that simply identifies some 'preferred solutions' out of the transfinite number of the possible ones without

Figure 2. Portion of the metabolic network of a cell

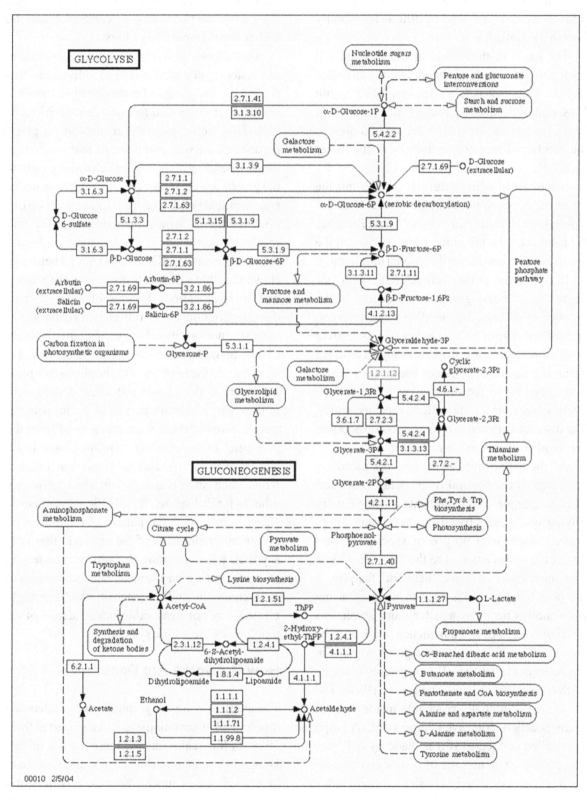

ever thinking of describing the structural equations on behind. This kind of attitude is normally known as 'statistics'.

The basic mathematical model to approach the topological study of networks is the so called 'graph'. The graph is defined as a tuple (V,E), with V as a set of vertices (or nodes) and E as a set of edges (or arrows, arcs). The degree of a node is the number of arcs connected to it (Palumbo et al. 2006).

In the case of a directed graph', or *digraph*, the set of edges is composed by directed arcs and is defined as a -tuple (i,j) of vertices where i denotes the head and j the tail of the edge. Arrows on the arcs are used to encode the directional information.

In a directed graph, vertices have both 'in-degree' and 'out-degree': the in-degree is the number of distinct arcs leading to that vertex, and the out-degree is the number of arcs leading away from that vertex. A *walk* through a directed graph is a sequence of nodes connected by arcs corresponding to the order of nodes in the sequence; a *path* is a walk with no repeated nodes. The distance between two vertices corresponds to the number of arcs in the minimum path.

All the applications of the network paradigm are based on the possibility to operate some sort of classification of the elements of the network relying on features based on their connectivity pattern alone, with no use of specific properties of the nodes external to the network wiring. The most basic of these 'network' features is the possibility to reach a given node i starting from another node j by a path along a graph: this possibility defines an equivalence relation 'to be connected to', that partitions a given graph G in equivalence classes called 'components' made by all the nodes that are connected among them. The set of nodes mutually reachable inside a given graph is called 'connected component'. A graph G is called connected if it is made by only one component . The number of distinct paths connecting two nodes can be considered as an 'index of connectivity' on the graph nodes: the greater

the number of paths connecting the two nodes, the greater the two nodes are correlated, and the higher their connectivity index.

This allows for a straightforward application of clustering algorithms able to individuate 'supernodes', i.e. groups of nodes highly connected among each other and forming functional modules. This metric property of topological graph representation was exploited in many different fields extending from organic chemistry (where the graphs are the molecules with atoms as nodes and chemical bonds as edges (Lukovits 2000), to protein domains where the nodes are aminoacid residuals and the edges the structural contiguity relation (Rao and Caflisch 2004), social networks (Freeman 2004). It is worth noting that the generation of classifications (families of nodes) derives directly from the pattern of mutual relations between the nodes without any explicit involvement of features of the nodes other than their connectivity pattern in the network. This implies a complete inversion of the classic reductionist approach: in the case of network paradigm the property of the elements of the system are derived from the properties of the entire system (the connectivity pattern of the graph) and not *viceversa* . In other words each node is completely identical to any other as for its 'nature': its specific determination stems from its peculiar pattern of relations with all the other elements of the network, that is to say that, when adopting the network modelling style, we opt for an intrinsic, context dependent geometry of the studied system in which the single elements are not measurable independently of the topology of the whole system.

How Networks Are Described

The study of complex graphs for which detailed topological information was lacking, started from 1950. In this realm, the pioneering work of two Hungarian mathematicians, Erdos and Renyi can be considered of much importance (Erdos and Renyi 1960, Palumbo et al. 2006): they introduced the concept of 'random graphs', in which the number of connections linking the different nodes is defined by stochastic variables. Each node of the graph can be defined by the number of nodes connected to it (degree): this gives rise to the degree distribution $P(k)$ describing the 'general wiring pattern' of the network having as abscissa the number k of connections and as y axis, the number of nodes having k connections. In analogy with statistical mechanics, these distributions are defined as 'scaling laws'. (Barabasi and Albert 1999)

The humanities scientists are acquainted with the Zipf's law linking the length of the words and their frequency of occurrence. This is another scaling law, whose specific shape allows us to make some inference on the system at hand (Perline 1996). Statisticians simply refer to these 'laws' as 'distributions' so wisely attenuating the arrogance of the term 'law' frankly exaggerated for what is simply an empirical observation. In the case of networks, what happens is that if the nodes are too many, it is impossible to enumerate the degree of connectivity of each single node and we need to perform some statistics, i.e. to use some meaningful summary of what's going on.

These statistical distributions can give us some useful information on the general shape of the analysed networks, Figure 3 shows two typical kinds of distributions: the panel on the left shows a Poisson distribution in which there is a privileged

scale of number of connections and a decreasing number of nodes having less than average or more than average links. Panel on the right depicts a so-called "*scale-free*" network (Palumbo et al. 2006), in which there is a huge majority of nodes with a low number of connections and a very small number of nodes having a huge number of links. These highly connected nodes are called "*hubs*". This kind of architecture often leads to a "small-world" property (Watts and Strogatz 1998), i.e. each node is, on average, "near" to any other in terms of number of arcs connecting them.

The Barabasi group (Albert et al. 2000) investigated the tolerance of both random and scale-free networks after the removal of several nodes. The deletion of a node causes the augmentation of the distance between the nodes in the network. The authors distinguish between two kinds of deletion: failure and attack. The former consists in removal of a randomly selected set of nodes, wile the latter consists in the deletion of the most connected nodes of the network. The robustness of a scale-free network is due to its particular connection distribution: as a few nodes are highly connected, an informed attack will provoke the deletion of a hub and, as a consequence, the isolation of many nodes. On the other hand, a random failure has only a small probability to significantly alter the structure of the scale-fee network, because the majority of the nodes have a few connections and the probability to damage a

Figure 3. Two types of distributions

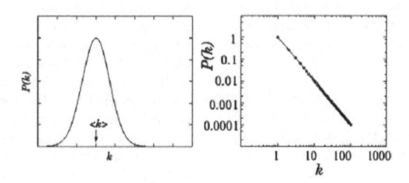

highly connected node (with consequently limited effects on the entire network) is quite high.

There is a vast debate about the different distributions present in biological networks (Palumbo et al. 2006); this debate stems from the lack of reliable experimental data or from the controversial definition of what a connection is. A particular enlightening example are protein interaction networks for which there is a big debate on how to measure a protein-protein interaction. Thus I think it is better to concentrate on the simple possibility to describe real networks by means of statistical indexes derived from P(k) distribution without paying attention to the classification of a network as "small-world" or "Poissonian": the relevant thing is that these indexes can give us some good prediction about the behaviour of the modelled system.

The tendency of having subsets of nodes strongly connected among them can be measured by the so-called aggregation coefficient. Let's consider a generic i node f the network having $k(i)$ edges connecting it to other $k(i)$ nodes. In order that these nodes possess the maximal connectivity (each ode connected to each other) we should have a total number of edges equal to:

$$k(i)*(k(i)-1)/2 \tag{1}$$

Expression (1) corresponds to the maximal number of connections among k(i) nodes when self connections are avoided. Thus, it is perfectly natural to define the *aggregation coefficient* in terms of the ratio between the number of actually observed Ei and the maximal number of connections expressed by (1). Thus, the aggregation coefficient relative to node i, Ci is expressed as:

$$Ci = 2*(Ei/k(i)*(ki-1)) \tag{2}$$

The aggregation coefficient for the entire network corresponds to the average of Ci over all the nodes. The operative counterpart of clustering tendency is the concept of modularity, that is the possibility to isolate portions of a more general network that can be considered as partially independent sub-networks, i.e. "modules" that can be studied as such, without necessarily referring to the whole network, given the by far greater relevance of 'inside-module' links with respect to the 'between-modules' ones. This is nothing different of the concept of 'stable classification' in classical multidimensional statistics, in which 'well behaved' clusters are defined collections of statistical units very near each other (in the network language having a lot of mutual connections) and distant from the elements of the other cluster (in the network language, having only few arcs connecting to elements of different modules).

A CASE STUDY

Let's shift now to an example in which a network based modelling allowed us to rationalize a relevant biochemical phenomenon: the essential character of a metabolic reaction (Palumbo et al. 2005). The metabolism of an organism (in this case the yeast *Saccharomyces Cerevisiae*) can be thought as a network in which the metabolites are the nodes and the arcs correspond to enzymes converting a metabolite i into a metabolite j, the elimination of an enzyme by a specific mutation corresponds to the elimination of the arc directly connecting the two metabolites at its ends. Adopting a purely 'network based' approach to the study of this system implied the task of inferring the lethal character of each mutation (i.e. the arcs whose elimination ends into the death of the microorganism) on the pure basis of its position into the wiring diagram, without any reference to the nature of the catalysed reaction.

The metabolic network of microorganisms, at odds with other biological networks like protein-protein interaction network or genetic regulation network, is very well understood and characterized. It corresponds to those Boeheringer's 'Charts of Metabolism' pinned on the walls of almost

Figure 4. Metabolic network

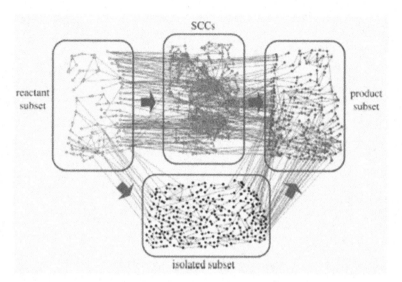

every biochemistry laboratory in the world, having enzymatic reactions as edges and metabolites as nodes.

A metabolic network can be imagined (Figure 4) as composed by four distinct classes of nodes. The first one is the *strong connected components* (SCC), made of nodes each other linked by direct paths; the *reactant subsets* consists of metabolites entering the system as reactants and called '*sources*' because they can reach SCC from the external environment. Another class is constituted by the *product subset*: such metabolites are positioned at the end of a given pathway and thus exiting the system as products (they are called *sinks* in opposition to the sources). The metabolites in the last class, called 'isolated subset', are inserted in autonomous pathways with respect to SCCs. This architecture can be found in many scale-free networks as World Wide Web, the electric power transmission grid and airplane connections (Crucitti et al. 2004).

Since an enzymatic reaction is catalysed by one or more enzymes, an arc represent the enzymes involved in the reaction. This opens the way to a straightforward analysis of the possibility to derive biologically meaningful features from network topology: relying on the existing data base of the experimentally verified effects of yeast mutations

(http://www-sequence.stanford.edu/group/ yeast_deletion_project/deletions3.html) we checked the possibility to pick up a connectivity descriptor able to unequivocally define essential enzymes (those enzymes whose lack provokes yeast death). If this can be done, this is a proof of the possibility to consider the 'whole metabolism' as a biological entity per se, from whose structure the biological relevance of the single elements of the system (the specific enzymes) derives. In other words, the biological role of a given enzyme is not fully definable in isolation from the whole set of interactions it is embedded into, so falsifying the basic tenet of a great part of scientific and technological applications of molecular biology.

Figure 5 is a graphic representation of the *Saccharomyces Cerevisiae* metabolic network, the labels of the nodes correspond to the codes of the different metabolites according to KEGG data base (Ma and Zeng 2003). Yellow bars show where essential enzymes are positioned in the network. Nodes coloured in blue, light blue, violet and green belong to the strong connected components of the network. These components

Figure 5. A graphic representation of the Saccharomyces Cerevisiae metabolic network

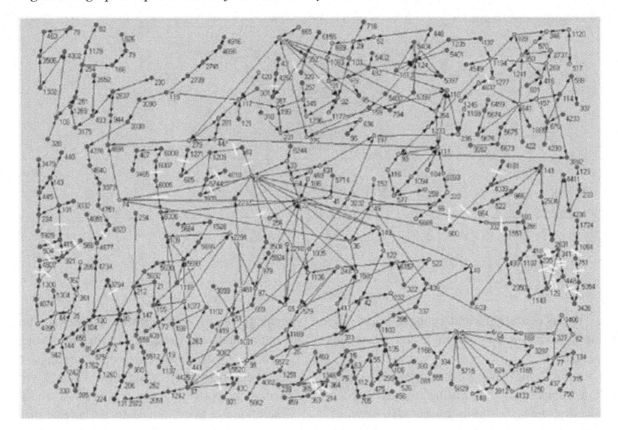

constitute the cores of the network and all of the nodes belonging to one of them can reach one another because they are fully connected.

Our conjecture was that the lethal mutations can unequivocally be defined by those isolating one or more nodes from the entire network: i.e. lethal mutations are those that do not allow for an alternative pathway to reach one or more nodes. This was actually the case, so pointing to a much more crucial role played by peripherical portions of the network with respect to hubs. As a matter of fact nodes in SCCs are protected by the redundancy of paths (high connectivity), thus it is extremely difficult that a single arc deletion can isolate a node an SCC, on the contrary a lateral node, due to its low connectivity, can be easily isolated by an arc deletion.

The demonstration of the possibility to exactly predict a biological phenomenon (essential character of an enzyme) from the sole analysis of connectivity pattern of the metabolic network without referring to any biochemical notion of single enzymes physiology is a strong proof of the possible usefulness of the network approach and of the feasibility of an holistic approach in biology.

Obviously, even if the results give the impression something we can call 'metabolic network' does in fact exist we must pay the maximal attention to the fact that all the things we speak about in science are not 'real entities' but (at their best) useful toy models of what does effectively exists. This is a basic point to keep in mind in order not to ingenerate the dangerous mistake of applying a successful model to anything in the world. The basic question is then:

Table 1. Possible network formalization

System	Nodes	arcs (an arc does exist when)
Building	Rooms	It is possible to go from room i to room j directly
Railway	stations	Station *j* can be reached from station *i* with no intermediate stop
Office	Clerks	Two clerks collaborate in the same job
Scientific Literature	authors	Author *i* and j have co-authored one or more papers
Lego	Bricks	Two bricks are directly connected with no intermediate brick
Computer Network	Computers	There is a physical connection between computers *i* and *j*
Internet	websites	There is a direct link between two sites *i* and *j*
Gene Expression	Genes	Genes *i* and *j* share the same promoter

When is it Convenient to Model Something like a Network?

Networks are everywhere ? Yes and no, clearly the basic definition of a network is sufficiently vague to be applied to anything by means of a minimal formalization effort, this is a relatively easy (and basically trivial) exercise developed in the Table 1.

Table 1 reports a possible network formalization (in terms of nodes and arcs) for eight different systems. The interested reader could both enlarge the reported list or invent more smart network formalizations for the reported examples (it is worth noting I can choose different nodes and arcs for the same object, depending on which of the multiple relations present in a given object I decide to assume as privileged view as in the case of Internet where a software view of the system instead of the hardware one was privileged). For each of these formalizations I can easily derive all the topological descriptors we discussed above and thus identifying hubs, non-hub connectors (the essential enzymes of the case study), measuring different connectivity indexes and so forth.

The basic question to decide if my network formalization is worth of is thus simply 'Can I derive some useful information from the topology of the network ?'. Let's try and play the game of useful/trivial for the above sketched examples:

- **Building:** Useful, but only if the building is very big (a lot of rooms) and you are the architect that must connect nodes families (modules) with different functions (let's think of a building hosting different work activities): the correspondence network modules / different activities is probably a useful optimization principle.
- **Railway:** Trivial if you are a passenger, this is the information you can derive from any railway book, the relevant information is the time needed to go from one place to another and so choosing the best travel schedule. Useful, if you must plan the railway, because you could optimise topology in relation to the traffic fluxes.
- **Office:** Useful, if two clerks pertaining to two different departments collaborate more often than two clerks of the same department, this can point to a wrong human resources allocation.
- **Scientific Literature:** Trivial, this kind of exercise is only useful to increase scientists pomposity (and this equates selling refrigerators at the North pole).
- **Lego:** Trivial, the bricks are basically interchangeable.
- **Computer Network:** Useful, this is very important for both optimising the connections in terms of physical location of computers and of shared work.

- **Internet:** Knowing the reciprocal links between different sites mirrors their relative arguments, it could be useful for someone that is interested in developing a study about the ecology of web users.
- **Gene Expression:** Debatable, even if the current vision seems to answer Trivial because sharing the same promoter or transcription factor does not seem to be as biologically meaningful as considered some years ago. Completely different it is the case described in the introduction (cell differentiation) where the network wiring is not associated to a specific molecular interaction (like Transcription Factors or DNA methylation patterns) but made it to emerge 'a posteriori' from the observed similarities in gene expression between different tissues. In this 'statistical' case the network metaphor appears very promising.

The 'useful/trivial' game of Table 1 was played by assuming an explicit semantic attitude, i.e. having in mind the use we can made of a network formalization, we could equally play a 'syntactic' version of the game, in which the decision of the relevance of the network modelling is based on how straightforward and natural is the 'network translation' of the specific system.

Basically a network is made of nodes and arcs: nodes are locations where activity (or energy, or matter, or whatsoever) is especially concentrated with respect to the rest of environment, arcs are links between these locations along which something happens (chemical transformations, flux of energy or of information, chemical bonding..). When this partition of the space is clear cut and unambiguous, network formalization is syntactically correct (..then obviously we must decide about its semantic justification). Thus it is perfectly fit to think of highway system as a network: the cities are the nodes, the highways connecting them are the arcs. The population density, function, landscape, and so forth inside

the cities (nodes) is basically different from that of the country along which the highways go: thus modelling the system as a network is perfectly natural and unambiguous. This is no more the case when we want to model the streets inside a town as a network: who plays the role of node ? who plays the role of arc ? We can decide for different choices but there is not a most natural one.

In conclusion network based modelling of complex systems is a potentially very powerful tool, the important thing to keep in mind is that is a 'tool' and not the real thing. So it is important to avoid unjustified philosophical speculations on its use and maintain an operational attitude on the use of this paradigm.

CONCLUSION

The message I tried to convey in this chapter, mainly oriented towards biochemical sciences given my specific research interests, is that network formalization are neither 'the brilliant new paradigm of the future' opening our minds to a different view of the world nor an abstruse and mathematically intensive tool to approach complex systems in the 'definitive' way. Simply they are analysis tools, like the more ordinary but equally effective (and extremely more versatile) multidimensional statistics that, instead of the philosophers enthusiasm, generally elicit boring expressions. Like any analysis tool we decide when using a network algorithm on the basis of the problem at hand, taking into consideration its structural characteristics beside of any epistemological or theoretical predisposition.

REFERENCES

Albert, R., Jeong, H., & Barabasi, A. L. (2000). Error and attack tolerance of complex networks. *Nature*, *406*, 378–382.

Barabasi, A. L., & Albert, R. (1999). Emergence of scaling in random networks. *Science, 286,* 509–512.

Bork, P., Jensen, L. J., Von Mering, C., Ramani, A. K., Lee, I., & Marcotte, E. M. (2004). Protein interaction networks from yeast to human. *Current Opinion in Structural Biology, 7,* 292–299.

Crucitti, P., Latora, V., Marchiori, M., & Rapisarda, A. (2004). Error and attack tolerance of complex networks. *Physica A, 340,* 388–394.

De Jong, H. (2002). Modeling and simulation of genetic regulatory systems: A literature review. *Journal of Computational Biology, 9,* 67–103.

Erdos, P., & Renyi, A. (1960). On the evolution of random graphs. *Publications of the Mathematical Institute of The Hungarian Academy of Sciences, 2,* 17–61.

Felli, N., Cianetti, L., Pelosi, E., Carè, A., Gong, C., & Liu, G. A. (2010). Hematopoietic differentiation: A coordinated dynamical process towards attractor stable states. *BMC Systems Biology, 4,* 85.

Freeman, L. C. (2004). *The development of social networks analysis: A study in the sociology of science.* Vancouver, Canada: Booksurge Publishing.

Gardner, T. S., & Faith, J. J. (2005). Reverse-engineering transcriptional control networks. *Physics of Life Reviews, 2,* 65–88.

Ingber, D. E. (2006). Mechanical control of tissue morphogenesis during embriological development. *The International Journal of Developmental Biology, 50,* 255–266.

Klipp, E., Herwig, R., Kowald, A., Wierling, C., & Lehrach, H. (2005). *Systems biology in practice.* Weinheim, Germany: Wiley-VCH.

Lassig, M., Bastolla, U., Manrubia, S. C., & Valleriani, A. (2001). Shape of ecological networks. *Physical Review Letters, 86,* 4418–4421.

Lukovits, I. (2000). A compact form of adjacency matrix. *Journal of Chemical Information and Computer Sciences, 40,* 1147–1150.

Ma, H. W., & Zeng, A. P. (2003). The connectivity structure, giant strong component and centrality of metabolic networks. *Bioinformatics (Oxford, England), 19,* 1423–1430.

Mc Mahon, S. M., Miller, K. H., & Drake, J. (2001). Networking tips for social scientists and ecologists. *Science, 293,* 1604–1605.

Nielsen, J. (1998). Metabolic engineering: Techniques of analysis of targets for genetic manipulations. *Biotechnology and Bioengineering, 58,* 125–132.

Palumbo, M. C., Colosimo, A., Giuliani, A., & Farina, L. (2005). Functional essentiality from topology features in metabolic networks: A case study in yeast. *FEBS Letters, 579,* 4642–4646.

Palumbo, M. C., Farina, L., Colosimo, A., Tun, K., Dhar, P., & Giuliani, A. (2006). Networks everywhere? Some general implications of an emergent metaphor. *Current Bioinformatics, 1*(2), 219–234.

Perline, R. (1996). Zipf's law, the central limit theorem, and the random division of the unit interval. *Physical Review E: Statistical Physics, Plasmas, Fluids, and Related Interdisciplinary Topics, 54,* 220–223.

Rao, F., & Caflisch, A. (2004). The protein folding network. *Journal of Molecular Biology, 342,* 299–306.

Waddington, C. H. (1956). *Principles of embriology.* London, UK: Allen and Unwin Ltd.

Watts, D. J., & Strogatz, S. H. (1998). Collective dynamics of 'small world' networks. *Nature, 393,* 440–442.

Chapter 9
Complexity, Emergence and Molecular Diversity via Information Theory

Francisco Torrens
Institut Universitari de Ciència Molecular, Universitat de València, Spain

Gloria Castellano
Universidad Católica de Valencia San Vicente Mártir, Spain

ABSTRACT

Numerous definitions for complexity have been proposed with little consensus. The definition here is related to Kolmogorov complexity and Shannon entropy measures. However, the price is to introduce context dependence into the definition of complexity. Such context dependence is an inherent property of complexity. Scientists are uncomfortable with such context dependence that smacks of subjectivity, which is the reason why little agreement is found on the meaning of the terms. In an article published in Molecules, Lin presented a novel approach for assessing molecular diversity based on Shannon information theory. A set of compounds is viewed as a static collection of microstates that can register information about their environment. The method is characterized by a strong tendency to oversample remote areas of the feature space and produce unbalanced designs. This chapter demonstrates the limitation with some simple examples and provides a rationale for the failure to produce results that are consistent.

INTRODUCTION

Complexity is conceptually impressive; it is a discipline that can be applied to energy packets, traffic, neurones, bourse markets, molecules inside the cell, *etc.*, to any system formed by elements that interact between them in an apparently random

way and then, without understanding why and how, something happens (Mitchell, 2009). The emergent properties are impressive; they leave us astonished and state two basic questions. (1) Is there a science that could arrive to describe in a satisfactory way the internal laws of complexity? (2) This new that appears, was it there before and is it a question of being more refined with the calculations or is it really unforeseen?

DOI: 10.4018/978-1-4666-2077-3.ch009

We shall give an example from chemistry (Pullman, 1994). Imagine that one knows everything on the structure of the water molecule. Can this person foresee the transition from liquid to ice? Or does it happen at a different level? We think that it is fundamentally different because the second law of thermodynamics, *e.g.*, appears when there are more than one particle not only one. Physicists are not used to like the statement because they think that if they go shaking out the system top-down, they could become to understand all its features. They are used to be more reductionist but we as chemists have a different approach. We at the laboratory build up new complex systems instead of deconstructing the ones existing already. Moreover we study them in a more holistic way.

In earlier reports the fractal hybrid-orbital analyses of the protein tertiary structure were carried out (Torrens, 2000, 2001). Valence topological charge-transfer indices for molecular dipole moments were obtained (Torrens, 2004). Information-entropy molecular classification was applied to local anaesthetics (Castellano & Torrens, 2009; Torrens & Castellano, 2006) and inhibitors of human immunodeficiency virus type 1 (Torrens & Castellano, 2009, 2010, in press, a). It was reported the structural classification of complex molecules by artificial intelligence techniques (Torrens & Castellano, 2012). It was published the structural classification of complex molecules by information entropy and equipartition conjecture (Torrens & Castellano, in press, b). It was performed the molecular diversity studies of the bond-based linear indices of the non-stochastic and stochastic edge adjacency matrix of the physicochemical properties of organic molecules (Marrero-Ponce *et al*., 2010) and novel coumarin-based tyrosinase inhibitors discovered by the Organisation for Economic Co-operation and Development (OECD) principles-validated quantitative structure–activity relationship (QSAR) approach from an enlarged balanced database (Le-Thi-Thu *et al*., 2011). The following subsections describe the problem of complexity,

the concept of emergence, the entropy as a case study of emergence and the complexity in the group method of data handling (GMDH)-type neural networks. Then the computational method is explained. In next sections the calculation results are presented and discussed. The final section summarizes the conclusions.

THE PROBLEM OF COMPLEXITY

The study of *complex systems* emerged as a field although a good definition eluded formulation (Standish, 2001). Attempts go back to Shannon's inception of *information theory* (Shannon, 1948ab). Edmonds (1999) provided a good historical survey of *complexity*. It is important the concept of *Kolmogorov algorithmic information complexity* (KC) introduced by Kolmogorov (1965), Chaitin (1966) and Solomonoff (1964ab). Given a particular universal Turing machine (UTM) U, KC of a string of characters is the length of the shortest program running on U that generates the description. It has two main problems. (1) The dependence on U as there is no unique way of specifying it. The invariance theorem guarantees that any two UTMs, U and V, will agree on the complexity of a string x up to a constant independent of x (Li & Vitányi, 1997). However, for any two descriptions x and y there will be two machines U and V disagreeing on whether x is more complex than y or vice versa. (2) Random sequences have maximum complexity, as by definition a random sequence can have no generating algorithm shorter than simply listing the sequence, which as Gell-Mann (1994) pointed out contradicts the notion that random sequences should contain no information. The first problem of what reference machine to choose is a symptom of context dependence of complexity. Given a description x any value of complexity can be chosen for it by choosing an appropriate reference machine. It would seem that complexity is in the eye of the beholder (Emmeche, 1996). Is complexity completely subjective? Is everything lost? Rather than trying to hide the context dependence above it would be preferred to make it a feature. Instead of asserting complexity is a property of some system it is a property of descriptions. An interpreter of the descriptions can answer the question of whether two descriptions are equivalent or not. Consider Shakespeare's *Romeo and Juliet*. In Act II,ii line 58 Juliet says, *My ears have yet not drunk a hundred words*. If one changes the word *drunk* to *heard* your average theatregoer will not spot the difference. Perhaps the only one to notice would be a professional actor who played the scene many times. Therefore, the different texts differing by the single word *drunk/heard* in this scene are considered equivalent by our hypothetical theatregoer. An equivalent *class* of texts would be considered to be *Romeo and Juliet* by our theatregoer. Once the set of all possible descriptions are given and an equivalence class between descriptions given, then one can apply Shannon entropy formula to determine the complexity of that description under that interpretation:

$$C(x) = \lim_{s \to \infty} s \log_2 N - \log_2 \omega(s, x) \qquad (1)$$

where $C(x)$ is the complexity (measured in bits), N the size of the alphabet used to encode the description and $\omega(s,x)$ the size of the class of all descriptions equivalent to x and of length less than s. We assume that the interpreter of a description is able to determine where a description finishes, so that a description y of length $l(y)$ is equivalent to all $N^{s-l(y)}$ length s descriptions having y as a prefix. If we choose our description set to be all bit strings and our equivalence class to be all bit strings that produce the same output when executed by a universal Turing machine U, then:

$$\omega(s, x) = \sum_{p \in \{p : U(p) = U(x) \ell(p) \leq s\}} 2^{s-\ell(p)} \qquad (2)$$

where $l(p)$ is the length of program p. As $s \to \infty$ the distribution (when normalized) is known as the *universal* a priori *probability*. By the *coding theorem* the complexity defined by Equation (1) is equal to KC up to a constant independent of x. The perspective helps understanding the problem of random strings having maximal complexity. In an equivalence class generated by a human observer one random string is pretty much the same as any other. Therefore the ω-term of a completely random string will large probably of comparable size to N^8. Therefore the complexity of a random string as interpreted by a human observer is low, exactly the property required of Gell-Mann *effective complexity*. Whilst context dependence would appear to open up the curse of subjectivity it need not necessarily do so. In many situations the equivalence relation is well defined; *e.g.*, the notion of species in biology. The principle was used in artificial-life studies for the evolution of complexity (Adami, 2000; Floreano *et al.*, 1999).

EMERGENCE

Emergence is that other area of complex systems study that experienced controversy. Its importance stems from the belief that emergence is the key ingredient that makes a system complex. Emergence is the concept of some new phenomenon arising in a system that was not in the system's specification to start with. There is debate as to how this happens or whether emergence can truly happen within a formal system, *e.g.*, an agent-based model (Funtowicz & Ravetz, 1994; Rosen, 1999). Let us illustrate the debate with the example of *gliders* in *The Game of Life*. We would contend that the phenomenon is emergent, in the sense that the glider concept is not contained within the cellular automaton (CA) implementation language (*i.e.*, states and neighbourhoods), which puts us at odds with Rosen, who would argue that gliders are but complicated combinations of simple machines (CAs) not examples of *complexity*. What is our definition of emergence? Let us introduce two descriptions of a system called the *micro* and *macrodescription* each coded in their own language. Ronald *et al.* used the terms $£_1$ and $£_2$ to refer to the micro and macrolanguage, respectively. They called the microlanguage the *language of design* in view of artificial-life applications. However the microdescription may equally well be our best description of what happens at the most fundamental level. To make it clear emergence is not because of the failure of the microdescription as a modelling effort, since the emergent property should still appear as the result of a computer simulation constructed using the microdescription. We also assume that the macrodescription is a *good theory*. There is in general a trade-off between the predictive power of a theory and its explanatory power. An emergent phenomenon is one that is described by atomic concepts available in the macrolanguage, but cannot be so described in the microlanguage. In the case of the glider in The Game of Life any attempt at describing a glider would involve the CA transition table, but also the specific pattern of cell states that make up the glider. However which pattern? A glider can appear at any location within the CA and may have one of four possible orientations. The description cannot represent the fact that two gliders separated diagonally by one cell in along each axis with the same orientation are temporally related. A glider as an object-in-itself is a pure macrodescription object. Ronald *et al.* focused on the element of *surprise* as a test of emergence. They captured emergence as some kind of dissonance between the micro and macrolanguages. They claimed only a test for emergence not a definition along the lines of the more famous Turing test. However, the surprise factor really only works when the macrolanguage is enlarged, in order to make the macrodescription a better model of the system. Once the emergence property was recognized by the observer the property is no longer surprising. The definition of emergence works regardless of whether the observer is still surprised or not. Of

considerable interest is given a system specified in its microlanguage, does it have emergent properties? There is no general procedure for answering the question. One must construct a macrodescription of the system. If the macrodescription contains atomic concepts that are not simple compounds of microconcepts, then one has emergent properties. Is there a best macrodescription for any given system? The question is outside of the scope of this report and needs to be answered by theories of how scientific theories are developed. However, in general it seems unlikely that there would be a *best description* as it depends on the motives of the person using the description; *e.g.*, we alluded to the tension between predictive power and explanatory power. It is worth making a few comments on how this report connects with Holland's book on emergence (Holland, 1999). (1) Holland restricted his attention to the systems with a formal specification, precisely the ones in which Rosen would deny emergence. In the systems the microdescription is exactly equivalent to the real system as opposed to being a good approximation. (2) He defined all his examples in terms of *constrained generating procedures*, which are really equivalent formulation of Turing machines, which gives a dynamical flavour to the models he considered, which is perhaps unnecessary. The emergence of the Mandelbrot set from its definition in terms of an iterative map is not dynamic yet can be generated by a dynamic procedure, *e.g.*, a computer program. However, not until chapter 10 does he begin to tackle the nature of emergence itself introducing *levels of description* with the *micro, macrodistinction*. We believe this report make plain what Holland was struggling to express in the book.

Entropy as a Case Study of Emergence

Thermodynamics provides an excellent case study in emergence, as it is well understood theory, and illustrates the link between emergence and complexity. Thermodynamics is a macroscopic description of material systems expressed in terms of concepts, *e.g.*, temperature, pressure and entropy. It is related to the microscopic description of molecular dynamics *via* the reductionist theory of *statistical mechanics*. Within thermodynamics entropy is defined by differences along a reversible path:

$$\Delta S = \frac{\Delta Q}{T}$$

Within the framework of thermodynamics the quantity is objectively defined, up to an additive constant (usually assumed to be such that entropy vanishes at absolute zero). Within statistical mechanics entropy in the microcanonical ensemble is given by the Boltzmann formula:

$$S = k_b \ln W \tag{3}$$

where k_B is the Boltzmann constant (giving entropy in units of joules per kelvin), and W the number of microstates accessible to the system for a particular macrostate. The formula is similar to the information-based complexity formula (1), which led Jaynes (1965) to remark that entropy *measures our degree of ignorance as to the unknown microstate*. Denbigh and Denbigh (1987) are at pains to point out that entropy is fully objective, as it only depends on the macroscopic quantities chosen to define the macroscopic state (temperature, pressure, *etc.*) and is not dependent on any extraneous observer-related property. Provided two observers choose the same microscopic and macroscopic description of the system, they will agree on the value of entropy. By our previous definition of emergence entropy is an emergent quality of the system. The example illustrates how context-dependent emergent properties can be fully objective. With entropy defined by Equation (3) the well-known H-theorem holds. As a consequence the macroscopic (thermodynamic)

description is time irreversible whereas the microscopic description reversible. Time irreversibility is likewise an emergent property of the system. The clear relation between the Boltzmann-Gibbs entropy (Equation 3) and complexity (Equation 1) indicates that complexity is itself an emergent concept. If the micro and macroscopic languages were identical, corresponding to a situation of no emergence, complexity of descriptions degenerates to the trivial measure of description length.

Complexity in Group Method of Data Handling (GMDH)-Type Neural Networks

The traditional group method of data handling (GMDH)-algorithm was developed by Ivakhnenko in 1967 (Madala & Ivakhnenko, 1994). Like *neural networks* the GMDH approach is based on: (1) the black-box method as a principle approach to analyze systems on the basis of input-output data samples and (2) the connectionism as a representation of complex functions *via* networks of elementary functions. Separate lines of development starting from the scientific foundations are the theory of *neural networks* (NNs) and the theory of *statistical learning networks* (SLNs). The GMDH, as the most important representative of SLNs, was designed from a more cybernetical perspective and implemented a stronger behaviouristic power than NNs because of consideration of a third, unique principle: induction. The principle consists of (1) the cybernetic principle of self-organization as an adaptive creation of a network without given subjective points, (2) the principle of external complement enabling an objective selection of a model of optimal complexity and (3) the principle of regularization of ill-posed tasks. To realize a self-organization of models on the basis of a finite number of input-output data samples, the following conditions must be fulfilled: (1) a simple initial organization which enables *via* its evolution the description of a large class of systems, (2) a selection criterion for validation and measure of the usefulness of an organization relative to its intended task and (3) an algorithm for mutation of the initial or already evolved organization of a population. In conjunction with an inductive generation of many variables, a network is a function represented by a composition of many transfer functions. Typically they are nonlinear functions of a few variables or linear functions of many variables (Farlow, 1984; Lebart & Fenelon, 1971; Lebart *et al.*, 1977; Lemke, 1997; Lemke & Müller, 1997; Müller & Lemke, 1995).

The Race for Complexity

It must be recalled the theme of *complexity*, which most outstanding feature is the emergence of complexity *as is*. It is something well studied the appearance of new properties, *e.g.*, superconductivity, quantum Hall effects, critical phenomena (Domb & Green, 1976), deterministic chaos, *etc.*, but specific conditions that unleash such emergence are not known yet, so that this area is a hot subject in the theoretical and experimental research of current science.

COMPUTATIONAL METHOD

Lin (1996) proposed a new method for assessing molecular diversity based on the principles of information theory formalized by Shannon. In Lin method a collection of compounds is viewed as a static molecular collection of microstates, which can register information about their environment at some predetermined capacity. Molecular diversity is directly related to the information content of collection I as:

$$I = S_{max} - S \tag{4}$$

where S is the *entropy* of the system given by the von Neumann-Shannon expression:

$$S = \sum_{i=1}^{n} p_i \ln p_i \tag{5}$$

where n is the total number of microstates in the system and p_i the probability or frequency of the *i-th* microstate, subject to constraint:

$$\sum_{i=1}^{n} p_i = 1$$

The central concept in Lin approach is that each compound collection represents a finite number of distinguishable molecular species. In this case the entropy of the system is given by:

$$S(m,n) = \sum_{j=1}^{n} \sum_{i=1}^{m} p_{ij} \ln p_{ij} \tag{6}$$

where m is the number of species, n the number of individuals in the population and p_{ij} the probability of finding the *i-th* individual in the *j-th* species. Again the probabilities p_{ij} must satisfy constraint:

$$\sum_{j=1}^{n} \sum_{i=1}^{m} p_{ij} = 1$$

in which case the maximum entropy of Equation (4) is given by:

$$S_{max}(m,n) = -n \ln m$$

As evident from the equation, the information content of the collection rises as the number of species that are represented by that population decays. The difficulty with the approach stems from the fact that in a typical application m is unknown. In this case each member of the population can be treated as a unique, distinguishable species and the entropy of the system can be related to the *distinguishability* of the species, rather than their similarity to some *a priori* known set of prototypes. Under the formalism Equation (6) is replaced by:

$$S(n,n) = \sum_{j=1}^{n}\sum_{i=1}^{n} p_{ij} \ln p_{ij} \tag{7}$$

subject to the usual constraint:

$$\sum_{j=1}^{n}\sum_{i=1}^{n} p_{ij} = 1$$

and S_{max} becomes:

$$S_{max}(n,n) = -n \ln n$$

In Equation (7) the values of the p_{ij}'s can be computed directly from a molecular similarity table. Several methods for quantifying molecular similarity appeared in the literature most of which assign scores in interval [0,1] (Johnson & Maggiora, 1990; Kubinyi, 1993). Lin method involves computing the similarity table ρ_{ij}, using any established method, and applying a normalization factor to derive the actual probabilities. The factor is given by:

$$c = \frac{1}{\displaystyle\sum_{j=1}^{n}\sum_{i=1}^{n} \rho_{ij}}$$

and the actual probabilities by:

$$p_{ij} = c\rho_{ij}$$

According to Lin as the probability values draw closer the species become less indistinguishable, the entropy of the system decays and the information registered by the population rises.

CALCULATION RESULTS

While the use of information theory to quantify molecular diversity has certain intellectual appeal, the actual implementation has some important limitations (Agrafiotis, 1997ab, 1998). We shall first demonstrate the limitations using some simple examples and then discuss the reasons in the context of the underlying theory. We must point out that the following discussion is based on Lin definitions of entropy and *information* unless noted otherwise. As we argue toward the end of this report, it is the exact mathematical definition of the concepts that is responsible for the failures described below.

Consider the following example. Figure 1 shows two different sets of three imaginary compounds plotted against a uniform properly scale. The distances between pairs of points are $d_{13} = d_{23} = 0.5$ and $d_{12} = 1.0$. As usual the distance between two points d_{ij} is taken as a direct measure of their similarity ρ_{ij}. Two different popular methods are used to perform the transformation:

$$\rho_{ij} = \alpha - d_{ij} \tag{8}$$

and:

Figure 1. Two different sets of three imaginary compounds plotted against a uniform properly scale (in Figure 1b points 2 and 3 coincide).

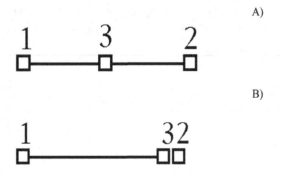

A)

B)

$$\rho_{ij} = \frac{1}{1 + \alpha d_{ij}} \tag{9}$$

where α is a constant (in this case 1.0). Using Equation (7) we can compute the following *entropies* for each method and set:

$$S_a = -1.887$$

and:

$$S_b = -1.609$$

using the linear form [Equation (8)] and:

$$S_a = -2.163$$

and:

$$S_b = -2.144$$

using the reciprocal form [Equation (9)] where a and b refer to the sets on the left- and right-hand sides of Figure 1, respectively. According to this and Equation (4), one would conclude that the diversity of set a is greater than the one of set b and that this is true, regardless of the functional form used to derive the similarities. For all practical purposes the result is suspicious.

Let us take the argument above a step further. Figure 2 shows the entropy of the same three-point set shown in Figure 1 *vs.* the position of one of the points relative to the other two. The two extremes represent the cases where the third point coincides with one of the two reference points (Figure 1b), while the middle represents the situation depicted in Figure 1a. The profile is based on the reciprocal function shown in Equation (9) but similar results are obtained with Equation (8). As we can see, the entropy function is at a minimum when the third point is located halfway between the two reference points and monotonically increases as the point moves away from the centre in either direction.

Figure 2. Entropy as a function of x

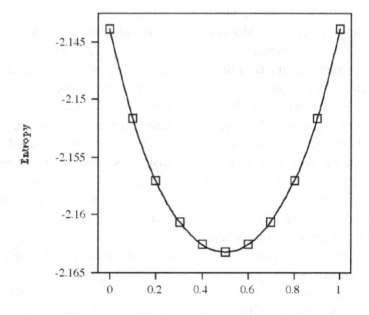

Distance 1-3

DISCUSSION

The reasons for the behaviour above can be traced back to Equations (3) and (4) and the definitions of entropy and information. As Lin correctly acknowledges, the pursuit of molecular diversity aims at maximizing our knowledge about the system under investigation. Clearly we are interested in compound collections that render *more* information about the underlying system, not *less*. However, there are many different types of information and the precise meaning depends on the context in which the term is used. In Shannon theory, information is used to measure the uncertainty associated with an event that is transmitted across a communication channel, which consists of a source that generates signals from some predefined set of possible signals and a receiver that receives the signals with some degree of uncertainty that depends on the characteristics of the source and communication line. Consider a device that can produce three possible symbols: A, B or C. As one waits at the receiving end one is uncertain as to which symbol will appear next. Once the signal is received one's uncertainty decays and one gains some information, which corresponds to a drop in *uncertainty*. Shannon entropy equation measures the uncertainty and represents the average *surprisal* for an infinite string of events produced by the source.

The extension of the concepts above to the study of molecular systems is straightforward. Indeed every collection of compounds can be viewed as a string of independent events, produced by an imaginary source and related to one another by virtue of a similarity metric. Shannon entropy expression can be used to measure one's ability to predict the events that are generated by that source. Clearly if one knows that the collection contains similar compounds, one can predict the overall structure of each compound with sufficient accuracy once one saw the first few. If on the other hand the collection contains diverse compounds, the element of surprise rises and one's

ability to predict their structures decays. Increase in diversity results in an *increase* in entropy not a decay as Lin suggested. Therefore, what is the type of information that one seeks to maximize in a diversity design? Gatlin, in her book on biological information theory, called this type of information *potential information* to distinguish it from *stored information* or the *what I do say* in Weaver statement (Gatlin, 1972). Since it varies directly with entropy high entropy leads to high potential information.

However there are some mathematical errors; *e.g.*, to satisfy the normality condition in Equation (7) the summation in equation $\Sigma_{j=1}^{N} \Sigma_{i=1}^{N} p_{ij} = 1$ should be over both i and j. The improper normalization may have serious numerical consequences. Moreover the coefficient c in equation $c = 1/(\Sigma_{j=1}^{N} \Sigma_{i=1}^{N} \rho_{ij})$ should be index-dependent. As pointed out by Maggiora (personal communication), joint probabilities are not necessarily symmetric while most similarity indices are. Equation $p_{ij} = c\rho_{ij}$ violates this, implying that similarity and probability are symmetric and linearly related by a single scalar parameter, which is not true. Would correcting the errors above lead to the *correct* response? The answer is no and the reason can be found again in Equations (7), $c = 1/(\Sigma_{j=1}^{N} \Sigma_{i=1}^{N} \rho_{ij})$ and $p_{ij} = c\rho_{ij}$. Entropy is minimized when the probability values become identical, which occurs when all the compounds in the collection become equidistant, which actually is another interesting consequence of the approach, *i.e.*, the fact that based on indistinguishability alone one cannot distinguish between two different, *e.g.*, tetrahedra, since the diversity is the same regardless of the size of the tetrahedron. If one is interested in a uniform sampling of the property space, one needs to consider only the immediate neighbourhoods of each compound. Although one may argue that some of the properties of Lin metric could be useful in a different context, it is clear that it cannot produce the kinds of uniform distributions that one typically requires in diversity designs. Lin concepts of indistinguishability and entropy bear a striking resemblance to similar ones used in fuzzy clustering (Bezdek, 1981). Indeed if one considers each member of the collection as a singleton cluster, the probabilities in Equation (7) become fuzzy cluster membership values and the entropy expression is identical to the fuzzy entropy of the system. In this context a critical comparison of two different clustering methods would be most constructive (Barni *et al.*, 1996; Krishnapuram & Keller, 1993, 1996).

CONCLUSION

From the previous discussion the following conclusions can be drawn.

1. Attributing complexity to only models and not to natural systems and relativizing its conception to the chosen framework, one arrives at an analytically useful conception of complexity. The conception not only captures much of the intuitive idea of complexity, but also allows the meaningful comparison of many different formulations of complexity and throwing some new light on some philosophical problems.

2. We focused on a particular measure of complexity to capture the difficulty of decomposing expressions and sketched a possible formal structure to relate different formal languages to the analysis of the sources of complexity in specific systems, which also provided a framework for the study of systematic methods simplification. This work is foundational in that it could form part of a new *science of complexity* (Casti, 1992). Much more can be done in this regard. (a) Further investigation into the relation between syntactic structures and complexity of expressions. (b) The development of automatic/semiautomatic methods of simplification. (c) The integration of this work into others' work in the field of *complex systems*, especially with regard to identifying possible *causes* of complexity. (d) The further development of measures of complexity for different purposes. (e) The use of this work as the synthesis of many formulations of complexity. Perhaps the most important way this work could be extended is towards a model of the process of modelling itself, which would involve extending and formalizing a semantic picture of modelling and could be seen as an extension of measure theory to nonnumeric structures (Tomasi, 1988). As Badii and Politi (1993) put it in their conclusion to their book on complexity: *The natural extension of the study of complexity... seems, therefore, to point inevitably to a theory of model inference.*

3. Self-organizing modelling technologies are a powerful approach to extract hidden knowledge from data serving for decision support of real-world problems. They are often an alternative choice to statistics, *neural networks* or *neurofuzzy* methods since they create optimal complex models automatically, fast and systematically and they provide an explanation component *via* explicit visible model descriptions.

4. This report describes our experience with the use of a new approach for assessing molecular diversity based on information theory. As we demonstrated with some simple examples, the method has a strong tendency to oversample remote areas of the feature space and produce unbalanced designs, which is because of the use of a certain type of information, whose mathematical definition is inappropriate for the study of molecular diversity.

5. Structure-based subcellular pharmacokinetics models the behaviour and the effects of chemicals in biosystems, as determined by the physicochemical properties and structures of chemicals and biosystems. Usually absorption, distribution, metabolism, excre-

tion and toxicity are, in practice, predicted using empirical modelling with molecular descriptors selected from large pools using exclusively statistical criteria, without paying much attention to the mechanisms of involved steps. The approaches try to capture the complexity of the pharmacokinetics processes *via* the unjustified use of a plethora of descriptors, rather than by focusing on the relevant chemicobiological interactions and building mechanistic models, which are often nonlinear in optimized coefficients.

ACKNOWLEDGMENT

G.C. belongs to the Catedra Energesis Tocnologia Interdisciplinar. F.T., acknowledges financial support from the Spanish Ministerio de Ciencia e Innovación (Project No. BFU2010–19118).

REFERENCES

Adami, C. (2000). Physical complexity of symbolic sequences. *Physica D. Nonlinear Phenomena, 137*, 62–69.

Agrafiotis, D. K. (1997a). On the use of information theory for assessing molecular diversity. *Journal of Chemical Information and Computer Sciences, 37*, 576–580.

Agrafiotis, D. K. (1997b). Stochastic algorithms for maximizing molecular diversity. *Journal of Chemical Information and Computer Sciences, 37*, 841–851.

Agrafiotis, D. K. (1998). Molecular diversity. In *Encyclopedia of computational chemistry*. New York, NY: Wiley.

Badii, R., & Politi, A. (1993). *Complexity: Hierarchical structures and scaling in physics* (p. 280). Cambridge, UK: Cambridge University Press.

Barni, M., Cappellini, V., & Mecocci, A. (1996). Comments on 'A possibilistic approach to clustering'. *IEEE Transactions on Fuzzy Systems, 4*, 393–396.

Bezdek, J. C. (1981). *Pattern recognition with fuzzy objective function algorithms*. New York, NY: Plenum Press.

Castellano, G., & Torrens, F. (2009). Local anaesthetics classified using chemical structural indicators. *Nereis, 2*, 7–17.

Casti, J. (1992). The simply complex: Trendy buzzword or emerging new science? *Bulletin of the Santa Fe Institute, 7*, 10–13.

Chaitin, G. J. (1966). On the length of programs for computing finite binary sequences. *Journal of the ACM, 13*, 547–569.

Denbigh, K. G., & Denbigh, J. (1987). *Entropy in relation to incomplete knowledge*. Cambridge, UK: Cambridge University Press.

Domb, C., & Green, M. S. (1976). *Phase transition and critical phenomena*. London, UK: Academic Press.

Edmonds, B. (1999). *Syntactic measures of complexity*. Unpublished doctoral dissertation, University of Manchester, Manchester.

Emmeche, C. (1996). *The garden in the machine: The emerging science of artificial life*. Princeton, NJ: Princeton University Press.

Farlow, S. J. (Ed.). (1984). *Self-organizing methods in modeling. GMDH type algorithms*. New York, NY: Marcel Dekker.

Floreano, D., Nicoud, J.-D., & Mondada, F. (Eds.). (1999). *Advances in artificial life: 5ᵗʰ European Conference, ECAL 99, Lecture Notes in Computer Science No. 1674*. Berlin, Germany: Springer.

Funtowicz, S., & Ravetz, J. (1994). Emergent complex systems. *Futures, 26*, 568–582.

Gatlin, L. (1972). *Information theory and the living system.* New York, NY: Columbia University Press.

Gell-Mann, M. (1994). *The quark and the jaguar: Adventures in the simple and the complex.* San Francisco, CA: Freeman.

Holland, J. (1999). *Emergence: From chaos to order.* Reading, MA: Perseus.

Jaynes, E. T. (1965). Gibbs vs Boltzmann entropies. *American Journal of Physics, 33,* 391–398.

Johnson, M. A., & Maggiora, G. M. (Eds.). (1990). *Concepts and applications of molecular similarity.* New York, NY: Wiley-Interscience.

Kolmogorov, A. N. (1965). Three approaches to the quantitative definition of information. *Problems of Information Transmission, 1,* 1–7.

Krishnapuram, R., & Keller, J. M. (1993). A possibilistic approach to clustering. *IEEE Transactions on Fuzzy Systems, 1,* 98–110.

Krishnapuram, R., & Keller, J. M. (1996). The possibilistic c-means algorithm: Insights and recommendations. *IEEE Transactions on Fuzzy Systems, 4,* 385–393.

Kubinyi, H. (1993). *QSAR: Hansch analysis and related approaches* (p. 172). Weinheim, Germany: VCH.

Le-Thi-Thu, H., Casañola-Martín, G. M., Marrero-Ponce, Y., Rescigno, A., Saso, L., & Parmar, V. S. (2011). Novel coumarin-based tyrosinase inhibitors discovered by OECD principles-validated QSAR approach from an enlarged balanced database. *Molecular Diversity, 15*(2).

Lebart, L., & Fenelon, J.-P. (1971). *Statistique et informatique appliqués* (p. 195). Paris, France: Dunod.

Lebart, L., Morineau, A., & Tabard, N. (1977). *Techniques de la description statistique.* Paris, France: Dunod.

Lemke, F. (1997). *Knowledge extraction from data using self-organizing modeling technologies.* Paper presented at eSEAM'97 Conference, MacSciTech organization.

Lemke, F., & Müller, J. A. (1997). Self-organizing data mining for a portfolio trading system. *Journal of Computational Intelligence and Finance, 5,* 12–26.

Li, M., & Vitányi, P. (1997). *An introduction to Kolmogorov complexity and its applications.* New York, NY: Springer.

Lin, S.-K. (1996). Molecular diversity assessment: Logarithmic relations of information and species diversity and logarithmic relations of entropy and indistinguishability after rejection of Gibbs paradox of entropy of mixing. *Molecules (Basel, Switzerland), 1,* 57–67.

Madala, H. R., & Ivakhnenko, A. G. (1994). *Inductive learning algorithms for complex systems modelling.* Boca Raton, FL: CRC.

Maggiora, G. M. (personal communication).

Marrero-Ponce, Y., Martínez-Albelo, E. R., Casañola-Martín, G. M., Castillo-Garit, J. A., Echeverría-Díaz, Y., & Romero Zaldivar, V. (in press). Bond-based linear indices of the non-stochastic and stochastic edge adjacency matrix. 1. Theory and modeling of *ChemPhys* properties of organic molecules. [in press]. *Molecular Diversity.*

Mitchell, M. (2009). *Complexity: A guided tour.* New York, NY: Oxford University.

Müller, J.-A., & Lemke, F. (1995). Self-organizing modelling and decision support in economics. *System Analysis Modeling Simulation, 18-19,* 135–138.

Pullman, B. (Ed.). (1994). *The emergence of complexity in mathematics, physics, chemistry and biology. Pontificiae Academiae Scientiarum Scripta Varia No. 89.* Vatican City, Vatican: Pontificia Academia Scientiarum.

Rosen, R. (1999). *Essays on life itself.* New York, NY: Columbia University Press.

Shannon, C. E. (1948a). A mathematical theory of communication: Part I, discrete noiseless systems. *The Bell System Technical Journal, 27,* 379–423.

Shannon, C. E. (1948b). A mathematical theory of communication: Part II, the discrete channel with noise. *The Bell System Technical Journal, 27,* 623–656.

Solomonoff, R. J. (1964a). A formal theory of inductive inference. Part I. *Information and Control, 7,* 1–22.

Solomonoff, R. J. (1964b). A formal theory of inductive inference. Part II. *Information and Control, 7,* 224–254.

Standish, R. K. (2001). On complexity and emergence. *Complexity International, 9,* 1–6.

Tomasi, J. (1988). Models and modeling in theoretical chemistry. *Journal of Molecular Structure, 179,* 273–292.

Torrens, F. (2000). Fractal hybrid orbitals in biopolymer chains. *Russian Journal of Physical Chemistry, 74,* 115–120.

Torrens, F. (2001). Fractals for hybrid orbitals in protein models. *Complexity International, 8,* 1–13.

Torrens, F. (2004). Valence topological charge-transfer indices for dipole moments. *Molecular Diversity, 8,* 365–370.

Torrens, F. (2002). Fractal hybrid-orbital analysis of the protein tertiary structure. *Molecules, 7,* 26-37

Torrens, F., & Castellano, G. (2006). Periodic classification of local anaesthetics (procaine analogues). *International Journal of Molecular Sciences, 7,* 12–34.

Torrens, F., & Castellano, G. (2009). Classification of complex molecules. In Hassanien, A.-E., & Abraham, A. (Eds.), *Foundations of computational intelligence* (*Vol. 5,* pp. 243–315). Berlin: Springer Studies in Computational Intelligence.

Torrens, F., & Castellano, G. (2010). Table of periodic properties of human immunodeficiency virus inhibitors. *International Journal of Computer Intelligence. Bioinformatics and Systems Biology, 1,* 246–273.

Torrens, F., & Castellano, G. (2011). Using chemical structural indicators for periodic classification of local anaesthetics. *International Journal of Chemoinformatics and Chemical Engineering. 1*(2), 15-34

Torrens, F., & Castellano, G. (in press, a). Periodic classification of human immunodeficiency virus inhibitors. In A. S. Sidhu, T. Dillon, & M. Bellgard (Eds.), *Biomedical data and applications.* Berlin, Germany: Springer Studies in Computational Intelligence.

Torrens, F., & Castellano, G. (2012). Structural classification of complex molecules by artificial intelligence techniques. In E. D. Castro & A. K. Haghi (Eds.), *Advanced methods and applications in chemoinformatics: Research methods and new applications.* Hershey, PA: IGI Global.

Torrens, F., & Castellano, G. (in press, b). Structural classification of complex molecules by information entropy and equipartition conjecture. In M. V. Putz (Ed.), *Chemistry information and computation in 21st Century.* New York, NY: Nova.

Chapter 10
Recurrence Indicators for the Estimation of Characteristic Size and Frequency of Spatial Patterns

Chiara Mocenni
University of Siena, Italy

Angelo Facchini
University of Siena, Italy

ABSTRACT

In this chapter, the authors propose a method for the estimation of the characteristic size and frequency of the typical structure in systems showing two dimensional spatial patterns. In particular, they use several indicators caught from the nonlinear framework for identifying the small and large scales of the systems. The indicators are applied to the images corresponding to the instantaneous realization of the system. The method assumes that it is possible to capture the main system's properties from the distribution of the recurring patterns in the image and does not require the knowledge of the dynamical system generating the patterns neither the application of any image segmentation method.

1. INTRODUCTION

Recurrence Plot (RP) and Recurrence Quantification Analysis (RQA) have been widely used as visual and quantitative tools for the analysis of nonlinear time series. In fact, they give a visual insight of the system dynamics when complex behaviors, such as deterministic chaos, are observed.

DOI: 10.4018/978-1-4666-2077-3.ch010

In recent years, RPs found a wide range of applications in the time series analysis of nonstationary phenomena, such as biological systems (P. Kaluzny, 1993, N. Thomasson, 2001, N. Marwan, 2002, J. P. Zbilut, 2004), speech analysis (L. Matassini, 2002, A. Facchini, 2005), financial time series (F. Strozzi, 2007), and earth sciences (N. Marwan, 2001, N. Marwan, 2003). The popularity of RPs lies in the fact that their structures are visually appealing, and that they allow for the investigation of high dimensional dynamics by means of a simple two-dimensional plot.

Furthermore, Recurrence Plots and Recurrence Quantification Analysis have been used for the detection of structural changes in the dynamics of complex nonlinear systems. For example, the relationship between the RP and sequences of bifurcations in the logistic equation has been discussed by (L.L. Trulla, 1996) for the detection of bifurcations without making any a priori assumption on the underlying equations of motion. (J. Gao, 2000) cope with the problem of identifying true bifurcation sequences and the causes of possibly false bifurcation points. They also give indications on how to choose suitable embedding parameters so that the bifurcation detection may still work when the signal is heavily corrupted by noise.

Recently, several extensions of RP and RQA to spatio-temporal systems have been proposed. (D.B. Vasconcelos, 2006) give a first definition of Spatial Recurrence Plot (SRP) and show that SRP allows one to detect some spatial patterns, like the roughness in metallic materials. They finally argue that SRP works well for recognizing other more general kinds of spatial structures. The extension of the RP to *d*-dimensional data sets, i.e. the Generalized Recurrence Plot (GRP) and Generalized Recurrence Quantification Analysis (GRQA), has been proposed by (N. Marwan, 2007(a)) with an application to the analysis of the bone structure from Computer Tomography images.

Recently, the GRP has been exploited for the characterization of spatially distributed systems (A. Facchini, 2009(a)) and investigation of pattern formation in chemical systems (A. Facchini, 2009(b)). A further application of this method to the analysis of and detection of bifurcations in spatially distributed systems has been recently published in (C. Mocenni, 2010), while analogies and differences between RP and GRP for spatial domains are discussed in (C. Mocenni, 2011).

This letter investigates the relationship between the recurrence measures and the pattern size and distribution in two dimensional domains. In section 2 the Recurrence Plots and the Recurrence Quantification analysis are introduced. Section 3 describes the experimental set-up and states the main results. Finally, concluding remarks and future work are reported in section 4.

2. RECURRENCE ANALYSIS OF COMPLEX SPATIALLY DISTRIBUTED SYSTEMS

In order to achieve a better understanding of the spatial extension, a short introduction on RP is given in the following, for a deeper treatment the reader is referred to (N. Marwan, 2007).

2.1 Time Series Analysis Based on Recurrence Plots

Let x_t be a time series and $S_m \subseteq R^m$ the associated *m*-dimensional embedded state space, reconstructed using the Takens delay Theorem ((F. Takens, 1981)). The Recurrence Plot is essentially a two dimensional binary diagram indicating the recurrences that occur in the space S_m within a fixed threshold ε at different times *i,j*. The RP is easily expressed as a two dimensional square matrix $R = \{r_{ij} : i, j = 1, ..., N\}$, with:

$$r_{ij} = \tau(\varepsilon - \left\| \vec{x}_i - \vec{x}_j \right\|) \tag{1}$$

where $x_i, x_j \in S_m$, *i,j*=1,...,*N*, *N* is the number of the measured states $\vec{x}_i$, $\tau(\cdot)$ is the step function, and $\|\cdot\|$ is a norm. In the graphical representation, each non-zero entry of the RP matrix **R** is marked by a black dot in the position (*i,j*). Since any state is recurrent with itself, the RP matrix **R** fulfills $r_{i,i} = 1$, i.e. the RP contains the diagonal, called *Line of Identity* (LOI).

The structures that can be identified in the RP give insights about the underlying dynamics are:

(a) Isolated points: the state does not persist for a long time; (b) Diagonal lines of length *l*: the trajectory visits the same portion of the phase space at different times; (c) Vertical and horizontal lines: the state changes very slowly in time.

In the global appearance of the RP, a homogeneous distribution of points is usually associated with stationary stochastic processes, e.g. gaussian or uniform white noise. On the other side, periodic structures, like long diagonal lines parallel to the LOI, indicate periodic behaviors, while drifts in the structure of the recurrences are often due to a slow variation of some parameter of the system and white areas or bands indicate non stationarity and abrupt changes in the dynamics. Recently, curved macrostructures have been related to very small frequency variations in periodic signals ((A. Facchini, 2007)).

Because of the limited screen resolution and the length of the time series, it is difficult to analyze the RP only by means of visual inspection (which is anyway useful to detect simple nonstationarities). To cope with this problem, the RQA offers a set of indicators computed on the structures of the RP. In the following we will briefly introduce only a subset of the RQA indicators (for an extensive discussion of other RQA measures the reader may refer to (A. Marwan, 2007(b))).

Let us now briefly describe the recurrence measures that will be used (see below for the mathematical description): the Recurrence Rate (*RR*), the Determinism (*D*) and the Recurrence Entropy (*RE*). Roughly speaking, the *RR* is the fraction of recurrent points with respect to the total number of possible recurrences. *D* is the fraction of recurrent points forming diagonal structures with respect to all the recurrences, and the *RE* is a complexity measure of the distribution of the diagonal lines in the GRP. The RR is a density measure of the RP, a typical value ranges between 10 and 20% ((A. Marwan, 2007(b))). The indicator *D* is introduced as a measure of the predictability of the system, because it accounts for the diagonal structures in the RP. In the one dimensional case,

i.e. time series, a line of length *l* indicates that, for *l* time steps, the trajectory in the phase space has visited the same region at different times. High values of *D* (60-70% or more) usually indicate the presence of periodicities in the data. The indicator *RE* represents a complexity measure of the RP. It refers to the Shannon entropy with respect to the probability of finding a diagonal line of length exactly equal to *l*. For periodic signals or uncorrelated noise the value is small (~0.2−0.8), while for chaotic systems, e.g. Lorenz, *RE*~3−4. The computation of the indicators based on the diagonal lines and their distribution provides valuable information about the structure of the RP and the underlying dynamics of the system under investigation.

2.2 Recurrence Plot of Spatially Distributed Systems

Recurrence Plots may be used for the analysis of systems showing complex patterns in time and space. In ((N. Marwan, 2007(a))) the authors introduce the Generalized Recurrence Plot for a *d*-dimensional data-set as the 2*d*-dimensional RP specified by the matrix **R**, whose elements are:

$$r_{\vec{i},\vec{j}} = \tau\left(\varepsilon - \left\| x_{\vec{i}} - x_{\vec{j}} \right\| \right) \qquad (2)$$

where $\vec{i} = i_1, i_2, ..., i_d$ is the *d*-dimensional coordinate vector and $\vec{x}_{\vec{i}}$ is the associated phase-space vector. This GRP accounts for recurrences between the *d*-dimensional state vectors. Although it cannot be visualized anymore, its quantification is still possible. Furthermore, as in the one-dimensional case, the LOI is replaced by a linear manifold of dimension *d* for which $R_{\vec{i},\vec{j}} = 1, \forall \vec{i} = \vec{j}$.

In a recent paper, (A. Facchini, 2009(a)) propose the application of Generalized Recurrence Plots and GRQA analysis to the analysis of complex images and introduce the *D*−*RE* diagram. In that context, an image represents the snapshot of an unknown dynamical system in steady state conditions and the signature of its dynamics is identified by the position of the image in the $D-RE$ space.

From the mathematical point of view, an image is a two-dimensional cartesian object composed of scalar values and in this special case the elements of the matrix **R** in the GRP are:

$$r_{i1,i2,j1,j2} = \tau\left(\varepsilon - |x_{i1,i2} - x_{j1,j2}|\right), \qquad i_1, j_1, i_2, j_2 = 1, ..., N \tag{3}$$

where each black dot represents a spatial recurrence between two pixels, and every pixel is identified by its coordinates (i_1, i_2), being i_1 and i_2 the row and the column index respectively. In this case, the recurrence plot is a four-dimensional RP and contains a two-dimensional identity plane, defined by setting $i_1 = j_1$ and $i_2 = j_2$.

2.3 Generalized Recurrence Quantification Analysis of Images

Since the GRP of an image is four dimensional, in principle its visual inspection is possible by projections in three or two dimensions. In practice, Generalized Recurrence Plots loose their visual appeal. Despite this drawback, RQA can still be performed since the structures described before (as isolated points and lines parallel to the LOI) can be easily extracted. In the following we describe how to generalize the structures formed by recurrences.

Denoting by l the length of a line structure, we build the histogram $P(l)$ of the line lengths and define the GRQA measures as in the one dimensional case. In particular, we focus on Recurrence Rate (RR), Determinism (D) and Recurrence Entropy (RE), defined as follows:

$$RR = \frac{1}{N^2} \sum_{i_1, i_2, j_1, j_2}^{N} r_{i_1, i_2, j_1, j_2} = \frac{1}{N^2} \sum_{l=1}^{N} lP(l),$$

$$D = \frac{\sum_{l=l_{\min}}^{N} lP(l)}{\sum_{l=1}^{N} lP(l)},$$

$$RE = -\sum_{l=l_{\min}}^{N} p(l) \log p(l), \quad p(l) = \frac{P(l)}{\sum_{l=l_{\min}}^{N} P(l)} \tag{4}$$

where $l_{\min}$ is the minimum length considered for the diagonal structures.

Other two indicators recently introduced are (C. Mocenni, 2011):

$$L^{*;D} = \arg\min_l \cdot [D(l)]^0 :^0 D(l) \geq D(l_{\max}) \tag{5}$$

$$L^{*;E} = \arg\min_l \cdot [E(l)]^0 :^0 E(l) \geq E(l_{\max}) \tag{6}$$

defined as the minimum line length for which the values of the indicators lay above a certain threshold (here assumed as 95% of the final values) and characterize the saturation velocity of D and E and are related to the size of the patterns present in the domain.

3. EXPERIMENTAL SETUP AND MAIN RESULTS

In (C. Mocenni, 2011) the relationship between the spot size and the critical lengths $L^{*;D}$ and $L^{*;E}$ are discussed. In particular, the above indicators are shown to represent reliable estimations of the average diameter of the spots. In this letter, the relationship between these measures and the number and size of the spots in a two dimensional patterned space is more deeply investigated. To this aim, a set of artificial data has been set-up by generating several images with spot numbers varying from 4 to 128 and other with spot whose radius varies in the range 9-50 pixels.

Figure 1. Images showing spots of different number and size: (a), (b) fixed size (R=16) and increasing N; (c),(d) Increasing R

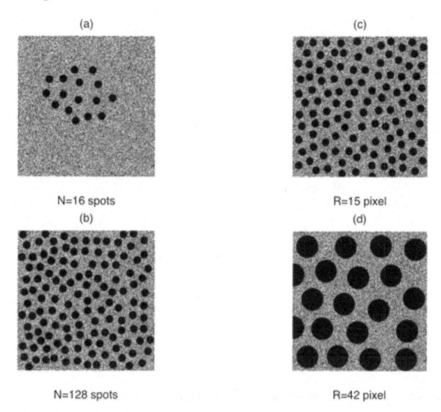

Panels (a),(b) of Figure 1 show two different spot distributions, while panels (c),(d) refer to different spot size. The background of the images has been set to noise to avoid any misleading contributions since the value of the recurrence indicators does not significantly differ from zero in the case of noise.

The recurrence indicators $D, RE, L^{*;D}$ and $L^{*;E}$ have been evaluated and the results are reported in the following.

In the case of increasing N, the results are reported in Figures 2(a),(b) and 3(a),(b). Referring to Figure 2(a),(b), one can notice that D and RE are increasing with the number of the spots, and that RE show a saturation effect for spot number larger that 32. This is not surprising since by increasing the size of the spots a constant increase of both D and RE and of the corresponding saturation

indicators is observed. Under the point of view of D, this is explained by noticing that a greater size increases the number and the lengths of the diagonal lines, therefore increasing the fraction of recurrent points organized in lines. On the other hand, recurrence entropy saturates because the distribution of the spots in the image does not change significantly when the number of the spots is high enough.

Another interesting result concerns the strong saturation of the line indicators $L^{*;D}$ and $L^{*;E}$ shown in Figure 3(a),(b). Both these integer measures are constant for spots number greater than 32. The saturating values correspond approximately to the spot dimension in the images (see Figure 1), showing that the above indicators provide reliable estimates of the typical structure of the patterns. A not meaningful number of spots in the image,

Figure 2. (a),(b) Determinism and recurrence entropy for different frequencies spotted patterns; (c),(d) Determinism and recurrence entropy for different size spotted patterns

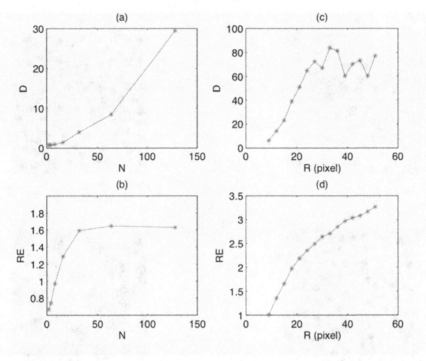

Figure 3. Evolution of the saturation indicators for N and R increasing

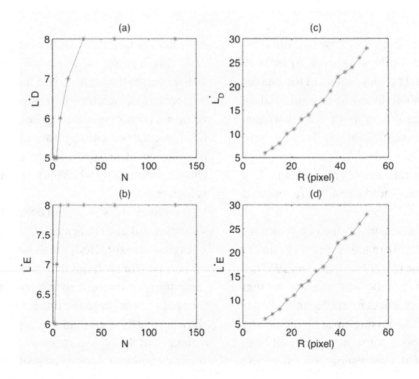

e.g. 4-16 spots, does not allow one to get the same conclusions, and introduces transient points before saturation.

Figures 2(c),(d) and 3(c),(d) report the results obtained in the case of increasing size. By inspection of Figure 2(c),(d) one can notice that D and RE increase with the dimension of the spots. The same increase is shown by $L^{*;D}$ and $L^{*;E}$, indicating approximately the typical structure of the spotted patterns. It is worth noticing that, after $R\sim30$, D saturates. This may be due to the finite size effect of the image, while RE do not seem affected by this phenomenon.

Finally, in order to compare the proposed method to standard image analysis techniques, a spatial fast fourier transform (fft) has been implemented for all the images used in the work. Figure 4 shows the computation of the 2D-FFT transform of the images for N and R increasing. As one can see, only small differences can be noticed by inspection of the transforms. This is mainly

due to the very simple nature of the images and to the fact that, the large amount of noise in the background corrupts the power spectrum.

4. CONCLUSION

The above results show that the spatial extension of the nonlinear recurrence methods used in this study provides a powerful tool for the analysis of spatial patterns allowing one to catch information on the typical structure of the pattern and on the frequency distribution of the spots in the pattern itself. One of the main features of the proposed method is that it does not require the knowledge of the systems equations describing the spatio-temporal dynamics, but it work on the time series. Furthermore, it is not based on the application of any image segmentation technique avoiding the drawbacks of very small or dense patterns. Finally, the analysis is not sensitive to the presence of

Figure 4. 2D-FFT transform of the images for N and R increasing

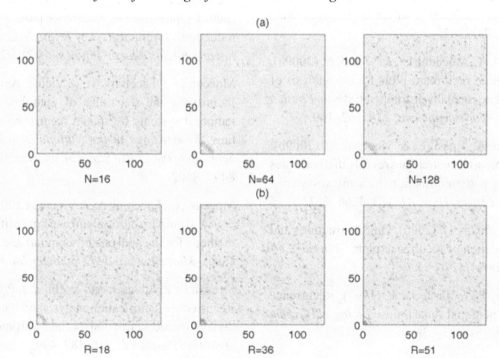

noise in the image, because it poorly contributes to the recurrence indicators estimation.

The comparison with the 2D-FFT transform of the images did not give valuable information about the nature of the patterns, since the noise present in the background corrupts the estimation of the power spectrum. In this sense, when dealing with this kind of images, and, in general, when dealing with real-world images, the presence of noise does not significantly affects the analysis of the patterns present in the domain, allowing for the identification of the patterns without the help of any segmentation tool.

REFERENCES

Facchini, A., & Kantz, H. (2007). Curved structures in recurrence plots: The role of the sampling time. *Physical Review E: Statistical, Nonlinear, and Soft Matter Physics, 75*, 36215.

Facchini, A., Kantz, H., & Tiezzi, E. (2005). Recurrence plot analysis of nonstationary data: The understanding of curved patterns. *Physical Review E: Statistical, Nonlinear, and Soft Matter Physics, 72*, 21915.

Facchini, A., Mocenni, C., & Vicino, A. (2009a). Generalized recurrence plots for the analysis of images from spatially distributed systems. *Physica D. Nonlinear Phenomena, 238*, 162–169.

Facchini, A., Rossi, F., & Mocenni, C. (2009b). Spatial recurrence strategies reveal different routes to Turing pattern formation in chemical systems. *Physics Letters. [Part A], 373*, 4266–4272.

Gao, J., & Cai, H. (2000). On the structures and quantification of recurrence plots. *Physics Letters. [Part A], 270*, 75–87.

Kaluzny, P., & Tarnecki, P. (1993). Recurrence plots of neuronal spike trains. *Biological Cybernetics, 68*(6), 527–534.

Marwan, N., Kurths, J., & Saparin, P. (2007a). Generalised recurrence plots analysis for spatial data. *Physics Letters. [Part A], 360*, 545–551.

Marwan, N., Romano, M. C., Thiel, M., & Kurths, J. (2007b). Recurrence plots for the analysis of complex systems. *Physics Reports, 438*, 237–329.

Marwan, N., Thiel, M., & Nowaczyk, N. R. (2002). Cross recurrence plot based synchronization of time series. *Nonlinear Processes in Geophysics, 9*(3/4), 325–331.

Marwan, N., Trauth, M. H., Vuille, M., & Kurths, J. (2003). Comparing modern and Pleistocene ENSO-like influences in NW Argentina using nonlinear time series analysis methods. *Climate Dynamics, 21*(3-4), 317–326.

Marwan, N., Wessel, N., Meyerfeldt, U., Schirdewan, A., & Kurths, J. (2002). Recurrence-plot-based measures of complexity and their application to heart-rate-variability data. *Physical Review E: Statistical, Nonlinear, and Soft Matter Physics, 66*(2), 026702.

Matassini, L., Kantz, H., Holyst, J., & Hegger, R. (2002). Optimizing of recurrence plots for noise reduction. *Physical Review E: Statistical, Nonlinear, and Soft Matter Physics, 65*(2), 021102.

Mocenni, C., Facchini, A., & Vicino, A. (2010). Identifying the dynamics of complex spatiotemporal systems by spatial recurrence properties. *Proceedings of the National Academy of Sciences of the United States of America, 107*(18), 8097–8102.

Mocenni, C., Facchini, A., & Vicino, A. (2011). (in press). Comparison of recurrence quantification methods for the analysis of temporal and spatial chaos. *Mathematical and Computer Modelling*.

Strozzi, F., Zaldivar, J.-M., & Zbilut, J. P. (2007). Recurrence quantification analysis and state space divergence reconstruction for financial time series analysis. *Physica A, 376*, 487–499.

Takens, F. (1981). *Detecting strange attractors in turbulence. Lecture Notes in Mathematics, 898.* New York, NY: Springer.

Thomasson, N., Hoeppner, T. J., Webber, C. L. Jr, & Zbilut, J. P. (2001). Recurrence quantification in epileptic EEGs. *Physics Letters. [Part A], 279,* 94–101.

Trulla, L. L., Giuliani, A., Zbilut, J. P., & Webber, C. L. Jr. (1996). Recurrence quantification analysis of the logistic equation with transients. *Physics Letters. [Part A], 223,* 255–260.

Vasconcelos, D. B., Lopes, S. R., Viana, R. L., & Kurths, J. (2006). Spatial recurrence plots. *Physical Review E: Statistical, Nonlinear, and Soft Matter Physics, 73,* 1–10.

Zbilut, J. P., Mitchell, J. C., Giuliani, A., Colosimo, A., Marwan, N., & Webber, C. L. (2004). Singular hydrophobicity patterns and net charge: A mesoscopic principle for protein aggregation/folding. *Physica A, 343,* 348–358.

Chapter 11
The Residence Time of the Water in Lake MAGGIORE:
Through a Eulerian–Lagrangian Approach

Leonardo Castellano
Matec Modelli Matematici, Italy

Nicoletta Sala
Università della Svizzera Italiana, Switzerland

Angelo Rolla
CNR – Institute for Ecosystem Study, Italy

Walter Ambrosetti
CNR – Institute for Ecosystem Study, Italy

ABSTRACT

This chapter describes a study designed to evaluate the spectrum of the residence time of the water at different depths of a deep lake, and to examine the mechanisms governing the seasonal cycle of thermal stratification and destratification, with the ultimate aim of assessing the actual exchange time of the lake water. The study was performed on Lake Maggiore (depth 370m) using a multidimensional mathematical model and computer codes for the heat and mass transfer in very large natural water bodies. A 3D Eulerian time-dependent CFD (Computational Fluid Dynamics) code was applied under real conditions, taking into account the effects of the monthly mean values of the mass flow rates and temperatures of all the tributaries, mass flow rate of the Ticino effluent and meteorological, hydrological, and limnological parameters available from the rich data-base of the CNR-ISE (Pallanza). The velocity distributions from these simulations were used to compute the paths of a large number of massless markers with different initial positions and evaluate their residence times in the lake.

DOI: 10.4018/978-1-4666-2077-3.ch011

INTRODUCTION

The findings presented here are the result of a two-year simulation and may be briefly summarized as follows: a) much of the water arriving in the lake from tributaries and/or from depths from 0.0 to around 50-70 m below the free surface has probable residence time values between 250 days and 2 years or more; b) the water flowing below 150-180 m shows some movement but is very unlikely to rise vertically; c) we can make no general hypothesis as to the fate of the water flowing in the intermediate zone. The fate of the intermediate water mass is linked to the fact that this water undergoes the year-to-year impact of the vertical winter mixing, and its renewal time depends on the extent to which it is involved in the circulatory system.

One of the major problems in theoretical and applied limnology is to establish the mean actual residence time of the water in a complex lake such as Lake Maggiore (Ambrosetti et al. 2003). Taking account also of the ongoing climate changes, it is only by determining this mechanism in real terms that that the velocity of the processes of concentration, dilution and permanence of substances in the lake can be assessed, with the resulting implications for water quality and the planning of effective policies to protect the environmental resources of the whole territory. The actual water exchange time can only be determined through an evaluation of the hydrodynamics of the lake. This means creating a numerical-mathematical model which can come as close as possible to making an exact evaluation of the residence time of the water in Lake Maggiore and which takes account primarily of its internal circulation, as well as the hydrology of its drainage basin. By "internal circulation" we mean the quantitative assessment of the longitudinal, transverse and vertical movements of the lake water at the various bathymetric depths in relation to its thermal structure and the meteorological and hydrological parameters responsible for the process.

The creation and study of a multidimensional mathematical model and calculation codes for the transfer of heat and mass in very large natural free surface water bodies has been one of the most pioneering applications of applied research and advanced engineering in the field of fluid dynamic methods. The problem was treated some decades ago by Orlob (1967), Cheng and Tung (1970), Dailey and Harleman (1972), Castellano and Dinelli (1975), while recent researchers have included Rueda and Schladow (2005), Yue et al. (2004), Leon *et al.* (2005), Pham Thi et al. (2005), Wang et a*l.* (2005), Castellano et al. (2008). Advances made so far are mainly due to the huge increase in computer calculating power, allowing researchers to use several hundred million calculation cells. With the quantity of input available, this has enabled us to develop a useful model for limnological studies, making it possible to work on the whole volume of a lake by dividing it into thousands of cells, and within time intervals ranging from a few months to years – an impossible enterprise in the past. Each of the simulations presented here, performed by applying our model, has required the use of extremely powerful processors and elaboration times which may go on for several days without interruption.

We should stress that the research performed so far represents a preliminary, if essential, study, aimed at fine-tuning and using the guidelines of a campaign of numerical simulations developed to study the time scales of the hydrodynamics and transport phenomena in Lake Maggiore. This work, continuing previous research, documents the capacities of the computer code used and shows evaluations of major importance regarding the fate of massless Lagrangian markers inserted at different locations in the lake at zero time of a biennial simulation. This process is a necessary preliminary to understanding the overall hydrodynamics of Lake Maggiore, an essential premise for the assessment of the actual exchange time of its water, which was our aim.

2. MODEL USED

The model used in this study is based on Computational Fluid Dynamics (CFD) as a reference code. This code, used in the study of processes of fluid dynamics and heat and mass exchange in surface water bodies, is employed by large research groups and those working in advanced engineering on problems in the industrial and environmental sectors (see Loga-Karpinska et al. (2003); Shen & Haas (2004); Jouon et al. (2006); Wilde et al. (2006); Liu et al. (2008)). The industrial use of the model by a number of bodies involves applying it in the smallest possible area of a water body and for a very short time period. To use the model for our purposes, some major modifications were necessary; the resulting model, which we called TRIM_LM (Three-dimensional Model Lake Maggiore) is described in detail in Castellano et al. (2008). For limnological studies, especially those on lake hydrodynamics, the model (as specified above) requires calculations on the whole volume of the lake and for time intervals ranging from some months to years. The ultimate aim of the TRIM_LM model is to evaluate the spectrum of the actual residence time of the water at different depths. The number of parameters to be used is high, and as emerges from the most exhaustive studies published in the specialised technical literature by Laval et al. (2003), Leon et al. (2005) Leon et al. (2006), among others, this is the major problem to be solved. In any case the level of accuracy of the results will depend on how good the mathematical and numerical model is, but also on the time scales, and the number and correctness of the experimental values available for the parameters.

One of the most important hydrodynamical features of deep lakes in temperate regions, especially sub-alpine lakes, is holo-oligomixis. Turbulence, transport and vertical mixing define the environmental characteristics in which bio-geochemical reactions take place (Salmaso, 2005; Rueda, 2006 Ambrosetti et al. 2010). They determine complex phenomena such as the oxygenation of the deep layers, nutrient recycling, the distribution of particulate and dissolved substances, the vertical migration of plankton with effect on the subsequent production, and so on. For example, some phyto-zooplanktonic species display high sensitivity to dynamic processes, which can produce in these populations a marked instability that can last for their whole annual cycle (Manca et al, 2000; Manca et al, 2009).

In deep lakes, and in Lake Maggiore in particular, the limited depth reached by the vertical mixing of its water by convective movements at the end of the limnological winter is of major importance. The global warming of recent decades is one of the causes that have contributed to the increase in the quantity of heat present, causing an increase in conditions of stability and static persistence of the deep hypolimnion, increasing the capacity for resistance of the water mass to the vertical circulation, inhibiting its complete homogenization and conditioning the overall hydrodynamics of the lake (Ambrosetti & Barbanti, 1999; Ambrosetti & Barbanti, 2002; Ambrosetti et al., 2007; Ambrosetti et al. 2010).

3. EVALUATION OF THE RESIDENCE TIME OF LAKE WATER

The TRIM_LM model, devised in 2008 and described in detail in Castellano et al (2008), was employed and fine-tuned for our purposes.

Over the last two years we have performed a series of simulations to study the sensitivity and behaviour of the lake hydrodynamics in the face of the demands of the hydro-meteorological parameters in order to refine the response and the validity of the model and adapt it with greater precision to the current state of our knowledge of physical limnology. We would emphasise that our results for the second year (2009) were markedly better than those of the previous year, due primarily to two factors:

a.   The increase in resolutive power of the integration grid mesh, from 400,000 to 877,500 cells;

b.   A more realistic calibration of the turbulence model.

The greater precision of these two factors produced a closer agreement between measurements and simulations, and a finer evaluation of the exchange coefficients across the free surface and of the associated reference temperatures. The resulting numerical simulations, obtained under simplified conditions compared to the complexity of natural conditions, provide a realistic picture of the hydrodynamic sensitivity of the lake to variations in all the major parameters, from meteorological values to the volume and temperature of the tributaries, and equivalent volumes of rainfall and runoff.

Fine-tuning the model enabled us to make numerical experiments to determine the residence times by observing the convective-diffusive trans-port of a conservative (i.e. not reactive) tracer. It should be stressed that there are no conceptual difficulties in this research: the difficulties are merely "technical", in so far as complete annual simulations must be performed for each hypothetical "spread" of tracer initially located at different points and at different depths, and each scenario requires considerable time for its performance.

The discrete model of the lake used in this study is given in Figure 1, and shows how the water body has been ideally subdivided into calculation cells with horizontal dimensions of 250x250 mt, while vertically it has been divided into 50 layers, closer together towards the top, to an overall total of 877,500 cells. The figure also shows that the "longitudinal direction", indicated with the symbol Y, is positive from S (outflowing Ticino) to N (inflowing Ticino), with the zero point located at the lake's incile ; the "transverse direction", indicated with the symbol X, is positive from W to E, with zero at the Toce outlet; the "vertical direction", indicated with the symbol

Figure 1. Grid mesh over the whole geometry of Lake Maggiore used in this study

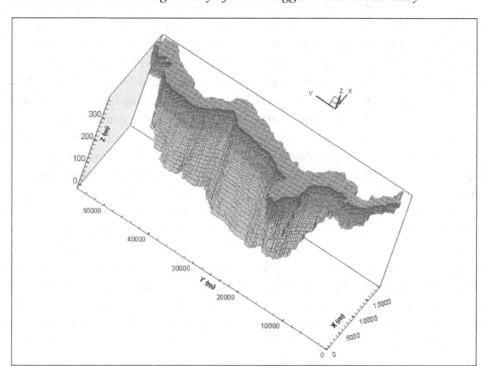

Z, has its zero at the point of maximum depth of the lake, so the positive sense is upwards. These indications are important as they make it possible to observe the position and the route of the markers represented in the subsequent figures.

This study monitors the movements of 72 massless Lagrangian markers inserted in different positions in Lake Maggiore at zero time of a multi-annual simulation. The application of the massless (non-reactive) marker method transported from 3D motion fields calculated using CFD (Computational Fluid Dynamics) systems may be regarded as a "recent approach" (Castellano, Ambrosetti, & Sala, 2008; Dinelli, Tozzi, 1977).

The markers were duly placed at t=0.0 of 1 January 2002 and monitored over a time period of 2 years. The markers are without mass and volume, so that they move solely at the local (calculated) velocity of the lake. The equations of their motion are purely "cinematic" (Lagrangian) and have the following form: where (x,y,z) are the coordinates (respectively transverse i.e. from west to east; longitudinal i.e. from south to north, and vertical) of the generic marker p; δt is the time increment; the superscript t stands for the variables evaluated in the "preceding" period; superscript t + δt stands for the variables in the "current" period; (u,v,w) are the Cartesian components of the velocity of the lake water provided at each point and instant by instant by the simulation (for each increment δt of time): in the context of (1.1)-(1.3) these velocities are those calculated for the computational cell containing the marker p at the instant "preceding" t.

The simulations are performed at time increments of 120 seconds.

As can be seen in Tables 1 and 2, two types of markers are used: "environmental markers", which had their starting position in the lake, and "tributary markers", which had their starting position at the outlet of the various tributaries. Note that the first 31 environmental markers were placed at different depths in the northernmost part of the lake, near where the River Ticino discharges into the lake, while the rest were placed at increasing depths moving in a southerly direction.

Only 5 of the 31 environmental markers (M5, M8, M10, M19, M31) with a starting position near the mouth of the inflowing Ticino reached the area of the outflowing Ticino and so may be regarded as having exited the lake. The resulting residence time values are between around 350 days (for the particles which started only a few metres below the free surface) and around 500 days (for the particles with a deeper starting position).

Of those reaching the outflow, marker M5 (Figure 2A), which left at the level of Locarno at a depth of 9.0 m (Table 1) followed a sinuous course, initially moving towards the western part of the lake before continuing towards the outflow. In the first 320 days it stayed at a depth within the top 25 m, subsequently rising to the surface before exiting the lake after around 500 days.

The exception in this series of markers was M31 (Figure 2B), which, starting from a depth of -100 m, succeeded in rising to the surface after a year, when it was located at the level of the deepest part of the lake (Ghiffa), subsequently exiting. The rise of this marker to the top may be connected with the fact that at the beginning of the two-year period (winter 2001-2002) the vertical convective mixing had reached a depth of only 100 m, so that the marker remained in its starting position for the whole of the annual cycle. The next winter the winter mixing exceeded a depth of 120 m, reaching the marker and carrying it up towards the surface.

It is interesting that the surface markers exiting the lake all had a tendency to move towards the western shore. This appears to be due not so much to an effect of the Coriolis force (negligible if we consider the relatively narrow width of the lake) as to the distinctive morphology of the lake valley, which tends to force the north winds (locally the strongest) to blow in a SSW direction.

Table 1. Position of environmental markers

Markers	X (m)	Y (m)	Z (m)	Markers	X (m)	Y (m)	Z (m)
M_1	16875.	55375.	-1.0	M_26	""	""	-80.0
M_2	""	""	-3.0	M_27	""	""	-84.0
M_3	""	""	-5.0	M_28	""	""	-88.0
M_4	""	""	-4.0	M_29	""	54625.	-92.0
M_5	""	""	-9.0	M_30	""	""	-96.0
M_6	""	""	-11.0	M_31	""	""	-100.5
M_7	""	""	-13.5	M_32	12375.	50500.	-106.0
M_8	""	""	-16.5	M_33	""	""	-112.0
M_9	""	""	-19.5	M_34	""	""	-120.0
M_10	""	""	-22.5	M_35	""	""	-128.0
M_11	16625.	55375.	-25.5	M_36	""	""	-138.0
M_12	""	""	-25.5	M_37	""	50000.	-150.0
M_13	16875.	55375.	-28.5	M_38	""	""	-162.0
M_14	""	""	-34.5	M_39	""	""	-174.0
M_15	""	""	-37.5	M_40	12875.	49125.	-189.0
M_16	""	""	-40.5	M_41	""	""	-207.0
M_17	""	""	-44.0	M_42	12625.	47275.	-225.0
M_18	""	""	-48.0	M_43	""	""	-243.0
M_19	""	55125.	-52.0	M_44	11375.	46875.	-261.0
M_20	""	""	-56.0	M_45	""	""	-279.0
M_21	""	""	-60.0	M_46	10875.	44125.	-298.5
M_22	""	54875.	-64.0	M_47	12875.	39125.	-319.5
M_23	""	""	-68.0	M_48	""	""	-340.5
M_24	""	""	-72.0	M_49	14875.	36375.	-361.5
M_25	""	""	-76.0	M_50	""	35625.	-370.0

Table 2. Position of tributary markers

Markers	fiume	X (m)	Y (m)	Z (m)	Markers	fiume	X (m)	Y (m)	Z (m)
M_51	Ticino	18875.	53375.	-1.0	M_62	Cannobino	9375.	42875.0	-7.0
M_52	""	18875.	53375.	-7.0	M_63	Maggia	14875.	51375.0	-1.0
M_53	Vevera	11875.	4875.	-1.0	M_64	""	14875.	51375.0	-7.0
M_54	""	11875.	4875.	-7.0	M_65	Verzasca	18625.	55125.0	-1.0
M_55	Erno	10625.	9625.	-1.0	M_66	""	18625.	55125.0	-7.0
M_56	""	10625.	9625.	-7.0	M_67	Tresa	15125.	32375.0	-1.0
M_57	Toce	875.	20875.	-1.0	M_68	""	15125.	32375.0	-7.0
M_58	""	875.	20875.	-7.0	M_69	Boesio	10875.	21125.0	-1.0
M_59	S.Bernard.	7125.	22125.	-1.0	M_70	""	10875.	21125.0	-7.0
M_60	""	7125.	22125.	-7.0	M_71	Bardello	12875.	14875.0	-1.0
M_61	Cannobino	9375.	42875.	-1.0	M_72	""	12875.	14875.0	-7.0

*The horizontal and vertical movement of all the markers indicated in the two tables are given in the appendix.

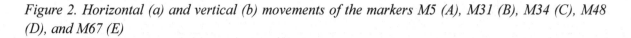

Figure 2. Horizontal (a) and vertical (b) movements of the markers M5 (A), M31 (B), M34 (C), M48 (D), and M67 (E)

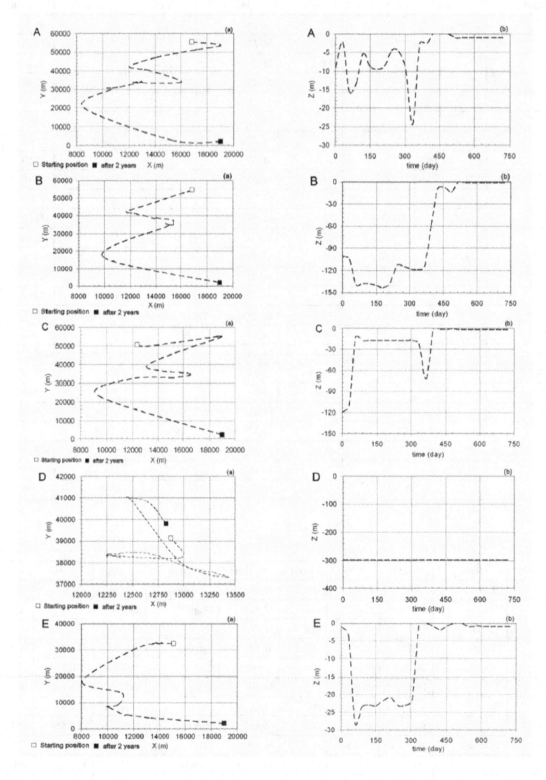

The 26 remaining particles in this series, which started out with almost the same horizontal co-ordinates and a vertical position between -1 and -128.5 m, followed different routes: M17, M22, M24, M30 travelled up and down over a relatively extensive area of the lake before returning almost to their initial position; M25 was lost, exiting from the calculation domain (this can be regarded as an undesired numerical effect); all the others covered around half of the whole nominal North-South distance, sometimes rising towards the free surface, sometimes sinking towards the bottom, and sometimes floating freely at their initial depth.

Of the 19 environmental markers with a starting position more than 130 m below the free surface, only the one labelled M34 (Figure 2C) reached the area of the outflowing Ticino; its initial position at the level of the Maggia delta probably affected its progress. Its residence time was around 400 days. Of the others: markers M40, M41, M42, M44, M46, M47, M48 (Figure 2D) tended to return to their initial position after more or less wide-ranging up and down movements through the waterbody. The movements of M36 and M37 were very short. M43, M45, M50 were lost from the calculation domain (numerical accidents). M36, M37 and M39 tended to move in a northerly direction. The others covered around one third of their nominal distance from the South but with more or less the same vertical position as they started with.

The stationary behaviour of this group of markers may be attributed to the fact that they were placed in the lake hypolimnion, an isolated and stable zone where water movements do not generally exceed one centimetre per second, except during certain events, mostly in winter, connected with the convective mixing or other mechanisms of oxygenation of the deepest layer. It has been shown that these mechanisms are not able to transfer masses of water from the bottom to the surface, and above all, during the two years of the simulation no water penetrated the layers of the hypolimnion (Ambrosetti et al., 2010).

Only 6 of the 22 tributary markers can be regarded as having exited the lake with the water of the outflowing Ticino: M53-M54 (from the Vevera), M56 (second marker from the Erno), M67-M68 (Tresa, Figure 2E), M72 (second marker from the Bardello). The residence time values were around 2 years for Vevera and Erno, and around 350 and 400 days for Tresa and Bardello respectively. Markers M57 and M58 from the Toce covered almost 80% of their nominal distance to the outlet. The others showed varying behaviours: the trajectories of markers M59-M60 (S. Bernardino) and M63-M64 (Maggia) tended to move in a SW direction, in contrast to M55 (Erno, first marker), M65-M66 (Verzasca), M69 (Boesio, first marker), M71 (Bardello, first marker), which travelled in a NE direction; M61 and M62 (Cannobino) both moved W but one towards N and the other towards S. Finally, the first marker of the Ticino tributary, M51, covered more than its nominal N-S distance to the outlet, while the second Ticino marker, M57, showed only a movement towards W.

The striking differences in behaviour between the tributary markers, even between single pairs, can be interpreted only in the light of the diverse thermal characteristics of the inflowing waters and the water present in the lake.

A first observation is that all the exiting markers had their starting position in the mouth of tributaries draining basins with low altitudes, i.e. with water whose temperature allows it to penetrate only the most superficial levels of the lake. In contrast, the tributaries flowing down from basins with higher mean altitudes, specifically the inflowing Ticino, the Maggia, and the Toce, are in general colder, and may also carry a load of glacial silt, which increases their density and allows them to penetrate deeper layers of the lake. Nevertheless, these markers do not in their subsequent route through the lake exceed a depth of 100 m, probably because they mix with the receiving water. Confirmation of the fact that vertical mixing did not occur and that the markers did not reach the lake bottom is provided by the fact that in the two years of the simulation no increase of oxygen was recorded in the hypolimnion; on the contrary, the oxygen decreased (Ambrosetti et al, 2010).

As for the different behaviour noted between single pairs from the same tributary mouth, the fact that they were inserted at two different depths (1 and 7 m) may have meant that each time they were inserted into streamlines with completely different dynamic characteristics, determined not only by the different penetration depths of the inflowing waters, but also by local morphological conditions.

CONCLUSION

In this chapter we have looked at the problems connected with the creation of models expressly designed for an understanding of lake dynamics. In particular we have focused on the movement of the water layers contained in the 0 to 370 metres depth of Lake Maggiore, with the aim of evaluating the actual exchange time of the water in deep lakes.

What we have decribed can be regarded as merely an introduction to a wider study on the possibility of using the Eulerian-Lagrangian methods of CFD (Computational Fluid Dynamics) to evaluate the hydraulic residence time of a large southern Alpine lake like Lake Maggiore.

The results of the study may be briefly summarized as follows:

1. Much of the water arriving in the lake from tributaries and/or from depths from 0.0 to around 50-70 m below the free surface has probable residence time values between 250 days and 2 years or more;
2. The water flowing below 150-180 m shows some movement but is very unlikely to rise vertically;
3. We can make no general hypothesis as to the fate of the water flowing in the intermediate zone.

These first conclusions about the residence time of Lake Maggiore water are fully confirmed by the mechanisms of mixing and deep water oxygenation described by Ambrosetti et. al. (2007) and Ambrosetti et al. (2009), in the winter, the water in the top layer (generally 100-150 m, in conformity with the convective activity of the last 40 years) is able to circulate freely. In contrast, the water in the deepest layers remains isolated, and though it may have a low degree of internal movement, it can be regarded as "still". The fate of the intermediate water mass is linked to the fact that this water undergoes the year-to-year impact of the vertical winter mixing, and its renewal time depends on the extent to which it is involved in the circulatory system.

Confirmation of these observations also comes from an analysis of the vertical distributions of thermal stability, which shows the distinct separation existing between upper mixed layers, upper hypolimnion and deep hypolimnion (Ambrosetti et al, 2009).

The study underlines both the potential and the difficulties involved in this approach. Whatever its degree of sophistication, from a theoretical standpoint a 3D mathematical model always offers a huge number of investigation probabilities. This can easily be deduced from the structure of equations (1.1)-(1.3), which represents a model of medium complexity; further comments are unnecessary.

Any difficulties will lie in the actual possibility of exploiting the potentiality of these models at a sufficiently high degree of precision. From a practical view point this means that the number of markers used will have to be large enough to yield statistically significant results, on a sufficiently fine discretization of the water body. This may be easily deduced from the quite marked differences observed in the trajectories of particles with relatively close starting positions, and in particular between the two particles associated with the same tributaries.

We are firmly convinced of the effectiveness of this approach, and are equally firm in our determination to make it a reality (Castellano et al., 2008; Castellano et al., 2010), but we are also quite certain of the need for increasingly detailed knowledge of the mechanisms regulating the complexity of systems like lakes of great area and depth, to prevent the application of these models being reduced to a purely numeric exercise.

In the light of these remarks, current research is proceeding as follows: a) an extension of the simulations described above to a period of more than 4 years; b) a new series of comparisons with more detailed discussion and 200 markers. The new discrete model and the starting position of the Lagrangian particles have been adjusted on the basis of the results described in the preceding section.

REFERENCES

Ambrosetti, W., & Barbanti, L. (1999). Deep water warming in lakes; an indicator of climatic change. *Journal of Limnology, 58*(1), 1–9.

Ambrosetti, W., & Barbanti, L. (2002). Phisycal limnology of Italian lakes. 2. Relationship between morphometric parameters, stability and Birgean work. *Journal of Limnology, 61*(2), 159–1167.

Ambrosetti, W., Barbanti, L., & Carrara, E. A. (2007). Riscaldamento delle acque profonde nei laghi italiani: Un indicatore di cambiamenti climatici. *Clima e Cambiamenti climatici le attività del CNR* (pp. 601-608).

Ambrosetti, W., Barbanti, L., & Carrara, E. A. (2010). Mechanism of hypolimnion erosion in a deep lake (Lago Maggiore, N.Italy). *Journal of Limnology, 69*(1), 3–14.

Ambrosetti, W., Barbanti, L., & Sala, N. (2003). *Residence time and physical processes in lake.* International Conference on Residence Time in Lakes: Science, Management, Education. September 29th- October 3rd Bolsena Viterbo.

Castellano, L., Ambrosetti, W., Barbanti, L., & Rolla, A. (2010). The residence time of the water in Lago Maggiore (N. Italy), first result from an Eulerian-Lagrangian approach. *Journal of Limnology, 69*(1), 15–28.

Castellano, L., Ambrosetti, W., & Sala, N. (2008). About the use of computational fluid dynamic (CFD) in the framework of physical limnological studies on a Great Lake . In *Reflexing interfaces* (pp. 257–277). Hershey, PA: Information Science Reference.

Castellano, L., & Dinelli, G. (1975). *Experimental and analytical evaluation of thermal alteration in the Mediterranean.* International Conference on Mathematical Models far Environinental Problems.

Cheng, R. T., & Tung, C. (1970). Wind-driven lake circulation by finite clement method. *Proceedings of the 13'x'Conference on Great Lakes Research,* (pp. 891-903).

Dailey, J. E., & Harleman, D. R. F. (1972). *Numerical model far the prediction of transient water quality in estuary networks* (Rep. No. MITSG 72-15). Cambridge, MA: MIT, Department of Civil Engineering.

Dinelli, G., & Tozzi, A. (1977). Three-dimensional modelling of the dispersion of pollutants in Mediterranean coastal waters. *XVII International Congress of IAHR,* August 1977, Baden Baden (Germany), (pp. 52-61).

Jouon, A., Douillet, P., Ouillon, S., & Fraunié, P. (2006). Calculations of hydrodynamic time parameters in a semi-opened coastal zone using a 3D hydrodynamic model. *Continental Shelf Research, 26,* 1395–1415.

Laval, B., Imberger, J., Hodges, B., & Stocker, R. (2003). Modeling circulation in lakes: Spatial and temporal variations. *Limnology and Oceanography, 48*(3), 983–994.

Leon, L. F., Lam, D., Schertzer, W. M., & Swayne, D. A. (2005). Lake and climate models linkage: A 3-D hydrodynamic contribution. *Advances in Geosciences, 4*, 57–62.

Leon, L. F., Lam, D. C. L., Schertzer, W. M., & Swayne, D. A. (2006). A 3D hydrodynamic lake model: Simulation on Great Slave Lake. *Proceedings International Modelling and Software Society Biennial Conference,* Burlington, VT.

Liu, W.-C., Chen, W.-B., Kuo, J.-T., & Wu, C. (2007). Numerical determination of residence time and age in a partially mixed estuary using three-dimensional hydrodynamic model. *Continental Shelf Research, 28*(8), 1068–1088.

Loga-Karpinska, M., Duwe, K., Guilbaud, C., O'Hare, M., Lemmin, U., & Umlauf, L. ... Mahnke, P. (2003). *D24: Realistic residence times studies, integrated water resource management for important deep European lakes and their catchment areas.* Eurolakes, FP5_Contract No.: EVK1-CT1999-00004

Manca, M., & DeMott, W. R. (2009). Response of the invertebrate predator Bythotrephes to a climate-linked increase in the duration of a refuge from fish predation. *Limnology and Oceanography, 54*(4).

Manca, M., Morabito, G., & Cavicchioni, N. (2000). First observations on the effect of a complete, exceptional overturn of Lake Maggiore on Plankton and primary production. *International Review of Hydrobiology, 85*(2-3), 209–222.

Orlob, G. T. (1967). *Prediction of thermal energy distribution in streams and reservoirs (Tech. Rep.).* Walnut Creek, CA: Water Resources Engineers, Inc.

Pham Thi, N. N., Huisman, J., & Sommeijer, B. P. (2005). Simulation of three-dimensional phytoplankton dynamics: Competition in limited environments. *Journal of Computational and Applied Mathematics, 174*(1), 57–77.

Rueda, F. J., & Cowen, E. A. (2005). Residence time of a freshwater embayment connected to a large lake. *Limnology and Oceanography, 50*(5), 1638–1653.

Rueda, F. V. (2006). Basin scale transport in stratified lakes and reservoirs: Towards the knowledge of freshwater ecosystem. *Limnetica, 1-2*, 33–56.

Salmaso, N. (2005). Effects of climatic fluctuations and vertical mixing on the interannual trophic variabilità of Lake Garda, Italy. 2005. *Limnology and Oceanography, 50*, 553–565.

Shen, J., & Haas, L. (2004). Calculating age and residence time in the Tidal York River using three-dimensional model experiments. *Estuarine, Coastal and Shelf Science, 61*(3), 449–461.

Wang, P., Song, Y. T., Chao, Y., & Zhang, H. (2005). Parallel computation of the regional ocean modeling system. *International Journal of High Performance Computing Applications, 19*(4), 375–385.

Wilde, J., Mierzwa, M., & Suits, B. (2006). *Using particle tracking to indicate Delta Residence Time.* California Water and Environmental Modeling Forum, 2006 Annual Meeting, February 28-March 2, 2006, Pacific Grove, California.

Yue, W., Lin, C.-L., & Patel, V. C. (2004). Large eddy simulation of turbulent open-channel flow with free surface simulated by level) set method. *Physics of Fluids, 17*(2), 1–12.

APPENDIX

Horizontal and vertical movement of all environmental and tributary markers in Tables 1 and 2.

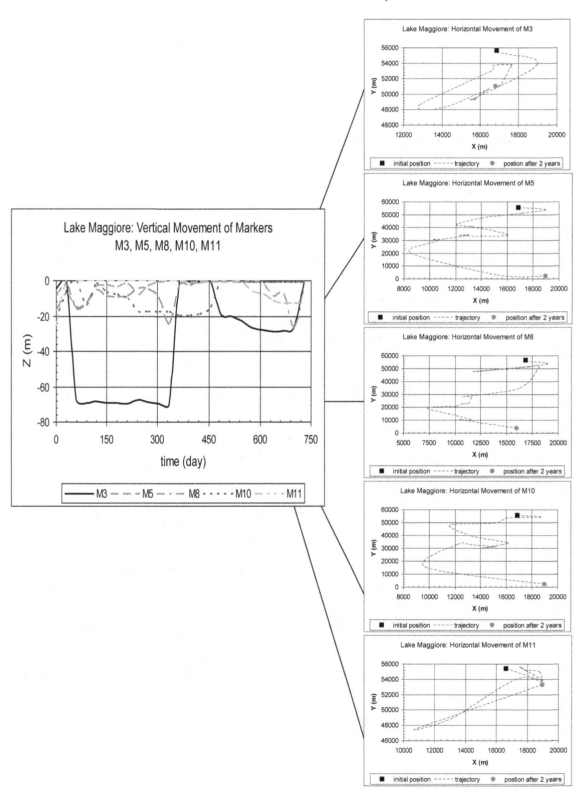

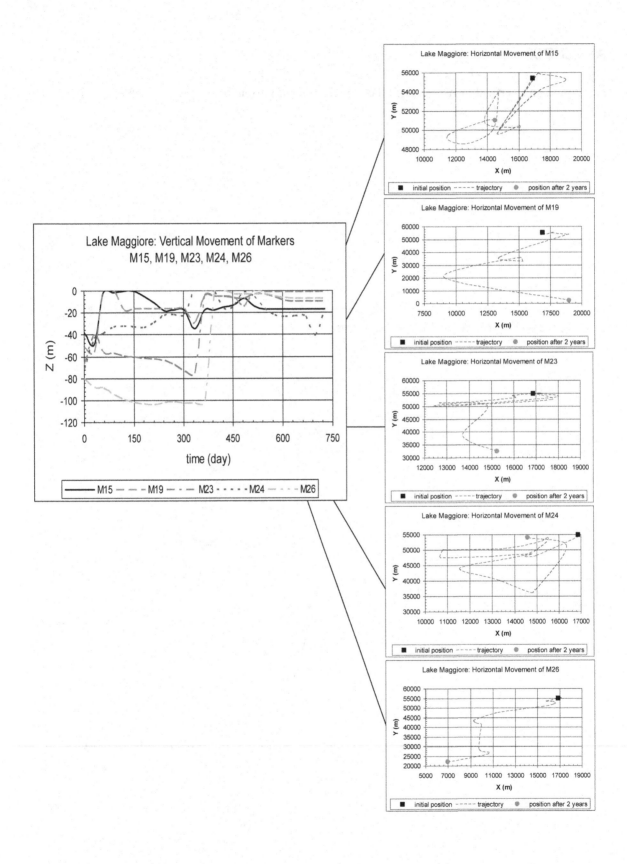

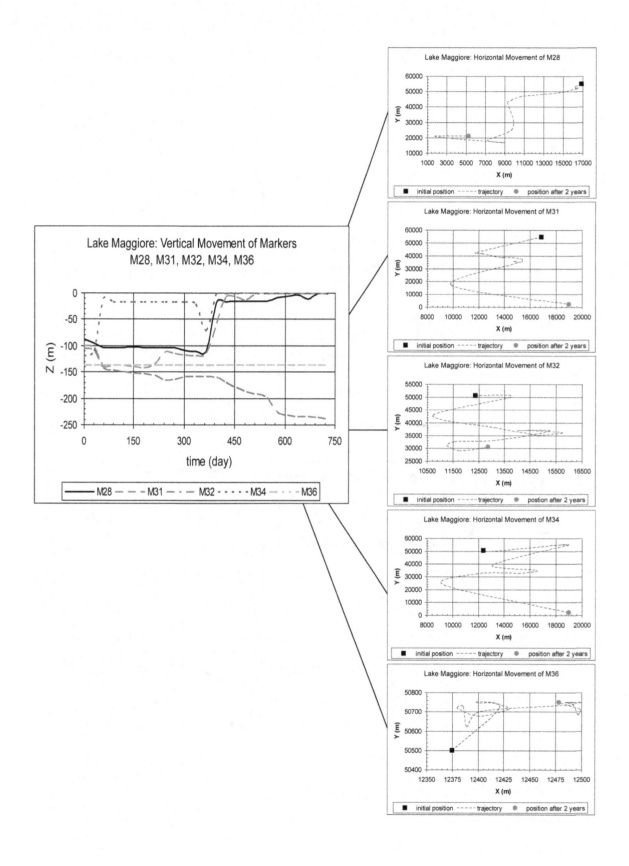

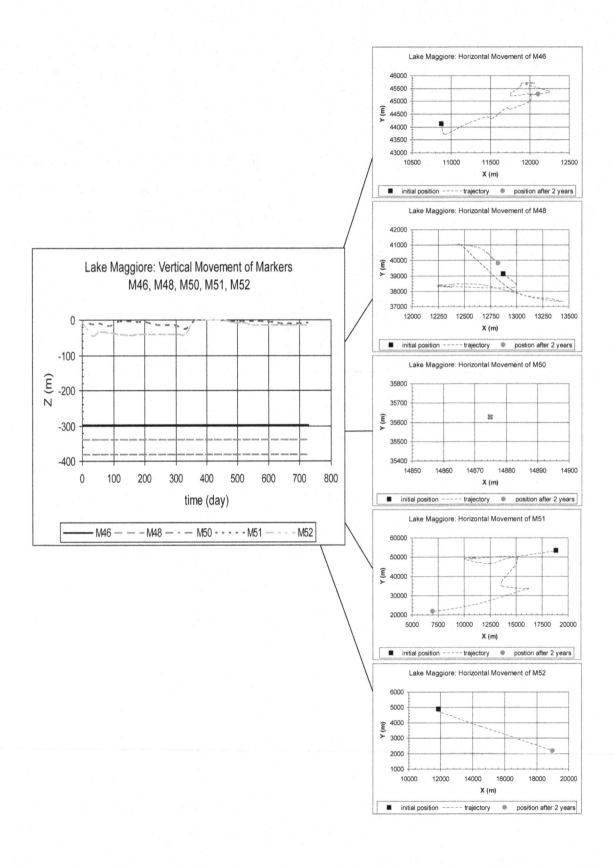

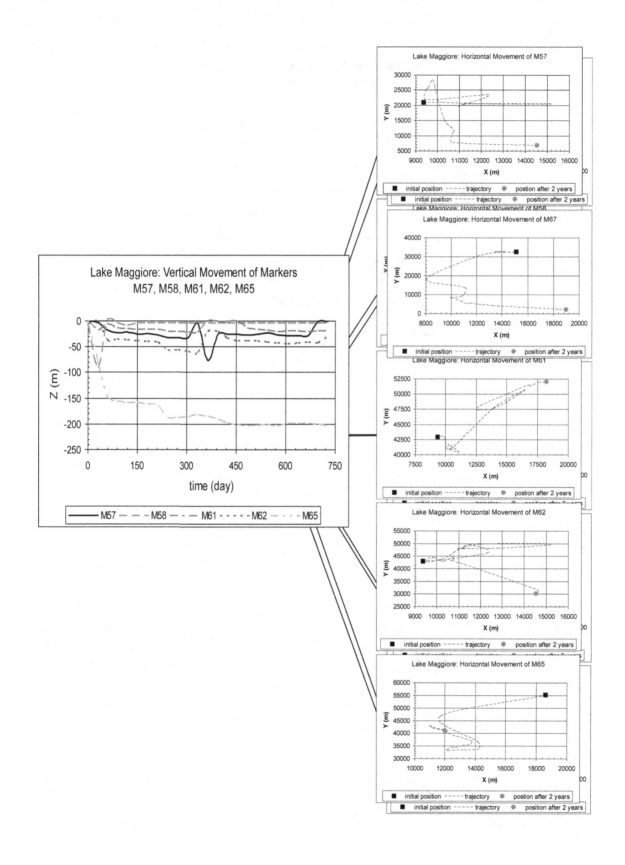

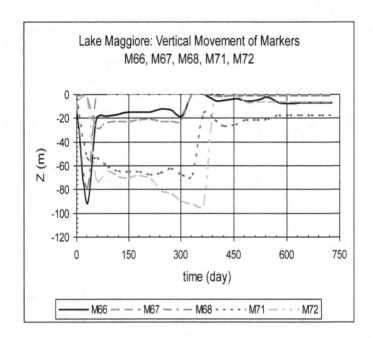

Chapter 12
Possibility of Fractal Aesthetics

Ljubiša M. Kocić
University of Niš, Serbia

ABSTRACT

Fast development of computer networking contributes to the global spreading and popularizing of the notion of fractals and complex patterns in their use in computer-aided design and computer art. This chapter looks for answers to the following questions: How are fractals perceived? Are fractals predominantly man-made or natural objects? How do fractals relate to the overall visual art experience of mankind? What are the main problems in using fractals in arts? What are the experiences from the visual art-history? Do Nature and artists use the same algorithm? What fractal experts can do to help artists?

1. INTRODUCTION

There is a geometry in the humming of the strings
-Pythagoras

Inspired by Alex Raymond's and Dan Barry's *Flash Gordon*, this author, in his teenage years, tried to produce his own SF cartoon. Supplied by the modest knowledge of Euclidean geometric forms, a small bottle of black China ink of acceptable quality and a sheet of *hammer* paper, he started making up his pictorial story. The main characters had been invented; the space ships had been already designed, when a major problem arose. How to draw starry skies, this unavoidable

scenery of space adventures? After many trials based on leaving white dots and blackening all the rest, the solution appeared by itself. Another bottle of China ink had to be provided, this time a white one. It turned out that the new technique was worth every penny. Not only the stars themselves but the whole Milky Way was very authentic! The author was captured by the beauty of chaotic scattered white dots all over the black background. Step by step, the author's attitude towards geometrically irregular forms was changing. Moreover, he became aware of importance of such forms in art expression. And soon, an unexpected feeling of the beauty of irregular and amorphous started to be a new reality. No wander when, about twenty years latter, looking at the newly published Barnsley's book (Barnsley, 1988), the old feeling resurrected.

DOI: 10.4018/978-1-4666-2077-3.ch012

Now, after nearly twenty years, this author is still fascinated by the effects chaotic patterns may cause on our senses, and continues looking for the answer why it is so.

Anticipation of chaos and fractals as "portraits of chaos" occurs many years before the first computing machine was ever built. But not earlier than the mid 60-es, with the help of the first computers with graphical capabilities, did the new exciting forms of chaotic patterns and fractal constructions started appearing. Still, broad science-oriented public becomes aware of the new, waste world of hyper-complex forms and colors upon Mandelbrot's publishing his famous books (Mandelbrot, 1975), (Mandelbrot, 1982). Many classic problems, once put away due their cumbersome mathematics, were revisited and solved using new techniques of Chaos theory and Fractals. It turns that the simple pendulum may be a source of practically endless, fantastic patterns. Geometrically very complicated shapes reveal a strict order in apparently disordered blueprint. Visually curious, these shapes look even more attractive due to their inner logic stemming in iron laws that govern the behavior of deterministic chaos. The new geometry based on a peculiar mathematical background, took the experts of different fields by storm. If the first reason was its high scientific interest and all-embracing nature, the second for sure was its *beauty*. Not long after, this non-scientific contested term, *beauty* will appear more and more frequently by the name of fractals, usually without any explanation. An especially strong connection has been established between fractals and Computer Graphics, but also between fractals and Computer Science in general. The aesthetic value of fractals has rarely been disputed. Instead, many authors began investigating of participation of fractal patterns and chaotic configurations in art. Let us remind of some fractal-oriented titles involving visual arts, music, poetry or architecture as well: (Emmer, 1993), (Peitgen & Richter, 1986), (Pollard-Gott, 1986), (Mandelbrot, 1989), (Hsti & Hsti, 1990),

(Prusinkiewicz, Lindenmayer, 1990), (Musgrave & Mandelbrot, 1991), (Gardner, 1992), (Shearer, 1992), (Peak & Frame, 1994), (Shearer, 1995), (Pickover, 1995), (Kocić, 2002), (Kocić, 2003), (Kocić, Stefanovska, 2005), (Kappraff, 2007), (Fulton, 1999), (Burkle-Elizondo et al., 2007), etc.

Many books on Chaos theory contain chapters devoted to aesthetic moment of different graphs concerning complex or chaotic dynamics. Orbits in phase space, strange attractors, basins of attractions, bifurcation diagrams etc, are compared with colored patterns of butterfly wings, with figures made by polar light, textile designs, plans of cities and so on. See (Schroeder, 1991), (Moon, 1992), (Zaslavsky et al. 1991). In the next section there is an analysis of how we perceive fractal images.

2. PERCEPTION OF FRACTALS

Since perception precedes any aesthetical judgment, it will be the first subject of our concern. We will restrict ourselves to *visual* component of perception only due to understandable reasons. But, before any discussion about how we perceive fractals, one needs to know as clearly as possible what *fractal* is. And here is the first problem. *Fractal* seems to be as fundamental concept as *space*, *life*, *truth*, *number* etc, and fails to undergo any strict and concise definition. According to Falconer (Falconer, 1990) (see also (Fisher, 1995)) only a descriptive definition is possible (we combine Falconer's and Fisher's version):

Definition 1: (Descriptive) The set A is a *fractal* if: (*i*) A has detail at every scale. (*ii*) A is exactly, approximately or statistically *self-similar*. (*iii*) Usually, the *fractal dimension* (properly defined) of A is greater than its topological dimension. (*iv*) There is a simple *algorithmic description* of A (possible recursively).

What in this definition is of interest concerning our perception? From (*i*) we may understand that

Figure 1. Ice cubes: Computer generated self-similar constructions

"having detail at every scale", means that fractal is too irregular to be described in traditional geometric language, both locally and globally (Falconer, 1990). So, the first formal characteristic of a fractal set is *high irregularity and complexity*.

The second property (from *ii*) is self-similarity. The term "similarity" should not be mixed with the notion of *similitude* familiar from Euclidean geometry. As it is known, two sets A_1 and A_2 from R^n are *similar* if one is image of the other, $A_1 = f(A_2)$, where $f : R^n \to R^n$ is transformation of similitude, which means that it has the form

$$f(x) = Ax + b, \quad x \in R^n, \quad (1)$$

where A is an $n \times n$ *orthogonal* real matrix, and b is a translation vector of length n. Being orthogonal, for A means satisfying $A^T A = \rho^2 I$, $\rho \in R$, and the corresponding transformation *f* is then a compositions of *translation, rotation, homogenous scaling* and *symmetries*. The set A is called *strictly self-similar* (Falconer, 1990), (Peitgen et al. 1992) if it satisfies

$$A = \cup_i w_i(A), \quad A \subset R^n, \quad (2)$$

where $\{w_i\}$ is the finite set of similitude mappings $w_i : R^n \to R^n$. Sets with the property of strict self-similarity are shown in Figure 1. Such property is not so easy to recognize by simple observation. But, there are both easier and more difficult examples. The easiest case is a regular self-similar subdivision, when the set A is subdivided into the set of equal shapes $w_i(A)$. An example is when a square is subdivided into 2^m sub-squares. This situation occurs in the case of self-similar tilings and ornaments. Such forms are pleasing for observer's eyes by the aesthetic rule known as *law of identity*. Examples in architecture can be found in classic temples (Egypt, Babylon, Assyria, Greece, Rome) in the rows of identical columns, in friezes and ornamental decorations.

If orthogonal transformations w_i have different scaling factors, ρ_i, the subsets $w_i(A)$ are more difficult to identify. This is case in Figure 1. Architecture exploits such strict self-similarity as another canon of beauty called *law of similitude*. Examples are buildings that have side wings being reduced copy of the central part (churches, cathedrals…).

If the matrix A in (1) is an arbitrary $n \times n$ real matrix and (2) is satisfied, then A is *self-affine* set. Here is a case that may, from the perceptive point of view, belong to law of similar, although

Figure 2. Self-affine architecture- Above: Facade of a Fourth Dynasty house (from the sarcophagus of Khûfû Poskhû); Below: Three stages of self-affine pre-fractal constructions

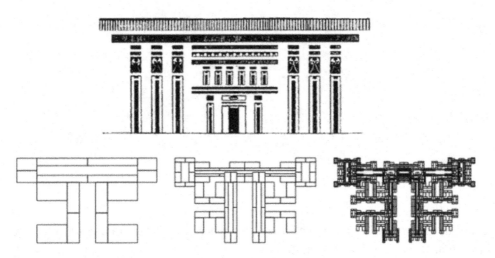

none of w_i are necessary orthogonal. This is when corresponding matrices A_i are *non-homogenous scaling* (*stretch*) (diagonal matrices). These transformations map rectangle into rectangle. In pictures of modern cityscapes, such kind of self-affinity is dominated. In fact, typical modern buildings are copies of each other upon orthogonal affine transformations extended by non-homogenous scaling. Some examples of such architectonic constructions are shown in Figure 2.

The case of general self-affinity, when skew (shear) transformations also participate is more difficult to distinguish by simple observation. But in some cases it is alsol possible. The case when it is very difficult or even impossible at all is when w_i are nonlinear mappings. This is the case of *exact* self-similarity, mentioned in point (*ii*) of Definition 1. An example of a fractal set being exactly self-similar upon a set of three contractive nonlinear mappings is given in Figure 3.

Let us discuss other two categories of generalized self-similarity mentioned in Definition 1. These are: *approximate* and *statistic* self-similarity.

These types of self-similarities are impossible to determine by visual observation. For example, Brownian motion is statistically self-similar (Peit-

gen, 1992, p. 494), and this property can not be registered by human eye. Also, Mandelbrot and Julia sets are approximate (or asymptotically) self-similar, which is also unnoticeable, except in some *intuitive* manner.

Self-similar sets are nicely represented by Iterated Function Systems (IFS) (Barnsley, 1988), (Barnsley, Demko, 1985), which consists of a metric space, say (R^n, d) and a collection of *contractive* mappings $w_i : R^n \rightarrow R^n$. (The mapping w is called *contractive* if there exists a real number $c \in (0, 1)$, such that the inequality $\|w(x) - w(y)\| \leq c \|x - y\|$ is *exact* one for some norm $||\cdot||$ in R^n). So, the IFS is given by

$$\mathbf{S} = \left\{ R^n; \ w_1, w_2, ..., w_k \right\}, \tag{3}$$

and the operator (sometimes called Hutchinson operator), defined by

$$W(\cdot) = \cup_i w_i(\cdot), \tag{4}$$

is closely related to **S**. The operator W is applied on H, the set of nonempty compact subsets of R^n. Denote by $W^{\circ m} = W(W^{\circ(m-1)})$ the m-th auto

Figure 3. Construction of "water plant" fractal by IFS that consists of 3 nonlinear contractions given in Appendix A1

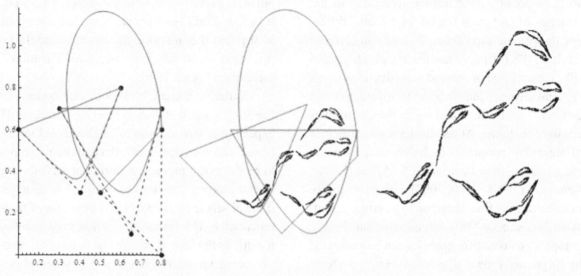

composition of W. Then, starting by an arbitrary set $B \in H$, the sequence

$$B, \ W(B), \ W^{\circ 2}(B), \ ..., \ W^{\circ m}(B), ... \qquad (5)$$

converges, provided all w_i are contractions. According to Banach theorem, the limit of (5) is the unique set $A \in H$, called *attractor* of S, the *fixed point* of the operator W. Thus,

$$A = W(A), \qquad A \in H, \qquad (6)$$

which is another form of (2). By the rule, attractors are fractal sets.

Much more than just definition, the notion of IFS is of wider importance. Barnsley in (Barnsley, 2010), correctly named the concept of Iterated Systems a "creative system". He compared self-similar fractals with plants and the IFS code with DNA bio-codes.

The next observation concerning Definition 1, includes fractal dimension (see any fractal book for definition). It is commonly known that formally very different fractal sets may have the same fractal dimension. For example, boundary of the Mandelbrot set, Sierpinski tetrahedron, Harter-Heighway dragon, Peano and Hilbert curve share fractal dimension 2. The only "communication" with different fractal dimension might be only intuitive and qualitative. The notion of intuitive perception has been developed by Carl Jung as a tool for investigating different psychological types. But it is for sure that fractal dimension, as measure of complexity may be important parameter for aesthetic perception. Many classic artworks were analyzed upon their fractal dimension (Voss, Wyatt, 1993), (Taylor et al., 1999), (Taylor, 1999).

If at all be possible, we can speak of having different "feeling" of three types of IFS (Barnsley, 1988): 1. *Totally disconnected*; 2. *Just touching* and 3. *Overlapping*. The first type results in what is generally named "Cantor dust". These fractals are dust-like. *Just touching* type leaves impression of very complicated ornaments, while the Overlapping IFS attractors looks "fat" and "heavy".

Finally, we came to the last descriptive characteristic of fractals, recursive algorithm.

Here, a lot can be said. First, different stages of the algorithm results in different pictures with an open possibility of deeper perception of the structure of particular fractal set. Second, different algorithmic approaches, like deterministic or random, IFS (affine or nonlinear), graph-guided IFS, context free or context sensitive L-systems (Prusinkiewicz, Lindenmayer, 1990) etc, result in different visual effects and widen the spectrum of possible outcomes. At last, the recursive structure of algorithm permeates including shape parameters like in affine invariant IFS (AIFS) (Kocić, Simoncelli, 1998, 2000, 2002) with a possibility to influence the final shape up to a certain extent. With the sentence "This fact is that astonishingly complex and beautiful graphics can be generated by surprisingly plain algorithms. Hence the term *algorithmic art*, which I use at present." Mandelbrot (Mandelbrot, 1989) clearly underlines the importance of algorithmic structure of fractal formulas.

So, these are perceptive elements that could have been extracted from the loose definition of fractal sets by a "fractal artist". At the end of this section at first sight opposite perceptions by two experienced experts will be quoted. The first one, the opinion of "the father of fractals", Benoit Mandelbrot (Mandelbrot, 1989).

Statement 1: (B. Mandelbrot) *The resulting balanced co-existence of order and chaos (in fractal sets) was found almost invariably to be beautiful.*

Now, the attitude, probably common to everyone who has ever experimented with generation of fractal images, was expressed by Michael Barnsley (Barnsley, 1988, p. 108), (Klein, M. et al., 1998):

Statement 2: (M. Barnsley) *"Typical" fractals are not pretty.*

This statement may look opposite to Statement 1, but in fact, it is complementary since it does not exclude the existence of beautiful fractals. It just introduces a simple truth: *Beauty is not an intrinsic quality of the fractal object.* Or, to put it in Sigmund Freud's way: "One feels inclined to say that the intention that fractals should be 'beautiful' is not included in the plan of 'Creation'" (according Freud, 1930).

Similarly, Statement 1 does not contradict Barnsley's one. It obviously refers to "successful" experiments when "balance" is already achieved. Note that "co-existence of order and chaos" seems to be the main impression during observation of fractal images. This impression is even stronger if the observer participates in the process of fractal creation. If a fractal attractor is very chaotic, it exhibits the lack of beauty due to its configuration being not orderly enough and thus amorphous (Figure 4, left). If otherwise, its formula contains a lot of regular geometry, the resulting fractal may look too ornamentally (lack of chaoticity, Figure 4, right).

To recapitulate that among several qualities of fractal attractors, it is reasonable to accept irregularity, complexity and strict self-similarity as directly perceptive. Also, from Statements 1 and 2 follows that typical fractals are not beautiful, but many of them are, and this beauty is mainly caused by "balanced co-existence of order and chaos". And all of this concerns what may be absorbed from fractal images by direct visual perception.

The second, intellectual component that contributes very much in creating our aesthetic judgment is elaborated in the next chapter.

3. FRACTALS AND AESTHETICS

It is difficult to overlook that contemporary internet sites are crowded with amateur "fractal art" of different quality. The amount of works is amazing compared to amateur "classic art". Explanation for this phenomenon seems to hide in the fact that it is much easier to "create" an

Figure 4. Fractal dimension: a) Boundary of the Mandelbrot set; b) Sierpinski tetrahedron; c) Harter-Heighway dragon; d) Hilbert curve

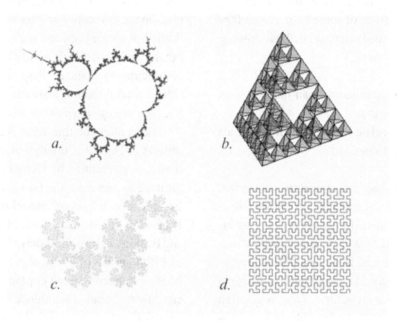

Figure 5. Approximations of two fractals: The "snowflake" code is given in Appendix A2

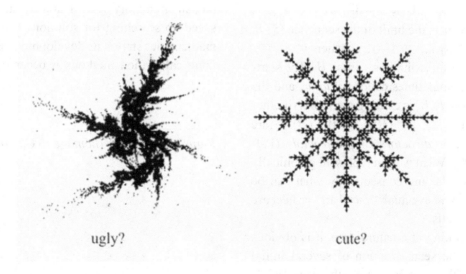

ugly?   cute?

attractive picture by automatic algorithm than to make time-consuming trials that usually result in failure. Professional artists are not so eager to use computer technology but the number of those using it steadily increases. Art galleries, exhibition facilities and different competitions accept the new visual form: *giclee prints*. These are prints from a digital source using ink-jet printing. Considerable artists' giclees started appearing in art galleries. The natural question of aesthetic values of these new trans-geometric forms is posed. The answer is not so simple, and we leave it to specialists in the area of aesthetics. Yet, some our ideas and experiences concerning relationship of fractals and aesthetics might be of some help. But before this discussion we need to answer to the following preliminary questions:

Q1: Are fractals predominantly man-made objects or natural objects?

Q2: How fractals relate to the overall visual art experience of mankind?

Let us discuss the first question. Like ideal lines or spheres, ideal fractals can not be found in Nature. Never mind if they are as large as intergalactic cloud of dust, they are of finite structure. What we can find in Nature *almost everywhere* are *pre-fractals*. Looking back at formula (6), we see that the attractor A (which is often fractal) is the fixed point of the Hutchinson operator W, which is a union of a finite collection of contractive mappings, see (4). In other words, A is the solution of the equality $A = \cup_i w_i(A)$, and it is given as the limit of the sequence (5) B, $W(B)$, $W^{\circ 2}(B),...,$ $W^{\circ k}(B),....$ when $k \to +\infty$, provided B is an arbitrary set from H. The starting set B is sometimes called *initiator*, and the first iteration $F(B)$ is called *generator*. All other iterations $W^{\circ 2}(B)$, $W^{\circ 3}(B)$, ..., $W^{\circ k}(B),...,$ are known as *pre-attractors* or *pre-fractals* (Falconer, 1990). What we can represent graphically are pre-fractals, and consequently what can be include in some eventual "fractal art" project are also pre-fractals.

Now, looking at a natural tree, it is obvious that it can be seen as union of several initial members of the sequence (5): B is the trunk, $W(B)$ is the set of major branches so that $B \cup W(B)$ is the trunk together with the branches along the trunk. Next, the set, $B \cup W(B) \cup W^2(B)$ contains trunk, major branches and smaller boughs, and so on, until the last leaf and leaf's hair. Thus, the whole natural tree can be seen as the union of 10 to 20 pre-fractal "generations". It is similar to other irregular forms: rocks, river networks,

clouds, live tissues, almost everything, from quantum structure of matter to distribution of mass in the universe and galactic clusters motion. Although natural objects are not (ideal) fractals but rather pre-fractals of different levels (and complexness) instead, they are still closer to (ideal) fractal than to a simple Euclidean shape. So, they are *approximately fractals*.

The reason for this omnipresence of fractal objects in Nature is the dynamics of the Nature, the state appreciated by Heraclites and latter formulated as *panta rei*, the famous phrase that have became a paradigm of eternal dynamics. By the expansion of exact sciences, Physics, Chemistry and Biology before all, at the turn of centuries (end of 19th to midst of 20th), many phenomena have been evidenced with no explanation or with very complicated ones. Turbulence of fluids, diffusion processes, atmosphere heath transfer, three-body problem, "reversible" chemical reactions, deposit processes (Figure 6), burst of viruses in epidemics, human circulatory system, and so on. In order to speed-up searching for solutions the numerical mathematics started its development. By formalizing calculation methods it became clear that

Figure 6. Haystack (homage to Claude Monet)

Figure 7. Natural fractal: Dendrite, a ready-made zinc deposit on ceramic plate, formed by electrolytic process

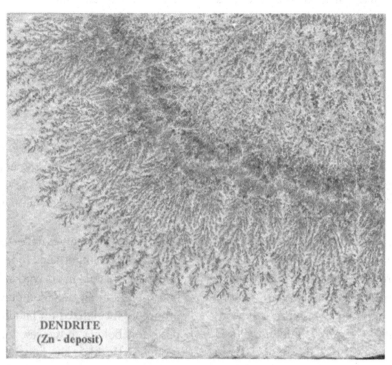

many problems can be solved by employing fast automatic arithmetic machines.

Consequently, the answer to the first question is likely to be that fractals are the inseparable ingredients of the architecture of the Universe and human intelligence has nothing to do with it. But it is not quite so. The invention of computer helped to clear up the lag of unsolved problems. The mathematical "monster" objects, anticipated by Weierstrass, Cantor, Peano, Hilbert, Julia, Poincaré, von Koch, Lévy, Sierpinski and others, started appearing on a surface of printing paper as strange clusters of pale dots. Although for a modest small picture of some Julia set the computer had to work several hours, nobody could stop the revolution.

At the end of 20th century, with the new computer generations of speed and memory increased up to million times, Chaos becomes one of the most popular disciplines, and fractals are well investigated.

Possible answer to Q1. Fractals are consequence of natural lows and natural dynamics. But, they could not be discovered and investigated without fast computers allowing visualization of this dynamics. Similar to Saturn rings, radiation, dinosaurs or Black holes, fractals are product of Nature, brought to day light thanks to collective intellectual efforts of a mankind.

How do men participate in the process of discovering, looking from the angle of art? Is an art photographer *creator* of the object in his photo? Of course not! Photographer's role is shifted from the sphere of *creation* to the sphere of *choice*. He/she chooses the right object in the right moment and adjusts the right parameters on the camera. It is true that the chosen object exists independently of the picture. But, on the other hand, without a skilled photographer no wider public would be able to enjoy the beauty of the object, moment, atmosphere... The similar story goes on with fractals. To be brought on the computer screen, somebody must do good programming job and perform it on the machine which, like camera or microscope, is a result of a collective intellectual contributions of many anonymous people. So, the situation with fractals is quite similar to *ready-made* objects (*objet trouvé*) being introduced in art during the Dadaistic movement by Marcel Dushamp (*Bicycle Wheel*, 1913), and also exploited by some other artists, not only Dadaists. They used to pick up an object from a store, from scrap yard or from nature, and, possibly after minor intervention, proclaim this object an original art creation.

This opinion is as well shared by Umberto Eco (Eco, 2004) who even uses the term "fractal aesthetics" to distinguish such *ready-made* characteristics of fractals.

The next approval comes in an unexpected and interesting manner from two art history books (Janson, 1969) and (Janson and Janson, 1977). These authors surely could not know about fractals at times when the books where being prepared, but guess what they use in their introductory chapters as very first illustrations? In *History of Art*, ((Janson, 1969)), Janson started his Introduction with the ready-made *Bull's head* by Picasso. In other book, *The Story of Painting*, as their first illustration in the introducing section "How Painting Began", Jansons put *Ink blot on folded paper* with the hint that "it is not too difficult to find two galloping animals" (in this blot). It is superfluous to say that ink blots are tightly connected with fractals (see the next section). According to author's opinion, these two illustrations show two evolution points of the Art: The beginning point, when man's admiration over strange forms obtained by hand prints against the cave's wall (the ink blot is just more articulated issue), and the point of mature art, at the end of a circle, when the artist understands that the best art is if it is *recognized* in everyday surrounding. This recognizing is the same process mentioned by Michelangelo in his famous claim "*I saw the angel in the marble and carved until I set him free*". And here we have a

Possible answer to Q2. Fractals relate to the visual arts in the analogue way as *ready-made* objects (introduced in the period of Dada movement) to visual art.

Now, these answers might be combined in the following

Statement 3: *Fractals are natural objects being discovered by collective intellect of mankind. This moment makes them similar to ready-made objects known from recent art history.*

This statement gives us two pieces of information of crucial importance for a person intending to exploit fractals in art works. First, this person has to be familiar with computers and computer programs specialized for handling fractals. Such programs belong to the category of ready-made products. Besides, an elementary knowledge of the topic is necessary. Second, they will have to *adjust* their artistic idea to the fractal object getting as program's output. This always goes this way with ready-made objects. The artist can not come with an *a priori* idea about how his future work will be designed. The idea comes with the *objet trouvé*, in our case with a particular fractal or a set of fractals. The program he/she uses usually offers some kind of a catalogue so the artist will have some preliminary vision, but the shortcoming is that catalogues contain a limited number of forms, and the artist risks being non-authentic.

A better solution for them is to make programs of their own. But this approach needs a more skillful programmer. In addition, the output gains on unpredictability. But, on the other hand, the joy of experimenting is much higher.

Immediately upon their appearance fractals have imposed their impact on visual arts. From the field of representational art, fractal technique (sometime called *fractalism*), spread out on painting, graphics, sculptures, installations, assem-

Figure 8. Four fractal "plants"

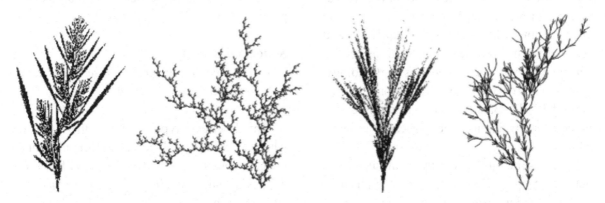

blages, architecture (Sala, 2002), poetry (Fulton, 1999) and music (Risset, 1986). This fact by itself proves that fractals do possess aesthetic values. How can we distinguish these features? How can we "measure" their importance or influence? Can we at all discuss about 'beauty of fractals' without looking at concrete 'fractal art' works?

Well, against Fiedler (Fiedler, 1887), aesthetic problem exists independently of art. This means that experts may discuss the aesthetic value of fractal objects regardless if it is used as an element of art or not. Acceptance of Fiedler's statement justifies our discussion here. Further deepening of the problem of beauty necessary leads to a labyrinth of very different philosophic standing points that do not agree about the fundamental question: "What is Beauty". Some philosophic schools have even antipodal opinions. Plato's metaphysical concept of "beautiful by itself" ($\alpha\nu\tau o$ τo $\chi\alpha\lambda o\nu$) is a nice attempt to formulate what the fundamental aesthetic problem really is. But, good formulation is one thing, the solution is another.

Modern aesthetics is not an exact discipline like Mathematics or Computer Science. It is positioned somewhere between philosophy and science. The aesthetical knowledge floats between rational and emotional, between induction and deduction. There are many aesthetic schools, many different standpoints, and many approaches. During the history of mankind two main aesthetical

Figure 9. Two visual representations of Farey tree of rational numbers

branches have been formed: The philosophical branch and the scientific branch. The first one (started with Pythagoreans (presumptively) and with Plato) is trying to deduce aesthetic principles from higher philosophic categories like Ontology, Anthropology or Gnoseology. The second, (started with Alexander Baumgarten) is using inductive methods and trying to establish aesthetics as an exact science.

But, despite such diversity of attitudes and methods, properties of fractal constructions may be recognized in many of these opinions. One of the oldest definitions of *beauty* goes back to Pythagoras: "*it is unity among diversity*". And it perfectly fits the notion of fractal! The fractal set is completely defined by a simple, compact formula that creates waste diversity, and this diversity is united by this formula, this DNA!

And this concept of Pythagoras has appeared many times in the opinions of other philosophers. The most important are Plato, St. Augustine and Leibniz.

Aristotle was also very close to geometry of fractals when mentioned *order* and *symmetry* as characteristics of beauty. Indeed, *order* is one of features of fractal sets sometimes being considered as ordered chaos. When speaking of symmetry, the defining equation (6) for a typical fractal set, $A = W(A)$ is in fact an equation of symmetry: symmetry upon the Hutchinson operator (4).

At the end of this section, we consider some aspects concerning the fact that fractals are not so easy to use as a resource for art production. The following statements might be of interest in illuminating of this problem.

Statement 4: *Except in some simple or trivial cases, one can not predict the fractal's form from the given code (unless it is not some of classic fractals).*

Really, an *a priori* knowledge or even anticipation from mathematical formula or physical analog model is impossible. Who can predict the shape of the close-up of the Mandelbrot set around the point $z = 0.551077 - i\,0.626566$?

Statement 5: *Fractal that we generate for the first time usually does not meet our idea but may satisfy our demands.*

This describes a typical situation that everyone who ever tried to produce fractal fitting his inner image. In other words, fractals are not "free form objects". Under the phrase *free form object* we understand geometric objects whose shape can be predicted. Such objects are *free form curves*, *surfaces* or *volumes* constructed over *Bernstein-Bezier basis* or over *B-spline bases* of different kinds. On the other hand, fractal attractor is *a strongly stable attractive fixed point* of the dynamical system defined by operator W (Barnsley, 2010), and thus unpredictable at all.

Statement 6: *Given fractal of a certain amount of beauty, finding the method for increasing this amount is an open problem.*

This statement is related to the previous one. Lack of manipulative abilities prevents the designer from improving the aesthetic value of a particular fractal object.

The negative determinants of the Statements 4-6 can be partly explained by the remark of Poincaré (Poincaré, 1943): "The space as it has been perceived by our senses is absolutely different than the space as defined by geometry". Together with Statement 3, these convey an idea that fractals are difficult for expressing artistic ideas in the domain of visual art. We have no reason to believe that in the field of music or poetry, the situation is any better.

Escapism, as described by Mark Rothko (Rothko, 2004) defines art as a form of escape from action. May as well "fractal art" be seen as a kind of escapism from responsibility of being geometrically incorrect?

4. FRACTAL ART THROUGH CENTURIES

Digital computers are not the only tools someone can produce fractals with. Many diverse fractals can be produced by analogue machines as well. A simple pendulum with an iron bob, swinging over a pair of magnets is an endless source of fractal patterns. Such an approach is used by the most popular *informel* artist, Jackson Pollock (Taylor et al., 1999), (Taylor, 2007). Folding a strip of paper may produce a fractal known as *Harter-Heighway dragon* (Mandelbrot, 1982) (or *paper-folding dragon*). One can go even simpler, to crumple a piece of paper. The obtained paper ball is a nice example of a 3D pre-fractal set. In fact such a "device" is invented and applied in painting as a peculiar analogue "machine" that leaves an irregular trace if being rolled over the fresh painted surface. Such experiments emphasize the fact that fractals can be retrieved from nature by taking some minimal human action, which means that man's in-between role is minimized. Even worse! Some fractals may be created by nature itself.

A classic Greek author Philostratos, in his dialog between Apolonius and Damis, argues about "images in the clouds". His conclusion is that observer's mind is enough to make these images, while an artist has to use both mind and hands to mimic the Nature. Plinius noticed that a sponge, impregnated by color and hit to the wall sometimes produces nice effects. These are first examples of the mentioning complex or fractal shapes in visual arts. According to (Hombrich, 1977), the Chinese painter Sung Ti (XI Century) suggested the method known as *Chinese occlusion* to invent nice landscapes. A piece of white silk should be placed over an old, decrepit wall. Looking through it early morning or in evening, one can see "landscapes" that can remember and then transfer to their own artworks.

The Italian renaissance painter Andrea Mantegna experimented with clouds having form of human faces (Hombrich, 1977). In his famous *Treatise of Painting*, Leonardo da Vinci gave the most extensive treatment of what now is called *Leonardo's method* or *blotting method*. Possibly inspired by Pietro del Kosimo, da Vinci emphasized power of "messy forms" like stains on old walls, clouds or muddy water in "favoring mind on various discoveries". Hoogstraeten, the XVII century writer, testified that the Dutch painter Jan Van Goyen was capable of getting out a picture with "small efforts" from stains of colors (Figure 10).

Figure 10. Left: Van Goyen, Two Men on a Footbridge over a Stream, 1655, oil on panel (detail); right: The "cloud" generated by an Iterated Function System

In XVIII century, a landscape painter, Alexander Cozens, author of a textbook of drawing *"A New Method of Assisting the Invention in Drawing Original Compositions of Landscape"* used and further developed *blotting method*. He was aware of the importance of having *a priori* knowledge of different schemes of skylines. These schemes including precise copy of mountain ranges had been first isolated and studied by Cozens. If the ink stains can be seen as fractal forms in painting, these skylines are *fractal curves* that have been described in the form of *fractal interpolating functions* by Barnsley (Barnsley, 1988). The upper part of Figure 11 shows one of Cozens drawings. From his skyline, ten points were selected and a fractal interpolation curve was constructed, by using interpolating method given in (Barnsley, 1988). Two curves are compared in the lower part of Figure 11. Importance of the Cozens method becomes obvious by its influence on famous John Constable. Alexander's' relative, John Robert Cozens also uses this method.

Not only do painters use blots of ink or color to improve their inspiration. A German poet Julius Kerner used blots of ink on a folded paper to recognize live figures or "ghosts", and then he wrote poems about these figures. Latter, such ink blots were exploited by Hermann Rorschach for his famous psychological test. William Turner, English landscape painter, was the next famous artist who used amorphous stains of color to gain vibrant and dramatic treatment of natural light and atmospheric effects in land and marine subjects. It is widely accepted that his work had a direct influence on the development of impressionism. In fact, impressionists also used freely formed colored spots to depict subtle variations in color of sky, water or vegetation.

By atomizing color grains, impressionism went to its pointillist stage, with Georges Seurat, and Paul Signac as main representatives. A specific and original approach in using stochastically distributed blots of color was performed by a French painter Odilon Redon. Besides exploring more or less amorphous and chaotically scattered particles

Figure 11. Above. Alexander Cozens, Streaky Clouds at the Bottom of the Sky (c.1785), drawing on paper; Below. Fractal interpolation: The fractal curve interpolating the Cozens skyline in 10 points

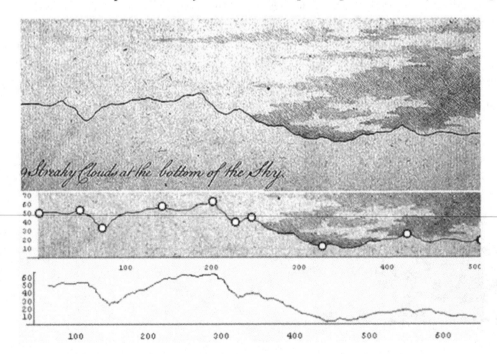

of color, there is another, more "mechanical" method for producing effects of natural patterns. This is *frottage* or *fratting method*, known from children's game of reproducing a coin relief on a piece of paper, by pencil rubbings over the paper keeping fixed over the coin. This technique, applied to different surfaces, like wood grain, fabric, or leaves, brings visual effects that are different from the one produced by "blotting method". Frottage was used by Gustave Moreau and some surrealists: Max Ernst, Salvador Dali and others. Ernst invented his *decalcomania method*, which is transferring of paint from one surface to another by pressing them together. These techniques are readable in a series of drawings (*Histoire naturelle* from 1926) and in many paintings such as *The Great Forest* (1927) and *The Temptation of St. Anthony* (1945). Salvador Dalì is a particular story. Blotting and different frottage effects keep appearing in his works permanently. Dalì also developed a few new techniques that can be viewed as imaginative variations of a blotting method. For example he used explosions to scatter nails or metal particles all over the surface, like in *Pieta - From The Apocalypse of St. John*, from 1959. Then, he used technique of scorching and smoking paper by candle (*Sfumato*, 1972). Futher, he invented a fancy variation of da Vinci method by 'recognizing' figures and genre scenes in white empty spaces between newspaper lines. In the period between 1934 and 1938, he used blots of India ink as well as frottage in many designs (*Portrait of Rene Crevel, The vertebrate Grotto - Transfer Series, Woman's Head with Shoe, Gradiva, Fantastic Beach Scene with Skeleton and Parrot*, etc.) A lot of his blotting-fratting experience was used in his famous *Tuna Fishing*, from 1967.

Salvador Dalì is apparently the first artist that explicitly painted a fractal. It was his *Visage of War*, an oil from 1940, the time that fractals were not yet discovered. It shows a hallucinating vision of skulls nested inside skulls using 'Russian doll' geometry. It is generated by three contractions with approximate contractive factor about 0.21.

Using well-known formula (Barnsley, 1988) the fractal dimension of *Visage of War* is about 0.705. This fractal is relative to *Sierpinski triangle* and falls to the family of so called *Cantor dusts* (Mandelbrot, 1982).

Different variations of blotting-fratting technique were used by many other surrealist painters: Andre Mason, Oscar Dominiguez, Raoul Ubac, Jacques Herold etc. Even smooth 'objects' are given 'fuzzy' structure. The nice example is *La tasse en fourrure* an object from 1936 made by Meret Oppenheim. It extends the subtle flickering sensibility of sculptures, introduced by Boccioni (*Unique Forms of Continuity in Space*, 1913). There are different techniques in Computer graphics that introduce 'fuzziness' into smooth objects. But, none is as expressive as fractal one. The *Haystack* in Figure 6, composed by three 'furry' variation of Sierpinski triangle is inspired by Oppenheim's construction. The tiny 'fur hair' is a consequence of having at least one unstable component added in the known Sierpiski fractal construction, making the related Hutcinson operator an expansion instead of contraction. Upon these conditions, the fixed point does not exist, but a limited number of pre-fractals are still bounded sets having divergent parts of trajectories heading outwards and giving 'fur effect'. By differently adjusted parameters, other effects are also possible, like 'rays of light', 'lines of fast movement', 'explosions' etc.

One important line of modern art is the so called *Art informel*. The form of such paintings/sculptures is compatible with the notion of *emotional vortex* used by Italian painter and sculptor Umberto Boccioni who said that "all creative art is produced from an emotional vortex". This 'emotional vortex' might be a possible answer to 'inner tensions in the soul of artist' as it formulated by Wassily Kandinsky. The protagonists of Art informel are *action painting* or *abstract expressionism* artists like Jackson Pollock, Norman Bluhm, James Brooks, Samuel Lewis Francis, Lee

Krasner, Clyfford Still, Sam Francis, Mark Tobey, Jean-Paul Riopelle, Peter Brüning and others.

All mentioned artists were convinced of beauty hidden in informal blots and stains of colors that are made or by swift movement of artistic brushes, knives or taking colors directly from tube (probably first used by van Gogh). In this way they introduce the external force, usually a chaotic one which stays in balance with inner "emotional vortex".

5. **Do artists and Nature use the same algorithm?** Now, we will focus on something else that keeps *Chaos* in a strong relationship with art in general. This relationship is not limited to visual arts, but for the sake of simplicity, we will explain it on the examples of drawing and painting.

Statement 7: *The algorithm used by artists in producing their works is meaningfully identical to baker's algorithm explaining the horseshoe map of Chaos theory.*

To explain Statement 7, consider an artist that started his drawing by copying some object, say the classic head of Athena (Figure 12). As we know, the drawing progresses in the sequence actions that alternate each other. These actions are: Observation of the object, taking proper measures "by eye", making the first sketch (Figure 12.1), again observation, adjusting measures and adding new details to the sketch (Figure 12.2), and so on until, the design is satisfactorily good (Figure 12.6). The algorithm is as follows:

Consider now the algorithm of calculating fractal attractor that approximates given set S. According to *Collage Theorem*, (Barnsley, Demko, 1985), (Barnsley, 1988), the initial set B

Figure 12. Head of Athena Promachos in six stages (pencil drawing by the author)

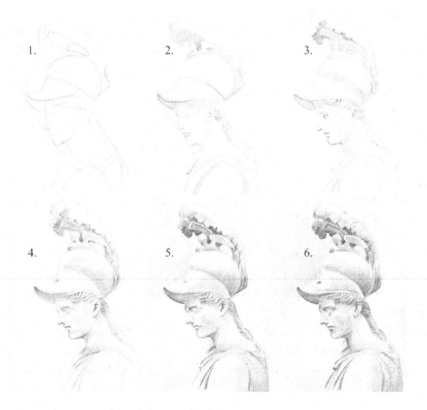

Algorithm 1.

Begin;
    1 Observe the object and make **drawing** (sketch);
    2 Compare object with the **drawing**;
    Satisfactory?
    If not, continue;
    If yes, go to End;
    3 Make changes in the **drawing**;
    4 Go to 2;
End;

that closely approximates S is chosen. The closeness of sets S and B are estimated by Hausdorff metric $h(S, B)$ (Barnsley, 1988). Construct the IFS

$$\{R^2;\ w_1, ..., w_k\},$$

such that the set $W(B) = \cup_i w_i(B)$ minimize the distance $h\left(S,\ W(B)\right)$. Calculate

$$W^{\circ 2}(B),\ W^{\circ 3}(B),\ ...,\ W^{\circ m}(B)$$

until $W^{\circ m}(B)$ will be satisfactory close to S.

The next table gives the pseudo-code of the Collage algorithm. Notations are illustrated by maple leaf being the target set S. Note that there is an amazing similarity with Algorithm 1.

As we know from Chaos theory, every new application of W in Algorithm 2 corresponds to stretching and folding R^2 space. Schematically, it is shown in Figure 13. This process, named *baker's algorithm* due to its similarity to kneading of dough, defines so called *horseshoe map* which correlates to convergence of the sequence { $W^{\circ m}(B)$ } to the attractor.

We can find elements of Baker's transform in the Algorithm 1, which means in the process of making an art piece, like drawing, painting or sculpture. Let us make it clearer. Consider an artist painting an object from his surrounding. He

Algorithm 2.

$S \simeq B$

$W^{\circ m}(B)$

Begin;
    1 Observe the object(target set **S**) and choose another set **B** as an approximation of S; Calculate **drawing:=** $W(B)$, the first sketch;
    2 Compare S with the **drawing** by calculating Hausdorff distance $h(S,$ **drawing);**
     Satisfactory?
    If not, continue;
    If yes, save **drawing** and go to End;
    3 Make changes in the **drawing**, by making substitution **drawing:=**$W($drawing$)$;
    4 Go to 2;
End;

Figure 13. Self-similar fractals and Baker's algorithm

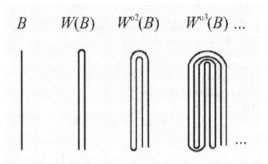

$$B \quad W(B) \quad W^{o2}(B) \quad W^{o3}(B) \ldots$$

defines a virtual frame (we will call it *world window*), that borders his object and prepares the area on his painting pad (*viewport*), Figure 14. Then he proceeds according to Algorithm 1. Thus, he has to pass the loop 2-3-4-2 many times. Each time, he compares object from *world window* with the picture from the *viewport*, and being unsatisfied he adds or removes tiny details or slightly changes colors or whatever in agreement with his vision he has formed in his mental or psychological space (ψ-space). This space among other material contains his knowledge and experience

Figure 14. Artist's Baker's transformation

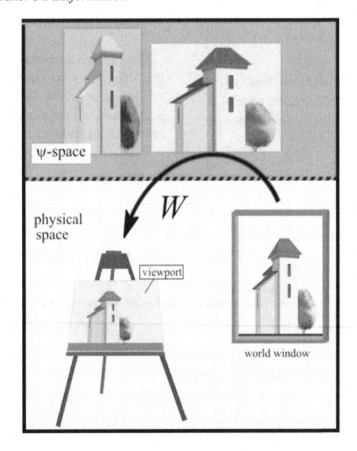

in the field of painting. What he sees is being modified according to his understanding of art work, composition, lines, surfaces, colors, shadows, etc. Every time his visual impression must pass though the sieve of his personal mode of painting. In this way, the vision, being refreshed every time he looks at the *world window*, is transformed into concentrated visual information being composed out of many similar situations he has stored in the memory. This transformation is similar to application of the Hutchinson operator *W*, on a pre-fractal set, in order to get better issue being closer to the target set.

The illustrations on Figures 15 and 16 may help in figuring out artist's baker's transformation in more details. The model is a simple dew-drop on a blue background. Watercolor paintings are used. The six stages were presented out of many. In stage 1, the background has been wetted and colored by the first layer of blue, leaving the empty oval place for the drop to be formed latter. After dying the paper, the drop is added as a separate object modeled a bit by coloring the drop's edge that is further from the light source slightly lighter. Near the other edge, a small white dot is left uncolored, for the reflex from the light. So, an elementary advanced knowledge about

Figure 15. A drop of dew, step by step (watercolor drawing by the author)

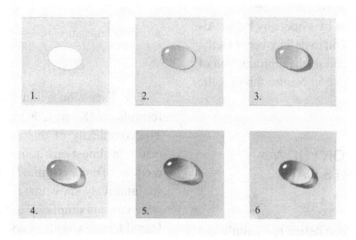

Figure16. A drop of dew explanation by Baker transform

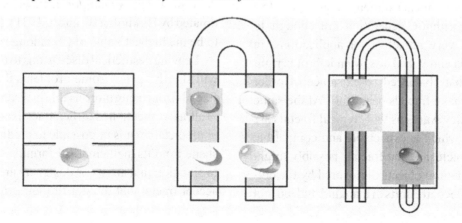

how to paint the water drop is obviously necessary in order to make the painting correctly. This means that much bigger content concerning the appearance of the water drop is needed than only having a 'sharp eye'. The knowledge about procedure of removing color from an already painted surface will help to produce proper half moon-like shadow being broken by a tinny light spot in the middle. Every progress towards the final image is one 'bending' of the imago-space, as shown in Figure 16.

So, the final picture is the result of adding or removing which is more massive at the beginning and very tinny at the end. A similar procedure is applied by sculptors. They start by a hip of clay and then model their object by adding or removing superfluous material in smaller and smaller amounts as the work approaches to end.

We close this section by a quote by Edgar Allan Poe: "Were I called on to define, very briefly, the term Art, I should call it 'the reproduction of what the Senses perceive in Nature through the veil of the soul."

6. CONCLUSION OR "HOW FRACTAL EXPERTS CAN CONTRIBUTE?"

Fractals are impossible to define in a simple and concise way. But some formal characteristics like high irregularity, self-similarity (of different kinds), non-integer dimension and (usually) simple, algorithmic generation are enough to make them very attractive for applications, in visual media and visual arts. Mandelbrot is right in saying that "balanced co-existence of order and chaos make fractals beautiful". At the same time, Barnsley warns us that "typical fractals are not pretty" which is expectable and compatible with our conclusion that fractals possibly might be seen as natural objects discovered by the collective intellectual efforts of mankind. Indeed, not

everything in Nature is pretty. This means that fractals fall into category of *ready-made* objects. They are rather natural objects than art works. But, as Malcolm Budd said (Budd, 1998): "Both work of art and natural objects can possess specifically aesthetic properties, such as beauty and gracefulness". In addition, discursive reasoning about aesthetic values of fractal formations is an awkward task. For Pythagoras and a number of latter philosophers (Plato, St. Augustine, Leibniz, Hemsterhuis, Voltaire), "beauty" is "unity among diversity" which sounds like very concise description of fractal object. Thus, fractals are ideal candidates for natural aesthetic objects. The criterion of "unity among diversity" seems incoherent with *aesthetic measure* defined by mathematician George Birkhoff (Birkhoff, 1931) as

$$\text{aesthetic measure} = \frac{\text{measure of order}}{\text{measure of complexity}}, \quad (7)$$

For discussion about deduction of Birkhoff formula see (Kocić, 2003); see also (Sala, 2007). The complexity of fractals is very high, which results in almost zero quotient in (7), provided the measure of order is limited to a small constant. But we intuitively know that the "measure of order", which means simplicity of the generating rule of fractal formula, is also very high compared to the huge complexity it produces. Anyway, the result in (7) should presumably be much over 1.5 which is the value for the *square form*, experimentally estimated by Birkhoff, (Birkhoff, 1931), that turned to be the highest value of (7) among polygons.

Leaving aesthetical discussions to experts, we will shortly review some problems that prevent fractals from being more usable in visual arts. First of all, as we mentioned earlier, fractals are formally unpredictable. It is impossible to predict fractal's shape from its mathematical formula. This leads to situation that artists or designers are forced to accept fractal that did not fit their original idea.

Figure 17. Continuous bending of Barnsley fern

Figure 18. Continuous "rotating" of Barnsley fern

Figure 19. Spline interpolating curve as border-fractal attractor

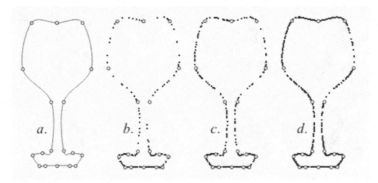

They as well have no means to improve beauty of the obtained fractal. For these reasons, artists and designers expect from the fractal experts to upgrade the existing algorithms or models so as to be suitable for modeling. For fractals, this means to be flexible, like for example free-form models of curves, surfaces or volumes, based on Bézier or spline schemes. Many projects are in progress concerning this matter. Affine IFS are generalized in different directions. In (Barnsley, 2010) some new methods are presented that introduce new degrees of freedom: Projective and bilinear IFS, blending of different attractors, fractal homeomorphism, V-variability and superfractality. Other methods exploit nonlinear IFS's or affine invariant IFS (AIFS) (Kocić, Simoncelli, 1998), (Kocić, Simoncelli, 2002). The examples of almost-predictable continuous deformation of Barnsley fern are given in Figures 17 and 18. Almost-predictable control is not as strict as free-form control exhibiting by Bézier or spline surfaces.

Other techniques use subdivision of smooth curves/surfaces in order to construct the IFS's and AIFS's that have exactly these curves/surfaces as attractors. Although these are not proper fractals since their fractal dimension are integer numbers, they are called *border fractals*. A border fractal, in the form of a cubic spline interpolant is presented in Figure 19. The "glass" contour (*a.*) is rendered as a cubic interpolation spline. Designs

(*b.*), (*c.*) and (*d.*), are obtained by random algorithm (chaos game) with 10, 20 and 40 points per segment.

At the end of this text, the following question makes sense: Do fractals impose a new way of looking at aesthetics? Maybe it is necessary to revise fundaments of aesthetics on the whole? Or even to establish a completely new Aesthetics? Or, taking into account that fractals interlace with an entire reality, even a new Axiology? In the meantime, the challenge of turning simple mathematical formulae into unpredictable amazing pictures will continue to intrigue.

REFERENCES

Barnsley, M. (1988). *Fractals everywhere*. San Diego, CA: Academic Press.

Barnsley, M. (2010). The life and survival of mathematical ideas. *Notices of the AMS*, *57*(21), 10–22.

Barnsley, M. F., & Demko, S. G. (1985). Iterated function systems and the global construction of fractals. *Proceedings of the Royal Society of London. Series A: Mathematical and Physical Sciences*, *399*, 243–275.

Birkhoff, G. D. (1931). A mathematical approach to aesthetics. *Scientia*, 133–146.

Budd, M. (1998). Aesthetics. In E. Craig (Ed.), *Routledge encyclopedia of philosophy*. London, UK: Routledge. Retrieved from http://www.rep.routledge.com/article/M046

Burkle-Elizondo, G., Valdez-Cepeda, R. D., & Sala, N. (2007). Complexity in the mesoamerican artistic and architectural works. In Sala, N. (Ed.), *Chaos and complexity in the arts and architecture* (pp. 119–128). New York, NY: Nova Science Publishers, Inc.

Eco, U. (2004). *Storia della Belleza*. Bompiani, Italy: RCS Libri S.p.A.

Emmer, M. (Ed.). (1993). *The visual mind: Art and mathematics*. The MIT Presss.

Falconer, K. (1990). *Fractal geometry: Mathematical foundations and applications*. John Wiley.

Fiedler, K. (1876). *Über die Beurteilung von Werken der Bildenden Künst*. Leipzig.

Fisher, Y. (Ed.). (1995). *Fractal image compression: Theory and application*. New York, NY: Springer Verlag.

Freud, S. (1930). *Civilization and its discontents (Das Unbehagen in der Kultur)*. London, UK: Penguin.

Fulton, A. (1999). Fractal amplifications: Writing in three dimensions. *The Kenyon Review New Series, 21*(2), 124–139.

Gardner, M. (1992). *Fractal music, hypercards, and more*. New York, NY: W.H. Freeman.

Hombrich, E. H. (1977). *Art and illusion*. London, UK: Phaidon Press.

Hsti, K., & Hsti, A. (1990). Fractal geometry of music. *Proceedings of the National Academy of Sciences of the United States of America, 87*, 938–941.

Janson, H. W. (1969). *History of art*. New York, NY: Harry N. Abrams, Inc.

Janson, H. W., & Janson, D. J. (1977). *The story of painting*. New York, NY: Harry N. Abrams, Inc.

Kappraff, J. (2007). Complexity and chaos theory in art. In Sala, N. (Ed.), *Chaos and complexity in the arts and architecture* (pp. 3–24). New York, NY: Nova Science Publishers, Inc.

Klein, M. (1998). Toward a better understanding of fractality in nature. In Pickover, C. A. (Ed.), *Chaos and fractals: A computer graphical journey*. Elsevier Science B.V.

Kocić, L. (2002). Art elements in fractal constructions. *Visual Mathematics, 4*(1). Retrieved from http://www.mi.sanu.ac.rs/vismath/ljkocic/index.html

Kocić, L. (2003). *Mathematics and esthetics* (in Serbian). Niš, Serbia: Niš Cultural Center.

Kocić, L., & Simoncelli, A. C. (1998). Towards free–form fractal modelling. In Daehlen, M., Lyche, T., & Schumaker, L. L. (Eds.), *Mathematical methods for curves and surfaces II* (pp. 287–294). Nashville, TN: Vanderbilt University Press.

Kocić, L., & Stefanovska, L. (2005). Complex dynamics of visual arts. In N. Sala (Ed.), *Chaos and Complexity Letters, 1*(2), 207-235.

Kocić, L. M., & Simoncelli, A. C. (2000). Fractal interpolation in creating prefractal images. *Visual Mathematics, 2*(2). Retrieved from http://www.mi.sanu.ac.rs/vismath/kocic1/index.html

Kocić, L. M., & Simoncelli, A. C. (2002). Shape predictable IFS representations. In Novak, M. M. (Ed.), *Emergent nature* (pp. 435–436). World Scientific.

Mandelbrot, B. (1975). *Les objets fractals: Forme, hasard et dimension*. Paris, France: Flammarion.

Mandelbrot, B. (1989). Fractals and an art for the sake of science. *Leonardo, Supplemental Issue Computer Art in Context*, 21-24.

Mandelbrot, B. B. (1982). *The fractal geometry of nature*. San Francisco, CA: W.H. Freeman.

Moon, F. (1992). *Chaotic and fractal dynamics*. Wiley & Sons, Inc.

Musgrave, K., & Mandelbrot, B. (1991). The art of fractal landscapes. *IBM Journal of Research and Development,* September.

Peak, D., & Frame, M. (1994). *Chaos under control: The art and science of complexity*. New York, NY: Freeman.

Peitgen, H.-O., Jurgens, H., & Saupe, D. (1992). *Chaos and fractals: New frontiers of science*. New York, NY: Springer-Verlag.

Peitgen, H.-O., & Richter, P. (1986). *The beauty of fractals: Images of complex dynamical systems*. New York, NY: Springer-Verlag.

Pickover, C. A. (Ed.). (1995). *The pattern book: Fractals, art, and nature*. World Scientific.

Poincaré, H. (1943). *La science et l'hypothèse*. Paris, France: Flammarion.

Pollard-Gott, L. (1986). Fractal repetition in the poetry of Wallace Stevens. *Language and Style, 19*, 233–249.

Prusinkiewicz, P., & Lindenmayer, A. (1990). *The algorithmic beauty of plants*. New York, NY: Springer-Verlag.

Risset, J.-C. (1986). Pitch and rhythm paradoxes: Comments on auditory paradox based on a fractal waveform. *The Journal of the Acoustical Society of America, 80*, 961–962.

Rothko, M. (2004). *The artist's reality: Philosophies of art* (Rothko, C., Ed.). New Haven, CT: Yale University Press.

Sala, N. (2002). The presence of the self-similarity in architecture: Some examples. In Novak, M. M. (Ed.), *Emergent nature* (pp. 273–282). World Scientific.

Sala, N. (2007). Preface. In *Chaos and complexity in the arts and architecture* (pp. vii–xiv). New York, NY: Nova Science Publishers, Inc.

Schroeder, M. (1991). *Fractals, chaos, power laws: Minutes from an infinite paradise*. New York, NY: W. H. Freeman.

Shearer, R. (1992). Chaos theory and fractal geometry: Their potential impact on the future of art. *Leonardo, 25*, 143–152.

Shearer, R. (1995). From flatland to fractaland: New geometries in relationship to artistic and scientific revolutions. *Fractals, 3*, 617–625.

Taylor, R. (2007). Pollock, Mondrian and nature: Recent scientific investigations. In Sala, N. (Ed.), *Chaos and complexity in the arts and architecture* (pp. 25–37). New York, NY: Nova Science Publishers, Inc.

Taylor, R., Michlich, A., & Jones, D. (1999). Fractal analysis of Pollock's drip paintings. *Nature, 399*, 422.

Voss, R., & Wyatt, J. (1993). Multifractals and the local connected fractal dimension: Classification of early Chinese landscape painting. In Crilly, A., Earnshaw, R., & Shaw, H. (Eds.), *Applications of fractals and chaos: The shape of things* (pp. 171–184). New York, NY: Springer Verlag.

Zaslavsky, G. M., Sagdeev, R. Z., Usikov, D. A., & Chemikov, A. A. (1991). *Weak chaos and quasiregular structures*. Cambridge University Press. 8.

APPENDIX

A1. *The mappings of the IFS with the attractor as in Figure3.*

$$w_1(x,\ y) = \left(\frac{(0.7 - 4\ x)\ y^2 + (4\ x - 0.2)\ y + 0.1}{(2 - 10\ x)\ y^2 + (10\ x - 2)\ y + 1},\ \frac{(1.4 - 3\ x)\ y^2 + (3\ x - 1.2)\ y + 0.6}{(2 - 10\ x)\ y^2 + (10\ x - 2)\ y + 1} \right),$$

$$w_2(x,\ y) = \left(\frac{(1.1 - 2.6\ x)\ y^2 + (2.6\ x - 0.6)\ y + 0.3}{(2\ - 4\ x)\ y^2 + (4\ x - 2)\ y + 1},\ \frac{(1.4 - 0.4\ x)\ y^2 + (0.4\ x - 1.4)\ y + 0.7}{(2\ - 4\ x)\ y^2 + (4\ x - 2)\ y + 1} \right),$$

$$w_3(x,\ y) = \left(\frac{(2.26 - 9.96\ x)\ y^2 + (3.59\ x - 1.84)\ y + 0.53}{(3.2 - 1.2\ x)\ y^2 + (1.2\ x - 3.2)\ y + 1},\ \frac{0.9\ y^2 - 0.6\ y + 0.3}{(3.2 - 1.2\ x)\ y^2 + (1.2\ x - 3.2)\ y + 1} \right),$$

A2. *The L-system for the "snowflake" in Figure 5 (right), in usual notation*

Axiom:	(F)+(F)+(F)+(F)+(F)+(F)+(F)+(F)
Rule:	F→F(+FF)(–FF)FF(+F)(–F)FF
Angle:	$\delta = 45$ deg.
Starting angle:	$\alpha = 0$ deg.
No of Iter.:	$n = 3$

Chapter 13
Parametric Generator for Architectural and Urban 3D Objects

Renato Saleri Lunazzi
École Nationale Supérieure d'Architecture de Lyon, France

ABSTRACT

The main goal of this chapter is to present a research project, developed by Map-Aria research team, which consists in applying automatic generative methods in design processes.

The Map-Aria research team of the School of Architecture of Lyon develops modeling assistants within the process of architectural conception. They run specific heuristics dramatically reducing time-consuming tasks of wide scale architectural and urban modeling by the implementation of bio-mimetic and/or parametric generative processes. Prior experiments implemented rule-based generative grammars with interesting results.

The authors developed and finalized a specific tool able to model the global structure of architectural objects through a morphological and semantic description of its finite elements. This discrete conceptual model - still in study - was refined during the geometric modeling of the "Vieux Lyon" district, containing a high level of morpho-stylistic disparity. Future developments should allow increasing the genericity of its descriptive efficiency, permitting even more sparse morphological and\or stylistic varieties. Its general purpose doesn't consist in creating a "universal modeler," but to offer a simple tool able to quickly describe a majority of standard architectural objects compliant with some standard parametric definition rules.

DOI: 10.4018/978-1-4666-2077-3.ch013

INTRODUCTION: SETTING UP THE PROBLEMATIC

Following upon the research work led for several years in the field of the paramétric modeling and generative approaches (Herr, 2002; Galanter, 2002; Saleri, 2005), this study aims at setting up a tool allowing to generate quickly exploitable architectural objects in the workflow of computer generated images.

This research task follows and focuses on a former investigation described in "Urban and architectural 3D fast processing" in *Reflexing interfaces: the complex evolution of information technology ecosystems* (Saleri, 2008).

We implemented more accurate modeling functions in order to upgrade the visual precision of 3D enactments (visible on Google Earth portal, not uploaded yet). Visual improvement enhances global 3D model on general volumetric definition, roofing structure and facade definition. Most of remarkable architectural masterpieces are still made through classic 3D modeling workflow; for instance, the Thomassin House, the "Temple du Change", the Saint Jean Cathedral exceed the descriptive model of the described tool and were modeled with traditional Maya geometric built-in routines.

MODEL

The general idea consists in a quick description of an architectural object by informing predefined fields, matching the characteristics of objects to be modelled through a fast and coherent description of the facade, the cross-section type and the plan.(checkboxes or scrolling menus which we can spread on demand by a direct observation of objects to be reproduced). The difficulty consists in the definition of an abstract model as precise as possible but generic enough to cover a wide variety of architectural elements (for example, ergodicity of descriptive model vs final resemblance of the produced models).

We can further discuss about the complexity mode of such a model, according to Rescher description (Rescher, 1998), and we can summarize overall compositional (ontological) complexity, which is only part of the "models of complexity" described as "epistemic modes (formulaic complexity), ontological (compositional and structure complexity) and functional complexity, as follows:

- Constitutional complexity (number of elements of a system)
- Taxonomical complexity (heterogeneity, number of types of elements in a system).

Figure 1. Visual enhancement of architectural models on the same block, comparing former and present version. The Thomassin House (visible on the right picture foreground) was modeled with traditional 3D construction sets. Obviously the polygon count is dramatically increased in the new model, consisting in 16.467 triangles (611 in the previous low-poly solution). In real-time applications both models are used for a LOD (Levels Of Detail) implementation.

When defining such a conceptual model the balance between genericity and specificity is essential; multiplying the describing parameters could certainly serve a more accurate description but also dramatically increases the user interactive process.

The goal is to split the descriptive elements in a pertinent set of discriminant parameters able to match as close as possible the encountered actual models.

Such a model is not obviously complete, and the huge variety of architectural objects around the world reflects the impossibility to define a "universal" descriptor. However, the underlying structural model is consistent enough to generate a wide morphological variety despite the homological similarity between every produced object.

General purpose is to ease the time-consuming task of geometric architectural modeling "from scratch" with an intuitive description of their major constituent elements; the interface, allows to define the most discriminating parameters able to characterize most of architectural morphotypes. We implemented a set of descriptors allowing to approach architectural variety by a parametric description in facade, cross section and plan.

Façade

The "spans / floors" model seems at first sight a strongly discriminating character for the description of an architectural model; its descriptive impact is however limited within the architectural examples met in the ancient districts of the "Vieux Lyon": indeed it seems that according to the land plotting previous to the XVIth century, the supporting walls are perpendicular to the street, freeing the facade openings from a strict vertical alignement (Paulin 1995). So far, this peculiar condition - when encountered - overflows the capabilities of the parametric descriptor. However, in most cases, the regularity of spans allows a "direct" description of the observed objects.

More specifically, the structure of the facade consists of 4 different parts, having each, when invoked, their specific parametric descriptors:

- The base
- The entresol (in yellow)
- The current floors (in green)
- The attique floor (in blue).

Figure 2 shows an example of structure of the facade.

Figure 2. The structure of the facade: by acting on the respective parameters it is possible to describe an infinite variety of different morphotypes.

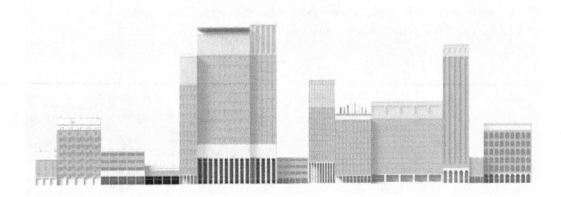

Figure 3. It is possible to modify or to switch descriptive characteristics; besides, a "random function" exists and provides random architectural combinations. In this example, the authors played facade variants having the same spans/floors ratio. The chimney generator is at the moment a random function that however respects some logical construction positioning.

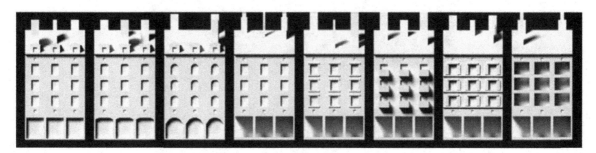

The window itself presents three different typological varieties and vary according to its width, its height and its depth:

- Straight girder
- Lowered bow
- Bow girder (to verify)

A specific treatment of the base also makes the "crossing covered portico" possible.

Cross Section

In the same way we predefined 8 types of standard roofs able to cover a big variety of architectural morphologies. These preset models are modifiable and scalable according to the model needs.

Plan

A wide urban area analysis allowed us to limit considerably the number of geometrical models occurrences, according to the met configurations;

Figure 4. 8 initial sets of roofing; when applied to "vieux Lyon" they allowed to describe most of the existing buildings

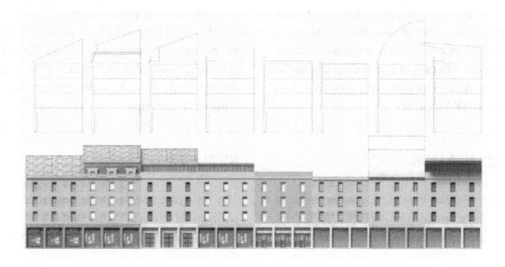

Figure 5. 4 types of articulation of the built in plan are enough for describing most of the met configurations. An experimental block generator - integrating consistent sets of basic shapes according to local configurations - is on study.

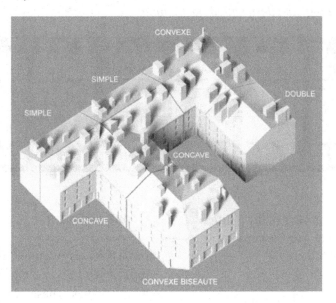

so, and except some rare particular case, it is possible to describe most of the articulations of the urban plots by using 4 basic shapes, called "concave", "convex", "simple" and "double".

To note a particular case of convexity which is a beveled variant of the convex preset: it meets a peculiar scenario often encountered in the Hausmannian land-plot of Lyon.

A finer adaptation of the outcoming models is necessary in particular where some specific road networks are found: especially in historical areas where distributive sets of land plotting are held by topological or constructive constraints: most of all, tortuous alleys and local steep slopes. In this case we take benefit of deformation functions offered by MAYA tools set.

(Maya Embedded Language) code sent to an active Maya application. A pre-load of environmental presets within Maya is however necessary as it contains basic textural primitives, invoked during the generative process. The self-contained dataset is downloadable and refers to a textural database created from actual pictures of "vieux Lyon" existing buildings.

Further improvements will extend the number of related elements in order to provide a wider set of combinational possibilities.

This specific workflow allows an on-line execution of the program (a local Maya licence is however required) and permits a "live support" through frequent code improvements and underlying databases upgrades.

IMPLEMENTATION

The workflow of the system runs under a simple GUI and Maya interaction. A HTML/Javascript environment is able to generate a formatted MEL

RESULTS

The full-scale testing of the described tool - experimented on a wide portion of the "*Vieux Lyon*" district - permitted to refine the underlying abstract

Figure 6. The synthetic version of one of the existing blocks, modelled with the described tool

Figure 7. The user interface providing a "simple" and an "expert" mode that can be unfolded (on the right). In plain mode one can generate preset configurations only by scrolling and clicking a few interactive commands. The "expert" mode allows some more precise positioning and dimensioning of preset elements

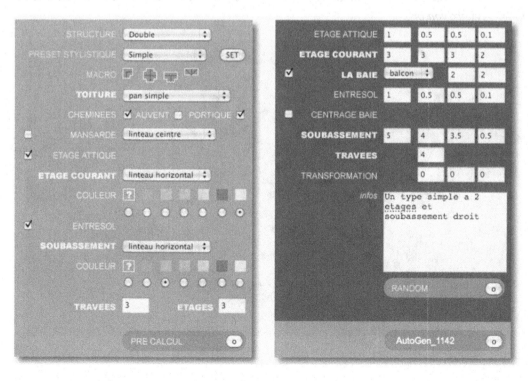

model and to adapt it to upcoming needs. Among the advantages of the depicted system we note that the overall genericity of the abstract models allows a fine description of most of the met cases.

A work of preliminary morphological factorization indeed allowed to establish the most discriminating elements in terms of structural and morphological description of the built elements.

It's a very exploitable tool within the 3D modeling workflow because for its simplicity and the extensibility of the domain of validity of the conceptual model. We presently experiment a cross-platform implementation with the research team of Gamer7 company, very interested in the specific "architectural" approach of the described method.

They develop an "out of the box" interface for game designers able to quickly supply realistic 3D immersive environments. The specific approach of our tool should next upgrade their own city builders in order to provide more realistic urban and architectural design environments.

CONCLUSION

In this chapter we have described a research project, developed by Map-Aria research team, which consists in automatic generative methods in design processes. The project consists in a specific tool able to model the global structure of architectural objects through a morphological and semantic description of its finite elements. The discrete conceptual model was refined during the geometric modeling of the "Vieux Lyon" district, containing a high level of morpho-stylistic disparity. Future developments should allow to increase the generalization of its descriptive efficiency, permitting even more morphological and\or stylistic varieties. It's important to consider that its general purpose does not consist in creating a "universal modeler" but to offer a simple tool able to quickly describe a majority of standard architectural objects compliant with some standard parametric definition rules.

Figure 8. A global view of the "Vieux Lyon" district, modelled with the developed tool. The previous version of the 3D model is visible on Google Earth portal, the updated detailed version can be found here: © www.vieuxlyon.org.

REFERENCES

Duprat, B., & Paulin, M. (1995). *Les systèmes de la façade et de la baie: Maisons à loyer urbaines du XIXe siecle*. Laboratoire d'Analyse des Formes, bureau de la recherche architecturale.

Galanter, P. (2002). *Complexity theory as a context for art theory.* In Generative Art 2002. Retrieved May 20, 2009, from http://www.vieux-lyon.org/vues-3d_f07700.htm

Herr, C. M. (2002). *Generative architectural design and complexity theory.* In Generative Art 2002. Retrieved June 10, 2009, from http://www.mendeley.com/research/generative-architectural-design-complexity-theory/#page-1

Rescher, N. (1998). *Complexity, a philosophical overview*. New Brunswick, NJ: Transaction Publishers.

Saleri, R. (2005). Pseudo-urban automatic pattern generation. *Chaos and Complexity Letters, 3*, 357–365.

Saleri, R. (2008). Urban and architectural 3D fast processing . In Orsucci, F., & Sala, N. (Eds.), *Reflexing interfaces: The complex evolution of information technology ecosystems*. Hershey, PA: IGI Global.

Chapter 14
Fractals, Computer Science and Beyond

Nicoletta Sala
Università della Svizzera Italiana, Switzerland

ABSTRACT

In the modelling of the natural shapes (clouds, ferns, trees, shells, rivers, mountains), the limits imposed by Euclidean geometry can be exceeded by the fractals. Fractal geometry is relatively young (the first studies are the works by the French mathematicians Pierre Fatou (1878-1929) and Gaston Julia (1893-1978) at the beginning of the 20th century), but only with the mathematical power of computers has it become possible to realize connections between fractal geometry and the other disciplines. It is applied in various fields now, from the biology to the architecture. Important applications also appear in computer science, because the fractal geometry permits to compress the images; to reproduce, in the virtual reality environments, the complex patterns and the irregular forms present in nature using simple iterative algorithms execute by computers. Recent studies apply this geometry for controlling the traffic in the computer networks (LANs, MANs, WANs, and the Internet) and in the realization of virtual worlds based on World Wide Web. The aim of this chapter is to present fractal geometry, its properties (e.g., the self similarity), and their applications in computer science (starting from the computer graphics, to the virtual reality).

INTRODUCTION

Fractal geometry is a recent discovery. It is also known as "Mandelbrot's geometry" in honour to its "father" the Polish-born Franco-American mathematician Benoit Mandelbrot, that showed how fractals can occur in many different places in both mathematics and elsewhere in nature.

DOI: 10.4018/978-1-4666-2077-3.ch014

Fractal geometry is now recognized as the true Geometry of Nature. Before Mandelbrot, mathematicians believed that most of the patterns of nature were far too irregular, complex and fragmented to be described mathematically. Mandelbrot's geometry replaces Euclidian geometry which had dominated our mathematical thinking for thousands of years.

The Encyclopaedia Britannica introduces the fractal geometry as follow (2007): "In mathematics, the study of complex shapes with the property of self-similarity, known as fractals. Rather like holograms that store the entire image in each part of the image, any part of a fractal can be repeatedly magnified, with each magnification resembling all or part of the original fractal. This phenomenon can be seen in objects like snowflakes and tree bark… This new system of geometry has had a significant impact on such diverse fields as physical chemistry, physiology, and fluid mechanics; fractals can describe irregularly shaped objects or spatially nonuniform phenomena that cannot be described by Euclidean geometry".

The multiplicity of the application fields had a central role in the diffusion of fractal geometry (Mandelbrot, 1982; Nonnenmacker et al., 1994; Eglash, 1999; Barnsley et al., 2002; Sala, 2004; Sala, 2006; Sala, 2008; Vyzantiadou et al., 2007).

BACKGROUND: WHAT IS A FRACTAL?

A fractal could be defined as a rough or fragmented geometric shape that can be subdivided in parts, each of which is approximately a reduced-size copy of the whole (Mandelbrot, 1988).

"Fractal" is a term coined by Benoit Mandelbrot (b. 1924) to denote the geometry of nature, which traces inherent order in chaotic shapes and processes. The term derived from the Latin verb "frangere", "to break", and from the related adjective "fractus", "fragmented and irregular". This term was created to differentiate pure geometric figures from other types of figures that defy such simple classification. The acceptance of the word "fractal" was dated in 1975. When Mandelbrot presented the list of publications between 1951 and 1975, date when the French version of his book was published, the people were surprised by the variety of the studied fields: linguistics, cosmology, economy, games theory, turbulence, noise on telephone lines (Mandelbrot, 1975). Fractals are generally self-similar on multiple scales. So,

all fractals have a built-in form of iteration or recursion. Sometimes the recursion is visible in how the fractal is constructed. For example, Koch snowflake, Cantor set and Sierpinski triangle are generated using simple recursive rules. The self similarity, the Iterated Function Systems and the Lindenmayer System are applied in different fields of computer science (e.g., in computer graphics, in virtual reality, and in the traffic control of computer networks).

The Self-Similarity

The self-similarity, or invariance against changes in scale or size, is a property by which an object contains smaller copies of itself at arbitrary scales. Mandelbrot defined the self-similarity as follow:" When each piece of a shape is geometrically similar to the whole, both the shape and the cascade that generate it are called self-similar" (Mandelbrot, 1982, p. 34).

A fractal object is self-similar if it has undergone a transformation whereby the dimensions of the structure were all modified by the same scaling factor. The new shape may be smaller, larger, translated, and/or rotated. "Similar" means that the relative proportions of the shapes' sides and internal angles remain the same. As described by Mandelbrot (1982), this property is ubiquitous in the natural world. Oppenheimer (1986) used the term "fractal" exchanging it with self-similarity, and he affirmed that the geometric notion of self-similarity is evolving in a paradigm for modelling the natural world, in particular in the world of botany.

Self-similarity appears in objects as diverse as leaves, mountain ranges, clouds, and galaxies. Figure 1a shows a snowflake which is an example of self-similarity in the nature. Figure 1b illustrates a Koch snowflake, it is built starting from an equilateral triangle, removing the inner third of each side, building another equilateral triangle at the location where the side was removed, and then repeating the process indefinitely. This

Figure 1. A snowflake a) is a natural fractal object and Koch snowflake b) is a fractal generated using simple geometric rules

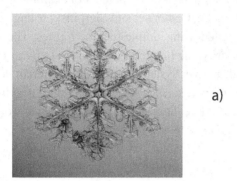

a)

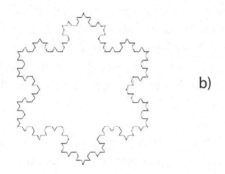

b)

fractal object represents an attempt to reproduce complex shapes present in the nature, using few simple geometric rules.

The Koch snowflake is an example of a shape with a finite area enclosed within an infinite boundary. This seems contrary to geometric intuition, but this is characteristic of many shapes in nature. For example, in the human body all the arteries, veins, capillaries and bronchial structures occupy a relative small fraction of the body. Thus, inside the human body there is the presence of fractal geometry using two different points of view: spatial fractals and temporal fractals. Spatial fractals refer to the presence of self-similarity, for instance, the small intestine repeats its form, observed to various enlargements. Spatial fractals also refer to the branched patterns that are present inside the human body for enlarging the available surface for the absorption of the substances (in

the intestine), and the distribution and the collection of the solutes (in the blood vessels, and in the bronchial tree).

Temporal fractals are present in some dynamic processes, for example in the cardiac rhythm. The long-term variability of heart rate observed over a wide range of time scales with scale-invariant power-law characteristics has recently been associated with the fractal scaling behaviour and long-range correlation properties (Meyer, 2002).

The Iterated Function System

Iterated Function System (IFS) is another fractal that can be applied in computer science. Barnsley (1993, p. 80) defined the Iterated Function System as follow: "A (hyperbolic) iterated function system consists of a complete metric space $(\mathbf{X}, d)$ together with a finite set of contraction mappings $w_n: \mathbf{X} \rightarrow \mathbf{X}$ with respective contractivity factor s_n, for n = 1, 2,.., N. The abbreviation "IFS" is used for "iterated function system". The notation for the IFS just announced is $\{ \mathbf{X}, w_n, n = 1, 2,.., N\}$ and its contractivity factor is $s = \max \{s_n: n = 1, 2, …, N\}$." Barnsley put the word "hyperbolic" in parentheses because it is sometimes dropped in practice. He also defined the following theorem (Barnsley, 1993, p. 81): "Let $\{\mathbf{X}, w_n, n = 1, 2, …, N\}$ be a hyperbolic iterated function system with contractivity factor s. Then the transformation W: $H(\mathbf{X}) \rightarrow H(\mathbf{X})$ defined by:

$$W(B) = \cup_{n=1}^{n} w_n(B) \qquad (1)$$

For all $B \in H(\mathbf{X})$, is a contraction mapping on the complete metric space $(H(\mathbf{X}), h(d))$ with contractivity factor s. That is:

$$H(W(\text{B}), W(C)) \leq s \cdot h(B,C) \qquad (2)$$

for all $B, C \in H(\mathbf{X})$. Its unique fixed point, $A \in H(\mathbf{X})$, obeys

$$A = W(A) = \cup_{n=1}^{n} w_n(A) \qquad (3)$$

and is given by $A = \lim_{n \to \infty} W^{on} (B)$ for any B $\in$ H(**X**)."

The fixed point A $\in$ H(**X**), described in the theorem by Barnsley is called the "attractor of the IFS" or "invariant set".

Bogomolny (1998) affirms that two problems arise. One is to determine the fixed point of a given IFS, and it is solved by what is known as the "deterministic algorithm".

The second problem is the inverse of the first: for a given set A$\in$H(**X**), find an iterated function system that has A as its fixed point (Bogomolny, 1998). This is solved approximately by the Collage Theorem (Barnsley, 1993, p. 94).

The Collage Theorem states: "Let (**X**, d), be a complete metric space. Let L$\in$H(**X**) be given, and let $\varepsilon \geq$ o be given. Choose an IFS (or IFS with condensation) {**X**, (w_n), w_1, w_2,..., w_n} with contractivity factor $0 \leq s \leq 1$, so that

$$h(L, \cup_{\substack{n-1 \\ (n-0)}}^{n} w_n(L)) \leq \varepsilon \qquad (4)$$

where h(d) is the Hausdorff metric. Then

$$h(L, A) \leq \frac{\varepsilon}{1-s} \qquad (5)$$

where A is the attractor of the IFS. Equivalently,

$$h(L, A) \leq (1, s)^{-1} h(L, \cup_{\substack{n-1 \\ (n-0)}} w_n(L)) \qquad (6)$$

for all L$\in$H(**X**)."

The Collage Theorem describes how to find an Iterated Function System whose attractor is "close to" a given set, one must endeavour to find a set of transformations such that the union, or collage, of the images of the given set under transformations is near to the given set.

Figure 2. Fern leaf created using the IFS

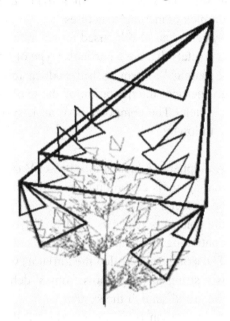

The Collage Theorem states that an Iterated Function System must be like in order to represent an image.

Next Figure 2 shows a fern leaf created using the IFS. The IFS is produced by polygons, in this case: triangles, that are put in one another. The final step of this iterative process shows a fern which has high degree of similarity to real one.

L-Systems

An L-system or Lindenmayer system is an algorithmic method for generating branched forms and structures such as plants. L-systems were invented in 1968 by Hungarian biologist Aristid Lindenmayer (1925-1989) for modelling biological growth. He worked with filamentous fungi and studied the growth patterns of various types of algae, for example the blue/green bacteria Anabaena catenula. Originally the L-systems were devised to provide a formal description of the development of such simple multicellular organisms, and to illustrate the neighbourhood relationships between plant cells. Later on, this system was extended to describe higher plants and complex branching structures.

L-systems can also be used to generate self-similar fractals that are a particular type of symbolic dynamical system with the added feature of a geometrical interpretation of the evolution of the system. The components of an L-system are the following:

- An alphabet which is a finite set V of formal symbols containing elements that can be replaced (variables).
- the constants which is a set S of symbols containing elements that remain fixed.
- The axiom (also called the initiator) which is a string ω of symbols from **V** defining the initial state of the system.
- A production (or rewriting rule) P that is a set of rules or productions defining the way variables can be replaced with combinations of constants and other variables. A production consists of two strings - the predecessor and the successor.

The rules of the L-system grammar are applied iteratively starting from the initial state.

L-systems are also commonly known as parametric L systems, and they are defined as a tuple **G** = {V, S, ω, P}.

Lindenmayer's original L-system for modelling the growth of algae and the blue-green bacteria (anabaena catenula) is the following (Prusinkiewicz and Lindenmayer, 1990, pp. 3 – 4):

- Variables: a b
- Constants: none
- Start (axiom): b
- Rules: (a → ab), (b → a)

The rule (a → ab), means that the letter a is to be replaced by the string ab, and the rule (b → a) means that the letter b is to be replaced by a. The symbols a and b represent cytological states of the cells (their size and readiness to divide). It produces:

- n = 0: b
- n = 1: a
- n = 2: ab
- n = 3: aba
- n = 4: abaab
- n = 5: abaababa

This is the simplest class of L-systems, those which are deterministic and context-free, called DOL-systems. Using geometric interpretation of strings it is possible to generate schematic images of Anabaena catenula.

L-system can be also defined as a formal grammar (a set of rules and symbols) most famously used for modelling the growth processes of plant development, and it has been thought able for modelling the morphology of a variety of organisms. The differences between L-systems and Chomsky grammars are well described by Prusinkiewicz and Lindenmayer that affirmed: "The essential difference between Chomsky grammars and L-systems lies in the method of applying productions. In Chomsky grammars productions are applied sequentially, whereas in L-systems they are applied in parallel and simultaneously replace all letters in a given word. This difference highlights the biological motivation of L-systems. Productions are intended to capture cell divisions in multicellular organisms, where many divisions may occur at the same time. Parallel production application has an essential impact on the formal properties of rewriting systems" (Prusinkiewicz and Lindenmayer, 1990, pp. 2 – 3). Strings generated by L-systems may be interpreted geometrically in different ways. For example, L-system strings serve a drawing commands for LOGO-style turtle. The turtle interpretation of parametric L-systems was introduced by Szilard and Quinton (1979), and extended by Prusinkiewicz (1986, 1987) and Hanan (1988, 1992). Prusinkiewicz and Lindenmayer defined a state of the turtle as a triplet (x, y, α), where the Cartesian coordinates (x, y) represent the turtle's position, and the angle α, called the heading, is interpreted as the direction in which the turtle is facing. Given the step

Table 1. Commands for LOGO-style turtle derived by L-systems

Symbols	Meaning
F	Move forward a step of length s. The state of the turtle changes, now it is (x', y', α), where x' = x +s ·cos α and y'= y + s ·sin α. A segment between (x, y), starting point, and the point (x', y') is drawn.
f	Move forward a tep of length s without drawing a line.
+	Turn left by angle δ. The positive orientation of angles is counterclockwise, and the next state of the turtle is (x, y, α+δ).
-	Turn right by angle δ. The next state of the turtle is (x, y, α - δ).
[	Push the current state of the turtle onto a pushdown operations stack. The information saved on the stack contains the turtle's position and orientation, and possibly other attributes such as the color and width of lines being drawn.
]	Pop a state from the stack and make it the current state of the turtle. No line is drawn, although in general the position of the turtle changes.

size s and the angle increment δ, the turtle can respond to commands represented by the symbols in the Table 1.

The Koch snowflake can be simply encoded as a Lindenmayer system with initial string "F--F--F", string rewriting rule F → F+F--F+F, and angle 60°. Figure 3 shows an example of plant-like structures generated by bracketed L-systems

Figure 3. Plant-like structures generated by L-system

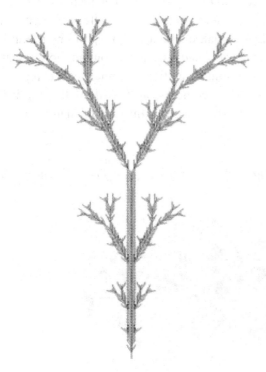

with the axiom Y (angle δ= 25.7°), and the replacement rules X→ X[-FFF][+FFF]FX and Y →YFX[+Y][-Y].

FRACTALS GEOMETRY IN COMPUTER SCIENCE

Fractal geometry is one of the most exciting frontiers in the fusion between mathematics and computer science. Mandelbrot's geometry permits to compress the images, to reproduce in computer graphics and in virtual reality environments the textures and the irregular forms present in nature (e.g. mountains, clouds and trees) using simple iterative or recursive algorithms. Recent studies also apply this geometry in the control of the traffic in the computer networks.

Fractal Geometry in Computer Graphics

The terms fractals has been generalized by the computer graphics community and it includes objects outside Mandelbrot's original definition (Foley et al., 1997). It means anything that has a substantial measure of exact or statistical self-similarity. In the case of statistical fractals it is the probability density that repeats itself on every scale. An application field of fractal geometry is in the compression of images (fractal compression).

A fractal compressed image can be defined as follow: it is an encoding that describes (i) the grid partitioning (the range blocks), and (ii) the affine transformations (one per range block) (Shulman, 2000). Research on fractal image compression derived from the mathematical ferment on chaos and fractals in the years 1978–1985. Barnsley was the principal researcher who worked on fractal compression. The basic idea was to represent by an Iterated Function System (IFS) of which the fixed point is close to that image (Barnsley, 1988; Barnsley et al., 1988). This fixed point is also known as "fractal" (Fisher, 1995). Each IFS is coded as a contractive transformation with coefficients. The Banach fixed point theorem (1922), also known as the contraction mapping theorem or contraction mapping principle, guarantees the existence and uniqueness of fixed points of certain self maps of metric spaces, and provides a constructive method to find those fixed points.

An image can be represented using a set of IFS codes rather than pixels. In this way, a good compression ratio could be achieved. This method was good for generating almost real images based on simple iterative algorithms. The inverse problem, going from a given image to an Iterated Function System that can generate the original (or at least closely resemble it), was solved by Jacquin according to Barnsley in March 1988. He introduced a modified scheme for representing images called Partitioned Iterated Function Systems (PIFS). The main characteristics of this

approach were that (i) it relied on the assumption that image redundancy can be efficiently exploited through self-transformability on a block-wise basis, and (ii) it approximated an original image by a fractal image (Jacquin, 1992). In a PIFS, the transformations do not map from the whole image to the parts, but from larger parts to smaller parts. In the Jacquin's method, the small areas are called "range blocks", the big areas are called "domain blocks" and the pattern of range blocks was called the "partitioning of an image". Every pixel of the original image has to belong to one range block. This system of mappings is contractive, thus when iterated it quickly converge to its fixed point image. Thus, the key point for this algorithm is to find fractals which can best describe the original image and then to represent them as affine transformations.

All methods are based on the fractal transform using iterated function systems which generate a close approximation of a scene using only few transformations (Peitgen and Saupe, 1988; Wohlberg and de Jager, 1999; Zhao and Liu, 2005).

Fractal compression is a lossy compression method (compressing data and then decompressing it retrieves data that may well be different from the original, but is close enough to be useful in some way), and most lossy compression formats suffer from generation loss: repeatedly compressing and decompressing the file will cause it to progressively lose quality (as shown in Figure 4).

Figure 4. Fractal compression: repeatedly compressing and decompressing the file will cause it to progressively lose quality

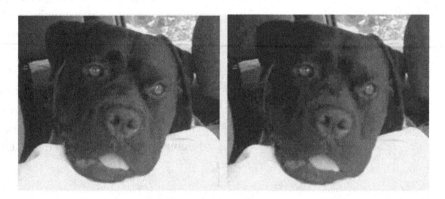

Mandelbrot's geometry and chaos theory can create beautiful images, 2D and 3D, as well as realistic natural looking structures, and fractal textures are used to add visual interest to relatively simple and boring geometric model (Ebert et al., 2003). Fractal algorithms can also be used in computer graphics to generate complex objects using Iterated Function Systems.

Smith (1984) was the first to prove that L-systems were useful in computer graphics for describing the structure of certain plants, in his paper: "Plants, Fractals, and Formal Languages". He claimed that these objects should not be labeled as "fractals" for their similarity to fractals, introducing a new class of objects which Smith called "graftals". This class had of great interest in the Computer Imagery (Smith, 1984; Foley et al., 1997).

Fractal Geometry for Modelling Landscapes

Other interesting application of fractal geometry in computer science is for modelling landscapes. Fournier et al. (1982) developed a mechanism for generating a kind of fractal mountains based on recursive subdivision algorithm for a triangle. Here, the midpoints of each side of the triangle are connected, creating four new subtriangles. Figure 5a shows the subdivision of the triangle into four smaller triangle, Figure 5b illustrates how the midpoints of the original triangle are perturbed in the y direction (Foley et al., 1997). To perturb these points, can be use the properties of the self-similarity, and the conditional expectation properties of fractional Brownian motion (abbreviated to fBm). The fractional Brownian motion was originally introduced by Mandelbrot and Van Ness in 1968 as a generalization of the Brownian motion (Bm). Figure 5 shows a recursive subdivision of an initial polygon using triangles. Other polygons can be used to generate the grid (e.g., squares and hexagons).

This method evidences two problems, which are classified as internal and external consistency problems (Fournier et al., 1982, pp. 374-375). Internal consistency is the reproducibility of the primitive at any position in an appropriate coordinate space and at any level of detail, so the final shape is independent of the orientation of the subdivided triangle. This is satisfied by a Gaussian random number generator which depends on the point's position, thus it generates the same numbers in the same order at a given subdivision level. The external consistency concerns the midpoint displacement at shared edges and their direction of displacement. This process, when iterated, produces a deformed grid which represents a surface; and after the rendering phase (that includes: hidden line, coloured, and shaded) can appear realistic fractal mountains, as shown in Figure 7 (Sala, 2009).

Figure 5. The subdivision of a triangle into four smaller triangle a). Perturbation in the y direction of the midpoints of the original triangle b)

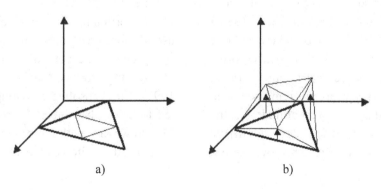

a)   b)

Figure 6. Grid of triangles generated by a recursive subdivision and applying the fractional Brownian motion

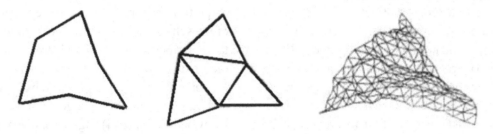

Figure 7. Fractal mountains generated using the recursive subdivisions

Last examples describe how to create fractal mountains but not their erosion. Musgrave et al.. (1989) introduced techniques which are independent of the terrain creation. The algorithm can be applied to already generated data represented as regular height fields require separate processes to define the mountain and the river system. Prusinkiewicz and Hammel (1993) combined the midpoint-displacement method for mountain generation with the squid-curve model of a non-branching river originated by Mandelbrot (Mandelbrot, 1978; 1979). Their method created one non-branching river as result of context sensitive L-system operating on geometric objects (a set of triangles). Three key problems remained open (i) the river flowed at a constant altitude, (ii) the river flowed in an asymmetric valley, and (iii) the river had no tributaries. Figure 8 shows an ex-

ample of a squid-curve construction (recursion levels 0–7) (Prusinkiewicz and Hammel, 1993, p. 177)

Maràk et al. (1997) reported a method for synthetical terrain erosion, that is based on rewriting process of matrices representing terrain parts. They found a rewriting process which was context sensitive. It was defined as a set of productions A → B, where A and B were matrices of numbers of type: N ×N, where N>0.

The terrain parts were rewritten using certain user-defined set of rules which represented an erosion process. The method consisted in three kinds of rewriting process (Maràk et al., 1997; Maràk, 1997). The "absolute rewriting" which permitted to erode the objects in predefined altitude. The "rewriting with the reference point" which could erode arbitrary object in any altitude. The

Figure 8. Squid-curve construction (recursion level 0-7)

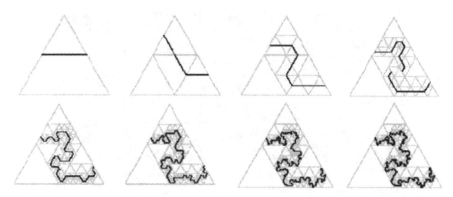

third kind of rewriting process which permitted to erode some shapes in any scale. Its advantage was that the algorithm could be controlled by some external rules and it could simulate different kinds of erosion (Maràk et al., 1997).

Guérin et al. (2002) proposed an interesting model for fractal curves and surfaces. This method, called "projected IFS", combined two classical models: a fractal model (IFS attractors) and a Computer Aided Geometric Design model (CAGD). The model based on Iterated Function System generates a geometrical shape or an image with an iterative process. This method permitted to reconstruct smooth surfaces, and not only rough surfaces, using real data. The original surface generated has been extracted from a geological database (found at the United States Geological Survey Home page, http://www.usgs.org).

Fractals, Virtual Reality, and Cyberspace

Virtual Reality (VR) is a technology which permits to create 3D space generated by the computer. The terms "virtual reality" were coined by Jaron Lanier.

VR could be classify in according to its methods of display; we have: a) immersive VR (which involves a high degree of interactivity and high cost peripheral devices, for example the head mounted displays), and b) non-immersive VR (often called desktop VR which is in the form of a windows into a virtual world displayed on a computer's monitor).

Fractal geometry is used in 3D virtual worlds for creating special effects (e.g., water, fog, clouds), textures, mountains and sets; an example is shown in Figure 9.

Virtual Reality is connected to the World Wide Web with Virtual Reality Modelling Language (VRML). VRML is a 3D graphics language used on the World Wide Web for producing "virtual worlds" that appear on the display screens using an appropriate VRML browser. Using fractal algorithms in VRML is possible to create virtual mountains as shown in Figure 10. This example shows that the connections between fractal geometry, "virtual worlds" and the World Wide Web exit.

This example shows that VRML can open opportunities for using fractal geometry in the Internet based virtual worlds (for example, AlphaWorld and Second Life) (Sala, 2009).

AlphaWorld was one of the oldest collaborative virtual world on the Internet that hosted some millions of people from all over the world. Since 1995, AlphaWorld has rapidly grown in size, and now exceeds 60 million virtual objects.

Second Life (SL) is an Internet-based virtual world launched in the summer of 2003. It was developed by Linden Research, Inc (also referred as Linden Lab).

Figure 9. Fractal computer-generated landscape

Figure 10. Virtual mountains realized in VRML using fractal algorithms

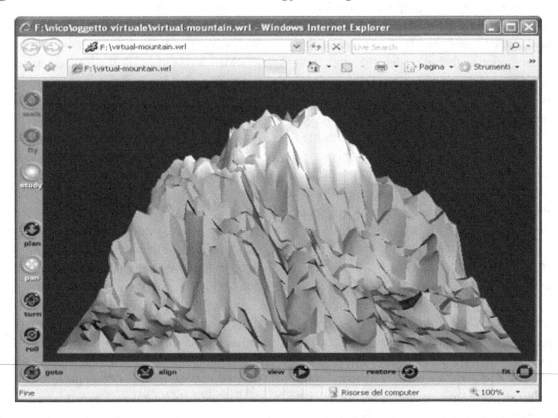

Figure 11. Tree automatically generated from a base shape (2005) and copying it in different scales a),
"Hilbert Cube" (2007) created in 3D using few iterations b) (http://www.segerman.org/2ndlife.html)

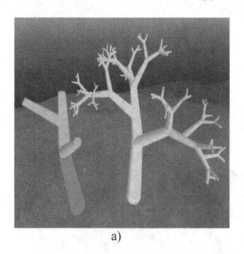

a)

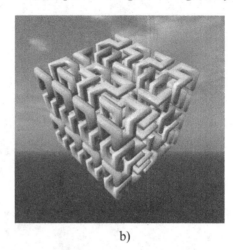

b)

Its users can interact with each other through avatars, providing an advanced level of a social network service combined with general aspects of a metaverse.

Avatars in Second Life are three-dimensional representations of the user. They are controlled and maintained by the user for the purpose of having agency within the virtual environment.

In Second Life, fractal geometry is present for creating suggestive landscapes, mountains, trees, sculptures and other fractal shapes using simple algorithms, useful for a quick 3D visualization. Figures 11a and 11b show two different applications of fractal geometry for realizing a fractal tree generated on a base shape, and a "Hilbert Cube" (Segerman, 2005, 2007).

Bourke (2007) presented and interacted in Second Life with 3D geometry derived mathematically or from datasets. The aim of Bourke's work was to explore the representation of various kinds of fractal forms, the applicability to a range of geometric representations was investigated with the view to using Second Life as a way of visualising scientific data in a interactive collaborative environment, which permits remote collaborative exploration of scientific datasets (Bourke, 2008).

Figure 12 shows an example of fractal objects created in Second life (Bourke, 2007).

Fractals for Controlling Network Traffic

Different models on the nature of network traffic have been proposed in the literature, but in contrast to traditional models the network traffic presented a kind of "fractality" (Norros, 1994; 1995, Park and Willinger, 2000; Liu J., 2006, Sala, 2008).

In the last decades, many fractal traffic processes were described, but the fractality in the traffic was a complex concept, and different approaches were developed. Early models included: fractional Brownian motion (Norros, 1994; 1995; Lévy Véhel and Riedi, 1997), zero-rate renewal process model (Veitch, 1992, 1993; Erramilli et al., 1993) and deterministic chaotic maps (Erramilli and Sigh, 1992; Erramilli et al., 1994; Mondragon et al. 1999).

Many studies have shown that the classical Markovian models were not able to describe the real behaviour of the traffic in the networks. These models made unacceptable mistakes in the quantitative design in the allocation of the resources, in the connection and in admission control, in the scheduling and in the traffic regulation. Markovian models supposed an autocorrelation which was decaying in an exponential way, but real examples showed a different behaviour (Norros, 1995).

Figure 12. Fractal objects in Second Life

Other studies based on fractal geometry, in particular referring to the property of the self-similarity, were realized. Self-similarity is an important notion for understanding the problems connected to the network traffic, including the modeling and the analysis of network performances (Norros, 1994; Fowler and Leland, 1994; Norros, 1995; Lévy Véhel and Riedi, 1997; Park and Willinger, 2000).

Leland et al. (1993; 1994) reported that the Ethernet Local Area Network (LAN) traffic was statistically self-similar. In fact, the Ethernet LAN data were not only consistent with self-similarity at the level of aggregate packet traffic, but they were also in agreement with the self-similarity in terms of the basic characteristics of the individual source-destination pair traffics that make up the self-similar aggregate trace. None of the other traffic models was able to describe this fractal behaviour, that has serious implications for the design, control, and analysis of high-speed networks, and that aggregating streams of such traffic typically intensifies the self-similarity ("burstiness") instead of smoothing it.

Figure 13 shows the Bellcore pOct traffic trace, famous fractal trace, with Hurst parameter of 0.78 (Norros, 1995).

Figure 13. Bellcore pOct traffic trace with Hurst parameter of 0.78 (Norros, 1995)

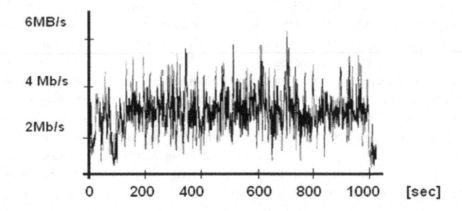

Klivansky, et al.(1994) presented an examination of packet traffic from geographically dispersed locations on the National Science Foundation Network (NSFNET) backbone. The analyses indicated that packet-level traffic over NSFNET core switches exhibited long-range dependence (LRD), and a subset of these showed the property of self-similarity (an asymptotic second order self-similarity).

Willinger et al. (1995), using an approach suggested by Mandelbrot (1969), showed that the superposition of many ON/OFF sources, each of which exhibited a phenomenon called the "Noah Effect", resulted in self-similar aggregate network traffic approaching fractional Brownian motion (the so-called "Joseph Effect").

Giordano et al. (1995) reported some realistic traffic scenarios in the analysis of broadband telecommunication networks. They described the performance evaluation of a broadband network which provided a best effort, asynchronous interconnection of several remote LANs, observing some relevant effects of the arrival processes on network performances considering a model of the Distributed Queue Dual Bus (DQDB) IEEE 802.6 network. The analysis of real traffic in LANs and in Metropolitan Area Networks (MANs) and of its long range dependence confirmed a self similar nature of the traffic offered to a broadband network.

Paxson and Floyd (1994, 1995) reported the results of measurement and analysis on Wide Area Network (WAN) traffic (TCP traffic), for applications like TELNET and FTP. Millions of connections and TCP packets from different sites, with traces ranging from 1 hour to 30 days, were collected. These studies showed the self-similar nature of WAN traffic.

Crovella and Bestavros (1995, 1996) reported that the World Wide Web (WWW) traffic is self-similar. They observed that: i) the traffic patterns generated by browsers have a self-similar nature, ii) every Web browser is modelled as an ON-OFF source model and data fits well the Pareto distribution, iii) the files available via the Web over the Internet seem to have a heavy-tailed size distribution (bimodal distribution).

Lévy Véhel and Riedi (1997) reported that the fractional Brownian motion, which has been used to model the long range dependence of traffic traces, showed the property of self-similarity. They noticed that the multi-fractal approach to the traffic was natural because it was a process of positive increments.

All these studies highlight that "fractal traffic" in LANs, in MANs, in WANs, and in WWW has a correlation existing at multiple time scales, a kind of self correlation that decays in low power way (as shown in Figure 14). This self correlation has an important impact on network performance.

The Hurst parameter H is able to show the "degree" of self-similarity (for example, the degree of persistence of the statistical phenomenon under test). H has a value range of $0.5 \leq H \leq 1.0$. A value of H= 0.5 indicates the lack of self-similarity, a value for H close to 1.0 indicates a large degree of self-similarity or long-range dependence in the process.

Zhang et al. (1997) applied the Hurst parameter to capture the fractal behaviour of the network traffic. They also made some interesting considerations of the multi-fractal behaviour and the value of the Hurst parameter when the traffic is merged.

The fractal characterization of the Internet traffic has an exhaustive description by Park and Willinger in their book: *Self-Similar Network Traffic and Performance Evaluation* (2000).

More recently, Salvador et al. (2004) addressed the modeling of network traffic using a multi-time-scale framework. They evaluated the performance of two classes of traffic models: Markovian and Lindenmayer-Systems based traffic models. These traffic models included the notion of time scale using different approaches: indirectly in the model structure, through a fitting of the second-order statistics, in the case of the Markovian models or directly in the model structure, in the case of the Lindenmayer-Systems based models.

Figure 14. Self-similarity in the traffic trace

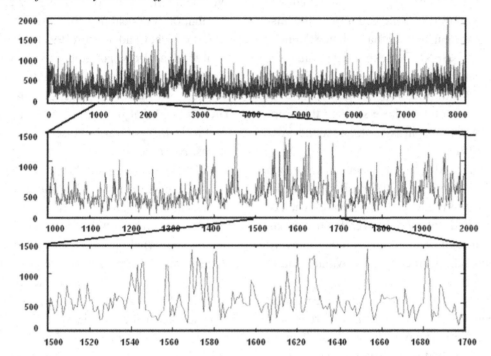

FUTURE TRENDS

In the field of the compression of images novel methods are studied. For example, van Wijk and Saupe (2004) present a fast method to generate fractal imagery based on Iterated Function Systems. The high performance derives from three factors: (i) all steps are expressed in graphics operations which can be performed quickly by hardware, (ii) frame to frame coherence is exploited, (iii) only a few commands per image have to be passed from the CPU to the graphics hardware, avoiding the classical CPU bottleneck.

Wang et al. (2006) present an interactive progressive fractal decoding method, where the compressed file can be transmitted incrementally and reconstructed progressively at users' side. The method requires no modification to encoder or decoder of any fractal image compression algorithm, and it provides the user-controlled decoding procedure with the inherited fractal fast decoding feature. Their experimental results shown that the method can be applied to various

fractal compression techniques and in particular where the transmission bandwidth is relevant.

Other studies are based on the idea for integrating Spiral Architecture (SA) and fractal compression (He et al., 2006a; Liu D., 2006). SA is an approach to machine vision system (Sheridan et al., 1991; Sheridan, 1996). It is inspired from anatomical consideration of the primate's vision system (Schwartz, 1980). The natural data structure that emerges from geometric consideration of the distribution of photo receptors on the primate's retina has been called the Spiral Honeycomb Mosaic (SHM) (Sheridan and Hintz, 1999). Spiral Architecture, inspired by the natural SHM, is an image structure on which images are displayed as a collection of hexagonal pixels placed in hexagonal grid (as shown in Figure 15a). Each hexagonal pixel has six neighbouring pixels that have the same distance to the centre hexagon of unit of vision. In this way, SA has the possibility to save time for local and global processing. In the human eye, these hexagons would represent the relative position of the rods and cones on the

Figure 15. Hexagonal grid a), rectangular grid b)

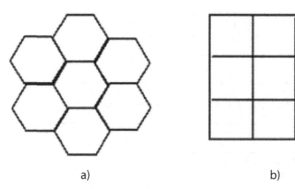

a)   b)

retina. This arrangement is different from the traditional rectangular image architecture, a set of 3×3 rectangles used as unit of vision, where each pixel has eight neighbour pixels (in Figure 15b).

This hexagonal representation has special computational features that are useful to the vision process, and it has features of higher degree of circular symmetry, uniform connectivity, greater angular resolution, and a reduced need of storage and computation in image processing operations.

Sheridan et al. (2000) introduced a one-dimensional addressing scheme for a hexagonal structure, together with the definitions of two operations: Spiral Addition and Spiral Multiplication, that correspond to image translation and rotation respectively. This hexagonal structure is called the Spiral Architecture. Each pixel on the Spiral Architecture is identified by a designated positive number, called Spiral Address. Figure 16a shows a Spiral Architecture and the Spiral Addresses. The numbered hexagons form the cluster of size

7^n. In Figure 12a there is a collection of $7^2 = 49$ hexagons with labelled addresses. Every collection of seven hexagons are labelled starting from the centre address as it was done for the first seven hexagons. The collection of hexagons, in Figure 16a, grow in powers of seven with uniquely assigned addresses. It is this pattern of growth of addresses that generates the Spiral, in fact the hexagons tile the plane in a recursive modular manner along the spiral direction (Figure 16b).

Wu et al. (2004) construct a virtual hexagonal structure which represents an important innovation in this field. Using Virtual Spiral Architecture, rectangular structure can be smoothly converted to Spiral Architecture. Virtual Spiral Architecture exists only during the procedure of image processing which creates virtual hexagonal pixels in the computer memory. The data can be reorganized in rectangular architecture for display. The term "virtual" refers to the characteristic that the hexagonal pixels do not physically exist.

Figure 16. Spiral architecture a) and spiral addressing b)

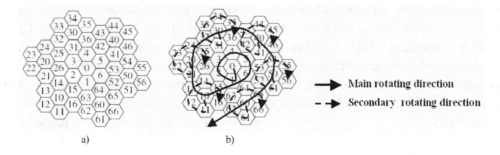

a)   b)

Figure 17. Image processing on virtual spiral architecture (He et al., 2006b, p. 572)

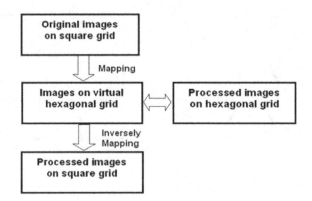

Figure 17 shows the phases of the image processing on virtual spiral architecture (He et al., 2006b, p. 572). The accuracy and efficiency of image processing on SA have been demonstrated in many recently published papers (Wu et al., 2004; Bobe and Schaefer, 2006; He et al, 2006a; He et al, 2006b). Spiral Architecture applied into fractal image compression improve the compression performance in compression ratio with little suffering in image quality. The methods presents the following advantages: little, if any, distortion is introduced, and regular pixels are divided up into sub-pixels.

In the field of modeling landscapes, the future trends are oriented to use fractal geometry, in particular IFS, generating terrain from real data extracting from geological data base. This is useful in the reconstruction of real terrain and landscapes (Guérin et al., 2002; Guérin, and Tosan, 2005).

Fractal geometry also offers an alternative approach to conventional planetary terrain analysis. For example, Stepinski et al. (2004) describe Martian terrains, represented by topography based on the Mars Orbiter Laser Altimetry (MOLA) data, as a series of drainage basins. Fractal analysis of each drainage network, computationally extracts some network descriptors that are used for a quantitative characterization and classification of Martian surfaces.

Other recent application of desktop VR is to create virtual worlds and virtual environments connected to the WWW. Second Life (SL) is an example in this field. SL could begin a "territory" where is possible to try interesting virtual building, an example is shown Figure 18. It has been realized using fractal algorithms in laboratory activities connected to the course of New Media at the Academy of Architecture – Mendrisio (USI, Switzerland) (Sala, 2011).

Other interesting application is in the generation of a fractal urban scenery. Li and Miller (2010) investigate how fractal theory can be used to mathematically simulate the multi-level hierarchical urban structure corresponding to various land use property probabilities of city regions. They found inspiration by modern fractal city theory (Batty and Longley, 1994; Tannier and Pumain 2005, Lagarias, 2007). They propose a system which automatically generates multi-level fractal urban scenery on a large scale. Theoretical foundation is based on the Central Place Theory (Christaller, 1933; Berliant, 2005), while fractal geometry is use to provide the computational substrate of the simulation system. This study is a tentative of an automatic solution to the problem of cityscape construction. The positive aspect is the reduction of the implementation. The probabilities were modelled theoretically based on hypothetical concepts, but the proposed probability map allows use of real-world data or drawing

Figure 18. Virtual building realised using fractal algorithms in Second Life

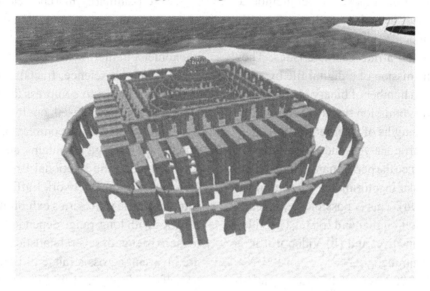

data where available. Figures 19a and 19b respectively show examples of the functional city blocks, and the land plots (Li and Miller, 2010, p. 11)

In the field of the network control traffic, recent studies intend to check the fractal behaviour of network traffic supporting new applications and services (Chakraborty et al., 2004). Internet traffic being extremely variable and bursty in a wide range of time scales is usually characterised by a self-similarity, which describes its statistics depending on the scales of resolution.

Figure 19. Functional city block a). Land plots b)

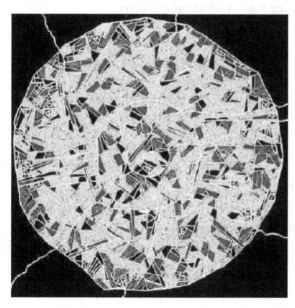

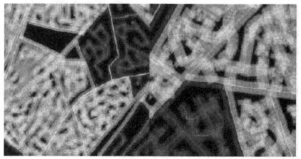

a)   b)

Marie et al. (2006) report a novel method to capture the fractal behaviour of Internet traffic adopting the Random Scaling Fractal model (RSF) to simulate its self-affine characteristics. They realize the transmission of a digital file by splitting the file into a number of binary blocks (files) whose size and submission times are compatible with the bursty lengths of Internet traffic.

The fractal traffic analyses and their results will be useful to enhance the performance of real-time traffic, in particular in multimedia video applications (Liu J., 2006). This is possible because: (i) Video traffic is self-similar and fractal, (ii) Video traffic is time-sensitive, and (ii) Video traffic is bandwidth-consuming.

Wang et al. (2009) report the fractal statistical characteristics of wireless network traffic which are studied using the Hurst parameter. They compared the parameter estimation values of fractal wireless network traffic using three different statistical approaches. Their simulation results demonstrated that wireless network traffic has fractal characteristics. These results could be useful for the performance improvement and the system design optimization of wireless network.

CONCLUSION

This chapter has described some applications of fractals in computer science. The fascination that surrounds fractal geometry seems to have two reasons. First, it is based on simple rules. The other reason is that fractal geometry is very suitable for simulating many phenomena. For example, the fractal behaviour and long-range dependence have been observed in the field of fluctuations in different systems, from black holes to quasars, rivers to fault lines, financial networks to computer networks and brains to hearts, these and many other kinds of complex systems have all exhibited power law scaling relations in their behaviours.

The self-similarity, that characterizes the fractal objects, is a unifying concept. In fact, it is an attribute of many laws of nature and innumerable phenomena in the world around us.

In computer science, fractals can be applied in different fields: to compress the images using simple algorithms based on Iterated Function Systems, for modelling complex objects in computer graphics (e.g., mountains, and rivers) using L-systems and the fractional Brownian motion, for controlling the network traffic. In particular, Internet traffic time series exhibit fractal characteristics with long-range dependence. This is due to the existence of several statistical properties that are invariant across a range of time scales, such as self-similarity, and multifractality, that have an important impact on network's performances. The traffic self-similarity existent in network and application traffic seems to be an ubiquitous phenomenon that is independent of technology, protocol and environment. Therefore, traffic models must be able to include these properties in their mathematical structure and parameter inference procedures.

Fractals in virtual reality can help to realize new forms which exceed the limits imposed by the "old" Euclidean geometry.

REFERENCES

Barnsley, M. F. (1988). *Fractals everywhere*. Boston, MA: Academic Press.

Barnsley, M. F. (1993). *Fractals everywhere* (2nd ed.). Boston, MA: Academic Press.

Barnsley, M. F., Jacquin, A. E., Malassenet, F., Reuter, L., & Sloane, A. D. (1988). Harnessing chaos for image synthesis. *SIGGRAPH, 1988*, 131–140.

Barnsley, M. F., Saupe, D., & Vrscay, E. R. (Eds.). (2002). *Fractals in multimedia*. Berlin, Germany: Springer.

Batty, M., & Longley, P. (1994). *Fractal cities: A geometry of form and function*. London, UK: Academic Press.

Berliant, M. (2005). *Central place theory*. Urban/Regional 0505001, EconWPA, 2005.

Bobe, S., & Schaefer, G. (2006). Image processing and image registration on spiral architecture with saLib. *International Journal of Simulation Systems, Science & Technology, Special Issue on. Vision & Visualisation, 7*(3), 37–43.

Bogomolny, A. (1998). *The collage theorem*. Retrieved September 15, 2005, from: http://www.cut-the-knot.org/ctk/ifs.shtml

Bourke, P. (2007). *Representing and modelling geometry in Second Life*. Retrieved December 11, 2008, from http://local.wasp.uwa.edu.au/~pbourke/fractals/secondlife/

Bourke, P. (2008). Evaluating Second Life as a tool for collaborative scientific visualisation.

Chakraborty, D., Ashir, A., Suganuma, G., Mansfield, K., Roy, T., & Shiratori, N. (2004). Self-similar and fractal nature of Internet traffic. *International Journal of Network Management, 14*(2), 119–129.

Christaller, W. (1933). *Die zentralen Orte in Süddeutschland*. Jena, Germany: Gustav Fischer.

Computer Games and Allied Technology. Singapore, April 28-30, 2008. Retrieved December 14, 2008, from http://local.wasp.uwa.edu.au/~pbourke/papers/cgat08/paper.pdf

Crovella, M. E., & Bestavros, A. (1995). *Explaining World Wide Web traffic self-similarity. Technical Report: TR-95-015*. Computer Science Department, Boston University.

Crovella, M. E., & Bestavros, A. (1996). Self-similarity in World Wide Web Traffic: Evidence and possible causes. *Proceedings of ACM SIGMETRICS'96*.

Ebert, D. S., Musgrave, F. K., Peachy, D., Perlin, K., & Worley, S. (2003). *Texturing and modeling: A procedural approach* (3rd ed.). US: Morgan Kaufmann Publishers Inc.

Eglash, R. (1999). *African fractals: Modern computing and indigenous design*. Piscataway, NJ: Rutgers University Press.

Erramilli, A., Gosby, D., & Willinger, W. (1993). Engineering for realistic traffic: A fractal analysis of burstiness. *Proceedings of ITC Special Congress*, Bangalore, India, 1993.

Erramilli, A., Pruthi, P., & Willinger, W. (1994). *Modelling packet traffic with chaotic maps. ISRN KTH/IT/R-94/18-SE*. Sweden: Stockholm-Kista.

Erramilli, A., & Singh, R. P. (1992). *An application of deterministic chaotic maps to model packet traffic*. Bellcore Technical Memorandum.

Fisher, Y. (1995). *Fractal image compression: Theory and application*. New York, NY: Springer-Verlag.

Foley, J. D., van Dam, A., Feiner, S. K., & Hughes, J. F. (1997). *Computer graphics: Principles and practice* (2nd ed.). New York, NY: Addison Wesley.

Fournier, A., Fussel, D., & Carpenter, L. (1982). Computer rendering of stochastic models. *Communications of the ACM, 25*, 371–384.

Fowler, H., & Leland, W. (1994). Local area network traffic characteristics, with implications for broadband network congestion management. *IEEE Journal on Selected Areas in Communications, 9*(7), 1139–1149.

Fractal geometry. (2007). In *Encyclopædia Britannica*. Retrieved February 26, 2007, from http://concise.britannica.com/ebc/article-9364797/fractal-geometry

Giordano, S., Pierazzini, G., & Russo, F. (1995). *Multimedia experiments at the University of Pisa: From videoconference to random fractals.* Retrieved October 10, 2006, from http://www.isoc. org/HMP/PAPER/109/html/paper.html

Guérin, E., & Tosan, E. (2005). Fractal inverse problem: Approximation formulation and differential methods. In Lévy-Véhel, J., & Lutton, E. (Eds.), *Fractal in engineering: New trends in theory and applications* (pp. 271–285). London, UK: Springer.

Guérin, E., Tosan, E., & Baskurt, A. (2002). Modeling and approximation of fractal surfaces with projected IFS Attractors. In Novak, M. M. (Ed.), *Emergent nature: Patterns, growth and scaling in the science* (pp. 293–303). New Jersey: World Scientific.

Hanan, J. S. (1988). *PLANTWORKS: A software system for realistic plant modelling.* Master's thesis, University of Regina.

Hanan, J. S. (1992). *Parametric L-systems and their application to the modelling and visualization of plants.* PhD thesis, University of Regina.

He, X., Hintz, T., Wu, Q., Wang, H., & Jia, W. (2006b). A new simulation of spiral architecture. *Proceedings of 2006 International Conference on Image Processing, Computer Vision, & Pattern Recognition (IPCV'06)* (pp. 570-575). Las Vegas, USA, Jacquin, A. E. (1992). Image coding based on a fractal theory of iterated contractive image transformations image processing. *IEEE Transactions, 1*(1), 18 – 30.

He, X., Wang, H., Wu, Q., Hintz, T., & Hur, N. (2006a). Fractal image compression on spiral architecture. *International Conference on Computer Graphics, Imaging and Visualisation (CGIV'06)*, (pp. 76-83).

Klivansky, S. M., Mukherjee, A., & Song, C. (1994). *On long-range dependence in NSFNET traffic. CC Technical Report; GIT-CC-94-61.* Georgia Institute of Technology.

Lagarias, A. (2007). Fractal analysis of the urbanization at the outskirts of the city: Models, measurement and explanation. *Cybergeo.* Retrieved from http://cybergeo.revues.org/8902

Leland, W. E., Taqqu, M. S., Willinger, W., & Wilson, D. V. (1993). On the self-similar nature of ethernet traffic. *Proceedings of the ACM/SIG-COMM'93*, (pp. 183-193). San Francisco, CA.

Leland, W. E., Taqqu, M. S., Willinger, W., & Wilson, D. V. (1994). On the self-similar nature of ethernet traffic (Extended Version). *IEEE/ACM Transactions on Networking, 2*(1), 1–15.

Lévy Véhel, J., & Riedi, R. (1997). Fractional Brownian motion and data traffic modeling: The other end of the spectrum. In Lévy Véhel, J., Lutton, E., & Tricot, C. (Eds.), *Fractals in engineering* (pp. 185–202). London, UK: Springer.

Li, B., & Miller, J. (2010). Fractal cityscape. *The International Journal of Virtual Reality, 9*(4), 7–12.

Liu, D. (2006). A parallel computing algorithm for improving the speed of fractal image compression based on spiral architecture. *Proceedings of 2006 International Conference on Image Processing, Computer Vision, & Pattern Recognition (IPCV'06)* (pp. 563-569). Las Vegas, USA.

Liu, J. (2006). *Fractal network traffic analysis with applications.* Ph-D Thesis, School of Electrical and Computer Engineering Theses and Dissertations, Georgia Tech Theses and Dissertations. Retrieved January 10, 2007, from http://hdl. handle.net/1853/11477

Mandelbrot, B. (1975). *Les objects fractals. Forme, hasard et dimension.* Paris, France: Nouvelle Bibliothèque Scientifique Flammaron.

Mandelbrot, B. (1982). *The fractal geometry of nature*. W.H. Freeman and Company.

Mandelbrot, B. B. (1969). Long-run linearity, locally Gaussian processes, H-spectra and infinite variances. *International Economic Review, 10*, 82–113.

Mandelbrot, B. B. (1978). Les objets fractals. *La Recherche, 9*, 1–13.

Mandelbrot, B. B. (1979). Colliers all'eatoires et une alternative aux promenades aux hasard sans boucle: Les cordonnets discrets et fractals. *CR (East Lansing, Mich.), 286A*, 933–936.

Maràk, I. (1997). *On synthetic terrain erosion modeling: A survey*. Retrieved April 14, 2005, from http://www.cescg.org/CESCG97/marak/

Marák, I., Benes, B., & Slavík, P. (1997). Terrain erosion model based on rewriting of matrices. *Proceedings of WSCG-97*, Vol. 2, (pp. 341-351).

Marie, R. R., Bez, H. E., Blackledge, J. M., & Datta, S. (2006). *On the fractal characteristics of network traffic and its utilization in covert communications*. Retrieved January 2, 2007, from http://ima.org.uk/Conferences/mathssignalprocessing2006/Marie.pdf

Meyer, M. (2002). Fractal scaling of heartrate dynamics in health and disease. In Losa, G. A., Merlini, D., Nonnenmacher, T. F., & Weibel, E. R. (Eds.), *Fractal in biology and medicine* (*Vol. III*, pp. 181–193). Basel, Switzerland: Birkhauser.

Mondragon, R. J., Arrowsmith, D. K., & Pitts, J. M. (1999). Chaotic maps for traffic modelling and queueing performance analysis. *Performance Evaluation, 43*(4), 223–240.

Musgrave, F. K., Kolb, C. E., & Mace, R. S. (1989). The synthesis and rendering of eroded fractal terrain. *Computer Graphics, 23*(3), 41–50.

Nonnenmacher, T. F., Losa, G. A., Merlini, D., & Weibel, E. R. (Eds.). (1994). *Fractal in biology and medicine*. Basel, Switzerland: Birkhauser.

Norros, I. (1994). A storage model with self-similar input. *Queueing Systems Theory and Applications, 16*(3-4), 387–396.

Norros, I. (1995). On the use of fractional Brownian motion in the theory of connectionless networks. *IEEE Journal on Selected Areas in Communications, 13*(6), 953–962.

Oppenheimer, P. (1986). Real time design and animation of fractal plants and trees. *Computer Graphics, 20*(4), 55–64.

Park, K., & Willinger, W. (2000). *Self-similar network traffic and performance evaluation* (1st ed.). London, UK: John Wiley & Sons.

Paxson, V., & Floyd, S. (1994). Wide area traffic: The failure of Poisson modeling. *Proceedings of ACM SIGCOMM'94* (pp. 257-268).

Paxson, V., & Floyd, S. (1995). Wide area traffic: The failure of Poisson Modeling. *IEEE/ACM Transactions on Networking, 3*(3), 226–244.

Peitgen, H., & Saupe, D. (1988). *The science of fractal images*. New York, NY: Springer-Verlag.

Prusinkiewicz, P. (1986). Graphical applications of L-systems. *Proceedings of Graphics Interface '86 - Vision Interface '86*, (pp. 247–253).

Prusinkiewicz, P. (1987). Applications of L-systems to computer imagery. In H. Ehrig, M. Nagl, G. Rozenberg, & A. Rosenfeld (Eds.), *Graph-Grammars and Their Application to Computer Science 3rd International Workshop, Lecture Notes in Computer Science, Vol. 291,* Warrenton, Virginia, USA, December 1986, (pp. 534–548). Heidelberg, Germany: Springer-Verlag.

Prusinkiewicz, P., & Hammel, M. (1993). A fractal model of mountains with rivers. *Proceeding of Graphics Interface, 93*, 174–180.

Prusinkiewicz, P., & Lindenmayer, A. (1990). *The algorithmic beauty of plants*. New York, NY: Springer-Verlag. Retrieved September, 2006, from http://algorithmicbotany.org/papers/abop/abop.pdf

Sala, N. (2004). Fractal geometry in the arts: An overview across the different cultures. In Novak, M. M. (Ed.), *Thinking in patterns: Fractals and related phenomena in nature* (pp. 177–188). Singapore: World Scientific.

Sala, N. (2006). Complexity, fractals, nature and industrial design: Some connections. In Novak, M. M. (Ed.), *Complexus mundi: Emergent pattern in nature* (pp. 171–180). Singapore: World Scientific.

Sala, N. (2008). Fractal geometry in computer science. In Orsucci, F., & Sala, N. (Eds.), *Reflexing interfaces: The complex coevolution of information technology ecosystems, information science reference* (pp. 308–328). Hershey, PA: IGI Global.

Sala, N. (2009). Fractal geometry in artificial world and in Second Life. *Chaos and Complexity Letters, 4*(1), 23–34.

Sala, N. (2011). Virtual reality in architecture, engineering and beyond. In Abu-Taieh, E., El Sheikh, A., & Jafari, M. (Eds.), *Technology engineering and management in aviation: Advancements and discoveries*.

Salvador, P., Nogueira, A., Valadas, R., & Pacheco, A. (2004). Multi-time-scale traffic modeling using Markovian and L-Systems models. *Proceedings of 3rd European Conference on Universal Multiservice Networks, Lecture Notes in Computer Science, Vol. 3262*, Porto, Portugal, October 25-27, 2004, (pp. 297-306). Heidelberg, Germany: Springer-Verlag.

Schwartz, E. (1980). Computation anatomy and functional architecture of striate cortex: A spatial mapping approach to perceptual coding. *Vision Research, 20*, 645–669.

Segermann, H. (2008). *Second Life*. Retrieved December 18, 2008, from http://www.segerman.org/2ndlife.html

Sheridan, P. (1996). *Spiral architecture for machine vision*. PhD thesis, University of Technology, Sydney.

Sheridan, P., & Hintz, T. (1999). Primitive image transformations on hexagonal lattice. Technical report, Charles Sturt University, Bathurst, NSW.

Sheridan, P., Hintz, T., & Alexander, D. (2000). Pseudo-invariant image transformations on a hexagonal lattice. *Image and Vision Computing, 18*, 907–917.

Sheridan, P., Hintz, T., & Moore, W. (1991). Spiral architecture in machine vision. *In T. Bossamier (Ed.), Australian Occam and Transputer Conference. Amsterdam, The Netherlands: IOS Press.*

Shulman, J. A. (2000). *Fractals and Benoit Mandelbrot: A computer science discovery often considered kind to prime numbers*. American Computer Science Association (ACSA). Retrieved December 28, 2006, from http://www.acsa2000.net/frac/

Smith, A. R. (1984). Plants, fractals, and formal languages. *Proceedings of the 11th Annual Conference on Computer Graphics and Interactive Techniques*, (pp. 1–10).

Stepinski, T. F., Collier, M. L., McGovern, P. J., & Clifford, S. M. (2004). Martian geomorphology from fractal analysis of drainage networks. *Journal of Geophysical Research, 109*(2), E02005.1-E02005.12

Szilard, A. L., & Quinton, R. E. (1979). An interpretation for DOL systems by computer graphics. *The Science Terrapin, 4*, 8–13.

Tannier, C., & Pumain, D. (2005). Fractals in urban geography: A theoretical outline and an empirical example. *Cybergeo, Systems, Modeling, Geostatistics*. Retrieved from http://cybergeo.revues.org/3275

van Wijk, J. J., & Saupe, D. (2004). Image based rendering of iterated function systems. *Computers & Graphics*, *28*(6), 937–943.

Veitch, D. (1992). Novel models of broadband traffic. *Proceedings 7ᵗʰ Australian Teletraffic Research Seminar*, Murray River, Australia, 1992.

Veitch, D. (1993). Novel models of broadband traffic. *IEEE Global Telecommunications Conference, 1993, including a Communications Theory Mini-Conference, Technical Program Conference Record, IEEE in Houston, GLOBECOM '93*, Vol. 2 (pp. 1057-1061).

Vyzantiadou, M. A., Avdelas, A. V., & Zafiropoulos, S. (2007). The application of fractal geometry to the design of grid or reticulated shell structures. *Computer Aided Design*, *39*(1), 51–59.

Wang, H., Wu, Q., He, X., & Hintz, T. (2006). A novel interactive progressive decoding method for fractal image compression. *First International Conference on Innovative Computing, Information and Control (ICICIC '06)*, Vol. III (pp. 613-617).

Wang, T., Yu, Q., & Mao, Y. (2009). Fractal characteristics analysis of wireless network traffic based on Hurst parameter. *International Conference on Communications, Circuits and Systems (ICCCAS)*, 2009, (pp. 173-176).

Willinger, W., Taqqu, M. S., Sherman, R., & Wilson, D. V. (1995). Self-similarity through high-variability: Statistical analysis of ethernet LAN traffic at the source level. *ACM Sigcomm*, *95*, 100–113.

Wohlberg, B., & de Jager, G. (1999). A review of the fractal image coding literature. *IEEE Transactions on Image Processing*, *8*(12), 1716–1729.

Wu, Q., He, X., & Hintz, T. (2004). Virtual spiral architecture. *Proceedings of the International Conference on Parallel and Distributed Processing Techniques and Applications*, Vol. 1 (pp. 399-405).

Zhang, H. F., Shu, Y. T., & Yang, O. W. W. (1997). Estimation of Hurst parameter by variance time plots. *Proceedings IEEE Pacrim 97*, Vol. 2 (pp. 883-886).

Zhao, E., & Liu, D. (2005). Fractal image compression methods: A review. *ICITA 2005. Third International Conference on Information Technology and Applications*, Vol. 1 (pp. 756 – 759).

292

Compilation of References

Abramson, G. (2000). Long transients and cluster size in globally coupled maps. *Europhysics Letters*, *52*(6), 615–619.

Adami, C. (2000). Physical complexity of symbolic sequences. *Physica D. Nonlinear Phenomena*, *137*, 62–69.

Adler, R. L., Konheim, A. G., & McAndrew, M. H. (1965). Topological entropy. *Transactions of the American Mathematical Society*, *114*, 309–319.

Agrafiotis, D. K. (1997a). On the use of information theory for assessing molecular diversity. *Journal of Chemical Information and Computer Sciences*, *37*, 576–580.

Agrafiotis, D. K. (1997b). Stochastic algorithms for maximizing molecular diversity. *Journal of Chemical Information and Computer Sciences*, *37*, 841–851.

Agrafiotis, D. K. (1998). Molecular diversity. In *Encyclopedia of computational chemistry*. New York, NY: Wiley.

Aiello, L. C., & Wheeler, P. (1995). The expensive-tissue hypothesis. *Current Anthropology*, *36*, 199–221.

Albert, R., Jeong, H., & Barabasi, A. L. (2000). Error and attack tolerance of complex networks. *Nature*, *406*, 378–382.

Alfinito, E., Viglione, R., & Vitiello, G. (2001). *The decoherence criterion*. Retrieved from http://arxiv.org/PS_cache/quant-ph/pdf/0007/0007020v2.pdf

Ambrose, S. H. (2001). Paleolithic technology and human evolution. *Science*, *291*, 1748.

Ambrosetti, W., Barbanti, L., & Carrara, E. A. (2007). Riscaldamento delle acque profonde nei laghi italiani: Un indicatore di cambiamenti climatici. *Clima e Cambiamenti climatici le attività del CNR* (pp. 601-608).

Ambrosetti, W., Barbanti, L., & Sala, N. (2003). *Residence time and physical processes in lake*. International Conference on Residence Time in Lakes: Science, Management, Education. September 29th - October 3rd Bolsena Viterbo.

Ambrosetti, W., & Barbanti, L. (1999). Deep water warming in lakes; an indicator of climatic change. *Journal of Limnology*, *58*(1), 1–9.

Ambrosetti, W., & Barbanti, L. (2002). Phisycal limnology of Italian lakes. 2. Relationship between morphometric parameters, stability and Birgean work. *Journal of Limnology*, *61*(2), 159–1167.

Ambrosetti, W., Barbanti, L., & Carrara, E. A. (2010). Mechanism of hypolimnion erosion in a deep lake (Lago Maggiore, N.Italy). *Journal of Limnology*, *69*(1), 3–14.

American Art Therapy Association. (2008). *About us.* Retrieved from http://www.americanarttherapyassociation.org/aata-aboutus.html

American Psychiatric Association – APA. (1994). *Diagnostic and statistical manual of mental disorders*. Washington, DC: Author.

Amos, L. A., & Amos, W. B. (1991). *Molecules of the cytoskeleton*. London, UK: MacMillan Press.

Amos, L. A., & Schlieper, D. (2005). Microtubules and MAPs. *Advances in Chemistry*, *71*, 257.

Ancoli, S., & Green, K. F. (1977). Authoritarianism, introspection, and alpha wave biofeedback training. *Psychophysiology*, *14*(1), 40–44.

Ancoli, S., & Kamiya, J. (1978). Methodological issues in alpha biofeedback training. *Biofeedback and Self-Regulation*, *3*(2), 159–183.

Anderson, C., & Mandell, A. (1996). Fractal time and the foundations of consciousness: Vertical convergence of 1/f phenomena from ion channels to behavioral states. In Mac Cormac, E., & Stamenov, M. (Eds.), *Fractals of brain, fractals of mind* (pp. 75–126). Amsterdam, The Netherlands: John Benjamin.

Anderson, C., Mandell, A., Selz, K., Terry, L., Robinson, S., & Wong, C. (1998). The development of nuchal atonia associated with active (REM) sleep in fetal sheep: Presence of recurrent fractal organization. *Brain Research, 787*(2), 351–357.

Andreassi, J. L. (2000). *Psychophysiology: Human behaviour and physiological response* (4th ed.). Mahweh, NJ: LEA.

Angelakis, E., Stathopoulou, S., Frymiare, J. L., Green, D. L., Lubar, J. F., & Kounios, J. (2007). EEG neurofeedback: A brief overview and an example of peak alpha frequency training for cognitive enhancement in the elderly. *The Clinical Neuropsychologist, 21*(1), 110–129.

Aoki, K., & Feldman, M. V. (1987). Toward a theory for the evolution of cultural. *Proceedings of the National Academy of Sciences of the United States of America, 84*, 7164–7168.

Arbib, M. A. (2002). The mirror system, imitation, and the evolution of language. In Nehaniv, C., & Dautenhahn, K. (Eds.), *Imitation in animals and artifacts*. The MIT Press.

Arbib, M. A. (2005). From monkey-like action recognition to human language: An evolutionary framework for neurolinguistics. *The Behavioral and Brain Sciences, 28*, 105–167.

Arns, M., de Ridder, S., Strehl, U., Breteler, M., & Coenen, A. (2009). Efficacy of neurofeedback treatment in ADHD: The effects on inattention, impulsivity and hyperactivity: A meta-analysis. *Clinical EEG and Neuroscience, 40*(3), 180–189.

Ascalaph. (n.d.). Retrieved from http://www.agilemolecule.com/Products.html

Asimov, I. (1950). *I, robot*. Boston, MA: Gnome Press.

Badii, R., & Politi, A. (1993). *Complexity: Hierarchical structures and scaling in physics* (p. 280). Cambridge, UK: Cambridge University Press.

Barabasi, A. L., & Albert, R. (1999). Emergence of scaling in random networks. *Science, 286*, 509–512.

Barlow, J. S. (1993). *The electroencephalogram: Its patterns and origins*. Cambridge, MA: MIT Press.

Barni, M., Cappellini, V., & Mecocci, A. (1996). Comments on 'A possibilistic approach to clustering'. *IEEE Transactions on Fuzzy Systems, 4*, 393–396.

Barnsley, M. (1988). *Fractals everywhere*. San Diego, CA: Academic Press.

Barnsley, M. (2010). The life and survival of mathematical ideas. *Notices of the AMS, 57*(21), 10–22.

Barnsley, M. F. (1988). *Fractals everywhere*. Boston, MA: Academic Press.

Barnsley, M. F. (1993). *Fractals everywhere* (2nd ed.). Boston, MA: Academic Press.

Barnsley, M. F., & Demko, S. G. (1985). Iterated function systems and the global construction of fractals. *Proceedings of the Royal Society of London. Series A: Mathematical and Physical Sciences, 399*, 243–275.

Barnsley, M. F., Jacquin, A. E., Malassenet, F., Reuter, L., & Sloane, A. D. (1988). Harnessing chaos for image synthesis. *SIGGRAPH, 1988*, 131–140.

Barnsley, M. F., Saupe, D., & Vrscay, E. R. (Eds.). (2002). *Fractals in multimedia*. Berlin, Germany: Springer.

Basch-Kahre, E. (1985). Patterns of thinking. *The International Journal of Psycho-Analysis, 66*(4), 455–470.

Bates, E., & MacWhinney, B. (1987). Competition, variation and language learning. In MacWhinney, B. (Ed.), *Mechanisms of language acquisition*. Erlbaum.

Bateson, G. (1979). *Mind and nature: A necessary unity*. Toronto, Canada: Bantam.

Batty, M., & Longley, P. (1994). *Fractal cities: A geometry of form and function*. London, UK: Academic Press.

Bazanova, O. M., & Lubomir, A. (2006). Learnability and individual frequency characteristics of EEG alpha activity. *Vestnik Rossiiskoi Akademii Meditsinskikh Nauk, 5*(6), 30–33.

Bazanova, O. M., Verevkin, E. G., & Shtark, M. B. (2007). Biofeedback in optimising psychomotor reactivity: II. The dynamics of segmental alpha-activity characteristics. *Human Physiology, 33*(6), 695–700.

Beatty, J. (1971). Effects of initial alpha wave abundance and operant training procedures on occipital alpha and beta wave activity. *Psychosomatic Science, 23*(3), 197–199.

Beatty, J., Greenberg, A., Diebler, W. P., & O'Hanlon, J. F. (1974). Operant control of occipital theta rhythm affects performance in a radar monitoring task. *Science, 183*(4127), 871–873.

Berkovic, S. F., Mulley, J. C., Scheffer, I. E., & Petrou, S. (2006). Human epilepsies: Interaction of genetic and acquired factors. *Trends in Neurosciences, 29*, 391–397.

Berliant, M. (2005). *Central place theory.* Urban/Regional 0505001, EconWPA, 2005.

Bezdek, J. C. (1981). *Pattern recognition with fuzzy objective function algorithms.* New York, NY: Plenum Press.

Binder, L. I., & Rosenbaum, J. L. (1978). The in vitro assembly of flagellar outer doublet tubulin. *The Journal of Cell Biology, 79*, 500–515.

Birbaumer, N. (1999). Slow cortical potentials: Plasticity, operant control, and behavioural effects. *The Neuroscientist, 5*(2), 74–78.

Birkhoff, G. (1967). *Lattice theory.* Providence, RI: American Mathematical Society.

Birkhoff, G. D. (1931). A mathematical approach to aesthetics. *Scientia*, 133–146.

Bobe, S., & Schaefer, G. (2006). Image processing and image registration on spiral architecture with saLib. *International Journal of Simulation Systems, Science & Technology, Special Issue on. Vision & Visualisation, 7*(3), 37–43.

Bodmer, W. F., & Cavalli-Sforza, L. L. (1976). *Genetics, evolution and man.* Freeman.

Bogomolny, A. (1998). *The collage theorem.* Retrieved September 15, 2005, from: http://www.cut-the-knot.org/ctk/ifs.shtml

Bohm, D., & Peat, F. D. (1987). *Science, order, and creativity.* New York, NY: Bantam.

Bollobas, B. (2001). *Random graphs.* Cambridge, UK: Cambridge University Press.

Bollobas, B., & Rasmussen, S. (1989). First cycles in random directed graph processes. *Discrete Mathematics, 75*(1-3), 55–68.

Bork, P., Jensen, L. J., Von Mering, C., Ramani, A. K., Lee, I., & Marcotte, E. M. (2004). Protein interaction networks from yeast to human. *Current Opinion in Structural Biology, 7*, 292–299.

Bourbaki, N. (1952). *Éléments de mathématique.* Paris, France: Actualités Scientifiques et Industrielles.

Bourke, P. (2007). *Representing and modelling geometry in Second Life.* Retrieved December 11, 2008, from http://local.wasp.uwa.edu.au/~pbourke/fractals/secondlife/

Bourke, P. (2008). Evaluating Second Life as a tool for collaborative scientific visualisation.

Boyd, R., & Richerson, P. J. (1985). *Culture and the evolutionary process.* University of Chicago Press.

Branigan, H. P., Pickering, M. J., & Cleland, A. A. (2000). Syntactic co-ordination in dialogue. *Cognition, 75*, B13–B25.

Breuer, J., & Freud, S. (1976). Studies on hysteria. In J. Strachey (Ed. & Trans.), *The standard edition of the complete psychological works of Sigmund Freud* (Vol. 2). London: Hogarth Press. (Original work published 1893-1895).

Brolund, J. W., & Schallow, J. R. (1976). The effects of reward on occipital alpha facilitation by biofeedback. *Psychophysiology, 13*(3), 236–241.

Bucci, W. (1997). *Psychoanalysis and cognitive science.* New York, NY: Guilford Press.

Budd, M. (1998). Aesthetics. In E. Craig (Ed.), *Routledge encyclopedia of philosophy.* London, UK: Routledge. Retrieved from http://www.rep.routledge.com/article/M046

Burkle-Elizondo, G., Valdez-Cepeda, R. D., & Sala, N. (2007). Complexity in the mesoamerican artistic and architectural works. In Sala, N. (Ed.), *Chaos and complexity in the arts and architecture* (pp. 119–128). New York, NY: Nova Science Publishers, Inc.

Burton, P. R., & Himes, R. H. (1978). Electron microscope studies of pH effects on assembly of tubulin free of associated proteins. *The Journal of Cell Biology, 77*(1), 120–133.

Campbell, P. J. (1974). Biological reference materials in microampoules. *Journal of Biological Standardization, 2*, 269–270.

Capra, F. (1975). *The Tao of physics*. Boulder, CO: Shambhala.

Carbonara, D. (Ed.). (2005). *Technology literacy applications in learning environments*. Hershey, PA: Idea Group.

Carlson-Sabelli, L. (2005). Co-creation practice: Education, nursing and psychodrama. In H. Sabelli (Ed.), *Bios: A study of creation* (609-618). Singapore: World Scientific.

Carlson-Sabelli, L., Sabelli, H., Zbilut, J., Patel, M., Messer, J., & Walthall, K. … Zdanovics, O. (1994). How the heart informs about the brain. A process analysis of the electrocardiogram. In R. Trappl, (Ed.), *Cybernetics and Systems '94*. Singapore: World Scientific.

Carlson-Sabelli, L., & Sabelli, H. (1992 a). Phase plane of opposites: A method to study change in complex processes, and its application to sociodynamics and psychotherapy. *The Social Dynamicist, 3*, 1–6.

Carlson-Sabelli, L., Sabelli, H., Patel, M., & Holm, K. (1992 b). The union of opposites in sociometry: An empirical application of process theory. *The Journal of Group Psychotherapy, Psychodrama and Sociometry, 44*, 147–171.

Carroll, S. B. (2001). Chance and necessity: the evolution of morphological complexity and diversity. *Nature, 409*, 1102–1109.

Castellano, L., & Dinelli, G. (1975). *Experimental and analytical evaluation of thermal alteration in the Mediterranean*. International Conference on Mathematical Models far Environinental Problems.

Castellano, G., & Torrens, F. (2009). Local anaesthetics classified using chemical structural indicators. *Nereis, 2*, 7–17.

Castellano, L., Ambrosetti, W., Barbanti, L., & Rolla, A. (2010). The residence time of the water in Lago Maggiore (N. Italy), first result from an Eulerian-Lagrangian approach. *Journal of Limnology, 69*(1), 15–28.

Castellano, L., Ambrosetti, W., & Sala, N. (2008). About the use of computational fluid dynamic (CFD) in the framework of physical limnological studies on a Great Lake. In *Reflexing interfaces* (pp. 257–277). Hershey, PA: Information Science Reference.

Casti, J. (1992). The simply complex: Trendy buzzword or emerging new science? *Bulletin of the Santa Fe Institute, 7*, 10–13.

Chabot, R. J., di Michele, F., Prichep, L., & John, E. R. (2001). The clinical role of computerized EEG in the evaluation and treatment of learning and attention disorders in children and adolescents. *The Journal of Neuropsychiatry and Clinical Neurosciences, 13*(2), 171–186.

Chaisson, E. J. (2001). *Cosmic evolution*. Cambridge, MA: Harvard University Press.

Chaitin, G. J. (1966). On the length of programs for computing finite binary sequences. *Journal of the ACM, 13*, 547–569.

Chakraborty, D., Ashir, A., Suganuma, G., Mansfield, K., Roy, T., & Shiratori, N. (2004). Self-similar and fractal nature of Internet traffic. *International Journal of Network Management, 14*(2), 119–129.

Chan, P. A., & Rabinowitz, T. (2006). A cross-sectional analysis of video games and attention deficit hyperactivity disorder symptoms in adolescents. *Annals of General Psychiatry, 5*, 16.

Cheng, R. T., & Tung, C. (1970). Wind-driven lake circulation by finite clement method. *Proceedings of the 13'x'Conference on Great Lakes Research*, (pp. 891-903).

Cho, M. K., Jang, H. S., Jeong, S., Jang, I., Choi, B., & Lee, M. T. (2008). Alpha neurofeedback improves the maintaining ability of alpha activity. *Neuroreport, 19*(3), 315–317.

Chomsky, N. (1975). *Reflections on language*. New York, NY: Pantheon.

Chrétien, D. (2000). Microtubules switch occasionally into unfavorable configuration during elongation. *Journal of Molecular Biology, 298*, 663–676.

Chrétien, D., Metoz, F., Verde, F., Karsenti, E., & Wade, R. H. (1992). Lattice defects in microtubules: Protofilament numbers vary within individual microtubules. *The Journal of Cell Biology, 117*(5), 1031–1040.

Chrétien, D., & Wade, R. H. (1991). New data on the microtubule surface lattice. *Biology of the Cell, 71*(1-2), 161–174.

Christaller, W. (1933). *Die zentralen Orte in Süddeutschland*. Jena, Germany: Gustav Fischer.

Clarke, A. R., Barry, R. J., McCarthy, R., & Selikowitz, M. (1998). EEG analysis in attention-deficit/hyperactivity disorder: A comparative study of two subtypes. *Psychiatry Research, 81*(1), 19–29.

Clarke, A. R., Barry, R. J., McCarthy, R., Selikowitz, M., & Brown, C. R. (2002). EEG evidence for a new conceptualisation of attention deficit hyperactivity disorder. *Clinical Neurophysiology, 113*(7), 1036–1044.

Clayton, S., & Brook, A. (2005). Can psychology help save the world? A model for conservation psychology. *Analyses of Social Issues and Public Policy (ASAP), 5*, 1–15.

Cohen, I., Navarro, V., Clemenceau, S., Baulac, M., & Miles, R. (2002). On the origin of interictal activity in human temporal lobe epilepsy *in vitro. Science, 298*, 1418–1421.

Cohen, J., & Stewart, I. (1995). *The collapse of chaos*. New York, NY: Penguin.

Computer Games and Allied Technology. Singapore, April 28-30, 2008. Retrieved December 14, 2008, from http://local.wasp.uwa.edu.au/~pbourke/papers/cgat08/paper.pdf

Corbin, H. (1979). *Spiritual body and celestial earth: From Mazdean Iran to Shi'ite Iran*. Princeton, NJ: Princeton University Press.

Cram, J. R., Kohlenberg, R. J., & Singer, M. (1977). Operant control of alpha EEG and the effects of illumination and eye closure. *Psychosomatic Medicine, 39*(1), 11–18.

Crovella, M. E., & Bestavros, A. (1996). Self-similarity in World Wide Web Traffic: Evidence and possible causes. *Proceedings of ACM SIGMETRICS'96*.

Crovella, M. E., & Bestavros, A. (1995). *Explaining World Wide Web traffic self-similarity. Technical Report: TR-95-015*. Computer Science Department, Boston University.

Crucitti, P., Latora, V., Marchiori, M., & Rapisarda, A. (2004). Error and attack tolerance of complex networks. *Physica A, 340*, 388–394.

Dailey, J. E., & Harleman, D. R. F. (1972). *Numerical model far the prediction of transient water quality in estuary networks* (Rep. No. MITSG 72-15). Cambridge, MA: MIT, Department of Civil Engineering.

Dale, R., & Spivey, M. J. (2006). Unravelling the dyad: Using recurrence analysis to explore patterns of syntactic coordination between children and caregivers in conversation. *Language Learning, 56*, 391–430.

Damasio, A. R. (1999). How the brain creates the mind. *Scientific American, 281*, 112–117.

Davidson, R. J. (1988). EEG measures of cerebral asymmetry: Conceptual and methodological issues. *The International Journal of Neuroscience, 39*(3), 71–89.

Dawkins, R. (1982). *The extended phenotype*. Freeman.

De Jong, H. (2002). Modeling and simulation of genetic regulatory systems: A literature review. *Journal of Computational Biology, 9*, 67–103.

Del Giudice, E., Doglia, M., & Milani, M. (1982). Self-focusing of Fröhlich waves and cytoskeleton dynamics. *Physical Review Letters, 90A*, 104–106.

Del Giudice, E., Doglia, S., Milani, M., & Vitiello, G. (1983). Spontaneous symmetry breakdown and boson condensation in biology. *Physical Review Letters, 95A*, 508–510.

Dempster, T., & Vernon, D. (2009). Identifying indices of learning for alpha neurofeedback training. *Applied Psychophysiology and Biofeedback, 34*, 309–318.

Denbigh, K. G., & Denbigh, J. (1987). *Entropy in relation to incomplete knowledge*. Cambridge, UK: Cambridge University Press.

Dennett, D. C. (1978). *Brainstorms*. Cambridge, MA: MIT Press/Bradford Books.

Dennett, D. C. (1991). *Consciousness explained*. Boston, MA: Little, Brown and Co.

Dewar, M. J. S., & Sabelli, N. L. (1962). The split p-orbital (SPO) method. *Physical Chemistry, 66*, 2300–2316.

Dietzgen, J. (1906). *The positive outcome of philosophy* (Unterman, E., Trans.). Chicago, IL: Charles H. Kerr & Company.

Dietzgen, J. (2010). *The nature of human brain work: An introduction to dialectics.* Oakland, CA: PM Press.

Dinelli, G., & Tozzi, A. (1977). Three-dimensional modelling of the dispersion of pollutants in Mediterranean coastal waters. *XVII International Congress of IAHR,* August 1977, Baden Baden (Germany), (pp. 52-61).

Domb, C., & Green, M. S. (1976). *Phase transition and critical phenomena.* London, UK: Academic Press.

Donald, M. (1997). Origins of the modern mind: Three stages in the evolution of culture and cognition. *The Behavioral and Brain Sciences, 16*(4), 737–791.

Donchin, E., & Coles, M. G. H. (1988). Is the P300 component a manifestation of context updating. *The Behavioral and Brain Sciences, 11*, 406–425.

Dunn-Snow, P., & Joy-Smelie, S. (2011). Teaching art therapy techniques: Mask-making, a case in point. *Art Therapy, 17*(2), 125–131. doi:doi:10.1080/07421656.2000.10129512

Duprat, B., & Paulin, M. (1995). *Les systèmes de la façade et de la baie: Maisons à loyer urbaines du XIXe siecle.* Laboratoire d'Analyse des Formes, bureau de la recherche architecturale.

Dyson, F. (1982). A model for the origin of life. *Journal of Molecular Evolution, 18*, 344–350.

Dyson, F. (1985/1999). *Origins of life.* Cambridge, UK: Cambridge University Press.

Ebert, D. S., Musgrave, F. K., Peachy, D., Perlin, K., & Worley, S. (2003). *Texturing and modeling: A procedural approach* (3rd ed.). US: Morgan Kaufmann Publishers Inc.

Eckmann, J.-P., Kamphorst, S. O., & Ruelle, D. (1987). Recurrence plots of dynamical systems. *Europhysics Letters, 5*, 973–977.

Eco, U. (2004). *Storia della Belleza.* Bompiani, Italy: RCS Libri S.p.A.

Edelman, G. M. (1992). *Bright air, brilliant fire. On the matter of the mind.* London, UK: Penguin Group.

Edmonds, B. (1999). *Syntactic measures of complexity.* Unpublished doctoral dissertation, University of Manchester, Manchester.

Eglash, R., & Broadwell, P. (1989). Fractal geometry in traditional African architecture. *Dynamics Newsletter,* June.

Eglash, R. (1999). *African fractals: Modern computing and indigenous design.* New Brunswick, NJ: Rutgers University Press.

Egner, T., & Gruzelier, J. (2003). Ecological validity of neurofeedback: Modulation of slow wave EEG enhances musical performance. *Neuroreport, 14*(9), 1221–1224.

Egner, T., & Gruzelier, J. H. (2001). Learned self-regulation of EEG frequency components affects attention and event-related brain potentials in humans. *Neuroreport, 12*(18), 4155–4159.

Egner, T., Strawson, E., & Gruzelier, J. H. (2002). EEG signature and phenomenology of alpha/theta neurofeedback training versus mock feedback. *Applied Psychophysiology and Biofeedback, 27*(4), 261–270.

Egner, T., Zech, T. F., & Gruzelier, J. (2004). The effects of neurofeedback training on the spectral topography of the healthy electroencephalogram. *Clinical Neurophysiology, 115*, 2452–2460.

Ellis, G. F. R. (2004). *Science in faith and hope: An interaction.* Philadelphia, PA: Quaker Books.

Ellis, G. F. R. (2005). Physics, complexity and causality. *Nature, 435*, 743.

Emmeche, C. (1996). *The garden in the machine: The emerging science of artificial life.* Princeton, NJ: Princeton University Press.

Emmer, M. (Ed.). (1993). *The visual mind: Art and mathematics.* The MIT Presss.

Engel, A. K., & Singer, W. (2001). Temporal binding and the neural correlates of sensory awareness. *Trends in Cognitive Sciences, 5*(1), 16–25.

Erdelyi, M. H. (1985). *Psychoanalysis: Freud's cognitive psychology.* New York, NY: W. H. Freeman & Company.

Erdos, P., & Renyi, A. (1960). On the evolution of random graphs. *Publications of the Mathematical Institute of The Hungarian Academy of Sciences, 2*, 17–61.

Erramilli, A., Gosby, D., & Willinger, W. (1993). Engineering for realistic traffic: A fractal analysis of burstiness. *Proceedings of ITC Special Congress*, Bangalore, India, 1993.

Erramilli, A., Pruthi, P., & Willinger, W. (1994). *Modelling packet traffic with chaotic maps. ISRN KTH/IT/R-94/18-SE*. Sweden: Stockholm-Kista.

Erramilli, A., & Singh, R. P. (1992). *An application of deterministic chaotic maps to model packet traffic*. Bellcore Technical Memorandum.

Faber, J., Portugal, R., & Rosa, L. P. (2006). Information processing in brain microtubules. *Bio Systems, 83*(1), 1–9.

Facchini, A., & Kantz, H. (2007). Curved structures in recurrence plots: The role of the sampling time. *Physical Review E: Statistical, Nonlinear, and Soft Matter Physics, 75*, 36215.

Facchini, A., Kantz, H., & Tiezzi, E. (2005). Recurrence plot analysis of nonstationary data: The understanding of curved patterns. *Physical Review E: Statistical, Nonlinear, and Soft Matter Physics, 72*, 21915.

Facchini, A., Mocenni, C., & Vicino, A. (2009a). Generalized recurrence plots for the analysis of images from spatially distributed systems. *Physica D. Nonlinear Phenomena, 238*, 162–169.

Facchini, A., Rossi, F., & Mocenni, C. (2009b). Spatial recurrence strategies reveal different routes to Turing pattern formation in chemical systems. *Physics Letters. [Part A], 373*, 4266–4272.

Falconer, K. (1990). *Fractal geometry: Mathematical foundations and applications*. John Wiley.

Farlow, S. J. (Ed.). (1984). *Self-organizing methods in modeling. GMDH type algorithms*. New York, NY: Marcel Dekker.

Farmelo, G. (Ed.). (2003). *It must be beautiful*. London, UK: Granta Books.

Feldman, M. W., & Laland, K. N. (1996). Gene-culture coevolutionary theory. *Trends in Ecology & Evolution, 11*, 453–457.

Felli, N., Cianetti, L., Pelosi, E., Carè, A., Gong, C., & Liu, G. A. (2010). Hematopoietic differentiation: A coordinated dynamical process towards attractor stable states. *BMC Systems Biology, 4*, 85.

Fell, J., Elfadil, H., Klaver, P., Roschke, J., Elger, C. E., & Fernandez, G. (2002). Covariation of spectral and nonlinear EEG measures with alpha biofeedback. *The International Journal of Neuroscience, 112*, 1047–1057.

Feynman, R. P. (1996). *Feynman lectures on computation* (Hey, A. J. G., & Allen, R. W., Eds.). Reading, MA: Addison-Wesley.

Feynman, R. P. (1998). *Statistical mechanics: A set of lectures*. Boulder, CO: Westview Press.

Fiedler, K. (1876). *Über die Beurteilung von Werken der Bildenden Künst*. Leipzig.

Fisher, Y. (1995). *Fractal image compression: Theory and application*. New York, NY: Springer-Verlag.

Fisher, Y. (Ed.). (1995). *Fractal image compression: Theory and application*. New York, NY: Springer Verlag.

Floreano, D., Nicoud, J.-D., & Mondada, F. (Eds.). (1999). *Advances in artificial life: 5th European Conference, ECAL 99, Lecture Notes in Computer Science No. 1674*. Berlin, Germany: Springer.

Fodor, J. A. (1983). *The modularity of mind*. Cambridge, MA: MIT Press.

Foerster von, H. (1953). Cybernetics: Circular causal and feedback mechanisms in biological and social systems. *Southern Medical Journal, 46*, 726–737.

Foley, J. D., van Dam, A., Feiner, S. K., & Hughes, J. F. (1997). *Computer graphics: Principles and practice* (2nd ed.). New York, NY: Addison Wesley.

Fonagy, P., & Target, M. (1997). Attachment and reflective function: Their role in self-organization. *Development and Psychopathology, 9*, 679–700.

Fournier, A., Fussel, D., & Carpenter, L. (1982). Computer rendering of stochastic models. *Communications of the ACM, 25*, 371–384.

Fowler, H., & Leland, W. (1994). Local area network traffic characteristics, with implications for broadband network congestion management. *IEEE Journal on Selected Areas in Communications, 9*(7), 1139–1149.

Fractal geometry. (2007). In *Encyclopædia Britannica*. Retrieved February 26, 2007, from http://concise.britannica.com/ebc/article-9364797/fractal-geometry

Freeman, L. C. (2004). *The development of social networks analysis: A study in the sociology of science*. Vancouver, Canada: Booksurge Publishing.

Freeman, W. J. (1975). *Mass action in the nervous system*. New York, NY: Academic Press.

Freeman, W. J., & Vitiello, G. (2006). Nonlinear brain dynamics as macroscopic manifestation of underlying many-body field dynamics. *Physics of Life Reviews*, *3*(2), 93–118.

Freud, S. (1920). *Beyond the pleasure principle. Standard Edition, 18*, 1-64. London, UK: Hogarth Press.

Freud, S. (1891). *(n.d.-a). On aphasia: A critical study*. New York, NY: International University Press.

Freud, S. (1930). *Civilization and its discontents (Das Unbehagen in der Kultur)*. London, UK: Penguin.

Freud, S. (n.d.-b). Project for a scientific psychology. In Strachey, J. (Trans. Ed.) *The standard edition of the complete psychological works of Sigmund Freud (Vol. 1*, pp. 295–391). London, UK: Hogarth Press. (Original work published 1895)

Freud, S. (n.d.-c). Screen memories. In Strachey, J. (Trans. Ed.) *The standard edition of the complete psychological works of Sigmund Freud (Vol. 3*, pp. 301–322). London, UK: Hogarth Press. (Original work published 1899)

Freud, S. (n.d.-c). The aetiology of hysteria. In Strachey, J. (Trans. Ed.) *The standard edition of the complete psychological works of Sigmund Freud (Vol. 3*, pp. 187–221). London, UK: Hogarth Press. (Original work published 1896)

Freud, S. (n.d.-d). Psychopathology of everyday life. In Strachey, J. (Trans. Ed.) *The standard edition of the complete psychological works of Sigmund Freud (Vol. 6)*. London, UK: Hogarth Press. (Original work published 1901)

Freud, S. (n.d.-e). Totem and taboo. In Strachey, J. (Trans. Ed.) *The standard edition of the complete psychological works of Sigmund Freud (Vol. 3*, pp. 187–221). London, UK: Hogarth Press. (Original work published 1913)

Freud, S. (n.d.-f). From the history of an infantile neurosis. In Strachey, J. (Trans. Ed.) *The standard edition of the complete psychological works of Sigmund Freud (Vol. 17*, pp. 1–124). London, UK: Hogarth Press. (Original work published 1918)

Freud, S. (n.d.-g). The 'uncanny. In Strachey, J. (Trans. Ed.) *The standard edition of the complete psychological works of Sigmund Freud (Vol. 17*, pp. 217–256). London, UK: Hogarth Press. (Original work published 1910)

Freud, S. (n.d.-h). Remarks on the theory and practice of dream-interpretation. In Strachey, J. (Trans. Ed.) *The standard edition of the complete psychological works of Sigmund Freud (Vol. 19*, pp. 107–122). London, UK: Hogarth Press. (Original work published 1923)

Freud, S. (n.d.-i). Civilization and its discontents. In Strachey, J. (Trans. Ed.) *The standard edition of the complete psychological works of Sigmund Freud (Vol. 21*, pp. 57–146). London, UK: Hogarth Press. (Original work published 1930)

Friel, P. N. (2007). EEG biofeedback in the treatment of attention deficit/hyperactivity disorder. *Alternative Medicine Review*, *12*(2), 146–151.

Fuchs, T., Birbaumer, N., Lutzenberger, W., Gruzelier, J. H., & Kaiser, J. (2003). Neurofeedback treatment for attention-deficit/hyperactivity disorder in children: A comparison with methylphenidate. *Applied Psychophysiology and Biofeedback*, *28*(1), 1–12.

Fukushige, T., Siddiqui, Z. K., Chou, M., Culotti, J. G., Gogonea, C. B., Siddiqui, S. S., & Hamelin, M. (1999). MEC-12, an α-tubulin required for touch sensitivity in C. elegans. *Journal of Cell Science*, *112*, 395–403.

Fulton, A. (1999). Fractal amplifications: Writing in three dimensions. *The Kenyon Review New Series*, *21*(2), 124–139.

Funtowicz, S., & Ravetz, J. (1994). Emergent complex systems. *Futures*, *26*, 568–582.

Gabora, L. (2000). Conceptual closure: Weaving memories into an interconnected worldview. In G. Van de Vijver & J. Chandler (Eds.), *Closure: Emergent organizations and their dynamics: Annals of the New York Academy of Sciences, 901*, 42-53.

Gabora, L. (2010b). Recognizability of creative style within and across domains: Preliminary studies. *Proceedings of the Annual Meeting of the Cognitive Science Society* (pp. 2350-2355). August 11-14, 2010, Portland, Oregon.

Gabora, L. (under revision). *The honing theory of creativity*, in press.

Gabora, L., O'Connor, B., & Ranjan, A. (in press). *The recognizability of individuals styles within and across domains*. Submitted.

Gabora, L. (2006). Self-other organization: Why early life did not evolve through natural selection. *Journal of Theoretical Biology, 241*(3), 443–450.

Gabora, L. (2008). The cultural evolution of socially situated cognition. *Cognitive Systems Research, 9*(1-2), 104–113.

Gabora, L. (2010a). Revenge of the 'neurds': Characterizing creative thought in terms of the structure and dynamics of human memory. *Creativity Research Journal, 22*(1), 1–13.

Gabora, L. (2011). Five clarifications about cultural evolution. *Journal of Cognition and Culture, 11*, 61–83.

Gabora, L., & Aerts, D. (2009). A model of the emergence and evolution of integrated worldviews. *Journal of Mathematical Psychology, 53*, 434–451.

Gaddini, E. (1989). Fenomeni PSI e processo creativo. In *Scritti*. Milan, Italy: Cortina. (Original work published 1969)

Gaddini, E. (1992). On imitation. In Limentani (Ed.), *A psychoanalytic theory of infantile experience*. London, UK: Routledge. (Original work published 1969)

Gaddini, E. (1969). On imitation. *The International Journal of Psycho-Analysis, 50*, 475–484.

Galanter, P. (2002). *Complexity theory as a context for art theory.* In Generative Art 2002. Retrieved May 20, 2009, from http://www.vieux-lyon.org/vues-3d_f07700.htm

Galatzer-Levy, R. (1988). On working through: a model from artificial intelligence. *Journal of the American Psychoanalytic Association, 38*(1), 125–151.

Gal-Or, B. (1972). The crisis about the origin irreversibility and time anisotro. *Science, 176*, 11–17.

Gao, J., & Cai, H. (2000). On the structures and quantification of recurrence plots. *Physics Letters. [Part A], 270*, 75–87.

Gardner, M. (1992). *Fractal music, hypercards, and more.* New York, NY: W.H. Freeman.

Gardner, T. S., & Faith, J. J. (2005). Reverse-engineering transcriptional control networks. *Physics of Life Reviews, 2*, 65–88.

Gatlin, L. (1972). *Information theory and the living system.* New York, NY: Columbia University Press.

Gauthier, Y. (1984). Hegel's logic from a logical point of view. In Cohen, R. S., & Wartofsky, M. W. (Eds.), *Hegel and the sciences* (pp. 303–310). New York, NY: D. Reidel Publishing.

Gazzaniga, M. S. (2005). *The ethical brain.* USA: The Dana Press.

Gell-Mann, M. (1994). *The quark and the jaguar: Adventures in the simple and the complex.* San Francisco, CA: Freeman.

Georgescu-Roegen, N. (1971). *Entropy: A new worldview.* New York, NY: Bantam Books.

Gerdes, P., & Arrancar, O. (1983). *Karl Marx: Arrancar o véu misterioso à matemática.* Maputo, Mozambique: Universidade Eduardo Mondlane.

Gibson, J. J. (1979). *The ecological approach to visual perception.* New Jersey, USA: Lawrence Erlbaum Associates.

Gifford, R. (in press). *The dragons of inaction: Psychological barriers that limit climate change mitigation and adaptation.*

Gifford, R. (2006). *Environmental psychology: Principles and practice.* Optimal Books.

Giordano, S., Pierazzini, G., & Russo, F. (1995). *Multimedia experiments at the University of Pisa: From videoconference to random fractals.* Retrieved October 10, 2006, from http://www.isoc.org/HMP/PAPER/109/html/paper.html

Glanville, R. (1998). A (Cybernetic) musing: The gestation of second order cybernetics, 1968-1975 – A personal account. *Cybernetics & Human Knowing, 5*(2), 85–95.

Gleiser, P. M., & Zanette, D. H. (2006). Synchronization and structure in an adaptive oscillator network. *Europhysics Journal B, 53*, 233–238.

Greenberg, J. R., & Mitchell, S. A. (1983). *Object relations in psychoanalytic theory*. Cambridge, MA: Harvard University Press.

Greenberg, L. (1987). An objective measure of methylphenidate response: Clinical use of the MCA. *Psychopharmacology Bulletin, 23*(2), 279–282.

Green, C. S., & Bavelier, D. (2003). Action video game modifies visual selective attention. *Nature, 423*.

Griffiths, M. (2000). Does internet and computer "addiction" exist? Some case study evidence. *Cyberpsychology & Behavior, 3*(2), 211–218.

Grim, P., Mar, G., & St. Denis, P. (1998). *The philosophical computer: Exploratory essays in philosophical computer modeling*. Cambridge, MA: The MIT Press.

Gruzelier, J. (2009). A theory of alpha/theta neurofeedback, creative performance enhancement, long distance functional connectivity and psychological integration. *Cognitive Processing, 10*(1), 101–109.

Guastello, S., & Bond, R. W. (2007). A swallowtail catastrophe model for the emergence of leadership in coordination-intensive groups. *Nonlinear Dynamics Psychology and Life Sciences, 11*, 235–251.

Guérin, E., & Tosan, E. (2005). Fractal inverse problem: Approximation formulation and differential methods. In Lévy-Véhel, J., & Lutton, E. (Eds.), *Fractal in engineering: New trends in theory and applications* (pp. 271–285). London, UK: Springer.

Guérin, E., Tosan, E., & Baskurt, A. (2002). Modeling and approximation of fractal surfaces with projected IFS Attractors. In Novak, M. M. (Ed.), *Emergent nature: Patterns, growth and scaling in the science* (pp. 293–303). New Jersey: World Scientific.

Hagan, S., Hameroff, S. R., & Tuszynski, J. A. (2002). Quantum computation in brain microtubules: Decoherence and biological feasibility. *Physical Review E: Statistical, Nonlinear, and Soft Matter Physics, 65*, 061901–061911.

Hameroff, S. R. (2007a). The brain is both neurocomputer and quantum computer. *Cognitive Science, 31*, 1035–1045.

Hameroff, S. R. (2007b). Orchestrated reduction of quantum coherence in brain microtubules. *NeuroQuantology, 5*(1), 1–8.

Hameroff, S. R., & Penrose, R. (1996a). Orchestrated reduction of quantum coherence in brain microtubules: A model for consciousness. *Mathematics and Computers in Simulation, 40*, 453–480.

Hameroff, S. R., & Penrose, R. (1996b). Conscious events as orchestrated space-time selection. *Journal of Consciousness Studies, 3*, 36–53.

Hanan, J. S. (1988). *PLANTWORKS: A software system for realistic plant modelling*. Master's thesis, University of Regina.

Hanan, J. S. (1992). *Parametric L-systems and their application to the modelling and visualization of plants*. PhD thesis, University of Regina.

Hanslmayr, S., Sauseng, P., Doppelmayr, M., Schabus, M., & Klimesch, W. (2005). Increasing individual upper alpha power by neurofeedback improves cognitive performance in human subjects. *Applied Psychophysiology and Biofeedback, 30*(1), 1–10.

Hardt, J. V., & Gale, R. (1993). Creativity increases in scientists through alpha EEG feedback training. *Proceedings of the Association for Applied Psychophysiology and Biofeedback*, 24th Annual Meeting, Los Angeles, CA, March 25-30.

Hardt, J. V., & Kamiya, J. (1976). Conflicting results in EEG alpha feedback studies: Why amplitude integration should replace percent time. *Biofeedback and Self-Regulation, 1*, 63–75.

He, X., Hintz, T., Wu, Q., Wang, H., & Jia, W. (2006b). A new simulation of spiral architecture. *Proceedings of 2006 International Conference on Image Processing, Computer Vision, & Pattern Recognition (IPCV'06)* (pp. 570-575). Las Vegas, USA, Jacquin, A. E. (1992). Image coding based on a fractal theory of iterated contractive image transformations image processing. *IEEE Transactions, 1*(1), 18 – 30.

He, X., Wang, H., Wu, Q., Hintz, T., & Hur, N. (2006a). Fractal image compression on spiral architecture. *International Conference on Computer Graphics, Imaging and Visualisation (CGIV'06)*, (pp. 76-83).

Hempel, C. G. (1945). Studies in the logic of confirmation I. *Mind, 54*, 1–26.

Hennessey, B. A., & Amabile, T. (2010). Creativity. *Annual Review of Psychology, 61*, 569–598. doi:doi:10.1146/annurev.psych.093008.100416

Herr, C. M. (2002). *Generative architectural design and complexity theory.* In Generative Art 2002. Retrieved June 10, 2009, from http://www.mendeley.com/research/generative-architectural-design-complexity-theory/#page-1

Hofstadter, D. (1979). *Gödel, Escher, Bach: An eternal golden braid.* New York, NY: Vintage.

Hofstadter, D. (2007). *I am a strange loop.* New York, NY: Basic Books.

Holland, J. (1999). *Emergence: From chaos to order.* Reading, MA: Perseus.

Holmes, D. S., Burish, T. G., & Frost, R. O. (1980). Effects of instructions and biofeedback on EEG-alpha production and the effect of EEG-alpha biofeedback training for controlling arousal in a subsequent stressful situation. *Journal of Research in Personality, 14*, 212–223.

Hombrich, E. H. (1977). *Art and illusion.* London, UK: Phaidon Press.

Hoyle, F. (1981). Hoyle on evolution. *Nature, 294*, 105.

Hsti, K., & Hsti, A. (1990). Fractal geometry of music. *Proceedings of the National Academy of Sciences of the United States of America, 87*, 938–941.

Huang, X.-R., & Knighton, R. W. (2005). Microtubules contribute to the birefringence of the retinal nerve fiber layer. *Investigative Ophthalmology & Visual Science, 46*(12), 4588–4593.

Husserl, E. (1980). *Collected works.* Boston, MA: The Hague

Hyams, J. S., & Lloyd, C. W. (Eds.). (1994). *Microtubules.* New York, NY: Wiley-Liss.

Iannaccone, P., & Khokha, M. (Eds.). (1996). *Fractal geometry in biological systems.* New York, NY: CRC Press.

Ingber, D. E. (2006). Mechanical control of tissue morphogenesis during embriological development. *The International Journal of Developmental Biology, 50*, 255–266.

Jackson, W. (2004). *Heaven's fractal net: Retrieving lost visions in the humanities.* Bloomington, IN: Indiana University Press.

James, W. (1967). *The writings of William James* (McDermott, J. J., Ed.). New York, NY: Random House.

Janson, H. W. (1969). *History of art.* New York, NY: Harry N. Abrams, Inc.

Janson, H. W., & Janson, D. J. (1977). *The story of painting.* New York, NY: Harry N. Abrams, Inc.

Jasper, H. H. (1958). Report of the committee on methods of clinical examination in electroencephalography. *Electroencephalography and Clinical Neurophysiology, 10*, 370–375.

Jaynes, J. (1995). The diacronicity of consciousness. In G. Trautteur (Ed.), *Consciousness: Distinction and reflection.* Napoli, Italia: Bibliopolis, 1995.

Jaynes, E. T. (1965). Gibbs vs Boltzmann entropies. *American Journal of Physics, 33*, 391–398.

Jaynes, J. (1976). *The origin of consciousness in the breackdown of bicameral mind.* New York, NY: Houghton Mifflin.

Jibu, M., Hagan, S., Hameroff, S. R., Pribram, K. H., & Yasue, K. (1994). Quantum optical coherence in cytoskeletal microtubules: Implications for brain function. *Bio Systems, 32*, 195–209.

Johnson, M. A., & Maggiora, G. M. (Eds.). (1990). *Concepts and applications of molecular similarity.* New York, NY: Wiley-Interscience.

Johnson, R., & Meyer, R. (1974). The locus of control construct in EEG alpha rhythm feedback. *Journal of Consulting and Clinical Psychology, 42*(6), 913.

Joja, A. (1969). *La lógica dialéctica y las ciencias* (Pérez, M. S., Trans.). Buenos Aires, Argentina: Juárez.

Jouon, A., Douillet, P., Ouillon, S., & Fraunié, P. (2006). Calculations of hydrodynamic time parameters in a semi-opened coastal zone using a 3D hydrodynamic model. *Continental Shelf Research, 26*, 1395–1415.

Jung, C. G. (1971). *Four archetypes* (Hull, R. F. C., Trans.). Princeton, NJ: Princeton University Press.

Kaluzny, P., & Tarnecki, P. (1993). Recurrence plots of neuronal spike trains. *Biological Cybernetics, 68*(6), 527–534.

Kamiya, J. (1968). Conscious control of brain waves. *Psychology Today, 1*, 57–60.

Kaneko, K. (1993). *Theory and applications of coupled map lattices*. Chichester, UK: Wiley.

Kaneko, K. (1994). Relevance of clustering to biological networks. *Physica D. Nonlinear Phenomena, 75*(1-3), 55–73.

Kappraff, J. (2007). Complexity and chaos theory in art. In Sala, N. (Ed.), *Chaos and complexity in the arts and architecture* (pp. 3–24). New York, NY: Nova Science Publishers, Inc.

Karkou, V., & Sanderson, P. (2006). *Arts therapies: A research based map of the field*. London, UK: Elsevier Churchill Livingstone.

Kauffman, L. (2001). *Knots and physics*. Singapore: World Scientific.

Kauffman, L. (2001). Virtual logic – Reasoning and playing with imaginary Boolean values. *Cybernetics & Human Knowing, 8*(3), 77–85.

Kauffman, L. (2004). Non-commutative worlds. *New Journal of Physics, 6*, 173–210.

Kauffman, L. H. (2004). Bio-logic. *AMS Contemporary Mathematics Series, 304*, 313–340.

Kauffman, L., & Sabelli, H. (1998). The process equation. *Cybernetics and Systems, 29*, 345–362.

Kauffman, L., & Sabelli, H. (2003). Mathematical bios. *Kybernetes, 31*, 1418–1428.

Kauffman, L., & Sabelli, H. (forthcoming). Riemann's zeta function displays a biotic pattern of diversification, novelty, and complexity. *Cybernetics and Systemics Journal.*

Kauffman, L., & Varela, F. (1980). Form dynamics. *Journal of Social and Biological Structures, 3*, 171–206.

Kauffman, S. (1986). Autocatalytic sets of proteins. *Journal of Theoretical Biology, 119*, 1–24.

Kauffman, S. (1993). *Origins of order*. New York, NY: Oxford University Press.

Kauffman, S. A. (1993). *The origins of order, self organization and selection in evolution*. New York, NY: Oxford University Press.

Kauffman, S. A. (1995). *At home in the universe. The search for laws of self-organization and complexity*. New York, NY: Oxford University Press.

Kauffman, S. A. (2000). *Investigations*. Oxford, UK: Oxford University Press.

Keizer, A. W., Verment, R. S., & Hommel, B. (2010). Enhancing cognitive control through neurofeedback: A role of gamma-band activity in managing episodic retreival. *NeuroImage, 49*(4), 3404–3413.

Keizer, A. W., Vershoor, M., Verment, R. S., & Hommel, B. (2010). The effect of gamma enhancing neurofeedback on the control of feature bindings and intelligence measures. *International Journal of Psychophysiology, 75*(1), 25–32.

Kelso, J. A. S. (1995). *Dynamic patterns: The self-organization of brain and behavior*. Cambridge, MA: MIT Press.

Kernberg, P. F. (2007). *Beyond the reflection: The role of the mirror paradigm in clinical practice*. New York, NY: Other Press.

Klein, M. (1998). Toward a better understanding of fractality in nature. In Pickover, C. A. (Ed.), *Chaos and fractals: A computer graphical journey*. Elsevier Science B.V.

Klimesch, W. (1999). EEG alpha and theta oscillations reflect cognitive and memory performance: A review and analysis. *Brain Research. Brain Research Reviews, 29*(2-3), 169–195.

Klimesch, W., Schimke, H., Ladurner, G., & Pfurtscheller, G. (1990). Alpha frequency and memory performance. *Psychophysiology, 4*, 381–390.

Klimesch, W., Schimke, H., & Pfurtscheller, G. (1993). Alpha frequency, cognitive load and memory performance. *Brain Topography, 5*(3), 241–251.

Klipp, E., Herwig, R., Kowald, A., Wierling, C., & Lehrach, H. (2005). *Systems biology in practice*. Weinheim, Germany: Wiley-VCH.

Klivansky, S. M., Mukherjee, A., & Song, C. (1994). *On long-range dependence in NSFNET traffic. CC Technical Report; GIT-CC-94-61*. Georgia Institute of Technology.

Knill, E. (2010). Quantum computing. *Nature, 463*, 441–443.

Knox, S. S. (1980). Distribution of 'criterion' alpha in the resting EEG: Further argument against the use of an amplitude threshold in alpha biofeedback training. *Biological Psychology, 11*, 1–6.

Kocić, L. (2002). Art elements in fractal constructions. *Visual Mathematics, 4*(1). Retrieved from http://www.mi.sanu.ac.rs/vismath/ljkocic/index.html

Kocić, L. (2003). *Mathematics and esthetics* (in Serbian). Niš, Serbia: Niš Cultural Center.

Kocić, L. M., & Simoncelli, A. C. (2000). Fractal interpolation in creating prefractal images. *Visual Mathematics, 2*(2). Retrieved from http://www.mi.sanu.ac.rs/vismath/kocic1/index.html

Kocić, L., & Stefanovska, L. (2005). Complex dynamics of visual arts. In N. Sala (Ed.), *Chaos and Complexity Letters, 1*(2), 207-235.

Kocić, L. M., & Simoncelli, A. C. (2002). Shape predictable IFS representations. In Novak, M. M. (Ed.), *Emergent nature* (pp. 435–436). World Scientific.

Kocić, L., & Simoncelli, A. C. (1998). Towards free–form fractal modelling. In Daehlen, M., Lyche, T., & Schumaker, L. L. (Eds.), *Mathematical methods for curves and surfaces II* (pp. 287–294). Nashville, TN: Vanderbilt University Press.

Koger, S., & Winter, D. D. (2010). *The psychology of environmental problems: Psychology for sustainability* (3rd ed.). New York, NY: Taylor & Francis.

Kohonen, T. (1990). The self-organizing map. *Proceedings of the IEEE, 78*, 1464–1480.

Kolmogorov, A. N. (1965). Three approaches to the quantitative definition of information. *Problems of Information Transmission, 1*, 1–7.

Konareva, I. N. (2006). Correlations between the psychological peculiarities of an individual and the efficacy of a single neurofeedback session. *Neurophysiology, 38*(3), 201–208.

Kondo, C. Y., Travis, T. A., & Knott, J. R. (1975). The effect of changes in motivation on alpha enhancement. *Psychophysiology, 12*(4), 388–389.

Koppens, F. H. L., Buizert, C., Tielrooij, K. J., Vink, L. T., Nowack, K. C., & Meunier, T. (2006). Driven coherent oscillations of a single electron spin in a quantum dot. *Nature, 442*, 766–771.

Kornhuber, H. H., & Deecke, L. (1965). Hirnpotentialänderungen bei Willkürbewegungen und passiven Bewegungen des Menschen: Bereitschaftspotential und reafferente Potentiale. *Pflügers Arch. ges. Physiol, 284*, 1–17.

Kosok, M. (1984). The dynamics of Hegelian dialectics, and nonlinearity in the sciences. In R. S. Cohen & M. W. Wartofsky (Eds.), *Hegel and the sciences* (311-348). New York, NY: D. Reidel Publishing.

Kotchoubey, B., Schleichert, H., Lutzenberger, W., & Birbaumer, N. (1997). A new method for self-regulation of slow cortical potentials in a timed paradigm. *Applied Psychophysiology and Biofeedback, 22*, 77–93.

Krauhs, E., Little, M., Kempf, T., Hofer-Warbinek, R., Ade, W., & Postingl, H. (1981). Complete amino acid sequence of β-tubulin from porcine brain. *Proceedings of the National Academy of Sciences of the United States of America, 78*, 4156–4160.

Krishnapuram, R., & Keller, J. M. (1993). A possibilistic approach to clustering. *IEEE Transactions on Fuzzy Systems, 1*, 98–110.

Krishnapuram, R., & Keller, J. M. (1996). The possibilistic c-means algorithm: Insights and recommendations. *IEEE Transactions on Fuzzy Systems, 4*, 385–393.

Kroto, H. W., Heath, J. R., O'Brien, S. C., Curl, R. F., & Smalley, R. E. (1985). C_{60}: Buckminsterfullerene. *Nature, 318*, 162–163.

Kubinyi, H. (1993). *QSAR: Hansch analysis and related approaches* (p. 172). Weinheim, Germany: VCH.

Kuhlman, W. N., & Klieger, D. M. (1975). Alpha enhancement: effectiveness of two feedback contingencies relative to a resting baseline. *Psychophysiology, 12*(4), 456–460.

Kuhn, T. S. (1962). *The structure of scientific revolutions*. Chicago, IL: University of Chicago Press.

Kurz, M. (2002). The psychology of environmentally sustainable behavior: Fitting together pieces of the puzzle. *Analyses of Social Issues and Public Policy (ASAP)*, *2*(1), 257–278.

Lacan, J. (1937). The mirror stage. In *Ecrits*. W. W. Norton, new edition (2005)

Ladd, T. D., Jelezko, F., Laflamme, R., Nakamura, Y., Monroe, C., & O'Brian, J. L. (2010). Quantum computers. *Nature*, *464*, 45–53.

Lagarias, A. (2007). Fractal analysis of the urbanization at the outskirts of the city: Models, measurement and explanation. *Cybergeo*. Retrieved from http://cybergeo.revues.org/8902

Lakatos, I. (1976). *Proofs and refutations*. New York, NY: Cambridge University Press.

Laland, K. N., Odling-Smee, J., & Feldman, M. W. (2000). Niche construction, biological evolution, and cultural change. *The Behavioral and Brain Sciences*, *23*, 131–175.

Landauer, R. (1961). Irreversibility and heat generation in the computing process. *IBM Journal of Research and Development*, *3*, 183–191.

Landers, D. M., Petruzzello, S. J., Salazar, W., Crews, D. J., Kubitz, K. A., & Gannon, T. L. (1991). The influence of electrocortical biofeedback on performance in pre-elite archers. *Medicine and Science in Sports and Exercise*, *23*(1), 123–129.

Lang, K. R., & Gingerich, O. (1979). *A source book in astronomy and astrophysics, 1900-1975*. Cambridge, MA: Harvard University Press.

Lanyon, B. P., Weinhold, T. J., Langford, N. K., Barbieri, M., James, D. F. V., Gilchrist, A., & White, A. G. (2007). Experimental demonstration of a compiled version of Shor's algorithm with quantum entanglement. *Physical Review Letters*, *99*, 250505–3.

Lassig, M., Bastolla, U., Manrubia, S. C., & Valleriani, A. (2001). Shape of ecological networks. *Physical Review Letters*, *86*, 4418–4421.

Laval, B., Imberger, J., Hodges, B., & Stocker, R. (2003). Modeling circulation in lakes: Spatial and temporal variations. *Limnology and Oceanography*, *48*(3), 983–994.

Lawvere, F. W. (1996). Unity and identity of opposites in calculus and physics. *Applied Categorical Structures*, *4*, 167–174.

Lawvere, F. W., & Schanuel, S. H. (1982). *Categories in continuum physics: Lectures given at a workshop held at SUNY, Buffalo 1982*. New York, NY: Springer.

Lawvere, F. W., & Schanuel, S. H. (1997). *Conceptual mathematics: A first introduction to categories*. New York, NY: Cambridge University Press.

Lebart, L., & Fenelon, J.-P. (1971). *Statistique et informatique appliqués* (p. 195). Paris, France: Dunod.

Lebart, L., Morineau, A., & Tabard, N. (1977). *Techniques de la description statistique*. Paris, France: Dunod.

LeDoux, J. E. (2002). *Synaptic self: How our brains become who we are*. New York, NY: Viking.

Lefebvre, H. (1969). *Logique formelle, logique dialectique*. Paris, France: Editions Anthropos.

Leland, W. E., Taqqu, M. S., Willinger, W., & Wilson, D. V. (1993). On the self-similar nature of ethernet traffic. *Proceedings of the ACM/SIGCOMM'93*, (pp. 183-193). San Francisco, CA.

Leland, W. E., Taqqu, M. S., Willinger, W., & Wilson, D. V. (1994). On the self-similar nature of ethernet traffic (Extended Version). *IEEE/ACM Transactions on Networking*, *2*(1), 1–15.

Lemke, F. (1997). *Knowledge extraction from data using self-organizing modeling technologies*. Paper presented at eSEAM'97 Conference, MacSciTech organization.

Lemke, F., & Müller, J. A. (1997). Self-organizing data mining for a portfolio trading system. *Journal of Computational Intelligence and Finance*, *5*, 12–26.

Leon, L. F., Lam, D. C. L., Schertzer, W. M., & Swayne, D. A. (2006). A 3D hydrodynamic lake model: Simulation on Great Slave Lake. *Proceedings International Modelling and Software Society Biennial Conference*, Burlington, VT.

Leon, L. F., Lam, D., Schertzer, W. M., & Swayne, D. A. (2005). Lake and climate models linkage: A 3-D hydrodynamic contribution. *Advances in Geosciences*, *4*, 57–62.

Le-Thi-Thu, H., Casañola-Martín, G. M., Marrero-Ponce, Y., Rescigno, A., Saso, L., & Parmar, V. S. (2011). Novel coumarin-based tyrosinase inhibitors discovered by OECD principles-validated QSAR approach from an enlarged balanced database. *Molecular Diversity, 15*(2).

Levenson, E. (1983). *The ambiguity of change*. New York, NY: Basic Books.

Lévy Véhel, J., & Riedi, R. (1997). Fractional Brownian motion and data traffic modeling: The other end of the spectrum. In Lévy Véhel, J., Lutton, E., & Tricot, C. (Eds.), *Fractals in engineering* (pp. 185–202). London, UK: Springer.

Levy, A., Alden, D., & Levy, C. (2006). Biotic patterns in music presented at the society for chaos theory in psychology & life sciences. 16th Annual International Conference 4-6 August 2006 Baltimore MD, USA.

Levy-Carciente, S., Sabelli, H., & Jaffe, K. (2004). Complex patterns in the oil market. *Interciencia, 29*, 320–323.

Lewontin, R. C. (1983). Gene, organism, and environment. In Bendall, D. S. (Ed.), *Evolution from molecules to men*. Cambridge University Press.

Li, B., & Miller, J. (2010). Fractal cityscape. *The International Journal of Virtual Reality, 9*(4), 7–12.

Libet, B. (1993). *Neurophysiology of consciousness: Selected papers and new essays*. Boston, MA: Birkhauser.

Libet, B., Freeman, A., & Sutherland, K. (1999). *The volitional brain: Towards a neuroscience of free will*. Thorverton, UK: Imprint Academic.

Lieberman, P. (1991). *Uniquely human: The evolution of speech, thought, and selfless behavior*. Cambridge, MA: Harvard University Press.

Li, M., & Vitányi, P. (1997). *An introduction to Kolmogorov complexity and its applications*. New York, NY: Springer.

Linck, R. W., & Langevin, G. L. (1981). Reassembly of flagellar B (αβ) tubulin into singlet microtubules: Consequences for cytoplasmic microtubule structure and assembly. *The Journal of Cell Biology, 89*, 323–337.

Linden, M., Habib, T., & Radojevic, V. (1996). A controlled study of the effects of EEG biofeedback on cognition and behaviour of children with ADD and LD. *Biofeedback and Self-Regulation, 21*(1), 35–49.

Lin, S.-K. (1996). Molecular diversity assessment: Logarithmic relations of information and species diversity and logarithmic relations of entropy and indistinguishability after rejection of Gibbs paradox of entropy of mixing. *Molecules (Basel, Switzerland), 1*, 57–67.

Liu, D. (2006). A parallel computing algorithm for improving the speed of fractal image compression based on spiral architecture. *Proceedings of 2006 International Conference on Image Processing, Computer Vision, & Pattern Recognition (IPCV'06)* (pp. 563-569). Las Vegas, USA.

Liu, J. (2006). *Fractal network traffic analysis with applications*. Ph-D Thesis, School of Electrical and Computer Engineering Theses and Dissertations, Georgia Tech Theses and Dissertations. Retrieved January 10, 2007, from http://hdl.handle.net/1853/11477

Liu, W.-C., Chen, W.-B., Kuo, J.-T., & Wu, C. (2007). Numerical determination of residence time and age in a partially mixed estuary using three-dimensional hydrodynamic model. *Continental Shelf Research, 28*(8), 1068–1088.

Loga-Karpinska, M., Duwe, K., Guilbaud, C., O'Hare, M., Lemmin, U., & Umlauf, L. ... Mahnke, P. (2003). *D24: Realistic residence times studies, integrated water resource management for important deep European lakes and their catchment areas*. Eurolakes, FP5_Contract No.: EVK1-CT1999-00004

Lowe, J., & Amos, L. A. (1998). Crystal structure of the bacterial cell-division protein FtsZ. *Nature, 391*, 203–206.

Lowe, J., Li, H., Downing, K. H., & Nogales, E. (1998). Refined structure of αβ-Tubulin at 3.5 A° resolution. *Journal of Molecular Biology, 313*, 1045–1057.

Lubar, J. F., & Shouse, M. N. (1976). EEG and behavioral changes in a hyperkinetic child concurrent with training of the sensorimotor rhythm (SMR): A preliminary report. *Biofeedback and Self-Regulation, 1*(3), 293–306.

Lubar, J. F., Swartwood, M. O., Swartwood, J. N., & O'Donnell, P. H. (1995). Evaluation of the effectiveness of EEG neurofeedback training for ADHD in a clinical setting as measured by changes in T.O.V.A. scores, behavioural ratings, and WISC-R performance. *Biofeedback and Self-Regulation, 20*(1), 83–99.

Lu, C. Y., Browne, D. E., Yang, T., & Pan, J. W. (2007). Demonstration of a compiled version of Shor's quantum factoring algorithm using photonic qubits. *Physical Review Letters, 99*, 250504–250508.

Lukovits, I. (2000). A compact form of adjacency matrix. *Journal of Chemical Information and Computer Sciences, 40*, 1147–1150.

Lynch, J. J., & Paskewitz, D. A. (1971). On the mechanisms of the feedback control of human brain wave activity. *The Journal of Nervous and Mental Disease, 153*(3), 205–217.

Madala, H. R., & Ivakhnenko, A. G. (1994). *Inductive learning algorithms for complex systems modelling.* Boca Raton, FL: CRC.

Maggiora, G. M. (personal communication).

Ma, H. W., & Zeng, A. P. (2003). The connectivity structure, giant strong component and centrality of metabolic networks. *Bioinformatics (Oxford, England), 19*, 1423–1430.

Malchiodi, C. (2007). *The art therapy sourcebook.* New York, NY: McGraw-Hill.

Manca, M., & DeMott, W. R. (2009). Response of the invertebrate predator Bythotrephes to a climate-linked increase in the duration of a refuge from fish predation. *Limnology and Oceanography, 54*(4).

Manca, M., Morabito, G., & Cavicchioni, N. (2000). First observations on the effect of a complete, exceptional overturn of Lake Maggiore on Plankton and primary production. *International Review of Hydrobiology, 85*(2-3), 209–222.

Mandelbrot, B. (1989). Fractals and an art for the sake of science. *Leonardo, Supplemental Issue Computer Art in Context*, 21-24.

Mandelbrot, B. (1975). *Les objects fractals. Forme, hasard et dimension.* Paris, France: Nouvelle Bibliothèque Scientifique Flammaron.

Mandelbrot, B. (1977). *The fractal geometry of nature.* New York, NY: W. H. Freeman.

Mandelbrot, B. (1982). *The fractal geometry of nature.* W.H. Freeman and Company.

Mandelbrot, B. B. (1969). Long-run linearity, locally Gaussian processes, H-spectra and infinite variances. *International Economic Review, 10*, 82–113.

Mandelbrot, B. B. (1978). Les objets fractals. *La Recherche, 9*, 1–13.

Mandelbrot, B. B. (1979). Colliers all'eatoires et une alternative aux promenades aux hasard sans boucle: Les cordonnets discrets et fractals. *CR (East Lansing, Mich.), 286A*, 933–936.

Mandelbrot, B. B. (1982). *The fractal geometry of nature.* San Francisco, CA: W.H. Freeman.

Mandelkow, E. M., Mandelkow, E., & Milligan, R. A. (1991). Microtubules dynamics and microtubules caps: A time-resolved cryoelectron microscopy study. *The Journal of Cell Biology, 114*, 977–991.

Mann, C. A., Lubar, J. F., Zimmerman, A. W., Miller, C. A., & Muenchen, R. A. (1992). Quantitative analysis of EEG in boys with attention-deficit-hyperactivity disorder: Controlled study with clinical implications. *Pediatric Neurology, 8*(1), 30–36.

Maràk, I. (1997). *On synthetic terrain erosion modeling: A survey.* Retrieved April 14, 2005, from http://www.cescg.org/CESCG97/marak/

Marák, I., Benes, B., & Slavík, P. (1997). Terrain erosion model based on rewriting of matrices. *Proceedings of WSCG-97*, Vol. 2, (pp. 341-351).

Marie, R. R., Bez, H. E., Blackledge, J. M., & Datta, S. (2006). *On the fractal characteristics of network traffic and its utilization in covert communications.* Retrieved January 2, 2007, from http://ima.org.uk/Conferences/mathssignalprocessing2006/Marie.pdf

Marks-Tarlow, T. (1995). The fractal geometry of human nature. In R. Robertson & A. Combs (Eds.), *Proceedings from the First Conference of the Society for Chaos Theory in Psychology and the Life Sciences.* Mahweh: NJ: Erlbaum.

Marks-Tarlow, T. (2002). Fractal dynamics of the psyche. In B. Goertzel & A. Combs (Eds.), *Dynamical psychology: An international, interdisciplinary e-journal of complex mental affairs*. Retrieved from http://www.goertzel.org/dynapsyc/2002/FractalPsyche.htm

Marks-Tarlow, T. (1999). The self as a dynamical system. *Nonlinear Dynamics Psychology and Life Sciences, 3*(4), 311–345.

Marks-Tarlow, T. (2005). Semiotic seams: Fractal dynamics of reentry. *Cybernetics & Human Knowing, 11*(1), 49–62.

Marks-Tarlow, T. (2008). *Psyche's veil: Psychotherapy, fractals and complexity*. New York, NY: Routledge.

Marks-Tarlow, T., Robertson, R., & Combs, A. (2002). Varela and the Uroboros: The psychological significance of reentry. *Cybernetics & Human Knowing, 9*(2), 31–47.

Marrero-Ponce, Y., Martínez-Albelo, E. R., Casañola-Martín, G. M., Castillo-Garit, J. A., Echeverría-Díaz, Y., & Romero Zaldivar, V. (in press). Bond-based linear indices of the non-stochastic and stochastic edge adjacency matrix. 1. Theory and modeling of *ChemPhys* properties of organic molecules. [in press]. *Molecular Diversity*.

Marshall, M. S., & Bentler, P. M. (1976). The effects of deep physical relaxation and low-frequency-alpha brainwaves on alpha subjective reports. *Psychophysiology, 13*(6), 505–516.

Marwan, N. (2003). *Encounters with neighbours*. Doctoral dissertation, University of Potsdam.

Marwan, N., Kurths, J., & Saparin, P. (2007a). Generalised recurrence plots analysis for spatial data. *Physics Letters. [Part A], 360*, 545–551.

Marwan, N., Romano, M. C., Thiel, M., & Kurths, J. (2007b). Recurrence plots for the analysis of complex systems. *Physics Reports, 438*, 237–329.

Marwan, N., Thiel, M., & Nowaczyk, N. R. (2002). Cross recurrence plot based synchronization of time series. *Nonlinear Processes in Geophysics, 9*(3/4), 325–331.

Marwan, N., Trauth, M. H., Vuille, M., & Kurths, J. (2003). Comparing modern and Pleistocene ENSO-like influences in NW Argentina using nonlinear time series analysis methods. *Climate Dynamics, 21*(3-4), 317–326.

Marwan, N., Wessel, N., Meyerfeldt, U., Schirdewan, A., & Kurths, J. (2002). Recurrence-plot-based measures of complexity and their application to heart-rate-variability data. *Physical Review E: Statistical, Nonlinear, and Soft Matter Physics, 66*(2), 026702.

Marx, K., & Engels, F. (1978). *The Marx and Engels reader* (Tucker, R. C., Ed.). New York, NY: Norton and Company.

Masson, J. M. (Ed.). (1985). *The complete letters of Sigmund Freud to Wilhelm Fliess 1887-1904*. Cambridge, MA: Belknap.

Matassini, L., Kantz, H., Holyst, J., & Hegger, R. (2002). Optimizing of recurrence plots for noise reduction. *Physical Review E: Statistical, Nonlinear, and Soft Matter Physics, 65*(2), 021102.

Mathiak, K., & Weber, R. (2006). Toward brain correlates of natural behavior: fMRI during violent video games. *Human Brain Mapping, 27*(12), 948–956.

Matte Blanco, I., & Raynor, E. (1998). *The unconscious as infinite sets*. London, UK: Karnac Books.

Maturana, H. (2002). *Autopoiesis, structural coupling and cognition: A history of these and other notions in the biology of cognition*. Instituto Matriztico, Internet publication.

Maturana, H. R., & Varela, F. J. (1980). *Autopoiesis and cognition, the realization of the living*. Dordrecht, Holland: D. Reidel Pub. Co.

Mavromatos, N. (2000). *Cell microtubules as cavities: Quantum coherence and energy transfer?* Retrieved from http://arxiv.org/pdf/quant-ph/0009089

Mavromatos, N., Mershin, A., & Nanopoulos, D. V. (2002). *QED-cavity model of microtubules implies dissipationless energy transfer and biological quantum teleportation*. Retrieved from http://arxiv.org/pdf/quant-ph/0204021

Mc Mahon, S. M., Miller, K. H., & Drake, J. (2001). Networking tips for social scientists and ecologists. *Science, 293*, 1604–1605.

McCulloch, W. S., & Pitts, W. (1943). A logical calculus of the ideas immanent in nervous activity. *The Bulletin of Mathematical Biophysics, 5*, 115–133.

Meares, R. (2006). *The metaphor of play*. New York, NY: Routledge.

Meyer, M. (2002). Fractal scaling of heartrate dynamics in health and disease. In Losa, G. A., Merlini, D., Nonnenmacher, T. F., & Weibel, E. R. (Eds.), *Fractal in biology and medicine* (*Vol. III*, pp. 181–193). Basel, Switzerland: Birkhauser.

Michette, A. G., Mavromatos, N., Powell, K., Holwill, M., & Pfauntsch, S. J. (2004). Nanotubes and microtubules as quantum information carriers. *Proceedings of the Society for Photo-Instrumentation Engineers, 522*, 5581.

Mindell, A. (2000). *Quantum mind: The edge between physics and psychology*. Portland, OR: Lao Tse Press.

Mino, G. (Ed.). (2001). *Bruno G. Corpus iconographicum*. Milan, Italy: Adelphi.

Minsky, M. (1985). *The society of mind*. New York, NY: Simon & Schuster.

Mitchell, M. (2009). *Complexity: A guided tour*. New York, NY: Oxford University.

Mocenni, C., Facchini, A., & Vicino, A. (2010). Identifying the dynamics of complex spatio-temporal systems by spatial recurrence properties. *Proceedings of the National Academy of Sciences of the United States of America, 107*(18), 8097–8102.

Mocenni, C., Facchini, A., & Vicino, A. (2011). (in press). Comparison of recurrence quantification methods for the analysis of temporal and spatial chaos. *Mathematical and Computer Modelling*.

Monastra, V. J., Lynn, S., Linden, M., Lubar, J. F., Gruzelier, J., & La Vaque, T. J. (2005). Electroencephalographic biofeedback in the treatment of attention deficit/hyperactivity disorder. *Journal of Neurotherapy, 9*(4), 5–34.

Monastra, V. J., Monastra, D. M., & George, S. (2002). The effects of stimulant therapy, EEG biofeedback and parenting style on the primary symptoms of attention deficit/hyperactivity disorder. *Applied Psychophysiology and Biofeedback, 27*(4), 231–249.

Monderer, R. S., Harrison, D. M., & Haut, S. R. (2002). Neurofeedback and epilepsy. *Epilepsy & Behavior, 3*, 214–218.

Mondragon, R. J., Arrowsmith, D. K., & Pitts, J. M. (1999). Chaotic maps for traffic modelling and queueing performance analysis. *Performance Evaluation, 43*(4), 223–240.

Moon, B. (1999). The tears make me paint: The role of responsive artmaking in adolescent art therapy. *Art Therapy: Journal of the American Art Therapy Association, 16*(2), 78–82. doi:doi:10.1080/07421656.1999.10129671

Moon, B. (2009). *Existential art therapy: The canvas mirror*. Springfield, IL: Charles C. Thomas Publisher, Ltd.

Moon, F. (1992). *Chaotic and fractal dynamics*. Wiley & Sons, Inc.

Morowitz, H. J. (2002). *The emergence of everything: How the world became complex*. New York, NY: Oxford University Press.

Müller, J.-A., & Lemke, F. (1995). Self-organizing modelling and decision support in economics. *System Analysis Modeling Simulation, 18-19*, 135–138.

Musgrave, K., & Mandelbrot, B. (1991). The art of fractal landscapes. *IBM Journal of Research and Development*, September.

Musgrave, F. K., Kolb, C. E., & Mace, R. S. (1989). The synthesis and rendering of eroded fractal terrain. *Computer Graphics, 23*(3), 41–50.

NANO-D. (n.d.). Retrieved from http://nano-d.inrialpes.fr/

Nanopoulos, D. V. (1995). Theory of brain function, quantum mechanics and superstrings. Retrieved from http://arxiv.org/abs/hep-ph/9505374

Nanopoulos, D. V., & Mavromatos, N. (1996). *A non-critical string (Liouville) approach to brain microtubules: State vector reduction, memory coding and capacity*. Retrieved from http://arxiv.org/abs/quant-ph/9512021

Nickerson, R. S. (2003). *Psychology and environmental change*. Mahwah, NJ: Lawrence Erlbaum Associates.

Nielsen, J. (1998). Metabolic engineering: Techniques of analysis of targets for genetic manipulations. *Biotechnology and Bioengineering, 58*, 125–132.

Nielsen, M. A., & Chuang, I. L. (2000). *Quantum computation and quantum information*. New York, NY: Cambridge University Press.

Nogales, E. (1998). Structure of the αβ-tubulin dimer by electron crystallography. *Letters to Nature, 391*, 192–203.

Nogales, E., Whittaker, M., Milligan, R. A., & Downing, K. H. (1999). High-resolution model of the microtubule. *Cell, 96*, 79–88.

Nonnenmacher, T. F., Losa, G. A., Merlini, D., & Weibel, E. R. (Eds.). (1994). *Fractal in biology and medicine*. Basel, Switzerland: Birkhauser.

Norman, D. A. (1988). *The design of everyday things*. New York, NY: Doubleday.

Norman, D. A. (1999). Affordances, conventions, and design. *Interaction, 6*(3), 38–41.

Norris, S. L., Lee, C., Burshteyn, D., & Cea-Aravena, J. (2001). The effects of performance enhancement training on hypertension, human attention, stress, and brain wave patterns: A case study. *Journal of Neurotherapy, 4*(3), 29–44.

Norros, I. (1994). A storage model with self-similar input. *Queueing Systems Theory and Applications, 16*(3-4), 387–396.

Norros, I. (1995). On the use of fractional Brownian motion in the theory of connectionless networks. *IEEE Journal on Selected Areas in Communications, 13*(6), 953–962.

Nowlis, D. P., & Kamiya, J. (1970). The control of electroencephalographic alpha rhythms through auditory feedback and the associated mental activity. *Psychophysiology, 6*(4), 476–484.

Oldenbourg, R., Salmon, E. D., & Tran, P. T. (1998). Birefringence of single and bundled microtubules. *Biophysical Journal, 74*, 645–654.

Oppenheimer, P. (1986). Real time design and animation of fractal plants and trees. *Computer Graphics, 20*(4), 55–64.

Orlob, G. T. (1967). *Prediction of thermal energy distribution in streams and reservoirs (Tech. Rep.)*. Walnut Creek, CA: Water Resources Engineers, Inc.

Orsucci, F. (2006b). The paradigm of complexity in clinical neuro-cognitive science. *The Neuroscientist – SAGE, 12*(4), 1-10.

Orsucci, F., Giuliani, A., Webber, C., Zbilut, J., Fonagy, P., & Mazza, M. (2006). Combinatorics & synchronization in natural semiotics. *Physica A: Statistical Mechanics and its Applications, 361*, 665–676.

Orsucci, F. (2009). *Mind force: On human attractions*. River Edge, NJ: World Scientific Publishing.

Orsucci, F. (Ed.). (1998). *The complex matters of the mind*. Singapore: World Scientific.

Orsucci, F., Giuliani, A., & Zbilut, J. (2004). Structure & coupling of semiotic sets. *Experimental Chaos, American Institute of Physics. AIP Proceedings, 742*, 83–93.

Orsucci, F., & Sala, N. (2005). Virtual reality, telemedicine and beyond. In Carbonara, D. (Ed.), *Technology literacy applications in learning environments* (pp. 755–757). Hershey, PA: Idea Group.

Orsucci, F., Walters, K., Giuliani, A., Webber, C. Jr, & Zbilut, J. (1999). Orthographic structuring of human speech and texts. *International Journal of Chaos Theory and Applications, 4*(2), 80–88.

Ott, E., Grebogi, C., & Yorke, J. A. (1990). Controlling chaos. *Physical Review Letters, 64*(11), 1196.

Pais, A. (1989). George Uhlenbeck and the discovery of electron spin. *Physics Today, 42*, 30–40.

Palumbo, M. C., Colosimo, A., Giuliani, A., & Farina, L. (2005). Functional essentiality from topology features in metabolic networks: A case study in yeast. *FEBS Letters, 579*, 4642–4646.

Palumbo, M. C., Farina, L., Colosimo, A., Tun, K., Dhar, P., & Giuliani, A. (2006). Networks everywhere? Some general implications of an emergent metaphor. *Current Bioinformatics, 1*(2), 219–234.

Pampaloni, F., & Florin, E. L. (2008). Microtubule architecture: inspiration for novel carbon nanotube-based biomimetic materials. *Trends in Biotechnology, 26*(6), 302–310.

Papa, M. A. (2008). Progress towards gravitational wave astronomy. *Classical and Quantum Gravity, 25*, 114009–11401.

Park, K., & Willinger, W. (2000). *Self-similar network traffic and performance evaluation* (1st ed.). London, UK: John Wiley & Sons.

Patapievici, H.-R. (2004). *Ochii Beatriceii. Cum arata cu adevarat lumea lui Dante?* Bucuresti, Romania: Humanitas.

Patel, M., & Sabelli, H. (2003). Autocorrelation and frequency analysis differentiate cardiac and economic bios from 1/F noise. *Kybernetes, 32*, 692–702.

Paxson, V., & Floyd, S. (1994). Wide area traffic: The failure of Poisson modeling. *Proceedings of ACM SIGCOMM'94* (pp. 257-268).

Paxson, V., & Floyd, S. (1995). Wide area traffic: The failure of Poisson Modeling. *IEEE/ACM Transactions on Networking, 3*(3), 226–244.

Peak, D., & Frame, M. (1994). *Chaos under control: The art and science of complexity.* New York, NY: Freeman.

Pecora, L. M., & Carroll, T. L. (1990). Synchronization control of chaos. *Physical Review Letters, 64*, 821.

Peitgen, H.-O., Jurgens, H., & Saupe, D. (1992). *Chaos and fractals: New frontiers of science.* New York, NY: Springer-Verlag.

Peitgen, H.-O., & Richter, P. (1986). *The beauty of fractals: Images of complex dynamical systems.* New York, NY: Springer-Verlag.

Peitgen, H., & Saupe, D. (1988). *The science of fractal images.* New York, NY: Springer-Verlag.

Penrose, R. (2005). *The road to reality.* New York, NY: Knopf.

Peper, E., & Mullholland, T. (1970). Methodological and theoretical problems in the voluntary control of electroencephalographic occipital alpha by the subject. *Kybernetik, 7*(1), 10–13.

Perline, R. (1996). Zipf's law, the central limit theorem, and the random division of the unit interval. *Physical Review E: Statistical Physics, Plasmas, Fluids, and Related Interdisciplinary Topics, 54*, 220–223.

Pessa, E. (2007). Phase transition in biological matter. In Licata, I., & Sakaji, A. (Eds.), *Physics of emergence and organization* (pp. 165–228). Singapore: World Scientific.

Pessa, E., & Vitiello, G. (2004). Quantum noise induced entanglement and chaos in the dissipative quantum model of brain. *International Journal of Modern Physics B, 18*(6), 841–858.

Petitot, J. (1999). *Naturalizing phenomenology, issues in contemporary phenomenology and cognitive science.* Stanford, CA: Stanford University Press.

Pham Thi, N. N., Huisman, J., & Sommeijer, B. P. (2005). Simulation of three-dimensional phytoplankton dynamics: Competition in limited environments. *Journal of Computational and Applied Mathematics, 174*(1), 57–77.

Piaget, J. (1950). *Introduction à l'épistémologie génétique.* Paris, France: Presses Universitaires de France.

Pickover, C. A. (Ed.). (1995). *The pattern book: Fractals, art, and nature.* World Scientific.

Pierson, G. B., Burton, P. R., & Himes, R. H. (1978). Alterations in number of protofilameCNTs in microtubules assembled in vitro. *The Journal of Cell Biology, 76*, 223–228.

Pizzi, R., Inama, G., Durin, O., & Pedrinazzi, C. (2007). Non.invasive assessment of risk for severe tachyarrhythmias by means of non-linear analysis techniques. *Chaos and Complexity Letters, 3*(3).

Pizzi, R., Strini, G., Fiorentini, S., Pappalardo, V., & Pregnolato, M. (in press). Evidences of new biophysical properties of microtubules. [in press]. *NanoBiotechnology.*

Planty-Bonjour, G. (1965). *Le categories du materialisme dialectique.* Paris, France: Presses Universitaires de France.

Plotkin, W. B. (1976). On the self-regulation of the occipital alpha rhythm: Control strategies, states of consciousness, and the role of physiological feedback. *Journal of Experimental Psychology. General, 105*(1), 66–99.

Poincaré, H. (1943). *La science et l'hypothèse.* Paris, France: Flammarion.

Politzer, G. (1928). *Critique des fondements de la psychologie.* Paris, France: Le Editions Rieder.

Politzer, G. (1948). *Principes élémentaires de philosophie.* Paris, France: Messidor Scandéditions.

Pollard-Gott, L. (1986). Fractal repetition in the poetry of Wallace Stevens. *Language and Style, 19*, 233–249.

Popper, K. R. (1992). *The logic of scientific discovery.* New York, NY: Routledge.

Popper, K. R. (2003). *Conjectures and refutations: The growth of scientific knowledge.* New York, NY: Routledge.

Port, R., Tajima, K., & Cummins, F. (1999). *Non-linear analysis of developmental processes* (van der Maas, L. J., & van Geert, P., Eds.). Amsterdam, The Netherlands: Elsevier.

Postingl, H., Krauhs, E., Little, M., & Kempf, T. (1981). Complete amino acid sequence of α-tubulin from porcine brain. *Proceedings of the National Academy of Sciences of the United States of America, 78*, 2757–2761.

Prahalad, C. K., & Ramaswamy, V. (2000, January 1). Co-opting customer competence. *Harvard Business Review, 78*(1), 79–87.

Prewett, M. J., & Adams, H. E. (1976). Alpha activity suppression and enhancement as a function of feedback and instructions. *Psychophysiology, 13*(4), 307–310.

Prigogine, I. (1980). *From being to becoming.* San Francisco, CA: Freeman.

Prigogine, I. (1984). *Order out of chaos.* Boston, MA: Shambhala Publications.

Protein Data Bank. (n.d.). Retrieved from http://www.rcsb.org/pdb/home/home.do

Prusinkiewicz, P. (1986). Graphical applications of L-systems. *Proceedings of Graphics Interface '86 - Vision Interface '86,* (pp. 247–253).

Prusinkiewicz, P. (1987). Applications of L-systems to computer imagery. In H. Ehrig, M. Nagl, G. Rozenberg, & A. Rosenfeld (Eds.), *Graph-Grammars and Their Application to Computer Science 3rd International Workshop, Lecture Notes in Computer Science, Vol. 291,* Warrenton, Virginia, USA, December 1986, (pp. 534–548). Heidelberg, Germany: Springer-Verlag.

Prusinkiewicz, P., & Lindenmayer, A. (1990). *The algorithmic beauty of plants.* New York, NY: Springer-Verlag. Retrieved September, 2006, from http://algorithmicbotany.org/papers/abop/abop.pdf

Prusinkiewicz, P., & Hammel, M. (1993). A fractal model of mountains with rivers. *Proceeding of Graphics Interface, 93,* 174–180.

Prusinkiewicz, P., & Lindenmayer, A. (1990). *The algorithmic beauty of plants.* New York, NY: Springer-Verlag.

Pullman, B. (Ed.). (1994). *The emergence of complexity in mathematics, physics, chemistry and biology. Pontificiae Academiae Scientiarum Scripta Varia No. 89.* Vatican City, Vatican: Pontificia Academia Scientiarum.

Rao, F., & Caflisch, A. (2004). The protein folding network. *Journal of Molecular Biology, 342,* 299–306.

Rasey, H. W., Lubar, J. F., McIntyre, A., Zoffuto, A. C., & Abbott, P. L. (1996). EEG biofeedback for the enhancement of attentional processing in normal college students. *Journal of Neurotherapy, 1*(3), 15–21.

Ravelli, R., Gigant, B., Curmi, P. A., Jourdain, I., Lachkar, S., Sobel, A., & Knossow, M. (2004). Insight into tubulin regulation from a complex with colchicine and a stathmin-like domain. *Letters to Nature, 428,* 198–202.

Regestein, Q. R., Pegram, G. V., Cook, B., & Bradley, D. (1973). Alpha rhythm percentage maintained during 4- and 12- hour feedback periods. *Psychosomatic Medicine, 35*(3), 215–222.

Rescher, N. (1996). *Process metaphysics.* Albany, NY: State University of New York.

Rescher, N. (1998). *Complexity, a philosophical overview.* New Brunswick, NJ: Transaction Publishers.

Richardson, D. C., & Dale, R. (2005). Looking to understand: The coupling between speakers' and listeners' eye movements and its relationship to discourse comprehension. *Cognitive Science, 29,* 39–54.

Riegel, K. (1979). *Foundations of dialectical psychology.* London, UK: Academic Press.

Riley, S. (1999). Brief therapy: An adolescent intervention. *Art Therapy: Journal of the American Art Therapy Association, 16*(2), 83–86. doi:doi:10.1080/07421656.1999.10129669

Risset, J.-C. (1986). Pitch and rhythm paradoxes: Comments on auditory paradox based on a fractal waveform. *The Journal of the Acoustical Society of America*, *80*, 961–962.

Ritter, H., & Schulten, H. (1988). Convergence properties of Kohonen's topology conserving maps: Fluctuations, stability, and dimension selection. *Biological Cybernetics*, *60*, 59–71.

Rizzolatti, G., & Arbib, M. A. (1998). Language within our grasp. *Trends in Neurosciences*, *21*, 188–194.

Robertson, R. (1989). The evolution of number: Self-reflection and the archetype of order. *Psychological Perspectives*, *20*(1), 128–141.

Robertson, R. (1995). *Jungian archetypes*. York Beach, ME: Nicholas-Hay.

Robertson, R. (2000). The evolution of Jung's archetypal reality. *Psychological Perspectives*, *41*, 66–80.

Roche, S., Akkermans, E., Chauvet, O., Hekking, F., Issi, J.-P., & Martel, R. … Poncharal, P. (2006). *Transport properties. understanding carbon nanotubes*. In A. Loiseau, P. Launois, P. Petit, S. Roche, & J.-P. Salvetat (Eds.), *Lecture Notes in Computer Science, 677*, 335–437.

Rosen, R. (1999). *Essays on life itself*. New York, NY: Columbia University Press.

Rossi, E. L. (1996). The psychobiology of mind-body communication: The complex, self-organizing field of information transduction. *Bio Systems*, *38*, 199–206.

Rothko, M. (2004). *The artist's reality: Philosophies of art* (Rothko, C., Ed.). New Haven, CT: Yale University Press.

Rueda, F. J., & Cowen, E. A. (2005). Residence time of a freshwater embayment connected to a large lake. *Limnology and Oceanography*, *50*(5), 1638–1653.

Rueda, F. V. (2006). Basin scale transport in stratified lakes and reservoirs: Towards the knowledge of freshwater ecosystem. *Limnetica*, *1-2*, 33–56.

Ruelle, D. (1981). Small random perturbations of dynamical systems and the definition of attractors. *Communications in Mathematical Physics*, *82*, 137–151.

Sabelli, A. (1952). *Escritos*. Private edition, Buenos Aires.

Sabelli, H. (1971). An attempt to formalize some aspects of dialectic logic, Beyer. In R. Wilhelm (Ed.). *Hegel-Jahrbuch* (211-213). Meisenheim am Glan, Germany: Verlag Anton Hain.

Sabelli, H. (1989). *Union of opposites: A comprehensive theory of natural and human processes*. Lawrenceville, NJ: Brunswick.

Sabelli, H. (1994). Entropy as symmetry: Theory and empirical support. In B. Brady & L. Peeno (Eds.), *Proceedings International Systems Society 38th Annual Meeting* (pp. 1483-1496).

Sabelli, H. (1995). Non-linear dynamics as a dialectic logic. *Proceedings of International Systems Society* (pp. 101-112).

Sabelli, H. (2008). Bios theory of innovation. *The Innovation Journal: The Public Sector Innovation Journal, 13*. Retrieved September 1, 2010, from http://www.innovation.cc/scholarly_style-articles.htm

Sabelli, H. (2008). How medicine informs informatics: Information is asymmetry, not entropy. *The Open Cybernetics and Systemics Journal, 2*, 93-108. Retrieved from http://www.bentham.org/open/tocsj/openaccess2.htm

Sabelli, H., & Kovacevic, L. (2003). *Biotic expansion of the universe*. International Conference on Advances in Internet, Processing, Systems, and Interdisciplinary Research. Electronic Publication IPSI-2003.

Sabelli, H., Kauffman, L., Patel, M., Sugerman, A., Carlson-Sabelli, L., Afton, D., & Konecki, J. (1997). How is the universe, that it creates a human heart? Part II. Co-creation, evolution and entropy. In Y. P. Rhee & K. D. Bailey (Eds.), *Systems thinking, globalization of knowledge, and communitarian ethics: Proceedings of the International Systems Society* (pp. 924-935). Seoul, South Korea.

Sabelli, H., Thomas, J., Kovacevic, L., Lawandow, A., & Horan, D. (2010). Biotic dynamics of galactic distribution, gravitational waves, and quantum processes. A causal theory of cosmological evolution. In A. D. Wachter & R. J. Propst (Eds.), *Black holes and galaxy formation*. New York, NY: Nova Science Publishers. Retrieved from https://www.novapublishers.com/catalog/product_info.php?products_id=19328

Sabelli, H. (1964). A pharmacological strategy for the study of central modulator linkages. In Wortis, J. (Ed.), *Recent advances in biological psychiatry* (pp. 145–182). New York, NY: Plenum Press.

Sabelli, H. (1972). A pharmacological approach for modeling neuronal nets. In Drischeland, H., & Dattmar, P. (Eds.), *Biocybernetics* (pp. 1–9). Jena, Germany: Veb Gustav Fischer Verlag.

Sabelli, H. (1984). Mathematical dialectics, scientific logic and the psychoanalysis of thinking. In Cohen, R. S., & Wartofsky, M. W. (Eds.), *Hegel and the sciences* (pp. 349–359). New York, NY: D. Reidel Publishing.

Sabelli, H. (1998). The union of opposites: From Taoism to process theory. *Systems Research, 15*, 429–441.

Sabelli, H. (2000). Complement plots: analyzing opposites reveals Mandala-like patterns in human heartbeats. *International Journal of General Systems, 29*, 799–830.

Sabelli, H. (2001). Novelty, a measure of creative organization in natural and mathematical time series. *Nonlinear Dynamics Psychology and Life Sciences, 5*, 89–113.

Sabelli, H. (2001). The co-creation hypothesis. In Ragsdell, G., & Wilby, J. (Eds.), *Understanding complexity*. London, UK: Kluwer Academics Publishers.

Sabelli, H. (2003). Mathematical development: A theory of natural creation. *Kybernetes, 32*, 752–766.

Sabelli, H. (2005). *Bios. A study of creation*. Singapore: World Scientific.

Sabelli, H. (forthcoming). Biothermodynamics. *Open Cybernetics and Systemics Journal*.

Sabelli, H. (forthcoming). The biotic pattern of prime numbers. *Cybernetics and Systemics Journal*.

Sabelli, H., & Abouzeid, A. (2003). Definition and empirical characterization of creative processes. *Nonlinear Dynamics Psychology and Life Sciences, 7*, 35–47.

Sabelli, H., & Carlson-Sabelli, L. (1991). Process theory as a framework for comprehensive psychodynamic formulations. *Genetic, Social, and General Psychology Monographs, 1*, 5–27.

Sabelli, H., & Carlson-Sabelli, L. (1996). *As simple as one, two, three. Arithmetic: A simple, powerful, natural and dynamic logic* (pp. 543–554). Louisville, Kentucky: Proceedings International Systems Society.

Sabelli, H., & Carlson-Sabelli, L. (2005). Bios, a process approach to living system theory. *Systems Research and Behavioral Science, 23*, 323–336.

Sabelli, H., Carlson-Sabelli, L., Patel, M., Zbilut, J., Messer, J., & Walthall, K. (1995). Psychocardiological portraits: A clinical application of process theory. In Abraham, F. D., & Gilgen, A. R. (Eds.), *Chaos theory in psychology* (pp. 107–125). Westport, CT: Greenwood.

Sabelli, H., & Kauffman, L. (1999). The process equation: Formulating and testing the process theory of systems. *Cybernetics and Systems, 30*, 261–294.

Sabelli, H., & Kauffman, L. (2004). Bios and bipolar feedback: Mathematical models of creative processes. *Journal of Applied System Studies, 5*, 21–34.

Sabelli, H., & Kovacevic, L. (2006). Quantum bios and biotic complexity in the distribution of galaxies. *Complexity, 11*, 14–25.

Sabelli, H., & Kovacevic, L. (2008). Biotic complexity of population dynamics. *Complexity, 13*, 47–55.

Sabelli, H., & Kovacevic, L. (forthcoming). Economic bios. *Kybernetes*.

Sabelli, H., & Lawandow, A. (forthcoming). Homeobios: The pattern of heartbeats in newborns, adults, and elderly persons. *Nonlinear Dynamics Psychology and Life Sciences*.

Sabelli, H., Lawandow, A., & Kopra, A. R. (2010). Asymmetry, symmetry and beauty. *Symmetry, 2*, 1591–1624.

Sabelli, H., Patel, M., & Sugerman, A. (2004). Flux and action: Process statistics. *Journal of Applied System Studies, 5*, 54–66.

Sabelli, H., Patel, M., Sugerman, A., Kovacevic, L., & Kauffman, L. (2004). Process entropy, a multidimensional measure of diversity and symmetry. *Journal of Applied System Studies, 5*, 129–143.

Sabelli, H., Patel, M., & Venkatachalapathy, V. K. (2004 c). Action and information: Repetition, rise and fall. *Journal of Applied System Studies, 5*, 67–77.

Sabelli, H., Sugerman, A., Kovacevic, L., Kauffman, L., Carlson-Sabelli, L., Patel, M., & Konecki, J. (2005). Bios data analyzer. *Nonlinear Dynamics Psychology and Life Sciences, 9*, 505–538.

Sabelli, H., & Thomas, G. (2008). The future quantum computer: Biotic complexity. In Orsucci, F., & Sala, N. (Eds.), *Reflecting interfaces: The complex coevolution of information technology ecosystems*. Hershey, PA: IGI Global.

Sabelli, H., Zarankin, S., & Carlson-Sabelli, L. (2004 a). Opposition: The phase space of opposites in psychology, sociology and economics. *Journal of Applied System Studies, 5*, 78–93.

Sala, N. (2002). The presence of the self- similarity in architecture: Some examples. In Novak, M. M. (Ed.), *Emergent nature* (pp. 273–283). Singapore: World Scientific.

Sala, N. (2004). Fractal geometry in the arts: An overview across the different cultures. In Novak, M. M. (Ed.), *Thinking in patterns: Fractals and related phenomena in nature* (pp. 177–188). Singapore: World Scientific.

Sala, N. (2006). Complexity, fractals, nature and industrial design: Some connections. In Novak, M. M. (Ed.), *Complexus mundi: Emergent pattern in nature* (pp. 171–180). Singapore: World Scientific.

Sala, N. (2007). Preface. In *Chaos and complexity in the arts and architecture* (pp. vii–xiv). New York, NY: Nova Science Publishers, Inc.

Sala, N. (2008). Fractal geometry in computer science. In Orsucci, F., & Sala, N. (Eds.), *Reflexing interfaces: The complex coevolution of information technology ecosystems, information science reference* (pp. 308–328). Hershey, PA: IGI Global.

Sala, N. (2009). Fractal geometry in artificial world and in Second Life. *Chaos and Complexity Letters, 4*(1), 23–34.

Sala, N. (2010). Fractals in architecture, hyperarchitecture …and beyond. *Chaos and Complexity Letters. International Journal on Dynamical System Research, 4*(3), 147–180.

Sala, N. (2011). Virtual reality in architecture, engineering and beyond. In Abu-Taieh, E., El Sheikh, A., & Jafari, M. (Eds.), *Technology engineering and management in aviation: Advancements and discoveries*.

Saleri, R. (2005). Pseudo-urban automatic pattern generation. *Chaos and Complexity Letters, 3*, 357–365.

Saleri, R. (2008). Urban and architectural 3D fast processing. In Orsucci, F., & Sala, N. (Eds.), *Reflexing interfaces: The complex evolution of information technology ecosystems*. Hershey, PA: IGI Global.

Salmaso, N. (2005). Effects of climatic fluctuations and vertical mixing on the interannual trophic variabilità of Lake Garda, Italy. 2005. *Limnology and Oceanography, 50*, 553–565.

Salvador, P., Nogueira, A., Valadas, R., & Pacheco, A. (2004). Multi-time-scale traffic modeling using Markovian and L-Systems models. *Proceedings of 3rd European Conference on Universal Multiservice Networks, Lecture Notes in Computer Science, Vol. 3262*, Porto, Portugal, October 25-27, 2004, (pp. 297-306). Heidelberg, Germany: Springer-Verlag.

Sapmaz, S., Meyer, C., Beliczynski, P., Jarillo-Herrero, P., & Knowenhoven, L. P. (2006). Excited state spectroscopy in carbon nanotube double quantum dots. *Nano Letters, 6*(7), 1350–1355.

Saunders, P. T. (1980). *An introduction to catastrophe theory*. New York, NY: Cambridge University Press.

Savage, C., Hamelin, M., Culotti, J. G., Coulson, A., Albertson, D. G., & Chalfie, M. (1989). MEC-7 is a β-tubulin gene required for the production of 15-protofilament microtubules in Caenorhabditis elegans. *Genes & Development, 3*, 870–881.

Scalzone, F., & Zontini, G. (2001). The dream's navel between chaos and thought. *The International Journal of Psycho-Analysis, 82*(2), 263–282.

Schroeder, M. (1991). *Fractals, chaos, power laws*. New York, NY: Freeman.

Schuster, P. (2010). Origins of life: Concepts, data, and debates. *Complexity, 15*(3), 7–10.

Schwartz, E. (1980). Computation anatomy and functional architecture of striate cortex: A spatial mapping approach to perceptual coding. *Vision Research, 20*, 645–669.

Searle, J. R. (1980). Minds, brains, and programs. *The Behavioral and Brain Sciences, 3*, 417–424.

Segermann, H. (2008). *Second Life*. Retrieved December 18, 2008, from http://www.segerman.org/2ndlife.html

Segré, D., Ben-Eli, D., Deamer, D. W., & Lancet, D. (2001). The lipid world. *Origins of Life and Evolution of the Biosphere, 31*, 119–145.

Segré, D., Ben-Eli, D., & Lancet, D. (2000). Compositional genomes: Prebiotic information transfer in mutually catalytic noncovalent assemblies. *Proceedings of the New York Academy of Science USA, 97*, 4112–4117.

Segré, D., Shenhav, B., Kafri, R., & Lancet, D. (2001). The molecular roots of compositional inheritance. *Journal of Theoretical Biology, 213*, 481–491.

Shannon, C. E. (1940). *A symbolic analysis of relay and switching circuits*. Massachusetts Institute of Technology, Department of Electrical Engineering.

Shannon, C. E. (1948a). A mathematical theory of communication: Part I, discrete noiseless systems. *The Bell System Technical Journal, 27*, 379–423.

Shearer, R. (1992). Chaos theory and fractal geometry: Their potential impact on the future of art. *Leonardo, 25*, 143–152.

Shearer, R. (1995). From flatland to fractaland: New geometries in relationship to artistic and scientific revolutions. *Fractals, 3*, 617–625.

Shen, J., & Haas, L. (2004). Calculating age and residence time in the Tidal York River using three-dimensional model experiments. *Estuarine, Coastal and Shelf Science, 61*(3), 449–461.

Sheridan, P. (1996). *Spiral architecture for machine vision*. PhD thesis, University of Technology, Sydney.

Sheridan, P., & Hintz, T. (1999). Primitive image transformations on hexagonal lattice. Technical report, Charles Sturt University, Bathurst, NSW.

Sheridan, P., Hintz, T., & Moore, W. (1991). Spiral architecture in machine vision. *In T.* Bossamier (Ed.), *Australian Occam and Transputer Conference. Amsterdam, The Netherlands: IOS Press.*

Sheridan, P., Hintz, T., & Alexander, D. (2000). Pseudo-invariant image transformations on a hexagonal lattice. *Image and Vision Computing, 18*, 907–917.

Shockley, K., Santana, M.-V., & Fowler, C. A. (2003). Mutual interpersonal postural constraints are involved in cooperative conversation. *Journal of Experimental Psychology. Human Perception and Performance, 29*, 326–332.

Shor, P. W. (1997). Polynomial-time algorithms for prime factorization and discrete logarithms on a quantum computer. *SIAM Journal on Scientific Computing, 26*, 1484–1509.

Shulman, J. A. (2000). *Fractals and Benoit Mandelbrot: A computer science discovery often considered kind to prime numbers*. American Computer Science Association (ACSA). Retrieved December 28, 2006, from http://www.acsa2000.net/frac/

Siegel, D. J. (2007). *The mindful brain*. New York, NY: Norton.

Smerz, K. E., & Guastello, S. (2008). Cusp catastrophe model for binge drinking in a college population. *Nonlinear Dynamics Psychology and Life Sciences, 12*, 205–224.

Smith, A. R. (1984). Plants, fractals, and formal languages. *Proceedings of the 11th Annual Conference on Computer Graphics and Interactive Techniques*, (pp. 1–10).

Solomonoff, R. J. (1964a). A formal theory of inductive inference. Part I. *Information and Control, 7*, 1–22.

Somers, D., & Kopell, N. (1995). Waves and synchrony in networks of oscillators of relaxation and non-relaxation type. *Physica D. Nonlinear Phenomena, 89*, 169–183.

SONNIA. (n.d.). Retrieved from http://www.molecular-networks.com/

Spencer-Brown, G. (1969). *Laws of form*. London, UK: Allen and Unwin.

Spencer-Brown, G. (1979). *Laws of form* (rev. ed.). New York, NY: E. P. Dutton.

Standish, R. K. (2001). On complexity and emergence. *Complexity International, 9*, 1–6.

Stepinski, T. F., Collier, M. L., McGovern, P. J., & Clifford, S. M. (2004). Martian geomorphology from fractal analysis of drainage networks. *Journal of Geophysical Research, 109*(2), E02005.1-E02005.12

Sterman, M. B. (1973). Neurophysiologic and clinical studies of sensorimotor EEG biofeedback training: some effects on epilepsy. *Seminars in Psychiatry, 5*(4), 507–525.

Sterman, M. B. (1996). Physiological origins and functional correlates of EEG rhythmic activities: Implications for self-regulation. *Biofeedback and Self-Regulation, 21*(1), 3–33.

Sterman, M. B. (2000). Basic concepts and clinical findings in the treatment of seizure disorders with EEG operant conditioning. *Clinical EEG (Electroencephalography), 31*(1), 45–55.

Sterman, M. B., & Friar, L. (1972). Suppression of seizures in an epileptic following sensorimotor EEG feedback training. *Electroencephalography and Clinical Neurophysiology, 33*(1), 89–95.

Sterman, M. B., & Macdonald, L. R. (1978). Effects of central cortical EEG feedback training on incidence of poorly controlled seizures. *Epilepsia, 19*(3), 207–222.

Sterman, M. B., Macdonald, L. R., & Stone, R. K. (1974). Biofeedback training of the sensorimotor electroencephalogram rhythm in man: Effects on epilepsy. *Epilepsia, 15*(3), 395–416.

Stern, D. (1985). *The interpersonal world of the infant.* New York, NY: Basic Books.

Straker, L. M., Pollock, C. M., Zubrick, S. R., & Kurinczuk, J. J. (2006). The association between information and communication technology exposure and physical activity, musculoskeletal and visual symptoms and socioeconomic status in 5-year-olds. *Child: Care, Health and Development, 32*(3), 343–351.

Strozzi, F., Zaldivar, J.-M., & Zbilut, J. P. (2007). Recurrence quantification analysis and state space divergence reconstruction for financial time series analysis. *Physica A, 376*, 487–499.

Sugerman, A., & Sabelli, H. (2003). Novelty, diversification and nonrandom complexity define creative processes. *Kybernetes, 32*, 829–836.

Szilard, A. L., & Quinton, R. E. (1979). An interpretation for DOL systems by computer graphics. *The Science Terrapin, 4*, 8–13.

Takens, F. (1981). *Detecting strange attractors in turbulence. Lecture Notes in Mathematics, 898.* New York, NY: Springer.

Tan, G., Thornby, J., Hammond, D. C., Strehl, U., Canady, B., Arnemann, K., & Kaiser, D. A. (2009). Meta-analysis of EEG biofeedback in treating epilepsy. *Journal of Clinical EEG & Neuroscience, 40*(3), 173–179.

Tannier, C., & Pumain, D. (2005). Fractals in urban geography: A theoretical outline and an empirical example. *Cybergeo, Systems, Modeling, Geostatistics.* Retrieved from http://cybergeo.revues.org/3275

Tausk, V. (1933). On the origin of the "influencing machine" in schizophrenia. *Psychoanalytic Quarterly, 2*, 519-556. (Original work published 1919)

Taylor, R. (2007). Pollock, Mondrian and nature: Recent scientific investigations. In Sala, N. (Ed.), *Chaos and complexity in the arts and architecture* (pp. 25–37). New York, NY: Nova Science Publishers, Inc.

Taylor, R., Michlich, A., & Jones, D. (1999). Fractal analysis of Pollock's drip paintings. *Nature, 399*, 422.

Tegmark, M. (2000a). The importance of quantum decoherence in brain processes. *Physical Review E: Statistical Physics, Plasmas, Fluids, and Related Interdisciplinary Topics, 61*(4), 4194–4206.

Tegmark, M. (2000b). Why the brain is probably not a quantum computer. *Information Science, 128*(3-4), 155–179.

Thomas, G. H., Sabelli, H., Kovacevic, L., & Kauffman, L. (2006). *Biotic patterns in Schrödinger's equation and the evolution of the universe.* Retrieved April 26, 2011, from http://www.necsi.edu/events/iccs6/papers/b7794439dbc6b0515c7659d6088d.pdf

Thomas, G. H. (2006). *Geometry, language and strategy.* Singapore: World Scientific.

Thomasson, N., Hoeppner, T. J., Webber, C. L. Jr, & Zbilut, J. P. (2001). Recurrence quantification in epileptic EEGs. *Physics Letters. [Part A]*, *279*, 94–101.

Thompson, L., & Thompson, M. (1998). Neurofeedback combined with training in metacognitive strategies: Effectiveness in students with ADD. *Applied Psychophysiology and Biofeedback*, *23*(4), 243–263.

Thompson, W. I. (1996). *Coming into being: Artefacts and texts in the evolution of consciousness*. New York, NY: St. Martin's Press.

Thom, R. (1983). *Mathematical models of morphogenesis*. Chichester, UK: Ellis Horwood.

Thom, R. (1994). *Structural stability and morphogenesis*. Boulder, CO: Westview Press.

Tomasello, M. (2003). *A usage-based theory of language*. Cambridge, MA: Harvard University Press.

Tomasi, J. (1988). Models and modeling in theoretical chemistry. *Journal of Molecular Structure*, *179*, 273–292.

Torrens, F. (submitted for publication). Fractal hybrid-orbital analysis of the protein tertiary structure. *Molecules, 7*.

Torrens, F., & Castellano, G. (in press, b). Periodic classification of human immunodeficiency virus inhibitors. In A. S. Sidhu, T. Dillon, & M. Bellgard (Eds.), *Biomedical data and applications*. Berlin, Germany: Springer Studies in Computational Intelligence.

Torrens, F., & Castellano, G. (in press, c). Structural classification of complex molecules by artificial intelligence techniques. In E. D. Castro & A. K. Haghi (Eds.), *Advanced methods and applications in chemoinformatics: Research methods and new applications*. Hershey, PA: IGI Global.

Torrens, F. (2000). Fractal hybrid orbitals in biopolymer chains. *Russian Journal of Physical Chemistry*, *74*, 115–120.

Torrens, F. (2001). Fractals for hybrid orbitals in protein models. *Complexity International*, *8*, 1–13.

Torrens, F. (2004). Valence topological charge-transfer indices for dipole moments. *Molecular Diversity*, *8*, 365–370.

Torrens, F., & Castellano, G. (2006). Periodic classification of local anaesthetics (procaine analogues). *International Journal of Molecular Sciences*, *7*, 12–34.

Torrens, F., & Castellano, G. (2009). Classification of complex molecules. In Hassanien, A.-E., & Abraham, A. (Eds.), *Foundations of computational intelligence* (*Vol. 5*, pp. 243–315). Berlin: Springer Studies in Computational Intelligence.

Torrens, F., & Castellano, G. (2010). Table of periodic properties of human immunodeficiency virus inhibitors. *International Journal of Computer Intelligence. Bioinformatics and Systems Biology*, *1*, 246–273.

Torrens, F., & Castellano, G. (in press). a). Using chemical structural indicators for periodic classification of local anaesthetics. *International Journal of Chemoinformatics and Chemical Engineering*.

Trautteur, G. (1987, February). *Intelligenza umana e intelligenza artificiale*. Paper presented at Centro Culturale San Carlo of Milano, Milan.

Trautteur, G. (1997-1998). Distinzione e riflessione. *ATQUE*, *16*, 127–141.

Travis, T. A., Kondo, C. Y., & Knott, J. R. (1974). Parameters of eyes-closed alpha enhancement. *Psychophysiology*, *11*(6), 674–681.

Travis, T. A., Kondo, C. Y., & Knott, J. R. (1975). Alpha enhancement research: A review. *Biological Psychiatry*, *10*(1), 69–89.

Treisman, A. (1996). The binding problem. *Current Opinion in Neurobiology*, *6*(2), 171–178.

Trulla, L. L., Giuliani, A., Zbilut, J. P., & Webber, C. L. Jr. (1996). Recurrence quantification analysis of the logistic equation with transients. *Physics Letters. [Part A]*, *223*, 255–260.

Turing, A. M. (1964). *Minds and machines*. Englewood Cliffs, NJ: Prentice Hall. (Original work published 1950)

Turkle, S. (1988). Artificial intelligence and psychoanalysis: A new alliance. *Daedalus*, *117*(1), 241–268.

Tuszynski, J. A., Brown, J. A., & Hawrylak, P. (1998). Dielectric polarization, electrical conduction, information processing and quantum computation in microtubules: Are they plausible? *Philosophical Transactions of the The Royal Society of London A, 356*(1743), 1897–926.

Tuszynski, J. A., Brown, J. A., Crawford, E., & Carpenter, E. J. (2005). Molecular dynamics simulations of tubulin structure and calculations of electrostatic properties of microtubules. *Mathematical and Computer Modelling, 41*, 1055–1070.

Tuszynski, J. A., Trpišová, B., Sept, D., & Satarić, M. V. (1997). The enigma of microtubules and their self-organization behavior in the cytoskeleton. *Bio Systems, 42*, 153–175.

Tuszynski, J., Hameroff, S. R., Satarić, M. V., Trpišová, B., & Nip, M. L. A. (1995). Ferroelectric behavior in microtubule dipole lattices: Implications for information processing, signaling and assembly/disassembly. *Journal of Theoretical Biology, 174*, 371–380.

Tyson, P. D. (1982). The choice of feedback stimulus can determine the success of alpha feedback training. *Psychophysiology, 19*(2), 218–230.

Valle, R. S., & DeGood, D. E. (1977). Effects of state-trait anxiety on the ability to enhance and suppress EEG alpha. *Psychophysiology, 14*(1), 1–7.

van Wijk, J. J., & Saupe, D. (2004). Image based rendering of iterated function systems. *Computers & Graphics, 28*(6), 937–943.

Vandersypen, L. M. K., Matthias, S., Gregory, B., Yannoni, C. S., Sherwood, M. H., & Chuang, I. L. (2001). Experimental realization of Shor's quantum factoring algorithm using nuclear magnetic resonance. *Nature, 414*, 883–887.

Vandervert, L. (1990). Systems thinking and neurological positivism: Further elucidations and implications. *Systems Research, 7*(1), 1–17.

Varela, F. (1975). A calculus for self-reference. *International Journal of General Systems, 2*, 5–24.

Varela, F. (1979). *Principles of biological autonomy*. New York, NY: North Holland.

Varela, F. J., Thompson, E., & Rosch, E. (1991). *The embodied mind, cognitive science and human experience*. Cambridge, MA: MIT Press.

Vasas, V., Szathmáry, E., & Santos, M. (2009). Lack of evolvability in self-sustaining autocatalytic networks: A constraint on metabolism-first path to the origin of life. *Proceedings of the National Academy of Sciences of the United States of America, 107*(4), 1470–1475.

Vasconcelos, D. B., Lopes, S. R., Viana, R. L., & Kurths, J. (2006). Spatial recurrence plots. *Physical Review E: Statistical, Nonlinear, and Soft Matter Physics, 73*, 1–10.

Veitch, D. (1992). Novel models of broadband traffic. *Proceedings 7th Australian Teletraffic Research Seminar*, Murray River, Australia, 1992.

Veitch, D. (1993). Novel models of broadband traffic. *IEEE Global Telecommunications Conference, 1993, including a Communications Theory Mini-Conference, Technical Program Conference Record, IEEE in Houston, GLOBECOM '93*, Vol. 2 (pp. 1057-1061).

Vernon, D. (2005). Can neurofeedback training enhance performance? An evaluation of the evidence with implications for future research. *Applied Psychophysiology and Biofeedback, 30*(4), 347–364.

Vernon, D. (2008). Neurofeedback: using computer technology to alter brain functioning. In Orsucci, F., & Sala, N. (Eds.), *Reflexing interfaces: The complex coevolution of information technology systems* (pp. 94–108). New York, NY: Information Science Reference.

Vernon, D. (2009). *Human potential: Exploring techniques used to enhance human performance*. London, UK: Routledge.

Vernon, D., Dempster, T., Bazanova, O., Rutterford, N., Pasqualini, M., & Andersen, S. (2009). Alpha neurofeedback training for performance enhancement: Reviewing the methodology. *Journal of Neurotherapy, 13*(4), 214–227.

Vernon, D., Egner, T., Cooper, N., Compton, T., Neilands, C., Sheri, A., & Gruzelier, J. (2003). The effect of training distinct neurofeedback protocols on aspects of cognitive performance. *International Journal of Psychophysiology, 47*(1), 75–85.

Vernon, D., Frick, A., & Gruzelier, J. (2004). Neurofeedback as a treatment for ADHD: A methodological review with implications for future research. *Journal of Neurotherapy, 8*(2), 53–82.

Vernon, D., & Gruzelier, J. (2008). Electroencephalographic biofeedback as a mechanism to alter mood, creativity and artistic performance. In DeLuca, B. N. (Ed.), *Mind-body and relaxation research focus* (pp. 149–164). Nova Science.

Vetsigian, K., Woese, C., & Goldenfeld, N. (2006). Collective evolution and the genetic code. *Proceedings of the New York Academy of Science USA, 103*, 10696–10701.

Vitiello, G. (1995). Dissipation and memory capacity in the quantum brain model. *International Journal of Modern Physics B, 9*(8), 973–989.

Vlek, C., & Steg, L. (Eds.). (2007). Human behavior and environmental sustainability. *The Journal of Social Issues, 63*(1), 1–231.

von Neumann, J. (1958). *The computer and the brain*. London, UK: Yale University Press.

Voss, R., & Wyatt, J. (1993). Multifractals and the local connected fractal dimension: Classification of early Chinese landscape painting. In Crilly, A., Earnshaw, R., & Shaw, H. (Eds.), *Applications of fractals and chaos: The shape of things* (pp. 171–184). New York, NY: Springer Verlag.

Vyzantiadou, M. A., Avdelas, A. V., & Zafiropoulos, S. (2007). The application of fractal geometry to the design of grid or reticulated shell structures. *Computer Aided Design, 39*(1), 51–59.

Wächtershäuser, G. (1992). Groundwork for an evolutionary biochemistry: The iron-sulfur world. *Progress in Biophysics and Molecular Biology, 58*, 85–201.

Wacker, M. S. (1996). Alpha brainwave training and perception of time passing: Preliminary findings. *Biofeedback and Self-Regulation, 21*(4), 303–309.

Waddington, C. H. (1956). *Principles of embriology*. London, UK: Allen and Unwin Ltd.

Wang, H., Wu, Q., He, X., & Hintz, T. (2006). A novel interactive progressive decoding method for fractal image compression. *First International Conference on Innovative Computing, Information and Control (ICICIC'06)*, Vol. III (pp. 613-617).

Wang, T., Yu, Q., & Mao, Y. (2009). Fractal characteristics analysis of wireless network traffic based on Hurst parameter. *International Conference on Communications, Circuits and Systems (ICCCAS)*, 2009, (pp. 173-176).

Wang, P., Song, Y. T., Chao, Y., & Zhang, H. (2005). Parallel computation of the regional ocean modeling system. *International Journal of High Performance Computing Applications, 19*(4), 375–385.

Wang, Y., Kempa, K., Kimball, B., Carlson, J. B., Benham, G., & Li, W. Z. (2004). Receiving and transmitting light-like radio waves: Antenna effect in arrays of aligned carbon nanotubes. *Applied Physics Letters, 85*(13), 2607–2609.

Watson, J. D., & Crick, F. H. C. (1953). A structure for deoxyribose nucleic acid. *Nature, 171*, 737–738.

Watts, D. J., & Strogatz, S. H. (1998). Collective dynamics of 'small world' networks. *Nature, 393*, 440–442.

Webber, C. L. Jr, & Zbilut, J. P. (1994). Dynamical assessment of physiological systems and states using recurrence plot strategies. *Journal of Applied Physiology, 76*, 965–973.

Weber, B. H. (2000). Closure in the emergence and evolution of life: Multiple discourses or one? In J. L. R. Chandler & G. Van de Vijver (Eds.), *Closure: Emergent organizations and their dynamics, Annals of the New York Academy of Sciences, 901,* 132-138.

Weber, B. H. (1998). Emergence of life and biological selection from the perspective of complex systems dynamics. In van de Vijver, G., Salthe, S. N., & Delpos, M. (Eds.), *Evolutionary systems: Biological and epistemological perspectives on selection and self-organization*. Dordrecht, The Netherlands: Kluwer.

Weber, B. H., & Depew, J. D. (1996). Natural selection and self-organization. *Biology and Philosophy, 11*(1), 33–65.

Weber, E., Koberl, A., Frank, S., & Doppelmayr, M. (in press). Predicting successful learning of SMR neurofeedback in healthy participants: methodological considerations. *Applied Psychophysiology and Biofeedback*.

Wheeler, J. A. (1957). Assessment of Everett's "relative state" formulation of quantum theory. *Reviews of Modern Physics, 29,* 463–465.

Wilde, J., Mierzwa, M., & Suits, B. (2006). *Using particle tracking to indicate Delta Residence Time.* California Water and Environmental Modeling Forum, 2006 Annual Meeting, February 28-March 2, 2006, Pacific Grove, California.

Williams, R. J. P., & Frausto da Silva, J. J. R. (1999). *Bringing chemistry to life: From matter to man.* Oxford, UK: Oxford University Press.

Williams, R. J. P., & Frausto da Silva, J. J. R. (2002). The systems approach to evolution. *Biochemical and Biophysical Research Communications, 297,* 689–699.

Williams, R. J. P., & Frausto da Silva, J. J. R. (2003). Evolution was chemically constrained. *Journal of Theoretical Biology, 220,* 323–343.

Willinger, W., Taqqu, M. S., Sherman, R., & Wilson, D. V. (1995). Self-similarity through high-variability: Statistical analysis of ethernet LAN traffic at the source level. *ACM Sigcomm, 95,* 100–113.

Winnicott, D. (1974). *Playing and reality.* Harmondsworth, UK: Penguin.

Winnicott, D. W. (1987). *The child, the family, and the outside world.* Reading, MA: Addison-Wesley Pub. Co.

Winter, D. D., & Koger, S. M. (2004). *The psychology of environmental problems* (2nd ed.). Mahwah, NJ: Lawrence Erlbaum Associates.

Wisdom, J. O. (1961). A methodological approach to the problem of hysteria. *The International Journal of Psycho-Analysis, 42,* 224–237.

Woese, C. R. (2002). On the evolution of cells. *Proceedings of the National Academy of Sciences of the United States of America, 99*(13), 8742–8747.

Woese, C. R. (2004). A new biology for a new century. *Microbiology and Molecular Biology Reviews, 68*(2), 173–186.

Wohlberg, B., & de Jager, G. (1999). A review of the fractal image coding literature. *IEEE Transactions on Image Processing, 8*(12), 1716–1729.

Wolf, F. (1994). *The dreaming universe: A mind expanding journey into the realm where psyche and physics meet.* New York, NY: Simon and Schuster.

Woolf, N. J., & Hameroff, S. R. (2001). A quantum approach to visual consciousness. *Trends in Cognitive Sciences, 5*(11), 472–478.

Wu, Q., He, X., & Hintz, T. (2004). Virtual spiral architecture. *Proceedings of the International Conference on Parallel and Distributed Processing Techniques and Applications,* Vol. 1 (pp. 399-405).

Xu, L. D., & Li, L. X. (1989). Complementary opposition as a systems concept. *Systems Research, 6,* 91–101.

Yoo, H. J. (2004). Attention deficit hyperactivity symptoms and internet addiction. *Psychiatry and Clinical Neurosciences, 58*(5), 487–494.

Yue, W., Lin, C.-L., & Patel, V. C. (2004). Large eddy simulation of turbulent open-channel flow with free surface simulated by level) set method. *Physics of Fluids, 17*(2), 1–12.

Zanette, D. H., & Morelli, L. G. (2003). Synchronization of coupled extended dynamical systems. *International Journal of Bifurcation and Chaos in Applied Sciences and Engineering, 13*(4).

Zaslavsky, G. M., Sagdeev, R. Z., Usikov, D. A., & Chemikov, A. A. (1991). *Weak chaos and quasiregular structures.* Cambridge University Press. **8.**

Zbilut, J. P., Mitchell, J. C., Giuliani, A., Colosimo, A., Marwan, N., & Webber, C. L. (2004). Singular hydrophobicity patterns and net charge: A mesoscopic principle for protein aggregation/folding. *Physica A, 343,* 348–358.

Zeilinger, A., Weihs, G., Jennewein, T., & Aspelmeyer, M. (2005). Happy centenary, photon. *Nature, 433,* 230–238.

Zhang, H. F., Shu, Y. T., & Yang, O. W. W. (1997). Estimation of Hurst parameter by variance time plots. *Proceedings IEEE Pacrim 97,* Vol. 2 (pp. 883-886).

Zhao, E., & Liu, D. (2005). Fractal image compression methods: A review. *ICITA 2005. Third International Conference on Information Technology and Applications,* Vol. 1 (pp. 756 – 759).

About the Contributors

Franco Orsucci received his first degree in Medicine and second degree in Psychiatry at La Sapienza University in Rome (Italy). He has been a researcher at the Italian National Research Council. Now he is Professor of Clinical Psychology and Psychiatry at the Catholic University and Gemelli University Hospital in Rome. He is also a research fellow at the London University College, and founder and Editor in Chief of *Chaos and Complexity Letters: International Journal of Dynamical System Research* (Nova Science, New York). His last published books are *Changing Mind, Transitions in Natural and Artificial Environments* (World Scientific, Singapore, 2002) and *Bioethics in Complexity* (Imperial College Press, London, 2004). He has also published more than 80 scientific articles on neuroscience and cognitive science.

Sala Nicoletta received the degree in Physics ("Laurea"), Applied Cybernetics, at the University of Milan (Italy), Ph.D. in Communication Science at Università della Svizzera italiana of Lugano (USI, Lugano, Switzerland), Postgraduates (two years for each) in: "Didactics of the communication and multimedia technologies" and "Journalism and mass media." She is Professor in Information Technology and in Electronics and she teaches at University of Lugano (Mendrisio, Switzerland). She is founder and co-editor of *Chaos and Complexity Letters: International Journal of Dynamical System Research* (Nova Science, New York). Her research interests concern various scientific topics from an interdisciplinary point of view and comprise the following areas: fractal geometry and complexity; mathematics in arts, architecture and industrial design; new media and IT in the learning environments; and virtual reality in education. She has authored 20 mathematics and information technology books, and edited 10 others. She has written 300 scientific papers.

* * *

Walter Ambrosetti is working at the I.S.E-C.N.R. ("Istituto per lo Studio degli Ecosistemi" - "Institute for Ecosystem's Study") in Pallanza and he has always been researching in different branches of physical limnology; the main topics can be summarised as follows: 1) building of an integrated knowledge concerning geology, geography and geomorphology of lakes watersheds, and their influence on water bodies; 2) definition of the climatological conditions of lakes environments and analysis of those meteorological parameters closely related to physical-limnological phenomena; 3) analysis of the main factors influencing lakes hydrodynamics; 4) thermal characterization of lakes, giving particular attention to energy exchanges between a lake and the atmosphere and to its heat budgets; 4) study of lacustrine water movements: deep and superficial currents, turbulence, internal seiches, and vertical mixing; 6) analysis of physical aspects concerning eutrophication in lakes: testing of the presence of mechanisms other than convection responsible of the oxygenation of deep water in lakes. He is author or co-author of 210 scientific papers, most of them published on international journals.

Gloria Castellano is PhD in Chemistry, and Full-time Associated Professor in Organic Chemistry of the Universidad Católica de Valencia *San Vicente Mártir* in the Faculty of Experimental Sciences. She is head of the Research Group in Methods and Numerical Simulation for the Development of Inter-disciplinary Technologies in the Chair Energesis of the Universidad Católica de Valencia *San Vicente Mártir*. She is Editor-in-Chief of *Nereis: Latin American Journal of Methods, Modelling and Simulation in Interdisciplinary Technology*. She has 21 research articles published in indexed journals.

Leonardo Castellano, graduated in Physics at the University of Milan (Italy) with a thesis entitled "A Quasi-Three Dimensional Model for the Thermal Pollution of the Po River." Encouraged by interna-tional success of the above model, he initiated a long career as consultant of the most important Italian and European research centers in the field of the mathematical modelling for any sort of environmental and industrial processes and systems. He has published over 100 scientific papers. For many years he served as invited Professor at the Department of General Physics of the University of Milan; from 1998 is invited Professor at the Department of Computer Science. He passed away in the Spring of 2012.

Tammy Dempster has a BSc in Psychology and is currently working in the Department of Applied Social Sciences at Canterbury Christ Church University. Having worked in both the cognitive and social psychology fields, her research interests are varied, but her main field of interest is neurofeedback and in particular its use on healthy participants for the purposes of optimal performance. She is currently in the final year of her PhD, for which she is investigating the methodological variations in the use of neurofeedback to train the alpha brainwaves of healthy populations. She is particularly interested in trying to establish if there is an optimum methodology for alpha neurofeedback training and what effect such training has on areas of cognition such as memory and creativity as well as personality variables such as locus of control.

Angelo Facchini was born in Siena 1973. In 2001 he earned the Laurea Degree in Telecommunications Engineering and the PhD in Physical chemistry in 2005, both from the University of Siena. His work is focused on nonlinear time series analysis and complex system. Research interests include: recurrence plot of time series and spatio-temporal systems, pattern formation, and analysis of biophysical phenomena.

Silvia Fiorentini received a Master in Medical Biotechnology in 2003 and a PhD in Computer Science in 2011 at the University of Milan. From 2003 to 2008 she was Research Fellow at the National Tumour Institute of Milan and at the IFOM (Firc Institute of Molecular Oncology) of Milan, Nanotechnology Unit, then at the PTP (Lodi Technopark), working in the animal genomic and bioinformatics units. Cur-rently she carries on her research work for a multinational corporation.

Liane Gabora is an Associate Professor of Psychology at the University of British Columbia. She researches the cognitive mechanisms underlying creativity, how creative ideas evolve through culture, and how humans came to be so creative, using computational and mathematical models, as well as studies involving human participants. She also works on the comparison of biological and cultural evolution, and the development of a general theory of evolution that encompasses both. She has proposed that culture evolves through a non-Darwinian process of self-organization and communal exchange similar to that by which biologists now believe the earliest forms of life likely evolved. Her theory of creativity, referred to as honing theory, posits that our creative abilities reflect the tendency for minds to self-organize in order to regain dynamical equilibrium, and highlights the actualization of potential through interaction with a context. Dr. Gabora has over 100 papers published in scholarly books and journals, has given lectures worldwide, and has over a million dollars in research grants. She was awarded the 2011 Berlyne Award from Division 10 of the American Psychological Association for outstanding achievement by a junior scholar. She is also an artist, a published fiction writer, and an accomplished composer of music and lyrics for piano.

Alessandro Giuliani is Senior Scientist at Environment and Health Dept., Computational and experimental carcinogenesis unit, at Istituto Superiore di Sanità (Italian NIH). He is mainly involved in the generation and testing of soft physical and statistical models for life sciences, with a special emphasis on the elucidation of mesoscopic complex systems like protein sequence/structure prediction, quantitative structure/activity relations in medicinal chemistry, analysis of physiological time series, analysis of ecological systems. He is in the editorial board of *Current Bioinformatics, Systems and Synthetic Biology Springer,* and *BMC Applied Informatics.* He acts as a reviewer for the subsequent journals: *American Journal of Physiology, Journal of Medicinal Chemistry, Chemical Toxicology, Medical and Biological Engineering and Computing, Physics Letters A, Journal of Chemical Information and Computer Science, Chemical Research in Toxicology, Biophysical Journal, Neuroscience Letters, Bioinformatics, Biopolymers, FEBS Journal,* and *Genome Biology.*

Louis Kauffman was born in Potsdam, New York on Feb. 3, 1945. He graduated from Norwood-Norfolk Central High School in 1962 as valedictorian. He received the degree of B.S. in Mathematics from MIT in 1966. Kauffman was awarded a PhD. in Mathematics by Princeton University in 1972. He has been teaching at the University of Illinois at Chicago since January 1971, with visiting appointments at the University of Michigan, Universidad de Zaragoza, Spain, Universita di Bologna, Bologna, Italy and the Institute des Hautes Etudes Scientifiques in Bures Sur Yvette, France, and others. Kauffman is the author of four books on knot theory (three in Princeton University Press and one in World Scientific Press), a book on map coloring and the reformulation of mathematical problems, *Map Reformulation* (Princelet Editions; London and Zurich (1986)) and is the editor of the World-Scientific 'Book Series on Knots and Everything'. He is the Editor in Chief and founding editor of the *Journal of Knot Theory and its Ramifications.* Kauffman is the recipient of a 1993 University Scholar Award by the University of Illinois at Chicago and he is the 1993 recipient of the 1993 Warren McCulloch Memorial Award of the American Society for Cybernetics for significant contributions to the field of Cybernetics and the 1996 award of the Alternative Natural Philosophy Association for his contribution to the understanding of discrete physics. He was Polya Lecturer for the Mathematical Association of America from 2008 to 2010 and President of the American Society for Cybernetics from 2005 to 2008.

Ljubiša M. Kocić is full Professor with the Faculty of Electronic Engineering, University of Niš (Serbia). He was born 1952, and received a PhD degree in 1985 from the University of Niš in applied mathematics. His fields of interest include chaos theory, fractal geometry, computer-aided design, and approximation theory. He is a member of AMS and different national scientific forums, and a member of editorial board of *Chaos and Complexity Letters*. His hobby is painting, especially in watercolor technique.

Terry Marks-Tarlow, Ph.D., is a Clinical Psychologist in private practice in Santa Monica, California (www.markstarlow.com). Dr. Marks-Tarlow teaches advanced sequencing yoga workshops, while adopting a strong mind/body focus clinically. During long-term psychotherapy with patients, she specializes in productive blocks and highlights creative expression. As a visual artist, she specializes in figure drawing (www.contemporary-art-gallery.de). Her first book, "Creativity Inside Out: Learning through Multiple Intelligences" (1996; Addison-Wesley; forward by Howard Gardner) is a creativity curriculum for educators. Her book in progress, "Psyche's Fractal Veil: Complexity and Psychotherapy," combines nonlinear science with the art of psychotherapy.

Maegan Merrifield is currently pursuing her PhD in Art Therapy at the University of British Columbia. She is a PhD student at the University of British Columbia. She has a Master's of Science in Clinical Psychology and has spent her career working with adolescents and young adults. As a Doctoral student she is specializing in Expressive Arts Therapy and is researching the connection between the creative process and emotional health and healing. She has been published in the journal *Educational Psychologist* on the subject of art therapy.

Chiara Mocenni, since 2002, is Assistant Professor at the Department of Information Engineering of the University of Siena, where she teaches Complex Dynamical Systems. She received her Laurea Degree in Mathematics from the University of Siena in 1992's. Before joining the Systems and Control Group at DII in 1998 as Research Associate, Chiara Mocenni received the PhD in Physical Chemistry. From the 2000s, she serves on the Board of Directors of the Center for the Study of Complex Systems. Main research interests are complex systems, mathematical modeling and identification of dynamical systems, spatio-temporal time series analysis, systems biology, qualitative and bifurcation analysis, and behavioral models.

Rita Pizzi received the degree in Physics at the University of Milan and the Ph.D. in Electronic and Information Engineering at the University of Pavia. From 1986 to 1996 she collaborated with the CNR - Institute of Advanced Biomedical Technologies, and from 1996 to 2001, she worked at the National Institute of Neurology C. Besta. Currently, she works at the Department of Information Technologies of the University of Milan, where she is Senior Research Fellow and Aggregate Professor, teaching courses of Artificial Intelligence, Medical Informatics, Statistics, Information Systems, Information Theory, and Probabilistic Methods. Her research interests are concerned with Artificial Intelligence applied to the biomedical field and with computational physics. Currently she coordinates the Living Networks Lab, which is concerned with the study of the computational aspects of natural neural networks. Her major research result is the development of the first human-electronic creature: a living network of human neurons connected to a robotic body.

Massimo Pregnolato is Professor of "Medicinal Chemistry" and "Synthesis of Drugs" within the "Pharmaceutical Chemistry and Technology" degree course at the Faculty of Pharmacy, University of Pavia. Author of more than 60 scientific publications on medicinal chemistry and catalysis and inventor in 10 patents in the field of protein engineering and enzyme biocatalysts for the preparation of drugs. He is Chief Editor of *Quantum Biosystems*, Chairman of Quantum Paradigms of Psychopathology (QPP), Member of Scientific Commitee of Istituto di Ricerca "Paolo Sotgiu" in Psichiatria e Cardiologia Quantitativa ed Evoluzionistica, Università L.U.de.S. of Lugano, Switzerland," 2010 "Giorgio Napolitano" Medal Prize winner, Advisory Board Member of *DNA Decipher Journal,* Director of the QuantumBioLab, Founder of the Quantumbionet international network for the advancement of studies in quantum biology, and for the reunion of Arts and Science and quantIP for the management of intellectual property. He is also Founder of the Consortium of Italian Biocatalysis Center in July 2007, Creative Class Knowledge Manager, member of the Open Network for Science & Art of Virtual Enterprises and the QuantumArtGroup.

Angelo Rolla is working with the C.N.R.- I.I.I. on problems of water physics, with particular reference to lake hydrodynamics, and has co-authored 150 publication with the C.N.R. researcher participating in the proposed project. He is responsible for preparing software for the collection of historical data, which is homogenized, standardized, and proposed in terms of derived parameters with database structures adequate for the subsequent analyses, and aimed in particular a trend evaluation, periodicity, and interrupted time series analysis.

Hector Sabelli, M.D., Ph.D., an Argentine-born, American scientist and psychiatrist, is the former Director of the Institute of Pharmacology, University of Litoral, Argentina; Professor and Chairman, Pharmacology, Health Sciences University, Chicago, and Pharmacology Professor, and Associate Professor of Psychiatry, Rush University, Chicago. He studies creative processes from mathematical, empirical, and clinical perspectives. Earlier work includes the discovery of phenylethylamine, a stimulant neurohormone reduced in depression. He was awarded several research and clinical prizes (Bennett Award, Society of Biological Psychiatry, 1963; Scientific Research Award, Interstate Postgraduate Medical Association of North America, 1970; Best Teacher of the Year Award, The Chicago Medical School, 1975; Clinical Research Award, American Academy of Clinical Psychiatrists, 1984; Manic Depressive and Depressive Association of Northwest Indiana Award for Community, Education and Service, 1991; Zerka Moreno Award in Psychodrama, American Society of Group Psychotherapy, Sociometry and Psychodrama, 1993; Manic Depressive and Depressive Association of Northwest Indiana Award, 1994) and a Doctor Honoris Causa from the University of Rosario, Argentina in 1994. He is the author of 200 scientific articles in medicine, physics, sociology, and psychology, and 6 books: Chemical Modulation of Brain Function, 1973; Union of Opposites: A Comprehensive Theory of Natural and Human Processes, 1989; Personalization: A New Vision for the Millennium, 1991; Caos Argentino: Diagnóstico y Enfoque Clínico, 1991; María / Mary, Bilingual play, 1992; and Bios: A Study of Creation, 2005. He is currently writing a work titled "Medical Reasoning: Physical Priority and Psychological Supremacy in Clinical Care, Science, and Society."

Renato Saleri Lunazzi is born in 1964. He lived in Belgium, Switzerland, Italy, and currently in France. He has been Architect, Post Graduate in Industrial Design and Informatics productive processes. He has joined the MAP (Modèles et simulations pour l'Architecture, l'urbanisme et le Paysage) ARIA research team in 1995. He is recently involved in automatic generative design processes research tasks.

Franco Scalzone was born in Napoli where he graduated in Medicine and Surgery; he specialised in Psychiatry in Roma. He worked in Public Psychiatric Centres. He is a member of the Italian Psycho-analytical Society (SPI) and currently practises as private psychoanalyst. His main fields of interest are the hysteria syndrome and the interchange between psychoanalysis and neuroscience. He is the author of several scientific papers such as "Notes for a dialogue between psychoanalysis and neuroscience" and was the Editor, together with Dr. G. Zontini, of the anthology: *Perché l'isteria?* (Liguori, Napoli, 1999).

Giuliano Strini was born in Rome, Italy, September 9, 1937. He is an Associate Professor in Experimental Physics and has been teaching a course on Quantum Computation at Università di Milano, for several years. From 1963, he has been involved in the construction and development of the Milan Cyclotron. His publications concern nuclear reactions and spectroscopy, detection of gravitational waves, quantum optics, and more recently, quantum computers. He is a member of the Italian Physical Society, and also of the Optical Society of America.

Gerald H. Thomas holds a PhD in theoretical physics, and has practiced at CERN, Geneva and at Argonne National Laboratory, USA. He has extensive experience as senior manager from Fortune 500 companies to small venture companies, building a wealth of knowledge about real world decisions and strategies He currently teaches computer engineering at Milwaukee School of Engineering. He has published numerous research articles on high energy physics in international journals, and more recently, a book on decision theory.

Francisco Torrens is BSc, Universitat de València, 1984, MSc, 1987, PhD, 1990 (talent prize 1991, grant 1987-91), Editor-in-Chief of *Meeting in Science, Technology, Education and Gender*, editor of *Molecules, MATCH Communications in Mathematical and in Computer Chemistry, Research Journal of BioTechnology, Research & Reviews in BioSciences, Asian Journal of Biochemistry, Asian Journal of Scientific Research, Biotechnology, International Journal of Biological Chemistry, Current Drug Discovery Technologies, Journal of WSCG, African Journal of Biochemistry Research, Molecular Diversity, African Journal of Pure and Applied Chemistry, African Journal of Pharmacy and Pharmacology, International Journal of Liquid State Sciences, International Journal on Analytical Proteomics, Research in Pharmaceutical Biotechnology, IETE Technical Review, Der Pharma Chemica, Journal of Nanoscience and Nanotechnology, Journal of Electromagnetic Analysis and Applications, Journal of Integrated OMICS, Nereis, Journal of Life Sciences,* and *Internatonal Journal of Bochemistry Research & Review*. He is a member of 62 scientific societies, 26 research projects, 6 visitor professor responsible, and lecturer U.V., 1995-present.

David Vernon, PhD, is a Senior Lecturer in Psychology at Canterbury Christ Church University. His interests include exploring techniques used to enhance human performance and he has recently finished a book which examines a range of both passive and active approaches. His research has focused on the use of electroencephalographic (EEG) biofeedback and more recently cortical entrainment using binaural beats and he has published a number of papers exploring the effects of these techniques and attempting to refine the methodology.

Gemma Zontini was born in Napoli where graduated in Medicine and Surgery and specialised in Psychiatry. She is a full member of the Italian Psychoanalytical Society (SPI) and Director of a Centre for Diagnosis and Treatment. Her interest are hysteria and the relation between psychoanalysis and neuroscience. She published several scientific papers as, with F. Scalzone, "The dream's navel between chaos and thought", and papers on the Psychiatry–Medicine relation. She edited with F. Scalzone the anthology *Tra psiche e cervello* (Liguori, Napoli (Italy), 2004), an introduction to a dialogue between psychoanalysis and neuroscience.

Index